BLACK EARTH

THE HOLOCAUST AS HISTORY AND WARNING

TIMOTHY SNYDER

NEW YORK

Published in the United States by Tim Duggan Books, an imprint of the Crown Publishing Group, a division of Penguin Random House LLC, New York.
timdugganbooks.com

Tim Duggan Books and the Crown colophon are registered trademarks of Penguin Random House LLC.

Originally published in slightly different form in hardcover in the United States by Tim Duggan Books, an imprint of the Crown Publishing Group, a division of Penguin Random House LLC, New York, in 2015.

Library of Congress Cataloging-in-Publication Data is on file with the Library of Congress.

ISBN 978-1-101-90347-6
eBook ISBN 978-1-101-90346-9

Printed in the United States of America

Book design by Lauren Dong
Maps by Beehive Mapping
Cover design by Christopher Brand
Cover photograph © Alex Majoli/Magnum Photos

10 9

BLACK EARTH

ALSO BY TIMOTHY SNYDER

Nationalism, Marxism, and Modern Central Europe: A Biography of Kazimierz Kelles-Krauz

Wall Around the West: State Borders and Immigration Controls in the United States and Europe (ed. with Peter Andreas)

The Reconstruction of Nations: Poland, Ukraine, Lithuania, Belarus, 1569–1999

Sketches from a Secret War: A Polish Artist's Mission to Liberate Soviet Ukraine

The Red Prince: The Secret Lives of a Habsburg Archduke

Bloodlands: Europe Between Hitler and Stalin

Thinking the Twentieth Century (with Tony Judt)

Stalin and Europe: Imitation and Domination, 1928–1953 (ed. with Ray Brandon)

Ukrainian History, Russian Policy, and European Futures (in Russian and Ukrainian)

The Politics of Life and Death (in Czech)

The Balkans As Europe: The Nineteenth Century (ed. with Katherine Younger, forthcoming)

Praise for
BLACK EARTH

"Snyder's historical account has a vital contemporary lesson. . . . It's a testament to his intellectual and moral resources that he can so deeply contemplate this horrific past in ways that strengthen his commitment to building a future based on law, rights, and citizenship."

—*The Washington Post*

"Timothy Snyder's bold new approach to the Holocaust links Hitler's racial worldview to the destruction of states and the quest for land and food. This insight leads to thought-provoking and disturbing conclusions for today's world. *Black Earth* uses the recent past's terrible inhumanity to underline an urgent need to rethink our own future."

—Ian Kershaw

"An impressive reassessment of the Holocaust, which steers an assured course [and] challenges readers to reassess what they think they know and believe . . . *Black Earth* will prove uncomfortable reading for many who hew to cherished but mythical elements of Holocaust history."

—*The Economist*

"*Black Earth* elucidates human catastrophe in regions with which a Western audience needs to become familiar."

—*The New York Times Book Review*

"Part history, part political theory, *Black Earth* is a learned and challenging reinterpretation."

—Henry Kissinger

"A very fine book . . . Snyder identifies the conditions that allowed the Holocaust—conditions our society today shares. . . . He certainly couldn't be more right about our world."

—*The New Republic*

"In this unusual and innovative book, Timothy Snyder takes a fresh look at the intellectual origins of the Holocaust, placing Hitler's genocide firmly in the politics and diplomacy of 1930s Europe. *Black Earth* is required reading for anyone who cares about this difficult period of history."

—Anne Applebaum

"Timothy Snyder is now our most distinguished historian of evil. *Black Earth* casts new light on old darkness. It demonstrates once and for all that the destruction of the Jews was premised on the destruction of states and the institutions of politics. I know of no other historical work on the Holocaust that is so deeply alarmed by its repercussions for the human future. This is a haunted and haunting book—erudite, provocative, and unforgettable."

—Leon Wieseltier

"*Black Earth* is provocative, challenging, and an important addition to our understanding of the Holocaust. As he did in *Bloodlands*, Timothy Snyder makes us rethink those things we were sure we already knew." —DEBORAH LIPSTADT

"Excellent in every respect . . . Although I read widely about the Holocaust, I learned something new in every chapter. The multilingual Snyder has mined contemporaneous Eastern European sources that are often overlooked."
—STEPHEN CARTER, *BLOOMBERG*

"Timothy Snyder's *Black Earth* is not only a powerful exposure of the horrors of the Holocaust but also a compelling dissection of the Holocaust's continuing threat." —ZBIGNIEW BRZEZINSKI

"In *Black Earth,* a book of the greatest importance, Snyder now forces us to look afresh at these monumental crimes. Written with searing intellectual honesty, his new study goes much deeper than *Bloodlands* in its analysis, showing how the two regimes fed off each other." —ANTONY BEEVOR, *THE SUNDAY TIMES*

"Timothy Snyder argues, eloquently and convincingly, that the world is still susceptible to the inhuman impulses that brought about the Final Solution. This book should be read as admonition by presidents, prime ministers, and in particular by anyone who believes that the past is somehow behind us."
—JEFFREY GOLDBERG

"Snyder is both a great historian and a lively journalist. . . . If we understood the Nazi horror more clearly, we might be less susceptible to those who misremember the past to mislead us in the present. Snyder's *Black Earth*, like *Bloodlands* before it, is an indispensable contribution to that clearer understanding." —*COMMENTARY*

"Snyder writes elegant, lucid, powerful prose. He has read widely in literatures not widely read. In *Black Earth* he has synthesized previous work into a narrative of the Holocaust that recasts the familiar in unfamiliar terms that challenge the thinking of experts and non-experts alike." —*HAARETZ*

"No matter how many histories, biographies, and memoirs you may have already read, *Black Earth* will compel you to see the Holocaust in a wholly new and revelatory light." —*THE JEWISH JOURNAL*

For K. and T.

Im Kampf zwischen Dir und der Welt,
sekundiere der Welt.

In the struggle between you and the world
take the side of the world.

—Franz Kafka, 1917

Ten jest z ojczyzny mojej.
Jest człowiekiem.

He is from my homeland.
A human being.

—Antoni Słonimski, 1943

Schwarze Milch der Frühe wir trinken sie abends
wir trinken sie mittags und morgens wir trinken sie nachts
wir trinken und trinken

The black milk of daybreak
we drink in the evening
in the afternoon in the morning in the night
we drink and we drink

—Paul Celan, 1944

לכל איש יש שם
שנתנו לו המזלות
ונתנו לו שכניו

Every man has a name
given by the stars
given by his neighbors.

—Zelda Mishkovsky, 1974

Contents

Prologue

In the fashionable sixth district of Vienna, the history of the Holocaust is in the pavement. In front of the buildings where Jews once lived and worked, ensconced in sidewalks that Jews once had to scrub with their bare hands, are small square memorials in brass bearing names, dates of deportation, and places of death.

In the mind of an adult, words and numbers connect present and past. A child's view is different. A child starts from the things.

A little boy who lives in the sixth district observes, day by day, as a crew of workers proceeds, building by building, up the opposite side of his street. He watches them dig up the sidewalk, just as they might in order to repair a pipe or lay some cable. Waiting for his bus to kindergarten one morning, he sees the men, directly across the street now, shovel and pack the steaming black asphalt. The memorial plaques are mysterious objects in gloved hands, reflecting a bit of pale sun.

"Was machen sie da, Papa?" "What are they doing, Daddy?" The boy's father is silent. He looks up the street for the bus. He hesitates, starts to answer: *"Sie bauen . . ."* "They are building . . . " He stops. This is not easy. Then the bus comes, blocking their view, opening with a wheeze of oil and air an automatic door to a normal day.

Seventy-five years earlier, in March 1938, on streets throughout Vienna, Jews were cleansing the word "Austria" from the pavement, unwriting a country that was ceasing to exist as Hitler and his armies arrived. Today, on those same pavements, the names of those very Jews reproach a restored Austria that, like Europe itself, remains unsure of its past.

Why were the Jews of Vienna persecuted just as Austria was removed from the map? Why were they then sent to be murdered in Belarus, a thousand kilometers away, when there was evident hatred of Jews in Austria itself? How could a people established in a city (a country, a continent) suddenly have its history come to a violent end? Why do strangers kill strangers? And why do neighbors kill neighbors?

In Vienna, as in the great cities of central and western Europe generally, Jews were a prominent part of urban life. In the lands to the north, south, and east of Vienna, in eastern Europe, Jews had lived continuously in towns and villages in large numbers for more than five centuries. And then, in less than five years, more than five million of them were murdered.

Our intuitions fail us. We rightly associate the Holocaust with Nazi ideology, but forget that many of the killers were not Nazis or even Germans. We think first of German Jews, although almost all of the Jews killed in the Holocaust lived beyond Germany. We think of concentration camps, though few of the murdered Jews ever saw one. We fault the state, though murder was possible only where state institutions were destroyed. We blame science, and so endorse an important element of Hitler's worldview. We fault nations, indulging in simplifications used by the Nazis themselves.

We recall the victims, but are apt to confuse commemoration with understanding. The memorial in the sixth district of Vienna is called *Remember for the Future.* Should we be confident, now that a Holocaust is behind us, that a recognizable future awaits? We share a world with the forgotten perpetrators as well as with the memorialized victims. The world is now changing, reviving fears that were familiar in Hitler's time, and to which Hitler responded. The history of the Holocaust is not over. Its precedent is eternal, and its lessons have not yet been learned.

An instructive account of the mass murder of the Jews of Europe must be planetary, because Hitler's thought was ecological, treating Jews as a wound of nature. Such a history must be colonial, since Hitler wanted wars of extermination in neighboring lands where Jews lived. It must be international, for Germans and others murdered Jews not in Germany but in other countries. It must be chronological, in that Hitler's rise to power in Germany, only one part of the story, was followed by the conquest of Austria, Czechoslovakia, and Poland, advances that reformulated the Final Solution. It must be political, in a specific sense, since the German destruction of neighboring states created zones where, especially in the occupied Soviet Union, techniques of annihilation could be invented. It must be multifocal, providing perspectives beyond those of the Nazis themselves, using sources from all groups, from Jews and non-Jews, throughout the zone of killing. This is not only a matter of justice, but of understanding. Such a reckoning must also be human, chronicling the attempt to survive as well as the attempt to murder, describing Jews as they sought to live as well as those few non-Jews who sought to help them, accepting the innate and irreducible complexity of individuals and encounters.

A history of the Holocaust must be contemporary, permitting us to experience what remains from the epoch of Hitler in our minds and in our lives. Hitler's worldview did not bring about the Holocaust by itself, but its hidden coherence generated new sorts of destructive politics, and new knowledge of the human capacity for mass murder. The precise combination of ideology and circumstance of the year 1941 will not appear again, but something like it might. Part of the effort to understand the past is thus the effort needed to understand ourselves. The Holocaust is not only history, but warning.

Introduction: Hitler's World

Nothing can be known about the future, thought Hitler, except the limits of our planet: "the surface area of a precisely measured space." Ecology was scarcity, and existence meant a struggle for land. The immutable structure of life was the division of animals into species, condemned to "inner seclusion" and an endless fight to the death. Human races, Hitler was convinced, were like species. The highest races were still evolving from the lower, which meant that interbreeding was possible but sinful. Races should behave like species, like mating with like and seeking to kill unlike. This for Hitler was a law, the law of racial struggle, as certain as the law of gravity. The struggle could never end, and it had no certain outcome. A race could triumph and flourish and could also be starved and extinguished.

In Hitler's world, the law of the jungle was the only law. People were to suppress any inclination to be merciful and be as rapacious as they could. Hitler thus broke with the traditions of political thought that presented human beings as distinct from nature in their capacity to imagine and create new forms of association. Beginning from that assumption, political thinkers tried to describe not only the possible but the most just forms of society. For Hitler, however, nature was the singular, brutal, and overwhelming truth, and the whole history of attempting to think otherwise was an illusion. Carl Schmitt, a leading Nazi legal theorist, explained that politics arose not from history or concepts but from our sense of enmity. Our racial enemies were chosen by nature, and our task was to struggle and kill and die.

"Nature knows," wrote Hitler, "no political boundaries. She places life forms on this globe and then sets them free in a play for power." Since politics was nature, and nature was struggle, no political thought was possible. This conclusion was an extreme articulation of the nineteenth-century commonplace that human activities could be understood as biology. In the 1880s and 1890s, serious thinkers and popularizers influenced by Charles Darwin's idea of natural selection proposed that the ancient questions of political thought had been resolved by this breakthrough in zoology. When Hitler was young, an interpretation of Darwin in which competition was identified as a social good influenced all major forms of politics. For Herbert Spencer, the British defender of capitalism, a market was like an ecosphere where the strongest and best survived. The utility brought by unhindered competition justified its immediate evils. The opponents of capitalism, the socialists of the Second International, also embraced biological analogies. They came to see the class struggle as "scientific," and man as one animal among many, instead of a specially creative being with a specifically human essence. Karl Kautsky, the leading Marxist theorist of the day, insisted pedantically that people were animals.

Yet these liberals and socialists were constrained, whether they realized it or not, by attachments to custom and institution; mental habits that grew from social experience hindered them from reaching the most radical of conclusions. They were ethically committed to goods such as economic growth or social justice, and found it appealing or convenient to imagine that natural competition would deliver these goods. Hitler entitled his book *Mein Kampf—My Struggle*. From those two words through two long volumes and two decades of political life, he was endlessly narcissistic, pitilessly consistent, and exuberantly nihilistic where others were not. The ceaseless strife of races was not an element of life, but its essence. To say so was not to build a theory but to observe the universe as it was. Struggle was life, not a means to some other end. It was not justified by the prosperity (capitalism) or justice (socialism) that it supposedly brought. Hitler's point was not at all that the desirable end justified the bloody means. There was no end, only meanness. Race was real, whereas individuals and classes were fleeting and erroneous constructions. Struggle was not a metaphor or an analogy, but a tangible and total truth. The weak were to be dominated by the strong, since "the world is not there for the cowardly peoples." And that was all that there was to be known and believed.

Hitler's worldview dismissed religious and secular traditions, and yet relied upon both. Though he was no original thinker, he supplied a certain resolution to a crisis of both thought and faith. Like many before him he sought to bring the two together. What he meant to engineer, however, was not an elevating synthesis that would rescue both soul and mind but a seductive collision that destroyed both. Hitler's racial struggle was supposedly sanctioned by science, but he called its object "daily bread." With these words, he was summoning one of the best-known Christian texts, while profoundly altering its meaning. "Give us this day," ask those who recite the Lord's Prayer, "our daily bread." In the universe the prayer describes, there is a metaphysics, an order beyond this planet, notions of good that proceed from one sphere to another. Those saying the Lord's Prayer ask that God "forgive us our debts, as we also have forgiven our debtors. And lead us not into temptation, but deliver us from evil." In Hitler's "struggle for the riches of nature," it was a sin not to seize everything possible, and a crime to allow others to survive. Mercy violated the order of things because it allowed the weak to propagate. Rejecting the biblical commandments, said Hitler, was what human beings must do. "If I can accept a divine commandment," he declared, "it's this one: 'Thou shalt preserve the species.'"

Hitler exploited images and tropes that were familiar to Christians: God, prayers, original sin, commandments, prophets, chosen people, messiahs—even the familiar Christian tripartite structure of time: first paradise, then exodus, and finally redemption. We live in filth, and we must strain to purify ourselves and the world so that we might return to paradise. To see paradise as the battle of the species rather than the concord of creation was to unite Christian longing with the apparent realism of biology. The war of all against all was not terrifying purposelessness, but instead the only purpose to be had in the universe. Nature's bounty was for man, as in Genesis, but only for the men who follow nature's law and fight for her. As in Genesis, so in *My Struggle*, nature was a resource for man: but not for all people, only for triumphant races. Eden was not a garden but a trench.

Knowledge of the body was not the problem, as in Genesis, but the solution. The triumphant should copulate: After murder, Hitler thought, the next human duty was sex and reproduction. In his scheme, the original sin that led to the fall of man was of the mind and soul, not of the body. For Hitler, our unhappy weakness was that we can think, realize that others belonging to other races can do the same, and thereby recognize them as fellow human beings. Humans left Hitler's bloody paradise not because of carnal knowledge. Humans left paradise because of the knowledge of good and evil.

When paradise falls and humans are separated from nature, a character who is neither human nor natural, such as the serpent of Genesis, takes the blame. If humans were in fact nothing more than an element of nature, and nature was known by science to be a bloody struggle, something beyond nature must have corrupted the species. For Hitler the bringer of the knowledge of good and evil on the earth, the destroyer of Eden, was the Jew. It was the Jew who told humans that they were above other animals, and had the capacity to decide their future for themselves. It was the Jew who introduced the false distinction between politics and nature, between humanity and struggle. Hitler's destiny, as he saw it, was to redeem the original sin of Jewish spirituality and restore the paradise of blood. Since homo sapiens can survive only by unrestrained racial killing, a Jewish triumph of reason over impulse would mean the end of the species. What a race needed, thought Hitler, was a "worldview" that permitted it to triumph, which meant, in the final analysis, "faith" in its own mindless mission.

Hitler's presentation of the Jewish threat revealed his particular amalgamation of religious and zoological ideas. If the Jew triumphs, Hitler wrote, "then his crown of victory will be the funeral wreath of the human species." On the one hand, Hitler's image of a universe without human beings accepted science's verdict of an ancient planet on which humanity had evolved. After the Jewish victory, he wrote, "earth will once again wing its way through the universe entirely without humans, as was the case millions of years ago." At the same time, as he made clear in the very same passage of *My Struggle,* this ancient earth of races and extermination was the Creation of God. "Therefore I believe myself to be acting according to the wishes of the Creator. Insofar as I restrain the Jew, I am defending the work of the Lord."

Hitler saw the species as divided into races, but denied that the Jews were one. Jews were not a lower or a higher race, but a nonrace, or a counterrace. Races followed nature and fought for land and food, whereas Jews followed the alien logic of "un-nature." They resisted nature's basic imperative by refusing to be satisfied by the conquest of a certain habitat, and they persuaded others to behave similarly. They insisted on dominating the entire planet and its peoples, and for this purpose invented general ideas that draw the races away from the natural struggle. The planet had nothing to offer except blood and soil, and yet Jews uncannily generated concepts that allowed the world to be seen less as an ecological trap and more as a human order. Ideas of political reciprocity, practices in which humans recognize other humans as such, came from Jews.

Hitler's basic critique was not the usual one that human beings were good but had been corrupted by an overly Jewish civilization. It was rather that humans were animals and that any exercise of ethical deliberation was in itself a sign of Jewish corruption. The very attempt to set a universal ideal and strain towards it was precisely what was hateful. Heinrich Himmler, Hitler's most important deputy, did not follow every twist of Hitler's thinking, but he grasped the conclusions: Ethics as such was the error; the only morality was fidelity to race. Participation in mass murder, Himmler maintained, was a good act, since it brought to the race an internal harmony as well as unity with nature. The difficulty of seeing, for example, thousands of Jewish corpses marked the transcendence of conventional morality. The temporary strains of murder were a worthy sacrifice to the future of the race.

Any nonracist attitude was Jewish, thought Hitler, and any universal idea a mechanism of Jewish dominion. Both capitalism and communism were Jewish. Their apparent embrace of struggle was simply cover for the Jewish desire for world domination. Any abstract idea of the state was also Jewish. "There is no such thing," wrote Hitler, "as the state as an end in itself." As he clarified, "the highest goal of human beings" was not "the preservation of any given state or government, but the preservation of their kind." The frontiers of existing states would be washed away by the forces of nature in the course of racial struggle: "One must not be diverted from the borders of Eternal Right by the existence of political borders."

If states were not impressive human achievements but fragile barriers to be overcome by nature, it followed that law was particular rather than general, an artifact of racial superiority rather than an avenue of equality.

Hans Frank, Hitler's personal lawyer and during the Second World War the governor-general of occupied Poland, maintained that the law was built "on the survival elements of our German people." Legal traditions based on anything beyond race were "bloodless abstractions." Law had no purpose beyond the codification of a *Führer*'s momentary intuitions about the good of his race. The German concept of a *Rechtsstaat*, a state that operated under the rule of law, was without substance. As Carl Schmitt explained, law served the race, and the state served the race, and so race was the only pertinent concept. The idea of a state held to external legal standards was a sham designed to suppress the strong.

Insofar as universal ideas penetrated non-Jewish minds, claimed Hitler, they weakened racial communities to the profit of Jews. The content of various political ideas was beside the point, since all were merely traps for fools. There were no Jewish liberals and no Jewish nationalists, no Jewish messiahs and no Jewish Bolsheviks: "Bolshevism is Christianity's illegitimate child. Both are inventions of the Jew." Hitler saw Jesus as an enemy of Jews whose teachings had been perverted by Paul to become one more false Jewish universalism, that of mercy to the weak. From Saint Paul to Leon Trotsky, maintained Hitler, there were only Jews who adopted various guises to seduce the naive. Ideas had no historical origins and no connection to the succession of events or to the creativity of individuals. They were simply tactical creations of the Jews, and in this sense they were all the same.

Indeed, for Hitler there was no human history as such. "All world-historical events," he claimed, "are nothing more than the expression of the self-preservation drive of the races, for better or for worse." What must be registered from the past was the ceaseless attempt of Jews to warp the structure of nature. This would continue so long as Jews inhabited the earth. "It is Jewry," said Hitler, "that always destroys this order." The strong should starve the weak, but Jews could arrange matters so that the weak starve the strong. This was not an injustice in the normal sense, but a violation of the logic of being. In a universe warped by Jewish ideas, struggle could yield unthinkable outcomes: not the survival of the fittest, but the starvation of the fittest.

From this it followed that Germans would always be victims so long as Jews existed. As the highest race, Germans deserved the most and had the most to lose. The unnatural power of Jews "murders the future."

Though Hitler strove to define a world without history, his ideas were altered by his own experiences. The First World War, the bloodiest in history, fought on a continent that thought itself civilized, undid the broad confidence among many Europeans that strife was all to the good. Some Europeans of the Far Right or the Far Left, however, drew the opposite lesson. The bloodshed, for them, had not been extensive enough, and the sacrifice incomplete. For the Bolsheviks of the Russian Empire, disciplined and voluntarist Marxists, the war and the revolutionary energies it brought were the occasion to begin the socialist reconstruction of the world. For Hitler, as for many other Germans, the war ended before it was truly decided, the racial superiors taken from the battlefield before they had earned their due. Of course, the sentiment that Germany should win was widespread, and not only among militarists or extremists. Thomas Mann, the greatest of the German writers and later an opponent of Hitler, spoke of Germany's "rights to domination, to participate in the administration of the planet." Edith Stein, a brilliant German philosopher who developed a theory of empathy, considered "it out of the question that we will now be defeated." After Hitler came to power she was hunted down in her convent and murdered as a Jew.

For Hitler, the conclusion of the First World War demonstrated the ruin of the planet. Hitler's understanding of its outcome went beyond the nationalism of his fellow Germans, and his response to defeat only superficially resembled the general resentment about lost territories. For Hitler, the German defeat demonstrated that something was crooked in the whole structure of the world; it was the proof that Jews had mastered the methods of nature. If a few thousand German Jews had been gassed at the beginning of the war, he maintained, Germany would have won. He believed that Jews typically subjected their victims to starvation and saw the British naval blockade of Germany during (and after) the First World War as an application of this method. It was an instance of a permanent condition and the proof of more suffering to come. So long as Jews starved Germans rather than Germans starving whom they pleased, the world was in disequilibrium.

From the defeat of 1918 Hitler drew conclusions about any future conflict. Germans would always triumph if Jews were not involved. Yet since

Jews dominated the entire planet and had penetrated the minds of Germans with their ideas, the struggle for German power must take two forms. A war of simple conquest, no matter how devastatingly triumphant, could never suffice. In addition to starving inferior races and taking their land, Germans needed to simultaneously defeat the Jews, whose global power and insidious universalism would undermine any such healthy racial campaign. Thus Germans had the rights of the strong against the weak, and the rights of the weak against the strong. As the strong, they needed to dominate the weaker races they encountered; as the weak, they had to liberate all races from Jewish domination. Hitler thus united two great motivating forces of the world politics of his century: colonialism and anti-colonialism.

Hitler saw both the struggle for land and the struggle against the Jews in drastic, exterminatory terms, and yet he saw them differently. The struggle against inferior races for territory was a matter of the control of parts of the earth's surface. The struggle against the Jews was ecological, since it concerned not a specific racial enemy or territory but the conditions of life on earth. The Jews were "a pestilence, a spiritual pestilence, worse than the Black Death." Since they fought with ideas, their power was everywhere, and anyone could be their knowing or unknowing agent. The only way to remove such a plague was to eradicate it at the source. "If Nature designed the Jew to be the material cause of the decline and fall of the nations," said Hitler, "it provided these nations with the possibility of a healthy reaction." The elimination had to be complete: If one Jewish family remained in Europe, it could infect the entire continent.

The fall of man could be undone; the planet could be healed. "A people that is rid of its Jews," said Hitler, "returns spontaneously to the natural order."

Hitler's views of human life and the natural order were total and circular. All questions about politics were answered as if they were questions about nature; all questions about nature were answered by reference back to politics. The circle was drawn by Hitler himself. If politics and nature were not sources of experience and perspective but empty stereotypes that exist only in relation to each other, then all power rested in the hands of he who circulated the clichés. Reason was replaced by references, argumentation by incantation. The "struggle," as the title of the book gave away, was "mine": Hitler's. The totalistic idea of life as struggle placed all power to interpret any event in the mind of its author.

Equating nature and politics abolished not only political but also scientific thought. For Hitler, science was a completed revelation of the law of racial struggle, a finished gospel of bloodshed, not a process of hypothesis and experiment. It provided a vocabulary about zoological conflict, not a fount of concepts and procedures that allowed ever more extensive understanding. It had an answer but no questions. The task of man was to submit to this creed, rather than willfully impose specious Jewish thinking upon nature. Because Hitler's worldview required a single circular truth that embraced everything, it was vulnerable to the simplest of pluralisms: for example, that humans might change their environment in ways that might, in turn, change society. If science could change the ecosystem such that human behavior was altered, then all of his claims were groundless. Hitler's logical circle, in which society was nature because nature was society, in which men were beasts because beasts were men, would be broken.

Hitler accepted that scientists and specialists had purposes within the racial community: to manufacture weapons, to improve communications, to advance hygiene. Stronger races should have better guns, better radios, and better health, the better to dominate the weaker. He saw this as a fulfillment of nature's command to struggle, not as a violation of its laws. Technical achievement was proof of racial superiority, not evidence of the advance of general scientific understanding. "Everything that we today admire on this earth," wrote Hitler, "the scholarship and art, the technology and inventions, are nothing more than the creative product of a few peoples, and perhaps originally of a single race." No race, however advanced, could change the basic structure of nature by any innovation. Nature had only two variants: the paradise in which higher races slaughter the lower, and the fallen world in which supernatural Jews deny higher races the bounty they are due and starve them when possible.

Hitler understood that agricultural science posed a specific threat to the logic of his system. If humans could intervene in nature to create more food without taking more land, his whole system collapsed. He therefore denied the importance of what was happening before his eyes, the science of what was later called the "Green Revolution": the hybridization of grains, the distribution of chemical fertilizers and pesticides, the expansion of irrigation. Even "in the best case," he insisted, hunger must outstrip crop improvements. There was "a limit" to all scientific improvements. Indeed, all of "the scientific methods of land management" had already been tried and had failed. There was no conceivable improvement, now or in the future, that would allow Germans to be fed "from their own land and territory." Food could only be safeguarded by conquest of fertile territory, not by science that would make German territory more fertile. Jews deliberately encouraged the contrary belief in order to dampen the German appetite for conquest and prepare the German people for destruction. "It is always the Jew," wrote Hitler in this connection, "who seeks and succeeds in implanting such lethal ways of thinking."

Hitler had to defend his system from human discovery, which was as much of a problem for him as human solidarity. Science could not save the species because, in the final analysis, all ideas were racial, nothing more than aesthetic derivatives of struggle. The contrary notion, that ideas could actually reflect nature or change it, was a "Jewish lie" and a "Jewish swindle." Hitler maintained that "man has never conquered nature in any matter." Universal science, like universal politics, must be seen not as human promise but as Jewish threat.

The world's problem, as Hitler saw it, was that Jews falsely separated science and politics and made delusive promises for progress and humanity. The solution he proposed was to expose Jews to the brutal reality that nature and society were one and the same. They should be separated from other people and forced to inhabit some bleak and inhospitable territory. Jews were powerful in that their "un-nature" drew others to them. They were weak in that they could not face brutal reality. Resettled to some exotic locale, they would be unable to manipulate others with their unearthly concepts, and would succumb to the law of the jungle. Hitler's first obsession was an extreme natural setting, "an anarchic state on an island." Later his thoughts turned to the wastes of Siberia. It was "a matter of indifference," he said, whether Jews were sent to one or the other.

In August 1941, about a month after Hitler made that remark, his men began to shoot Jews in massacres on the scale of tens of thousands at a time, in the middle of Europe, in a setting they had themselves made anarchic, over pits dug in the black earth of Ukraine.

1

Living Space

Although Hitler's premise was that humans were simply animals, his own very human intuition allowed him to transform his zoological theory into a kind of political worldview. The racial struggle for survival was also a German campaign for dignity, he maintained, and the restraints were not only biological but British. Hitler understood that Germans were not, in their daily life, beasts who scratched food from the ground. As he developed his thought in his *Second Book,* composed in 1928, he made clear that securing a regular food supply was not simply a matter of physical sustenance, but also a requirement for a sense of control. The problem with the British naval blockade during the First World War had not simply been the diseases and death it brought during the conflict and in the months between armistice and final settlement. The blockade had forced middle-class Germans to break the law in order to acquire the food that they needed or felt that they needed, leaving them personally insecure and distrustful of authority.

The world political economy of the 1920s and 1930s was, as Hitler understood, structured by British naval power. British advocacy of free trade, he believed, was political cover for British domination of the world. It made sense for the British to parlay the fiction that free exchange meant access to food for everyone, because such a belief would discourage others from trying to compete with the British navy. In fact, only the British could defend their own supply lines in the event of a crisis, and could by the same token prevent food from reaching others. Thus the British blockaded their enemies during war—an obvious violation of their own ideology of free trade. This capacity to assure and deny food, Hitler emphasized, was a form of power. Hitler called the absence of food security for everyone except the British the "peaceful economic war."

Hitler understood that Germany did not feed itself from its own territory in the 1920s and 1930s, but also knew that Germans would not actually have starved if they had tried. Germany could have generated the calories to feed its population from German soil, but only by sacrificing some of its industry, exports, and foreign currency. A prosperous Germany required exchange with the British world, but this trade pattern could be supplemented, thought Hitler, by the conquest of a land empire that would even the scales between London and Berlin. Once it had gained the appropriate colonies, Germany could preserve its industrial excellence while shifting its dependence for food from the British-controlled sea lanes to its own imperial hinterland. If Germany controlled enough territory, Germans could have the kinds and the amounts of food that they desired, with no cost to German industry. A sufficiently large German empire could become self-sufficient, an "autarkic economy." Hitler romanticized the German peasant, not as a peaceful tiller of the soil, but as the heroic tamer of distant lands.

The British were to be respected as racial kindred and builders of a great empire. The idea was to slip through their network of power without forcing them to respond. Taking land from others would not, or so Hitler imagined, threaten the great maritime empire. Over the long term, he expected peace with Great Britain "on the basis of the division of the world." He expected that Germany could become a world power while avoiding an "Armageddon with England." This was, for him, a reassuring thought.

It was also reassuring that such an alteration of the world order, such a reglobalization, had been achieved before, in recent memory. For generations of German imperialists, and for Hitler himself, the exemplary land empire was the United States of America.

America taught Hitler that need blurred into desire, and that desire arose from comparison. Germans were not only animals seeking nourishment to survive, and not only a society yearning for security in an unpredictable British global economy. Families observed other families: around the corner, but also, thanks to modern media, around the world. Ideas of how life should be lived escaped measures such as survival, security, and even comfort as standards of living became comparative, and as comparisons became international. "Through modern technology and the communication it enables," wrote Hitler, "international relations between peoples have become so effortless and intimate that Europeans—often without realizing it—take the circumstances of American life as the benchmark for their own lives."

Globalization led Hitler to the American dream. Behind every imaginary German racial warrior stood an imaginary German woman who wanted ever more. In American idiom, this notion that the standard of living was relative, based upon the perceived success of others, was called "keeping up with the Joneses." In his more strident moments, Hitler urged Germans to be more like ants and finches, thinking only of survival and reproduction. Yet his own scarcely hidden fear was a very human one, perhaps even a very male one: the German housewife. It was she who raised the bar of the natural struggle ever higher. Before the First World War, when Hitler was a young man, German colonial rhetoric had played on the double meaning of the word *Wirtschaft:* both a household and an economy. German women had been instructed to equate comfort and empire. And since comfort was always relative, the political justification for colonies was inexhaustible. If the German housewife's point of reference was Mrs. Jones rather than Frau Jonas, then Germans needed an empire comparable to the American one. German men would have to struggle and die at some distant frontier, redeeming their race and the planet, while women supported their men, embodying the merciless logic of endless desire for ever more prosperous homes.

The inevitable presence of America in German minds was the final reason why, for Hitler, science could not solve the problem of sustenance. Even if inventions did improve agricultural productivity, Germany could not keep pace with America on the strength of this alone. Technology could be taken for granted on both sides; the quantity of arable land was the variable. Germany therefore needed as much land as the Americans and as much technology. Hitler proclaimed that permanent struggle for land was nature's wish, but he also understood that a human desire for increasing relative comfort could also generate perpetual motion.

If German prosperity would always be relative, then final success could never be achieved. "The prospects for the German people are bleak," wrote an aggrieved Hitler. That complaint was followed by this clarification: "Neither the current living space nor that achieved through a restoration of the borders of 1914 permits us to lead a life comparable to that of the American people." At the least, the struggle would continue as long as the United States existed, and that would be a long time. Hitler saw America as the coming world power, and the core American population ("the racially pure and uncorrupted German") as a "world class people" that was "younger and healthier than the Germans" who had remained in Europe.

While Hitler was writing *My Struggle,* he learned of the word *Lebensraum* (living space) and turned it to his own purposes. In his writings and speeches it expressed the whole range of meaning that he attached to the natural struggle, from an unceasing racial fight for physical survival all the way to an endless war for the subjective sense of having the highest standard of living in the world. The term *Lebensraum* came into the German language as the equivalent of the French word *biotope,* or "habitat." In a social rather than biological context it can mean something else: household comfort, something close to "living room." The containment of these two meanings in a single word furthered Hitler's circular idea: Nature was nothing more than society, society nothing more than nature. Thus there was no difference between an animal struggle for physical existence and the preference of families for nicer lives. Each was about *Lebensraum.*

The twentieth century was to bring endless war for relative comfort. Robert Ley, one of Hitler's early Nazi comrades, defined *Lebensraum* as "more culture, more beauty—these the race must have, or it will perish." Hitler's propagandist Joseph Goebbels defined the purpose of a war of extermination as "a big breakfast, a big lunch, and a big dinner." Tens of millions of people would have to starve, but not so that Germans could survive in the physical sense of the word. Tens of millions of people would have to starve so that Germans could strive for a standard of living second to none.

"One thing the Americans have and which we lack," complained Hitler, "is the sense of vast open spaces." He was repeating what German colonialists had said for decades. By the time Germany had unified in 1871, the world had already been colonized by other European powers. Germany's defeat in the First World War cost it the few overseas possessions it had gained. So where, in the twentieth century, were the lands open for German conquest? Where was Germany's frontier, its Manifest Destiny?

All that remained was the home continent. "For Germany," wrote Hitler, "the only possibility of a sound agrarian policy was the acquisition of land within Europe itself." To be sure, there was no place near Germany that was uninhabited or even underpopulated. The crucial thing was to imagine that European "spaces" were, in fact, "open." Racism was the idea that turned populated lands into potential colonies, and the source mythologies for racists arose from the recent colonization of North America and Africa. The conquest and exploitation of these continents by Europeans formed the literary imagination of Europeans of Hitler's generation. Like millions of other children born in the 1880s and 1890s, Hitler played at African wars and read Karl May's novels of the American West. Hitler said that May had opened his "eyes to the world."

In the late nineteenth century, Germans tended to see the fate of Native Americans as a natural precedent for the fate of native Africans under their control. One colony was German East Africa—today Rwanda, Burundi, Tanzania, and a bit of Mozambique—where Berlin assumed responsibility in 1891. During an uprising in 1905, the Maji Maji rebellion, the Germans applied starvation tactics, killing at least seventy-five thousand people. A second colony was German Southwest Africa, today Namibia, where about three thousand German colonists controlled about seventy percent of the land. An uprising there in 1904 led the Germans to deny the native Herero and Nama populations access to water until they fell "victim to the nature of their own country," as the official military history put it. The Germans imprisoned survivors in a camp on an island. The Herero population was reduced from some eighty thousand to about fifteen thousand; that of the Nama from about twenty thousand to about ten thousand. For the German general who pursued these policies, the historical justice was self-evident. "The natives must give way," he said. "Look at America." The German governor of the region compared

Southwest Africa to Nevada, Wyoming, and Colorado. The civilian head of the German colonial office saw matters much the same way: "The history of the colonization of the United States, clearly the biggest colonial endeavor the world has ever known, had as its first act the complete annihilation of its native peoples." He understood the need for an "annihilation operation." The German state geologist called for a "Final Solution to the native question."

A famous German novel of the war in German Southwest Africa united, as would Hitler, the idea of a racial struggle with that of divine justice. The killing of "blacks" was "the justice of the Lord" because the world belonged to "the most vigorous." Like most Europeans, Hitler was a racist about Africans. He proclaimed that the French were "niggerizing" their blood through intermarriage. He shared in the general European excitement about the French use of African troops in the occupation of Germany's Rhineland district after the First World War. Yet Hitler's racism was not that of a European looking down at Africans. He saw the entire world as an "Africa," and everyone, including Europeans, in racial terms. Here, as so often, he was more consistent than others. Racism, after all, was a claim to judge who was fully human. As such, ideas of racial superiority and inferiority could be applied according to desire and convenience. Even neighboring societies, which might seem not so different from the German, might be defined as racially different.

When Hitler wrote in *My Struggle* that Germany's only opportunity for colonization was Europe, he discarded as impractical the possibility of a return to Africa. The search for racial inferiors to dominate required no long voyages by sea, since they were present in eastern Europe as well. In the nineteenth century, after all, the major arena of German colonialism had been not mysterious Africa but neighboring Poland. Prussia had gained territory inhabited by Poles in the partitions of the Polish-Lithuanian Commonwealth in the late eighteenth century. Formerly Polish lands were thus part of the unified Germany that Prussia created in 1871. Poles made up about seven percent of the German population, and in eastern regions were a majority. They were subjected first to Bismarck's *Kulturkampf*, a campaign against Roman Catholicism whose major object was the elimination of Polish national identity, and then to state-subsidized internal colonization campaigns. A German colonial literature about Poland, including best sellers, portrayed the Poles as "black." The Polish peasants had dark faces and referred to Germans as "white." Polish aristocrats, fey and useless, were endowed with black hair and eyes. So were the beautiful Polish women, seductresses who, in these stories, almost invariably led naive German men to racial self-degradation and doom.

During the First World War, Germany lost Southwest Africa. In eastern Europe the situation was different. Here German arms seemed to be assembling, between 1916 and 1918, a vast new realm for domination and economic exploitation. First Germany joined its prewar Polish territories to those taken from the Russian Empire to form a subordinate Polish kingdom, which was to be ruled by a friendly monarch. The postwar plan was to expropriate and deport all of the Polish landholders near the German-Polish border. In early 1918, after the Bolshevik Revolution had taken Russia from the war, Germany established a chain of vassal states to the east of Poland, from the Baltic to the Black Sea, the largest of which was Ukraine. Germany lost the war in France in 1918, but was never finally defeated on the battlefield in eastern Europe. This new east European realm was abandoned without, it could seem to Germans, ever having been truly lost.

The complete loss of the African colonies during and after the war created the possibility for a vague and malleable nostalgia about racial mastery. Popular novels about Africa with titles such as *Master, Come Back!* could make sense only after such a complete break. Germans could continue to see themselves as good colonizers, even as the realm of colonization itself became fluid and vague, projected into the future. Hans Grimm's novel *A People Without Space,* which sold half a million copies in Germany before the Second World War, concerned the plight of a German who had left Africa only to be frustrated by confinement within a small Germany and an unjust European system.

The problem suggested its own solution. Since racism was an asserted hierarchy of rights to the planet, it could be applied to Europeans who lived east of Germany. Africa as a place was lost, but "Africa" as a form of thinking could be universalized. The experience in eastern Europe had established that neighbors could also be "black." Europeans could be imagined to want "masters" and yield "space." After the war, it was more practical to consider a return to eastern Europe than to Africa. Here, as in so many other cases, Hitler drew vague sentiments to remorselessly tight conclusions. He presented as racial inferiors the largest cultural group in Europe, Germany's eastern neighbors, the Slavs.

"The Slavs are born as a slavish mass," wrote Hitler, "crying out for their master." He meant primarily the Ukrainians, who inhabited a stretch of very fertile land, as well as their neighbors—Russians, Belarusians, and Poles. "I need the Ukraine," he stated, "in order that no one is able to starve us again, like in the last war." The conquest of Ukraine would guarantee "a way of life for our people through the allocation of *Lebensraum* for the next hundred years." This was a matter of natural justice: "It is inconceivable that a higher people should painfully exist on a soil too narrow for it, whilst amorphous masses, which contribute nothing to civilization, occupy infinite tracts of a soil that is one of the richest in the world." As their land was taken, Ukrainians could be given, said Hitler, "scarves, glass beads, and everything that colonial peoples like." A single loudspeaker in each village would "give them plenty of opportunities to dance, and the villagers will be grateful to us." Nazi propaganda would simply remove Ukrainians from view. A Nazi song for female colonists described Ukraine thus: "There are neither farms nor hearths, there the earth cries out for the plough." Erich Koch, chosen by Hitler to rule Ukraine, made the point about the inferiority of Ukrainians with a certain simplicity: "If I find a Ukrainian who is worthy to sit with me at table, I must have him shot." Even in the racial murder threats, the dining room was the backdrop.

When German occupation came in 1941, Ukrainians themselves made the connection to Africa and America. A Ukrainian woman, literate and reflective in a way that Nazi racism could not have contemplated, recorded in her diary: "We are like slaves. Often the book *Uncle Tom's Cabin* comes to mind. Once we shed tears over those Negroes, now obviously we ourselves are experiencing the same thing." Yet in one respect, colonialism in eastern Europe had to differ from the American slave trade or the conquest of Africa. It required two feats of imagination: the wishing away not just of peoples but also of political entities that were similar to the German state. Hitler's preoccupation with the racial struggle for nature occluded both nations and their governments. It was always legitimate to destroy states; if they were destroyed, that meant that they should have been destroyed.

Some states, claimed Hitler, were inviting attack. Lower races were incapable of state building, so what appeared to be their governments was illusory—a façade for Jewish power. Hitler maintained that the Slavs had never governed themselves. The lands east of Germany had always been ruled by "foreign elements." The Russian Empire had been the creation of an "essentially German upper class and intelligentsia." Without this tradition of German leadership, "the Russians would still be living like rabbits." Ukrainians were by nature a colonial people and, as German colonial administrators would say, "blacks." After Germany was forced in 1918 to withdraw its troops and cede its new empire, most of Ukraine, like most of the lands of the Russian Empire, was consolidated within a new communist state known as the Union of Soviet Socialist Republics (Soviet Union, USSR). Hitler claimed that the USSR was an expression of a Jewish "worldview." The idea of communism was simply a deception that led Slavs to accept their "new leadership in Jewry."

Communism was the proximate example of Hitler's claim that all universal ideas were Jewish and all Jews were the servants of universal ideas. The proclaimed identity of Jews with communism—the Judeobolshevik myth—was for Hitler the apposite demonstration of both the supernatural strength and the earthly weakness of Jews. It demonstrated that Jews could win destructive power over the masses with their unnatural ideas. "Bolshevism of international Jewry attempts from its control point in Soviet Russia to rot away the very core of the nations of the world," he wrote. Yet this apparent misfortune was in fact an opportunity. In killing the strongest members of the Slavic races inside the Soviet Union, Jews were doing the work that Germans would have to do in any event. Jewish communism was in this sense, Hitler wrote, "fortunate for the future." The Bolshevik Revolution of 1917, thought Hitler, was therefore "merely a preparation" for the later return of "German domination."

Hitler's interpretation of the Bolshevik Revolution as a Jewish project was far from unusual: Winston Churchill and Woodrow Wilson saw it the same way, at least at first. A *Times* of London correspondent saw Jews as the leading force of the world Bolshevik conspiracy. What was unusual was Hitler's relentlessly systematic conclusion that Germany could gain global power by eliminating east European Jews and overturning their supposed Soviet citadel. This was nothing more than self-defense, he maintained, since Bolshevism's victory by whatever insidious means would bring the "destruction, indeed the final extermination, of the German people." In a direct confrontation, though, the Jewish threat could be eliminated. The destruction of Soviet Jews would cause the Soviet Union to "immediately break up." It would prove to be a "house of cards" or a "giant with feet of clay." The Slavs would fight "like Indians," with the same result. Then, in the East, "a similar process will repeat itself for the second time, as in the conquest of America." A second America could be created in Europe, after Germans learned to see other Europeans as they saw indigenous Americans or Africans, and learned to regard Europe's largest state as a fragile Jewish colony.

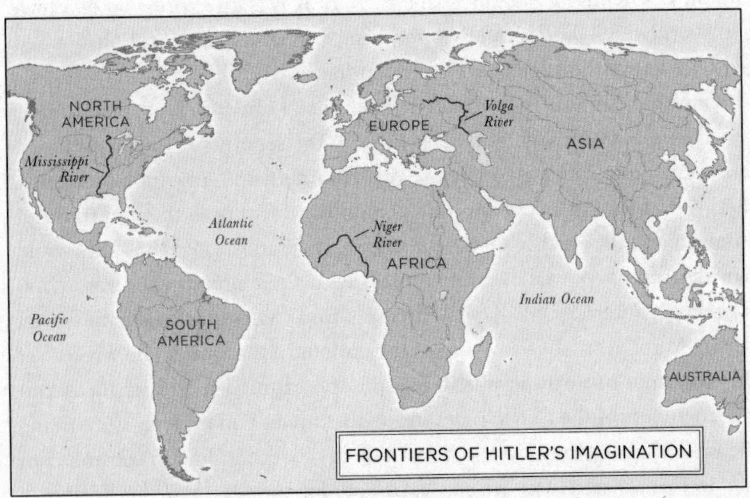

FRONTIERS OF HITLER'S IMAGINATION

In this racist collage Europeans were interspersed with Africans and Native Americans. Hitler compressed all of imperial history and a total racism into a very short formulation: "Our Mississippi must be the Volga, and not the Niger." The Niger River, in Africa, was no longer accessible to German imperialism after 1918, but Africa remained a fount of the images and the colonial longing. The Volga, the eastern border of Europe, was where Hitler imagined the outer limit of German power. The Mississippi was not only the river that runs from north to south through the middle of the United States. It was also the line beyond which Thomas Jefferson wanted all Indians expelled. "Who," asked Hitler, "remembers the Red Indians?" For Hitler, Africa was the source of the imperial references but not the actual site of empire; eastern Europe was that actual site, and it was to be remade just as North America had been remade.

The destruction of the Soviet Union, thought Hitler, would allow the right master race to starve the right subhumans for the right reasons. Once the Germans replaced the Jews as the colonial masters, food from Ukraine could be directed away from the useless Soviet populations towards grateful German cities and a submissive Europe. Hitler's axiom that life was a starvation war and his proposal for a hunger campaign against the Slavs were reflected in policy documents formulated after his rise to power in Germany in 1933. A Hunger Plan created under the authority of Hermann Göring foresaw that "many tens of millions of people in this territory will become superfluous and will die or must emigrate to Siberia." Then, according to a second round of plans, designed under the authority of Heinrich Himmler, colonization by Germans could begin.

The Judeobolshevik conception allowed Hitler's portrait of a planetary ecosystem polluted by Jewish ideas to crystallize as planning. The Judeobolshevik myth seemed to define the point where the application of German force could win an empire and restore the planet. It also permitted a politics of war and extermination that would be decisive for Jews and, in a different way, for Germans. The idea that Jewish power was global and ideological seemed to make the Jewish hold on territory weaker rather than stronger. If Jews could be eliminated, then they could no longer purvey their false ideas of human solidarity, and would have to yield their planetary dominion. Thus the Judeobolshevik myth courted the warriors by promising an easy triumph.

If the war did not proceed as planned, if the Soviet Union could not be so easily destroyed, then the idea of Jewish hegemony over the entire planet could return to the forefront of rhetoric and policy. If the Jews were not weakened by a first strike on Soviet territory, then the war against them would have to be escalated. If Germany had to fight a global enemy, there would seem to be no alternative to a total campaign against Jews, since in a long war the Jews could strike from any point at any time. The Jews behind the lines, in places under German control, would have to be exterminated. This latent potential within Hitler's ideas was realized in practice: Jews were not killed in large numbers first in Berlin, but on the frontiers of German power in the Soviet East. As the tide of war turned, the mass killing moved west from the occupied Soviet Union to occupied Poland and then to the rest of Europe.

The Judeobolshevik myth seemed to justify a preemptive strike on a certain valuable territory against an inherently planetary enemy. It linked the elimination of the Jews to the subjugation of the Slavs. If this connection could be established in theory and Germans thrust eastward into war, Hitler could hardly fail in practice. Failure to conquer Slavs would make the case for exterminating Jews.

The Judeobolshevik idea, a major source of the Second World War, had its origins in the First. It reached Hitler's mind after a peculiar German experience during the collapse of the Russian Empire, on the eastern front of the First World War.

From the perspective of Berlin, the First World War was fought on a western front against France (and Britain, and later the United States) and on an eastern front against the Russian Empire. Germany was surrounded by enemies on both sides and had to try to eliminate one quickly in order to defeat the other. The attack on France in 1914 failed, condemning Germans to a long two-front war. Under these circumstances, German diplomats sought nonmilitary means of removing the Russian Empire from the conflict, such as fomenting revolution. In April 1917, after a first revolution in Russia had already taken place, Germany arranged the transport of Vladimir Lenin, the leader of the Bolsheviks, from Zurich to Petrograd in a sealed train. He succeeded, along with his comrades, in organizing a second revolution in November. He then withdrew the Russian Empire from the war. This appeared at first to be a tremendous German victory.

Before the revolutions of 1917, the Russian Empire had been the homeland of more Jews than any other country in the world—and an actively antisemitic state. Jews were subject to official forms of discrimination and targeted in pogroms of increasing intensity and frequency. These were not organized by the state, but the Russian imperial subjects who perpetrated them believed that they were following the will of the tsar. Jews were almost two hundred times more likely than ethnic Russians to emigrate from the Russian Empire, in part because they were more likely to want to leave, and in part because imperial authorities were glad to see them go. During the First World War, Jews were largely excluded from the body politic.

Jews inhabited the western regions of the Russian Empire, through which Russian imperial soldiers advanced and retreated as they engaged their German and Austrian enemies. As Russian troops marched into the lands of the Habsburg monarchy in autumn 1914, they found Jews who owned farms (which was illegal in the Russian Empire) and promptly expropriated them. In January 1915, official imperial circulars blamed Jews for sabotage. That month the Russian imperial army expelled some hundred thousand Jews from forty towns near Warsaw. Local Poles took the Jews' property and kept it. When the Germans drove the Russians back east in 1915, Russian imperial soldiers blamed Jews and carried out about a hundred pogroms. The head of the right faction of the Russian parliament (later the minister of internal affairs) explained setbacks by referring to the plans of an international Jewish oligarchy. Meanwhile, the Russian Empire deported about half a million Jews from their homes, on the logic that they might collaborate with the invaders. The army was the agent of deportations, so soldiers and officers could loot Jews, their fellow Russian imperial subjects. This mass expulsion from the Jewish heartland, accompanied by systematic theft and frequent violence, was one of the greatest disruptions of traditional Jewish life in history.

In the minds of Europeans, the Russian deportation altered the Jewish question. Tens of thousands of Jews fled the Russian Empire, creating an impression in European cities that Jews from the East were suddenly everywhere. The deportations shaped the lives of many of the major Jewish revolutionaries of the twentieth century, both of the Right and the Left. As very young boys both Menachem Begin and Avraham Stern, later right-wing radicals, were displaced. Within the Russian Empire, Jews deported from the front made for the major cities, such as Moscow, Petrograd, and Kyiv, where they were often shunned as spies and denied employment and shelter. After the February 1917 Revolution, as the empire lurched towards becoming a republic, the Jews were formally emancipated and became citizens. Of the sixty thousand or so Jews in Moscow at this time, about half were refugees. Many of them joined Lenin in his second Russian revolution that November. Lenin thanked Jews for their decisive support in the city that he would make his capital.

As of November 1917, Jews were suddenly equal members of a new revolutionary state rather than a repressed religious minority in an empire. The vast majority of Jews tried in 1918 to return to their homes, only to find them, very frequently, inhabited by other people. The Jews' neighbors did not want to return what they had taken, and often attacked the Jews instead. As one regime gave way to another, Jews were targeted by everyone involved. The first pogroms after the revolution were carried out by the Red Army; but the ideology of their commanders was internationalist, and officers usually tried to stop anti-Jewish violence.

The other side generally did not show such restraint. The men who took up arms against Lenin's revolution represented no coherent movement; the closest thing to an ideology of counterrevolution was antisemitism. Opponents of the new regime, seeking to draw support from the population, wed traditional religious antisemitism to a present sense of threat, portraying the Bolsheviks as a modern Satan. As the civil war ground on, killing millions of people, journalists and propagandists who opposed revolution developed the Judeobolshevik myth. They drew some of their ideas from the *Protocols of the Elders of Zion.* The notion of global Jewish power seemed to explain the double catastrophe of revolution and military defeat. It transformed the victory of a universal over a national idea into a plot of an identifiable group of people who could be punished.

Germany backed the revolutionaries in 1917, only to find itself on the side of the counterrevolutionaries not long thereafter. During the chaos that followed Lenin's revolution, Germany was able to build a chain of client states between the Baltic and the Black Sea. The most important of these was Ukraine. The German plan for 1918 was to recall troops from the east to fight a final battle on the western front while feeding Germans from Ukrainian grain. The Germans called the treaty they signed with the Ukrainian state in February 1918 the "Bread Peace," and it was very popular

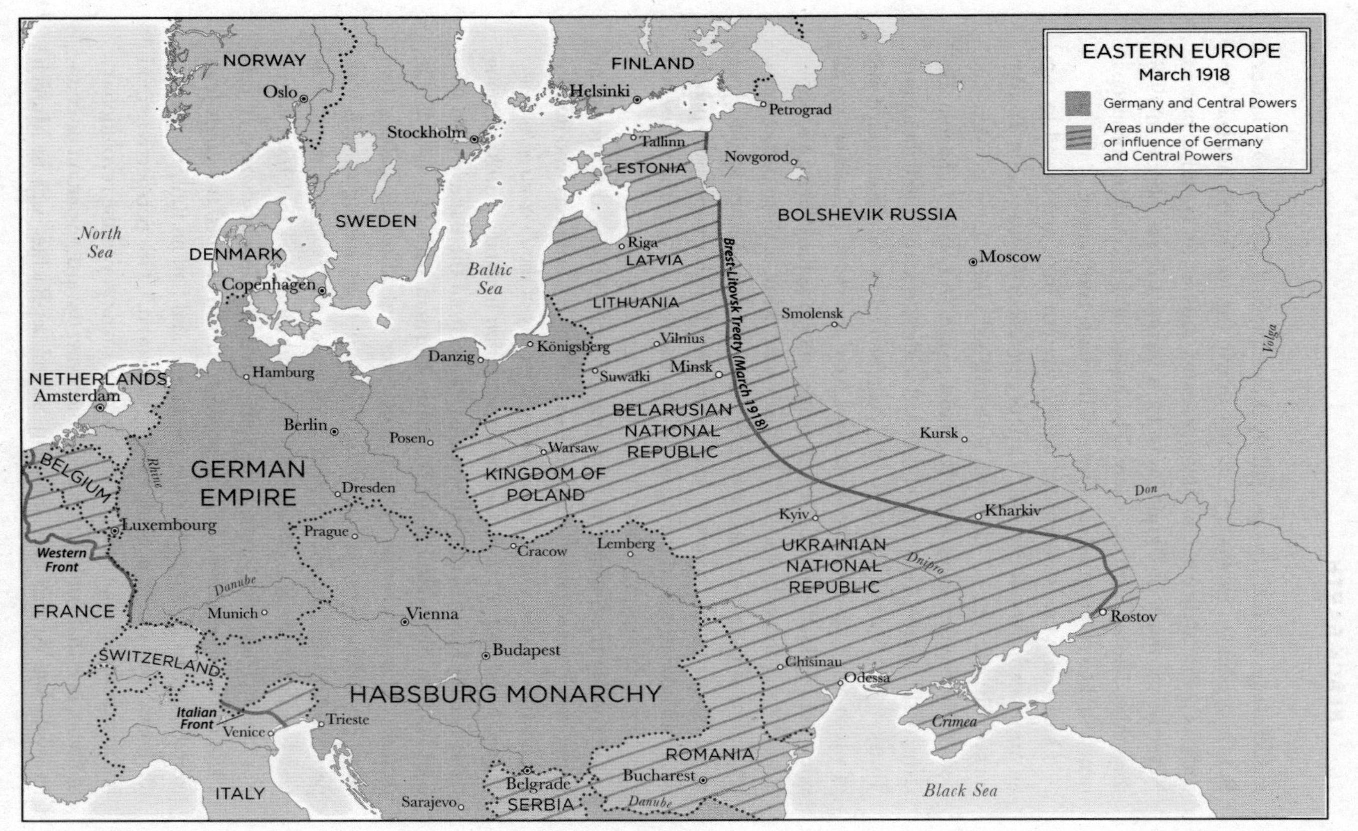
EASTERN EUROPE
March 1918
Germany and Central Powers
Areas under the occupation or influence of Germany and Central Powers
NORWAY
Oslo
SWEDEN
Stockholm
FINLAND
Helsinki
Petrograd
Tallinn
ESTONIA
Novgorod
BOLSHEVIK RUSSIA
Moscow
Riga
LATVIA
LITHUANIA
Smolensk
Vilnius
Minsk
Königsberg
Suwałki
Brest-Litovsk Treaty (March 1918)
Volga
North Sea
DENMARK
Copenhagen
Baltic Sea
Danzig
Hamburg
NETHERLANDS
Amsterdam
Berlin
Posen
BELARUSIAN NATIONAL REPUBLIC
Warsaw
Kursk
BELGIUM
Rhine
GERMAN EMPIRE
Dresden
KINGDOM OF POLAND
Don
Kyiv
Kharkiv
Luxembourg
Prague
Cracow
Lemberg
UKRAINIAN NATIONAL REPUBLIC
Dnipro
Western Front
Danube
FRANCE
Munich
Vienna
Rostov
Budapest
SWITZERLAND
Chisinau
Odessa
HABSBURG MONARCHY
Italian Front
Trieste
Venice
Crimea
ROMANIA
Belgrade
Bucharest
ITALY
Sarajevo
SERBIA
Danube
Black Sea

in Germany. German troops quickly drove the Red Army from Ukraine. But the scheme to exploit the country to win the war failed, not least because of the resistance of Ukrainian peasants, militias, and political parties. Nevertheless, much of Ukraine was, for a memorable six months in 1918, something like a German colony. The image of a Ukrainian cornucopia penetrated German minds at a time of blockade and hunger.

Once Germany was defeated on the western front and forced to sign an armistice in November 1918, Lenin's commissar for war, Leon Trotsky, turned his attention to Germany's abandoned client states in what had been the western reaches of the Russian Empire. In Latvia, Lithuania, Belarus, and Ukraine, German officers and soldiers remained to fight against Trotsky's Red Army. Ukraine in 1919 collapsed into a complicated civil war in which some hundred thousand Jews were murdered by soldiers on all sides: Bolsheviks, the anti-Bolshevik armies known as the Whites, and above all soldiers of the independent Ukrainian state. Most of these perpetrators, regardless of their identities or loyalties, had learned violence against Jews in the Russian imperial army. Very often their Jewish victims were people who had been deported during the war by the Russian imperial policy and therefore lacked security and connections where they were.

The vanquished adherents of the Judeobolshevik thesis were among the hundreds of thousands of defeated Russian imperial subjects who flooded defeated Germany. One of them brought a copy of the *Protocols of the Elders of Zion*, which appeared in German translation in January 1920. Among those fleeing Lenin's triumph were Germans from the Baltic region who could convey the Judeobolshevik idea in German without a text. These included Max Erwin von Scheubner-Richter and Alfred Rosenberg, two early Nazi influences on Hitler. In 1919 and 1920, having spoken with people who knew the *Protocols* and having read the *Protocols* himself, Hitler assimilated the Judeobolshevik myth and the notion that Jews kill by starvation. These ideas were at the time a matter of intense debate. In July 1920, the representative of Soviet power in Berlin claimed that most Jews were bourgeois, had opposed the revolution, and had no future on Soviet territory. They would not rule but be "destroyed." This perspective could not persuade Germans who were seeking a single key to the revolutionary moment, one that could be turned either way, toward revolution or counterrevolution. At this very moment, Scheubner-Richter was in Munich gathering money and men to mount an armed expedition against the Bolsheviks, with special emphasis on liberating Ukraine.

The Judeobolshevik idea has a specific historical origin: an extension of the antisemitism of official Russia, an adaptation of Christian apocalyptic visions during a time of crisis, an explanation of the collapse of the ancient imperial order, a battle cry during a civil war, and a form of consolation after defeat. When the Nazi movement began, armed counterrevolution was under way in Russia and Ukraine, and its victory was still a real prospect in the minds of people who mattered to Hitler. For a brief moment in 1920, the Red Army seemed to be on its way to Germany. As the soldiers of Bolshevism advanced on Warsaw that August, it seemed that a final confrontation of the forces of revolution and counterrevolution would soon take place. But after a surprising and decisive Polish victory in that battle and the war, and with the consolidation of the European system that followed in 1921, the character of the problem changed.

Scheubner-Richter's attempt to assemble an anti-Bolshevik army collapsed in 1922. When he marched arm in arm with Hitler in Munich in 1923, the Nazi putsch was, for him, a final lurch towards the East. When Scheubner-Richter was killed and Hitler was imprisoned, some Nazis saw the failure as a triumph not so much of the young Weimar Republic in Germany as of the Judeobolshevik power they believed they were opposing. As Hitler composed *My Struggle* in prison in 1924, the Bolsheviks became less a concrete group of political rivals and more a way to connect his ideas about Jews to a piece of territory. For Hitler, who knew little about the Russian Empire, and who thought in grand abstractions, the Judeobolshevik idea was not the end of a Russian struggle but the beginning of a German crusade, not a myth arising from painful events but the glimmering light of eternal truth.

The Judeobolshevik myth seemed to provide the missing piece of Hitler's entire scheme, uniting the local with the planetary, the promise of victorious colonial war against Slavs with a glorious anti-colonial struggle against Jews. A single attack on a single state, the Soviet Union, could solve all the problems of the Germans at the same time. The destruction of Soviet Jews would mean the removal of Jewish power, which would allow the creation of an eastern empire, which would mean the replay of American frontier history in eastern Europe. The racial German empire would revise the global order and begin the restoration of nature on a planet polluted by Jews. If the war was won, Jews could be eliminated as convenient. If Germans were somehow held back by inferior Slavs, then Jews would bear the consequences. Either way, the pursuit of racial empire would bring the politics of Jewish eradication.

In Hitler's ecology, the planet was despoiled by the presence of Jews, who defied the laws of nature by introducing corrupting ideas. The solution was to expose Jews to a purified nature, a place where bloody struggle rather than abstract thought mattered, where Jews could not manipulate others with their ideas because there would be no others. The exotic deportation sites that Hitler imagined for the Jews, Madagascar and Siberia, would never fall under German power. Much of Europe, however, would. Not so very long after Hitler published his ideas about daily bread and the commandment of self-preservation, Europeans were forcing Jews to recite the Lord's Prayer and killing them when they could not. Europe itself became the anti-garden, a landscape of trenches.

During a death march, Miklós Radnóti wrote a poem, meant to be discovered in his clothing when his remains were excavated from a death pit: "I the root was once the flower / under these dim tons my bower / comes the shearing of the thread / deathsaw wailing overhead."

2

Berlin, Warsaw, Moscow

A worldview is not a plan for taking power. The Judeobolshevik myth supplied an image of the enemy, but not a foreign policy. *Lebensraum* was a summons to empire, not a military strategy. The problem for Hitler the thinker was that German politics, neighboring states, and the European order could not be abolished by the stroke of a pen. After he left prison in 1924, Hitler learned some practical lessons, without ever changing his mind about the theory. As a young veteran of the First World War, Hitler could imagine that a dramatic gesture, a coup attempt in Munich in 1923, would suffice to transform Germany. In this he was wrong. He was defeated, and his comrade Scheubner-Richter was killed, by the forces of the state. Yet Hitler did come to power, a much cannier politician, ten years after his failed putsch. Then he and his party comrades, with considerable popular support, transformed the German state. Hitler could imagine that the Soviet Union was a cowardly Jewish coven. In this he was mistaken. Yet he did manage, eight years after winning power in Germany, to make war on Moscow and begin a Final Solution.

For Hitler's worldview to change the world, he had to become a new type of politician, practicing a new type of politics. For anarchy in theory to become extermination in practice, the German state had to be refashioned, and neighboring states had to be destroyed. For the Jews of Europe to be murdered, the states destroyed had to be the ones where Jews were citizens. The vast majority of European Jews lived beyond Germany, the largest number of them in Poland. Poland was not only the major homeland of the Jews, but also the country that separated Germany from the

Soviet Union. In one way or another, Poland had to figure in Hitler's plans to destroy the Jews and the Soviet state.

In the six years after Hitler came to power, he succeeded in altering the German state, but failed to recruit a Polish partner for his wars. Had Poland and Germany fought as allies against the Soviet Union in 1939, the result would no doubt have been disastrous for the Jews of Europe. The Holocaust as we know it, however, followed instead a German-Soviet war against Poland. That the Second World War began as and when it did—as a campaign of state destruction and national extermination against Poland in September 1939—was a result of Hitler's success at home, his failure to sway Poland to his dream of foreign conquest, and the willingness of the Soviet leadership to join in a war of aggression.

At first glance, a German-Polish alliance would seem more plausible than a German-Soviet alliance. The Nazis and the Soviets spent the second half of the 1930s in a vituperative contest of propaganda, each presenting the other as the ultimate evil. Warsaw and Berlin seemed, by contrast, to have much in common. From 1935 to 1938, both Germany and Poland were central European states pressing territorial claims on their neighbors while boasting a grand rhetoric of global transformation. Leaders in both Berlin and Warsaw faulted the world order for constraining flows of food, raw materials, and human beings. Both placed the Jewish question at the center of their diplomatic rhetoric, suggesting that its resolution in Europe was a matter of international justice. Both emphasized the threat of Soviet communism.

Often the German decision to attack Poland in 1939 is explained in the terms provided by Hitler and his propagandists: by Berlin's campaign for adjustments to the border, or by Warsaw's resistance to them. This had almost nothing to do with it. In fact, the war between Germany and Poland resulted from deep differences on the Jewish and Soviet questions that were shrouded for years by Polish diplomacy. Hitler was willing to treat Warsaw as an ally in his grander campaigns against Moscow and against Jews, and also willing to destroy it entirely when such an alliance came to seem implausible, as it did in early 1939. Either way, Hitler saw Poland only as an element in his own master plan: as a helper in his grand eastern war, or as a territory from which that war could be launched. Hitler gave much more thought to the first variant than to the second, which was an improvisation that followed rapidly upon the surprising failure of German-Polish diplomacy in early 1939. All the while, Poland was an actor with its own aims and purposes. Germany and Poland ended up thwarting each other because German and Polish foreign policy were built upon a very different analysis of global politics and the role of the state.

Berlin's global position after Hitler's rise to power might be characterized as *recolonial*. Empires as such were just and good; the best empires were racial; Britain and America were rival exemplars of racial mastery; a German empire would restore balance to the world. The globe was naturally a world of competing empires; what was unnatural was the existence of a Jewish empire—the Soviet Union—and Jewish influence in London, Washington, Paris, and elsewhere. Germany would make a redeemingly racial empire by displacing a decadent Jewish dominion. In Hitler's mind, Poland's place in such a recolonial project was to help Germany: during the war as an ally or benign neutral, afterward as a satellite or puppet. In this conception no violent changes in the German-Polish border were needed, since Poland could grant territory to Germany in exchange for some of the booty in their joint conquest of the USSR. In the end this would be meaningless since Poland would fall under the thrall of Germany during the war itself.

Warsaw's global attitude, by contrast, might be called *decolonial*. Poland's history was one of destruction of an ancient Polish-Lithuanian Commonwealth by surrounding empires in 1795 and the creation of a nation-state in 1918. As Poles saw matters, empires had no special legitimacy, and as a matter of historical logic and justice were giving way to nation-states. Empires might be destroyed, as the Nazis thought; but if so, they would be replaced by nation-states rather than racial regimes. All nations were more or less equal actors in history, striving towards freedom. Most leading Polish politicians were attached to the nation-state as an intrinsic value and a collective achievement of the recent past. The unglamorous conservative definition of the state, the monopolist of violence and the enforcer of laws, was for many Poles a precious and unlikely achievement. No Polish leader, despite a grandiosity of rhetoric about foreign policy, imagined that Poland would displace one of the world powers.

Unlike Hitler and some of the Nazis, the Polish leadership had no theory about the secret leadership of the USSR or all empires by Jews, and no illusions about the hidden fragility of the great powers. The imperial system, of which the USSR was a more or less normal part, would eventually give way to national liberation. In the meantime, maritime empires such as Britain and France had to open themselves to the resettlement of millions of Polish Jews. Warsaw hoped that Polish Jews would rebel against empires and form Polish-Jewish states that would somehow extend Polish influence in any site of settlement—least implausibly Palestine. Israel was as far as Warsaw's dreaming went.

Both Berlin and Warsaw supported the removal of millions of Jews from Europe. For Hitler, this was part of a vast project of ecological restoration, in which the elimination of Jews after a German victory would repair the planet. The German state was a means to an end; it could and would be mutated and then put at risk. Antisemitism likely had more popular resonance in Poland than in Germany, at least before 1933, but no one with ideas similar to Hitler's came close to achieving power in Warsaw. Whereas German policy involved the destruction of states where Jews lived, Polish policy sought the creation of a state for the Jews. The covert essence of German foreign policy in the late 1930s was the ambition to build a vast racial empire in eastern Europe; the covert essence of Polish foreign policy was to create a State of Israel in Palestine from the territories granted by a League of Nations mandate to the British Empire.

The Nazi recolonial and the Polish decolonial mindsets were each, in their different ways, quite radical. Each was a challenge to the imperial order as it stood, the first envisioning its refoundation on the racial principle, the second its inevitable replacement by postcolonial states. The foreign policies they generated could seem rather similar, especially to a *Führer* in Berlin who thought that he needed allies. At a crucial level of political theory, however, the opposition could hardly have been more basic: rejection versus endorsement of the traditional state.

This fundamental difference in attitudes about the state arose in large measure from opposing experiences and interpretations of the First World War. It was a basic cause of the Second. For Polish patriots, 1918 was a year of miracles, when an independent Polish state, absent from the maps of Europe for more than a century, arose again. For Germans, 1918 was a year of the unimaginable military defeat, followed in 1919 by the Treaty of Versailles and humiliating territorial concessions—largely to the new Poland.

After the failure of his coup, Hitler learned to be politic, using the energy of German resentment to further his own extraordinary ambitions. He exploited the broad German consensus in favor of revising the European political order, even though his own goal was to destroy it. He presented himself as a determined advocate of national self-determination, even though he did not actually believe in national rights. Likewise, he learned to soften his presentation of the Jewish menace. He no longer said in public that Christianity was as Jewish as Bolshevism. German Christians would be allowed to modify their doctrine rather than be forced to abandon it, as they were drawn into the larger struggle that would drain it of all meaning. To Hitler, his fellow Germans were of interest only insofar as they could be rallied to join a mindless war for future racial prosperity. In other words, Germans were disappointingly frivolous as they pursued their petty preoccupations of the Weimar Republic of the 1920s. Hitler could hardly tell them that, and he did not.

After his release from prison, Hitler still sounded radical by comparison with the ruling German social democrats or traditional conservatives, but now his radicalism was in dialogue with political rivals and meant to attract German voters. Success came in the early 1930s, when the world economy was in depression, and capitalism and communism alike seemed to have failed. This left an opening for National Socialists to present capitalism and communism as mad and doomed alternatives and themselves as rescuers rather than as revolutionaries. Hitler did not emphasize at this time, as he had in *My Struggle,* that only the extermination of Jews could preserve Germans and the world from the two supposedly Jewish systems. In his election campaigns of 1932 and 1933, Hitler instead presented his own National Socialism as a recipe for stability and common sense to be contrasted to the insanity of capitalist and communist ideology.

In reality, National Socialism involved the aspiration to destroy communism in order to build a massive empire that would insulate Germany from the vicissitudes of global capitalism; there was nothing remotely conservative about that aim. Hitler presented his anti-communism not as a

WESTERN U.S.S.R.
1924
NORWAY
Oslo
SWEDEN
Stockholm
FINLAND
Helsinki
Petrograd
Tallinn
ESTONIA
Novgorod
North Sea
DENMARK
Copenhagen
Baltic Sea
LATVIA
Riga
Moscow
LITHUANIA
Kaunas
Wilno
Smolensk
U.S.S.R.
RUSSIAN S.F.S.R.
Volga
NETHERLANDS
Amsterdam
Hamburg
Danzig
Königsberg
Suwałki
Minsk
Białystok
BELARUSIAN S.S.R.
Berlin
Poznań
Warsaw
Łódź
POLAND
Kursk
BELGIUM
Rhine
GERMANY
Dresden
Don
Luxembourg
Łuck
Kyiv
Kharkiv
Tsaritsyn
Prague
Cracow
Lwów
Zhytomyr
Dnipro
CZECHOSLOVAKIA
UKRAINIAN S.S.R.
FRANCE
Danube
Kamianets-Podilskyi
Stalino
Munich
Vienna
Bratislava
Rostov
SWITZERLAND
AUSTRIA
Budapest
HUNGARY
Chisinau
Odessa
ROMANIA
Crimea (R.F.S.R.)
Venice
Trieste
YUGOSLAVIA
Belgrade
Bucharest
ITALY
Sarajevo
Danube
Black Sea
TRANSCAUCASIAN S.F.S.R.

military crusade against a great power, but as concern for the bottom line of German businesses and the full bellies of the electorate. In spring 1933, as the Soviet introduction of collective agriculture starved millions of peasants, Hitler used the specter of hunger to discourage Germans from voting for the Left. When he spoke at the Berlin *Sportpalast* of "millions of people being starved," he was appealing to the middle classes and their fears. When he continued by saying that Soviet Ukraine "could be a grain silo for the entire world," he was speaking to his Nazi followers. He veiled one sense of *Lebensraum,* the bloody conquest of habitat, behind the other, the promise of physical comfort.

In 1933, Hitler emerged triumphant from democratic elections during a long German constitutional crisis that had already centralized power in the office of the chancellor. His National Socialist party, which had won only twelve seats in parliament in 1928, claimed a staggering 230 in July 1932, falling to 196 in November 1932. Hitler was named chancellor of a coalition government in January 1933, supported by conservatives and nationalists who believed that they could control him. This was an error. Hitler used the arson of the parliament building in February to limit the rights of German citizens and create a permanent state of exception that permitted him to rule without parliamentary oversight.

In the weeks and months of Hitler's consolidation of power in spring 1933, his followers carried out pogroms and organized a boycott of Jewish-owned businesses. The fifty thousand or so Polish Jews in Germany were not subject to these repressions; their Polish citizenship protected them, as it would for the next five years, from Nazi oppression. This was all the more notable in that Polish Jews in Poland organized a counterboycott, refusing to trade with Germany. The boycotts and beatings of German Jews were barbarous in appearance, again by comparison with what had come before. But they were a weak foretaste of the political Armageddon that Hitler had in mind. He would need a war, and a special kind of war. For that he needed not just power in Germany, but also a reconfiguration of German power.

After Hitler's rise in 1933, he pursued domestic policy for more than six years before he began his first war. This is a long time without armed struggle for a man whose theory urgently demanded blood sacrifice for the restoration of nature. Hitler had learned tactics and even a certain kind of tact after the failure of his 1923 coup, but his electoral gambits did not qualify as a program. Disguising one's own ultimate aims to gain power is not the same thing as making daily decisions once power has been won. Hitler was no believer in institutions and could hardly have been satisfied simply by turning German administrative organs to his own purposes. He was not even a German nationalist. In his view, Germans were presumptively superior to all others, but the hierarchy was to be established in practice, by racial war. He would need special measures to direct Germans towards that war, and unusual techniques to direct their state to the purposes of generating anarchy.

These were mammoth tasks; his tactics were equal to them.

An initial inspiration, according to Hitler himself, was the *Balkan Model.* Like a number of other politicians of his era, he saw in the Balkan nation-states that had emerged from the declining Ottoman Empire in the nineteenth century the proper relationship between domestic and foreign policies. Serbia and the other Balkan states had shown how to achieve "a specific foreign policy goal" through "military conflicts." Balkan-style militarism featured a specific political economy. The leaders of nation-states with limited internal markets and primarily agricultural exports wanted larger economies. The justification for extending the national territory was the liberation of fellow nationals abandoned on the wrong side of the border. At home, voters were told that war was liberation; in fact, expansion broadened the tax base. The only purpose of domestic politics, Hitler claimed, was to mobilize the energy and resources necessary for achieving living space abroad.

Hitler was, to a point, a Balkan-style militarist. The case he made at home and abroad for the need to expand the military was the classic Balkan one of self-determination. Domestic politics thus became the art of accumulating resources and manipulating opinion such that war became possible and seemed inevitable. Although Hitler did not seem to personally care very much about the plight of Germans abroad, he recognized that nationalism of this kind could mobilize German emotion. Hitler built up the German armed forces beyond all previous limits and apparently beyond reason. Compulsory military service was reintroduced in 1935, and military budgets grew extraordinarily from year to year. In creating his war machine, Hitler accumulated debt that could be covered only by war, a condition that itself became an argument for the initiation of one. The old dilemma of budget priorities—guns or butter—could be solved in traditional Balkan style: butter through guns. As Hitler put it, "from the distress of war grows the bread of freedom."

He respected the Balkan Model but saw it as a first step rather than a final achievement. Although Hitler needed to control the German state, its expansion was not really his goal; although he understood the uses of German nationalism he was not really a nationalist. The national sentiments of his fellow Germans were what he called a "space-conquering force" that could propel them into the racial struggle where they could see and fulfill their higher destiny. Love of country had to be mobilized to get German men out of the country and into alien realms that they could master. As one German woman who understood Hitler would put it, the "inclination towards confined spaces clings like a sticky mass to the German people and must be overcome." For the far greater ambition of *Lebensraum,* Hitler introduced seven innovations to the Balkan Model: the *party-state,* the *entrepreneurship of violence,* the *export of anarchy,* the *hybridization of institutions,* the *production of statelessness,* the *globalization of German Jews,* and the *redefinition of war.*

Unlike the Balkan leaders to whom he paid a grudging respect, Hitler was not a king innovating from established notions of legitimacy and sovereignty. He was not the dynastic embodiment of a people with duties or interests, but rather a clear-sighted representative—as he saw matters—of a race doomed to bloody struggle until eternity. The apostle of nature had to accommodate traditional institutions to his own vision of the future, which meant transforming them before he made war. Beginning from the legal position of chancellor within a faltering republic, inheriting a host of institutions, Hitler and the Nazis created something new.

The theoretical reconciliation between the old and the new Germany was the *party-state.* Such a synthesis had been pioneered by Lenin in the Soviet Union a decade earlier. The Soviet state was present in every way a state might be: with an administration, a parliament, a judiciary, a government, an executive, even a constitution. In fact, the Soviet state was subordinate to the communist party, which was itself supposed to represent the workers and their interests. The communist party, in turn, was run by a central committee, which was run by a politburo of a few men and indeed usually dominated by a single man. Lenin had the advantages and disadvantages of revolution; Hitler's party did not. Thus the Nazi assimilation of state to party, the *Gleichschaltung,* took place gradually.

In 1934, Hitler was officially titled "*Führer* and Reich Chancellor." This vague designation indicated that Hitler was the head of a racial body as well as the head of government. Hitler was a racial colonialist in theory and an opponent of the Weimar Republic in practice. In the name of racial consolidation he destroyed the republic's basic freedoms and mocked its constitution. And yet its bureaucrats generally considered Hitler's rule as a legitimate continuity of administration.

Of course, the very notion of a party-state was self-contradictory. The Nazi party was founded on the assumption of endless racial conflict, whereas any traditional state asserts the right to control and limit violence. Conflict had to be maintained but at the same time channeled. The existence of the party-state depended, therefore, on Hitler's second innovation, the *entrepreneurship of violence.*

The classic definition of the state, provided by the German sociologist Max Weber, is the institution that seeks to monopolize legitimate violence. In the 1920s and the early 1930s, Hitler sought to discredit the Weimar Republic by demonstrating that it could not, in fact, do this. His armed guards, known as the SA and SS, functioned before his takeover of 1933 as de-monopolizers of violence. When they beat opponents or started brawls, they were demonstrating the weakness of the existing system. Following the example of Benito Mussolini after his rise to power in Italy, Hitler kept his paramilitaries after he himself had won power. Often after a revolution the professional miscreants are subordinated to the state and become servants of order rather than its violators. But the SA and SS remained party organizations even after the state had been won. Although their members wore uniforms and had ranks, these did not indicate a particular place in a state hierarchy. The SA and SS were organizations of power, but not of a power confined by a conventional state. Their final authority was the good of the race, as defined by their *Führer.* After the takeover of 1933, they became entrepreneurs of violence, looking for ways and means of murder that would serve the larger project of racial empire even as the German state came under Nazi control.

Yet this innovation, in its turn, posed a basic problem: How could the entrepreneurs propagate violence in Germany when what Hitler needed was a foreign war, and thus the strength within Germany to fight? How much blood could be shed in the very country that Hitler needed as his base for his global war in the name of race? If people accustomed to violence were to be trained in violence, where would that training be put to use? The rulers of the Soviet Union had earlier faced the same problems, and solved them elegantly. The conflict required by theory was to continue, but not on the lands controlled by the theorists. The communist party was meant to guide the workers through painful class conflict, but of course after the revolution such a thing could not be admitted to exist with the Soviet Union itself. The Bolsheviks therefore maintained that their state was a peaceful homeland of socialism that provided an example of future harmony for the rest of the world. Soviet foreign policy worked from the assumption that class conflict beyond the Soviet Union would eventually bring down world capitalism, and generate new allies. In the meantime, it was reasonable and legitimate for Soviet foreign policy to encourage this historical process. In other words, Soviet authorities monopolized violence within their own country, and exported the revolution.

Hitler's third innovation, *anarchy for export,* was a similar solution to the conundrum of legitimizing and cultivating violence while preserving one's own authority. After 1933, Nazi Germany was chiefly a base for further operations abroad, which would then transform Germany itself. German institutions were altered in part to transform Germans, but mainly to prepare the way for an unprecedented kind of violence beyond Germany. The revolution would proceed abroad, and when complete it would redeem Germans and allow them to elevate their own country. The German state had to be preserved precisely to allow the destruction of other states, an achievement that would establish the new racial order.

The outlines of this solution emerged in June 1934, a little more than a year after Hitler seized power, in the defeat of one set of violent entrepreneurs, the larger and more populist *Sturmabteilung* (SA), by another, the more elite bodyguard initially known as the *Schutzstaffel* (SS). The SA and its leader Ernst Röhm were faithful to Nazi ideology in its literal, antipolitical reading. Röhm imagined that his SA men would become a new kind of army, fomenting revolution inside Germany and abroad. He spoke of a second revolution to follow Hitler's takeover of 1933. Hitler, by contrast, understood that a period of political transformation in Germany would have to precede the completion of the revolution by foreign war. In the Night of the Long Knives, the SS arrested and executed Röhm and other leaders of the SA, while propaganda denounced the victims as homosexuals. As so often in Nazi actions, the apparent conservatism was a cover for something truly radical. The legal theorist Carl Schmitt explained that Hitler was protecting the one true law, that of the race, by asserting himself against law as conventionally understood. By suppressing the SA, Hitler was able to appease the commanders of the German armed forces, who had seen the SA as a threat.

Whereas the SA had stood for Hitler's youthful anarchism, the SS understood the need for a new sort of racial politics, radical but patient. The SS was not a direct rival to the German army nor a threat to order in Germany. Its commander Heinrich Himmler followed Hitler in seeing Germany as a realm of politics where change would come gradually. Rather than making claims for revolutionary power within Germany, then, the SS would take part in the destruction of states beyond Germany. This involved a future division of labor with the army rather than a present competition. The existence of useful German institutions had to be squared with the desirability of the law of the jungle; actions taken in the present in Germany had to prepare the way for the future conflict that was National Socialism's essence. The German army would prepare the way by defeating armies, and then the SS would restore the natural racial order by destroying states and eliminating human beings.

This mission of deferred supremacy allowed the young men who joined the SS to reconcile racism with elitism, and careerism with a sense of destiny. They could believe that they were defending what was best in

Germandom even as the existence of their organization transformed the German state.

After its triumph in the Night of the Long Knives, the SS implemented Hitler's fourth innovation, the *hybridization of institutions.* Crime was redefined; racial and state organizations were merged; and cadres were rotated back and forth. In 1935, in a significant reform, Himmler explicitly redefined the SS and the police apparatus as a single organ of racial protection. Himmler, who served a racial movement rather than a traditional state, personally directed both the SS and the German police from 1936. The investigative service of the SS, known as the *Sicherheitsdienst* (SD), proposed a new definition of political crime. It was not crime against the state; the state had validity only insofar as it represented the race. Since politics was nothing but biology, political crime was a crime against the German race. Himmler's deputy Reinhard Heydrich, whom Hitler called the "man with the iron heart," directed the SD.

In 1937, Himmler established the Higher SS and Police Leaders, a new top level of authority that would unify the two chains of commands under a few men chosen by and subordinate to Himmler. These new positions would become significant in territories beyond Germany during war. The Higher SS and Police Leaders were constrained by the thicket of police institutions and laws in Germany itself; later they could develop a new political order in the East without such encumbrances. In September 1939, Heydrich was placed at the head of a new institution known as the Reich Security Main Office, which unified his SD (a party and racial institution) with the Security Police (a state institution). It was Heydrich who would be charged with creating the *Einsatzgruppen* (task forces) that would follow German troops into conquered terrains. The *Einsatzgruppen* were also hybrid organizations, mixing SS members and others. The police forces themselves were hybridized from within, as police officers were recruited to the SS while SS officers were assigned to the police. The secret state police (Gestapo), the detectives of the Criminal Police (Kripo), and even the regular uniformed Order Police (Orpo) were to become Himmler's racial warriors.

Among the limited responsibilities of the SS in prewar Germany were the concentration camps, small stateless zones inside Germany itself. This *precedent of statelessness* was Hitler's fifth innovation. Himmler established the first camp at Dachau in 1933 as a place where the National Socialist party (as opposed to the German state) could punish people—extralegally, as party leaders deemed necessary. The political enemy and the social enemy were the racial enemy, and the camps were to hold all of these groups. Placing socialists, communists, political dissidents, homosexuals, criminals, and people presented as "work-shy" in the camps separated them from the normal protections of the state, and filtered them from the German national community. Their labor would help prepare Germany for a war that would destroy other states.

The most important aspect of the camps was the precedent they set. The concentration camp system within Germany in the 1930s was not very expansive—German colonial facilities in the 1890s were comparable, and the contemporary Soviet Gulag was more than a hundred times larger. German camps were chiefly important as a demonstration that organs of coercion could be separated by the *Führer*'s will and barbed wire from the law and the state. In this sense the concentration camps were training grounds for the more general SS mission beyond Germany: the destruction of states by racial institutions. Death rates in whole east European countries, in places where the SS would destroy the state, would be much higher than death rates in German concentration camps in the 1930s.

Hitler's sixth political innovation was the *globalization of German Jews.* In reality, Jews were a very small part of the population of Germany, under one percent. Most Jews were assimilated to German society in language and culture; indeed, the German high culture of the early twentieth century, including much of the modernism that remains celebrated today, was in significant measure a creation of Jews. Most Germans did not see Jews in their daily life, and were not particularly good at distinguishing Jews from non-Jews. To make a new racial optic was to consolidate the German national community, the *Volksgemeinschaft.*

After Hitler's takeover, membership in the German state followed the rules of membership in the Nazi party. In 1933, Jews were banned from public service and from serving as lawyers. By the terms of the Nuremberg Laws of 1935, Jews became second-class citizens. For the Nazi legal theorist Carl Schmitt, these laws were part of a "constitution of liberty," since they embodied the arbitrary distinction between friend and enemy that would make, in his view, normal politics possible. As of 1938, Jews could not exercise any commercial, medical, or juridical function in Germany. The steady disappearance of Jews from public life was meant to spur Jews to leave Germany and to revise the worldviews of Germans. In everyday life, measures directed against Jews forced Germans to think about Jews, to notice Jews, and to define themselves as "Aryans," as members of a group that excluded the Jews with whom they shared the country.

At the same time, Nazi propaganda aggressively included German Jews in an imaginary group, the international Jewish conspiracy. Often Jews were described not as individuals, but as members of *Weltjudentum*, world Jewry. When books were burned, the message was global: In Heidelberg those of "Jewish, Marxist, and similar origins" were put to the torch; in Göttingen books were set alight along with a sign bearing the name "Lenin," the founder of the Soviet state. In this way the Jew became the Bolshevik, the union consummated by the very act of burning. Not so very much later it would be not books but Jews themselves who would be burned bearing such signs.

The globalization of the German Jew in the 1930s was an important but limited achievement. The Jew, as Hitler saw matters, remained inside the German. The extraction of the Jew from the German could be achieved only by removing Jews from the planet, something that could not yet be articulated in any precise way. Experience would later show that for Jews to be killed, they would first have to be physically removed from Germany. With a few hundred exceptions, Germans would not kill German Jews on the territory of their common prewar homeland. Germans beyond Germany, invading and occupying neighboring countries, and meeting Jews in places where political authority had been removed and the Jews had no protection, often described them in the impersonal way prescribed by propaganda. Jews beyond Germany were the overwhelming majority of the victims of the Holocaust. The globalization of racism succeeded when combined with world war.

Hitler's final innovation was the *redefinition of war.* His version of militarism went beyond preparation for conventional wars, as in the Balkans. He intended not just to take territory that might be portrayed as ethnically contiguous, as in the Balkan Model, but to destroy entire states and master entire races. "Our border," as the SS slogan went, "is blood." In 1938, Hitler did away with the position of minister of war, and took personal command of the armed forces. Himmler, Göring, Heydrich, and the other Nazi leaders planned a war of extermination, starvation, and colonization in eastern Europe.

Oddly, this planning was not directed against Germany's actual eastern neighbor. Poland was unimportant in Hitler's writings of the 1920s and visible only as a desired ally in his policies after the seizure of power in 1933. This seems stranger still in light of the fact that Poland is where the Jews of Europe chiefly lived. About ten times as many Jews were citizens of Poland as were citizens of Germany. There were about as many Jews in individual Polish cities such as Warsaw and Łódź as there were Jewish citizens of Germany. And of course Poland was the country that lay between Germany and the Soviet Union, where Hitler's true revolution was to be made.

A war was always the object of Hitler's policy. The fact that one took place was above all a result of his designs and achievements within Germany. Yet Hitler made a mistake about Poland, imagining it only as an instrument in a larger German enterprise. Instead, Poland behaved as a political agent, a sovereign state.

The German calamity of 1918 was a Polish miracle. Virtually everything about the outcome of the First World War that was threatening for Germans was exhilarating for Poles. The Treaty of Versailles of 1919, a symbol of injustice in Germany, was a pillar of the legal order in which an independent Poland could exist. When German troops withdrew from the East, a new Polish army could fill the power vacuum. Poles fought the Red Army for the lands that had been German client states. Poland won the Polish-Bolshevik War, and the Treaty of Riga of 1921 established Poland's eastern border with the Soviet Union.

Poland was a new state drawing together territories from three former empires: Russian, Habsburg, and German. Jews were present in large numbers in almost the entire country, so interaction with them was a part of daily life for the other citizens of Poland. Jews were most of the doctors, lawyers, and traders, and so mediated in contacts with the broader worlds of knowledge, power, and money. Jews paid more than a third of the taxes in Poland, and firms owned by Jews were responsible for about half of the foreign trade. There were about as many assimilated Jews in Poland as there were in Germany; the difference was that for every assimilated Polish Jew there were ten more who spoke Yiddish and were religiously observant in one traditional form or another. Jews in Poland had parallel systems of schooling, a parallel press, and a parallel party system.

The question of loyalty to the Polish state was not resolved simply by answers to census questions about language or religion. It is to yield to ethnic nationalism to imagine that all people who spoke only Polish identified with the Polish state and that people of other backgrounds necessarily did not. Not everyone who spoke Polish was loyal to the new state or even identified with it. Most Poles were peasants, and most peasants awaited some gesture from the state that would arouse their loyalty. The Polish countryside was massively overpopulated, and rural unemployment was staggeringly high. Land reform was halting and insufficient. Rather than redistributing land from the large estates, the Polish state acted as a broker in negotiations for purchases and a source of credit for purchases. Peasants were dissatisfied by slow transactions, and hurt when credits were withdrawn during the Depression. Most peasants wanted both their own plot of land and their traditional rights to shared use of common land, desires that were contradictory in ideology but understandable in practice. When all land was treated as private property with defined owners, ancient rights to the use of pastures and forests could not be enforced. Polish peasants had been immigrating to America in large numbers for half a century, but in the 1920s and 1930s new American laws held them back. Independent Poland assimilated and integrated large numbers of peasants, but had to deal with considerable dissatisfaction in the countryside.

Polish patriotism spread outward from the intelligentsia, a large social group mostly composed of the children of noble landholders and of the rising middle classes, including the children of prosperous Jews. Polish political society was divided into two major orientations with opposing ideas about the design and purposes of the new polity. The most popular movement among Poles was known as National Democracy and led by Roman Dmowski. It favored land reform but only insofar as this helped Poles rather than Ukrainians and Belarusians, who were in some eastern regions of Poland more numerous and just as poor or poorer. The second major formation, descending from the Polish Socialist Party of Józef Piłsudski, supported land reform in principle, but in power yielded to the voices of the noble landholders it came to see as bastions of the state.

The differences between the two movements on the national and Jewish questions were fundamental. The National Democrats began from the idea that Polish traditions of toleration had doomed the old Polish-Lithuanian Commonwealth in the eighteenth century, and that only ethnic Poles could be trusted. National Democrats tended to emphasize the need to create a nation from Polish-speaking peasants, to regard Ukrainians and other Slavs (perhaps a quarter of the population) as possibly assimilable, but to see Jews (about a tenth of the population) as foreigners. Although the movement was founded by secular nonbelievers influenced by a Social Darwinist conception of life as struggle, with time it assimilated traditional religious antisemitic ideas, such as the responsibility of Jews for the death of Jesus. Like the Roman Catholic Church, National Democrats tended to associate Jews with Bolshevism. The significant presence of Jews in Poland made antisemitism more politically salient there than in Germany, but it also made it more difficult for antisemites such as Dmowski to present Jews in an entirely uniform, stereotyped way. Although conspiratorial thinking and the Judeobolshevik conception were certainly present in religious and secular propaganda, Polish antisemites tended to think of Jews as a Polish rather than a planetary problem.

Dmowski's opponent, Józef Piłsudski, began his conception of politics from the state rather than from the nation. He tended to value the traditions of the old Polish-Lithuanian Commonwealth, and to believe that its legacy of toleration was still applicable. He saw individuals as citizens of the state, with reciprocal obligations. He began as a socialist revolutionary, and even as he moved away from his youthful ideals he maintained the conviction that revolutionary violence was justified. Though his supporters were probably less numerous than Dmowski's, he usually had the tactical advantage of the initiative. Whereas Dmowski tended to think that the Polish nation had to be raised from its peasant roots before statehood could be achieved, Piłsudski was ready to rally the forces that were available at any given time.

Piłsudski's moment was the First World War. He had prepared for a European crisis by organizing Legions within the Habsburg monarchy. The idea was to fight alongside the regular Habsburg forces as long as that seemed to promise political gains for Poles within the multinational empire, and then use the military training for other purposes if and when it seemed warranted. While empires collapsed he also organized a secret Polish Military Organization tasked with winning independence and favorable borders. Piłsudski was able to take power in Warsaw and even lead a victorious war against Lenin's revolutionary state in 1919–1920. What he could not do was persuade a majority of Poles to accept his version of the state. An old socialist comrade, Gabriel Narutowicz, was elected Poland's first president and then was promptly assassinated by a nationalist fanatic. Piłsudski then withdrew from the politics of the state he had done much to create.

When Piłsudski returned to power, in 1926, it was by coup d'état against both the National Democratic Right and its dominance in Polish society, and against the threat of a communist Left which, he thought, the National Democrats only aided with their chauvinism. Rather than altering the constitution of the Polish republic, he manipulated its institutions, finding ways to generate pliable majorities in parliament. He formed an electoral entity, the Non-Party Bloc for Cooperation with the Government, which was supported by the national minorities, including traditional Jews. The orthodox Jewish party Agudat Yisrael became a bastion of support of his regime. Synagogues adopted resolutions to vote for Piłsudski's Bloc, and rabbis led their followers to the urns. Some of the people who ran the Bloc were secular Jews and Ukrainians.

Piłsudski brought a fake democracy combined with a pinch of renewed liberalism. His maintenance of the appearance of democratic procedures after 1926 was meant to preserve a sense of legitimacy while keeping the National Democrats from winning power. His authoritarian regime perhaps held off the worst. The years between Piłsudski's coup and his death saw world economic collapse, the rise of the Far Right across Europe, Hitler's seizure of power and the beginning of the *Gleichschaltung,* and Joseph Stalin's consolidation of power and the famines of Soviet collectivization. Piłsudski treated the state, in what was becoming an old-fashioned way, as the equal preserve of all citizens. His governments removed all legal discriminations against Jews, and created a legal basis for the local Jewish communes responsible for religious and cultural affairs.

Piłsudski's fundamental respect for the state, as opposed to Hitler's basic disdain for it, was visible in the fate of the organizations that Piłsudski had used to seize power. Just as Hitler had his SA and his SS, Piłsudski had his Legions and his Polish Military Organization. But the men and women who served in these Polish paramilitary formations were integrated into conventional state institutions, either after the war or when Piłsudski returned to power in 1926. Most of the men and women Piłsudski trusted in power had served in the Legions or the Polish Military Organization. They were sometimes involved in conspiracies of Piłsudski's making, but formed no alternative structure based in aspirations to zoological anarchy or the supposed superiority of their race (some of them, in any event, were Jewish). Veterans of the organizations certainly indulged in the romantic myth of Piłsudski as the savior of the nation, and in the general cult of secular messianism that was the spiritual element of his sort of patriotism. The essential idea was that Poles suffered on this earth so that Poles and others might be liberated—also on this earth.

With time, these ideas became nostalgic rather than energizing, as the Polish independence won in 1918 came under increasing threat from both east and west. By 1933, when Hitler came to power, Piłsudski's old comrades in arms—now diplomats, spies, and soldiers—were preoccupied with the state mainly as an achievement that had to be preserved from both Berlin and Moscow.

Józef Piłsudski was an enemy of the Soviet Union. He had beaten the Red Army on the battlefield in the Polish-Bolshevik War, and he regarded Stalin as a bandit. His feelings about the USSR, unlike Hitler's, were shaped by personal knowledge of the Russian Empire. Hitler, who exhibited strong convictions about Russian history and racial character, did not know the Russian language and never visited the Russian Empire or the USSR. Piłsudski was born a Russian imperial subject, and had learned to curse in Russian during five years of political exile in Irkutsk—a habit he retained to the end of his life. Piłsudski had been across the Ural Mountains, which for Hitler were as mythical as the Hyperboreans; Piłsudski had been deported to Siberia, where Hitler dreamed of deporting Jews.

For Piłsudski neither Russia nor the Left was an abstraction. As a student in Kharkiv in 1886, he moved with the Russian revolutionary populists of Narodnaia Volia, the movement that would inspire the Bolsheviks of the next generation. A year later his older brother plotted with Lenin's older brother in a conspiracy to assassinate the tsar. Piłsudski was accused of involvement as well, and sentenced to five years of Siberian exile. Upon his return he helped to establish the illegal Polish Socialist Party and edited its newspaper, *The Worker*. He was a Russian revolutionary, in that he and his comrades operated in an illegal underground along with Russians, Jews, and socialists of all possible origins in the Russian Empire.

Piłsudski was perfectly aware that there were Jews on the Left: Jews in the Russian socialist movement who opposed Polish independence; Jews who wanted Jewish autonomy with whom he cooperated; Jews in his own Polish Socialist Party. Jews were among the comrades and friends of his political youth and, in some measure, his political maturity. He knew the Polish Jews and other Poles who took part in the Bolshevik Revolution. These were, for him, individuals with names and pasts who had made a terrible mistake. He himself believed that statehood had to precede socialism. During and after the First World War he plotted with and fought alongside numerous Jewish members of his Legions and Polish Military Organization. In his circles the Judeobolshevik idea was known to be a folly. The Soviet Union was an actual foreign threat, whereas the Jewish question was a matter of domestic politics.

Piłsudski and his comrades tended to see empires as incubators of nations, and progress as national liberation. As people who had themselves built an independent nation-state from territories of the defunct Russian Empire, they tended to believe that the same process could be repeated within the Soviet Union. The major national question, to their minds, was Ukraine. Whereas Hitler and the Nazis tended to see Ukraine as a zone for settler colonization, Piłsudski and his comrades saw it as a neighboring country and a possible political asset. Indeed, for many Polish leaders Ukraine was home. Piłsudski was from Lithuania, but he studied in eastern Ukraine. Many of Piłsudski's lieutenants were Poles from Ukraine, and much of the 1919–1920 war with the Bolsheviks had been fought there. Thousands of Poles from Ukraine had been killed in battle there, as had thousands of Poles who were not. Poles from Ukraine regarded the country sometimes sentimentally and often condescendingly, but always as a place inhabited by human beings. Unlike the Nazis, no Polish statesman could see Ukraine as a blank slate or as a land without people.

After Piłsudski's return to power in 1926, some of his old comrades in the foreign ministry and in military intelligence began a project known as Prometheanism. Named after the titan of Greek mythology who blessed humanity with light and cursed humanity with hope, this policy involved the support of oppressed nations against empires, and in particular the support of the Ukrainian cause in the Soviet Union. The USSR had been established as a union of formally national republics. Soviet leaders imagined that new non-Russian and non-Jewish elites could be recruited through an acknowledgment of the existence of the other nationalities combined with affirmative action. Their optimism was grounded in a Marxist faith about the future triumph of the working class and the socialism it would bring. The Polish Prometheans, working from a different scheme of history, saw the Soviet nations rather than social classes as the historical actors that, with proper support, might weaken the Soviet Union. Prometheanism was the hidden part of Polish foreign policy, funded from secret budgets and carried out by trusted men and women. Its centerpiece was Poland's most Ukrainian province, Volhynia, where for several years a Ukrainian culture was officially supported in order to attract the attention and sympathy of Ukrainians within the Soviet Union.

Naturally, support of national movements within the Soviet Union, and the whole Promethean idea, were thought to serve Polish interests. Even so, many of those who took part in them also believed that they were continuing a certain ethical tradition, one of sacrifices made by one nation for the good of all. Their liberal nationalism had been confirmed rather than challenged by the outcome of the First World War. The slogan from the romantic patriots of the nineteenth century was "For your freedom and ours!" All would make sacrifices, and all could triumph in the end.

Piłsudski was right to see the USSR as a solid political edifice and as a continual threat to Poland, but wrong to view it as a kind of updated Russian Empire. Hitler grasped its novelty and radicalism, but mistakenly reduced the ideas and aims of its leaders to Jewish world domination. Soviet ideologists presented Piłsudski and Hitler together as "fascists," which overlooked the very significant differences between an authoritarian defender of statehood and a warmongering biological anarchist. But Marxists were right to notice that the private property regime that prevailed in both Poland and Germany was so different from the Soviet system as to make communism almost impossible to understand in both Warsaw and Berlin.

The Soviet, Polish, and German systems can be defined by their relationship to land. Communists, like capitalists, had to confront the basic dilemma of maintaining stability in the countryside while satisfying urban populations. In the Soviet Union in the 1920s, those urban populations were a largely theoretical working class inhabiting largely unbuilt cities, to be fed by real peasants who in some places, such as Ukraine, were very attached to their real plots of land. The Nazis exported the land question, treating it as a matter of foreign conquest. Polish governments tried and failed to resolve it in a more or less legal way. Stalin faced the issue squarely and drew a logical conclusion: The existing Soviet peasant and countryside could and would give way to a future of workers and cities. The Poles had no glorious vision of a peasant utopia; the Nazi agrarian vision of *Lebensraum* depended upon a foreign triumph. The Soviets believed that their revolution could be made at home, the costs borne precisely by the large peasant class—people who had no place in socialism in any case.

In Moscow, Warsaw, and Berlin, the land question was always international as well as domestic. If Germany was recolonial, planning to seize lands from another empire, and Poland was decolonial, hoping to liberate other empires for the emigration of its citizens, the Soviet Union was *self-colonial.* Stalin wished to apply to his own subjects the policies that he believed imperialists applied to native peoples. Since the Soviet Union was isolated from the capitalist world and yet needed to match capitalist development, the only hope was to exploit the resources, including the people, to be found within Soviet borders. Since the Soviet Union was the largest country in the world, covering a sixth of its landmass, such thinking was plausible in Moscow as it was not in Berlin or Warsaw. The centerpiece of Stalin's self-colonization was the collectivization of agriculture that began in earnest in 1930: the seizure of private farmland and the transformation of some peasants into controlled agricultural laborers and others into workers in the city or in the camps.

This policy brought massive resistance and then massive starvation: first in Soviet Kazakhstan, where more than a million people died in a mad dash to pin nomads to plots of land, which the state then took from them almost immediately, and then in southern Soviet Russia and the entirety of Soviet Ukraine, productive territories where peasants lost their land to the collective. In the second half of 1932, Stalin treated the starvation in Ukraine as a political problem, blamed the Ukrainians themselves, and claimed that the whole crisis was a result of Polish intelligence work. The Soviet leadership that autumn and winter applied a series of specific policies to Soviet Ukraine that ensured that starvation deaths were concentrated there rather than elsewhere. About 3.3 million inhabitants of Soviet Ukraine died horrible and unnecessary deaths of starvation and disease in 1932 and 1933.

From the beginning of collectivization, thousands of peasants fled Soviet Ukraine across the Polish border, entire villages at a time, begging for a war of liberation. One peasant promised that if "a war were to begin the mood of the people is such that if the Polish army came everyone would kiss the feet of the Polish soldiers and attack the Bolsheviks." Another expressed the hope that "Poland or some other state would come as quickly as possible to free them from their misery and oppression." The summary report of the Polish border guards assigned to interview the Soviet refugees read as follows: "The population longs for armed intervention from Europe."

A deliberate mass starvation in one of the earth's most fertile regions could hardly escape notice. But the reactions in Warsaw and Berlin were quite different. Even as they chronicled starvation, Polish border guards and intelligence officers reported that Soviet forces assembled along the borders after the first wave of flights and enforced the starvation campaign. Contemplating the lethal and unmistakably modern policy of collectivization, Polish Prometheans began to ask themselves whether they had, in fact, understood the Soviet Union. Given this new uncertainty, some began to wonder whether their prior attempts to use the national question were politically and morally sound. Polish foreign policy changed course. Poland had agreed in 1931 to a Soviet proposal to discuss a treaty of nonaggression, and one was signed in July 1932. This separated Poland from its previous Ukrainian clients and from the Ukrainian question. This too had its moral hazards.

Polish diplomats in Soviet Ukraine, in evident moral distress, observed the consequences of collectivization. The consul in Kharkiv, then the capital of Soviet Ukraine, estimated that five million people had died of hunger, which was a low estimate for the Soviet Union as a whole and a slightly high one for Ukraine itself. In February 1933, he reported that men came to his office to weep about their starving wives and children. "On the streets" of Kharkiv, another diplomat wrote, "one sees people in the last throes and corpses." Hundreds of dead bodies were removed each night; residents of Kharkiv complained that the militia was not clearing them quickly enough. Polish intelligence reported, correctly, that the starvation was even worse in the villages. Peasants were fleeing the countryside for Kharkiv to beg on the streets. The militia tried to move them out of sight; the quota for the number of children to be seized each day was two thousand. Even as the death toll moved from the hundreds of thousands to the millions, the head of Polish military intelligence wrote in March 1933 that "we want to be loyal" to the arrangement with the Soviets, "even though they continually provoke and blackmail us."

The withdrawal of the Poles from the Ukrainian question could be experienced by Ukrainians themselves as a betrayal, as indeed it was. The leading Polish expert on the nationalities question recorded one consequence of the Soviet-Polish agreement: "The signing of the pact annulled the hope of rescue from abroad, and so Soviet power in the conviction of the mass population became the absolute master of life and death. This was confirmed by the fact of the massive extinction of the rural population in spring 1933." The last hope of Ukrainian peasants, as they themselves said, was a German invasion of the Soviet Union and the destruction of the Soviet order.

The Polish diplomats, accustomed to seeing nationality and loyalty as political matters, began to ask themselves how the Germans would manage Soviet Ukraine if they did invade at some later point. As one wrote, the Germans "will have to think long and hard about their material and moral approach to the local population, what the slogans will be and how they will be realized." These nuances would have escaped Hitler. He was planning to invade the Soviet Union and seize Ukraine, but with the goal of racial colonization rather than of national liberation. He did not see Ukrainians or Soviet citizens as subjects of politics, or even as full human beings.

The political famine in Soviet Ukraine realigned the foreign relations of the major regional powers, setting the stage for the Second World War. In 1930, as mass collectivization began, Stalin and the Soviet leadership were alarmed by the consequences of their own policies and sought peace talks with Piłsudski to avoid Polish intervention during the collectivization chaos. The Polish leadership, cutting defense budgets during the Great Depression and troubled by the moral implications of intervention, was agreeable. Moscow and Warsaw signed their treaty of nonaggression in July 1932. Berlin was very sensitive to the possibility that this pact might be directed against its interests. Piłsudski assigned his new foreign minister, Józef Beck, appointed in November 1932, to balance this agreement with a similar accord with Germany. This initiative was timely. Piłsudski had tried (and failed) to arouse interest in Europe for a preemptive action against Hitler. Hitler was interested in rapprochement with Warsaw. In January 1934, Berlin and Warsaw signed a declaration of nonaggression, agreeing that their common border would not be changed by force.

For Polish leaders in 1933 and 1934, facing the rise of both Hitler and

Stalin, preserving the status quo was an end in itself. For Berlin the declaration was a first step towards the grand plan of eastern war and colonization of Soviet territory. Hitler knew that peace with Poland was unpopular in Germany, but he did not care: He saw the German-Polish territorial questions as a springboard to future eastern empire. He expected that a deal could be reached whereby Poland would voluntarily concede some territories in exchange for lands gained from the Soviet Union. In that scenario, traditional German revanchists would get what they wanted—and be drawn into the war that Hitler wanted. After the joint declaration, anti-Polish disinformation disappeared from German newspapers. Joseph Goebbels, Berlin's master of propaganda, lectured in Warsaw on the challenging subject of "National Socialist Germany as an Element of European Peace"; Beck promised to prevent an international congress of Jewish organizations from meeting in Poland. Piłsudski, now an old man in faltering health, began to figure in German military publications as the genius who had shown, back in 1920, how the Red Army could be beaten in rapid encirclement battles. His memoirs were published in German with a munificent foreword by the minister of defense. Hitler wondered aloud about what it would take to draw the Poles into a full military alliance and told his generals that this was what he wanted and expected.

Moscow had its own interpretation of the diplomatic realignment brought about by the Ukrainian catastrophe. Whereas Warsaw saw the nonaggression agreements with both Moscow and Berlin as proof of a policy of supporting the status quo, and Berlin saw its engagement with Warsaw as pointing towards a common campaign against the Soviet Union, Moscow saw the German-Polish rapprochement as a sign that Poland and the Soviet Union would never be allies. In the European war that Stalin expected, Poland would be either hostile or neutral toward the USSR. This meant that Polish statehood was of no possible value to the Soviet Union, and should be eliminated when the occasion arose. It then transpired that the large Polish minority in the western reaches of the USSR had been hostages to the possibility of some future Soviet-Polish accord. Once Stalin ceased to believe that Poland could ever be a Soviet ally, Soviet citizens of Polish nationality became disposable. Poles in the Soviet Union could be blamed for Soviet policy failures (such as the famine in Ukraine) and punished accordingly.

In the five years between the signing of the German-Polish declaration in January 1934 and the clear break in German-Polish relations that would come in January 1939, Poles in the Soviet Union were subjected to a campaign of ethnic cleansing. The first wave of deportations of Soviet Poles from border regions of Soviet Ukraine and Soviet Belarus began a few weeks after the German-Polish declaration was signed and continued until 1936. Then Polish communists in the Soviet Union were depicted as participants in a vast Polish conspiracy to undo the Soviet order. Their interrogation led to the "discovery" of this "plot," which then became the justification for the Polish Operation of 1937 and 1938—the largest and bloodiest of the Soviet ethnic actions during the Great Terror of those years. More than a hundred thousand Soviet citizens were shot as ostensible Polish spies. This was the largest peacetime ethnic shooting campaign in history.

As the Polish Operation began, Stalin said that he wanted the "Polish-espionage slime" to be destroyed "in the interests of the USSR." When the chance came to destroy the Polish state itself, he would seize it. Poland was the home of Europe's largest Jewish population, more than three million people. The annihilation of their polity would be crucial to their fate.

3

The Promise of Palestine

Naturally, there were Polish spies in the Soviet Union in the 1930s, some of them on a rather unusual assignment. On June 8, 1935, Polish military intelligence ordered its officers in Soviet Ukraine to make tours of all the battlefields of the Polish-Bolshevik War of 1919–1920. Their task was not to prepare some new campaign, but to commemorate a past one. Józef Piłsudski had died the month before, and a small bag of earth from each of the battle sites was to be discreetly gathered for his burial mound.

The end of a political life reopened the issue of the character of the Polish state. Piłsudski's authority had been personal, and the old comrades ("the colonels") who wished to succeed him had to contend with popular politics at a time of economic depression. Piłsudski's old enemies, the National Democrats, chose to exploit popular antisemitism to mount a challenge to the regime that his associates established after his death. Their encouragement of pogroms, at the same time an act of racism and a violation of the law, was understood by both sides as an attack on the state. The new regime enjoyed greater formal powers than had Piłsudski himself, since it exploited an authoritarian constitution that had been conceived while he was still alive. Although most of his successors were not antisemitic by conviction themselves, they tried to ride out the challenge from the National Democrats by adopting antisemitic public policy. In so doing, Piłsudski's successors compromised the basic moral premise of his politics: that Poland was a state and not a race.

In 1935, responsibility for Jewish affairs was transferred from the ministry of internal affairs to the ministry of foreign affairs. Jews were no longer normal citizens to be integrated and protected by the state, but somehow aliens: a matter for the world at large, objects whose future might be negotiated with foreign officials. Piłsudski's electoral organization, which had been popular with Jews, was replaced by a party of power which excluded them. This new Camp of National Unity (Obóz Zjednoczenia Narodowego, OZON), created in 1937, announced its preference for the emigration of about ninety percent of Poland's Jews. Such policies, regarded as a loathsome betrayal of tradition and principle by much of the Polish Center and Left, were meant to prevent the pogroms organized by nationalists. The leader of OZON had a Jewish wife, something unthinkable for a Nazi. Nevertheless, by the standards of previous Polish practice, the change after 1935 was fundamental and unmistakable.

The man responsible for Jewish policy was Wiktor Tomir Drymmer, a close collaborator of Polish foreign minister Józef Beck. With a background in military intelligence, Drymmer was formally in charge of both personnel and consular affairs in the foreign ministry. He was also the head of its emigration office, charged with arranging the exit of citizens. Poland's official position was that European maritime empires should either permit Poland access to resources in their overseas colonies or allow Polish citizens to migrate to such places. This analysis had a force that went beyond Jewish policy. At a time when rural unemployment exceeded fifty percent, Warsaw was pushing for the right of all of its citizens to emigrate. In the case of Jews, Polish diplomats pointed to the dramatic consequences of frozen migration routes. Before the First World War, roughly 150,000 Jews left Europe each year; in the 1930s the figure was a small fraction of this. In "trying to find an outlet for its surplus population" the Polish government had "in mind the Jews first of all."

The question of the settlement of European Jews was a general European one, in which Poland occupied a position somewhere between the Nazi one (Jews must be eliminated, and emigration seemed the practical way to achieve this) and the Zionist one (Jews had a right to a state, which would have to be created from an existing colony).

The question of where European Jews might settle had been open since the nineteenth century, and very different sorts of politicians and ideologues proposed the same places. The island of Madagascar, a colonial

French possession off the southeast African coast in the Indian Ocean, was introduced to the discussion by the antisemite Paul de Lagarde (actually a German named Bötticher) in 1885. This idea could be considered with greater or lesser hostility or sympathy. It had supporters in Great Britain and, of course, among Germans, including the Nazi leadership. Only in French could one say *"Madagassez les Juifs,"* but not all of those who considered the idea in France were enemies of the Jews. Zionists also considered Madagascar, although most rejected it.

Polish authorities also allowed themselves to be tempted by the prospect of colonizing Madagascar. The idea of settling Madagascar with Polish citizens was first raised in 1926; at that time the idea was the emigration of Polish peasants from the overpopulated countryside. A decade later, after Piłsudski's death, the idea returned in a Jewish variant. Beck proposed the emigration of Polish Jews to Madagascar to French prime minister Léon Blum in October 1936, and Blum allowed the Poles to send a three-man exploratory delegation to the island. The representative of the Polish government thought that about fifty thousand Jews could be settled immediately—a significant number, but not one that would have affected the population balance in Poland. The delegate from the Jewish Emigration Association thought that four hundred families might settle. The agricultural expert from Palestine thought that even this was too much. The inhabitants of Madagascar rejected any settlement from Poland. French nationalists, for their part, were concerned that the Polish colonization project would succeed and that the island would become Polish. Meanwhile, the pro-Madagascar propaganda of the Polish regime backfired: When told that the island was suitable for colonization, Polish nationalists demanded "Madagascar only for the Poles!"

Beck and Drymmer expressed a special interest in the future of Palestine, a former Ottoman possession that was under British authority. The decline and fall of the Ottoman Empire had been a lesson for many European statesmen. Whereas Hitler tended to see the creation of Balkan nation-states from the Ottoman Empire as a positive example of militarism, Poles understood the same history as national liberation that would spread from Europe to Asia. Whereas European territories taken from empires after the First World War generally became nation-states, Asian territories tended to become part of the French or British empires, sometimes in the form of "mandates" from the League of Nations. These were places judged not ready for sovereignty, and thus allotted to the great powers for political tutoring. Palestine, taken from the defunct Ottoman district of South Syria, was such a mandate. Although the territory had a rather small Jewish minority when the British took control in 1920, British policy presented Palestine as a future Jewish National Home. This was in line with the hopes of Zionists, who hoped that one day a deal for full statehood could be struck.

Hitler's Jewish policy forced all of the powers to clarify their position on the future of Palestine. About 130,000 German Jews emigrated in the years after Hitler came to power, some fifty thousand of them settling in Palestine. Their arrival reduced the demographic advantage of local Arabs, who tended to consider Palestine as part of some larger Arab homeland. Thinking that a continuation of Jewish immigration could lead

to the success of Zionism, Arab leaders organized political action: first riots in April 1936, then the formation of strike committees and a general strike that lasted through October. This meant that 1937 was the moment of truth for the European states with a declared interest in the future of Palestine: Great Britain, Nazi Germany, and Poland.

London at first reacted to the Arab disturbances with a proposal for the partition of Palestine. When this led to further political chaos, the British restricted Jewish immigration to a quota. As the world was seen from London, Palestine was only a tiny part of the vast Arab and Muslim territories of the British Empire. Pleasing Jews over Palestine could mean alienating Muslims throughout the Near East and southern Asia. Berlin specified in 1937 its own attitude toward Zionism and a possible State of Israel. Palestine had appealed to the Nazi regime as a place where Jews could settle so long as this had no clear political implications for the Near East. But in spring 1937 the German consul in Jerusalem was concerned lest the creation of a State of Israel from Palestine weaken Germany's position in the world. The German foreign minister circulated the official position to all embassies and consulates that June: Jewish statehood in Palestine was to be opposed, as a State of Israel would become a node in the world Jewish conspiracy.

The Polish position differed from both the British and the German. London favored Jewish statehood (at some distant and undefined point) but opposed much further Jewish migration for the time being. Berlin opposed Jewish statehood, but wanted Jews to leave Germany as soon as possible for some distant and undefined place. Warsaw wanted both massive emigration of Jews from Europe and a Jewish state in Palestine. In public the Polish foreign minister and other diplomats called upon the British to ease immigration restrictions and create a Jewish National Home as soon as possible. The Poles had very specific ideas of what such an entity should be: "A Jewish, independent Palestine, as large as possible, with access to the Red Sea." This meant both sides of the River Jordan; in private, Polish diplomats even raised with British colleagues the issue of the Sinai Peninsula, in Egypt. In 1937, the Polish armed forces began to offer arms and training to the Haganah, the main Zionist self-defense force in Palestine.

Zionism was the Jewish political movement, active for half a century, whose advocates identified the future of the Jewish people with the settlement of Palestine and the establishment of a state. As a general matter, Zionists believed that this would be achieved through cooperation with the British Empire and other great powers. Although its advocates held a variety of political positions and its factions were many, many Zionists in the 1930s were left-wing, envisaging agricultural communes that would transform both the ancient Jewish land and the modern Jewish people. In Poland, Zionism was the ideology of a whole range of political parties, from extreme Left through extreme Right. Much to the dismay of Zionist leaders in London and New York, the direction of the overall movement was much affected by the politics of Zionism within Poland.

The world Zionist movement split in September 1935, just as Polish policy on Jews was revised by Piłsudski's successors. Vladimir Jabotinsky emerged then from the General Zionist movement with a program of Revisionist Zionism. He urged Jews in Europe to consider massive and rapid emigration while calling for the immediate creation of a State of Israel in the Mandates of both Palestine and Trans-Jordan. This version of Zionism spoke to Poland's new leaders. In June 1936, Jabotinsky presented his "evacuation plan" to the Polish foreign ministry. He claimed that Palestine, over time, could absorb eight million Jews. When his initiative was announced in the Polish press a few weeks later, the specified goal was the settlement of Palestine on both sides of the River Jordan by 1.5 million Jews in the course of the following ten years.

Jabotinsky wanted Poland to inherit the Mandate of Palestine from Great Britain. He even proposed that Poland be given the Mandate of Syria, which it could then trade for the Mandate of Palestine or use as leverage against the Arabs generally. This sort of thinking about foreign policy was very much in the Polish diplomatic tradition: an imaginative attempt to turn nothing into leverage. Indeed, the easy agreement between Jabotinsky and Polish leaders was not simply a matter of common interests. Although Jabotinsky spoke French when he made his case in Warsaw, he like most Polish leaders was born a Russian imperial subject and had been educated in the Russian language. The idea of building a nation-state from empires that partitioned historic national lands was a common one.

Jabotinsky's power base by 1936 was Polish. Revisionism was a movement of youth, based in paramilitary organizations. By far the largest of these was Betar, the right-wing Jewish youth paramilitary in Poland, whose members promised to devote their lives "to the revival of the Jewish state with a Jewish majority on both sides of the Jordan." Betar's model was the Polish Legions of the First World War, which in the favorable conditions of war among empires had prepared the way for Polish independence. Like the Poles of the Legions, the Jews of Betar trained with weapons and awaited the opportune moment of general conflict. The vast majority of Betar members were products of the Polish school system, and imbibed its core message of secular messianism ("Our dream: to die for our people!"). When Betar brawled with Jewish leftist organizations, its members sang Polish patriotic songs—in Polish. Uniformed Betar members bearing firearms marched and performed at Polish public ceremonies alongside Polish scouts and Polish soldiers. Their weapons training was organized by Polish state institutions and provided by Polish army officers. Menachem Begin, one of Betar's leaders, called upon Betar members to defend the borders of Poland in the event of war. Betar members wrote in their newspapers of their two fatherlands, Palestine and Poland. They flew two flags, the Zionist and the Polish, until the end of their existence in Poland—in the ghetto uprising of 1943 they raised both banners from the building that served as their headquarters.

Both Menachem Begin and another promising Betar activist, Yitzhak Shamir, treasured the Polish Romantic poets of the nineteenth century and quoted them at Jewish gatherings. The great poet of the new Jewish Right, Uri Zvi Greenberg, spent the 1930s in Poland. The secular messianism of Begin and Shamir and the Betar movement bore a strong resemblance to the Polish version, developed during Poland's long period of statelessness in the nineteenth century: sacrifice on this earth for change on this earth.

After Piłsudski's death in May 1935, Polish spies were not the only ones sent on long missions to find the symbolically appropriate soil for his commemoration. Members of Betar brought clumps of earth from their own sacred site, Tel Hai in Palestine, where their own hero, Joseph Trumpeldor, had been killed by Arabs. ("Betar" was the site of the last stand in the Third Roman-Jewish War; the name was later reimagined as a Hebrew acronym for "Covenant of Joseph Trumpeldor.") In life, both Trumpeldor and Piłsudski had been subjects of the Russian Empire; both struggled to reconcile national and social justice; and both commanded legions that were meant to cultivate cadres for national armies and national states. Piłsudski had been victorious in his war of liberation against the Soviet Union in 1920; Trumpeldor was killed that same year. So their unity after death was perhaps not so strange. Betar members attended Piłsudski's open-air memorial service in large numbers, arriving in precision formation on motorcycles bearing Polish and Zionist flags. Jabotinsky spoke of "eternal, indestructible sacrifices on the altar of the fatherland." Piłsudski became a central cult figure of both traditions, that of Polish leaders and Jewish revolutionaries.

Yet disagreement about the meaning of Piłsudski's legacy was inevitable. Piłsudski had led a colorful life and had deployed violence in various settings. Which Piłsudski was the model for the Jewish future? Was it the Piłsudski of the Legions, nominally loyal to an empire, and preparing for a war in which that empire would have to make concessions? This was how Jabotinsky saw matters, and at first his vision defined that of Betar. As time passed, however, the Piłsudski of the Polish Military Organization, exploiting terror and propaganda, was ever more appealing to Jewish rebels. Each of these approaches has a political logic; each depends upon a judgment of the historical conjuncture. The logic of legions is that supporting an empire in times of war creates debts to be repaid in times of peace. The logic of terrorism is that fear can destroy a weak system and make way for a new one. In the late 1930s, Menachem Begin mounted a challenge to Jabotinsky, supporting political terrorism rather than legions. At a Betar congress in Warsaw in September 1938, Begin openly criticized Jabotinsky's judgment.

By 1938, the Polish ruling elite was supporting the most radical available option among the Revisionist Zionists, a conspiratorial National Military Organization operating in Palestine that favored terrorism to provoke the conjuncture rather than waiting for it. After the Arab riots and general strike of 1936, and the British concessions to the Arabs in 1937, members of the Haganah disagreed about the future. Younger, more right-wing, and more radical individuals left the Haganah to form the Irgun Tzvai Leumi, or National Military Organization, named and modeled after the Polish Military Organization, and usually known as Irgun. The core of the new Irgun were Jews from Poland who had been members of Betar. Under Begin, the leader of Betar in Poland from March 1939, the organization was increasingly a front for Irgun.

Irgun liaised with the Polish government through the Polish consul in Jerusalem, Witold Hulanicki. His general instructions were to present himself as "the representative of a state that has interests that are similar to Zionist aspirations and that can contribute to the realization of those aspirations." Hulanicki tended to know about Irgun's actions before they took place. From his perspective, Irgun was a "very comfortable and very much needed (by me) political instrument" and Avraham Stern, one of its leaders, was a Polish agent.

Avraham Stern was a child of revolution. He was born in Suwałki in 1907, in a Jewish-Polish town near the Augustów Forest in the western reaches of the Russian Empire. Deported as a boy along with his family and hundreds of thousands of other Jews, he became one of the young Jewish men radicalized by the Russian imperial collapse. He lived with his family in Bashkiria for about six years, then saw the great cities of postrevolutionary Russia and became a communist before returning to Suwałki in what had meanwhile become independent Poland. Stern came to revere Piłsudski and his new Polish state much as he had admired Lenin and his new Soviet state. He immigrated to Palestine in the 1920s, and began studies at the Hebrew University of Jerusalem. He was regarded by his professors as one of the great hopes of Jewish humanist studies. But he was without any means of subsistence, and in 1929 he was going hungry.

Although he was a talented linguist and writer, Stern opted in the 1930s for politics over literature. He traveled in Europe seeking support for an independent Jewish state, first from Mussolini's Italy and then in Piłsudski's Poland. Although he was an early emigrant from Poland and thus not a product of Betar, he was very comfortable in Polish culture. He wrote romantic poems about arousing hearts of stone and raising the dead—in Polish. As exercises for himself he composed poems simultaneously in his three revolutionary languages: Russian, Hebrew, and Polish. In a poem in Hebrew and Polish, he wrote of the tears shed for his happy childhood, his troubled youth, and his failed manhood. Stern grew to maturity in the middle of the great east European revolutionary forces: communist revolution, Polish state building, Zionism. He was a child of revolution who wanted to be a father of revolution. "Reality is not what it appears to be," he wrote, "but what force of will and longing for a goal make it."

Hulanicki, the Polish consul in Jerusalem, described Stern to his superiors in the foreign ministry as the "ideological leader" of the "extreme elements" of Irgun. In February 1938, Hulanicki wrote to Drymmer in Warsaw, asking him to meet Stern. The proposal that Stern brought to Drymmer, with Hulanicki's support, was that Poland train instructors for Irgun. The Irgun elites trained by Poland would then become the officer corps of a future Jewish revolutionary army that would conquer Palestine. The soldiers would be thousands of trained Betar fighters brought from Poland. One of the Irgun men imagined "armed soldiers, entire battalions from many ships, landing simultaneously at various points along the coast of Eretz Israel."

Drymmer endorsed the idea. Field training in the southeastern Polish region of Volhynia (where Betar had been trained by the Polish army for years) and staff training at Rembertów (a military base just outside of Warsaw) began within a few months. Volhynia became a staging area for the clandestine and illegal emigration of revolutionary Jews with military training to the British Mandate of Palestine. In Volhynia, where more than two-thirds of Jewish students attended Zionist schools, the regional governor, Henryk Józewski, was a sympathizer of Revisionist Zionism.

The first major encounter between German Jewish policy and Polish Jewish policy was not in Europe but in Asia. Nazi oppression led to the immigration of German Jews to Palestine, which led to the Arab riots that radicalized right-wing Zionism and created a new possibility for Polish foreign policy: the support of Irgun.

Although Polish leaders were responding to British, German, Arab, and Jewish actions over which they had little influence, their own policy did follow something like a consistent line. In a sense, the small group of

Poles who made foreign policy after 1935 were shifting from one form of Prometheanism to another. The initial Prometheanism, under Piłsudski, presumed that Warsaw could aid neighboring peoples to the east, above all Ukrainians, to gain their freedom from the dominion of Moscow. The emerging variant involved support of the Jewish nation against British rule in Palestine. As Polish authorities abandoned the anti-Soviet line that Hitler admired, they shifted to a pro-Zionist conspiracy that the Nazis would have found incomprehensible—had they known anything about it.

There was some continuity in personnel from the first to the second Prometheanism. The Volhynian governor who supported Revisionist Zionism, Józewski, had been the most important Promethean activist. His heroes were Piłsudski and Jabotinsky, whom he called "an apostle of the Jewish world." His province had been a departure point for Ukrainian spies in the early 1930s; it became a training ground for Jewish revolutionaries in the late 1930s. Drymmer, the high official of the foreign ministry charged with the Jewish question, had been a Polish Military Organization operative in Ukraine and a Promethean. Tadeusz Pełczyński, the director of Polish military intelligence who organized the training courses for Irgun, was also a veteran of the Polish Military Organization and a Promethean. Witold Hulanicki, the Polish consul in Jerusalem, was one more product of the Polish Military Organization.

The continuities were ideological as well as personal. For the men in power in Warsaw, supporting right-wing Jews meant supporting fellow anti-communists. Revisionist Zionists might one day lead millions of Polish Jews to Palestine; in the meantime they drew some young Jewish hotheads away from communism, beat up in brawls the young Jewish men who did opt for the Far Left, and supported the Polish government against the Soviet Union. All of these veterans of Polish conspiracy could see that Jews needed statehood as Poles once did. The younger Jewish men whom they supported and sometimes befriended were looking forward to statehood just as the older Poles were looking back nostalgically to its creation. Jewish Prometheanism was thus a chance for Poles to relive a youth whose accomplishments now seemed endangered. As one Polish diplomat explained the endorsement of the Revisionists to a bemused supporter of mainstream Zionism, "Emotionally, they appeal to us the most." From the Ukrainian to the Jewish Prometheanism extended the basic optimism that the liberation of nations from empires was a good to be expected from history. Poles preserved the same fundamental tradition of using the weapons of the weak to oppose empires and create states. They still embodied a certain elite romanticism of politics, the belief that deft techniques of state creation were a matter for the sensitive and courageous few, who would bring along the masses later, in good time. And they maintained the same preference for secret measures.

Yet there were some telling differences between the first and the second Prometheanism, corresponding to the fundamental shift in Polish Jewish policy in 1935. After 1935, the regime was much more pessimistic about the possibility for change in the Soviet Union. Poles who had worked for the Promethean movement either became liberal critics of the new regime or tacked to the new right-wing version of the idea. The first Prometheanism saw national minorities in someone else's country as a problem for that other country—the major example being Ukrainians in the Soviet Union. The first Prometheanism had also involved the Muslim nations of the USSR. Insofar as Prometheans had engaged Jerusalem before 1935, it was as a center of Islamic national movements. The second Prometheanism regarded a national minority in Poland as a burden for Poland. Jews were no longer seen as citizens of a republic, but a national problem that might be resolved here or there, or perhaps a national force that might be deployed abroad. Jerusalem was no longer a city of Muslims today but a city of (Polish) Jews tomorrow. There was no longer the solidarity expressed by the slogan "For your freedom and ours!" The slogan of the second Prometheanism might have been: "For our freedom from you!"

In the first Prometheanism, Poland was to endorse minority rights to set an example and destabilize neighboring regimes that did not. In the second Prometheanism, it was legitimate to create conditions under which Poland's own citizens would wish to emigrate. The Polish authoritarian regime after 1935 countenanced the use of economic pressure to encourage Jews to leave the country. The police stopped attempts at pogroms but treated boycotts of Jewish businesses as a legitimate economic choice. The parliament passed a ban on kosher slaughter, though it was never implemented. Civil society was moving in the same direction. Professional organizations in which Jews were prominent had to reregister their members. Most universities did nothing as Jewish students were beaten and intimidated until they sat in the last rows of the lecture halls, called "ghetto benches." Much of the clergy of the Roman Catholic Church, in Poland as elsewhere in Europe, continued to explain that Jews were responsible for the evils of modernity in general and communism in particular.

Unlike the Nazi regime, the Polish government did not present Jews as the hidden hand responsible for global crises and therefore for all of Poland's woes. Jews were portrayed, rather, as human beings whose presence was economically and politically undesirable. The vision of a future Poland without most of its Jews was certainly antisemitic, but this was not an antisemitism that identified Jews with the fundamental ecological or metaphysical evils of the planet. Unlike in Germany, there was meaningful opposition. The Polish Socialist Party, the largest political party in Warsaw, opposed the government line, as did the mayor of Warsaw. The Jewish political party known as the Bund, committed to socialism in Europe and to Jews remaining in Poland, did extremely well in the 1938 local elections. For that matter, the Jewish share in the Polish economy was greater in 1938 than it had been when the Great Depression began. The undeniable liveliness of Jewish commerce and politics as the 1930s came to an end made Poland quite different from Germany.

Nazi leaders saw in Poland what they wanted to see. A certain amount of misperception in Berlin was perhaps inevitable. Local Jewish success in Poland was invisible from Berlin, whereas official Polish restrictions on Jewish life were reported favorably in the German press. The more ambitious elements of Polish pro-Zionism were clandestine, whereas the official antisemitism was open. The Nazi leadership could read the evidence from Poland as a sign that the friendly German foreign policy initiated in 1934 had worked and could be extended.

This was a misunderstanding, although one that Polish diplomats, lacking any better ideas, cultivated for as long as they could. The German-Polish nonaggression declaration of January 1934 was for Piłsudski and then for Beck a counterpoint to the July 1932 treaty of nonaggression with the USSR. For Hitler, it was a platform for recruitment to a future anti-Soviet crusade. Like most of Hitler's policies in the 1930s, it was significant for what it promised about the future. In May 1934, Hitler was already wondering aloud what sort of commitment Poland would need to join in an alliance against the Soviet Union. Speaking to the Polish ambassador Józef Lipski that August, Hitler called Poland Germany's "shield in the east." The following January he pronounced that Germany and Poland would be compelled to make war together against the USSR. As Hitler explained to Beck later in 1935, the German-Polish declaration was to be understood as part of a German grand design.

It quickly became obvious in Warsaw what that design entailed. Hermann Göring, Hitler's plenipotentiary on Polish matters, was quite forthcoming with his Polish interlocutors. On a hunting trip in the Białowieża Forest with Polish officials in January 1935, Göring unveiled the grand scheme of a German-Polish invasion of the USSR, with Poland to get the spoils of Ukraine. Lipski, the Polish ambassador to Berlin, found this implausible and asked Göring not to repeat such ideas to Piłsudski when they all returned to Warsaw. Göring did so anyway, but was ignored; Piłsudski was in any event very ill. Göring made similar approaches on at least four more occasions after Piłsudski's death, sometimes offering land to the Poles from Soviet Ukraine, sometimes from northern Soviet Russia. No one in Warsaw would ever be persuaded by any of this, though the barrage of proposals from Göring and others continued for years.

Göring would later return to Białowieża to hunt—after the war began, after Poland was destroyed, after the SS cleared the woods of Jews.

Cults of personality are open to postmortem interpretation. Piłsudski's successors struggled to preserve the status quo by realizing what they saw as his political testament of 1932–1934: a diplomatic balance between Nazi Germany and the Soviet Union. People who wanted to change Europe recalled the young Piłsudski: Betar saw the legionary of the First World War in 1918, Irgun the conspiratorial state builder of the Polish Military Organization of 1919—and the Nazis the military commander who had beaten the Red Army in 1920. Hitler saw Piłsudski as the "great patriot and statesman" who having defeated the Bolsheviks once would surely have seized the chance to do so again. The Polish leadership, although happy to dabble in Jewish revolution in Palestine, had a much more conservative understanding of Piłsudski's European prescription for the 1930s. Poland was to keep an equal distance from both mortal threats, Nazi Germany and the Soviet Union.

The hope was that if Poland could stay neutral between what Piłsudski had called "totalistic states," no war could take place. Any war, the Poles liked to think, would have to involve Poland as an ally of either the Soviets or the Germans, since any war that involved them would have to take place on Polish territory. The plan was to stop all wars by refusing to join in them, to halt two mobile forces by standing still between them. Although Piłsudski himself understood that this was at best a strategy for a few years, his successors became attached to the leverage of neutrality and saw it as a doctrine. This prevented them from recognizing the scale of Hitler's ambition and from grasping that Stalin had dismissed the Polish state and was awaiting an offer from Hitler.

Right after Piłsudski's death, Göring proposed a common German-Polish invasion of the Soviet Union, an offer he repeated in February 1936. Throughout that year, Hitler made similar appeals to the Poles. Jan Szembek, Beck's number two in the Polish foreign ministry, reported upon his extensive conversations with Hitler at the Berlin Olympics of August 1936: "Hitler's policy to us is dictated by the conviction that Poland will be his natural ally in future conflicts with the Soviets and communism." That November, Germany and Japan initiated the Anti-Comintern Pact. Though ostensibly a defensive arrangement against international communism, this rather quickly became the basis for a military alliance. Berlin asked Warsaw to join the Pact in February 1937, a full six months before Italy became its third member. Warsaw refused this proposal then, as it did on at least five occasions thereafter.

This was a trying time for Polish diplomats. Unlike the Germans, Japanese, and Italians, the Poles had experience with communist power and a sense of what a conflict with the USSR would mean. Many of the Poles running the country in the late 1930s had fought the Soviets in 1919–1920 and had lost comrades to the Red Army and to the Soviet secret state police, back then called the Cheka. Some of them had seen the tortured bodies of friends and relatives in mass graves; such things were not forgotten. In 1936, Polish diplomats serving in the Soviet Union received instructions about how to comport themselves in the event of arrest by the NKVD, as the Soviet secret state police was by then known. Beginning in

GERMANY, POLAND, AND U.S.S.R.
1937
NORWAY
FINLAND
Helsinki
Leningrad
Stockholm
Tallinn
ESTONIA
Novgorod
SWEDEN
North Sea
DENMARK
Baltic Sea
LATVIA
Riga
Copenhagen
LITHUANIA
Moscow
RUSSIAN S.F.S.R.
Smolensk
Kaunas
Königsberg
Wilno
Danzig
East Prussia
Suwałki
Minsk
U.S.S.R.
Volga
NETHERLANDS
Amsterdam
Hamburg
Grodno
BELARUSIAN S.S.R.
Białystok
Hannover
Berlin
Kursk
Poznań
Warsaw
Pińsk
GERMANY
BELGIUM
Rhine
Łódź
POLAND
Leipzig
Dresden
Radom
Lublin
Don
Luxembourg
Równe
Kyiv
Kharkiv
Stalingrad
Prague
Zhytomyr
Cracow
Lwów
UKRAINIAN S.S.R.
CZECHOSLOVAKIA
Dnipro
Strasbourg
Danube
Kamianets-Podilskyi
Stalino
FRANCE
Munich
MOLDAVIAN A.S.S.R.
Rostov
Vienna
AUSTRIA
Budapest
SWITZERLAND
Chisinau
Tiraspol
HUNGARY
Cluj
Odessa
Trieste
Zagreb
ROMANIA
Crimea
Venice
Belgrade
YUGOSLAVIA
Bucharest
ITALY
Sarajevo
Danube
Black Sea
GEORGIAN S.S.R.

1937, Polish diplomats were filing or reading reports about the distressing number of ethnic Poles disappearing from Soviet Ukraine, Soviet Belarus, and the large cities of Soviet Russia.

General instructions from the Warsaw headquarters of Polish military intelligence made clear that the disastrous Polish position in the Soviet Union could not be improved by a German invasion. Poland had no capacity to intervene on Soviet territory, and a German intervention would only make matters worse. Poland's policy of equal distance meant that its territory was not only Germany's shield to the east, but the USSR's shield to the west. It was a dire situation, whose logic Polish diplomats, of course, did not explain to their German colleagues. They tried, as diplomats do, to make the most of what their interlocutors wanted, without acceding to it. When asked about a German-Polish alliance against the Soviet Union, they evaded the issue for as long as possible. When finally forced to issue a categorical response, they categorically refused.

In summer 1938, Göring was once again trying to tempt the Poles with the fertile soil of Ukraine. Matters came to a head that October, when Hitler presented the Poles with a "comprehensive solution" to all of the problems in German-Polish relations. Such a grand stroke was very much Hitler's style, and he could believe that he was offering Poland a more than reasonable arrangement. The claims he made on Poland's territory were mild by comparison with the German mainstream: that Danzig, a free city on the Baltic coast, be allowed to return to Germany; and that German authorities be allowed to build an extraterritorial autobahn across Polish territory between the main body of German territory and its noncontiguous Prussian districts. These two issues were negotiable, and indeed were negotiated. The real problem was what Poland would get "in return." As German foreign minister Joachim von Ribbentrop explained to Ambassador Lipski, the Germans envisioned for the near future "joint action in colonial matters, the emigration of Jews from Poland, and a joint policy to Russia on the basis of the Anti-Comintern Pact."

Ribbentrop made much of the gains of Ukrainian territory that Poland would supposedly win in the conquered Soviet Union. This fell on deaf ears. The decision against intervening in the Soviet Union had been made in Warsaw in 1933. Polish leaders had ceased to believe that Ukraine could be transformed easily by outside actors. They calculated that the Germans might take Moscow with Polish help, but did not see how a political victory could follow. They were keenly aware that a joint German-Polish invasion of the USSR would involve massive German troop movements around or through Poland, and anticipated that any such war would leave Poland a German satellite.

The side talk between German and Polish leaders during the critical weeks of late 1938 was about the Jewish question. Hitler had explained to Lipski in September that he anticipated a common anti-Jewish action by Germany, Poland, and Romania. In November, Hitler praised Polish authorities for undertaking the vital struggle against the Jews. At the time of his proposal of a "comprehensive solution" and in subsequent discussions with Polish diplomats, Hitler stressed the positive connection between an anti-Soviet alliance and the removal of the Jews from Europe, in the first instance from Poland and Romania. In his mind, the destruction of the Soviet Union was part of a larger campaign against the planetary Jewish threat. His Polish interlocutors did not follow this chain of reasoning.

In these negotiations the Germans and Poles seemed to be discussing the same desired outcome: an emigration of millions of European Jews to Madagascar. Although the two sides were apparently referring to the same island and the same action, something very different was meant. The Germans were perfectly correct that the Polish leadership feared the Soviet Union and wanted to be rid of most Polish Jews. The Poles saw these as distinct problems, where the attempt to solve one might create problems for the other. They were opposed to a war of aggression against the Soviet Union in any case. And they simply could not understand how the Germans meant to invade the Soviet Union while deporting the Jews of Europe. Any such mass deportation would have required the cooperation of the colonial powers, the British and the French, which would obviously not be proffered to countries that were trying to alter the world order by force. In simple logistical terms the idea also seemed to make no sense. How could Poland arrange a deportation of millions of Jews while the country was mobilized for war? Should the tens of thousands of Jewish officers and soldiers be pulled from the ranks of the Polish army? Insofar as the Poles understood German intentions, they were wary.

Most important was what the Poles did not understand. They could not grasp a special feature of Nazi thought: the aim to do something difficult or even impossible, in the secret knowledge that failure would prepare the way to something still more radical. The geopolitical vision of the Poles failed them here. They could not see that for the Nazis "Madagascar" was not simply a place, but a label, a bookmark in a burning book. It was synonymous with a Final Solution; or, in Himmler's words, with "the complete extirpation of the concept of Jews." For the Poles, Madagascar was an actual island in the actual Indian Ocean, an actual possession of the actual French empire, an actual site of an actual exploratory mission, a subject of actual political discussions, one of two places (along with Palestine) that were seriously considered as destination points for a mass migration of Polish Jewry. Polish leaders did not grasp that for the Nazis the issue was not the feasibility of one deportation plan, but the creation of general conditions under which Jews could be destroyed one way or another. Given their own obsession with the idea of statehood, Poles could not see that a bloody whirlwind of improvisation was coming, where German aggression would destroy polities, opening pathways toward the unthinkable. German leaders would later continue to speak of "Madagascar" even after their men had killed the Jews who were supposed to emigrate there.

Warsaw's political vision reached as far as the idea of a State of Israel. If a European crisis was coming, perhaps Jewish rebels such as Avraham Stern would be able to organize a revolt—one that would lead to a Jewish state that would welcome millions of Polish Jews. Polish officers had already begun to train the rebels of Irgun who were to lead such a revolt, and the young men of Betar who were to be its soldiers. As Hitler and Ribbentrop were pressing their "comprehensive solution" in December 1938, Drymmer issued instructions that made explicit the final purpose of Polish policy toward Betar and Irgun. Warsaw was supporting Irgun and Betar so that they would be ready to press forward with violence to Jewish statehood when the crisis came.

Over the course of 1938, European states were already collapsing under Nazi pressure. As the year came to an end, the crisis seemed to be coming.

4

The State Destroyers

"Overnight! This was all overnight." Years later, Erika M. still could not hide her astonishment at the collapse of Austria, at the end of her country, on the night of the eleventh of March, in the pivotal year of 1938.

The Austria where Erika had spent a very happy Jewish childhood, "the most wonderful existence a child can have," was perhaps an unlikely creation. In 1914, when the First World War began, "Austria" was simply the informal name of some German-speaking regions of the great power known as the Habsburg monarchy. When that war came to an end with the defeat of that empire, Austria was created as a new republic and the new homeland of those German-speaking people—including about 200,000 Jews, most of them inhabitants of the capital, Vienna. In the beginning, few believed that the small alpine country could survive. *Lebensunfähig*—incapable of life—was the verdict of economists and politicians alike. The population was only seven million, by comparison with the fifty-three million of the Habsburg domains. The richest lands of the old monarchy had fallen to the new state of Czechoslovakia. The separation of Austria from territories that fell to Poland, Hungary, Yugoslavia, and Romania destroyed a large and vibrant internal market. Most Austrians either had little sense of national identity or thought of themselves as Germans.

The leaders of the new country tried to found it as "German-Austria," including in its constitution a promise to seek unification with the larger German state to its north. This was exactly what the victors in the First World War—the Americans, the British, and, above all, the French—wished to prevent. It had been precisely an alliance between Vienna and Berlin that had begun, as Paris and London saw matters, the bloodiest war in the history of the world. More than a million French soldiers had not fallen so that Germany could end the war holding Austrian territories it had not possessed at the beginning. Thus the peace treaties applied to Germany and Austria, signed at Versailles and Saint-Germain in 1919, explicitly forbade each country from uniting with the other. This was, of course, a resented violation of the principle of national self-determination, the moral cause that the American president Woodrow Wilson had brought to the western allies when the United States joined the war on the western front in 1917.

The contradictory Austria of the early twentieth century was frozen in the mind of Hitler and many other Europeans throughout the succeeding two decades. Hitler had no sympathy for the Habsburg monarchy, the land of his birth, nor for cosmopolitan Vienna, where he had failed as a painter. He saw the city as an unhealthy mixture of races, held together only by the iniquitous plans of the Jews, who held true power. When he moved from Vienna to Munich in 1912, he believed that he had left a non-German city for a German one. It seems that he went to Germany to avoid mandatory military service in the Habsburg army, but in 1914 he volunteered for the German one, and served in the trenches as a messenger during the First World War. A German by choice, he shared the view of many German soldiers and politicians that the old multinational monarchy was doomed by its very nature. For Hitler, Austria had a past that was unworthy of Germans and a future that was unworthy of mention. He was an Austrian who had joined Germany; at some point all of the others (except the Jews, of course) would follow.

Although Hitler did not place Austria at the center of his concerns in the 1920s and 1930s—that place was always held by the Soviet Union—he took for granted that Austria and Germany would one day be united. His National Socialist Party, including its paramilitary arms, the SA and SS, were active in Austria as well as in Germany. In Austria especially, it was obvious that the work of these racial organizations was directed towards something more ambitious than an internal transformation of Germany; after all, Austria and Germany had never in history been united in a single national state. The prospect of their unification—*Anschluss*—was the part of the Nazi program that was most relevant to Austrians.

Yet for Erika M., a Jewish girl whose whole life had been spent in independent Austria, and whose whole world was changed forever on March 11, 1938, Austria was real. Over the course of the two decades after the First World War, an Austrian state was constructed, despite everything. Austria inherited from the old empire major political parties with experience in mass politics. The Social Democrats, the largest party when Austria was established after the war, were discredited immediately by their failed attempt to join the new republic to Germany. Yet the Social Democrats ruled without interruption in the Viennese metropolis, the first socialist party to govern a city of a million people or more on its own. They built a miniature welfare state known as "Red Vienna," which proved to be both popular and successful.

Beyond Vienna, the leading party was the Christian Socials, who, like their socialist rivals, had a rich history in democratic competition dating back to the monarchy. Unlike the Social Democrats, however, they had never believed in unification with some idealized Germany. They identified with the Roman Catholic religion, the one trait that distinguished most Austrians from most Germans. Some of them were monarchists, fondly recalling the old multinational empire.

Jews were relatively more numerous in Austria than in Germany, and functioned in both of the main Austrian political movements. Most Austrian Jews lived in Vienna, where most voted for the Social Democrats. Yet Jews were also to be found in conservative organizations. The leader of the Austrian monarchist movement, for example, was Jewish.

Austria's major political conflict was between these two native traditions, the Right and the Left. In 1927, the Social Democrats, who had just won elections, organized a general strike in the capital, but were unwilling to try to seize total power. In 1934, the Christian Socials backed right-wing paramilitaries in conflicts with left-wing paramilitaries, leading to clashes that became a brief civil war. The Austrian regular army backed the Right, and the Left was crushed. The symbolic end came as army artillery shelled the great public housing complexes, the pride of Red Vienna, from the hills beyond the city. The Social Democrats were then banned, and the Christian Socials reformed themselves as the largest part of a right-wing coalition known as the Fatherland Front. Austrian politicians and journalists associated with the Social Democrats fled the country, among them a considerable number of Jews.

The Nazis were never the largest party in Austria, and never won an election. They were a significant but distant third in popularity. But with the socialists humiliated and Hitler's model in display across the border after 1933, the Nazis could challenge the Austrian authoritarian regime. Austrian Nazis assassinated the Austrian chancellor Engelbert Dollfuß on July 25, 1934, but their coup did not lead to the national revolt they expected. On the contrary, the murderers were arrested and executed. Austrian Jews saw the Dollfuß regime as a barrier to National Socialism. Although the Fatherland Front looked very much like a fascist organization, complete with its own uniforms and salutes—and even its own version of a cross meant to compete with the Nazi *Hakenkreuz*—its politics were quite different. It identified Austria as "the better Germany" and Austrians as Germans, but did not identify Germans as a race. Although there were certainly antisemites in the movement, the Fatherland Front instituted no antisemitic policies on the model of Hitler. Despite considerable antisemitism on the Right and even on the Left, Jews continued to serve in Austrian ministries and to live more or less unhindered lives as Austrian citizens.

The rise of Hitler to power in Germany in 1933 raised the Austrian question in a new economic form. Germany's recovery from the Great Depression created an attraction that could not be reduced to tradition or nationalism. Austrians who found jobs in Germany were impressed. Like its east European neighbors, Austria was an agrarian country and as such had been wracked by the Great Depression. The Fatherland Front, despite its radical iconography, was among the most conservative European governments in its economic policy. Whereas Germany under the Nazis accumulated huge budget deficits, Austria under the Fatherland Front pursued a tight fiscal and monetary policy, jealously hoarding its foreign currency and gold reserves. From Hitler's perspective, this was one more reason, and an increasingly pressing one, why Austria needed *Anschluss* with the Reich. Germany needed the money.

As Germany asserted its place in Europe, Austria lost its allies. In 1934, during the failed Nazi coup in Austria, fascist Italy rallied to Austria's defense. Benito Mussolini, Italy's fascist *Duce,* was still hoping to create an Italian sphere of influence in the Balkans, Hungary, and Austria. Two years later, after Hitler had begun to rearm Germany, Mussolini had to accept the role of partner (and soon junior partner). He washed his hands of the Austrian question, leaving the matter to Hitler. Thus in 1936, in what was known as the "Gentlemen's Agreement," members of the Nazi party in Austria were amnestied, and some of them brought into government. Austrian Nazis used their access to the public sphere to press the case for an *Anschluss.* That October, Nazi Germany and fascist Italy announced their "Axis." For Vienna this meant political isolation. As the saying at the time went, the Axis was the spit upon which Austria was roasted.

In February 1938, Hitler summoned the Austrian chancellor, Kurt von Schuschnigg, to his residence in the Bavarian Alps. Like his predecessor Dollfuß, Schuschnigg represented the Christian Socials and the Fatherland Front—and thus the sovereign Austrian Right that was opposed to *Anschluss.* Hitler demanded concessions that would have meant the end of Austrian sovereignty. Schuschnigg was intimidated, but upon his return to Vienna he regained his spine. In defiance of Hitler, he called a referendum on Austrian independence. Hitler was using the language of self-determination to press a German claim on what Hitler thought were German territories, so let the Austrian people decide. Schuschnigg was sure that he would win the referendum: The question was full of so many desiderata as to make clear that the correct answer was "yes"; the voting was to be open rather than secret; ballots were to be issued with answers already printed; much of the Austrian population really did favor independence in 1938; and, in any event, his regime was an authoritarian one that could arrange the results as necessary.

The days of March 9 and 10, 1938, were devoted to propaganda in favor of Austrian independence, over the radio, in the newspapers, and, following Austrian traditions, in signs painted on the streets of Vienna. The main propaganda slogan was simply *Österreich*—Austria. Abandoned by its former ally Italy and ignored by Great Britain and France, the country had no external backers. In rallying internal support, Schuschnigg was hoping to make a case against Hitler's claims that European powers might heed. Hitler, understanding the risks, threatened to invade. Under this second round of threats, Schuschnigg yielded. No referendum took place.

Erika M. was right: Everything really did change overnight. On the evening of March 11, Austrians sat close to their radios to hear an important announcement from the chancellor. This was a Friday night, but Erika's family, like other observant Jews, broke the Sabbath to listen to the radio. Although this was probably not a case of immediate threat to a particular person, which would technically justify the violation of Jewish law, Viennese Jews were right to think that this radio address was a matter of life and death. At 7:57 p.m. Schuschnigg announced his decision not to defend Austria from Hitler. At that moment the Austrian state in effect ceased to exist. Formal power passed to an Austrian Nazi lawyer, Arthur Seyß-Inquart, whose program involved the termination of the entity he now governed. Popular opinion assimilated the meaning of the end of Austria far more quickly than even Nazis in Vienna or Berlin expected. That same evening crowds appeared on the streets, shouting Nazi slogans and looking for Jews to beat. That first night of lawlessness in Austria was more dangerous for Jews than the preceding two decades of Austrian statehood. Their world was gone.

The next morning the "scrubbing parties" began. Members of the Austrian SA, working from lists, from personal knowledge, and from the knowledge of passersby, identified Jews and forced them to kneel and clean the streets with brushes. This was a ritual humiliation. Jews, often doctors and lawyers or other professionals, were suddenly on their knees performing menial labor in front of jeering crowds. Ernest P. remembered the spectacle of the "scrubbing parties" as "amusement for the Austrian population." A journalist described "the fluffy Viennese blondes, fighting one another to get closer to the elevating spectacle of the ashen-faced Jewish surgeon on hands and knees before a half-dozen young hooligans with Swastika armlets and dog-whips." Meanwhile, Jewish girls were sexually abused, and older Jewish men forced to perform public physical exercise.

The symbolic destruction of Jewish status was accompanied by and enabled theft from Jews. On March 11, 1938, about seventy percent of the residential property on the *Ringstrasse*, the beautiful circular avenue that encloses Vienna's first district, had belonged to Jews. From the dawn of the twelfth of March, that percentage decreased by the hour. Jewish businesses were marked as such, and the automobiles of Jews were stolen. The SA had made lists of Jewish apartments that their members wanted for themselves, and this was their chance. Jewish professors and judges were driven from their offices. Austrian Jews began to commit suicide: seventy-nine in March, and then sixty-two more in April.

The "scrubbing parties" were also political. Jews were cleaning the streets at certain places, working with acid, brushes, and their bare hands to remove one sort of mark. They were erasing a word that had been painted on Vienna's avenues only a few days before: "Austria." That word had been the slogan of Schuschnigg's referendum propaganda, of which Jews could now be portrayed as the organizers. It was also the name of a state of which Jews had been citizens. Jews were unwriting Austria, and they were doing it within the circles of onlookers on the streets, under the gazes and the grins.

Austrians separated themselves from their fellow citizens and the disappearing state not only by their behavior and by their expressions, but also by their lapel pins—like the pavement propaganda, another example of Austrian political culture. Not only Nazis but also people who had been Social Democrats or Christian Socials before March 11 began to wear Nazi lapel pins. Standing by during the "scrubbing parties" was thus by no means a neutral position or a simple act of observation. The very act of spectating communicated the new group boundaries and assigned blame for the past. We watch, they perform. The Jews were responsible for Austria, for that old order, not us. Their punishment now is proof of their complicity then. Our separation is proof of our innocence. Thus responsibility was perfectly excised, in perfect bad faith. In an instant, violence organized by race replaced two decades of political experience.

The Austrian satirist Karl Kraus had written in 1922 that Austria was a laboratory for the end of the world. It now became a realm of experimentation for the Germans, with some surprising lessons. One Viennese Jew recalled that "Austrians became antisemites all of a sudden and taught the Germans how to treat Jews." There had been no Austrian Nuremberg Laws, no restrictions of Jews in public life, no exclusion of Jews from society. Until the day of Schuschnigg's address, Jews had been equal citizens.

Jews had an important role in the economy, and some had performed important functions in the regime. The end of the Austrian state brought violence against Austrian Jews in five weeks that was comparable to the suffering that German Jews had endured under Hitler over the course of five years. The organizers in Austria were usually Nazis, but they were operating in conditions of state collapse that allowed their revolution to proceed further and faster. Ironically, the SA, which had been humiliated in Germany in the Night of the Long Knives in 1934, did make something like the "second revolution" its murdered leaders had wanted—only in Austria rather than Germany.

What Austrian Nazis managed to achieve in a matter of hours and days was indeed an unexpected inspiration for German Nazis. Hitler himself was pleased and surprised by the immediate support for annexation. On the *Heldenplatz,* the grand square beneath the royal castle in Vienna, Hitler proclaimed the *Anschluss.* This was on March 15, four days after Schuschnigg's capitulation. Along with Hitler came the Nazi leaders who exploited the anarchy created by the SA and turned it to their own purposes. On March 28, Hermann Göring required an orderly redistribution of stolen Jewish property. Some four-fifths of Jewish businesses in Austria were aryanized by the end of 1938, far surpassing the pace in Germany itself. In August, Adolf Eichmann, the head of the Jewish section of Reinhard Heydrich's SD, established in Vienna a Central Office for Jewish Emigration.

In 1938, some sixty thousand Jews left Austria, as compared to some forty thousand who left Germany. And most of those German Jews emigrated after Nazis applied the lessons that had been learned in Vienna.

In 1935, German Jews had been reduced to second-class citizens. In 1938, some Nazis discovered that the most effective way to separate Jews from the protection of the state was to destroy the state. Any legal discrimination would be complicated by its unforeseen consequences for other aspects of the law and in bureaucratic practice. Even matters that might seem simple, such as expropriation and emigration, proceeded rather slowly in Nazi Germany. When Austria was destroyed, by contrast, Austria's Jews no longer enjoyed any state protection and were victimized by a majority that wished to distance itself from the past and align itself with the future. Statelessness opened a window of opportunity for those who were ready for violence and theft. By the very logic of *Anschluss,* the Nazi state itself had to close that window, since Austria was meant to become a part of Germany, and anarchy fomented by the SA would undo its own ability to rule. But even a moment of temporary statelessness had profound consequences. March 1938 was the first time that Nazis could do as they pleased with Jews, and the result was humiliation, pain, and flight.

Avraham Stern, the radical Zionist and client of the Polish regime, happened to be in central Europe at the time. He was visiting Warsaw for consultations with Polish authorities after a Revisionist Zionist congress in Prague in January 1938. On his way back from Poland to Palestine he stopped in Austria and spoke to the new Nazi authorities about the emigration of a few right-wing comrades to Palestine—one of the men he brought out believed that Stern had "negotiated with Eichmann." This was the kind of thing that Polish authorities had been hoping that Stern could do, though on a far larger scale.

On March 15, 1938, the day of the *Anschluss,* Polish diplomats were preparing a pro-Zionist request to the Americans. They asked the U.S. Department of State to pressure the British Foreign Office to open Palestine to Jewish migrants from Europe. In general the Poles urged American diplomats to support an independent Israel with the most expansive possible boundaries. The timing was no coincidence. The major consequence of *Anschluss* was exactly the opposite of what the Polish leadership desired. German policy and Polish policy both aimed to extrude Jews; now an enlarged Germany was dispatching Jews to Poland. Some twenty thousand of the Jews in Austria were Polish citizens, many of whom claimed and received the right to return to their country of origin. Since America and Palestine remained blocked (except to daredevils like Stern), Poland could expect ever more Jewish immigration as German power spread.

Polish diplomats worked unceasingly to open Palestine to Jewish settlement, but were in no position to force that issue. German repressions of Jews had led Britain not to soften but to harden its line on Jewish immigration to Palestine. The Polish foreign ministry asked the Polish parliament after the *Anschluss* for the right to review the documentation of all citizens who had resided abroad for longer than five years. This was granted on March 31, 1938. Although the law and most of the internal bureaucratic correspondence avoided the word "Jew," the purpose of the new policy was clear: to block the next wave of returning Polish Jews. As Drymmer himself put it, the goal was "excluding the unworthy and above all disposing of the destructive element," by which he certainly meant Jews. This was a qualitative change in Polish citizenship policy, occasioned by the pressure of *Anschluss* and immigration limits in Palestine and the United States, and inspired by German examples. Until 1938, Polish diplomats, whatever their personal feelings, had intervened on behalf of all Polish citizens, including Jews.

The Nazis understood the implications of the Polish initiative for the sixty thousand or so Jews of Polish citizenship residing in Germany in 1938. If these people lost their Polish citizenship while living in Germany, it would become very difficult to expel them later to Poland. Berlin asked Warsaw for a delay in the application of the Polish law, and the German coercive apparatus was mobilized for its greatest stroke thus far. With Himmler's approval, Heydrich arranged for the forcible expulsion of some seventeen thousand Jews of Polish citizenship across the German-Polish border on the night of October 28. This was a shockingly massive exercise of coercion by the standards of the day. It was also the first major action of such a kind by the SS, whose capacity for violence expanded rapidly at the German border. The surprise deportation of Jews from Germany to Poland was a strange contrast to the words of Hitler, who was speaking just at this time to the Polish government about a common Jewish policy.

In European capitals in 1938, state destruction could appear to be something that happened to other people, perhaps even as a beneficial correction of the postwar order. Neither the western powers nor the Poles concerned themselves with the passing of Austria. The Jewish perspective was different: Jews could see the beginning of a general process of separation from European states, and began to sense that they had nowhere to go. In July 1938, representatives of thirty-two countries, led by the United States, discussed Jewish emigration at Évian-les-Bains in France. Only the

Dominican Republic agreed to take any Jews. The various ways that Jews were separated from the state in Europe, meanwhile, began to interact and mutually reinforce. The German destruction of Austria brought Jews to Poland. Warsaw reacted by seeking to deny citizenship to Polish Jews living abroad. Berlin responded by expelling such people across the Polish border. By the standards of the time and place, this seemed to Jews like a catastrophe, above all to the individuals and families concerned. Very often these were people whose whole lives were in Germany and whose connections to Poland were quite limited.

The Grynszpan family, for example, had moved to Germany from the Russian Empire in 1911, seven years before Poland had regained independence. The children had been born in Germany, spoke German, and regarded themselves as Germans. They held Polish passports after 1918 because their parents hailed from a part of the Russian Empire that had become Poland. In 1935, the Grynszpans sent their son Herschel, then fifteen, to stay with an aunt and uncle in Paris. By 1938, his Polish passport and his German visa had both expired, and he had been denied legal residency in France. His aunt and uncle had to hide him in a garret so that he would not be expelled. On November 3, they showed him a postcard from his sister, mailed right after the family had been deported from Germany to Poland: "everything is finished for us." The next day Herschel Grynszpan bought a gun, took the metro to the German embassy, asked to meet a German diplomat, and shot the one who agreed to see him. It was, as he confessed to the French police, an act of revenge for the suffering of his family and his people.

Some of the top Nazis saw an opportunity to move toward a Final Solution on the territory of Germany. With Hitler's permission, Goebbels organized the coordinated attacks on Jewish property and synagogues on the night of November 9 that came to be known, as a result of all the broken glass, as *Kristallnacht.* The official pogroms were indeed a shattering experience for many German Jews. Some two hundred of them were killed or committed suicide. The deliberate violence in Germany itself in November 1938 was thus the closing of a circle that was opened with the destruction of the Austrian state. The *Anschluss* had led to the flight of Jews to Poland; this prompted new Polish restrictions on Jews living abroad; this led the Germans to expel Polish Jews; this caused an assassination in Paris that served as a pretext for organized violence in Germany. The *Kristallnacht* pogroms showed not only what the destruction of Austria had enabled, but also the limits of applying the violent side of the Austrian model within Germany. In Austria, public violence was possible during the interval between the end of Austrian authority and the consolidation of German authority. Such an opening could not really be created in Germany. The German state was to be mutated but not destroyed.

With *Kristallnacht,* Goebbels did show that the Austrian model of expropriation and emigration could function in Germany. It was only after violence had actually been delivered on a national scale that German Jews began to leave their homeland in large numbers. Nevertheless, disorderly violence within the Reich itself was revealed to be a dead end. Most of German public opinion was opposed to the chaos. Visible despair led to expressions of sympathy with Jews, rather than the spiritual distancing that Nazis expected. Of course, it was possible for Germans not to wish to see violence inflicted upon Jews while at the same time not wishing to see Jews at all. Göring, Himmler, and Heydrich immediately drew the conclusion that inspiring pogroms inside Germany had been a mistake. Not long after they would organize pogroms in much the same way as Goebbels had, but beyond the borders of Germany, in time of war, in places where German force had destroyed the state.

Hitler did nothing to defend Goebbels, whom he had unleashed in the first place, and said nothing in public about *Kristallnacht.* Three days after *Kristallnacht,* Göring said that Hitler would now approach the western powers with a Madagascar plan for the resettlement of Jews. Two weeks after *Kristallnacht,* Hitler was discussing the deportation of European Jews to Madagascar with confused Polish diplomats. The Poles could not understand how Germans could intend such a complicated logistical operation when all they seemed able to organize was chaos in Austria and Germany. Furthermore, in light of the consequences of previous German policy towards Jews, and in the context of the ongoing discussions of a "comprehensive solution" to the problems of German-Polish relations, the idea had a whiff of blackmail. More than thirty thousand Jews had been delivered by German policy to Poland thus far in 1938. If Poland agreed to improve relations with Germany on the terms proposed by Hitler, then Germany would stop sending Jews to Poland and instead cooperate in sending them somewhere else. The Jewish question had become a source of tension in German-Polish relations. German pressure was one reason Hitler's idea of a comprehensive solution of German-Polish problems, with its promise of joint policy on Jewish matters, was unattractive.

In Warsaw in 1938, Hitler's negotiating style, so effective in Vienna, had an effect opposite to what was intended.

Over the course of 1938, as Hitler was seeking, with success, to destroy the Austrian state, and working, without success, to recruit Poland as an ally, he was also trying to provoke a conflict over Czechoslovakia. The pretext was the status of the three million Czechoslovak citizens who identified themselves as Germans. In February 1938, as Hitler was threatening Austrian leaders, he also declared that the Germans of Czechoslovakia were under his personal protection. This had no legal meaning, but that was the point: States did not matter but races did; conventions did not matter but the personal decisions of the *Führer* did. When Austria fell in March 1938, the future of Czechoslovakia darkened.

Hitler had no sincere interest in the German minority question in Czechoslovakia or anywhere else. In his worldview, Germans were a race and had a right to what they could conquer for themselves. Hitler meant to use minority questions to confuse enemies and to foment the war in which all Germans would prove their racial mettle. He raised what he thought were impossible demands on behalf of Germans in Czechoslovakia, and was then frustrated when Czechoslovakia and its allies gave him everything that he said he wanted. The result was a second improvised destruction of a European state, further worsening the position of Europe's Jews.

Czechoslovakia, like Austria, was a creation of the peace treaties after the First World War. Whereas Austria, as a rump successor state of the Habsburg monarchy, was punished as an enemy, the new state of Czechoslovakia was meant as a reward to people seen as allies. Before the First World War, Czech politicians had always been rather comfortable within the Habsburg monarchy, whose multinational character and liberal constitution protected Czechs from domination by Germans. It was only when the monarchy's existence was threatened that they began to speak about an independent state. By the middle of the First World War, it seemed probable that the old monarchy was doomed whether it won or lost. If it won, it would be nothing more than a satellite of Germany, which would oppress the Czechs. If it lost, it would be destroyed by triumphant democracies of the West. In this situation, a few Czechs began to lobby for recognition in the western capitals. Because theirs was a small people, they claimed that Slovaks also belonged to the same nation. Because they wished their state to be defensible, they asked for mountain ranges inhabited mainly by Germans. Czechoslovakia was established on the principle of self-determination, with a generous admixture of political realism.

Czechoslovakia was thus like the old Habsburg monarchy: It was multinational and liberal. Unlike its neighbors, it maintained a democratic system through 1938. As Hitler sought to dismantle Czechoslovakia, he called the mountainous territories inhabited by Germans the invented name "Sudetenland," which falsely suggested that they had some historic unity. Although the region defined by Hitler had a German majority overall, it included zones that had Czech majorities. It also included Czechoslovakia's natural defenses, as well as the impressive fortifications built up by the Czechoslovak army. The Czechoslovak armaments industry was the best in Europe at the time, and Hitler's zone also included its major factories. The famous Škoda works, one of the most impressive industrial complexes in Europe, was three miles inside the border of the "Sudetenland."

Czechoslovakia was a creation of the western democracies and saw itself as one of them. It was an ally of France and enjoyed some sympathy in Britain, though perhaps less than it deserved. Wiser heads in Paris understood that Hitler's proclaimed defense of the Germans was a political preparation for an invasion of Czechoslovakia, which, if the French fulfilled their treaty obligation, would lead to a general European war. The Soviet Union now expressed an interest in the well-being of Czechoslovakia and made overtures to Paris. French leaders hoped for an arrangement with Moscow that might deter Hitler, or at least decrease the likelihood that France would have to face Germany alone.

Unfortunately for the French, at precisely this time the Soviet NKVD was in the midst of executing half of the higher officers of the Red Army in a tremendous wave of terror. Although the details were not known to the French general staff, French officers and diplomats did notice that their

Soviet interlocutors kept disappearing without a trace. Even absent this demoralizing development, the French would have needed to convince either Poland or Romania to allow Soviet forces to cross their countries. The USSR shared no border with Czechoslovakia, and so any intervention by the Red Army would involve the passage of Soviet troops through a third country. In Warsaw and Bucharest, the Czechoslovak crisis began to look like the pretext for a Soviet intervention in central Europe. The Poles and Romanians feared a Soviet invasion of their own countries more than a German invasion of Czechoslovakia.

In September, the second European crisis of 1938 reached its height. Hitler had ordered preparations for war with Czechoslovakia in May, with an expected invasion in October. He had also instructed the leaders of the German national minority to escalate their demands. On September 12, Hitler gave a rousing although factually absurd speech about the need to rescue Germans from Czech policies of extermination and to do away with Czechoslovakia generally. There was nothing at all inevitable about the fulfillment of his wishes. The Czechoslovak state was quite impressive in most respects; indeed, in its combination of prosperity and freedom, it was unmatched in central Europe and perhaps on the entire continent. Open talk of the destruction of Czechoslovakia made the destruction possible, especially insofar as European leaders could persuade themselves that yielding to such rhetoric somehow meant yielding to reason.

Even as London and Paris urged Prague to compromise, the Soviets provided indications of their willingness to intervene in central Europe to protect Czechoslovakia. Four Soviet army groups were moved to the Polish border. Three days after Hitler's speech, the Soviet regime accelerated the ethnic cleansing of its western borderlands. From September 15 onward Soviet authorities carried out swift mass executions in the Polish Operation without any sort of review. Local authorities formed "troikas"—groups of three—from the local party head, procurator, and ranking NKVD officer. The troikas could sentence people to death and carry out the sentence without awaiting any sort of confirmation. Oral instructions made clear that "Poles should be completely destroyed."

Throughout the territory of Soviet Ukraine, which bordered Poland, Polish men were shot in huge numbers in September 1938. In the city of Voroshilovgrad (today Luhansk), Soviet authorities considered 1,226 cases in the Polish Operation during the Czechoslovak crisis and ordered 1,226 executions. In September 1938, in the regions of Soviet Ukraine adjacent to the Polish border, Soviet units went from village to village as death squads. Polish men were shot, Polish women and children were sent to the Gulag, and reports were filed afterward. In the Zhytomyr region, which bordered Poland, Soviet authorities sentenced 100 people to death on September 22, 138 more on September 23, and 408 more on September 28.

That was the day that Hitler had set as the deadline for an invasion of Czechoslovakia. The German army was standing at the Czechoslovak border. The Red Army was standing at the Polish border; and the NKVD had cleared the hinterland of suspicious elements by massive shootings and deportations of Poles. A German invasion of Czechoslovakia would have provided the pretext for a Soviet invasion of Poland. Perhaps the Red Army would then have entered Czechoslovakia and sought to engage the German army. More likely it would have sought some truce with Germany that allowed it to take territory from Poland without having to engage the Germans. The suspicion is warranted, since the next time Soviet forces massed at the Polish border it was eleven months later, after Moscow had made just such a deal with Berlin. But this cannot be known for certain, since the crisis was resolved. At Munich on September 30, 1938, the leaders of Britain, France, Italy, and Germany decided that Czechoslovakia should cede the territories that Hitler wanted.

Czechoslovakia had no part in this Munich accord and was not legally bound by it. Abandoned by their friends and allies, its leaders decided not to fight the Germans alone. As Czechoslovak troops and police withdrew from the "Sudetenland" in October, political violence prevailed: mostly Germans attacking other Germans, pro-Nazis killing the rival Social Democrats whose orientation had been illegal in Nazi Germany for five years. In November the "Sudetenland" was joined to Germany—Germans, Czechs, mountains, fortresses, arms factories, and all. An *Einsatzgruppe* entered with the assignment of eliminating political opponents; its members were explicitly forbidden to kill. The thirty thousand or so Jews who had lived there, like the Jews of Austria a few months earlier, found themselves suddenly deprived of state protection. About seventeen thousand of them were deported by the Germans or fled; they lost their property. In what remained of Czechoslovakia, Jews rightly feared the total destruction of their state and thus the loss of their property rights. About a third of Czechoslovak banking and industrial capital was owned by Jews; much of this was acquired at tremendous discount by Germans in late 1938 and early 1939.

Poland bordered all parties most concerned by the crisis of state destruction of 1938: Germany, Czechoslovakia, and the Soviet Union. Warsaw had no sympathy for Prague, since the Czechoslovak army had seized some important industrial territory around Teschen in 1919 when the Polish army had been busy fighting the Soviets. Polish diplomats wrote of Czechoslovakia as an "artificial creation" and an "absurdity." While Berlin presented itself as the defender of the rights of the German minority in Czechoslovakia, Warsaw followed suit and presented itself as the protector of Poles in Czechoslovakia. When Germany seized the territories it called the Sudetenland, Poland exploited the moment to claim the Teschen region that Czechoslovakia had taken in 1919.

Poland looked like a German ally in these days, although its policy was, in fact, an independent one that Warsaw had to explain to Berlin. Poland wanted the Teschen region for some of the same reasons that Germany wanted the Sudetenland: It was rich in resources, rail connections, and industry. Teschen would help Poland prepare for war, but Germans could not be entirely sure on which side Poland would be fighting. Polish diplomats tried to get credit in Berlin for their "decided position" against the Soviet Union, with no effect. Hitler was consciously provoking a European war, and would have taken it in whatever form it came. He could not be impressed that Poland had proven to be a barrier to a Soviet intervention in Czechoslovakia when what he really wanted was an offensive war against the Soviet Union. He expected much more from the Poles than an imitation of German policy in these local crises, and he was telling them so.

By November 1938, Germany had absorbed Austria and much of Czechoslovakia. Some nine million people had been added to the Reich, along with Austria's gold and Czechoslovakia's arms. No doubt Hitler thought that these gains made his offer of a "comprehensive solution" to German-Polish problems more difficult for the Polish leadership to refuse. After all, Germany had shown that it could take what it wanted in any case. Hitler believed that Warsaw had no choice but to recognize common interests with respect to the Jews and the Soviet Union. But Warsaw saw the Jewish and the Soviet questions rather differently than did Berlin, and it viewed growing German power as a source of worry rather than as a reason for compromise. The Poles understood, since the Germans had said so for years, that territorial adjustments in central Europe were only a small part of a much larger plan.

The destruction of Austria and Czechoslovakia raised the Jewish and eastern questions in ways that were disturbing in Warsaw. The "scrubbing parties" and *Kristallnacht* had brought tens of thousands of Jews to Poland. The Munich accords, meanwhile, opened the issue of the future of all Czechoslovak territories, including the far eastern region known as Subcarpathian Ruthenia. Germany declared the region autonomous in October 1938. By the terms of the First Vienna Award of November 1938, a southern zone was ceded to Hungary, and Germany then recognized the remainder as a state. Warsaw had some influence in the new statelet for two weeks in October, until its men were displaced by Avgustyn Voloshyn and other Ukrainian nationalists. These were people who believed that the Polish state should be dismantled and a Ukrainian state created from its territories. German-backed Ukrainian revisionists were thus in control of a sensitive territory on Poland's border just as the future of German-Polish relations was being decided. During these last weeks of 1938, it appeared in Warsaw that Berlin was using Ukrainian nationalism against Poland—at the very moment that German diplomats were promising Poland Ukrainian territory from the Soviet Union.

Germany wanted Polish territorial concessions and promised three things in return: a war against the Soviet Union, a resolution of the Jewish question, and territory from Ukraine. Polish authorities wanted no war, and doubted German goodwill on all three issues. German proposals seemed either contradictory or made in bad faith. Uncertainty about Ukraine was a further reason, as 1938 came to a close, why Hitler's proposal of a "comprehensive solution" failed to find support in Warsaw.

As 1939 began, Hitler finally faced international resistance he could not overcome with words. On the fifth of January, Polish foreign minister

Józef Beck rejected Hitler's proposals after a personal conversation. The Poles were prepared to offer concessions on the issues of Danzig and the corridor, but these of course were not the issue. From Hitler's perspective these territorial matters were propaganda signals to German public opinion that his revisionism had something to do with what most Germans wanted. Beck was uninterested in Hitler's main offer: vague promises of resolving the Jewish question and territorial gains in Ukraine after a joint attack on the Soviet Union. Thus Poland was revealed to be a problem, a barrier rather than a bridge to Hitler's main object of dispatching Germans to a fateful war of racial destruction in the East. In these weeks the Poles did try to tilt their foreign policy back toward Moscow.

Hitler's problem was that his Polish interlocutors understood his foreign policy, if not well, then at least better than the German public did. The German foreign minister, Joachim von Ribbentrop, made a final effort on the twenty-fifth of January, a symbolic date, the five-year anniversary of the signing of the German-Polish nonaggression declaration. Once again Ukraine was the bait. Once again the Germans failed. Polish diplomats asked Ribbentrop not to claim in Berlin that any agreement had been or might be reached. On the very day of that conversation, the *New York Times* published an article in which Poland's foreign minister Beck presented the Soviet Union as an equal to Nazi Germany in its foreign policy. By calling both neighbors "allies" in front of the foreign press, Beck made clear that Poland would not join either in a war against the other. Ribbentrop returned to Berlin the next day with the certainty that Poland would never be a German ally against the Soviet Union.

The day of Ribbentrop's return from Warsaw was a Thursday; the following Monday, Hitler gave the most notorious speech of his career. On January 30, 1939, Hitler proclaimed to the German parliament that if the Jews began a world war, it would end with their extermination. Poland had always been a matter of practice rather than theory for Hitler, and now improvisation gave way to rage. The particular style of international politics he had developed in 1938, the destruction of neighbors with words rather than weapons, had failed. His specific calculation about Poland, that its leaders would join in an antisemitic crusade against the USSR, had proven wrong. Both promises and threats regarding Jewish and Ukrainian questions had failed. The Polish choice was the end of a Nazi illusion that had lasted for five years.

Hitler decided to eliminate Poland as an object of international relations. The sudden necessity he felt to invade Poland had tremendous implications for Hitler's plans. With Poland as an ally or benign neutral, Germany might have avoided the traditional problem of encirclement, its doom in the First World War. In such a scenario Germany could first invade France and remove the French army from the war, and then turn its attention to the real target, the riches of the Soviet Union. In Hitler's basic scheme, Germany was to smash the USSR and become a world power after France was beaten and as the British (and the Americans) sat by and watched. Having redeemed the German race, attained continental power, and begun the grand project of planetary salvation from the Jews, Germany could later confront the British and the Americans as necessary. But with Poland as an adversary, the entire calculus was altered. As of January

30, 1939, as a result of his determination to begin a war despite his Polish miscalculation, Hitler had to contemplate a global conflict that would begin not after but before he won his European war. A German invasion of Poland might bring France into a war against Germany, thus creating encirclement. Worse still, it might draw in the United Kingdom, an eventuality Hitler always hoped to avoid. If Germany had to fight a long war in the west it was then to be feared that the USSR might intervene from the east.

Of course, in Hitler's mind, any such insidious alliance against Germany would have to be the work of Jews. Since Jews, he believed, held the real power in foreign capitals, they would be the ones to determine whether or not a German invasion of Poland in 1939 actually did become a world war. If Jews could be made to understand that a world war was not in their interest, Hitler seems to have believed, then France and Britain and the Soviet Union would stay out of the initial conflict. If the Jews could be deterred with threats, then the German war against Poland could remain a local conflict in eastern Europe, a minor setback in Hitler's plans rather than a major disruption. Thus Hitler's failed Polish policy did not lead to warnings to the Poles. It led to warnings to the Jews.

Hitler's notion that a threat to exterminate Jews would influence the future policy of the great powers was erroneous. The January 30, 1939, "prophecy," as Hitler would call it in later speeches, had no resonance in Paris, London, or Moscow. What did matter was the continuation of German aggression in Czechoslovakia a few weeks later. On March 15, 1939, Germany moved forward to complete the destruction of that country, incorporating the Czech lands of Bohemia and Moravia as a "Protectorate" and creating an independent Slovak state that was to be an ally of Germany. Those who had betrayed Czechoslovakia to Germany at Munich in September 1938 were now betrayed by Germany in their turn. Since Hitler had taken lands that were populated by Czechs rather than Germans, it was clear that his claims to be interested only in national self-determination were lies. Those in London and Paris who had covered their complicity in the rape of Czechoslovakia with guilty references to the First World War realized that they had helped prepare the way for a Second. Paris and London in March 1939 now found themselves reaching the same conclusion as Warsaw had in December: Germany was about to undertake a massive war of aggression in which the only choices were resistance and submission.

On March 21, 1939, a few days after the destruction of Czechoslovakia, Germany unveiled its new propaganda line towards Poland. After five years of coordinating his propaganda with Warsaw, Goebbels could finally say what he, and no doubt many Germans, actually thought. From one day to the next Poland was again the ancient enemy, the oppressor of Germans, the grasping and monstrous creation of an unjust postwar settlement. Hitler's diplomatic misfortune with Warsaw was good luck in domestic politics. War was not popular with Germans in 1939. But a war against Poland for border territories, now apparently in the offing, was far less unpopular than a massive ideological war of aggression in alliance with Poland against the Soviet Union would have been.

On March 25, 1939, Hitler ordered preparations for a war of destruction against Poland. Aside from the political preliminaries directed to Germany and world public opinion, the planned campaign had nothing to do with Danzig or an extraterritorial corridor. Indeed, it had little to do with war as conventionally understood. What Hitler suddenly wanted was the complete annihilation of the Polish state and the physical elimination of all Poles who might be capable of building such a state. He would say as much, repeatedly, in the weeks to come. This radical plan to destroy a polity and a political nation was consistent with his general ideas about Slavs, and the invasion was a step eastward towards the Ukrainian breadbasket. It was however inconsistent both with his actions of the previous five years and with the announced reasons for German hostility now appearing in the press. The goal of the propaganda was to propel Germans, unknowingly, into a far greater conflict in the East.

The Poles were in a relatively good position to know what the war would be about. They knew that their choice was not between war and peace, as British prime minister Neville Chamberlain had thought at Munich, but between one kind of war and another: an offensive campaign as a German ally against the Soviet Union, or a defensive campaign against a German attack. If Poland had chosen a submissive alliance rather than a defiant resistance, thought Foreign Minister Beck, "We would have defeated Russia, and afterward we would be taking Hitler's cows out to pasture in the Urals." Beck, who after a long tenure as foreign minister had made many enemies in Europe, now made a hero of himself by resisting Hitler in public. On the fifth of May, 1939, responding to Hitler's speeches, he addressed the Polish parliament. He used the kind of language that, until that point, no statesman, including those enjoying greater safety and power, had directed to Hitler. There could be compromise on various issues. But there could be no compromise on sovereignty. "There is only one thing in the life of people, nations, and states that is without price," said Beck, "and that thing is honor."

Yet neither the collapse of German-Polish relations nor the threat of war with Germany had any effect on Polish policy towards its own Jews. That policy had always been a sovereign one, arising from popular antisemitism and mass unemployment, calculated from assumptions about Polish interests. From the Polish perspective, Germany was a confusing and unhelpful partner on the Jewish question, whose policies had closed the gates to Palestine and driven tens of thousands of Jews to Poland. When Britain responded to German aggression against Czechoslovakia by guaranteeing Poland's security, this opened, from Warsaw's perspective, the possibility of a promising new partnership in Jewish policy. Great Britain, after all, held the mandate to Palestine and determined how many European Jews could emigrate there.

Polish relations with Britain in the 1930s had been cool, and until spring 1939 diplomats had no good occasion to raise the Palestinian issue. In Geneva, at meetings of the League of Nations, Polish diplomats buttonholed their British counterparts and tried to explain the need for the immigration of Polish Jews to Palestine, but this could easily be turned aside. The closest thing the Poles had to an argument was that the world was focused only on the very small German Jewish population, while ignoring the much bigger Polish Jewish population. Polish diplomats cautiously made the case that an opening of Palestine only for German Jews (which did not, in any case, happen) would be seen inside Poland as unfair. In spring 1939 Polish diplomats could raise the matter of Jewish emigration apropos of something very important: the coming war.

When Beck flew to London in April 1939 for discussions that were supposed to concern the German threat to Europe, he treated the Jewish question as though it were the first order of business. Since Beck and the British foreign secretary, Lord Halifax, hardly knew each other, this priority led to a surreal exchange. Knowing of Beck's preoccupations, Halifax had tried to get his ambassador in Warsaw to explain to the Poles that the two states had no "colonial question" to discuss. Halifax paid no heed to Beck when he raised the Palestine question, and British policy was moving in a direction opposite to Polish preferences. That same month, Prime Minister Chamberlain said that if Britain had to anger one side in Palestine it should be the Jews rather than the Arabs. The loyalty of Arabs and Muslims was too important in the British Empire as a whole to be challenged, especially at a time of coming conflict. A British White Paper of May 1939 recommended that future Jewish immigration to Palestine be made subject to Arab approval. London had decided to protect Poland from the German threat and in this sense, indirectly, Poland's Jews. But the British were completely unmoved by the Polish idea that Palestine should be opened to massive Jewish settlement immediately.

Despite Warsaw's new relationship with London, the conspiratorial track of Poland's Palestine policy remained operative in spring 1939. Polish authorities maintained their friendly relationship with the Revisionist Zionist leader Vladimir Jabotinsky, who after *Kristallnacht* had hoped for an evacuation of a million Jews in 1939. He knew that his Polish patrons would make his case to the British. In the early months of the year, Jabotinsky, like his Polish partners, believed that the prospect of war might create an opening in London. He wanted to form Jewish legions that would fight for the British against the Germans, with the hope that the political capital thus earned could be converted into British support of a State of Israel after the war. Yet more and more of his followers were thinking not of the legionary but the terrorist strategy, whereby an empire weakened by war could be driven from the national homeland. Polish policy was aligned with the Jewish rebels whom the British had most reason to fear.

Between February and May 1939, at the very time that Britain and Poland joined forces against Germany, Polish military intelligence was training a select group of Irgun activists in a secret location near Andrychów. The Polish officers stressed the kinds of measures that Poles had used with success during and after the First World War: sabotage, bombings, and irregular warfare against an occupying army. The twenty-five Jews who were trained came from Palestine, but the language of instruction was Polish (with a Hebrew translation). At the end of the session Avraham Stern arrived and gave a rousing speech. In Polish he thanked the Polish officers for their support and noted the similarities between the Jewish and Polish liberation struggles. In Hebrew he described the future Jewish invasion of Palestine. As one of the participants later noted with a certain amount of understatement, "the Polish government's support of the Irgun could be viewed as an unfriendly act toward Britain, with whom Poland wanted to sign a treaty."

The men to whom Stern spoke became Irgun officers who would lead the revolt against the British. When they returned to Palestine in May 1939, just as the British White Paper was published, and right after Poland accepted a British security guarantee, these Jewish radicals began to employ their Polish weapons and training in operations against Poland's new ally. The British noticed the training and confiscated some of the weapons, but never made the connection to Warsaw.

Polish military intelligence officers excelled in the kinds of insurgency in which they trained Irgun, as they did in certain aspects of counterintelligence work. A special unit of military intelligence, for example, had broken the mechanized German code system known as "Enigma," and built duplicates of the machine in order to decode messages. In July 1939, Polish cryptologists passed on their knowledge and these duplicates to their British and French allies. This work would be important for the British later in the war, providing the basis for the decryption station at Bletchley Park. In their estimations of just how the war would unfold, however, the men and women of Polish intelligence committed a major error.

After 1933, Polish military intelligence, the Second Department of the General Staff, regarded both the Soviet Union and Nazi Germany as threats, with the Soviets seen as the more worrisome. The debate at the top of the Second Department was about whether a Soviet or a German invasion was more likely. Few if any officers recognized that Poland's own decision not to ally with Nazi Germany would lead to a rapid German invasion of Poland. Once Britain and France had guaranteed Poland's sovereignty, Germany faced encirclement from west and east. Hitler had lost, at least for the time being, any hope for the constellation he wanted: British indifference or support during a German war against the Soviet Union. Poland, which was not supposed to make a difference one way or the other, had altered the basic calculation of *My Struggle*. Logically, Germany's only chance to avoid encirclement lay to the east of Poland: the Soviet Union itself. And this was the logic that Hitler indeed followed.

The Poles could be forgiven for not expecting this. They strongly suspected that Germany planned to invade the Soviet Union. Yet few people in Warsaw or elsewhere could anticipate Hitler's rapid changes in tactics. Seeing only the final goal as important, he was capable of doing almost anything along the way. Thus after a whole career of anti-communism and after five years of recruiting Poland for a war against the Soviet Union, Hitler decided to ask the Soviet Union for a war against Poland. On August 20, 1939, he requested a meeting between his foreign minister, Ribbentrop, and the Soviet leadership. Stalin had been hoping for something like this. Berlin could offer what London and Paris could not: the remaking of eastern Europe. After German policy openly shifted against Poland in the spring, Stalin made a telling gesture towards Hitler. Knowing that Hitler had pledged never to make peace with Jewish communists, he fired his Jewish commissar for foreign affairs, Maxim Litvinov, a few weeks after the public break between Germany and Poland. Hitler told army commanders that "Litvinov's dismissal was decisive." When Ribbentrop arrived in Moscow he spoke with Viacheslav Molotov, a Russian.

The agreement signed by Ribbentrop and Molotov on August 23, 1939, was much more than a nonaggression pact. It included a secret protocol that divided Finland, Estonia, Latvia, Lithuania, and Poland into Soviet and German spheres of influence. Poland was split between the two, with the obvious implication that the Soviets would join the Germans in invading the country and cooperate in the destruction of the state and political society. The precise contents of the secret protocol did not have to be known for the meaning of the accord to be clear to intelligent observers. Peace with the Soviet Union meant, at the very least, a free hand for Hitler.

By chance the World Zionist Congress was in session in Geneva when news of the Molotov-Ribbentrop pact was reported by the world's press. The Jews gathered from Europe and the four corners of the world were shocked. The leader of the General Zionists, Chaim Weizmann, closed the congress with the words "Friends, I have only one wish: that we all remain alive." There was no melodrama in this. The regions covered by the secret protocol of the Soviet-German agreement were a heartland of world Jewry, continuously settled by Jews for half a millennium. This heartland was about to become the most dangerous place for Jews in their entire history. A Holocaust would begin there twenty months later. Within three years, most of the millions of Jews who lived there would be dead.

For Stalin, the deal with Hitler was a great relief. He and many of his comrades had read Hitler's writings and took them seriously. Stalin understood that Hitler aimed for the fertile farmland of Ukraine and said as much on a number of occasions. In agreeing to divide eastern Europe with Hitler, he hoped to divert the armed conflict to western Europe, where Britain and France would have to deal with the Germans. From a Soviet ideological perspective, this meant that the contradictions of capitalism were working themselves out on the battlefield, with the help of a nudge from Soviet diplomacy. From Stalin's tactical perspective, the best way to fight a war was to allow others to bleed themselves white, and then move to take the spoils.

Just as pertinent as Stalin's calculations about future conflict was his present community of interests with Hitler. In 1939, Hitler reached the same conclusion that Stalin had reached in 1934: Since Poland was no longer a conceivable ally in a European war, it had no reason to exist. Molotov spoke of Poland as the "ugly offspring" and Hitler of Poland as the "unreal creation" of Versailles. Stalin proclaimed a "common desire to get rid of the old equilibrium." He knew that the breaking of the old balance meant anarchy and pain for Jews. He was aware that dividing Poland in half meant giving two million Jews to Hitler. The Treaty on Borders and Friendship that the Soviets and Germans signed on September 28, 1939, shifted Warsaw, which capitulated that day to German siege, from the Soviet to the German zone. Stalin thus granted Europe's most important Jewish city to Hitler. The joint invasion of Poland, Stalin said, meant a friendship with Germany sealed "in blood." Much of the blood shed in wartime Poland would be that of Jewish civilians, including three hundred thousand Jews of Warsaw.

Aside from Soviet and German propagandists, working in harmony, few people could find anything good in the Molotov-Ribbentrop pact. One exception, thousands of miles away, was American evangelists, known as dispensationalists, who believed in a coming Armageddon in which they would be transported to heaven. They read the improbable accord between Nazis and Stalinists as the realization of a biblical prophecy (Ezekiel 38) of an alliance between Gog and Gomer that would attack the Land of Israel and thus fulfill one of the preconditions for the return of the messiah.

Avraham Stern in Palestine concluded from the Molotov-Ribbentrop pact that Hitler was more pragmatic than he appeared. If the *Führer* would deal with a Soviet Union that he had always condemned as a front for Jewish power, then why not with Jews themselves? Perhaps the coming conflict would, despite everything, provide Jews with some sort of opportunity for redemption. Stern, who had drunk deeply from the cup of secular messianism, was not so far away from the Americans who imagined Jesus returning as a savior bearing a sword rather than an olive branch, massacring his enemies rather than loving them. Stern's poetic inspiration Uri Zvi Greenberg wrote of the messiah arriving on a tank. Stern himself prophesied that the blood of Jews would be the red carpet for the messiah, adorned by the white lilies of the brains blown from their skulls.

Stern was about to lose a patron in a bloody tragedy that was equal to the darkest poetic fantasy. On August 22, 1939, Hitler told his generals that the "destruction of Poland" was "in the foreground. The goal is to destroy living forces, not to reach any particular line." Here was the opportunity, if unexpected, to begin a racial war. He continued: "Close your hearts to mercy. Brutal action. Eighty million people must get their due. Their existence must be secured. The stronger has the right." Germany was indeed much the stronger, in no small measure because of what Hitler had acquired without war from Austria and Czechoslovakia in 1938.

The invasion of Poland came from all sides: on September 1 from the north and west by German forces from Germany, from the south by German forces from what had been Czechoslovakia with the assistance of Slovak troops, and then on September 17 from the east by the Red Army. German and Soviet forces met at Brest and organized a joint victory parade, swastika followed by hammer and sickle, "Deutschland über Alles" followed by the Internationale. The Soviet commander invited German reporters to visit him in Moscow after the common "victory over capitalist Albion." Some of the German tanks admired on the streets of Brest were likely of Czechoslovak production; some of the German soldiers and SS men invading Poland were Austrian. German technical superiority, which Hitler saw as racial superiority, was a fact. When the German air force overflew the parade at Brest, its pilots were pausing from their terror bombing of Polish towns and cities. Bombing civilians was a tactic that Europeans generally saw as legitimate when used in colonial possessions; it was now applied in Europe itself. Far more Jews were killed in the German terror bombing of Warsaw in September 1939 than as a result of all prior German policies taken together in the six years since Hitler had come to power. Likewise, the seven thousand Jewish soldiers killed in action resisting the German invasion far outnumbered the Jews who had been killed in Germany to that point.

The German invasion of Poland was undertaken on the logic that Poland did not, had not, and could not exist as a sovereign state. Soldiers taken prisoner could be shot, since the Polish army could not really have existed as such. Once the campaign was over, what began was not an occupation, since by Nazi logic there was no prior polity whose territory could be occupied. Poland was a geographic designation meaning land to be taken. German international lawyers contended that Poland was not a state, but merely a place without a legitimate sovereign over which the Germans found themselves masters. Polish law was declared null and void—indeed, never to have existed. This state of affairs was based upon the simple will of the *Führer;* once war was under way this sufficed for important dispensations beyond the borders of prewar Germany. The true Nazi revolution had begun.

The nullification of statehood and law was no technicality, but rather a matter of life and death. Traditionally, European states understood one another's regimes as legitimate. Even when they were at war, they recognized one another's existence and the distinctiveness of one another's constitutional traditions. Citizenship is meaningful only when recognized reciprocally; Hitler was destroying the principle of citizenship when he destroyed a neighboring civitas, moving Germany along with Europe towards lawlessness. Germany was treating Poland as European states in their most destructive moments treated settler colonies: as a bit of earth inhabited by ungoverned and undefined beings. SS publications described Poland, a country where more than thirty million people lived, as "virgin territory." Italians quickly got the message, comparing Poland to Ethiopia, their own African conquest.

Coordinating this utopian colonial image with twentieth-century political reality in the middle of Europe required not just the subjugation of people, but also the destruction of the institutions that were, in fact, present. The bulk of Germany's imperial work in Poland would involve not so much the creation of something new, as the removal of what was actually there. Restoring the law of the jungle in a country where forests had been cleared a thousand years earlier would require an enormous amount of work.

The destruction of the Polish state was achieved in both ink and blood. As the lawyers worked their typewriters, the murderers worked their guns. Hitler called for a "massive extermination of the Polish intelligentsia." Insofar as Polish culture existed at all, thought Hitler, it would disappear with the physical elimination of its relatively few "bearers." Hitler foresaw a "resolution of the Polish problem" by the murder of those who might be regarded as fully human. The invasion of Poland gave the state destroyers of the SS the cover of war for their lawless mission. Heydrich organized the *Einsatzgruppen*, task forces of policemen and SS members usually led by party and SS members of long standing. He instructed his subordinates to murder the Polish leading classes in order to render Polish resistance impossible. Thus, for example, all veterans of the Polish Legions and the Polish Military Organization were to be found and killed. The major operation of the *Einsatzgruppen* was known as Tannenberg, the plan to murder some sixty-one thousand Polish citizens.

The *Einsatzgruppen* killed about as many people as expected in Poland in autumn 1939, although they were at first inept in the actual tracking of particular individuals. Nevertheless, they kept up the killing of targeted groups after military operations concluded in October and as they established themselves in Polish cities as the stationary German police. Heydrich expected the "liquidation of leading Poles" to be complete by November. When the shooting of tens of thousands of Poles in 1939 seemed not to suffice, further "leadership elements" were identified in order to be "liquidated" in mass shootings in forests outside the major cities in spring 1940. Heydrich imagined that the killing of the elites would leave the Poles as a mass of laborers. Himmler predicted that the very idea of a Polish nation would disappear.

The first thrust of the German offensive—military, political, and racial—was directed against Poland as a political entity rather than against its Jewish citizens. But the destruction of the Polish state had the greatest consequences for Poland's Jews. Minorities depend the most on the protection of the state and upon the rule of law, and it is usually they who suffer most from anarchy and war. The Jews of Poland, to be sure, had to fear official and popular antisemitism in Poland in the late 1930s. Yet they had much more to lose than other Polish citizens from the destruction of Poland. The annihilation of the Polish state by Nazi power was not a simple disappearance, but rather a shattering of existing institutions, and the resulting fragments had sharp, cutting edges.

The first fragmentation was that of *national authority*. The German-Soviet Treaty on Borders and Friendship of September 1939 spoke of "the collapse of the Polish state"; subsequent German legal language denied that there had ever been a Polish state. All at once Jews were no longer citizens of anything. For that matter, neither were Poles, Ukrainians, Belarusians, or anyone else with Polish documents (except members of the German minority, who were suddenly privileged). Much of the subject population adapted immediately to German racial expectations. The moment the Germans entered Polish cities to allocate food, some Poles pointed out the Jews waiting in line so that Poles would get more and Jews less (or nothing). Racism and materialism were intertwined right from the beginning.

With the principle of citizenship abolished and the principle of race established, no one wanted to be treated worse than the Jews.

Much of Poland's west was annexed to the Reich—or, officially, de-annexed back to the Reich. The new German districts drawn from Polish territories, the new *Gaue,* were governed by Hitler's cronies, old Nazi party men. These leaders had much more freedom of action than their colleagues in the prewar German districts, who always had to deal with the burdens of law and bureaucracy. The largest and most important of the new *Gaue* was the *Warthegau,* home to 4.2 million Poles, 435,000 Jews, and only 325,000 Germans. This was a new kind of German district. Prewar Germany was overwhelmingly German; here Germans were a colonial elite and the majority population were "protected subjects." Polish children, for example, were to be taught a pidgin German in school, so that they would be distinguishable as racial inferiors but capable of taking orders from Germans. Much of central Poland was transformed into a colony known as the "General Government." It was initially called the "General Government of the Occupied Polish Lands," but this qualification was dropped because of its suggestion that Poland had once existed. According to Nazi logic there was no occupation, but rather a colonization of legally "empty" territory. The degree of freedom was even greater here than in the new *Gaue*, since there was not even the pretense of German law.

In the annexed zones and in the General Government, Polish civil law was replaced by anti-Jewish repression, which accelerated at a pace impossible in prewar Germany. In October 1939, the Germans seized "the property of the former Polish state" and all Jewish property. Jews were banned from practicing professions, and Jewish males were required to report for labor. Jews lost the right to remain where they were. Both Heydrich and the new governor-general Hans Frank ordered ghettoization of Polish Jews. This proceeded differently in different regions; by the end of 1941 most Polish Jews were behind the walls of a ghetto. Crucial everywhere was the simple assumption that Jews could be separated from the protection of the law: They had no power to decide where their bodies would be, and no claim to possessions. Beginning in Poland, the Germans would establish ghettos in every country where they attempted to destroy a state, and in no country where they carried out a conventional occupation. The ghetto was the urban expression of state destruction.

The creation of ghettos in the cities meant a basic transformation of the Polish landscape. Jews, who had been almost everywhere in prewar Poland, were now concentrated in a small number of urban neighborhoods. This made possible the theft by Germans of all of the Jewish property that they could take (as well as the rape of Jewish girls and women). The signal to the surrounding population was unambiguous. Jews had often been beyond the world of moral concern in interwar Poland; now they were beyond the reach of law and indeed the ambit of daily life. By the time ghettos were established and Jews deported to them, their Polish neighbors had been pauperized by German rule for about a year. This presumably made Poles more likely to steal from Jews when the opportunity arose. As was the case everywhere, people in Poland tended to hate those from whom they stole because they had stolen from them.

For most Poles, the ghettoizations of 1940 and 1941 were the moment when Jews disappeared from their lives. Hundreds of years of mixed settlement were suddenly over, from one day to the next. Jews, once seen every day in every setting, were now seen only in work columns or through walls—or, very rarely, in hiding. Their houses in the villages and their apartments in the city were there for the taking. The traditionally Jewish vocations, in commerce and the professions, would now be performed by others. German occupation obviously did not mean social advancement for Poles as such, since educated Poles were killed and the rest were treated as a mute proletariat. Poles in the General Government were seized on the streets and sent to camps as forced labor. All of this created a setting of relative deprivation, wherein many Poles found it acceptable to seize what they could from Jews as the Jews disappeared. Polish theft of Jewish property did not make Poles allies of the Germans, but it did make them seek to justify what they had done and tend to support any policy that kept the Jews from regaining what had been theirs. In any event, helping Jews who left the ghettos was punishable by death in the General Government.

The second fragmentation brought by the German destruction of the Polish state was that of *local authority,* both that of the prewar village and county administrations and the prewar Jewish autonomous bodies. The Polish central government was destroyed, Polish law was abolished, and the Polish state was declared never to have existed. Polish local authorities did remain in place, but were now unmoored from prior law and tradition. Removed from the previous institutional hierarchy by German practice, their function was fundamentally altered by Nazi priorities. They no longer executed orders from central ministries or represented the interests of local citizens. There were no longer ministries and there were no longer citizens. Instead, local authorities were made personally responsible for the implementation of German racial policies. They oversaw the deportations of Poland's Jews to ghettos and the distribution of property not taken by the Germans.

The Jews sent to the ghettos were met there by a melancholy parody of interwar Jewish authorities: the *Judenrat,* established by order of Governor-General Frank in November 1939. Under Piłsudski, Poland's Jews had been allowed to choose local self-governing authorities, known as *kehillot* or *gminy*. These bodies took responsibility for matters of religion, marriage, burial, ritual slaughter, and in some measure for social welfare and education. Jewish communal authorities were authorized to receive money from abroad to fund these activities. Under the Germans, these local authorities, generally the same people, became the *Judenrat*, responsible for the execution of German orders. They were in no reciprocal relationship with the Polish state, which no longer existed, and were henceforth prevented from maintaining connections with other Jewish communities around the world. It was simplest for Germans just to take the *kehilla* as it was, just as it was simplest to take the Polish local mayors and county commissioners as they were. What was usually decisive was the destruction of the Polish state and the character of German policy, not the character of these individuals. Those who did leave could always be replaced by others.

New Jewish police forces, armed with clubs, were technically subordinate to the *Judenräte*, but in the crucial cases took orders from the Germans. The head of the two-thousand-strong Jewish police in the Warsaw ghetto was Józef Szeryński, who had served in the Polish police before the war. Young Jewish men from Betar, who had been trained in the use of weapons by the Polish state, also showed a certain inclination to join the Jewish police. Often Jewish policemen tried to resolve strife between Jews to prevent any recourse to German authority. From 1940, the Jewish police oversaw the mandatory labor required of all Jews. From 1941, they rounded up their fellow Jews for deportations from ghettos to labor camps; in 1942, to death facilities. The Jewish informers who offered their services to the Germans tended to be people who had a record as informers for the prewar Polish police. Naturally, they were now informing about different things.

The third fragmentation of the Polish state was the separation of a once-centralized institution from the shattered hierarchy: *the Polish police.* The regular Polish police had been a hierarchically organized institution subordinate to the Ministry of Internal Affairs. In the 1930s the Polish police were instrumental in defending Jewish life, commerce, and politics. Jewish tradesmen maintained friendly relationships, often by way of bribes, with the policemen charged with protecting town markets. The Polish police sometimes sided with Poles in fights between Poles and Jews, although Polish nationalists complained that policemen sided with Betar. Polish judges often found Jews guilty of provoking the violence that was directed against them. Yet on the whole, the Polish police were expected to prevent pogroms, and generally did so. In the Poland of the 1930s, a pogrom was a violation of public property and an attempt to demonstrate the weakness of the state. Most policemen, regardless of their views about Jews, understood their duties to the bourgeois order.

Then that order changed. A conventional state that sought to monopolize violence was destroyed by a racial regime that sought to channel anarchy. When the Polish state was destroyed in September 1939, its policemen no longer had superiors to instruct them. The highest authorities of the Polish state evacuated Warsaw, leaving policemen to decide their own course. It cannot be said that Polish policemen then sided with the Germans. Many policemen from throughout Poland chose to gather in Warsaw and fight the Germans as the Polish capital was besieged. After the capitulation, they faced the classical dilemma of forces of order. To leave their posts would provoke chaos and crime. To stay meant working for a foreign invader. Most Polish policemen chose the latter. The German Order Police then racialized the units that became the subordinate Polish Order Police (known as the Blue Police): Jews could not return to duty, and Poles could not arrest Germans. Whereas Germans were not usually punished for refusing orders to shoot civilians, Polish policemen could be shot. The Polish policemen were subordinated to a German structure that they could not at first hope to understand: to the German Order Police, which meant ultimately to Himmler. In coming years, some thirty thousand German Order Policemen would take part in the murder of Jews in Poland. The Polish police became, with time, a subordinate part of the German apparatus of racial war.

The Polish state was to be destroyed because in 1939 Hitler was angry and impatient and had no better way of approaching the Soviet border than by obliterating the country that lay between. Hitler was equipped by ideology to envision the destruction of states in the name of nature and had at his disposal an imposing army and special task forces whose essential mission was the destruction of institutions to permit racial war. The SS and the *Einsatzgruppen* first killed on a large scale in Poland—but their main target was Polish elites, not Jews.

Jews, not seen as a race, were to be removed from the habitat entirely. The new German lawlessness took its most striking form in the expulsion of Jews from their homes to ghettos in the cities. For the Germans, the ghettos were holding tanks where Jews were concentrated before deportation to some exotic place where nature would take its course. In the overpopulated ghettos, deaths outnumbered births by a factor of ten. Most of the people who died in the first months were Jews who had been deported from the countryside or from other towns and had few or no possessions and connections. The big ghettos, such as Warsaw, took on a kind of colonial appearance, as rickshaws replaced automobiles (stolen by the Germans) and the streetcar service (restricted by the Germans). The luster of subjugation attracted German tourists, who often returned home with a pleasant sense of imperial mastery. The problem for those responsible in Berlin was that there was no actual overseas colony to which Jews could be deported.

The Nazi racial policy of 1939 and 1940, the purification of the conquered Polish territories, was a cruel shambles. Himmler was given broad powers as a kind of racial commissar on October 7, 1939. His best idea was to deport Jews and Poles from the Polish territories annexed to Germany to the General Government. Even if this had somehow succeeded, which it did not, it would merely have displaced the racial enemies a short distance to the east. The vast number of Poles in the annexed territories made the scheme dystopian. In the territories annexed to the Reich, Poles outnumbered Germans about twenty to one, and even Jews slightly outnumbered Germans. The city of Łódź, incorporated into Nazi Germany, became, by population, its largest Jewish and its largest Polish city.

In practice, Himmler deported Poles first. They were regarded as the pertinent political enemy, and their farms could be given to Germans who were arriving from territories that the Soviet Union had invaded. Some 87,883 people were deported from the annexed territories in December 1939 and another 40,128 early the next year, most of them Poles. These numbers signify a vast amount of human suffering but hardly altered the demographic balance. The transport of Jews from the Reich to the General Government was pointless in conception and unachieved in practice. It was very exciting, however, to some Germans on the territory of the prewar Reich, who began to lobby for the deportation of Jews from their localities. Heydrich had to stop such local initiatives in December 1939. It was then, in January 1940, that Heydrich's subordinate Eichmann made an approach to Stalin: Perhaps the Soviet Union would be willing to take two million Jews from German-occupied Poland? Stalin was not interested in admitting masses of unscreened people to the USSR; receiving Jews seems to have been one of the few Nazi requests he declined during the period of his alliance with Hitler.

The ghettos became a holding pen for a much more ambitious deportation plan: the evacuation of Jews to Madagascar. This was the black hole for Jews that had received the most attention in Germany and throughout Europe before the war. It was the solution that Hitler had suggested to Polish leaders in 1938, who could not understand how he meant to combine it with war. A victory over France, German leaders hoped, would open up Madagascar, which was a French colonial possession. Having defeated Poland, Hitler returned to his basic scenario for the war: remove the French threat from the west to avoid the strategic problem of encirclement, and then attack the Soviet Union to achieve the war's aim, *Lebensraum*. After German troops entered Paris on June 14, 1940, Eichmann sent an envoy to look for the documentation of the 1936 Polish-French discussions about Madagascar. The new French government established in Vichy supported a Madagascar deportation. But shipping millions of people from Europe to the Indian Ocean was a project that would require the approval, and indeed the support, of the British Empire. When France fell, Britain remained in the war.

This was the latest surprise for Hitler, who was wrong about a number of strategic predictions. The western allies were supposed to defend Czechoslovakia but did not; Poland was not supposed to fight but it did; France was supposed to fight longer than it did; Britain was supposed to see the logic of peace if France fell but did not. Winston Churchill, who had succeeded Chamberlain as prime minister, was defiance itself. On July 10, 1940, Hitler began an air war with Britain, and expressed the conviction that the defeat of Britain would remove the final barrier to the Madagascar plan. But he was in no position to defeat the United Kingdom. The German air force was outfought by the British, who commissioned skilled Polish and Czech pilots. The German navy was too small to mount a serious amphibious assault on the British coast. Like so much else, the invasion had not really been thought through. An outline for a

Madagascar deportation was already out of date when completed in August 1940, since by then Hitler had abandoned any intention to occupy Great Britain.

When Hitler understood that Madagascar was impossible, his thoughts turned back to the Soviet Union. On July 31, 1940, just three weeks after he had begun his halfhearted British campaign, he asked his generals to review plans for the invasion of the Soviet Union. The war against the USSR would make sense, he reminded his generals, only if Germany could "smash the state" and that "in one blow." In December, he issued the formal directive for the submission of war plans to "crush Soviet Russia in a rapid campaign."

Thus the black hole for the Jews migrated from one obscure and exotic imperial locale to another, from the tropical maritime south to the frozen tundra of the north. Hitler imagined that the Soviet state would be crushed in a few weeks, and that its Jews, and perhaps other Jews as well, could then be dispatched to Siberia. About this, too, he was mistaken. But erring was an essential part of Nazi logic. The *Führer* could never be wrong; only the world could be wrong; and when it was, the fault would be borne by the Jews.

Nazi strategic predictions about the behavior of particular states were often mistaken, but the Nazis were learning a lesson about what happened in general when states were destroyed. Indeed, misunderstandings of neighboring peoples forced unexpected campaigns to destroy states, which, in turn, opened a realm of experimentation. The annexation of Austria accelerated the deportation of Jews, the invasion of Poland created a new opportunity for their ghettoization, and then the war of annihilation against the Soviet Union would permit a Final Solution. It was not a Final Solution of the type that had been considered, a deportation to some obscure and distant place seized from another empire. It was a Final Solution of mass murder, in the Jewish homeland itself, in eastern Europe.

The three million German men assembled to invade the Soviet Union in June 1941 found themselves in Polish territories that had been colonized and terrorized. The Poland these three million German soldiers saw had been utterly transformed, its Jews humiliated and ghettoized, the rest of its population subjected to an improvised anarchy of exploitation. When these three million men crossed the German-Soviet border on the twenty-second of that month, they first set foot in a very special zone: the territories that Germany had granted to the Soviet Union in September 1939. The German invasion of the Soviet Union thus began as a *reinvasion* of territories that had just been invaded. The German attack on the Soviet Union meant destroying a state apparatus, the new Soviet one, right after the Soviets had destroyed another set of state apparatuses, those of the independent states of the 1920s and 1930s. A double invasion by great powers would have been dramatic enough, though not quite unprecedented.

Double state destruction of this kind was something entirely new.

5

Double Occupation

During the war, the gifted political thinker Hannah Arendt glimpsed what was happening. A Jewish political emigrant from Germany, she understood how National Socialist ideology could be realized. If Jews were to be removed from the planet, they first had to be separated from the state. As she wrote later, "one could do as one pleased only with stateless people."

Like succeeding historians of the Holocaust, and in accord with the German Jewish experience she shared with some of them, she saw this separation from the state as the gradual deprivation of rights. As she observed, "the first essential step on the road to total domination is to kill the juridical person in man." Yet the easiest way to deprive a Jew of law and to instruct non-Jews in lawlessness was to destroy entire jurisdictions, as with Austria and Czechoslovakia. As Arendt came to realize, the Jews "were threatened more than any other by the sudden collapse of the system of nation states." Above all, Jews were placed in peril by the collapse of the states of which they were citizens. The war of 1939, the attack on Poland by Germany, brought new sorts of depravations as the state was fragmented along new, colonial lines. But even ghettoization and the proclamation of a colonial order were not enough to precipitate a Holocaust. Something more was needed: a double destruction of the state.

In 1939, when Hitler made his alliance with Stalin, he was undertaking to destroy states by proxy. Hitler had a vivid idea of what Soviet rule would mean for the places granted to Moscow by the German-Soviet Treaty on Borders and Friendship: the Baltic states of Lithuania, Latvia, and Estonia; and the eastern half of Poland. If anything, his notion of Soviet terror was exaggerated: the total elimination of all thinking people, the murder of tens of millions by starvation. Himmler wrote of the "Bolshevik method" of the "physical extermination of a nation." Hitler, in making his alliance with the Soviet Union, was always planning to invade the lands that he granted his ally. His invitation to Stalin in 1939 to destroy states would precede his own campaign in the same lands to follow in 1941. The German *Führer* was therefore contemplating the double destruction of states: first the crushing of interwar nation-states by Soviet techniques, seen as extraordinarily radical, and then the elimination of newly created Soviet state apparatus by Nazi techniques, still in the making.

Germans found the conditions where "one could do as one pleased," where they could kill Jews in large numbers for the first time, in 1941, as they invaded the Soviet Union. It was in the zone of double occupation, where Soviet rule preceded German, where the Soviet destruction of interwar states was followed by the German annihilation of Soviet institutions, that a Final Solution took shape. Almost all of the two million or so Jews who came under German rule in 1939 would die. The same was true of the two million Jews who came under Soviet rule in 1939 and 1940. Indeed, the Jews who initially fell under Soviet rule were the first to be murdered *en masse* by the Germans.

When the Germans and the Soviets undertook their joint invasion of Poland in September 1939, the Soviets were the senior partners in political violence. The Soviet secret state police, the NKVD, had experience in mass killing that was unrivalled by any German institution. Some 681,692 Soviet citizens had been arrested, shot, and buried in pits in the operations of the Great Terror of 1937–1938. The NKVD had shot twice as many Poles on its own territory while preparing for war in those years than the *Einsatzgruppen* shot when German forces actually invaded Poland in 1939. In proportional terms the contrast is far greater. The killing of 111,091 Soviet citizens in the Polish Operation of 1937–1938 changed the nationality structure of the western Soviet Union. A third of the male Soviet Poles of military age were killed before the war in this and other terror actions, their wives and children often sent to be denationalized at concentration camps or orphanages. The Soviet republics that bordered Poland, Soviet

Ukraine and Soviet Belarus, lost a considerable part of their Polish minority to murder and deportation: some 59,903 people in Ukraine, some 61,501 people in Belarus.

Stalin's rationale for the mass murder of Soviet citizens of Polish nationality was not racial but ethnostrategic. At Stalin's behest and under his guidance, the NKVD used interrogations to develop a theory of a vast Polish plot against the Soviet Union, directed by the Polish Military Organization. This was entirely false. While veterans of the Polish Military Organization were quite active in Polish military intelligence and in the higher reaches of the state, the institution as such no longer existed, and certainly not as assassins and saboteurs on Soviet territory. The veterans of the Polish Military Organization, insofar as they were plotting acts of conspiratorial violence in the late 1930s, were thinking of the British in Palestine. By the end of the Great Terror, however, the NKVD had assembled enough confessions by torture to compose a fictional narrative in which even leaders of the Soviet state were secret Polish agents. This proved to be quite risky for the NKVD itself. Since the imagined conspiracy grew from week to week in 1937 and 1938, NKVD commanders could always be charged with having neglected the Polish danger in the past.

In 1938, Stalin was able to turn the Soviet communist party, an early target of the purges, against the NKVD. When higher officers of the secret state police were themselves arrested and killed, younger ones took their places. As a consequence, the nationality structure of the NKVD was altered. It was no longer an exceptionally cosmopolitan elite with revolutionary prestige in which Jews (and Latvians and Poles) were highly represented. Polish officers were removed and often executed in the Polish Operation. Then the entire NKVD was purged: first for not being vigilant enough, then for being too vigilant. By the end of 1938, the NKVD had become an organization dominated by Russians (65 percent of high officers) and Ukrainians (17 percent of high officers). Russians were now overrepresented in the NKVD by comparison to their share in the general Soviet population. The percentage of Jews was down from nearly forty percent to less than four percent. There were no longer any Poles at all.

It was this NKVD, experienced in murder, humbled by Stalin, and russified, that was turned against Polish institutions and elites after the Soviet invasion of eastern Poland of September 17, 1939. An actual assault on potential resisters in eastern Poland was a much safer assignment for the NKVD than the Polish Operation inside the Soviet Union had been, since real enemies could be found among the Polish citizenry, and real progress could be reported. The collapse of Poland brought by German and Soviet arms generated real chaos that could demonstrably be mastered. In eastern Poland, Soviet soldiers beat men to death for their gold teeth and raped women in the knowledge that this would be dismissed as "children playing a little." Soviet invasion meant local uprisings by native communists, who often robbed and killed Poles who had been in authority, and by native nationalists, who often believed Soviet propaganda about national freedom to the east and national liberation by the Red Army. It meant attacks upon Polish officials and landowners, the score settling that is always to be expected when regimes change with sudden violence.

Against this backdrop the Soviet NKVD could bring to occupied eastern Poland calm and order of a certain sort. Unlike members of the *Einsatzgruppen*, who in 1939 were killing for the first time and who did so to create the conditions for a German racial triumph, NKVD officers were experienced administrators of life and death whose task was to establish the basis of a certain model of statehood. NKVD officers, generally Russians and Ukrainians, were transferred in large numbers to the newly conquered eastern Polish territories in late 1939. Over the course of 1940, the majority of arrests and imprisonments in the entire Soviet Union was made in occupied eastern Poland, a tiny percentage of Soviet territory. The typical sentence was eight years in the Gulag; some 8,513 people were sentenced to death in individual cases.

Unlike the Germans, the Soviets had mechanisms for and experience with large-scale deportations. Rather than colonial fantasies, they had time-tested destinations: the vast network of prison camps and special settlements known as the Gulag. Soviet internal colonization was inscribed in tundra and steppe. On December 5, 1939, Stalin ordered preparations for a first wave of deportations, to target the Polish state apparatus and its influential supporters. Some 139,794 people were accordingly forced from their homes onto trains and sent to the Gulag, usually to Soviet Kazakhstan, in February 1940. Polish Jews were deported as capitalists to the Gulag in large numbers in April 1940 and then still larger numbers in June 1940 for expressing the desire to retain their Polish citizenship. In

the months after the Soviet invasion, some 292,513 Polish citizens were deported to the Gulag in four major waves, along with perhaps another two hundred thousand in smaller actions or after individual arrests. In these four large actions, almost 60 percent of the victims were Poles (who were about 40 percent of the population in eastern Poland), just over 20 percent Jews (8 percent of the population), about 10 percent Ukrainians (about 35 percent of the population), and about 8 percent Belarusians (8 percent of the population).

One of the individuals who was apprehended and sentenced to the Gulag was a young writer from Kielce, Gustaw Herling-Grudziński. The accusation leveled against him by Soviet authorities was that he had illegally left Poland for Lithuania to fight against the USSR. He politely asked his interrogators to alter the charge to indicate that he had intended leaving Poland to fight against the Germans. They assured him that it amounted to the same thing. Herling later provided one of the most powerful accounts of life in a Soviet concentration camp, where hard-won solitude is the only substitute for impossible freedom, and where a personality integrated under entirely different conditions can be disassembled into its component parts. "There," in the Gulag, "it has been proved that when the body has reached the limit of its endurance, one cannot, as was once believed, rely on strength of character and conscious recognition of spiritual values; there is nothing, in fact, which man cannot be forced to do by hunger and pain." Herling became convinced "that a man can only be human under human conditions."

From the Soviet perspective the most dangerous Polish group was the officer class. It represented a threefold threat: It was the leadership of an enemy army; some of its senior officers were veterans of campaigns against the USSR; and its reserve officers represented the Polish educated classes. The Soviets saw the Polish educated classes as the basis for the Polish political nation. The immediate aim of the arrest and elimination of such people was to make political resistance more difficult. The officers of the Polish army who surrendered or were captured were placed in camps, where they were investigated and interrogated individually. Then NKVD director Lavrentii Beria sent a troika that judged the group collectively. "Each one of them," wrote Beria to Stalin, "is waiting to be released in order to be able to enter actively into the battle against Soviet power." He recommended "the supreme punishment—shooting." Stalin approved.

In April 1940, some 21,892 Polish officers and other Polish citizens were shot by NKVD officers in the Katyn Forest and at four other sites. Because the Polish army was an instrument of social mobility, many of the victims, about forty percent, were from peasant and working-class backgrounds. Because the Polish officer class was multinational, many of the victims were members of national minorities, including Jews. Henryk Strasman, a member of Irgun, was among those killed by a bullet at the base of the neck and buried in a mass grave at Katyn. Wilhelm Engelkreis, a doctor and reserve officer, was also murdered at Katyn. His daughter, writing later from Israel, recalled her childhood despair at the loss of her father. Hieronim Brandwajn, a doctor, was murdered at Katyn; his wife, Mira, died two years later in the Warsaw ghetto without knowing what had happened to her husband. Mieczysław Proner was a pharmacist and a chemist and a Jew and a Pole and a reserve officer and a combatant. He fought against the Germans in the Polish army, only to be arrested by the Soviets and murdered in the same action. A few months later his mother was ordered to the Warsaw ghetto; two years later she was deported to Treblinka and gassed.

With one exception, the 21,892 people murdered by the NKVD were men. Many of them, like these Polish Jews, had families in the German occupation zone, who now faced German repressions without heads of household. Since the Soviets were killing the same kinds of Polish citizens as the Germans—the educated elite—they were making the German task easier. When the families of the murdered officers were in the Soviet zone, the NKVD deported them to the Gulag. Surprised by a knock on the door, these people almost never escaped. One of the rare exceptions was the wife of a Polish officer who left her children with a trusted Jewish neighbor. But this was a rather isolated example of a failure of the NKVD. These Soviet deportations of 1940 repeated, on a smaller scale, the methods of the Great Terror. In the Polish Operation, Polish men had been shot and the families deported to be exploited and denationalized.

There was also continuity of personnel: Vasily Blokhin, one of the executioners of the Polish officers, had killed thousands of Soviet citizens during the Great Terror. Wearing a leather cap, apron, and gloves to the elbows, Blokhin personally shot about two hundred and fifty men each night. In the Soviet system, the number of executioners was very small, and they were officers. They followed clear written orders issued within a strict hierarchy. The Soviet system included within itself legal states of exception, which, once they had been used to justify the special measures needed for mass terror, could be terminated. In the German system, as it developed, innovations from below met wishes from above, orders were often unclear, and the officers tried to devolve the responsibility for the actual shooting to their men, or indeed to non-Germans who happened to be in the vicinity. The Soviet system was, therefore, much more precise and efficient in its campaigns of murder. But the German system was more efficient in creating large numbers of executioners.

The Soviets, at least some of them, believed in what they were doing. After all, they did it themselves and recorded what they did, in clear language, in official documents, filed in orderly archives. They could associate themselves with their deeds, because true responsibility rested with the communist party. The Nazis used grand phrases of racial superiority, and Himmler spoke of the moral sublimity involved in killing others for the sake of the race. But when the time came, Germans acted without plans and without precision, and with no sense of responsibility. In the Nazi worldview, what happened was simply what happened, the stronger should win; but nothing was certain, and certainly not the relationship between past, present, and future. The Soviets believed that History was on their side and acted accordingly. The Nazis were afraid of everything except the disorder they themselves created. The systems and the mentalities were different, profoundly and interestingly so.

Yet the two regimes acted in the same time and place. Whatever the Soviets did, and with whatever motives, they were doing to people who, if not killed or deported, would then face the Nazis and their methods. The damage that the NKVD inflicted was a matter of the deportation or death of human beings, and of the disruption of lives and the alteration of spirits. It was very important that the Soviets destroyed the Polish state in their half of Poland; it was very important that they physically removed those who were associated with Polish statehood. Yet perhaps most important was the way Soviet policies influenced those who survived and remained: these citizens of annihilated states, these new Soviet citizens, these people who would confront the *Wehrmacht* and the SS in 1941.

Like the Nazis, the Soviets began from the assumption that the Polish state created in 1918 had no right to exist and so could be eliminated by decree and then mocked. But the form of the mockery was tellingly different. The Soviets, like the Germans, destroyed Polish state symbols, but on the logic that they represented a "bourgeois," "reactionary," "white," or "fascist" Poland. The problem with the Polish state, in the Soviet view, was that it was a creation of the upper classes. This was very different from the Nazi view, which was that lower races such as the Poles did not deserve a political existence.

In western and central Poland, occupied by Nazi Germany, the higher Polish officials were hunted down, imprisoned in camps, and often killed, whereas the lower-level officials, such as the mayors, county commissioners, and village heads, were expected to follow new kinds of orders from German authorities. As Hans Frank, the head of the German colony known as the General Government, described the task: "The leadership elements we have now identified in Poland are what is to be liquidated." This was race war: extermination of the vital racial forces of the enemy, and then the exploitation of its lower elements.

An empire on Nazi principles required an open subordination of inferior races, and thus an extravagantly visible difference between the political existence of Germans and that of others. Soviet empire involved the territorial extension of the Soviet Union as it already was. In eastern Poland, occupied by the Soviet Union, higher Polish officials were treated much as they were in the German zone. But, for a time at least, their place was taken by people of humble social origins or even by imprisoned members of local communist parties. In one town after another, the political prisoners became the local authorities. This was a temporary but important phase in the change of regime, since it transferred the appearance of the responsibility for the Soviet revolution to local people. Some Polish citizens were thus implicated in Soviet-style class warfare: the decapitation of the bourgeois or feudal leadership of the enemy, the promotion of workers and peasants, and then the subordination of everyone to a larger order that proclaimed its own egalitarianism.

The Soviet decapitation of society was accompanied by a zombification of the social body. The Soviets took the possibility of Polish resistance much more seriously than the Germans did, since for them it represented one instance of the formidable power of international capitalism rather than the last gasps of a suffocating race. The NKVD applied far more sophisticated methods than the German Gestapo, usually observing resistance groups, arresting and recruiting their members one by one, and slowly trying to break the whole organization or, ideally, turn it to the Soviet side without its members realizing what was happening. Since resistance was for the Soviets by definition part of an international plot, the Soviet hope was always to follow the links from the Polish underground back to the Polish government-in-exile and to its British and French allies. In practice, Soviet rule meant the cultivation of distrust, as Polish citizens ready for conspiratorial work became unsure of one another and incapable of discerning which underground groups were legitimate and which were fronts for the NKVD. Thus equality in the Soviet sense emerged in occupied eastern Poland: Polish citizens learned to distrust one another equally. Everyone became a potential traitor, and appearances were not to be believed. This new reality undermined the old in a matter of weeks.

Whereas Germans excluded Polish citizens from participation in their new order, the Soviets forced Polish citizens to take part in Soviet political rituals, presented as exercises in liberation. The Soviets introduced their own version of democracy, in which participation was open and mandatory, and voters had no alternatives. On October 22, 1939, inhabitants of what had been eastern Poland were called upon to elect their representatives to national assemblies. In the Soviet zone of occupation, Poles were the largest national group, but not a majority. Ukrainians were a majority in the south, Belarusians in the north, and Jews were numerous everywhere. The Soviet notion was to divide most of the occupied lands between a Ukrainian zone in the south and a Belarusian zone in the north, which would then be attached to the existing Soviet Ukrainian and Soviet Belarusian republics. This is indeed what transpired.

After the obligatory, humiliating, and falsified vote, the national assemblies, meeting in the first days of November 1939, proclaimed the desire that their lands be incorporated into the Soviet Union. This opened the way for Soviet citizenship to be extended to all inhabitants of eastern Poland, a symbolic expression of equality that would have been unthinkable in the Nazi empire. Of course, it also opened the way for the arrival of thousands of Soviet officials from further east, mostly Russians and Ukrainians, who would hold the real power. Local people, usually communists and members of the Ukrainian, Belarusian, and Jewish minorities, had been useful as ostensible self-liberators. But their liberation simply meant inclusion in a powerful system with its own priorities, one of which was maintaining the alliance with Nazi Germany. To take one striking example: Jewish butchers lost ownership of their slaughterhouses and found themselves, as Soviet state employees, packing meat for the German troops fighting against the western democracies.

The Soviets behaved as if eastern Poland had been joined to their homeland of socialism forever. Of course, this would not be the case, since the leaders of Nazi Germany, the Soviet ally that allowed the new disposition of territory, were intending to attack the Soviet Union at the first opportunity. Stalin expected Hitler's betrayal, but believed in 1939, 1940, and even 1941 that his ally could be placated with outspoken loyalty and regular deliveries of goods. Thus the Soviet Union supplied Germany not only with security in the east but also with some of the physical resources used to fight the wars in western Europe in 1940: the oil, the minerals, the grain. The Royal Air Force proposed to bomb Soviet airfields as a way to slow Hitler's advance through western Europe. The peasants in Soviet Ukraine sang:

Ukraine is fertile
She gives her grain to the Germans
And she herself goes hungry.

In its newly acquired lands, the Soviet Union created material, psychological, and political resources for the Germans, openings for future Nazi power in eastern Europe that had not existed before 1939. Though the Soviets did not intend to create these resources, their availability was decisive for the course of events after the Germans invaded these lands. This was true in eastern Poland in 1939 and would be all the more true in the Baltic states after their occupation and annexation by the Soviet Union in summer 1940.

In putting an end to capitalism, the Soviets created a *material resource.* From the Soviet perspective the goal was equality, but equalization means losses for some and gains for others. Even before the Red Army arrived, local "communists went mad, carrying out revisions by night and robbing and killing Poles." Joel Cygielman, a Jew fleeing the German invasion in his own automobile, lost it to a Soviet officer who threatened him with a grenade. In Kovel, Jews who greeted the Red Army with flowers found that the soldiers were interested only in what was in their shops. Soviet soldiers at first stole what they could and then bought what remained on the strength of an overvalued ruble. Local communists placed in positions of authority used the pretext of arms searches to rob their neighbors.

The end of the Polish civil code was experienced by most people as the legalization of theft. If property could be taken by the state, perhaps it was permissible to take it back again. The lack of legal assurances to property made those who claimed new land or residences believe that they themselves had to make sure that the previous owners never came back. Jews had the most urban property to lose, and usually lost it: in the double sense of the nationalization of their goods and the deportation of their persons to Soviet Kazakhstan. The Soviet Union did not discriminate against Jews as such; it was an anti-antisemitic entity that criminalized ethnic discrimination. Given the social structure of the market economy in eastern Poland, however, Soviet measures against capitalism affected Jews more than others. To be sure, eastern Poland was generally a very poor territory, although its society was far more prosperous than that of the Soviet Union to which it was to be leveled. Mendel Szef, a dairyman from Łuck, put matters this way: "after the occupation of our country, it was said that all are equal, rich and poor, but it turned out that all are poor, since the rich were arrested and sent to the depths of Russia."

The massive scale of Soviet deportations and executions permitted a social revolution in both the countryside and the towns, as people scrambled for the tens of thousands of suddenly empty farms and homes. In the countryside of eastern Poland, where rural unemployment exceeded fifty percent in the 1930s, people were hungry for land. Not everyone took land from their neighbors, but many did. Here, as in all such cases, peasants knew that if they did not take a vacant farmstead, someone else would. Some Ukrainian peasants who refused to claim land from deported Polish neighbors were forced to do so at gunpoint. In many towns most of the good stone houses were owned by Jews, who were often deported to the Gulag. For their neighbors in wooden huts or hovels, a move to the center of town and residence in a stone house were the peak of imaginable social advancement. The Soviets did not expropriate Jews as a racial group. Even so, the fact of the prior expropriation of a large number of Jews created an opportunity, if an unexpected one, for the Germans who would later arrive. When Soviet power was replaced by German, non-Jews could try to get their property back, but Jews could not. The property that Jews had already lost could be claimed by others. The initial Soviet expropriations, swift and systematic, were racialized by the subsequent German arrival.

Most Jews in eastern Poland were of very humble means. Nevertheless, Jews provided the connection between peasants and markets, countryside and city. In other words, much of what Soviet officials would see as speculation, profiteering, and the like was commercial activity usually carried out by Jews. In Poland's Volhynia district, for example, 75 percent of the registered traders (14,587 of the 19,337) were Jews. The radical devaluation of the Polish currency and then its abolition in December 1939 destroyed the social position of Jews who had some savings or investments. The end of debts denominated in Polish currency was a relief for many but a burden upon Jewish lenders and, indeed, the removal of their source of authority in communities. The ceaseless Soviet propaganda against commerce as such was, in fact though not in intention, directed against Jews, and weakened their standing.

In altering the character of politics, the Soviets created a *psychological resource.* Jews were given the appearance but not the reality of power. After the arrival of the Red Army in September 1939, local Jews appeared in visible positions of responsibility in greater numbers than had ever been the case between the wars. The Polish central government had acted to make sure that even towns with a Jewish majority did not have a majority of Jews on the city council. Although there were a few Jews in the Polish police and the Polish administration generally, the tendency was to keep those numbers low. The change in autumn 1939 was, therefore, experienced as dramatic. The Soviets had no particular desire to promote Jews as such, although a few commanders and officials opined that Jews were more reliable than Poles. Still, Jews were among those who were available and exhibited the willingness and skills to take up new positions. Jews were never the majority of local collaborators with the Soviet regime; Belarusians and Ukrainians were overall far more numerous. Local Jews never held real power, with the exception of a few weeks in autumn 1939, and that on a very local scale, and alongside other, non-Jewish, collaborators. Nevertheless, the change of regime made Jews collectively vulnerable. When the Germans invaded, the actual administrators of the new Soviet territory, the Soviet officials from the east, could marshal the resources they needed to flee. But the local Jews, those who had collaborated with the Soviets and those who had not, generally remained behind.

In other ways Soviet policy created the conditions for acts of revenge.

In 1939, the Soviets had defeated, destroyed, and discredited traditional authorities, both secular and religious. They had presided over a moment of score settling and chaos in which many new scores were created that might be settled in the next moment of violent transition. They had deported or shot half a million people in lands where the total population was just over thirteen million, meaning that most families had been touched by the NKVD in some way. The rapid destruction of the Polish state was not simply a fact but a source of shame, a catastrophe that would beg for a scapegoat.

Even as Soviet power generated feelings of shame and resentment, it forced society to break the taboo of collaboration with a foreign power. Certain people had chosen, at the beginning, to collaborate; far more had collaborated simply by dint of continuing to hold their positions, fearful of deportation or worse if they did not demonstrate loyalty. With time, almost everyone had to engage with the Soviet regime in some way or another. The nature of the system demanded it. In seeking to transform eastern Poland into part of their own state, Soviet leaders included the local population in the process quite intensively: through coerced voting, through the encouragement of denunciations, through interrogation and torture and betrayal. Because the Soviet system was inclusive, there was often no clear line between victims and collaborators. Often the very experience that led to collaboration, such as torture and imprisonment, also meant victimhood. This refined the psychological resource in a special way. In Soviet conditions, victimhood and collaboration were widespread and hard to define, and so the next power holder would be the one to define them.

Finally, in destroying states, the Soviet Union created a *political resource.* As fragile and flawed as the Polish, Estonian, Latvian, and Lithuanian states might seem, they were the homelands of tens of millions of Europeans. The wholesale destruction of modern states with fully fledged political nations was an extraordinarily radical step. Of course, not all of the (former) citizens of these (former) states cared deeply about national independence, but many did. Insofar as the Soviets removed states that people wanted, and insofar as the Germans could pose as the ally of those who wished to restore them, the Germans could manipulate a powerful desire. The nature of this opportunity depended, of course, upon what leaders of national groups believed that they could gain or lose from occupiers. The joint German-Soviet invasion of Poland did not, for example, create much of a Polish political resource for the Germans. Having already invaded Poland once in 1939, they could hardly pose as a liberator of Poland when invading the Soviet Union from their Polish colony in 1941. Germans could take credit on a local scale for ending Soviet oppressions, but they could hardly promise political autonomy to Poland.

The perspective of some of the political leaders of Poland's ethnic minorities was quite different. Poland had been the largest homeland of Ukrainians beyond the Soviet Union and the largest homeland of Jews in the world. Almost all of Poland's Ukrainians and more than a third of Poland's Jews fell under Soviet rule in 1939. Neither Ukrainians nor Jews fared well in the enlarged Soviet Union; in general their experience was far worse than expected.

In the Ukrainian case, the opportunity this presented to the Germans was rather strong. The Ukrainian minority in Poland was substantial and territorially concentrated, adjacent to the Ukrainian republic of the Soviet Union. Although Ukrainian nationalism was never the dominant political orientation in Ukrainian political life in Poland, it did attract attention in neighboring capitals. All regional powers had tried to turn the Ukrainian question to their own ends in the 1920s and 1930s. The Soviets pursued a policy of affirmative action of Ukrainians in Soviet Ukraine in the 1920s and established a Communist Party of Western Ukraine on Polish territory in the hope of drawing Ukrainians from Poland toward the Soviet Union. The Poles imitated this policy in their Volhynian district in order to draw Ukrainians in the Soviet Union towards Poland. The Germans had cultivated Ukrainian agents within Poland, usually nationalists, who believed correctly that Germany was the only power that could possibly destroy both enemies: Poland and the Soviet Union.

That said, the Ukrainian nationalists associated with Germany knew perfectly well that a major source of their local support was the social question—chiefly the redistribution of farmland. And the Soviets were quite aware that the Communist Party of Western Ukraine had to address the national question. With nationalists concerned with expropriating large estates and communists flying national flags, a certain amount of ideological syncretism was the rule in the 1930s. For example, a local Ukrainian communist leader could be a Jewish woman named Fryda Szprynger, and one of her more successful underground activists could, meanwhile, use the pseudonym "Hitler."

The Soviet invasion of eastern Poland in 1939 meant the destruction of the mainstream Ukrainian political parties that had functioned legally in Poland: the Ukrainian National Democratic Alliance (UNDO), for example, which had tried to work within legal institutions and had opposed official antisemitism. Soviet rule created relatively favorable conditions for groupings that had been illegal: the nationalists and the communists—the first because they were accustomed to being underground, the second because they could emerge from underground and collaborate with the regime. Yet, as Jews and Poles tended to notice, often it was Ukrainian nationalists rather than communists (insofar as this distinction had meaning) who took up local positions of Soviet authority. Both Ukrainian nationalists and Ukrainian communists took the opportunity to denounce local Poles to Soviet authorities, no doubt from both political and self-interested motives. In most villages in southeastern Poland there was a Ukrainian activist who knew what categories of person the NKVD was looking for and was happy to supply an appropriate Pole. This created an empty homestead and farm; denunciation and deportation were a version of land reform.

During the first few months of Soviet rule, the social revolution from abroad attracted many Ukrainians. Polish authorities were often replaced by Ukrainians, although in meaningful positions these were Ukrainians from Soviet Ukraine. The handful of Jewish mayors were also replaced by Ukrainians from the east. The initial Soviet deportations chiefly concerned Poles and indeed Polish landowners, and so could be experienced as social advance for Ukrainian peasants. Soviet-style revolutions usually had two stages: first a gesture to the peasants, then the seizure of their land. In 1940, the Soviets began to collectivize agriculture in the territory they had annexed from Poland, just as they had done a decade earlier in the Soviet Union as a whole. Some Ukrainians recalled then the mass famine that had followed in the USSR. Virtually none wanted to concede land to the Soviet state. Collectivization discredited Ukrainian communists among the population and led some Ukrainian communists to shift toward nationalism.

Ukrainian nationalists, for their part, were hoping in 1940 for a German invasion of the Soviet Union that would create the possibility for a Ukrainian state. These were people who had been Polish citizens, and saw themselves as representatives of the millions of Ukrainians in Poland and the tens of millions of Ukrainians in the Soviet Union. From their perspective, only Germany could create the conditions for a Ukrainian state by destroying both Poland and the USSR. Poland was no more as of 1939; in 1940, some Ukrainian nationalists joined in the German preparations to annihilate the Soviet Union. The Germans used Ukrainian informers to prepare the way for the invasion known as Operation Barbarossa, and they recruited and trained hundreds of Ukrainians for advance groups to be used in Soviet Ukraine. In early 1941, the NKVD sensed the threat and began to arrest Ukrainians in high numbers. The fourth wave of Soviet deportations, in May and June 1941, was heavily Ukrainian. Many thousands of Ukrainians were also imprisoned. When the Germans did arrive in June 1941, they found the corpses of these people left behind in Soviet prisons.

All in all, Soviet occupation closed Jewish possibilities. Could it also have created a Jewish political resource for the Germans? As with the Ukrainians, there was a Jewish nationalist Right in interwar Poland, Betar, that was committed to building an independent national state by revolutionary and violent means. Unlike Ukrainian nationalists, however, Jewish nationalists were the clients and not the enemies of the Polish state. They wanted to leave Polish territory rather than claim it for their own. After the German invasion of September 1, 1939, leaders of Betar fled eastward from the Germans. They were then caught in the Soviet net. Jewish radicals, unlike Ukrainian radicals, had no experience of working underground. The Soviets quickly identified and arrested them. The NKVD was aware that Betar was a front for Irgun, and broke underground Irgun circles as well. Menachem Begin, the leader of Betar in Poland, fled from Warsaw to Vilnius and managed to hide for a time. He was eventually arrested by the NKVD—in the middle of a game of chess—and sentenced to eight years of hard labor at the camps of Vorkuta.

Betar was quickly powerless in occupied Poland. Its sister organization Irgun, based two thousand kilometers away in Palestine, was not. The conspirators of Irgun, most of them Polish Jews, found themselves in an unexpected predicament: considering the opportunities provided by war but deprived of the backer which had sought to prepare them for such a moment. They had received a certain amount of training from the Poles, as well as money and weapons. Yet the grand scheme for which all of that was mere preparation—a landing of thousands of Betar members in Palestine with Polish support—was now unthinkable. No further Polish help was coming. The Polish officers who had trained Irgun were dead or in camps or in hiding or in exile. The latest shipment of Polish weapons for Irgun in Palestine, on the docks in Gdynia in August 1939, was destroyed by German fire even as Poles scrambled to unpack the weapons to use them to defend themselves. Irgun had been preparing for a conflict with the British Empire, but not for one in which its Polish patron would be totally absent. As one Betar comrade wrote to another in distress in late 1939, "we feel that there is no one behind us."

Of the three European states with an active interest in Palestine in the 1930s, only two remained as the decade came to an end: Nazi Germany and Great Britain. They were at war with each other, which meant that Jewish fighters in Palestine might gain some leverage by siding with one or the other. Nazi Germany was the enemy of Jews in Europe (although to what extent was not fully clear, even in 1939). It was also the enemy of the British Empire, which controlled Palestine and prevented Jewish emigration. Irgun could not decide between the obligation to defend Jews and the obligation to fight for a Jewish state, so chose neutrality between Germany and Britain. Avraham Stern now led a split within Irgun, establishing a splinter group eventually known as Lehi. He was joined by Yitzhak Shamir, another Polish Jew who had hoped for further training in Poland but had run out of time. Lehi then did exactly what other Far Right groups did at the time: It made a proposal to Hitler.

The appeals sent by Jewish and Ukrainian nationalists to Hitler were very similar. The Organization of Ukrainian Nationalists used this language in June 1941: "The newly emerging Ukrainian State will cooperate closely with the Great Nazi German Reich, which under the guidance of its *Führer* Adolf Hitler is forming a new order in Europe and the world and which will help the Ukrainian Nation liberate itself from Muscovite oppression." In Palestine, Lehi saw the British much the same way as the Ukrainian nationalists saw the Soviets, and it drew the same practical conclusions. In January 1941, Stern proposed "cooperation between the New Germany and a renewed racial-national Hebrewdom," which would involve "the erection of a historical Jewish State on national and totalitarian foundations, which would stand in a treaty relationship with the German Reich, in the interest of the protection and strengthening of the future German power position in the Near East."

Stern assumed that Hitler wished to rid Europe of Jews and that a logical way to do so would be to send them all to Palestine. Perhaps misled by his contacts with Polish elites, he confused the Polish with the German approach. The Polish regime really had supported a mass Jewish emigration to Palestine and a Jewish state. Lehi could be trusted to make a Jewish state that would be a good partner for Nazi Germany, continued Stern, because "in its worldview and structure it is closely related to the totalitarian movements of Europe." Stern was asking Berlin to replace Warsaw as the patron of Lehi. The documents concerning Poland's official Zionism, he helpfully (and correctly) noted, could be found in the Polish archives, now under German control.

Neither of these nationalist proclamations, the Ukrainian or the Jewish, should be understood to express the desires of the nation concerned, or even for that matter the convictions of the authors. With the destruction of the Polish state and the advance of German power, an alliance with Nazis could seem logical, at least to radicals who expected the old order to collapse anyway. Of course, those who issued such appeals did not intend to be used by the Nazis but rather to use them for their own purposes, however unrealistic this calculation might have been. Even the expressions of ideological sympathy need not be taken too literally: Some Ukrainian nationalists had once been communists, and Lehi would shift towards a pro-Soviet orientation a few years later.

Every method of changing the world has advantages and disadvantages. Different tactics generate different needs. A group that chooses legions, as Jabotinsky was still urging Jews in Palestine to do, gambles that the occupying empire will win the war and will then owe something to the oppressed but supportive minority after the victory. A group that chooses terror needs the occupying empire to be destroyed, but almost always lacks the strength to carry out such a deed itself. Therefore it has an objective need for an outside backer. This need for help was the political resource available, in theory, to the Germans.

These Jewish and Ukrainian offers of collaboration with Nazi Germany had to fail, and did fail, and in a certain way failed together. In making their offer to Hitler, Ukrainian nationalists were revealing the political resource, a vulnerability that Hitler did exploit up to a point: the desire for a state. Because German forces really were going to enter lands inhabited by Ukrainians, it was possible for the German leadership to turn the desire of Ukrainian nationalists for a state towards their own purposes. With Jews in Palestine, matters were entirely different. No German troops would enter Palestine; and even if they had, they would have encountered an Arab rather than a Jewish majority. Insofar as the Germans wanted to exploit a local political force, it was far simpler for them to direct Arab nationalism against both the British and the Jews, as had been their practice already in the 1930s.

The Nazi leadership could reconcile, after its own fashion, the Jewish and the Ukrainian nationalist appeals. Hitler did favor the elimination of Jews from Europe, as Stern understood. But he had no desire to create a Jewish state, even beyond Europe, even as a way to draw Jews away from Europe. Germany was willing to use Ukrainians, as Ukrainian nationalists hoped. But that was only because the Germans were intent upon conquering Ukraine. The Nazis opposed Ukrainian statehood and would imprison the Ukrainian nationalists who declared independence. Insofar as Ukrainians collaborated with Germans, it would be as local administrators and policemen, with no political authority. It was precisely the murder of Jews that would become the Nazi substitute for political activity in Ukraine (and elsewhere). In 1941, the Nazis would tell aspiring political collaborators that the liberation to which they could contribute was liberation from the Jews, and that any future political cooperation would depend upon participation in this project. Thus Berlin addressed its Jewish and its Ukrainian problems together, twisting political aspirations toward racial murder and thereby beginning a murderous Final Solution.

In 1940, the application of Soviet power in eastern Europe during the German conquest of western Europe drove the Jews into an impossible position. Jews suffered as much or more than any other group under Soviet rule. They lost much from the end of Polish law, which was the basis of the commerce by which many made a living and of the property rights that gave their urban existence a foundation. They lost the communal autonomy that they had enjoyed under Polish rule and the associated rights to practice religion, run schools, and maintain contacts with Jews around the world. Jews were deported to the Gulag in large numbers in April and June 1940. The Jews of the second group were refugees of the German zone of Poland who imagined that the war would end and that they could return to their homes and businesses in places then occupied by the Germans. They thus declined Soviet citizenship, unaware that what they were being offered was a choice between that and the Gulag.

In the first half of 1940, when eastern Poland had been annexed by the Soviets but Lithuania was still an independent state, Jews fled from the enlarged USSR to Lithuania in the tens of thousands. Along with the large-scale attempts of Jews to return from the Soviet to the German occupation zone and the mass refusal by Jews of Soviet passports, this was another very strong sign that most Jews did not actually wish Soviet rule for themselves. The NKVD reported that Jewish refugees were particularly hostile to Soviet rule. But the Jews' options were narrowing. The German victory over France in June 1940 meant a long war and thus no immediate prospect for the restoration of Poland. The Soviet occupation of Lithuania that same month destroyed the possibility of shelter within a neighboring and relatively supportive state. Judging from how Jews voted with their feet, the general order of preferences had been (1) Lithuania, (2) Poland, (3) the Soviet Union, and (4) Nazi rule. As of summer 1940, the possible rulers of east European Jews were reduced to two: Nazi Germany and the Soviet Union. Since emigration was for most east European Jews all but unthinkable—Palestine and America being closed—their mental geography was now limited to these two options.

With the wider world unattainable, with conventional states destroyed, with Nazi Germany on the march, Jews had no choice but to see the USSR as the lesser evil. For most of them, this was indeed a choice between varieties of evil. The joke among Jews in Łuck was that the life preserved by Soviet power was life imprisonment. As one Galician Jew remembered, already under the Soviet regime "fathers of families had become like loosely hanging limbs. The framework of their lives was torn away; their families became unsteady; their desire for society disappeared; and the authority of Jewish conscience crumbled." The special Nazi enmity to Jews put them in a different position from all of their neighbors under Soviet power in 1939 and 1940, who could at least imagine that a German invasion would put Soviet repression to an end. The combination of a German threat and a Soviet reality left Jews doubly vulnerable. Given their greater fear of Nazi Germany, Jews could seem like the collective ally of the Soviet power that had in fact just dismantled their traditional communities and deported or killed many of their most active men and women.

The Jewish and Ukrainian questions are only a faint suggestion of the political resource that Soviet occupation delivered to Nazi Germany. The Organization of Ukrainian Nationalists and Lehi were fringe groups representing national minorities who could imagine that somehow the destruction of states provided opportunities. An infinitely greater political resource arose when the Soviet Union destroyed entire nation-states, such as Lithuania and Latvia. Soviet state destruction made the political perspective of people who had been marginal right-wing national terrorists seem like the mainstream.

Lithuanians and Latvians had enjoyed statehood between the wars, but lost it as a result of the Molotov-Ribbentrop pact. In this respect the Lithuanian and Latvian position was like the Polish one. Yet unlike Poland, which had been divided and destroyed by Nazi Germany and the Soviet Union together, Lithuania and Latvia were occupied and eliminated by the Soviet Union alone. Lithuanians and Latvians, unlike Poles, could therefore imagine a German liberation from Soviet power. Poles experienced a simultaneous double occupation, Lithuanians and Latvians a consecutive double occupation. During the German occupation, Jews in Lithuania and Latvia could thus be blamed for what happened during the Soviet period—not just for local oppressions, but for an entire national calamity. This was a tragically unique situation.

Before the consecutive Soviet-German occupation, Lithuanian and Latvian Jews had little reason to expect the fate that would befall them. Interwar Lithuania was a right-wing dictatorship, but not an antisemitic one. The dictator, Antanas Smetona, warned at home and abroad against racial and religious discrimination, and he campaigned in particular against what he called the "zoological nationalism and racism" of the Hitlerian variety. His enemies on the Far Right called him the "king of the Jews." Such people he generally had imprisoned. Not a single Jew was killed in a pogrom in interwar Lithuania. The one major case of anti-Jewish violence led to arrests, a trial, and prosecution.

By the standards of Europe in the late 1930s, Lithuania was a refuge for Jews. In 1938 and 1939, some 23,000 Jews fled to Lithuania, some from Nazi Germany, some from the Soviet Union. Among them was Rafał Lemkin, who later invented the term "genocide." In September 1939, Germany expelled some 1,500 Jews from Suwałki, a Polish town on the Lithuanian border that was to be incorporated into the Reich. This was the second time in a quarter century that such a thing had happened: Avraham Stern's family, and many others, had been deported from Suwałki by the Russian imperial army in 1915. These Suwałki Jews were welcomed and cared for by Lithuanian authorities. During the German-Soviet invasion of Poland, the German leadership tried to encourage Lithuania to make claims against Poland, which the Lithuanian leadership refused to do. This was all the more significant since the Lithuanian government had been claiming the city of Vilnius from Poland for twenty years. The independent Lithuanian state, unlike the Soviet Union, declined to be a German ally as the war began.

As a result of the German-Soviet victory and the destruction of the Polish state, however, Lithuania did make some territorial gains. The Soviet Union granted the city of Vilnius, taken from northeastern Poland, to Lithuania. This added about a hundred thousand more Jews to the Lithuanian population. Many Jews saw Lithuanian rule as less nationalist than Polish rule, as indeed it was, at least with respect to them. As Soviet forces withdrew from the city and Lithuanian forces entered in late October

1939, residents of the city, mostly Poles, attacked Jews. The Lithuanianization of the city that followed was directed against the Polish rather than the Jewish population. Lithuania set about making Vilnius its capital and transporting tens of thousands of ethnic Lithuanians to the city.

In late 1939 and early 1940, Zionists and religious Jews saw Vilnius, which was a major Jewish city inside what was still then an independent state, as a place of safety. Zionists fled the Soviet zone of Poland on the correct assumption that the Soviets would otherwise destroy their organizations and arrest them. For Jews seeking a refuge from the enlarging USSR, Vilnius held a special hope. The writer Benzion Benshalom recalled the mood of Jews seeking an escape from German and Soviet power: "Faces were aglow, eyes ablaze, hearts feverish. Vilna!" (Ironically, his brother was a communist.) The leadership of Betar fled from the German occupation zone through the Soviet occupation zone to Vilnius, which they then treated as their base. "Only then," as one of them remembered, "did we breathe more freely." In London, Jabotinsky referred to the Betar men who made it to Lithuania as the "saved."

The position of Jews in interwar Latvia was, if anything, somewhat better. Latvia was also ruled by a right-wing authoritarian regime, but not one that was oriented to race or antisemitism. The Latvian leader, Kārlis Ulmanis, a graduate of the University of Nebraska, took for granted the multinational character of his state. The main ethnic conflict in Latvia was not between Latvians and Jews but between Latvians and Germans. Nevertheless, Germans, like Jews, served as ministers of government in interwar Latvia. The Orthodox Jewish political party, Agudat Yisrael, had some sway with right-wing Latvian governments, as did the Jewish socialist party, the Bund, with left-wing governments. Latvia, like Lithuania, passed no racist or antisemitic legislation before the war, and took in Jewish refugees from Germany and Austria in the late 1930s. As in Lithuania there was a Far Right movement with an antisemitic stance in Latvia, and as in Lithuania it was illegal before the war.

Latvia and Lithuania were similar in that they were small countries (populations about two million and three million) with substantial Jewish populations governed by authoritarian regimes whose policies were tolerant by the standards of the Europe of the late 1930s. Their fates were brought together in June 1940, when the Soviet Union took advantage of

the terms of its alliance with Nazi Germany to occupy and annex them both. Very quickly the Soviets decapitated the Latvian and Lithuanian political classes, deporting to the Gulag most of the leaders who had not already fled.

The subsequent and rapid Soviet takeover of the two sovereign states created psychological, material, and especially political resources in Latvia and Lithuania on a scale far greater than in Poland. The material resource was enormous: Soviet rule quickly opened the question of the property rights of the entire nation. The Soviets expropriated Jews (not as Jews, but as businessmen), raising the question of the ultimate ownership of their property. The psychological resource was also of an extraordinary scale. The destruction of the two states generated feelings of shame, humiliation, and the desire for revenge. In both Lithuania and Latvia, an entire political order was destroyed and an entire population could imagine its return. By destroying the Lithuanian and Latvian states, the Soviets gave the Germans the ability to promise a war of liberation. This was the political resource in its purest form.

The political resource included the supply of cadres: people displaced by Soviet policy who could be exploited by the Germans. The fact that the Soviets controlled the capitals and decimated the political elite enabled the Germans to make a certain important selection. In the main, the men who had actually ruled Lithuania and Latvia were sent to the Gulag or killed. But some Lithuanian and Latvian nationalists who had fled the interwar regimes or Soviet power made their way to Berlin. Beyond that, a considerable number of Lithuanians and Latvians posed as Germans in 1940, which allowed them to be "repatriated" to Germany under a German-Soviet agreement. The Germans could then decide which of these people they would bring when they reinvaded Latvia and Lithuania.

The timing of the Soviet annexation of Latvia and Lithuania led to a tragic coincidence. By the time the Soviets had readied the trains for their major deportations of Lithuanian and Latvian citizens to the Gulag, the Germans had prepared their trains for an invasion of the Soviet Union. The deportations from Lithuania began in the early morning of June 14, 1941. About seventeen thousand people were loaded onto boxcars (of whom only about a third ever returned). The German invasion came a week later. Because the Soviets were preparing major repressions when the Germans invaded, the prisons were full. Stalin raged until the very last moment that all reports of a German invasion were propaganda. As a result, no one could make preparations for evacuation or defense, and, of course, prisoners were the last priority and considered dangerous. Most of them were shot by their guards, in Lithuania and Latvia and everywhere across the front. As a result, Germans who arrived in Lithuania and Latvia were able to display the fresh corpses as palpable evidence of Soviet terror. In June 1941 in the Baltics the Soviet project of state destruction met the German project of state destruction in time and in place.

For the German state destroyers, the men of the *Einsatzgruppen* arriving to begin a second occupation of eastern Poland, Lithuania, and Latvia in summer 1941, the encounter with Soviet power was an opportunity. They could not have known beforehand how bountiful the political resource would be, since they had not been trained to think of the Soviet Union as a polity nor of Slavs or Balts as people with political motivations. Because Germans could not know how deep the Soviet reach into occupied societies had been, the new politics after summer 1941 would be a spontaneous creation of Germans and the local peoples whose lands they reinvaded.

The German entrepreneurs of violence would react to a new situation and exploit its possibilities. They did not know what they would find and were mistaken in some of their expectations. What they brought was the yearning for anarchy that can only be brought to the stranger, what they learned was to exploit the experience of the Soviet occupation to further the most radical goals of their own, and what they invented was a politics of the greater evil. In the zone of double darkness, where Nazi creativity met Soviet precision, the black hole was found.

6

The Greater Evil

"The epoch of statehood has come to an end." So proclaimed the German legal theorist Carl Schmitt. Throughout Hitler's career, Schmitt had provided elegant theoretical support for his *Führer*'s actions, in domestic and then foreign policy, as Hitler mutated the German state and began to destroy its neighbors. The lesson that Hitler had drawn from the Balkans, Schmitt presented as a purely German idea: There is no such thing as domestic politics as such, since everything begins with the confrontation with a chosen foreign enemy. The definition of the domestic was that which had to be manipulated to destroy what is foreign. Germany itself had no content. The idea of the people, the *Volk*, was there to persuade Germans to throw themselves into their murderous destiny as a race. The people were only what they proved themselves to be, which without struggle was nothing.

Beyond manipulation itself there was no object or subject of politics. There was only the darkness that is consummate when gifted minds such as Schmitt's cloak evil with unreason. As Germany undid Austria and Czechoslovakia, as the Soviet Union occupied and annexed Lithuania, Latvia, and Estonia, and as the two together destroyed Poland, Schmitt prepared the legal theory of statelessness. It began from the axiom that international law arises not from norms but from power. Rules are interesting only insofar as they reveal who can make exceptions to them. For Schmitt, "obsolete interstate international law" was a masquerade, since all that mattered was who could destroy states. If Germany followed its *Führer* and ignored "the empty concept of state territory," German power would flow to its natural frontiers. The result would be a "sensibly divided earth," untroubled by the normative restraints on political and military action that Schmitt described as Jewish.

Schmitt believed that the German understanding of law had to be purged of the Jewish "infection," by which he meant principles that blocked conclusions such as his own. Affirming the end of the state meant applying the law of the jungle and presenting it as actual law. Might did make right, not just in practice, but as a matter of principle; and, of course, this conclusion came very close to abolishing the very idea of principle. The same case was made, in different ways, by other Nazi legal thinkers, such as Viktor Bruns and Edgar Tartarin-Tarnheyden. Arthur Seyß-Inquart, who presided over the end of the Austrian state and administered the occupied Netherlands, was a lawyer and doctor of law. In between those two assignments he was the assistant to Hans Frank, the governor-general of occupied Poland. In western Europe, said Seyß-Inquart, we have a function; in eastern Europe "we have a National Socialist mission."

Frank, Hitler's personal lawyer, never ceased to provide circular and specious defenses of the "legality" of what he was doing in occupied Poland: "The law is what serves the race, and lawlessness is what hurts the race." Non-racist norms were simply the work of Jews, "who instinctively saw in jurisprudence the best possibility to carry out their own racial work." Frank never forgot that racial triumph meant racial comfort, that *Lebensraum* was about the pleasures of his living room. He was the sort of man who not only stole a royal castle for his own residence, but actually made tours of other castles to steal their silver for his own table. He sent his wife to make shopping excursions to the Cracow ghetto, where the price was always right. When he left Poland he took its Rembrandts with him.

Lawyers were extremely prominent among those who exported anarchy from Germany. Bruno Müller, for example, commanded an *Einsatzgruppe* in Poland in 1939 and then an *Einsatzkommando* in the Soviet Union in 1941. He was a mass murderer of Poles and Jews in two campaigns to obliterate the state. At the first execution of his second campaign he lifted into his hands a two-year-old Jewish child and said: "You must die so that we can live."

This is what law for the race and against the state had become—and indeed had always meant.

Germany at war remained a state, if an altered one. For most Germans most of the time, law in its entirely traditional sense, implemented by state instances, still organized life. Policies directed chiefly against German citizens, such as the discrimination of Jews, were most significant as a preparation for a larger struggle. Policies that seemed to weaken the German state, such as the lawless zones of the concentration camps, were templates for the far larger stateless spaces that would arise in the East. Policies that seemed to transform the state, such as the creation of hybrid institutions that united both SS and traditional police, revealed their potential east of Germany, where prewar states were destroyed. Only beyond Germany could the exception truly become the rule, as Schmitt wished, because only beyond Germany could normal political life be obliterated and a new ethos of nihilistic power be created.

As the *Einsatzgruppen* followed the German army eastward into the doubly occupied lands and then into the prewar Soviet Union, their commanders sometimes communicated with Berlin. British authorities, aided by Polish cryptographers, had built for themselves a replica of the Enigma machine that the Germans used for encoding and decoding messages. As the British came to realize, what they were decoding were kill figures. "We are in the presence," said Winston Churchill, "of a crime without a name." Its perpetrators were human beings, operating with initiative and creativity in political circumstances of their own making. State destruction did not alter politics, but rather created a new form of politics, which enabled a new kind of crime.

The Holocaust has ingrained racial stereotypes in our own minds; but no stereotype can explain why and how, in the six months after the German invasion of the Soviet Union, a technique to kill Jews in large numbers was developed and some one million Jews were murdered. A stereotype of Germans is that they are orderly and follow plans. Yet when the invasion of the Soviet Union began on June 22, 1941, Berlin had no plan for the mass extermination of Soviet Jews, let alone for all Jews under German control. One notion was that Soviet Jews would be sent to Siberia after a quick and triumphant military campaign against the Red Army. There was no discussion of a Final Solution to take place during the war, nor could there have been, since German leaders took for granted that the war would take weeks and the Final Solution years.

Sometimes the *Einsatzgruppen* who followed the *Wehrmacht* into the Soviet Union are presented as unstoppable agents of evil with an unambiguous program of total killing. In this argument, the men of the *Einsatzgruppen* knew from the beginning, regardless of whether or not there was a plan, that they were supposed to kill all of the Jews. An image emerges of the *Einsatzgruppen* as special antisemitic units with perfect knowledge and exclusive responsibility. But this was not, in fact, the case. The *Einsatzgruppen* had orders to shoot some Jews from the beginning, but not to shoot them all; their initial instructions mentioned Jews as one category among others. Their basic task at the beginning of the invasion of the Soviet Union was to demolish the state, as they had done in Poland. Thus their targets were groups thought to be mainstays of the Soviet regime. In Poland this had meant educated Poles; in the Soviet Union this meant, as the Nazis saw matters, communists and Jewish males.

Antisemitism cannot fully explain the behavior of the members of the *Einsatzgruppen*. The *Einsatzgruppen* sent into Austria and Czechoslovakia in 1938 did not kill Jews. The *Einsatzgruppen* sent into Poland in 1939 killed far more Poles than Jews. Even the *Einsatzgruppen* sent into the USSR killed others besides Jews. Throughout the occupation of the Soviet Union they murdered the disabled, Gypsies, communists, and, in some regions, Poles. There were for that matter no Germans (or collaborators) whose only task was to shoot Jews; everyone who was expected to shoot Jews was also expected to shoot others, and did so. Among the thousands of members of the *Einsatzgruppen* and the tens of thousands of Germans who shot Jews there is no known perpetrator who agreed to kill Jews but refused to kill Gypsies or Belarusian civilians or Soviet prisoners of war. Nor were there perpetrators who agreed to kill Belarusian civilians or Soviet prisoners of war or Gypsies but not Jews. The people who killed people, killed people.

The *Einsatzgruppen* shot others besides Jews; and others besides the *Einsatzgruppen* shot Jews. Although the *Einsatzgruppen* were the first to shoot Jews in large numbers, they were a small minority of the German perpetrators. The myth of their total responsibility arose during postwar trials in the Federal Republic of Germany as a way to protect the majority of German killers and isolate the killing from German society as such. In fact, German policemen were far more numerous than the *Einsatzgruppen* on the eastern front and killed more Jews. These men usually lacked the special preparation of the *Einsatzgruppen,* but they had been a focus of Himmler and Heydrich's attempt to create hybrid institutions within Germany that would permit destruction and racial warfare beyond its borders. Policemen deemed unreliable had been removed from service. By the time of the invasion of the USSR, about a third of policemen with officer rank belonged to the SS, and about two-thirds belonged to the National Socialist party. Regardless of whether or not they were party or SS members, German policemen were dispatched to the East and murdered Jews. German soldiers also killed a large number of Jews, and assisted the *Einsatzgruppen* and the police in organizing ever larger mass shootings in 1941.

In 1941, the German members of the *Einsatzgruppen,* the German policemen, and the German soldiers worked together with a large number of local people of multiple nationalities who had experienced Soviet rule. Together these groups developed techniques of mass murder during the first six months after the German invasion. The techniques reflected no prior plan; indeed, some of them contravened initial orders. The *Einsatzgruppen* were doing what Himmler and Heydrich told them to do, but their commanders were also refining methods of killing and inventing rationalizations for killing. The commanders had to test whether their operations and rationalizations were acceptable to other German forces; they had to persuade their own men to kill women and children; and they had to find ways to generate local collaboration as the job became too large and difficult.

If the killing of 1941 involved locals, then perhaps it was a result of local antisemitism rather than German politics? This is a popular way to explain the Holocaust without politics: as a historically predictable outburst of the barbarity of east Europeans. This sort of explanation is reassuring, since it permits the thought that only peoples associated with extravagant antisemitism would indulge in disastrous violence. This comforting and erroneous thought is a legacy of Nazi racism and colonialism. The racist and colonial idea that the Holocaust began as an elemental explosion of primitive antisemitism arose as Nazi propaganda and apologetics. The Germans wished to display the killing of Jews on the eastern front as the righteous anger of oppressed peoples against their supposed Jewish overlords.

Even the most hidebound Nazis realized, once they had actually arrived in eastern Europe, that the situation was not so simple as this. The truly spontaneous score settling that followed the arrival of German troops was politically rather than racially motivated and killed a very small number of Jews—and also killed people who were not Jewish. The instructions conveyed to the *Einsatzgruppen* commanders were to create the appearance of local spontaneity, which, of course, suggests that the reality was absent. In practice, the Germans concluded within a few weeks that the stimulation of pogroms among people who had been ruled by the Soviet Union was not the way forward to a Final Solution. In consecutively occupied Lithuania, where the Holocaust began, less than one percent of the Jews who were murdered were victims of pogroms. For that matter, Germans were present at every single pogrom.

After the war, Soviet propaganda repeated the Nazi case. One unpleasant reality with which Soviet propagandists had to contend was that the Holocaust had begun precisely where the Soviet Union had brought its own new revolutionary order in 1939 and 1940. A second was that Soviet citizens of all nationalities, including considerable numbers of communists, had collaborated with the Germans in the killing of Jews everywhere that contact with Germans was made: both in the territories that the Soviets annexed in 1939 and 1940 and in the territories of the prewar Soviet Union, including Soviet Russia. Thus, Soviet propagandists tried with Orwellian precision to ethnicize history and to limit responsibility for the Holocaust to Lithuanians and Latvians, precisely the peoples whose states the Soviet Union had destroyed in 1940, and to west Ukrainians, whose national aspirations were also crushed by Soviet power. This export of moral responsibility seemed to justify the renewed Soviet takeover of these lands after the war. Thus the Nazis first and the Soviets later made efforts to direct responsibility for the killing of the Jews to the countries they both invaded.

Certainly there was abundant local antisemitism in eastern Europe. Hostility to Jews in the major Jewish homeland had been an important current in religious, cultural, and political life for hundreds of years. In interwar Poland in particular, the idea that Jews were alien to the national body and should leave the national territory was ever more popular in the 1930s. Yet the relationship between sentiment and killing is not straightforward. Age-old antisemitism cannot explain why pogroms began precisely in summer 1941. Such an explanation ignores the suggestive fact that pogroms were most numerous where Germans drove out Soviet power, and the obviously material fact that the instigation of pogroms in such places was explicit German policy. Pogroms and other forms of local collaboration in killing were less likely in Poland, where antisemitism had been more prevalent before the war, than they were in Lithuania and Latvia, where antisemitism was less prevalent. In the Soviet Union, where before the war antisemitism was a crime, there was much more direct collaboration in the killing of Jews than in Poland. In the occupied USSR, the killing of Jews began immediately upon contact with German forces. In occupied Poland, the Holocaust began more than two years after the German invasion and was largely isolated from the local population. In the occupied Soviet Union, the killing of Jews took place in the open air, in front of the population, with the help of young male Soviet citizens.

It is tempting to imagine that a simple idea in the minds of simple people decades past and thousands of miles away can explain a complex event. The notion that local east European antisemitism killed the Jews of eastern Europe confers upon others a sense of superiority akin to that the Nazis once felt. These people are quite primitive, we can allow ourselves to think. Not only does this account fail as an explanation of the Holocaust; its racism prevents us from considering the possibility that not only Germans and Jews but also local peoples were individual human agents with complex goals that were reflected in politics. When we fall into the trap of ethnicization and collective responsibility, we collude with Nazi and Soviet propagandists in the abolition of political thought and the lifting of individual agency.

What happened in the second half of 1941 was an accelerating campaign of murder that took a million Jewish lives and apparently convinced the German leadership that all Jews under their control could be eliminated. This calamity cannot be explained by stereotypes of passive or communist Jews, of orderly or preprogrammed Germans, of beastly or antisemitic locals, or indeed by any other cliché, no matter how powerful at the time, no matter how convenient today. This unprecedented mass murder would have been impossible without a special kind of politics.

The commencement of mass killing in the doubly occupied lands was the latest stage in the development of the new politics initiated eight years earlier, when Hitler came to power in Germany. Just as Nazis had to reach other Germans to develop biological politics within Germany, so Germans had to reach non-Germans for Nazi ideology to be realized beyond Germany.

In a way, the invasion of 1941 mirrored Hitler's takeover of power in Germany. A planetary vision of bloody racial struggle, something not inherently attractive to most people most of the time, was translated at moments of stress into concepts and images that could generate political support. In Germany in 1933, Hitler's notion that Jews were communists and communists were Jews was translated into the much more banal but accessible idea that rule from the Left would mean chaos and hunger for Germany. In eastern Europe in 1941, Judeobolshevism was also translated from vision into politics, but in lands where people had actually experienced Soviet rule. The key to this translation of ideology to politics in both cases was an effective appeal to human experience at the crucial time. In Germany in 1933, Hitler directed fear against the eastern neighbor, the Soviet Union. In 1941, in the doubly occupied lands, Germans directed the experience of Soviet occupation against Jewish neighbors.

In a dark irony, Nazis profited from their basic error. Their essential idea was that the Soviet Union was a Jewish empire, which would be destroyed by a German empire. When Germany invaded the Soviet Union in June 1941, however, the societies that German invaders encountered were not divided between Jewish rulers and Christian victims. For one thing, the Soviets had been more effective than the Germans in bodily removing their human targets from the scene. Half a million or so Polish, Lithuanian, and Latvian citizens, including many Jews and members of other national minorities, had been deported to the Gulag (where many of them had already died). The corpses of thousands more Polish, Lithuanian, and Latvian citizens, including Jews and members of other national minorities, were buried in hidden Soviet mass graves. All of these indisputable victims of Soviet rule were dead or thousands of miles away. Even the prisoners of the NKVD could not usually be recruited, since most of them were shot or deported just as the Germans arrived.

To a degree that the Germans could not imagine, the Soviets had integrated the local populations into their own system. This meant that people in the doubly occupied lands could see themselves as victims, even though or indeed precisely because they had exercised a certain amount of power in the Soviet regime. The psychological and political reasons to overcompensate by insisting on victimhood were strong. There were the people of the Left who had first supported the Soviet system and then changed their minds, and now wanted to forget their original commitments. There were the men and women who had at first resisted the Soviet system, and then allowed themselves to be recruited by it as agents and informers. Such people had escaped death or deportation by collaborating with the Soviets, and were thus still at home when the Germans arrived—and eager to purge their own pasts by collaborating again. There were the young men who had been drafted into the Red Army, and then deserted when the Germans arrived. There were the policemen who had served the interwar governments and then the Soviet regime, and thus had helped deport those who had actually resisted the Soviets. When the Germans arrived, such policemen had every reason to prove themselves cooperative. There were the people who had served the Soviet security apparatus at a very high level—so high that they knew others would remember. In those cases the people in question had to maintain an important position with the Germans in order to survive, and they sometimes did.

The Soviet system was not a Jewish conspiracy, and most communist party members, policemen, and collaborators had not been Jews. The Germans had to believe that they were, since the entire premise of the invasion was that a Jewish cabal would quickly crumble as its local Jewish collaborators were eliminated. Whatever local people might have said to save their own skins during the war or ethnicize their experiences thereafter, they generally knew that nothing of the kind was true, since they had actually experienced the Soviet system. The Soviet administration did employ Jews in higher numbers than the prewar regimes, and it did employ them disproportionately to their numbers. Nevertheless, Soviet power was based everywhere in the local majorities: be they Latvian, Lithuanian, Belarusian, Ukrainian, Russian, or Polish. Insofar as non-Jews made the claim that Jews were Soviet collaborators and that Soviet collaborators were Jews (and insofar as such claims are made today), they minimized the indispensable role that non-Jewish locals played in the Soviet regime. In defining communism as Jewish and Jews as communists, the German invaders in fact pardoned the vast majority of Soviet collaborators.

The involvement of essentially everyone in the Soviet system, which was the political reality, could be reduced to the idea of a few guilty Jews, which was a political fantasy. The Judeobolshevik myth confirmed the idea that the Nazis had to hold in order for their own invasion to make sense: that one blow to the Soviet Union could begin the undoing of the world Jewish conspiracy and that one blow to the Jews could bring down the Soviet Union. It simultaneously allowed the people who had actually partaken of Soviet power to separate the past from themselves, both in their own imaginations and in their interactions with the new anti-Soviet Nazi ruler. When Heydrich wrote of the need for "self-cleansing," he had in mind that communities could be spurred to cleanse themselves of Jews. In fact, insofar as locals sided, or pretended to side, with Nazi policies towards the Jews, they were cleansing themselves of their own past. German ignorance of the politics of Soviet rule and occupation created a certain opportunity for locals to exploit Germans.

As a result, the murderous politics that emerged was a joint creation of Germans and locals, each of whom was performing the undoing of Soviet power, but with different ideas of what that power had been, and with different interests. To be sure, the coordination of actors with different experiences, perceptions, and goals is what politics is about. But here, in this special time and place, where one extraordinarily severe regime gave way to another, where collaboration with the Soviets had been broad and where Nazi instructions for racial murder were general, there was no guiding source of political authority. The politics of the greater evil was a common creation at a time of chaos.

In a sense, 1941 was a reprise of 1938, of the *Anschluss* of Austria, the first Nazi success in state destruction. As some Nazis learned in Vienna, the suspension of state authority itself creates a political resource, since suddenly almost no one wishes to be identified with the old regime and everyone wishes to be supported, or at least spared, by the new one. When the new regime was a Nazi one, racism permitted much of the population to separate itself, by way of public performances, from its own actual political history. In the occupied Soviet Union in 1941, as in Austria in 1938, the collapse of the prior regime supplied aesthetic elements of a political scenography by which the local population performed Nazi ideology, reconciling its own interests and hopes with the perceived ideas of those who now held power. The public and ritual identification of Jews with the prior regime delegitimized both at the same time, in a closed circle of condemnation that left the majority outside and relatively safe. If the regime had collapsed, and the Jews were the regime, then their downfall was the logical consequence. Just as people must be concentrated before they can be murdered *en masse,* so must responsibility be concentrated before it can be abolished. Thus Jews and only Jews were to answer for the past. And when they were assembled and murdered, the responsibility went up in smoke.

In Austria in 1938 a large number of local Nazis had made their own plans for Austrian Jews, and so the actions taken when the state collapsed were immediate and racial. In doubly occupied eastern Poland, the first place reached by German forces in their reinvasion of June 1941, the reaction was not so precise, because locals could not be sure at first what the Nazis expected. Of course, the German displacement of Soviet power led to a good deal of local score settling, just as the Soviet displacement of Polish power had done twenty-one months before. The initial beatings, humiliations, and killings that commenced with the arrival of the Germans were not, however, organized by ethnicity, but rather driven by personal grievances during the occupation. In the days immediately after the Germans arrived, Poles did kill Jews, but they also killed other Poles. Large pogroms of Jews were not precipitated by the withdrawal of the Soviets but by the arrival of the Germans.

The Germans seemed to have conceived a basic scenography of regime change. Brought by the *Einsatzgruppen* and the German Order Police with the invasion of the USSR, it strongly resembled the ritual violence of the SA in Vienna. The equivalent of the "scrubbing parties" of spring 1938 was the ritualized destruction of Lenin and Stalin statues in the doubly occupied lands in summer 1941. Forcing Jews to remove propaganda was a way to blame them for it. Those who forced them to do so or who contemplated the scene were releasing themselves from responsibility for the old order and ingratiating themselves to the masters of the new one.

What local people expected from the German invasion of 1941 depended upon their experience of Soviet rule in 1940. And what the Soviet experience had meant depended, in turn, upon interwar politics. The various peoples of eastern Poland—Poles, Ukrainians, Belarusians, Jews—reacted very differently to the German invasion of June 1941 not because they belonged to various ethnicities, but because they had different hopes and aims arising from prior experiences. In southeastern Poland, there was more collaboration with the Germans in the early days and weeks of the invasion than in northeastern Poland, because in southeastern Poland there were Ukrainian nationalists who could believe that a German invasion would advance their political interests.

As Ukrainian nationalists helped organize pogroms in reinvaded southeastern Poland in summer 1941, they also helped the Germans to translate the experience of Soviet rule into a fantasy of Ukrainian innocence and Jewish guilt. When the corpses of prisoners were found inside an NKVD prison, German propaganda inevitably presented the executioners as Jews. When on June 30 the Germans removed some of the bodies of the thousands of prisoners shot by the NKVD in Lwów, Ukrainian nationalists helped them portray these killings as a Jewish crime against the Ukrainian nation. The actual NKVD officers who had performed the actual executions had gone, but the Jews of Lwów remained. Here, as elsewhere, corpses were put on display wherever they were found, the horror associated with the Jews. The shock of the moment helped transform a political crime into an ethnic one; an ethnic crime meant ethnic responsibility; murder of those held to be responsible was not so much revenge as a transformation of the past. Recent history became a racial fable, with murder as the moral. Of course, in individual cases, matters could be much simpler than this. One Ukrainian survivor of a Soviet prison shooting, for example, became a regional police commander for the Germans.

In Lwów on July 25, 1941, more than four weeks after the NKVD had shot its prisoners, Jews were killed in a pogrom organized by the Germans with the help of local nationalists. This was anything but a spontaneous reaction. Active assistance in pogroms in summer 1941 provided useful political cover for the large number of Ukrainians who had been communists or Soviet collaborators or both. The Judeobolshevik myth, spread locally by militias, provided the perfect escape route for most Soviet collaborators, who, in fact, were Ukrainian. Nationalists told fellow Ukrainians that they could purge themselves of the stain of collaboration with the Soviets by killing one Jew. Quite often, as in the town of Mizoch, some of the collaborators with Soviet rule were Ukrainian nationalists who, until summer 1941, had cooperated with Jews in the Soviet apparatus.

By reducing actual Ukrainian political experience to the abstraction of Judeobolshevism, the Germans gave Ukrainians who had collaborated with the Soviets a chance, which they quickly took. Again and again, Ukrainians identified Jews as communists and Soviet collaborators, thereby sheltering themselves and their families. In the town of Klevan, for example, Ukrainians went from Jewish house to Jewish house, pointing out supposed Soviet collaborators. In Dubno, where three-quarters of the population was Jewish, some of the Ukrainians allowed by the Germans to run the town in 1941 had offered their services to the Soviets in 1939. In other words, Ukrainians who spent the first two years of the war helping the local NKVD commander (who was Jewish) deport Poles, Jews, and Ukrainians shifted to helping the SS kill Jews, Ukrainians, and Poles whom they—actual Soviet collaborators—denounced as Soviet collaborators. The Germans were unable to process the rush of denunciations, and, falling back upon their own racial illusions, were often manipulated. Double collaboration was noticed by Jews and Poles in these places, but is absent in both Ukrainian and German histories of the war.

In doubly occupied northeastern Poland, where there was no national question and thus no political resource, the chain of events was rather different. In the weeks after the invasion, the Germans dedicated far more of their own resources to provoking violence against Jews, with far weaker results. Jews were killed by the Germans, and eventually also by Poles, but in smaller numbers and in fewer places.

DOUBLE OCCUPATION
August 1941
Doubly occupied by August 1941
NORWAY
Oslo
SWEDEN
Stockholm
FINLAND
Helsinki
KARELO-FINNISH S.S.R.
Leningrad
Tallinn
ESTONIAN S.S.R.
Novgorod
U.S.S.R.
Riga
LATVIAN S.S.R.
Moscow
RUSSIAN S.F.S.R.
North Sea
DENMARK
Baltic Sea
LITHUANIAN S.S.R.
Smolensk
Vilnius
Königsberg
Danzig
Minsk
Hamburg
NETHERLANDS
BELARUSIAN S.S.R.
Białystok
Berlin
Molotov-Ribbentrop Line
Posen
Vistula
Kursk
WARTHEGAU
Warsaw
BELGIUM
Rhine
GERMANY
Łódź
Dresden
Lublin
Don
Volga
GENERAL GOVERNMENT
Kyiv
Stalingrad
LUX.
Prague
Zhytomyr
Protectorate of Bohemia and Moravia
Cracow
Lviv
Alsace Lorraine
UKRAINIAN S.S.R.
Dnipro
Danube
Kamianets-Podilskyi
Stalino
FRANCE
SLOVAKIA
Munich
Bratislava
Vienna
MOLDAVIAN S.S.R.
Budapest
SWITZERLAND
HUNGARY
Chisinau
Odessa
VICHY FRANCE
CRIMEA (RSFSR)
ROMANIA
ITALY
CROATIA
Bucharest
Black Sea
SERBIA
GEORGIAN S.S.R.

In Białystok, a major city of northeastern Poland, the Germans began the mass killing themselves in June 1941. By this time the city had already been occupied twice. First had come the German army in September 1939, followed by the bloodiest German special unit of the Polish campaign, *Einsatzgruppe* IV, which killed Poles and Jews in the city. By the terms of the Treaty on Borders and Friendship between Nazi Germany and the Soviet Union of the twenty-eighth of that month, the *Wehrmacht* and SS withdrew from Białystok to be replaced by the Red Army and the NKVD. Under Soviet power, much of the city center was disassembled, and Jewish enterprises (along with all others) were closed. The Soviet occupation then continued until the German reinvasion of June 1941. On June 27, 1941, Order Police Battalion 329 entered Białystok, with general orders to eliminate Soviet stragglers and "enemies." What followed was a new type of German mass murder, perhaps meant as a prototype.

Jews were ordered to clear Białystok of Lenin and Stalin statues as Soviet music played in the background. German policemen spread through the city, with orders to seize all Jewish men of military age. They shot a number of them on the spot. German policemen shot ten Jews inside one of the city's many small synagogues and then left their corpses on its steps. They seized some women and children and well over a thousand men. Some Germans raped Jewish women. Meanwhile, other German policemen sealed the neighborhood around the synagogue and mounted a machine gun in front of it. The Germans then forced the Jews into the synagogue, poured gasoline on the exterior, and set it aflame. The screaming was punctuated by machine gun fire for about half an hour. The logic of this scenography was evident: The Jews were responsible for the Soviet occupation, and liberation meant killing them. This was no doubt clear enough to a population that was fully aware of the Judeobolshevik myth, which had been widespread on the Polish Right in the interwar period. Nevertheless, the German mass murder by immolation of June 27 did not lead to the immediate results the Germans seem to have expected.

In those days of late June and early July 1941, Poles were settling scores in northeastern Poland. Just as the arrival of the Red Army twenty months before had brought local violence, so, too, did the arrival of the German army. Some Poles killed some Jews, but some Poles also killed other Poles. These spontaneous individual killings followed no scenography. Poles did not immediately follow the Białystok example, as clear as it was. Two days after the mass murder in Białystok, Heydrich issued a specific order to his *Einsatzgruppen* to inspire pogroms while this was still possible, in the chaos of the collapse of Soviet power. These "self-cleansing efforts" were to be "provoked without leaving a trace, to be intensified when necessary, to be channeled into the proper course. The local 'self-defense' should be denied the possibility of later referring to political assurances."

If Heydrich's order was meant to bring about widespread pogroms in northeastern Poland, it failed. In contrast to southeastern Poland, where Ukrainian nationalists were at work, there was no obvious political question, no prior political organization, and no body of selected and trained emigrants to translate the German program into a local liberation. In early July 1941, northeastern Poland received unusually intense attention from the Nazi leadership and the German police. Heydrich repeated his orders to incite pogroms. Himmler, who was disappointed with the absence of pogroms in the region, came to Białystok and gave a similar order. Even Göring visited the region during these days and issued the same instructions himself.

The presence and preferences of three of the highest Nazi officials brought an unusually thick presence of German police forces to the region. They came from three different directions. Elements of *Einsatzgruppe* B returned from the east, police from the enlarged Reich arrived from the northeast, and police from Warsaw in the General Government arrived from the southwest. The members of all three of these units had a great deal of experience in the mass murder of Poles and Jews. Indeed, some of the policemen coming from Warsaw already had memories of prior murder in Białystok, since the Warsaw stationary police had been constituted from *Einsatzgruppe* IV, which had ravaged the city in 1939. Even this unusual attention by the top German leadership and the rally of German police forces from all sides could not compensate for the absence of the political resource. The Germans provoked about a dozen pogroms, and local Poles killed several thousand Jews. These results were far inferior, from the German perspective, to the killing in southeastern Poland, where politically motivated Ukrainians were at work.

The scale of the murder was also inferior to what the Germans were already achieving to the north and east, as they drove Soviet forces from

Lithuania and Latvia and occupied these countries themselves. Indeed, the return visit of German forces to northeastern Poland in early July 1941 was probably an attempt to match the results already achieved in Lithuania and Latvia. The pogroms in northeastern Poland began after Germans and Lithuanians were already killing Jews in Lithuania, one whole country to the north and east. For that matter, the pogroms in northeastern Poland began after Germans and Latvians were killing Jews in Latvia, two whole countries to the north and east. The killings in northeastern Poland, in this broader perspective, represented a de-escalation rather than an escalation, since murder in the region was much less widespread than in Lithuania and Latvia. And it stopped after a few weeks. Pogroms without a political resource were a blind alley.

The Germans were learning a new politics, and both success and failure were instructive. The distribution of pogroms, and the absence of truly spontaneous pogroms, demonstrated that the initial Nazi assumptions about local behavior were wrong. The Nazi logic was that the subhumans could be provoked to kill their Jewish exploiters. In fact, pogroms in northeastern Poland tended to take place where non-Jews had collaborated with the Soviet regime. In places where Jewish communists were numerous, pogroms were actually less common, since communism in a given locality meant contacts between Jews and non-Jews and a habit of conspiracy. Communist Jews had places to seek advice and places to hide. The same held for Piłsudski's interwar electoral bloc, which had been a multinational undertaking. When it was significant in a given community, Jews and Poles tended to have civil relations, and pogroms were less likely to take place.

The most notorious pogrom in northeastern Poland, at Jedwabne on July 10, 1941, demonstrated how little the Germans understood. German police returned to Jedwabne on that day, more than two weeks after the actual change of regime, and two weeks after the Białystok example. In Jedwabne, the Germans had, although they did not know this, the ideal conditions for a pogrom. In the interwar years communism and the Piłsudski movement had been weak in the area, which meant that there was little tradition of Jewish-Polish contacts. The person who had betrayed the anti-Soviet Polish underground in Jedwabne to the Soviets was a Pole, not a Jew. The Germans were offering, as the Poles understood even if the Germans did not, an opportunity for self-cleansing, in which responsibility for the Soviet regime could be placed upon the local Jews and then eliminated.

The scenography in Jedwabne followed closely that of Białystok, except that here Germans set the rules and Poles followed them. In the presence of German police, some local Poles forced some local Jews to remove the Lenin statue. Then about three hundred Jews, some carrying a red banner to symbolize their supposed link to communism, were marched to a barn and burned alive by some of their Polish neighbors. As in most such cases, individuals who had collaborated with communism were certainly killing individuals who had not. The mass murder created a collective stereotype, ethnicizing the guilt and rearranging the past. The Lenin statue was burned in the barn along with the Jews (much as Lenin signs were burned with "Jewish" books back in Germany). The lie that the Germans told to the Poles through posters and megaphones—that Jews were communists and communists Jews—was told back to the Germans by the Poles in cinders and ash.

In northeastern Poland, pogroms followed the Białystok choreography. Germans assembled Poles; Poles assembled Jews; Poles beat and humiliated Jews. Poles forced Jews to sing Soviet songs, carry Soviet flags, and destroy a nearby Lenin or Stalin monument when one was available. These murderous rituals were a reformulation of the experience of a shattering era that had now passed, but not an immediate and unreflective reaction to suffering. These pogroms were not spontaneous acts of revenge, but a joint effort, by Germans and locals, to reassemble the experience of the Soviet occupation in a way that was acceptable to both sides.

The Jedwabne method of killing Jews, horrible as it was, could not become a Final Solution because there was no political resource. The Germans could appeal to psychological and material resources: Poles could exculpate themselves from their own association with Soviet rule by killing Jews, and they could take Jewish property. In the Jedwabne region, where owning a mule was a mark of prosperity, this motive cannot be discounted. But Germany could not even pretend to offer Poland to the Poles. Germany had already invaded Poland once. Indeed, during the first invasion of September 1939, German forces had actually reached Jedwabne and the other places in northeastern Poland where the July 1941 pogroms took place. That first time around, in September 1939, German forces had mainly been interested in murdering Poles. After withdrawing from the region, the Germans had annexed and colonized much of western and central Poland, as everyone knew. When the Germans returned in 1941 they did not even bother to make political promises to Poles. In fact, the Germans intended to kill Poles after using them to kill Jews.

The presence or absence of pogroms in doubly occupied eastern Poland had to do with recent political history and thus with a political sensibility that Nazis did not believe that subhumans could possess. But the political learning came quickly. In Lithuania, where the political resource was vast, pogroms were training grounds for people who could be selected by the Germans for more organized methods of mass killing. By the time the Germans reached Latvia, they had understood that pogroms were useful mainly as a method of recruitment. Rather than being discouraged that the masses did not join in pogroms, they hired the people who seemed interested in leading them.

It was in the consecutively occupied lands of Lithuania and Latvia that the Holocaust began. Unlike in eastern Poland, in Lithuania and Latvia the apparently chaotic killing did escalate to a systematic Final Solution. At the end of 1941 the vast majority of Polish Jews were still alive, but almost all Lithuanian and Latvian Jews were dead.

The Germans understood that there was a Lithuanian question and came to grasp the full potential of the political resource. Lithuanians were Balts and therefore racially more valuable, from a Nazi perspective, than Slavs such as Poles. The Soviets had destroyed the Lithuanian state, and thousands of Lithuanian emigrants sought shelter in Germany. The Germans had a year between the Soviet destruction of Lithuania in June 1940 and their own invasion of the Soviet Union in June 1941 to screen and train these people, preparing a corps of locals to implement German policy. A Lithuanian Activist Front was founded in Berlin in November 1940. The Lithuanian politicians involved believed that they would be exploiting German military force to liberate Lithuania, whereas the Germans assumed they could channel Lithuanian political energies to their own purposes.

The Lithuanian activists arrived with the Germans in June 1941 and served as translators, literally and figuratively, of German intentions. Lithuanians hung German posters (in the Lithuanian language) identifying Jews with Soviet rule and Soviet crimes. This had a different resonance in Lithuania than it had in Germany: If communism could be limited to Jews, an exoneration was gifted to Lithuanians and all the other non-Jews who had collaborated with Soviet authorities. Germans did not understand, though Lithuanians did, that Soviet rule had already brought about the expropriation of Lithuanian Jews. Of the 1,593 businesses that the Soviets had nationalized in Lithuania in autumn 1940, Jews had owned 1,327, or 83 percent. With the Soviets gone, all of these businesses could be claimed by Lithuanians—provided that their previous Jewish owners did not reappear. Many of the wealthier Lithuanian Jews had been deported by the Soviets to the Gulag; those who remained would be vulnerable to Germans who wanted them killed and Lithuanians (and other inhabitants of Lithuania, including Poles and Russians) who were sitting in their businesses or offices. In the media and in person Lithuanians made the case to other Lithuanians that the German policy of murdering Jews was part of a transaction that would favor the revival of Lithuania and the renewal of its middle class. The Lithuanian Activist Front declared Lithuanian independence.

The politics of mass killing was a joint creation, a meeting of Lithuanian experiences and Nazi expectations. Lithuanians had been involved with Soviet rule, and so Nazi Judeobolshevism offered them an opportunity that the Germans themselves did not fully grasp. Members of all national groups in Lithuania, not just Lithuanians and Jews but also Poles and Russians, collaborated with the Soviet regime. Jews were somewhat more likely to do so than Lithuanians, but since Lithuanians were far more numerous, their role in the Soviet regime was much more important. Lithuanians quickly grasped that the Judeobolshevik myth amounted to a mass political amnesty for prior collaboration with the Soviets, as well as the general possibility to claim all of the businesses that the Soviets had taken from the Jews.

Actual political experience yielded to remorseless racial logic, not only in side switching but also in the accompanying violent actions. Lithuanian activists told known Soviet collaborators that a bloody absolution of their political sin was possible. In killing Jews, Lithuanians who had worked for the Soviet order could get a new start in politics in the eyes of other Lithuanians—the ones with German connections, the ones who now seemed to matter. The one group that had certainly supported the Soviet annexation of Lithuania, members of the Lithuanian Communist Party, were actually allowed to join the Lithuanian Activist Front—provided that they were not Jews. Non-Jewish communists were thus free to switch sides and thereby obliviate their Soviet collaboration. Lithuanian communist youth held in prison were told that the price of freedom was a certain demonstration of loyalty to their country: They had to kill one Jew. Jewish communists, like Jews in general, could not join the Lithuanian Activist Front. No matter how patriotic or loyal to Lithuania a Jew might have been, he was now excluded from Lithuanian politics. In summer and fall 1941, large numbers of Jews who had little to do with the Soviet occupation were murdered by large numbers of Lithuanians who had participated in it.

Where the Soviets had annihilated a nation-state, the Judeobolshevik myth functioned better than the Germans expected. For Nazis, Judeobolshevism was a description of the world, and Lithuanians who could be motivated to kill Jews were minor assistants in the healing of the planet. Any political promises were, of course, meant in bad faith. The German suggestion that killing Jews was part of a political transaction was mendacious. By the end of 1941, the Germans had banned all Lithuanian organizations. The political resource had been consumed. At that point, almost all of the Jews of Lithuania were dead.

For the Lithuanians themselves there was, of course, a deeper politics, invisible to the Germans. If the Jews were to blame for communism, then the Lithuanians could not have been. Individual Lithuanians who killed Jews were undoing their individual past under the Soviet regime. Lithuanians as a collectivity were erasing the humiliating, shameful past in which they had allowed their own sovereignty to be destroyed by the Soviet Union. The killing created a psychological plausibility with which it was difficult to negotiate: Since Jews had been killed they must have been guilty, and since Lithuanians had killed they must have had a righteous cause.

Double collaboration in Lithuania was the rule rather than the exception. The Germans were encountering a Sovietized population that they did not meaningfully alter before some of its members began killing Jews.

The Lithuanian soldiers who answered the call from the Lithuanian Activist Front to rebel were deserting from their Red Army units. The Lithuanian policemen who melted into the woods as anti-Soviet partisans had just been serving the Soviets and carrying out Soviet policies of repression. The Germans had neither the will nor the personnel to purge all of the hundreds of local administrations that had just been serving the Soviets—and certainly could not have done so in the brief time between their own arrival and the outbreak of anti-Jewish violence. The whole point of anti-Jewish violence, from a Lithuanian perspective, was to demonstrate loyalty before the Germans had time to figure out who had actually collaborated with the Soviets.

The Germans never did much alter the local administration; in general, the same people who enacted Soviet policy now enacted German policy. The Germans were concerned with removing top-level Soviet collaborators, but here they were rather hapless. Jonas Dainauskas, an officer of the prewar Lithuanian security police, had worked for the Soviet NKVD. When the Germans arrived he met with Franz Walter Stahlecker, the commander of *Einsatzgruppe* A, to arrange the participation of his men in the killing of Jews. Juozas Knyrimas, who had worked to help the Soviets deport Lithuanian citizens, now joined the Lithuanian police and killed Jews. Jonas Baranauskas, who had worked for the Soviet police, joined the Lithuanian partisans and killed Jews.

Vilnius, the Jerusalem of Lithuania, was home to nearly a hundred thousand Jews. Vilnius had been the Lithuanian capital between December 1939, when it was granted to Lithuania after the Soviet invasion of Poland, and June 1940, when the Soviet Union occupied and then annexed Lithuania. Between June 1940 and June 1941, it was the capital of the Lithuanian Soviet Socialist Republic. But throughout all of these political incarnations Vilnius was, in its population, a city of Poles and Jews. The Lithuanian Activist Front was more concerned with the Poles than the Jews in Vilnius, and tried with no success to persuade its German patrons that the Polish problem should be the higher priority. In fact, the Germans used Lithuanians to rid Vilnius of Jews. By July 1941, the main killing site was the Ponary Forest, just beyond the city. The murder operations there were led by Dr. Alfred Filbert, the commander of *Einsatzkommando* 9, and one of the young intellectuals of the SS. Filbert's men began very early to shoot Jewish women and children as well as Jewish men.

This innovation took place under the pressure of failure on the battlefield. If the Judeobolshevik myth worked as politics in lands where the Soviets had destroyed the state, it failed as the basis for a military strategy. The Germans were facing difficulties on the battlefield that the Lithuanians could not grasp and that they themselves could not admit. The Soviet Union had not collapsed like a "house of cards" or a "giant with feet of clay." Lithuania was the hinterland of Army Group North, which in the first weeks of the war was seen by Hitler, the author of those phrases, as the most important. The commanders of Army Group North were quite aware that their advance to Leningrad was not going as quickly as anticipated. By August 1941, Hitler was signaling to some of his closest collaborators, in the most indirect of ways, that the war was not going as planned. In Germany, Jews over the age of six were required to wear the Star of David that September, signifying their responsibility for the lost momentum of the military campaign. They were marked as hostages to the success of German soldiers, an extraordinary shift of responsibility that would be followed to its logical conclusion.

If the Soviet Union could not be brought down by a rapid attack against Jews, then Germany would have to be defended by a systematic campaign against the Jews under German control. Army commanders dropped whatever reservations they might have had about the activities of the *Einsatzgruppen*. Himmler began to order the murder of Jewish women and children. There was some difficulty in practice with this, even for some SS officers. Stahlecker, the commander of *Einsatzgruppe* A and thus the immediate superior of Filbert, recognized that the murder of civilians was an "emotional strain." Extra alcohol was given to German men who shot Jewish children, but this was not enough. Commanders had to explain to their men why they should violate a basic taboo. Though evidence of what they said is sketchy, educated SD officers such as Filbert, a doctor of law, presumably transmitted and adapted ideas making the rounds back in Germany. In the Nazi press, a key idea from Hitler's *My Struggle* was brought to public attention in July 1941: that the Jews must be annihilated because they wish to kill all Germans. This notion then quickly appeared

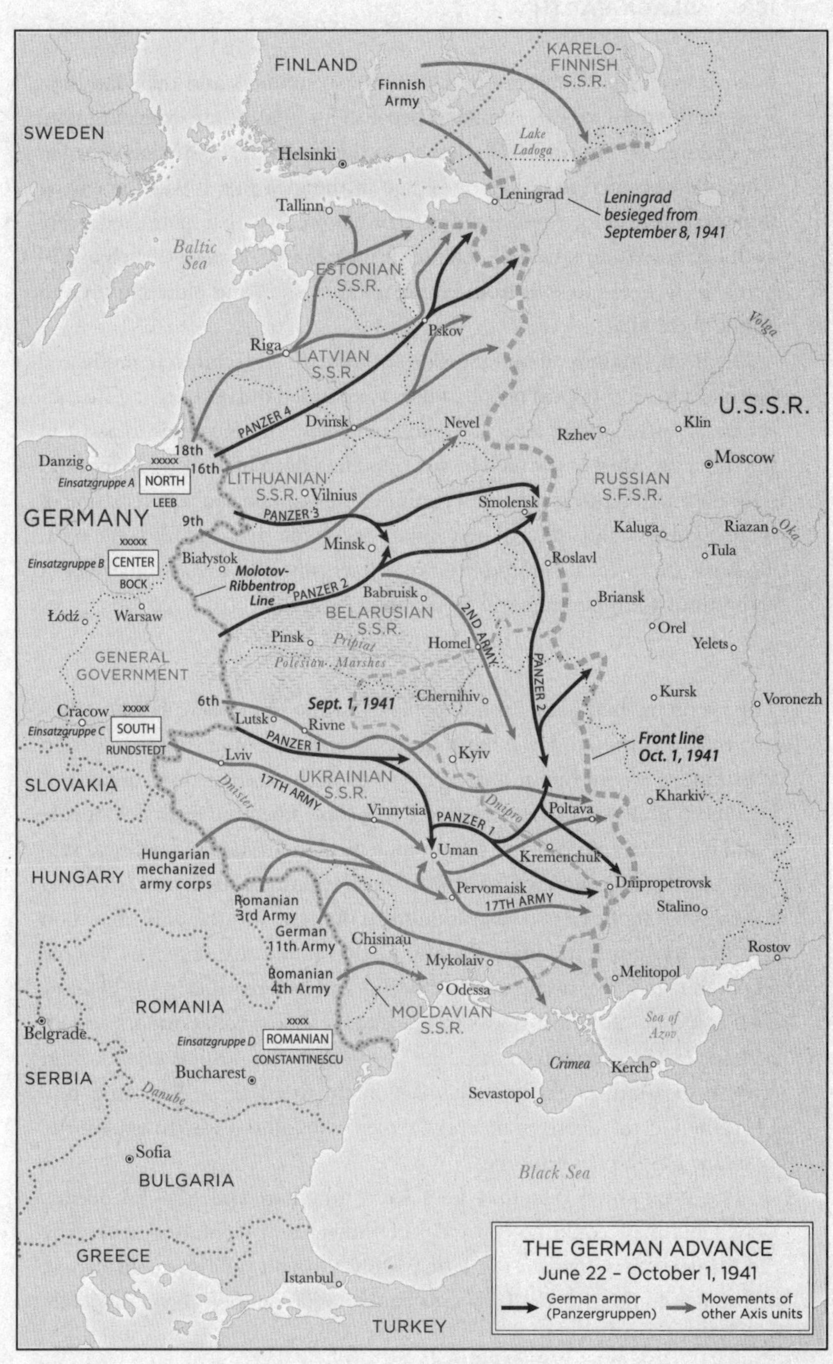
FINLAND
KARELO-FINNISH S.S.R.
Finnish Army
SWEDEN
Lake Ladoga
Helsinki
Leningrad
Leningrad besieged from September 8, 1941
Tallinn
Baltic Sea
ESTONIAN S.S.R.
Volga
Pskov
Riga
LATVIAN S.S.R.
U.S.S.R.
PANZER 4
Dvinsk
Nevel
Rzhev
Klin
18th
16th
Danzig
NORTH
Einsatzgruppe A
LEEB
Moscow
LITHUANIAN S.S.R.
Vilnius
RUSSIAN S.F.S.R.
GERMANY
9th
PANZER 3
Smolensk
Kaluga
Riazan
Oka
Minsk
Tula
Einsatzgruppe B
CENTER
BOCK
Białystok
Molotov-Ribbentrop Line
PANZER 2
Roslavl
Babruisk
Briansk
Łódź
Warsaw
BELARUSIAN S.S.R.
2ND ARMY
Pinsk
Pripiat
Homel
Orel
Yelets
Polesian Marshes
GENERAL GOVERNMENT
PANZER 2
6th
Sept. 1, 1941
Chernihiv
Kursk
Voronezh
Cracow
Einsatzgruppe C
SOUTH
RUNDSTEDT
Lutsk
Rivne
PANZER 1
Front line Oct. 1, 1941
Lviv
Kyiv
SLOVAKIA
Dnister
17TH ARMY
UKRAINIAN S.S.R.
Kharkiv
Dnipro
Vinnytsia
Poltava
PANZER 1
Hungarian mechanized army corps
Uman
Kremenchuk
HUNGARY
Dnipropetrovsk
Pervomaisk
17TH ARMY
Stalino
Romanian 3rd Army
German 11th Army
Chisinau
Rostov
Mykolaiv
Melitopol
Romanian 4th Army
Odessa
MOLDAVIAN S.S.R.
ROMANIA
Sea of Azov
Belgrade
Einsatzgruppe D
ROMANIAN
CONSTANTINESCU
Crimea
Kerch
SERBIA
Bucharest
Danube
Sevastopol
Sofia
BULGARIA
Black Sea
GREECE
Istanbul
TURKEY
THE GERMAN ADVANCE
June 22 – October 1, 1941
German armor (Panzergruppen)
Movements of other Axis units

in correspondence between the German executioners and their families: The enemy must be exterminated because his goal is our extermination; the children we murder suffer less than the children the Soviets murder. The killers seemed to be taking refuge in the idea that it was the enemy that was guilty of total policies of extermination, to which their deeds were nothing more than local self-defense. It took *Einsatzkommandos* such as Filbert's a few weeks to shift from killing a few women and older children to killing them all.

Their hesitations about murdering women and children motivated Germans to recruit local people. Filbert expanded the remit of the *Einsatzkommando* by engaging local Lithuanians, Poles, and Russians to assist in the shooting. Most of the men he recruited had been in the Red Army, and so had something to prove. Filbert himself had an unusual appreciation of these complex motivations, the need to overcome shadows from the past. He knew that not all communists were Jews, since his own brother was a communist who spent the war in German camps.

The Germans had come to understand that pogroms were not an effective way to eliminate Jews, but that the production of lawlessness was an appropriate way to find murderers who could be recruited for organized actions. Within weeks they grasped that people liberated from Soviet rule could be drawn into violence for psychological, material, and political reasons. Local people who returned with the Germans brought and amplified the German message that liberation from the Jews was the only liberation on offer, and a precondition for any further political discussions. People who had fled Soviet occupation for Berlin and new recruits in the country itself could be used in this way as translators. Local collaborators added, perhaps for their own purposes, the proposition that killing a Jew would remove the stain of Soviet collaboration. In this way, in June and July 1941, the German entrepreneurs of violence found the way to exploit the available post-Soviet resources.

The Nazi conviction that Jews were inhuman and east Europeans were subhuman could not provide anything like a technique to destroy the former and subjugate the latter. Only through politics could people be brought to do what the Germans could not do on their own: physically eliminate large numbers of Jews in a very brief period of time. Lithuania had shown what was politically possible; Latvia would reveal what was technically feasible. As with Lithuania, the Soviet destruction of the Latvian state in June 1940 opened an enormous political opportunity for the Germans, providing them with a pool of refugees from which to recruit. The Germans began their occupation of Latvia with about three hundred Latvians of their own choosing. One of these was the former head of the Latvian political police, whom they reinstalled. As in Lithuania, the arrival of the Germans was accompanied by a multimedia propaganda campaign in the local language. Newspapers published gruesome photos of prisoners killed by the NKVD, identifying the victims as Latvians and the perpetrators as Jews. Radio announcements and newspaper reports in the Latvian language associated the Soviet regime with the Jews, and liberation with their removal from Latvia.

By now Stahlecker, the commander of *Einsatzgruppe* A, had found a formula. As always the idea was, as he put it, to "make it appear that the indigenous populations reacted naturally" in attacking Jews and "carried out these measures of [their] own accord." He spoke of the need for "channeling" the experience of Soviet occupation into pro-German actions. As in Lithuania, the purpose of the local-language propaganda, delivered by media and by word of mouth, was to dig that channel. Stahlecker treated the pogroms that the Germans inspired as a kind of recruiting exercise. The result was a new model in doubly occupied Latvia: a shooting commando led by locals who, following German orders, would perform most of the killing. Its leader, Viktors Bernhard Arājs, would become one of the most accomplished mass murderers in the history of Europe.

Arājs was born in the Russian Empire in 1910 to a mother who spoke German and to a father who was repressed by Soviet authorities after the October Revolution. Like Stahlecker and other German mass murderers, Arājs was trained as a lawyer. He enrolled in law school in independent Latvia in 1932 and then joined the police two years later to pay the bills. He married an older woman for money to continue his studies, and then took a younger lover. When he returned to law school just before the war, he earned good marks in English constitutional law. His studies continued after the Soviets occupied and annexed Latvia. He adapted his biography to their ideological matrix, emphasizing in his applications to continue his studies his humble background and the journeyman labor he had performed. He earned his degree in Soviet Latvia, and therefore in Soviet law, with coursework on the Stalin constitution. He seems to have had some sympathy for the Soviet project and even for a time to have thought of himself as a communist. Then an employer he liked was repressed. As the Soviets retreated from the Germans in summer 1941, they seem to have killed Arājs's lover and her family. It is unclear whether he knew this at the time, or would have cared.

The major theme of the private and the public life of Arājs was social advancement. He served three quite different systems: the Latvian, the Soviet, and the German. He showed no sign of being pro-communist until the Soviets arrived, just as he showed no sign of being pro-Nazi until the Germans arrived. Indeed, as a policeman in independent Latvia he had arrested members of illegal right-wing groups. Arājs was able, perhaps by chance or perhaps by prior arrangement, to make contact with Stahlecker right after the German forces arrived. Stahlecker's personal translator was a German from Latvia who had known Arājs in the Latvian army before the war. Arājs and Stahlecker spoke on the first and second of July 1941, as anti-Jewish violence was under way in Riga. On July 3, Arājs and his men were already making their first arrests of Jews. The next day, they were burning the synagogues of Riga.

In Riga, Arājs was allowed to use the house of a Jewish banking family as his headquarters. The bankers had been expropriated and deported—not by the Germans, but by the Soviets. The wealthier Jews were already in the Gulag when the Germans arrived. This created a rather special material resource. Besides disposing of property rights as such, the Soviets had disposed of many of the property owners. If prior Jewish owners were still physically present, as some were, they would never regain their property under the Germans. If Jews even made a gesture toward Sovietized possessions they were treated by the Germans as looters. Non-Jewish inhabitants of Latvia—Latvians, Germans, and others—reasoned the way many people do in such situations: The only way to be sure about keeping stolen property is to make sure that no one with a legal claim can ever appear again. What had been the Sovietization of Jewish property now became, under the Germans, its Latvianization. The Germans, even as they claimed choice properties such as the banker family's house, could not possibly oversee this process throughout the country. The combination of Soviet expropriation and Nazi antisemitism created a clear material incentive for non-Jews to murder Jews.

On July 4, 1941, Arājs published advertisements, worded quite vaguely, encouraging Latvians to register for a new auxiliary police unit that would work for the Germans. He made no mention of Jews. Many of his first recruits were Red Army soldiers who had been soldiers of the Latvian army before that. Very likely these were men who wished to undo the double shame of losing Latvian independence and wearing the Soviet uniform. Volunteers who had served in the Soviet militias were probably also hoping to cleanse themselves of a Soviet past. Arājs also recruited with some success, following instructions from Stahlecker, among Latvians who had a grievance against Soviet rule. One new recruit, for example, had seen his parents deported by the Soviets. The largest age group among the new auxiliary policemen was between sixteen and twenty-one. For many such young people, the prior year of Soviet occupation, one way or another, must have been a decisive experience. Most of the new auxiliary policemen were working class. None of the first recruits knew in advance that his major duty would be to shoot Jews. Many of them did not volunteer at all, but were transferred from the regular police because the initial number of volunteers was insufficient. Certainly not all of these people were Latvian nationalists. Some of them were Russians.

The Arājs *Kommando,* the brainchild of Stahlecker, was overseen by his subordinates Rudolf Batz and Rudolf Lange. They taught its members how to assemble Jews and shoot them, and then passed responsibility for the killing to Arājs. He and his men shot Riga Jews in the forest of Bikernieki beyond the city. Then they traveled by an infamous blue bus throughout the countryside for six months, between July and December 1941, killing the Jews of the towns and villages. Of the sixty-six thousand or so Jews living in Latvia in summer 1941, the Arājs *Kommando* shot about twenty-two thousand, and then assisted in the killing of some twenty-eight thousand more. Like other murderers serving German policy, and like the

German murderers themselves, they killed whom they were assigned to kill. Like all of the mass murderers of Jews, they also murdered non-Jews. As they moved through the country, they shot patients of psychiatric hospitals, for example. After most of the Latvian Jews had been killed, the Arājs *Kommando* was dispatched to combat Soviet partisans, which in practice meant shooting Belarusian civilians.

Throughout all of this, Arājs was personally troubled that his legal credentials, assembled under Latvian and Soviet rule, were no longer valid. After his career of mass murder, he returned to university at Riga, where he completed a German degree in law.

The *Einsatzgruppen* were a hybrid institution, serving a state that was defined in racial terms, following ambiguous orders that allowed some room for maneuver. In Germany itself, the *Einsatzgruppen* existed only in training academies. Beyond Germany, they murdered and they pioneered. The Arājs *Kommando* represented a major innovation, developed within two weeks of the invasion itself: the organized use of substantial numbers of armed locals under German command to find, assemble, and kill Jews. Before the invasion there had been no thought of arming local people for any purpose; indeed, Hitler had explicitly forbidden this. Stahlecker and other commanders quickly saw and exploited the psychological, material, and political resources they inherited from the Soviets, thereby moving towards Hitler's grand design. By August 6, 1941, Stahlecker was able to contemplate "the unique possibility of a radical treatment of the Jewish question in the *Ostraum*," the East.

Aside from the *Einsatzgruppen*, the other German hybrid institution operative in the East was the Higher SS and Police Leaders. These men commanded both SS and police forces in a given zone of the occupied Soviet Union, bringing together racial and state organizations. In Germany, the Higher SS and Police Leaders had next to no meaning, but in the occupied Soviet Union they were Himmler's key subordinates. They reported directly to him, just as the *Einsatzgruppen* commanders reported directly to Heydrich. They, too, were expected to learn, experiment, and innovate. For example, Himmler could tell Friedrich Jeckeln, the Higher SS and Police Leader for Southern Russia (in practice, Ukraine), that Jewish children and women were to be shot, as he seems to have done on August 12, 1941. Just how this would be achieved was to be decided on the spot.

Jeckeln was the outstanding entrepreneur of violence among the Higher SS and Police Leaders. By the end of August 1941, he had determined that essentially all German units, be they SS, police, or army, could take part in mass coordinated shootings of Jews. Jeckeln's operations would show that even Germans who had no special preparation could participate in mass murder on a truly titanic scale.

Jeckeln's innovation was a result of the unexpected appearance of stateless Jewish refugees from Czechoslovakia in a zone of Soviet Ukraine under German occupation. The history of their death, which is also the history of the emergence of industrial killing, began years earlier with the destruction of their state. As Czechoslovakia was disassembled in 1938 and 1939, Czechoslovak Jews lost protection from their state. When Germany annexed the "Sudetenland" in November 1938, the Jews there either fled and abandoned their property or found themselves second-class citizens of the German Reich. Between November 1938 and March 1939, Jews were still citizens of the new truncated republic of Czecho-Slovakia. In March 1939, when Hitler moved to complete the destruction of the Czechoslovak state, these Jews were divided into different communities of fate. Jews from Bohemia and Moravia found themselves in a Protectorate

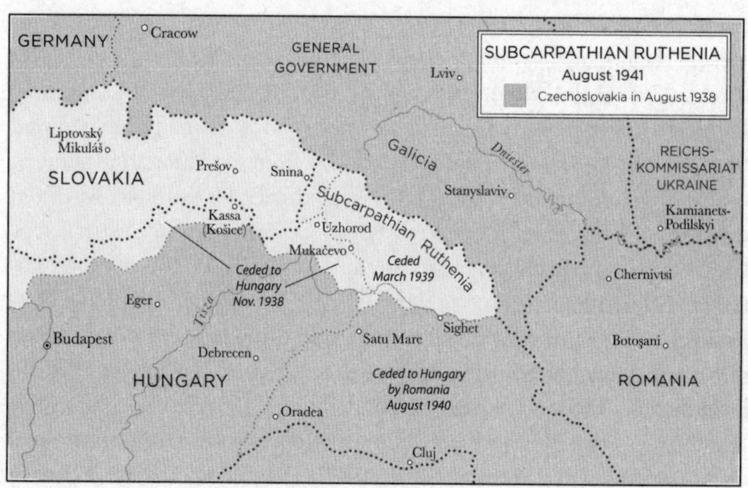

where only Germans were granted citizenship, subjected to the racial laws of the Reich. Jews of Slovakia found themselves at the mercy of lawmakers of a newly independent Slovak state.

The easternmost part of Czechoslovakia, Subcarpathian Ruthenia, underwent a different history. In October and November 1938, Germany had forced Czechoslovakia to cede southern Slovak territories as well as some of Subcarpathian Ruthenia to Hungary. In March 1939, when Czechoslovakia was completely dismantled, Hungary was granted the rest of the region. The Jews of Subcarpathian Ruthenia fell under Hungarian law. Jewish professionals and tradesmen were required to seek licenses, which often led to their losing their livelihoods. To become Hungarian citizens, Jews had to show that they or their families had been subjects of the Hungarian crown in 1918. In fact, Hungarian officials were instructed to treat Jews as "suspicious elements" regardless of what documents they assembled. Jews went to great trouble and expense to demonstrate their connection to the prior Hungarian state, but were excluded from state protection anyway. Hungary deported Jews and others from its new territories to Poland and to Slovakia as best it could beginning in March 1939. Not long after Germany invaded the Soviet Union in June 1941, Hungary began to deport populations regarded as undesirable, including but not limited to the Jews, to areas of Soviet Ukraine under German occupation.

Hungary made Jews stateless, and Germany killed them. What from the perspective of Budapest was an ethnic cleansing campaign became for Jeckeln the impulse towards a policy of industrial-scale killing. On August 26 and 27, 1941, Jeckeln oversaw a mass shooting operation in Kamianets' Podils'kyi designed to eliminate these stateless Jews who had been removed from Czechoslovak protection and excluded from the Hungarian state, as well as thousands of other local Jews. Vladimir P., for example, was from a family of local Jews. They were Soviet citizens who had experienced the risks and opportunities of the communist regime for two decades. His father had survived an arrest by the NKVD but did not escape the Germans. Vladimir himself slipped away only because he knew a local police officer, an acquaintance from Soviet times; all local collaborators, like all local victims, had been Soviet citizens. Vladimir's family were among the 23,600 Jews assembled and shot. The episode began with the conventional Nazi association of the communist and the Jew. Jeckeln chose a Jewish man at random and called him "Béla Kun," the name of the founder of a short-lived communist state in Hungary.

If the Judeobolshevik symbolism was the same for the pogroms and the mass killings, the scale and method were new. Crucially, Jeckeln learned that German Order Policemen would carry out mass shootings of thousands of innocent people who had not even been charged with a crime. For about half of the Order Policemen who served in the Soviet Union, the first stateless zone had been Poland after 1939. Such men had experience in murder of one kind or another. But roughly half came straight from Germany to the occupied USSR. The policemen learned to kill Jews very quickly, some writing letters home within weeks in which they took for granted the necessity of the murder of all Jews. The Germans themselves probably did not expect such rapid self-radicalization. Order Police officers quickly came to outnumber the *Einsatzgruppen* by a factor of ten: Some thirty-three thousand were on site by the end of 1941. Policemen carried out more shootings than members of the *Einsatzgruppen;* no mass shooting in the East would take place without them. At Kamianets' Podils'kyi, Jeckeln also demonstrated that the *Wehrmacht* would assist with supplies and coordination. In uniting SS, regular police, and soldiers, he developed a triumvirate that would persist in mass murder throughout the war.

Jeckeln's second major demonstration was in Kyiv, which had been the capital of Soviet Ukraine since 1934. Here the occasion for industrial-scale murder was not the unexpected appearance of stateless Jewish refugees but the surprise of Soviet sabotage. The Soviets had left bombs on timers in several major buildings in downtown Kyiv, which caused explosions that killed German officials and officers. This act of Soviet resistance was an opportunity for the Germans to claim and then stage Judeobolshevism. If the Soviets had attacked Germans, then Jews had to be held responsible.

On September 28, 1941, the German army printed and posted notices requiring Jews to appear at a certain intersection in western Kyiv with their documents and their valuables on the following day. Most of the Jews who had remained in Kyiv obeyed the order. People gathered early, before dawn, thinking that they would get the best seats on the trains. Elderly women wore strings of onions around their necks, food for the journey. Yom Kippur, the day of atonement, was two days away; people told themselves that they would be safe. At the screening point at the intersection non-Jews who had accompanied their families or friends were told to return home, and most did. From that point forward the Jews walked in a cordon made by German police and dogs to a ravine at Babyi Iar, where the German army had prepared trenches for mass shootings. There Germans, assisted by local collaborators, shot some 33,761 Jews over pits. They took some young Jewish women aside to be raped first. Jeckeln was improving upon his technique of killing. He now deployed what he called the "sardine method," in which people were forced to lie down in careful rows in a pit before they were shot. The next group was then forced to lie directly upon that layer of corpses, and so on. Once a pit was full, a German would tread over the pile of corpses, looking for signs of life, and firing bullets downward. This form of industrial murder, which allowed more than ten thousand individuals to be shot on a single day, was Jeckeln's personal invention. After the successful trial at Babyi Iar, he invited the Order Policemen who had assisted in the preparations to a drinking party where he explained the political logic of murder.

Many of the aged and infirm among Kyiv's Jews had been unable to gather as instructed by the posters printed by the German army. After the murder of their families and friends, they were left alone, helpless, in their apartments with their possessions. Some of them were then killed by their neighbors, until recently their fellow Soviet citizens, who took their property for themselves. In Soviet conditions multiple families crowded together in a single apartment, which meant that empty apartments were in high demand. Some of the pogromists in Kyiv were Soviet citizens who had suffered under Stalinism and who blamed the Jews. Very likely others were people who used the idea of Judeobolshevism as a retroactive justification of their own robbery. Throughout Europe, the murder of Jews created opportunities for theft, which in turn created a felt need for moral justification.

At the end of 1941, the murderous innovations were brought together. In November 1941, Jeckeln was transferred by Himmler from Ukraine to be the Higher SS and Police Leader of *Reichskommissariat Ostland,* which included Latvia. Ordered by Himmler to kill the remaining Jews of Riga, Jeckeln brought together his own technique of mass shooting with Stahlecker's technique of organizing locals. Using Germans as the shooters and the Arājs *Kommando* as the auxiliaries, Jeckeln had some fourteen thousand Riga Jews killed at pits in the Letbarskii Forest outside the city on November 30, 1941. The feat was repeated on December 8, 1941. The killing technology on display was conceived after the invasion, in the zone of consecutive occupation, by the Nazi entrepreneurs of violence.

Hundreds of thousands of Jewish children, women, and men were shot behind the lines, on what had been Soviet territory, as the German army battled the Red Army. The method of killing was perfected in late 1941, as the German attack upon the supposedly Jewish state was halted. The war on the Jews was being won, as the war against the USSR was being lost. The state destroyers of the SS could say that they were succeeding where all others had failed.

7

Germans, Poles, Soviets, Jews

"The East belongs to the SS!" So Heinrich Himmler liked to exclaim, and in a certain way he was right. It was not easy for the German civilian administrators, the men responsible for the zones known as *Reichskommissariat Ostland* and *Reichskommissariat Ukraine,* to exploit local laborers while stealing their food. Nor did it prove a simple task for the *Wehrmacht* to defeat the Red Army. The destruction of previous state authority gave Himmler's SS men a demonstrably achievable task in the military campaign and in the occupation. Clearing away previous institutions did not enable quick victory or colonization, but it did make possible the extermination of Jews. In the zone where the SS destroyed Soviet state structures, the vague concept of a Final Solution of the Jewish "problem" could become the specific project of killing Jews where they lived.

Himmler's subordinates, entrepreneurs of violence such as Stahlecker and Jeckeln, learned to exploit the resources left by Soviet rule, and invented the techniques they needed. It was already known that *Einsatzgruppen* could kill tens of thousands of people in cold blood; this they had done to Polish citizens in 1939. It was learned in 1941 that other Germans, with less training and weaker ideological preparation, could also kill in the tens of thousands. It transpired after June 1941 that almost every German who was ordered to shoot a civilian, Jewish or otherwise, would obey that order—even though asking to be spared from such duties brought no consequences beyond peer pressure. Although local populations disappointed Germans by not rising up as mindless hordes against local Jews, tens of thousands of local people could be recruited to auxiliary police or special commandos that, among other tasks, would shoot Jews in large numbers.

With this learning and these instruments in place, Himmler could travel through the occupied Soviet Union in August 1941 and urge the German forces who were slower to kill to keep up with those who were setting the pace. By September 1941, the killing shifted from shootings of Jewish men of military age to massacres of entire Jewish populations.

The invasion of summer 1941 was a special encounter of Nazi expectations with Soviet experiences. The more drastic the Soviet assault on prior politics, the greater the political resource, and the more extensive the field for Nazi innovation. Yet what the Germans learned about themselves and others turned out to have some application beyond the special zone of consecutive occupation where the Holocaust began. The double destruction of the state created the conditions for the crucial innovations. Once the concept of a Final Solution became the practice of mass murder, the new techniques of murder could be applied to the east of the zone, in the prewar Soviet Union.

Organized massacres involving multiple German institutions with local assistance began in the zone where the Soviets destroyed the interwar state and the Germans drove out Soviet power. The Germans continued the practice, with comparable success, in the lands that had been part of the USSR before 1939: prewar Soviet Belarus, prewar Soviet Ukraine, and prewar Soviet Russia. The death rate of Jews in the lands of the prewar Soviet Union occupied by Germany (95 percent) was almost as high as that in the doubly occupied lands where Soviet occupation of other sovereign states preceded German occupation (97 percent). Soviet citizens collaborated in the mass murder of Jews, regardless of whether they received Soviet passports in 1939 and 1940 or had spent their lives under Soviet rule. Communists collaborated with the Germans regardless of whether their party cards had been stamped a year or a decade before. There were, of course, some differences. Only in the prewar Soviet Union, it seems, did officers of the Soviet NKVD volunteer for the German police in order to kill enemies behind the front. Naturally, such people had to take part in the mass shootings of Jews, since not doing so would have drawn attention.

The Germans reached the prewar Soviet Union within a matter of weeks, but by then they had already learned from experience. By the time SS officers reached the prewar Soviet Union, they knew that the failure of the pogrom strategy did not really matter. In Estonia, the northernmost of the three Baltic states, and the last to be conquered, no pogroms at all were instigated—and yet almost all of the Jews who had not fled were found and killed by the Estonian Security Police under German authority. Pogroms did break out in the prewar Soviet Union, but usually in the aftermath of mass shooting rather than as a prelude. The Germans knew that they could exploit the local Soviet administrations, and they knew that they could recruit enough young men.

The prewar Soviet Union was far poorer than the Baltic states and even than eastern Poland, so every bit of property was all the more valued. Soviet policy in the annexed territories in 1939 and 1940 had created uncertainty about property; Soviet policy in the prewar Soviet Union had created widespread misery. Jews who lived in the lands of the prewar Soviet Union were farther to the east and therefore had more time to flee the German advance. This created a huge supply of houses and apartments, promptly appropriated by their Soviet neighbors. The very fact that some Jews were already gone and their residences already taken by others when the Germans arrived prompted the thought that more property would be available if the remaining Jews were removed. The acquisitive and the ruthless came to the fore. Soviet citizens were already classified by nationality in their internal passports, and Soviet culture was already one of ethnic denunciations. There had been no Jewish operation among the national operations of the Great Terror of 1937 and 1938. But the denunciatory frenzy had reached Jews nonetheless. In the interwar Soviet Union, Soviet Jews were accused of ritually murdering children and young women. In Moscow, Kharkiv, and Minsk, among other places, Soviet citizens partook in the blood libel. In Minsk, the man who accused Jews of ritual murder for Passover "to bake matzah" was a worker and a member of a communist party. This was in the capital of a Soviet republic in 1937, just as the Great Terror was beginning.

In an unhappy sequence, Soviet mass terror (1937–1938) was followed by an alliance with Nazi Germany (1939–1941), and then an invasion by Nazi Germany (1941). In the lands that German forces first reached after crossing through the new Soviet territories, in western Soviet Belarus and western Soviet Ukraine, the Great Terror had taken some three hundred thousand lives. Because shootings and deportations had removed much of the Polish minority from precisely this region, local Ukrainians,

Belarusians, and Russians had already seen a minority removed from their midst by state policy. The major settlements of Jews in the western Soviet Union had also been, almost without exception, major settlements of Poles. In 1939 and 1940, the Soviet alliance with Nazi Germany sowed ideological confusion among Soviet citizens. The Soviet press ceased to criticize German policies and began to publish Nazi speeches. Soviet citizens in public meetings occasionally misspoke, praising "Comrade Hitler" when they meant "Comrade Stalin" or calling for "the triumph of international fascism." Swastikas began to appear as graffiti in Soviet cities. When the Germans arrived in 1941, Soviet citizens who had denounced their Polish neighbors for their apartments three years before presumably had little hesitation about denouncing their Jewish ones. Soviet citizens—Russians, Ukrainians, Belarusians, and others—did hand over their Jewish neighbors to the Germans. The experience of running the errand of denunciation must have been very much the same. In Kyiv, Ukrainians and Russians helped the German Order Police find and register Jews before the mass shooting at Babyi Iar. Afterwards, the German police received the denunciations in what had been NKVD headquarters.

The Judeobolshevik myth, which worked as politics in the doubly occupied territories, could be applied with similar results when the Germans reached the prewar Soviet Union. Once developed, this technique of separating Jews from others could be applied anywhere in the Soviet space. The fact of past Soviet rule and the clarity of German anti-Jewish stereotypes combined to create an easy and callous excuse for murder, from the top of the system to the bottom. A Ukrainian policeman in the Galician town of Wiśniowiec could stop a Jew on the street and ask him: "Tell me, my friend, what did you do under the Soviet regime?" and then beat him regardless of the answer. The beating was the answer. As in the doubly occupied lands, in the prewar Soviet Union Jews were sacrificed for the holy lie of the collective innocence of others. In the end, it mattered little, from the Jewish perspective, whether a given territory had been ruled by the Soviets for a matter of decades or for a matter of months. Either way, Jews present on these territories when the Germans arrived were going to suffer and die.

In doubly occupied western Ukraine, the Germans could exploit the aspirations of Ukrainians to a national state. They could try to put to use the frustrations of two decades of Polish rule and two years of Soviet rule. In central and eastern Ukraine, under Soviet rule for two decades, nationalism had far less resonance. Although the Germans brought west Ukrainian nationalists with them, these collaborators found few interlocutors and were not usually instrumental in German policies in central and eastern Ukraine. Nevertheless, the killing of the Jews took place with the same efficiency.

In Zhytomyr, the major city of northwestern Soviet Ukraine, there was no memory of a recent Soviet occupation, but rather experience of two decades of Soviet rule. No deportations were under way when the Germans arrived, as had been the case in the lands the Soviets had annexed in 1939 and 1940. But, as in the doubly occupied regions, the NKVD had been holding Soviet citizens in prisons in the vicinity. In a number of cases the NKVD shot prisoners and left the corpses behind. As the inhabitants of Zhytomyr suspected, these very prisons had been sites of a much larger Soviet killing campaign not long before. In September 1938, the Red Army had gathered precisely in the Zhytomyr region as Soviet leaders spoke of a fraternal rescue of Czechoslovakia by way of an invasion of Poland. The NKVD meanwhile murdered large numbers of civilians, especially Polish men. The NKVD shot more than four hundred Soviet citizens in the area on the day that the Munich accords were signed, removing the occasion for war and an intervention in Poland. When war came a year later, the Soviet Union was an ally of Nazi Germany rather than an enemy; inhabitants of the Zhytomyr region, like all Soviet citizens, were then treated to almost two years of praise of Hitler's regime. This was followed from June 1941 by the Nazis' own propaganda: leaflets from airplanes equating Jews with communists.

When war came to Zhytomyr on July 9, 1941, in the form of a German invasion, the men of the SS had already passed through the lands that the Soviets had just annexed; they had their political formulas ready and could be confident of success. Wherever the Germans found corpses left by the NKVD, they blamed the Jews and usually shot some. On August 7, 1941, *Sonderkommando* 4a of *Einsatzgruppe* C undertook the simple scenography in Zhytomyr. Its members shot two Jews accused of working for the NKVD.

Then they asked the gathered public, mostly Ukrainians and Poles, "With whom do you have to settle a score?" The answer had already been given. The crowd responded: "The Jews!"

In this way the bulk of the Soviet population was released from its past, since essentially everyone in a city such as Zhytomyr had been associated with the Soviet regime. By appearing at the shooting and participating in an exchange with the German murderers, local people were doing their part in a bloody revision of history and general assignation of blame to the Jews. Here as everywhere, the lies and the killing were intimately connected. Although the Judeobolshevik myth also functioned within the Soviet Union itself, people in Zhytomyr generally knew that Jews were not responsible for communism. But once Soviet citizens had said out loud that Jews should be killed as punishment for communism, and watched as Jews were in fact killed, they could hardly admit that they had lied. In this way the killing itself drove forward the myth of Judeobolshevism. Mendacity supported murder; murder supported mendacity.

Kharkiv was the major city of northeastern Soviet Ukraine, near the border with Soviet Russia, with a significant Russian minority. Its inhabitants had suffered horribly in both the famine of 1932–1933 and in the Great Terror of 1937–1938. As a boy from a Jewish family remembered those years, "Every day kids would come over and say 'Mom's been arrested' or 'Dad's been arrested.'" In Kharkiv, as elsewhere in the prewar Soviet Union, arriving Germans were greeted with bread and salt. The Germans relied upon local collaborators who were placed in charge of largely unchanged local administrations. Although the Germans did bring a few west Ukrainian nationalists to Kharkiv, the collaborators were almost entirely Soviet citizens: Ukrainians, Russians, and others. The Germans appointed a mayor to head the Kharkiv administration and vice mayors for each of the city's nineteen districts, whose borders followed those of Soviet police precincts. Subordinate to the vice mayors were the building supervisors, in general the same people performing the same function that they had under Soviet rule: monitoring an apartment house and reporting on its residents.

In any large Soviet city, the Germans could install a local authority without Jews, but they could hardly manage without educated Soviet citizens—who were often members of the communist party. For most of the

Soviet population, the equation of Jews with communism was highly convenient, since it ethnicized Soviet history and thus liberated most Soviet citizens of any guilt for Soviet practices. When the Kharkiv Municipal Authority defined its role as "the final and utter defeat of the Jew-Bolshevik gangsters," it was expressing both the interest of the Germans in pretending that they were conquering communism by killing Jews and that of Soviet citizens in pretending that they had had nothing to do with communism. The politics of the greater evil meant proclaiming the destruction of Jewish communism while arranging for communists to kill Jews.

When the Kharkiv Municipal Authority decreed its right to distribute the property of Jews who had fled the German advance, it was transforming a German war of conquest into the possibility of relative social advancement for local Soviet citizens. Naturally, the capacity to redistribute extended also to the property of any Jews who might disappear for other reasons. The Kharkiv Municipal Authority ordered the building supervisors to carry out a census of their buildings, placing remaining Jews on a "yellow list." In early December 1941, the building supervisors created troikas to help them establish where the remaining Jews lived. On December 14, an announcement appeared around the city requiring Jews to report to a tractor factory the following day on pain of death. The following day, a long and miserable procession of Jews walked along Moskovs'kyi Prospekt, guided by local policemen and a few Germans. One woman stopped at the side of the road and gave birth, there and then, to twins; she and the babies were immediately shot. In the barracks of the tractor factory Jews were guarded by their fellow Kharkiv residents. These guards had the right to kill Jews, and sometimes did. The building supervisors reported that their houses were free of Jews and that apartments and movable property could be redistributed.

The mass shooting of the Jews of Kharkiv that began on December 27, 1941, was carried out by Germans: *Sonderkommando* 4a of *Einsatzgruppe* C along with Security Police Battalion 314. By January 2, 1942, the men of these units had murdered some nine thousand people. The bulk of the work that brought Jews to their places of death was done by their fellow Soviet citizens, working within institutions that resembled Soviet models and behaving much as they had under Soviet rule. A few of the local authorities acted from political conviction as anti-communists. Some residents of Kharkiv did hate Soviet rule as a result of the terror of the late 1930s and the famine of the early 1930s. The main political lesson of those experiences, however, had been submission. For the most part, the people who made the murder of Jews possible were simply products of the Soviet system, following a new line, adapting to a new master. The hunt for surviving Jews, ordered by the mayor, was carried out under the banner of the elimination of "Jewish-Communist and bandit-Bolshevik trash." This language is a hybrid of Soviet form and Nazi content.

No matter where the Germans arrived in the Soviet Union, the result was essentially the same: the mass murder of Jews who remained, planned by the Germans but achieved with much assistance from people of all Soviet nationalities. The Judeobolshevik myth separated Jews from other Soviet citizens and many Soviet citizens from their own pasts. The murder of Jews and the transfer of property eliminated the sense of responsibility for the past, creating a class of people who had gained from the German occupation, and seeming to promise relative social advance in a German future. Soviet Gypsies were not presented as an ideological enemy to the same extent, and did not provide the same degree of harmonization of German worldviews and local fears and needs. But they, too, were murdered in the occupied Soviet Union, and their property was also reallocated by the collaborating local administrations. In Kharkiv, the Gypsies were rounded up at the horse market.

Kharkiv, though a Russian-speaking city, was one of the cradles of Ukrainian culture; the same could not be said of the city named after the leader of the Soviet Union. Stalino, the major industrial city of southeastern Ukraine, known today as Donetsk, was something close to a model Soviet city. Its coal mines and industry, although they predated the Bolshevik Revolution, had been vastly expanded during Stalin's First Five-Year Plan of 1928–1933. Its hinterlands had been starved during the famine of 1932–1933 and resettled by people from throughout the Soviet Union. The growing city itself attracted workers from Soviet Russia and elsewhere. Stalino was a Soviet melting pot, a Russian-speaking city where Ukrainian national identity was far less present than in Kharkiv, and perhaps less so than anywhere else in Soviet Ukraine. The political identity seems to have been a Soviet one—if so, this was no more hindrance to collaborating with the Germans than anything else. The murder of Jews proceeded in Stalino much as elsewhere.

Because Army Group South of the *Wehrmacht* was slow to advance across Soviet Ukraine, Soviet authority in Stalino and the surrounding Donets Basin collapsed in stages rather than all at once. Communists tore up their party cards in expectation of the German arrival. Peasants were pleased because they expected that the Germans would abolish collective farming. Local men were sent to the front; their families had time to protest Soviet policies before the war came to Stalino. The NKVD tried to plant explosives in the mines to be tripped when the Germans arrived; women and children tried to stop this at Mine 4/21 in Stalino and were shot. The Red Army took livestock from the countryside when it retreated, and communist party members in Stalino absconded with food that was meant for the general population. The local militias, largely made up of miners, dispersed rather than fight the Germans. As the German army reached the Donbas region, *Einsatzgruppe* C killed Jews, sometimes alongside Gypsies, sometimes in mines.

In Stalino, as elsewhere, the stigmatization and murder of local Jews permitted a bridge between occupiers and occupied. The Germans quickly established a local administration in the city, headed by a longtime communist and largely staffed by communists. These new authorities recruited a local police force of some two thousand people, many of whom had also been members of the communist party. These local policemen assisted the Germans in the shooting of some fifteen thousand Jews in Stalino. In some considerable measure, the murder of Jews for their supposed communism was carried out by communists. By murdering the Jews, the local people of Stalino, like local people elsewhere, partook in a lie that emptied their own pasts of responsibility while providing a measure of protection from German rule. Whereas people in the doubly occupied lands were exorcising the specter of their own participation in a Soviet regime that lasted for a year or two, in places such as the Donbas the history that was evacuated was that of a whole generation.

Later, when Soviet power returned, people switched sides again. From that point forward the memory of typically Soviet places such as the Donets Basin has been dominated by a Soviet myth of anti-fascism, in which all Soviet citizens suffered equally under and struggled valiantly against German rule. This is just as true, which is to say just as false, as the wartime myth of anti-communism. The myth of Judeobolshevism in 1941 allowed Soviet citizens to separate themselves from their Jewish neighbors; the myth of the Great Fatherland War against Nazi Germany allowed them to separate themselves from their murder of their Jewish neighbors.

Belarus was the European republic of the USSR most altered by Soviet rule. It was a crucial test for German policy, since here—unlike in Lithuania, Latvia, or even parts of Ukraine—there was no national political resource. There was no meaningful Belarusian national question, and only a few Belarusian nationalists were brought by the German invaders from emigration or from one region of Belarus to another.

The initial German policy to Jews had been the same in Belarus as elsewhere. Indeed, the German mass murder of Jewish women and children began in Belarus on July 19, 1941, when Himmler ordered *Waffen*-SS troops behind Army Group Center to clear the Pripiat Marshes of Jews. On July 31, he indicated that the order included the murder of women. The *Waffen*-SS murdered some 13,788 children, women, and men. As of mid-August, *Einsatzgruppe* B, responsible for Belarus, had killed more Jews than any other *Einsatzgruppe*. But Arthur Nebe, its commander, had no recruitment opportunities comparable to those of Stahlecker in Lithuania and Latvia, since in Belarus there was no political resource. Local collaborators were generally Belarusians and Poles, usually people lacking any political motivation. Nebe also had less reinforcement by other German police units than Jeckeln to his south. In September 1941, the killing of Jews in Belarus fell behind that in the Baltics and in Ukraine.

With less local collaboration in the offing, the SS in Belarus in effect recruited the German army. Whereas Soviet citizens could be recruited by the equation of Bolsheviks and Jews, German army officers were sensitive to a modified logic: the triple equation of Jews, Bolsheviks, and partisans. If Jews were Bolsheviks, then a politically minded local might take part in their killing in order to prove that he was not a Bolshevik (and to profit from the dead Jew's property). If Jews were partisans, then German officers might want them dead in order to be able to fight a clean and victorious war. The army, which could not steal very much immobile property, also realized that killing Jews and allowing locals to take their houses was a kind of social policy. On September 18, 1941, at Krupki, northeast of Minsk, German soldiers of the Third Battalion of the 354th Infantry Division chose the site for the killing of Jews, and escorted them from the village to the awaiting SS. One soldier, presumably a father himself, allowed a Jewish mother to step away from the column for a moment to pull up her little boy's pants.

Not long afterwards, German soldiers would murder Jews in Belarus with no assistance from the SS. At a conference at Mahileu, where Army Group Center of the *Wehrmacht* had made its headquarters, Nebe and the Higher SS and Police Leader for the region, Erich von dem Bach-Zelewski, briefed army officers on partisan warfare. They even organized a demonstration. In a village where no partisans were actually found, Germans killed thirty-two Jews, most of them women. The message conveyed there was difficult to miss. Army officers reacted to the lessons of the conference, which took place on September 23–24, in different ways. But enough of them were willing or indeed eager to treat Jews as partisans that the default behavior of the army seemed to change.

By October 1941, the second major German offensive in the east, Operation Typhoon, was under way. There was never supposed to be a second German offensive, since Operation Barbarossa, launched in June, was expected to destroy the Soviet state by September. As terrifying as the initial German advance had been, it was far slower than the Germans had anticipated. The anxiety of delay was experienced first by Army Group North, which did not reach Leningrad. Army Group South made slower progress through Ukraine than expected. Hitler decided to send part of Army Group Center to help Army Group South in September. Once the breakthrough in Ukraine was achieved, Operation Typhoon was to follow: a final push toward Moscow by a regrouped and reinforced Army Group Center, gathering in Belarus almost two million soldiers.

Unlike Operation Barbarossa, which began in doubly occupied territory and reached prewar Soviet territory, Operation Typhoon was to begin and end in prewar Soviet territory. Nevertheless, it had the same basic consequences for Jews. After German troops advanced on September 30,

FINLAND
SWEDEN
Finnish Army
Lake Ladoga
Helsinki
Leningrad
Tallinn
Tikhvin
18th
Baltic Sea
18th
Novgorod
NORTH
LEEB
Front line Dec. 5, 1941
Pskov
Volga
16th
Riga
REICHSKOMMISSARIAT OSTLAND
Kalinin
Nevel
PANZER 3
Klin
Dvina
9th
Moscow
Danzig
Kaunas
4th
Vilnius
Vyazma
Smolensk
PANZER 4
Oka
GERMANY
Kaluga
Riazan
Minsk
Tula
Venev
CENTER
BOCK
2nd
Briansk
Warsaw
Oct. 1, 1941
PANZER 2
Łódź
Brest
Orel
U.S.S.R.
Pinsk
Pripiat
Homel
Polesian Marshes
GENERAL GOVERNMENT
Chernihiv
Kursk
Voronezh
Cracow
Lutsk
Rivne
Romny
Lviv
Zhytomyr
Kyiv
Belgorod
REICHSKOMMISSARIAT UKRAINE
Dniester
6th
Kharkiv
Don
Dnipro
17th
Vinnytsia
Poltava
SOUTH
Lozovaya
HUNGARY
RUNDSTEDT
Dnipropetrovsk
PANZER 1
Stalino
Don
Chisinau
Mykolaiv
Rostov
Mariupol
Odessa
11th ARMY
Melitopol
Sea of Azov
ROMANIA
Kerch
Bucharest
Crimea
Danube
Sevastopol
Sofia
BULGARIA
Black Sea
GREECE
Istanbul
TURKEY
THE GERMAN ADVANCE
October 1 – December 5, 1941
German armor (Panzergruppen)
German infantry

1941, Soviet Belarus became a killing zone very much like the Baltics and Ukraine. On October 2 and 3, Mahileu became the first sizable city in Belarus where all of the Jews were killed. Even as the German army was advancing east in huge numbers, the German killers presented their actions as defensive. To shoot Jewish babies in Mahileu was, as one German (Austrian) explained to his wife, to prevent something worse: "During the first try, my hand trembled a bit as I shot, but one gets used to it. By the tenth try I aimed calmly and shot surely at the many women, children, and infants. I kept in mind that I have two infants at home, whom these hordes would treat just the same, if not ten times worse. The death that we gave them was a beautiful quick death, compared to the hellish torments of thousands and thousands in the jails of the GPU. Infants flew in great arcs through the air, and we shot them to pieces in flight, before their bodies fell into the pit and into the water."

Once Operation Typhoon was under way, very little was needed to induce German soldiers to murder Jews. The Third Company of the 691st Regiment of the 339th Infantry Division had been serving the German occupation in France, stationed in the Loire Valley. A few days after its transfer to Belarus, on October 10, 1941, its men were sealing the village of Krucha, marching its Jews to pits, and shooting them all. The soldiers did not relish the task; the commanders seemed to wish to avoid the appearance of weakness in their new assignment. Whatever the reason, murder the soldiers did, although they were not punished if they asked to be excused from the shooting. This army unit, freshly arrived from French wine country, carried out the mass murder of the Jews of Krucha by themselves, with no assistance from the SS.

In Minsk, the capital of prewar Soviet Belarus, the Germans revealed a spectacular scenography of the Judeobolshevik myth. On November 7, 1941, the anniversary of the Bolshevik Revolution, Germans and local Belarusians and Russians forced the Jews of Minsk to carry Soviet flags and sing Soviet songs as they marched away from the city. Then the Jews were shot. The symbolism was obvious to all: The Jews were responsible for communism and for the Soviet Union; their elimination would mean its defeat, and of course the excision of responsibility for everyone else. The Germans repeated the performance in Minsk on other Soviet holidays such as Red Army Day and International Women's Day. As they established a civilian administration in occupied Soviet Belarus they could rely upon Soviet citizens, as they could in Soviet Ukraine and Soviet Russia. In Belarus, communists and members of the Komsomol, the communist youth group, joined the local police and took part in the mass shooting of Jews and other German policies.

With the advance of Operation Typhoon, Belarus became the hinterland of Army Group Center. With all of its swamps and forest, Belarus was well suited to partisan warfare. Even before the Soviets themselves grasped the utility of a partisan war behind the German lines, Germans had found the new ideological cover for the anti-partisan campaign to come: "a partisan is a Jew and a Jew is a partisan." Jews were first associated with the Soviet regime's creation, then with its predicted collapse, and then with an expected form of counterattack. Although the Germans had announced that they would not be observing the laws of war in the Soviet Union, and although German campaigns of mass killing were obvious violations of these laws, they were enormously sensitive to partisan campaigns directed against themselves. Any war by the rules must be a war the Germans were winning; so, if the Germans were not winning, someone else must be breaking the rules. Jews appear in this logic as the iniquitous force that seeks to thwart Germans who are struggling righteously for the triumph that nature owes them.

The policy of mass murder of Jewish women and children came slightly later to Belarus, and the Germans found it no easier. Here as elsewhere the imperative to kill women and children became an argument for involving locals—or auxiliary policemen already recruited in Lithuania or Latvia. It was also presumably one of the reasons that a new technique of killing was applied. The method of mass murder by carbon monoxide, already used in Germany and in occupied Poland against people deemed "unworthy of life," was applied in Belarus to Jews. Vans were adapted so that they pumped their exhaust into their own hold. Packing Jews, especially Jewish children, into these vans was a way to kill them without facing them directly. The children called the vehicles "black ravens." This is what their parents had called the NKVD vehicles that had taken people away during Stalin's Great Terror three years before.

By the end of 1941, the Germans, with help from Soviet citizens, had killed some one million Jews in the occupied Soviet Union. The *Einsatzgruppen* had improvised techniques of killing and perfected their political approach to local populations. Along with the Order Police and the *Wehrmacht,* they were moving imperceptibly toward a full implementation of the Judeobolshevik logic—which imperceptibly had become a way of covering defeat rather than of bringing about victory. They could not bring down the Soviet state, but they could kill Jews where they had demolished Soviet institutions. Otto Rasch, the commander of *Einsatzgruppe* C, noted in September 1941 that "the elimination of the Jews" was "practically easier" than the general campaign of colonial exploitation that had been the war's original aim.

The war proceeded differently along different fronts, with disappointment reaching first Army Group North, then Army Group South, and then Army Group Center. But everywhere the commanders of the *Einsatzgruppen, Wehrmacht,* and police knew that they were not as far east as they were supposed to be. The policemen were available in large numbers for killing Jews precisely because they could not fulfill their original assignment, which had been to control the much larger territory that was supposed to be conquered by the end of 1941. Army commanders were anxious. Soviet resistance was real. Only the *Einsatzgruppen,* and their SS commanders, seemed to have an answer: a war against the Jews in fact as well as in name.

The national identities of the peoples of the Soviet Union, so important to the mental world of German racists, and so prominent in later polemics, made very little difference to their behavior. The Soviet state was a barrier to German power, but no Soviet nation was. Jews died on the territories of the prewar Soviet Union in much the same ways and in much the same proportions as they did in the territories annexed by the Soviet Union in 1939 and 1940. The Germans were aided in their campaign of murder by members of all Soviet nationalities they encountered. When the Germans crossed the border from one Soviet republic to another, they paid little attention. Nor did they need to.

Whereas the Germans occupied Soviet Belarus and Soviet Ukraine in their entirety for much of the war, some 95 percent of the territory of Soviet Russia was spared German occupation. But in the parts of Soviet

Russia where German power did reach, Soviet citizens reacted much the same way as Soviet citizens elsewhere. Russians who had been prominent in the communist apparatus were informed by other Russians that they could clear their slate if they killed one Jew. Russian house managers, like house managers everywhere, provided the Germans with lists of Jews in their buildings. Russians (and others) served the Germans as policemen in Soviet Russia from the beginning. The Germans used Russian policemen in anti-Jewish actions in Soviet Russia as soon as they reached its territory. Russians in these auxiliary police forces tracked down Jews in Pskov, Briansk, and Kursk. Russian policemen were present at all of the mass shootings of Jews in occupied Soviet Russia, such as Rostov and Mineral'nye Vody. Russian policemen, like policemen everywhere, reported people who were hiding Jews in order to get their property. Russians informed on one another everywhere, including in the outskirts of besieged Leningrad. Russians were also present in the local police forces that killed Jews beyond Russia, for example, in Vilnius, Riga, Minsk, and Kharkiv.

In the cities of Soviet Russia that fell under German occupation, the local politics and the fate of Jews were the same as in Soviet Ukraine or Soviet Belarus. Army Group Center was held back for two months at Smolensk in western Russia, finally winning an encirclement battle on September 10, 1941. By this time, most of the local Jews, about ten thousand people, had been able to flee. Their Russian neighbors, some of whom had lost their own houses during the intense battle for the city, looted the Jews' property and took their apartments before the Germans arrived. The appropriation of mobile and immobile property was brought under control and regulated by the authorities installed by the Germans. The initial plunder created an appetite for more. The collaborating local administration of Smolensk, led by Russian communists with impressive records of service to the Soviet Union, ordered a census to record the place of residence of remaining Jews. They then provided the Germans with the personnel needed to place these people in a ghetto. This allowed the rapid seizure of the remaining Jewish property of the city. Once that was achieved, the residences of the ghetto itself could become the next object of desire. In May 1942, the Russian mayor, the noted Soviet jurist Boris Men'shagin, suggested to the Germans that clearing the ghetto would improve the living situation of Russians.

Local Russian policemen aided the Germans in murdering the remainder of the Jews of Smolensk a few weeks later.

If the war had gone as Hitler had expected, the winter of 1941 would have brought massive starvation throughout the western Soviet Union. Instead, Jewish children were being gassed in vans as war continued. The war of colonization against the Slavs, though it continued, was yielding to the war of elimination of the Jews.

In nature, thought Hitler, conflict was over food, and the weaker races were to starve. The objective of the Hunger Plan was precisely the starvation of supposedly inferior Slavs. After the defeat of the Red Army and the collapse of the Soviet state, food from the fertile parts of the western Soviet Union, above all Soviet Ukraine, was to feed German civilians. This reorganization of the European political economy was to make Germany self-sufficient and Germans secure and comfortable. Some thirty million Soviet citizens were supposed to starve in the winter of 1941, among them six million inhabitants of Soviet Belarus. This failed. Soviet citizens did indeed starve, and in large numbers: three million in prisoner-of-war camps, a million in Leningrad, tens of thousands more in Soviet Ukrainian cities such as Kharkiv and Kyiv. Yet the result was barely sufficient to feed the German soldiers fighting on the eastern front, and it did little to bring a new bounty home to Germany.

The German invasion of the USSR did create the possibility of distributing the hunger. As German soldiers were ordered to feed themselves and their animals (the Germans invaded with some 750,000 horses) from the land "like in a colonial war," the allocation of the foodstuffs that remained became a political problem. The result was the invention of a new politics in 1941 and 1942: the redistribution not of food in western and central Europe but of hunger in eastern Europe. Unable to reward civilians in Germany with plentiful food, German policy used food shortages to motivate peoples under their control and to enforce their own racial hierarchies. As early as September 1941, the Germans were no longer seeking to transform an entire region through starvation, but rather to allocate hunger in such a way as to help them win the war. People wanted Jewish property; they also wanted food rations better than those of the Jews.

Like the politics of Judeobolshevism, the politics of relative deprivation subdued resistance and generated collaboration. In the most drastic cases, people killed quickly in order to avoid dying slowly. Once released from starvation camps, Soviet prisoners of war were willing to do anything to stay out, including aiding Germans in the policy of the mass murder of Jews. Someone had to dig all of those pits. On December 7, Soviet prisoners of war were digging pits in the Letbarskii Forest so that Germans could shoot the Jews of Riga. Perhaps the Germans on the scene regarded this as the control of the Judeobolshevik menace. And yet, no matter how many battles the Germans seemed to win, and how many prisoners they took, starved, or exploited, the Red Army kept fighting.

The autumn of 1941 was eventful for ten-year-old Yuri Israilovich German. He was growing up in Kaluga, a city in Soviet Russia, about 190 kilometers southwest of Moscow. Two years earlier his father had disappeared in the middle of the night, arrested by the NKVD on charges of sabotage. A few weeks after the Germans invaded the Soviet Union, his father returned, emaciated and exhausted, from hard labor in the Soviet north. In September 1941, Yuri's father was mobilized, despite his condition, for the Red Army. With his father gone again, this time to fight the Germans, Yuri began to feel, for the first time, that he was being stigmatized as a Jew. A Russian neighbor said that the Germans would "deal with" people like him when they arrived. When German troops did reach the city in October 1941, Kaluga residents greeted them with bread and salt. Very quickly a local administration, following German orders, established a ghetto inside a cloister that had been closed under Soviet rule. Yuri and other children were forced to work in the fields, and to dig pits for murdered Jews. Some of the Jews inside the ghetto were shot, including those regarded as disabled and a kind teacher who had tried to help the children. Then, to everyone's surprise, shells began to burst around the city, and gunfire was heard. It was December 1941, and the Red Army had returned. In haste, the Germans tried to liquidate the ghetto, burning its buildings and shooting with machine guns at the Jews who tried to escape. Yuri and his mother were among the few survivors. They returned to their house, which had in the meantime been taken by an Orthodox priest.

The battle for Kaluga was part of the astonishing counterattack of the Red Army. In early December 1941, Soviet soldiers turned the tide at Moscow. Operation Typhoon had failed. On December 7, a German general, Hellmuth Stieff, wrote to his wife that he and his men were "fighting here for our own naked lives, daily and hourly, against an enemy who in all respects is far superior."

That very day the Japanese bombed Pearl Harbor, bringing the United States into the war. The global strategic catastrophe allowed Hitler to slip from one conception of his war to another. His very errors allowed him to radicalize his rhetoric. His misunderstanding of Poland had brought him a war with Britain. His underestimation of the Soviet Union meant that Germany now had to fight the British, the Soviets, and the Americans—all at once. Yet following the logic of his worldview, he could claim that the "common front" of capitalism and communism against Germany was the work of the Jews. A victory in the USSR might have allowed their deportation. A stalemate in the East and a long global conflict required something else. "The world war is here," said Hitler on December 12, 1941, recalling his "prophecy" of January 1939. "The annihilation of the Jews must be the necessary consequence."

In the occupied zones of the Soviet Union in the preceding six months, Germans had learned how this might be achieved: by mass shooting. By the time Hitler promised to annihilate the Jews in December 1941, a million Jews in the occupied Soviet Union had already been murdered. Even so, Governor-General Hans Frank had no idea how the Polish Jews packed into the ghettos of his General Government could be eliminated. After listening to Hitler in Berlin in December 1941, he returned to Cracow and spoke to his subordinates. "Gentlemen," he began, "I must ask you to rid yourselves of all feeling of pity. We must annihilate the Jews wherever it is possible, in order to maintain the structure of the Reich." He had understood what Hitler could not say: that the struggle was now defensive. The killing of the Jews was to substitute for a normal acknowledgment of defeat.

The lessons of the USSR could not be applied in Poland, at least not in the General Government and the lands annexed to the Reich, where Germany had been exercising power since 1939. Germany had invaded Poland more than two years earlier without beginning a Final Solution.

GERMANY AND THE GENERAL GOVERNMENT
June 1941
DENMARK
Copenhagen
SWEDEN
Baltic Sea
Memel
LITHUANIAN S.S.R.
Kaunas
Vilnius
Minsk
BELARUSIAN S.S.R.
Białystok
North Sea
Amsterdam
NETHERLANDS
Brussels
BELGIUM
Schleswig-Holstein
Hamburg
Mecklenburg
Weser-Ems
Ost-Hannover
Elbe
Hannover
Südhannover Braunschweig
Magdeburg-Anhalt
Berlin
Mark Brandenburg
Stettin
Pommern
Danzig
Danzig-Westpreußen
Königsberg
Sudauen
Ostpreußen
Vistula
Posen
WARTHELAND
Łódź
Warsaw
Warschau
Brest
Pinsk
U.S.S.R.
Westfalen Nord
Essen
Dortmund
Düsseldorf
Westfalen Süd
Köln
Köln-Achen
Kurhessen
Halle-Merseburg
Leipzig
GERMANY
Dresden
Nieder-Schlesien
Breslau
Oder
Radom
Lublin
GENERAL GOVERNMENT
Lutsk
Rivne
Hessen-Nassau
Thüringen
Sachsen
Sudetenland
Moselland
Frankfurt
Rhine
Mainfranken
Luxembourg
Westmark (planned)
Prague
Ober-Schlesien
Cracow
Krakau
UKRAINIAN S.S.R.
Lviv
Ternopil
Franken
Bayerische Ostmark
Protectorate of Bohemia and Moravia
(Elsaß)
Strasbourg
FRANCE
Württemberg-Hohenzollern
Danube
Stanyslaviv
Dnister
Kamianets-Podilskyi
SLOVAKIA
Baden
Schwaben
Munich
München-Oberbayern
Oberdonau
Niederdonau
Vienna
Bratislava
Chernivtsi
Salzburg
Bern
SWITZERLAND
Tirol-Vorarlberg
Steiermark
Budapest
Debrecen
HUNGARY
Iași
Lyon
Kärnten
Cluj
VICHY FRANCE
Milan
Venice
Trieste
Zagreb
ITALY
CROATIA
Brașov
ROMANIA

Einsatzgruppen had ravaged western and central Poland in 1939, but mostly in the hunt for educated Poles. There had been no promises of political liberation then, only the project of destroying the Polish state forever. No Poles had been used as political collaborators: not because none had offered (a few had), but because Berlin had no use for them. Though the Polish police had been preserved, no thought was given to arming enough Poles to carry out a Final Solution by shooting. Polish Jews had been placed in ghettos in 1940 and 1941, not to kill them but to prepare for some deportation. To be sure, tens of thousands of Jews had died of disease or malnutrition in the ghettos. Still, two million Jews were still alive in the western and central lands of Poland taken by Germany in 1939. How would these people be killed?

On January 30, 1942, Hitler spoke at the *Berliner Sportpalast* before masses of Germans. He recalled again, now publicly, his "prophecy" of January 30, 1939, issued right after his foreign minister had returned with the news that Poland would not join Germany in the war against the Soviet Union. He now misdated his "prophecy" to September 1, 1939, the date of the German invasion of Poland. Hitler had seen back then, it would seem, the logic of his own actions. If he won his war, he could defeat the Jews. And if he lost his war, he could characterize it as a planetary conflict and also defeat the Jews. In January 1942, he told Germans that Jews were to be held responsible for a world war. His "prophecy" would be fulfilled.

That same month, Hitler asked rhetorically why he should regard Jews any differently than he regarded Soviet prisoners of war. The comparison was a telling one. As of that point, the Germans had starved more non-Jewish Soviet citizens than they had shot Jews. That fall and winter something like two million Soviet citizens would die in the starvation camps, and another half a million in besieged Leningrad. Now this trend would reverse, and indeed some of the Soviet survivors of the starvation camps would be used to kill Jews. The threat of death by starvation turned the prisoner-of-war camps into factories of collaborators. About a million young men of the Soviet armed forces—Russians, Ukrainians, Belarusians, and others raised in communism and in anti-racism, most of them men of peasant or working-class origin aged between twenty and thirty—were chosen for new duties, directed against their homeland or against the Jews. Rather than killing the Slavs and then deporting the Jews, which had been the general idea, the Germans were finding ever new ways to exploit the Slavs against the Jews. They adapted the traditional African method of colonialism, exploiting a despised group against a still more despised one; they would even call these new collaborators *Askaren*. The *Askaren* had been local soldiers in German East Africa, first deployed in the 1888–1889 Abushiri rebellion, who had fought loyally in Africa under German command during the First World War. German East Africa was the only colony that had been defended until the end of the First World War, and so the legend of the *Askaren* was that of fidelity in a doomed but righteous struggle.

No one had to say that the war as originally conceived had been lost. No one had to explain that colonization of a particular territory inhabited by subhumans, as the Nazis saw matters, was yielding pride of place to the liberation of the planet from the domination of nonhuman Jews. When in October 1941 Himmler spoke with one of his enterprising lieutenants, Odilo Globocnik, the SS and Police Leader for the Lublin district of the General Government, there would have been no need for such explicit talk. The Lublin district lay at the eastern edge of the General Government, on what had been the border with Soviet Ukraine until June 1941; and it had been Globocnik's job in the six months after the invasion to prepare for the eastern empire. His Lublin district, thick with prisons and camps, perhaps the ghastliest part of the General Government, was originally meant as a kind of testing ground for the *Lebensraum* to the east. As the Soviets held the line and Hitler's priorities shifted, Himmler and Globocnik found the way to realize their *Führer*'s desires by murdering the Jews of Poland.

In the occupied Soviet Union in the second half of 1941, Globocnik's SS colleagues, men such as Stahlecker and Jeckeln, had improvised techniques of mass killing from the chaos created by the first weeks of a war of elimination against a state defined as Jewish. In the Lublin District of the General Government in late 1941 and early 1942, Globocnik was starting from very different initial conditions. Globocnik's innovation was to assemble the political fragments left by German policies of state destruction over the previous several years. From the east, he took the starved and demoralized Soviet prisoners of war. There are no known cases of anyone refusing to leave the starvation camps when offered a chance to do so, nor are any likely to be found. Trained at a camp known as Trawniki, Soviet citizens released from the starvation facilities (among them Belarusians, Chuvash, Estonians, Komi, Latvians, Lithuanians, Romanians, Russians, Tatars, Ukrainians, and at least one half Jew) would help build and guard the death factories at Bełżec, Sobibór, and Treblinka. Later they would be deployed to empty some of the larger ghettos, such as Warsaw. From the realities of occupied Poland, Globocnik would exploit the ghettos, their Jewish councils, the Jewish police, and Jewish and Polish informers.

From the west, from Germany itself, Globocnik would borrow the technique of mass murder through carbon monoxide. In Germany and in the annexed territories of Poland, German doctors had murdered with canisters of carbon monoxide; in occupied Soviet Belarus and Soviet Ukraine exhaust was pumped from vans into their own holds. Christian Wirth of Hitler's personal chancery, the man who had run the "euthanasia" program in Germany, found the technical solution that would be applied in these new facilities. He brought five young colleagues from the "euthanasia" program, most of them specialists in burning corpses, to Bełżec, where they experimented with methods of generating carbon monoxide in a closed space. They finally settled on a variation of the eastern technique: exhaust from internal combustion engines, pumped into sealed chambers. Some hundred more participants of the gassing program in Germany arrived in Globocnik's Lublin District in late 1941.

The program of mass killing developed by Himmler, Globocnik, and Wirth involved bringing these fragments together into a new whole, and that whole into murderous motion. Beginning in early 1942 in the Lublin District of the General Government, Globocnik's SS men would go from ghetto to ghetto, explaining the mission to the German stationary police. Under German supervision, the Jewish councils would order and the Jewish police would organize selections from the ghetto population to be taken to the trains. When the trains arrived at the new death facilities, the Jews would be murdered in gas chambers built and manned by Soviet citizens.

The practice of extermination was contingent in several ways upon the economics of scarcity. At the highest level, the failure of the German colonial campaign meant that the German leadership had to choose among victims. No tremendous bounty was produced by the starvation of Slavs, but Jews could be blamed for this failure. In the politics of relative deprivation, Poles who inherited Jewish property were all the more attached to what they had gained, and Soviet citizens were desperate to find a way to leave the starvation camps. In Nazi decisions about the fate of Polish Jews, one relevant calculation became Jewish productivity versus Jewish consumption of calories. At moments when food seemed more pressing, Jews were killed; at moments when labor seemed more urgent, Jews were spared. In such a dark market, in which Jews were nothing but economic units, the general tendency was toward extermination. In July 1942, when it became known that the General Government was to become a net food exporter, Himmler decided that all of its Jews should be killed by the end of the year.

Many Jews yielded to dreams of food when the Germans deliberately associated nourishment with deportations. In Cracow, where Governor-General Frank lived in his castle, the claim in 1942 was that Jews were being deported to the East to bring in the harvest in Ukraine. In Warsaw, in the largest ghetto in Frank's General Government, Jews were promised bread and jam if they reported to the *Umschlagplatz* for deportation. With time, as Jews came to understand what deportation meant, the politics of relative deprivation became the politics of the delay of death. Precisely because the Germans themselves were always uncertain as to whether they were more desperate for food or for labor, Jews could always persuade themselves that some of their number would be spared. The very fact of selection, as Warsaw Jews reported, meant "a division between the productive and the nonproductive" that "broke down the morale of the people of the ghetto." The hope of the individual for survival worked against the solidarity of the community. The Jewish policemen were assigned quotas of Jews to deliver to the trains, the fulfillment of which became their source of hope for themselves and their families and their alienation from others. As one of their number in Warsaw responded to the pleas of a fellow Jew: "That's your problem. My problem is to bring ten people."

Most likely there was never a definitive decision to murder all the Jews of Poland in death facilities. Once the process began in March 1942, however, the alternatives became infeasible, and for this reason unmentionable. As late as that February, Himmler and Heydrich were still discussing sending Jews to the Gulag. But absent a victory over the USSR in 1942, which was not forthcoming, this was impossible. Thus the deportations that began in the Lublin District spread throughout the General Government. At first Jews were sent from ghettos to Bełżec, then to Bełżec and Sobibór, and finally to Bełżec, Sobibór, and Treblinka. Over the course of 1942, some 1.3 million Polish Jews were murdered in these three death facilities. In Warsaw alone, in what was called the *Grosse Aktion*, some 265,040 Jews were deported to Treblinka and murdered and another 10,380 shot in the ghetto between July 23, 1942, and September 21, 1942. Tens of thousands remained, mostly young men, as the ghetto became a labor camp.

In Warsaw in late December 1942, some of those survivors, working together in a loose confederation known as the Jewish Combat Organization, began to assassinate the Jewish authorities of the ghetto. In January 1943, Himmler ordered that the ghetto be dissolved entirely. Jewish resistance prevented this deportation from being carried out. In February, Himmler renewed his order. When the Germans came again to the ghetto in larger numbers in April 1943, a significant number of Jews resisted. Some were from the Jewish Combat Organization, which included representatives of major Jewish parties such as the Bund as well as left-wing Zionists and communists; others fought within a Jewish Military Union that was dominated by the Revisionist Zionists of Betar. It was the Revisionists who, following old habit, raised both the Polish and the Zionist flags. The Warsaw Ghetto Uprising was the first major urban resistance to German rule in Europe. The Jews understood that they were not risking very much: In most cases, their families were already dead, and they believed, correctly, that the same fate awaited them. The rebellion led to the physical destruction of the Warsaw ghetto, as the Germans used flamethrowers to extract Jews from bunkers and then burned the entire district to the ground. The survivors were sent to other labor camps, as originally planned, where almost all of them were shot in 1944. This was the end of the most significant Jewish community in the world.

The man who suppressed the Warsaw Ghetto Uprising, Jürgen Stroop, believed that he was doing his part to win a war that would make Ukraine a German land of milk and honey. In fact, his superiors saw the extermination of Warsaw Jews as a necessity in July 1942 because of pressing food shortages. The logic was similar in the ghettos of the *Warthegau*, such as Łódż. German Jews were dispatched to the overcrowded ghetto there, then local German authorities were left to solve the problem of overpopulation by their own means.

In July 1941, the local head of the SD had proposed direct killing rather than slow starvation for the Jews of Łódż: "There is the danger this winter that the Jews can no longer all be fed. It is to be seriously considered whether the most humane solution might not be to finish off those Jews not capable of working by some sort of fast-working preparation. This would be in any event more pleasant than letting them starve." In a mental world where starvation was taken to be the norm, other forms of killing could be presented as a kindness.

That winter, Jews were indeed murdered by such a "preparation": the exhaust fumes that had already been tested in Belarus and in the east. The killing machines at Chełmno, where Jews from Łódż and elsewhere in the *Warthegau* were taken beginning in December 1941, were parked gas vans guarded by German Order Policemen. This was a modification of a technique earlier used to kill people designated as "unworthy of life." Immediately after the German invasion of Poland, the Germans had emptied Polish mental hospitals by gassing their patients. The SS commando responsible for these killings, led by Herbert Lange, was entrusted with the killing at Chełmno. There was also a certain amount of influence from the east. Otto Bradfisch had been the commander of *Einsatzkommando* 8 in Belarus, which painted Stars of David on its vehicles to proclaim its annihilatory task. In April 1942, he was assigned to Łódż, where he oversaw the continuing deportation of Jews to Chełmno.

As of the end of 1942, however, a large number of Jews were still alive in the Polish territories annexed to Germany, chiefly in Łódż. After the first selections, the ghetto there was transformed into a work camp, producing armaments. Tens of thousands of Jews would survive in Łódż until almost the end of the war, when they were deported to Auschwitz.

In the General Government, all of the major Jewish communities had been destroyed by autumn 1942. The Jews who were alive, with very few exceptions such as laborers in arms factories, were killed on sight by German police. Poles in the General Government who were caught aiding Jews were also subject to the death penalty, and villages where Jews were found were subject to collective retribution. In the last weeks of 1942, the main task of the German police in the General Government was what they called the "Jew hunts." There was so much shooting in the countryside that dogs on Polish farms ceased to react to the sound of gunfire.

In 1943 and 1944 in the General Government, German police sought to bring about the cooperation of Poles in the hunts. Himmler was at the top of the chain of command. His orders were passed through the Higher SS and Police Leader for Warsaw to the German Order Police. In turn, the German Order Police was to "involve in this action the broadest possible masses of Polish society." Thus, the German Order Police engaged two institutions that had existed in independent Poland, but which had been transformed by its destruction. The first was the Polish Order Police, which since 1939 had been purged, racialized, and subordinated to German purposes. The second were Polish local authorities, deprived of their previous relationship to state and law, but with two years of responsibility for German racial policy. Polish policemen and Polish local authorities were made personally responsible to their German superiors for ensuring that no Jews were left alive in their districts.

There was a politics to all this, but it was not a national politics. It is not clear in any event how many Polish-speaking peasants identified with the Polish nation and state in 1939. The social distance between peasants and Jews (although they lived in the same places) and between peasants and Polish officials (although they spoke the same language) was perhaps greater than nostalgic sentiment or wishful nationalism might suggest. What can be said with some confidence is that after three years of German rule, Polish-speaking peasants saw the Polish order as vanquished and lived within the German one. They were constantly told, and those who were literate could read, that their local authorities were responsible for keeping their village or county free of Jews. The village head had to post a notice promising death to Poles who aided Jews and rewards for those who turned them in. Jewish survivors remembered seeing such posters in every Polish village. If a Jew was hiding in a village, the village head could be denounced to the Germans by his own people, perhaps by a rival or someone bearing a grudge. In the Polish countryside people denounced one another quite regularly for all sorts of reasons; the presence of Jews was often just the pretext to settle a score. The legacy of prewar antisemitism, spread by both the secular Right and the Roman Catholic Church, was that Poles who wished to aid Jews feared other Poles. A village head could not organize or sanction a rescue of Jews unless he was sure that he could expect the solidarity of all villagers. This led to absurd situations in which village heads bribed their own villagers not to denounce them to the Germans.

Poles were not always executed for sheltering Jews, but they were often enough that the fear was real. In thousands of cases across the General Government, the German police carried out mass murders of Poles for one violation or another. In Krosno prison, a Polish woman was executed right after the Jew she had been sheltering was shot, her corpse pushed on top of his. All this took place in front of the other Polish prisoners, who could draw their own conclusions. When there was a denunciation, German policemen arrived to find and kill the Jews, and to punish the village if none were produced. In cases of uncertainty the villagers were required to join the Germans in the hunt for the reported Jews. During the "Jew hunt," the village leaders were made hostages and, in principle, could pay with their lives if the Jews were not found. The village night guard, men who in times of peace watched for fire or disorder, took part in the Jew hunts and were also made hostages. If they captured Jews, they would be rewarded. If they failed to find Jews, their lives were forfeit.

Sometimes Poles in the countryside would denounce Jews to the Polish police rather than directly to the Germans. This could seem less terrible than speaking directly to the foreign murderers. But once a Polish policeman had such knowledge, he became personally responsible for finding and delivering (or killing) the Jews in question. As of February 1943, the Polish police were under orders to kill "all Jews encountered, without warning." Sometimes the Polish police would indeed shoot the Jews themselves, for reasons as banal as the inconvenience of riding by horse cart to the nearest German gendarme station. Sometimes they took the Jews to the Germans. Sometimes they were then ordered by their German superiors to shoot the Jews. For Polish policemen, the penalty for refusing to obey such an order was death. (For German policemen there was no such punishment.) Even so, in some cases Polish policemen set Jews free or even helped them to survive.

In these conditions, with violence privatized and the peasant population mobilized, very few Jews survived in the Polish countryside. Thousands of Jews who were on the run and in hiding were caught and murdered, almost all after a denunciation.

Wherever the state had been destroyed, whether by the Germans, by the Soviets, or both, almost all of the Jews were murdered. The Holocaust began as mass shooting campaigns in lands where the state was destroyed twice in quick succession, first the prewar nation-state by the Soviets, then the Soviet apparatus by the Germans. The techniques developed in the zone of double statelessness—the recruitment of locals, the use of multiple German institutions, the open-air shootings—were also applied further east, everywhere in the Soviet Union that German power extended. In western and central Poland, where the Germans had been present since September 1939 but began the mass murder of Jews more than two years later, other techniques were applied: secret gassing facilities, deportation from the ghettos, Jew hunts. For the Jews of the Baltic states, eastern Poland, and the Soviet Union, there were bullets and pits; for the Jews of central and western Poland, there were exhaust fumes and ovens.

Most of the remaining Jews of Europe were destined for a place called Auschwitz.

8

The Auschwitz Paradox

Auschwitz symbolizes the intention to murder all Jews under German control, and Jews from every corner of the German empire were murdered in its gas chambers. Some Jews survived Auschwitz because it remained, to the end, a set of camps as well as a death facility, where Jews were selected for labor as they entered. Thus a story of survival at Auschwitz can enter collective memory. Almost literally no Jew who stood at the edge of a death pit survived, and almost literally no Jew who entered Treblinka or Bełżec or Sobibór or Chełmno survived. The word "Auschwitz" has become a metonym for the Holocaust as a whole. Yet the vast majority of Jews had already been murdered, further east, by the time that Auschwitz became a major killing facility. Yet while Auschwitz has been remembered, most of the Holocaust has been largely forgotten.

Auschwitz has been a relatively manageable symbol for Germany after the Second World War, significantly reducing the actual scale of the evil done. The conflation of Auschwitz with the Holocaust made plausible the grotesque claim that Germans did not know about the mass murder of the European Jews while it was taking place. It is possible that some Germans did not know exactly what happened at Auschwitz. It is not possible that many Germans did not know about the mass murder of Jews. The mass murder of Jews was known and discussed in Germany, at least among families and friends, long before Auschwitz became a death facility. In the East, where tens of thousands of Germans shot millions of Jews over hundreds of death pits over the course of three years, most people knew what was happening. Hundreds of thousands of Germans witnessed the killings, and millions of Germans on the eastern front knew about them. During the war, wives and even children visited the killing sites; and soldiers, policemen, and others wrote home to their families, sometimes with photographs, about the details. German homes were enriched, millions of times over, by plunder from the murdered Jews, sent by post or brought back by soldiers and policemen on leave.

For similar reasons, Auschwitz was a convenient symbol in the postwar Soviet Union and today in post-communist Russia. If the Holocaust is reduced to Auschwitz, then it can easily be forgotten that the German mass killing of Jews began in places that the Soviet Union had just conquered. Everyone in the western Soviet Union knew about the mass murder of the Jews, for the same reason that the Germans did: In the East the method of mass murder required tens of thousands of participants and was witnessed by hundreds of thousands of people. The Germans left, but their death pits remained. If the Holocaust is identified only with Auschwitz, this experience, too, can be excluded from history and commemoration.

Auschwitz was one of the few parts of the Holocaust to which Soviet citizens did not contribute. Soviet citizens were recruited by the Germans for the mass shootings of Jews, and Soviet citizens built and guarded the gassing facilities at Treblinka, Bełżec, and Sobibór. To be sure, all of this was possible because the Germans sought to destroy the Soviet state, and because the Soviet citizens in question were unmoored from prewar reality and in some cases trying to preserve their own lives. Yet after the war, Soviet propaganda was helpless to explain how so many people produced by the Soviet system had proven to be useful collaborators in the mass murder of so many other people produced by the Soviet system. It was enough of a problem, in the post-Stalin era that began with his death in 1953 and continues to this day, to explain why Soviet policy brought about the death of millions of Soviet citizens by famine and terror in the 1930s. This historical reality remains thoroughly politicized. The perhaps deeper problem, that tens of thousands of Soviet citizens could contribute to the murder of further millions of Soviet citizens on behalf of a totally alien system, has never been addressed. It has instead been displaced.

Auschwitz has also become the standard shorthand of the Holocaust because, when treated in a certain mythical and reductive way, it seems to separate the mass murder of Jews from human choices and actions. Insofar as the Holocaust is limited to Auschwitz, it can be isolated from most of the nations it touched as well as from the landscapes it altered. The gates and walls of Auschwitz can seem to contain an evil that, in fact, extended from Paris to Smolensk. Auschwitz, a German word defining a bit of territory that before and after the war was in Poland, does not seem like an actual place. It is surrounded by mental as well as physical barbed wire. Auschwitz calls to mind mechanized killing, or ruthless bureaucracy, or the march of modernity, or even the endpoint of enlightenment. This makes the murder of children, women, and men seem like an inhuman process in which forces larger than the human were entirely responsible. When the mass murder of Jews is limited to an exceptional place and treated as the result of impersonal procedures, then we need not confront the fact that people not very different from us murdered other people not very different from us at close quarters.

In the history of the Holocaust, Auschwitz was a place where the third technique of mass killing was developed, third in chronological order and also third in significance. The most important technique, because it came first, because it killed the most Jews, and because it demonstrated that a Final Solution by mass killing was possible, was shooting over pits. The next most important, and the next to be developed, was asphyxiation by the exhaust fumes of internal combustion engines. At around the time that these carbon monoxide facilities were coming into use, in early 1942, the policy of murdering all Jews was extended from the occupied Soviet Union and occupied Poland to all lands that fell under German control. Auschwitz became the major killing site for Jews in 1943 and 1944.

Auschwitz arose as a concentration camp, the seventh large one in the Reich, after Dachau, Sachsenhausen, Buchenwald, Flossenbürg, Mauthausen, and Ravensbrück. Its notorious greeting, *"Arbeit macht frei,"* arose from these German precedents. This new camp, unlike these antecedents, was located in the lands of occupied Poland annexed by the Reich and thus within the zone where the Nazi imagination flourished. Its original purpose in 1940 was to prepare the way for the larger eastern empire to come. Its first prisoners were Poles who were punished for their real or anticipated resistance. Its next major victim group was Soviet prisoners of war taken after the invasion of 1941. Insofar as Jews were admitted to Auschwitz in these early years, it was with the intention of marching them east in columns as slave laborers who would exhaust themselves building the German empire on conquered Soviet lands. Jews who lived near Auschwitz were actually among the last Polish Jews to be killed. They were first deported to Auschwitz as forced laborers, because that was Auschwitz's original mission. After the vast majority of Jews in the rest of Poland were already dead, murdered in pits or at Treblinka, Sobibór, Bełżec, or Chełmno, most Jews of the Auschwitz region were still alive.

The purpose of Auschwitz changed as the Nazi colonial mission gave way to the Final Solution, as the subjugation of Slavs was deprioritized and the murder of Jews became urgent. This general shift was evident across a whole range of Nazi endeavors: the shift by the *Einsatzgruppen* from killing some Jews to killing all of them; the use of German policemen originally assigned to other missions for the mass shooting of Jews; the recruitment of local people for auxiliary police; the release of some Soviet prisoners of war so that they could aid in the killing of Jews; the transformation of the Lublin District from a forepost of empire to an experimental ground for gassing facilities. In the case of Auschwitz, the shift from the dream of conquest to the reality of annihilation meant that a camp became a killing facility. The killing agent itself reveals the evolution. Hydrocyanic acid, sold under the trade name Zyklon B, was originally used to fumigate the barracks of the Polish prisoners. Then it was used to murder Soviet prisoners of war. Finally it would be used to murder nearly a million Jews.

Auschwitz was built in a zone of state destruction, after the invasion of Poland and as part of the attempt to obliterate the Polish political nation. Its original infrastructure was that of a Polish military barracks. As a territory it was conquered by Germany in September 1939 and granted to Germany by the terms of the German-Soviet Treaty on Borders and Friendship. Neither its construction nor its subsequent adaptations would have been thinkable, let alone possible, without the German campaign to eliminate rival polities and without the special talents and unusual goals of the state destroyers of the SS.

Auschwitz was unusual, however, in one important respect. Unlike the death pits in the doubly occupied zone and the occupied Soviet Union, unlike the death facilities at Bełżec, Sobibór, Treblinka, and Chełmno, it was the planned murder site for very large numbers of Jews who were still citizens of states that Germany recognized as sovereign. Its intended Jewish victims were generally people who lived beyond the German zone of state destruction and who were therefore much less vulnerable to the imposing power of the SS. Such individuals had to be abandoned by their governments or stripped of their citizenship and physically transported from their country of residence to Auschwitz. There was nothing automatic about this, and indeed it often proved to be difficult.

Hitler's fantasy of a planet without Jews was always present, and his desire to rid Europe of Jews was known to his subordinates no later than the spring of 1942. As of that moment, the policy of the mass murder of Jews, initiated the previous year in the Soviet Union, was general. Yet whether and to what extent that policy could be realized depended upon where Jews happened to live. Because the successful killing strategies were a result of prior decisions and actions that were specific to a certain part of eastern Europe, they could not be repeated with the same kind of success elsewhere. What happened to states in 1939, 1940, and 1941, in other words, was crucial for what would happen to Jews in 1942, 1943, and 1944. The Germans could not exploit the psychological, material, and political resources created by Soviet occupation in places where there had been no Soviet occupation. The Germans could not reassemble the fragments of destroyed states in places where they or the Soviets had not destroyed the state. The Germans could not apply the politics of relative deprivation in places where the war was not a campaign of racial mastery. In the museum at Auschwitz built in communist Poland after the war, its victims were classified by citizenship. This was designed to obfuscate the basic fact that the great majority of them were Jews, and murdered for no other reason. The emphasis on citizenship also obfuscated a more subtle but central fact: that the Jews who were killed were first separated from their states.

In many of the places from which the Jews were to be sent to Auschwitz, none of these conditions existed, and so Jews survived. Millions of European Jews who were condemned to die at Auschwitz survived because they never boarded a train. Jews under German control who were supposed to be sent to Auschwitz were more likely to survive than Jews under German control who were not supposed to be sent to Auschwitz. That is the Auschwitz paradox, and it can only be resolved by considering how states were and were not destroyed. These are the political particularities that explain the different outcomes within the universal design. Auschwitz demonstrates the universal design to kill Jews. It also demonstrates the general significance of statehood in protecting them.

A comparison between two countries under German occupation can suggest the significance of the political factor. Estonia and Denmark had a great deal in common when the Second World War began. Each was a small northern European state with a long Baltic coast, and each was home to a very small number of Jews. During the war both were under German occupation, both were subject to the Final Solution, and both were declared *judenfrei*—free of Jews—by their German occupiers. And yet the history of the Holocaust in each land could hardly have been more different. In Estonia, about 99 percent of the Jews who were present when German forces arrived were killed. In Denmark, about 99 percent of Jews who had Danish citizenship survived. The Jews of Denmark were marked for Auschwitz; the Jews of Estonia met their fate before Auschwitz became a death facility.

In no country under German occupation did a higher percentage of Jews die than in Estonia, and in none did a higher proportion survive than in Denmark. Given the totality of the German policy of killing Jews, this difference calls for an explanation. Surely the population of Estonia was known for its antisemitism? If anything, such a tradition is easier to document in Denmark. Surely the Estonians were governed by antisemites before the war? The double dictatorship of Konstantin Päts and Johan Laidoner was clearly conservative, but it came to power in a coup against the Far Right in 1934. In fact, Estonian Jews were equal citizens of the republic, which took in some Jewish refugees from Austria and Germany. Denmark, by contrast, turned away Jewish refugees after 1935.

Intuitions fail. The extremely different outcomes seem to have little to do with popular attitudes and prewar politics, and much to do with different experiences of war and occupation. Auschwitz reminds us of Hitler's vision of a world without Jews; it should also teach us of the importance of politics in hastening or hindering the realization of that vision.

Estonia shared the fate of Lithuania and Latvia in 1940. Like the other two Baltic states, it was granted by Germany to the Soviets by the terms of the Molotov-Ribbentrop pact, as modified and confirmed by the Treaty on Borders and Friendship of September 1939. The Soviet occupation of Estonia brought the complete destruction of the Estonian upper administration and political elite. President Päts, for example, was taken from his farm and deported to the Soviet Union, where he died. Laidoner, the commander in chief of the armed forces, also perished in exile after deportation. Of the eleven members of the last Estonian government, ten were imprisoned and nine of these killed (four by execution, five dying in Soviet camps).

Soviet law was applied retroactively in occupied Estonia, under the logic that the Estonian state not only did not exist, but had never existed. State service in the 1920s and 1930s was thus considered a crime. In what quickly became Soviet Estonia, the new Soviet authorities carried out some four hundred executions, and were preparing mass deportations as the German armed forces assembled to invade the Soviet Union in June 1941. On the night of June 14, the Soviet NKVD deported about 10,200 Estonian citizens, one percent of the entire population (and about ten percent of the Jewish minority, which was hugely overrepresented in Soviet repressions). A few days later, as German forces raced north through the Baltics to Estonia, the Soviets were shooting Estonian prisoners and leaving their corpses in the prisons.

The Germans arrived in Estonia in early July 1941 with their handpicked Estonians. As in Lithuania and Latvia, the Soviet occupation of Estonia had forced thousands of people to flee the country, many to Berlin. This left the Germans their choice of future collaborators. Many Estonians wished to return; the Germans could choose the ones they saw as most useful to their own purposes. The double occupation, here as elsewhere, meant a double filtering of the political elite. The Soviets destroyed the former ruling class; the Germans now prevented anyone who did not seem sufficiently pliable from returning. Naturally, the Nazi selection excluded the political Left and Center. As elsewhere that summer, the

Germans could exploit moral, material, and political resources created by the Soviet occupation.

As in Latvia and Lithuania, the political resource in Estonia was especially abundant. An entire state had been destroyed in humiliating and vicious fashion only a year earlier, so people were prepared for personal and political redemption. By July 1941, when *Einsatzgruppe* A reached Estonia, the Germans had perfected their argument that the liberation that they offered was from Jews and that local participation in such liberation was a precondition to political negotiations. As in Lithuania and Latvia, locals in Estonia served as translators of this message, adding the element that the Germans themselves would not have understood: that if Estonians collaborated with the second (German) occupier, their first (Soviet) collaboration would be forgotten. No pogroms of Jews took place in Estonia, nor were such seen as necessary by the Germans.

Double collaboration was quite widespread. Some of the Estonian anti-Soviet partisans known as the Home Guard killed Jews; the most zealous killers among those partisans were Estonian communists who had switched sides as the German invasion began in order to clear their names. The Estonian policemen who had collaborated in the Soviet deportations of Estonians and Jews now carried out the German murder of Estonians and Jews. Whereas the Soviets deported about ten thousand Estonian citizens, including about 450 Jews, under German occupation some ten thousand Estonian citizens were executed, among them 963 Jews. From the local perpetrator's perspective the work was not entirely different.

Former employees of the Soviet NKVD were especially significant in the mass murder of Jews in Estonia. Ain-Ervin Mere, for example, was an NKVD agent and director of a special department of the Estonian Rifle Corps, a Soviet unit that was supposed to defend Soviet Estonia from capitalist invasion. Instead he joined the Estonian Security Police under the Germans, serving as its commander from May 1942 through March 1943. The Estonian Security Police was the major agency charged with the murder of Jews. From April 1943 through the end of the war, Mere was a battalion commander in a *Waffen*-SS division. Ervin Viks, an Estonian policeman in the interwar period, worked for the NKVD in 1940 and 1941. Then he joined the Estonian Security Police under the Germans, where he ordered hundreds of executions of Jews and non-Jews. Alexander

Viidik had served in the Estonian Political Police before the war, then offered his services to the Soviet NKVD in 1940. After the German invasion he worked for the SD, the intelligence section of the SS, where he recruited his former Soviet contacts.

In Estonia, as everywhere else, the people who killed Jews under the German occupation also killed others. In occupied Lithuania, the policemen who took part in the shooting of more than 150,000 Jews in 1941 also guarded the camps where a similar number of Soviet prisoners of war starved. In Latvia, the commando that murdered the country's Jews also killed psychiatric patients and Belarusian civilians. Because there were very few Jews in Estonia, the murder of non-Jews was relatively more important than elsewhere. All of the 963 Estonian Jews murdered under German occupation were killed by Estonians, usually policemen. About ten times as many non-Jewish Estonians were also killed by those same Estonian policemen.

In Denmark almost everything was different. Unlike other northern European states such as Finland, Estonia, Latvia, and Lithuania, the Kingdom of Denmark shared no border with the Soviet Union, was not subject to the Molotov-Ribbentrop pact, and was not occupied by the Red Army. When the Second World War began with a German-Soviet invasion of Poland in 1939, Denmark was not involved. It suffered no Soviet invasion; its elites were untouched by Soviet practices of mass shooting and deportation. The political resource that was generated in Estonia could not be created in Denmark, since the Danish state was never destroyed. No double collaboration could be expected when there was only one occupation.

The German occupation of Denmark, when it came in April 1940, was mild. Denmark was, for Germany, neither an ideological enemy nor a racial target, and its territory was invaded for straightforward military reasons. The Germans did not declare, as they had already in Poland and would soon in the USSR, that the state they had attacked no longer existed. On the contrary, the German occupation proceeded on the explicit basis of Danish sovereignty. The Germans made clear that they did not "aim at disturbing the territorial integrity or the political independence of the Kingdom of Denmark." King Christian remained in Copenhagen and ruled as head of state. Democratic elections continued, parliament functioned, and governments changed according to the wishes of Danes. After 1941, during the unexpectedly long and fruitless German campaign in the East, Denmark's main task in the German empire was to provide food. Six thousand Danish men did serve in the *Waffen*-SS, some of them in the *Wiking* division alongside Estonians.

When the Final Solution was extended westward from the occupied Soviet Union to the rest of Europe in 1942, this created a problem in German-Danish relations. Danish authorities understood that yielding Jewish citizens to Germany would compromise Danish sovereignty. In December 1942, the United States, Great Britain, and the Soviet Union issued a warning that collaborators in the German crime of killing Jews would face consequences after the war. Sovereign governments, such as the Danish one, were in a position to heed such warnings. In early 1943, after the German surrender at Stalingrad, the tide of the war turned visibly against Germany. Copenhagen had ever less reason to participate in the Final Solution, while German authorities had ever less reason to alienate the Danes.

The elimination of the Jews nevertheless remained a constant priority in Berlin, and for Werner Best, the leader of the Nazi occupation authority in Denmark. In his initial communications with Berlin, Best maintained that a Final Solution in Denmark was impractical, since it would violate the constitution and lead to the fall of the government. This would force a massive German intervention and disrupt the favorable equilibrium that had been attained. But when the Danish government fell for other reasons, Best saw the opportunity to kill the Jews. It could be done, he thought, in the interval of instability, before a new government was formed. He made the appropriate proposal to Berlin in early September 1943.

There was a will but there was not a way. Rudolf Mildner was assigned to Copenhagen as the head of the Security Police and SD on September 20. He came directly from Katowice, in occupied Poland, where he had been the Gestapo chief with responsibility for Auschwitz. In other words, he was hardly a man without experience in the mass murder of Jews. Yet what he saw in Copenhagen convinced him that a Final Solution, at least of the sort that had been achieved in the stateless zone, was impossible in Denmark. He was confronted in Copenhagen with institutions that had been abolished further east: a sovereign state, political parties with convictions and support, local civil society in various forms, a police force that could not be expected to cooperate. Other German authorities had already drawn much the same conclusion. The local army commander refused to support the German police in any action against Jews. The local naval commander sent all of his ships for repairs on the day chosen for the roundup of Jews, October 2, 1943, so that the coast would be clear for whatever the Danes would wish to do. He also informed Social Democratic politicians of the date, and they in turn informed Danish Jews.

Denmark's neighbor Sweden, neutral in the war but complicit in the economic side of Germany's war effort, had every reason in 1943 to demonstrate a tilt towards the Allies. The Swedish government now proposed to Germany that Sweden take Denmark's Jews. It repeated the proposal over the radio on an open frequency, so that Danish Jews knew that they would be welcome in Sweden. Danes then arranged for a flotilla to ship their Jewish population to Sweden. The German police knew about this undertaking and did not stop it; the German navy watched the Danish boats float slowly by. The Danish citizens did this work at little risk to themselves, since helping their fellow citizens was not a crime in their own country. The German police raid of October 2 caught only 481 of the 6,000 or so Jews of Danish citizenship. The sovereign Danish government intervened with Berlin on behalf of these citizens. Some of them were released, and the rest were sent to Theresienstadt, a transit camp in what had been Terezín in Czechoslovakia, rather than to Auschwitz. Not a single one of them was gassed. Other Jews from other countries were however sent from Theresienstadt to Auschwitz and murdered to make room for the Danish Jews. German authorities took advantage of the presence of Danish Jews to make a propaganda film about the ostensibly good conditions for Jewish life in their camps.

Jews who were Danish citizens survived, which is not exactly the same thing as Jews in Denmark surviving. Danish authorities did not accept Jewish refugees after 1935, and they deported some of the ones who had arrived earlier back to Germany. The Jews who were denied state protection in Denmark shared the fate of Jews who lacked state protection in Estonia or, for that matter, everywhere else: death.

Occupied Estonia was part of the zone of statelessness where the entire Holocaust took place. In Estonia, Latvia, Lithuania, Poland, and the western Soviet Union, Hitler's vision of global racial struggle was converted, in conditions of statelessness, to new forms of politics. In each of these places the sequence of events that permitted the emergence of the Final Solution as mass killing was different. Nevertheless, a set of actions and absences can be identified.

The *actions* were the advance creation of racial or hybrid institutions whose major task was state destruction; the undertaking of aggressive war, permitting these institutions to fulfill their mission beyond their own homeland and in a permissive environment; the fact of state destruction, the removal of political capacity, the murder of leading classes, and the redefinition of such actions as law; the solicitation of collaboration, which was effective when it involved the exploitation of political resources created by an earlier state destroyer, but which always required the exploitation of existing local police forces, cut off from previous authority or eager to prove their loyalty after previous collaboration; the mobilization of psychological resources such as the release from humiliation and the gratification of the desire for revenge; the exploitation of greed, the material resource, enabled by ongoing or prior elimination of property rights; the recruitment of German institutions beyond those originally tasked with killing civilians; the exploitation of fragments of institutions remaining from earlier destructions of states.

After German (or Soviet and German) power destroyed states, the *absences* were the formal denial of sovereignty and the nullification of any connection by foreign policy to a larger world beyond German power; the lack of an overarching political entity that might protect its citizens, or motivate its citizens to protect it, and thus the disappearance of citizenship as a reciprocal relationship; the experience of the removal of traditional state protections in the form of laws and customs; the resulting spread of the dark market, the economic behaviors that arise in a free market without individual rights in which some people are treated as mere economic units to be consumed or sold; and the legal abyss, where all was permitted, where colonial thinking was natural, because international law in the traditional European sense did not apply.

These lists of actions and absences are both ways of characterizing the same extreme: the stateless zone where a Holocaust could be imagined, begun, and completed. At the other extreme during the Second World War were sovereign states that were untouched by German power. Although these generally pass unmentioned in analyses of the Holocaust, they are worth considering. After all, Hitler's racial theory was planetary, and his declaration of war against the Jews was global. There is no particular reason to think that antisemitism was more prevalent in Estonia, Latvia, or Lithuania between the wars than it was in the United States, Great Britain, or Canada.

Most Jews in the world were safe during the Holocaust for the simple reason that German power did not extend to the places they lived and did not threaten the states of which they were citizens. Jews with Polish passports were safe in countries that recognized the prewar Polish state, and killed in countries that did not. American and British Jews were safe, not just in their home countries but everywhere. The Germans did not contemplate murdering Jews who held American and British passports, and, with few exceptions, did not do so. Statehood, like statelessness, followed Jews wherever they went. Soviet Jews were killed, with few exceptions, if they were caught in the lands occupied by the Germans and where Germany fought its war of extermination. In these places the Germans behaved as if the Soviet state had been destroyed and sought to annihilate all of its traces. So long as Jews were in Soviet territory and east of the German occupation, however, they were preserved from the Final Solution—although they were of course subject to Soviet policies. Roughly fifteen percent of the Polish Jews deported by the NKVD in 1940 died in transit or in the Gulag; even so, at the end of the war these deportees were the largest surviving group of Polish Jews.

At one extreme of state destruction, the Holocaust took place; at the other extreme of state integrity, it did not. The middle cases, where the Nazi leadership sought but could not complete a Final Solution, are places where German power reached but where the state was not destroyed: the countries that were allied with Germany or occupied by Germany (or both). German policy was that Jews who inhabited such places were to be extracted, deported, and killed. Although a horribly high number of Jews from such countries were killed, and the fate of Jews in such places was always worse than that of their fellow citizens, more than half of the

Jews who had been citizens of these countries, taken together as a group, survived. The scale of suffering, almost one murder for every two Jews, exceeds that of any other category of people in the Second World War. Yet it is sufficiently different from the murder rate in the stateless zone, something like nineteen murders for every twenty Jews, to warrant serious attention. The history of each country that retained (some measure of) sovereignty despite German influence was, of course, distinct, but the logics of survival were everywhere the same: *citizenship, bureaucracy,* and *foreign policy.*

Citizenship is the name of a reciprocal relationship between an individual and a sheltering polity. When there was no state, no one was a citizen, and human life could be treated carelessly. Nowhere in occupied Europe were non-Jews treated as badly as Jews. But in places where the state was destroyed, no one was a citizen and no one enjoyed any predictable form of state protection. This meant that the other major German mass crimes, the starvation of prisoners of war and the murder of civilians—mostly Belarusians and Poles and Gypsies—also took place almost entirely within zones of statelessness. These policies together killed about as many people as the Holocaust, and they were implemented, and could only be implemented, in the same places. Where the state was not destroyed such extremes were impossible.

In states allied with Germany or states under more traditional occupation regimes, where the major political institutions remained intact, non-Jews who protected Jews were rarely punished for doing so. Non-Jews who were citizens of states could not simply be killed if they aided Jews. In the General Government and in the occupied western Soviet Union, however, the punishment for aiding Jews was death. More Poles were executed for aiding Jews in individual districts of the General Government than in entire west European countries. This is not because Poles were particularly inclined to rescue Jews, which they were not. It is because they were, in fact, sometimes executed for doing so, which rarely happened in western Europe. Indeed, in some places in German-occupied western Europe it was not even a punishable criminal offense to hide a Jew.

Compare the fates of Victor Klemperer, Anne Frank, and Emanuel

Ringelblum, three famous chroniclers of these years. Klemperer was a German scholar of Jewish origin who wrote a brilliant analysis of the language of the Third Reich. Frank was a German Jewish girl in hiding in the Netherlands who kept a diary that later became the most widely read text about the Holocaust. Ringelblum was a historian of Jewish life in Poland who, within the Warsaw ghetto, organized the assembly of an entire archive, creating one of the most important collections of sources of the Holocaust. "Collect as much as possible," said Ringelblum to a colleague in the project known as Oneg Shabbat. "They can sort it out after the war." Klemperer lived and so did the person who cared for him; Frank died but the people who tried to shelter her survived; Ringelblum was shot along with several people who had helped him. These fates reflect the different legal structures of Germany, the occupied Netherlands, and occupied Poland during the war.

Because Klemperer was a German citizen with a non-Jewish wife, he was not subject to the general policy of the deportation and murder of German Jews. Since his wife did not divorce him, he, like many such German Jewish men, survived. Anne Frank was also a German Jew, but in fleeing to the Netherlands she lost even the residual state membership available to her under the Nuremberg Laws. She and her family were eventually discovered and deported to Auschwitz. She died after a transfer to Bergen-Belsen, probably of typhus. The Dutch citizens who had hidden her family survived, since what they did was not subject to criminal prosecution in the Netherlands. Ringelblum's history was different. He was captured and rescued multiple times, aided by both Polish Jews and non-Jewish Poles. In the end, he and the Poles with whom he was hiding were all executed, probably together, in the ashes of the Warsaw ghetto. Most Poles who tried to aid Jews were not killed, but many of them were; and it was a risk that they all faced. This was the stateless predicament.

For Jews themselves, the existence of a state meant citizenship, even if only in an attenuated and humiliating form. Citizenship meant the legal possibility of emigration. Most German and Austrian Jews exploited this possibility, although they generally lost their possessions and their connections to their previous lives in doing so. Citizenship for Jews meant the existence of a civil code, even if sometimes a very discriminatory one, which allowed them claims to property. These could be traded, in ways that were obviously unjust, for the right to depart. The legal exploitation of Jews is often seen as a step towards their extermination, but this was not exactly the case. Even the most exploitative and painful forms of legal discrimination were much less risky to Jewish life than regime change or removal of state authority. In those situations, Jews were suddenly and totally vulnerable, since they lost their access to the civil code and thus their property rights. Rather than trading their property for their lives, they lost both.

Legal discrimination by antisemitic states did not bring an automatic downward spiral toward death, but state destruction did. Once a Jew lost access to a state he or she lost access to the protection of higher authorities and lower bureaucrats. Jews could live if they restored that access, but this was a difficult feat. Anton Schmid was a German (Austrian) soldier from Vienna who, in Vilnius, was responsible for the office that returned individual German soldiers to their units. He saved a Jewish man by providing him with a *Wehrmacht* uniform and paybook. He saved a Jewish woman in Vilnius by inventing for her a legal identity. With a bit of charm and bluster he generated a false baptismal certificate and moved her through the five necessary offices until she was fully documented. No Jew alone in the stateless zone could have done that. All in all, Schmid provided at least one hundred Jews with documents that gave them a chance to live.

Citizenship in modern states means access to *bureaucracy*. Bureaucracy has the reputation of killing Jews; it would be closer to the truth to say that it was the removal of bureaucracy that killed Jews. So long as state sovereignty persisted, so did the limits and possibilities afforded by bureaucracy. In most offices, time is slowed and matters are considered, perhaps with the help of petitions or bribes. When people in sovereign states beyond Germany wished to be noble, bureaucracy provided them with the opportunity to frame their arguments on behalf of individual Jews in the pragmatic or patriotic terms that employees of the state could understand and endorse. The bureaucracies beyond Germany also exhibited the typical tendencies of passing the buck, awaiting clear orders from higher authorities, and insisting on clarity of expression and proper paperwork. Many of the things that make bureaucracies annoying in daily life could and did mean survival for Jews.

Even German bureaucracy did not kill Jews by itself. Even after it was overlaid and penetrated by Nazi structures for six years, German bureaucracy was not capable of murdering the Jews of Germany. German officials were never even instructed, in any final and dispositive way, as to who among German citizens counted as a Jew. At the infamous Wannsee Conference in January 1942, the issue seems to have consumed more time than any other; but it was not resolved, either then or later. This was not for lack of desire: The lawyers concerned believed that Jewish "blood" had to be cleansed "from the German and indeed the entire European bloodstream." Such a thing could be undertaken only when neighboring European countries were invaded and their polities wrecked. German Jews died not because of bureaucratic precision in Germany but because of the destruction of bureaucracies in other countries. German Jews were not killed, with a very few exceptions, on the territory of prewar Germany. Instead they were extracted from Germany and deported to bureaucracy-free zones in the East, places where they would have been entirely safe before the war.

The killing sites of German Jews were places such as Łódż, Riga, and Minsk. If the Holocaust is recalled from the perspective of German Jews, as it usually is, these names evoke nothing but the horror of death amidst the unknown. In the minds of many Germans, and thus in many German sources, these cities are nothing more than improbable assemblages of subhumans in the colonial *Lebensraum*. The combination of Nazi and German Jewish sources can convey a misleadingly incomplete impression of these places.

Before the war, before the arrival of policies of state destruction, each of these cities was a model of Jewish civil society in Europe. Łódż, for example, was Poland's second largest city and its second largest Jewish city, with a sizable Jewish middle class. It was the birthplace of one of the most influential poets of the Polish language, Julian Tuwim, who was a Jew. It was annexed to the Reich after the 1939 invasion of Poland. Riga had been the capital of Latvia, where Jews enjoyed equal rights under the civil code, had sat in parliament, and were ministers of government. In the late 1930s, Riga was a site of refuge for a considerable number of Jews from Germany and Austria. It was altered first by Soviet state destruction in 1940 and then by German state destruction in 1941. Minsk, before the German invasion of the Soviet Union, had been the capital of the

Belarusian Soviet Socialist Republic. Rates of intermarriage were high, and Jewish and non-Jewish schoolchildren were often close friends. Jews had been executed in large numbers in the Soviet Great Terror of 1937, but not as Jews; most often they were taken away by the NKVD's black ravens and shot on false charges of espionage for Poland. Antisemitism was certainly present in Soviet Minsk; but it was a crime. Minsk had to be occupied by Germany, as it was in 1941, before it could become a place where people were murdered as Jews. Jewish urban civilization in eastern Europe had exhibited great variety; only the destruction of the state transformed cities with Jewish particularities into sites for a general policy of killing.

Bureaucracies in Germany could kill Jews only when bureaucracy-free zones elsewhere had been established. The elimination of Polish statehood at the beginning of the war was thus crucial for the entire course of the Holocaust, since it was on occupied Polish territory, in Germany's special colonial zone, that death facilities could be established. The Germans also considered creating a death facility in the occupied Soviet Union, in Mahileu. This was never undertaken; the crematoria designed for Mahileu were delivered instead to Auschwitz.

As a general matter, bureaucrats owed their salaries and their dignity to the sovereign state, and they understood that compromises over citizens meant compromises about citizenship, and that compromises over citizenship meant the weakening of sovereignty. Even when bureaucrats were implementing anti-Jewish measures, it mattered to them that these were policies that originated locally, rather than ones imposed from abroad. The thought "our Jews, our solution" was not noble, but it was typical. Then as now, sovereignty meant the visible ability to conduct foreign policy. In most places and times, the fundamental goal of foreign policy was to preserve the state. This required the ability to alter Jewish policy, since one Jewish policy or another might seem more strategically promising given the constellation of international power at a given moment. Even ethnic cleansers who were convinced that deporting Jews served the state did not lose sight of the fact that the Jewish question was only one issue among others.

For everyone making foreign policy who maintained the typical political focus on the state itself, the crucial question was always the likely outcome of the war. In general, states allied to Nazi Germany tacked towards Nazi policy through 1942 (although none of them followed it completely), and then toward Allied policy thereafter (while, of course, beginning from a position of antisemitic policy and sometimes a record of mass killing). Insofar as states were sovereign, policy was changed, and Jews sometimes survived as a result. Where sovereignty had been eliminated, foreign policy was no longer made.

Thus citizenship, bureaucracy, and foreign policy hindered the Nazi drive to have all European Jews murdered. Of course, each of the many states affected but not destroyed by German policy had its own history and its own particularities. Among the states that were not destroyed but were in some way dominated by Germany, three groups emerge: first, puppet states such as Slovakia and Croatia created in the wake of the destruction of other states; second, states that existed before the war and allied with Nazi Germany of their own accord, such as Romania, Hungary, Bulgaria, and Italy; and third, states whose territories were occupied by Nazi Germany after defeat on the battlefield and whose institutions were altered to various degrees without being completely destroyed, such as France, the Netherlands, and Greece. The variation among these countries was not as extreme as that between Estonia and Denmark. They supply points on the spectrum between the two points of double annihilation of sovereignty and mild German occupation. The history of their Jews confirms the connection between sovereignty and survival.

9

Sovereignty and Survival

Among Germany's allies, the puppets that arose from the wreckage of other states most closely resembled the zone of lawlessness where the Holocaust took place. A state had to be eliminated in order for such entities to be born, and both the end of the old and the creation of the new took place at Germany's behest. All of the citizens of that prior state lost the protection of the previous regime during the transition. The rulers of new states could then decide which of the people on their territory would be granted citizenship. When constitutions were written under German tutelage, it was unlikely that Jews would be granted full membership in the state. Germany was eager to receive the Jewish populations of these new states, first in labor camps and then in death facilities, which created an opportunity for local ethnic cleansers. Both of the puppet states that Germany created, Croatia from Yugoslavia and Slovakia from Czechoslovakia, were ruled by nationalists who could not have reached power without the destruction of multinational units. Over the long term, the puppets' factual dependence upon Nazi Germany meant that they did not engage in normal foreign policy and were not really sovereign. Since such entities had no prospects of surviving a Nazi defeat, their leaders could not really contemplate switching sides or trying to save their remaining Jews.

Germany invaded Yugoslavia in April 1941 after a coup took the country out of the Axis. The invasion was an Axis operation, with Italian, Hungarian, and Bulgarian troops taking part. Yugoslavia had been a centralized state dominated by Serbs; after its destruction Serbia became a district under German military occupation. Although a puppet government was appointed, it lacked every aspect of sovereignty. In Serbia,

Germans placed all male Jews capable of work into forced labor camps and announced that all sabotage would bring massive retaliation. As in the occupied Soviet Union, and on a similar timetable, German occupation forces opted for terror against civilians as the central method of control. Reprisals for any act of resistance were taken against Jews (and sometimes against Gypsies or communists), with a standard ratio of one hundred locals killed for every German death. By this method the vast majority of Serbia's Jews, about eight thousand, were dead by the end of 1941.

After Serbs, Croatians had been the next most numerous population of Yugoslavia. The prewar Kingdom of Yugoslavia had not been a federation divided into national territories; its electoral districts were gerrymandered to ensure the dominance of Serbs. For these and other reasons, Croatians had substantial grievances about rule from Belgrade, which were articulated by the Croatian Peasant Party. It differed from the radical Croatian nationalists of the Ustaše in that it opposed terrorism. It is impossible that the Ustaše could have come into power in Yugoslavia and extremely unlikely that it would have won elections in a democratic and independent Croatia. The Ustaše was, however, the chosen tool of the Germans. Its regime blamed Serbs and Jews for the existence and injustices of Yugoslavia and undertook a program of ethnic cleansing as a substitute for any actual domestic policy. The largest killing facility in wartime Croatia was the Jasenovac camp complex, a hundred kilometers south of Zagreb. The Serbs were by far the largest victim group there, though, in proportion to the size of their populations, the Gypsies and Jews suffered far more.

Croatia as a state had no hope of surviving a German defeat, and in this sense had no foreign policy and was not sovereign. Croatian authorities deported Jews to Auschwitz in August 1942 and again in May 1943, after most allies of Germany had ceased to do so. All in all about three-quarters of the Jews in wartime Croatia were murdered.

Slovakia was the other German puppet that arose from the wreckage of a multinational state destroyed by Germany. Czechoslovakia had been a multinational but not a federal state, and Slovaks had understandable grievances about the preponderance of Czechs in the administration of Slovak territories. These issues would almost certainly not have brought down democratic Czechoslovakia. In 1938, as he threatened Czechoslovakia with German nationalism in the "Sudetenland," Hitler also encouraged Slovak separatism. The result was that a nationalist fringe gained credibility and was able to join forces with the more mainstream Slovak parties in a campaign for autonomy from Prague. The Slovak state led by Jozef Tiso was created as a result of the German destruction of Czechoslovakia in March 1939. During the transition from Czechoslovak to Slovak law, Slovaks and others stole with enthusiasm from the Jews. Tiso and the leaders of the new state saw this as part of a natural process whereby Slovaks would displace Jews (and, in some measure, Slovak Catholics would displace Slovak Protestants) as the middle class. Laws expropriating Jews thus created an artificial Jewish question: what to do with all of these impoverished people?

Slovakia joined the Axis in November 1940 and participated in the

German invasion of the Soviet Union in June 1941. That September Slovakia passed its own discriminatory Jewish law. In October, Slovak leaders came to an accord with Heinrich Himmler on the deportation of their Jewish population to Auschwitz, and in December they received assurances that those deported would not return. Though some twenty-three thousand Jews did gain access to a bureaucratic exemption, about fifty-eight thousand were deported, most of whom were murdered. In March 1943, after the tide of war had turned, Slovak bishops intervened on behalf of Jewish converts to Christianity and Christians of Jewish origin. Slovak authorities then ceased deportations. In late August 1944, as Soviet forces entered eastern Slovakia, the Slovak resistance began an uprising against the Tiso regime. This brought a German invasion of the country by the German army and an *Einsatzgruppe,* and the murder of a further twelve thousand Jews. In the end, about three-quarters of the Jews of Slovakia were killed.

Romania, Germany's major military ally on the eastern front after 1941, was the only other state to generate an autonomous policy of the direct mass murder of Jews. Historically, antisemitism was far more integral to Romanian political life than to German. In the nineteenth century, state authorities had already identified and stigmatized Jews as a threat to Romanian security; only foreign pressure from the western powers that extended Romania's territory after the First World War brought the Jews inclusion as full citizens. Romania's policy to deport and kill Jews began during the Second World War in connection to a trauma of lost lands. Romania did not lose statehood during the war, but it did lose state territory. Regaining that land would become the central political obsession in Bucharest; Jews on the territory that Romania lost would later be the main victims of murderous new policies.

Romania had been regarded as one of the victor states after the First World War; along with admonitions about equal treatment for Jews had come massive territorial gains. Over the 1920s and 1930s, Bucharest's major institutional and political preoccupation was the romanianization of these new lands. In a matter of a few weeks in the summer of 1940, most of what had been gained was lost. The Soviet Union occupied northeastern

Romania (Bessarabia and northern Bukovina) in June and July 1940 and annexed these territories that August. That same month, Germany ordered Romania to grant northern Transylvania to Hungary. Shortly afterwards Romania lost southern Dobruja to Bulgaria. Thus, something like a third of the national territory and population vanished that summer. The monarchy paid the price. The Romanian king, who had declared himself to be a royal dictator, sought to divert the blame for his weakness to the Jews. Those who deposed him blamed both him and the Jews. In September 1940, General Ion Antonescu seized power with a program of territorial restoration, governing at first with the fascist Iron Guard.

Traditionally Romania had been a client of France, with whose culture Romanian elites identified, whose language was widely spoken, and whose foreign policy had brought Romania's territorial gains after the First World War. Germany had invaded and defeated France in spring 1940, and then forced Romania to cede territory to its neighbors. In this situation, Antonescu's only option, as he saw matters, was to ally with Germany, on the logic that Paris no longer counted and Berlin could alter borders. Romanian propaganda did not criticize German actions, but instead focused on Soviet aggression. Jews lost all of their rights in summer 1940. As part of Bucharest's courting of Berlin, Romanian law was modeled on German law. On January 7, 1941, Antonescu, visiting Berlin, became the first foreign leader to learn of Hitler's plan to invade the Soviet Union. Hitler took the Romanian army seriously; after the destruction of Poland, it was the only sizable force in eastern Europe that could be exploited against the Red Army. Understanding Hitler's intentions and enjoying Hitler's trust, Antonescu felt free to break with the Iron Guard and govern alone.

When on July 2, 1941, Romanian troops joined the German Eleventh Army in an attack on the USSR from Romanian territory, this was, like the German campaign generally, a reinvasion. Romanian troops first reached lands, northern Bukovina and Bessarabia, that had been part of Romania until a year before, when the Red Army had occupied them. As in the Baltic states, the Soviets were in the midst of mass deportations when the Romanian reinvasion took place. On the night of June 12, three weeks before the arrival of Romanian troops, the Soviet NKVD had deported at least 26,173 Romanian citizens and arrested about 6,250 more. Like Germany, Romania portrayed the Soviet Union as a Judeobolshevik state. Massive pogroms were initiated on Romanian territory in the days before the invasion, far exceeding anything possible in prewar Germany. As Romanian forces reinvaded the lands that had been lost to the Soviets, they shot a large number of Jews in the towns, killing some 43,500 in all.

The Romanian political rhetoric was similar to that presented by the Germans. Both Hitler and Antonescu proclaimed a liberation from Judeobolshevism. Germans were telling others (Poles, Ukrainians, Lithuanians, Latvians, Estonians, Belarusians, and Russians) that Jews were communists and communists were Jews. Romanians were telling this to other Romanians. The Germans were unaware at first that most collaboration with the Soviet order had not been Jewish. The Romanians knew that they were creating an alibi for their own people by blaming the Jews for Soviet rule. As elsewhere on the eastern front, the first reaction of local people was personal score settling, with little or no account taken of ethnicity. Romanian forces actually intended to protect local Soviet collaborators who were not Jewish and to punish those who were, and other Jews along the way. Their task was defined as "killing all Jews while protecting pro-Soviet gentiles from the rage of their neighbors." As local Romanians understood, "Nobody except Jews was persecuted at this time!" The ethnicization of guilt was fully planned and conscious.

Romanian soldiers quickly regained these prewar Romanian territories and occupied a good deal of the south of Soviet Ukraine. Like German soldiers, they were followed by special units whose initial assignment was to provoke pogroms. On July 6, 1941, an order from Romanian counterintelligence specified that pogroms were to be organized and given the appearance of spontaneity. In several cases, local populations, Romanians or Ukrainians, killed Jews before the arrival of Romanian troops. As elsewhere, however, most people watched passively. Romanian forces, like German ones in these same weeks, were frustrated that pogroms were not more widespread. After the initial pogroms came a general deportation of Jews from the recovered territories of Bessarabia and northern Bukovina further east to Romanian-occupied territories of the Soviet Union, known as "Transnistria." Some Jews were deported from one part of Transnistria to another. During these deportations, local Romanians and others took advantage of the obvious exclusion of Jews from legal protection. Some raped Jewish women. Others bribed gendarmes for the right to pick prosperous-looking Jews from the columns in order to murder them for their clothing. Nearly two hundred thousand Jews were assembled in makeshift camps created from pigpens, barns, and open fields, where they began to die almost immediately. Those who survived these camps recalled that they were helped by local people, especially women, who gave them food and water at risk to themselves. Romanian troops, meanwhile, carried out mass shootings of Jews as revenge for combat losses to the Red Army. After seventy thousand Romanian troops were lost in the battle for Odessa in October 1941, Romanian soldiers shot twenty-six thousand Jews beyond the city. All in all, this Romanian campaign of comprehensive deportation and sporadic massacre resembled the contemporary German idea of shipping the Jews to Siberia.

From the perspective of Bucharest, however, this anti-Jewish campaign was an attempt at the ethnic cleansing of one of several enemies of the Romanian state. It was carried out in zones where state territory had changed hands twice in two years, and where Jews could be blamed for defeat, scapegoated for collaboration, and eliminated under the cover of war. Romanian authorities also planned to deport Jews from the central part of the country untouched by war, but this proved difficult and in the end did not take place. Romanian Jews in central Romania had never lost their citizenship; there was no cover of war, nor any blame for communism to allocate. Of the 280,000 or so Jews killed as a result of Romanian policy, some 15,000 had lived in prewar Romania on territories that had not changed hands during the war. This was, of course, a significant number, but only about six percent of the total. Just as 97 percent of the Jews killed by Germany had lived beyond prewar Germany, so 94 percent of the Jews killed by Romania lived on territories Romania had lost to the USSR or had gained from the USSR.

In 1942, Romanian policy towards Jews, previously quite cooperative with the Germans, drifted in the other direction. Berlin wanted the remaining Jews under Romanian control sent to Auschwitz, but none were. Bucharest's refusal had to do with calculations of sovereignty. Romania was deporting and murdering Jews on the basis of its own reasoning and for its own purposes. Romanian leaders were annoyed by the high-handedness of the Germans sent to Bucharest to negotiate and vexed that they were asked to deport their Jews while Hungarian Jews and Italian Jews, citizens of other allies of Germany, remained at home. They worried that the removal of Jews would benefit the German ethnic minorities in towns in Transylvania and thus increase German influence in Romania. Above all, Romanians were displeased that their contribution to the war on the eastern front had not led to the return of northern Transylvania from Hungary.

Romanian policy was to murder Jews as a minority that could be removed during the war without larger political consequences. When this calculation changed, so did policy. Romanian policy had also been to deport and murder Gypsies under cover of war; since this policy was coordinated with Jewish policy, it was halted by a kind of accident. In October 1942, the Romanians halted their own deportations and ceased their own killing policies. They also ended discussions of sending Jews to Auschwitz. In 1943, Hitler tried and failed to change Antonescu's mind. Hitler's argument was that Romania's place in a future German Europe depended upon its current attitude towards Jews; Antonescu was of the opinion that the masses of Romanian corpses around Stalingrad were sacrifice enough. Rather than send Jews to Auschwitz in 1943, Bucharest once again extended its protection to Romanian Jews living abroad. The following year Romania reversed its alliances, and its armies finished the war fighting not alongside but against the Germans. All in all, about two-thirds of Romania's Jews survived.

The Romanian Holocaust began with the trauma of lost territory and an associated change not just of government but of regime, from monarchy to military dictatorship. It took place chiefly on the lands that the new regime believed it could win back by force from the Soviet Union. Romanian Jews in places where state territory did not change hands usually saw the end of the war. Romanian Jews at the site of a double regime change—where the Soviet Union destroyed Romanian state structures and then Romania did the same to Soviet structures—usually did not. The logic of the Romanian Holocaust was similar to that of the German Holocaust, with one major exception: Antonescu, unlike Hitler, saw his own state as worth protecting and thus considered the Jewish question, antisemite though he was, to be one issue among others. When the survival of the state was in question, Antonescu slowed the persecution of Jews. Hitler, who actually believed in a world of races rather than a world of states, did the opposite.

Under their longtime ruler, Regent Miklós Horthy, Hungarian leaders set a course towards an alliance with Germany, always keeping an eye on neighbor and rival Romania. Bucharest gained considerable territories after the First World War; its gains then were a part of Budapest's losses. Hungary, treated as a defeated power, lost most of its territory and population by the terms of the Treaty of Trianon of 1920. It recouped some of these losses thanks to Germany twenty years later. As a result of the destruction of Czechoslovakia, it was awarded southern Slovakia as well as Subcarpathian Ruthenia. Romania's loss of northern Transylvania in summer 1940 was Hungary's gain. All of these annexations, achieved without military effort, bound Hungary to Germany. If Hitler could award territory, he could also take it away. Romania fought alongside Germany against the USSR to regain territory; Hungary joined that invasion so as not to lose that same territory. Their war in the East was largely a contest for German favor in the Transylvanian Question.

Budapest passed anti-Jewish legislation on the German model as a signal of its loyalty to Berlin, but this did not, in itself, lead to mass killing. The Jews in greatest danger were the ones who inhabited territories newly acquired by the Hungarian state. Hungarian authorities deported Jews from Subcarpathian Ruthenia across the Soviet border just as Germany was invading the Soviet Union. These Jews were then the victims of the first large-scale shooting of the Holocaust, at Kamianets' Podils'kyi in August 1941. Hungary joined its German ally in the invasion of Yugoslavia in April 1941, and Hungarian forces shot a certain number of Jews there. The army also forced Jews into labor battalions, which then worked in dreadful conditions in the occupied Soviet Union. Some forty thousand Hungarian Jews perished in these units. All the same, the Hungarian leadership never showed any interest in deporting its Jewish citizens to Auschwitz. The government's general attitude was that a purge of national minorities could follow a victorious war.

As a result, some eight hundred thousand Jews were still alive on Hungarian territory in 1944. Since the vast majority of the three million or so Polish Jews had already by this point been murdered, Hungary's was now the most significant Jewish community of central and eastern Europe. In January and February 1943, the Hungarian army suffered huge losses as the Red Army retook the city of Voronezh. The Hungarian government began some clumsy attempts to make contact with the western powers. Learning of this, Hitler blamed the Jews of Hungary. On March 19, 1944, German troops entered Hungary; a few days later Döme Sztójay, who had been serving in Berlin as Hungarian ambassador, was named prime minister. It was this government, created in the unusual circumstances of German occupation and constrained in its freedom of action, which undertook to deport Hungarian Jews to German death facilities.

The German invasion of Hungary was a strange operation, since its purpose was to keep an allied state, and an allied army, in the war on the German side. The point was not to force Hungary to carry out the Final Solution, but rather to swing the balance of Hungarian politics sufficiently so that it might be carried out. The government that the Germans introduced in March 1944 was ideologically more antisemitic. The calculation of the new government, perhaps more important than its ideology, was that the deportation of Hungary's Jews was the price to be paid for the preservation of a Hungarian state. The German occupation was not meant to exploit Hungarians economically, but to divert economic calculations in such a way as to endanger Jews. Nazi ideology presented the murder of Jews as an end in itself. But the strategic calculation was that a Hungary culpable of murdering its Jews would be unable to switch sides.

The expropriation of Jews, as both the German occupiers and the Hungarian government understood, was an opportunity to gain a certain amount of support from the majority population in the strange new situation. That spring the Hungarian government announced a series of reforms that depended, as everyone could tell, on the robbery, and thus indirectly on the disappearance, of the Jews. The property of more than four million dead European Jews having changed hands by this point in time, the connection between expropriation and murder was clear to everyone; and if businesses and apartments were to be transferred, the government wanted to make the arrangements and get the credit. German state destroyers entered Hungary: a Higher SS and Police Leader alongside an *Einsatzgruppe,* the forces that organized the Final Solution in the East, as well as Adolf Eichmann, the SS deportation specialist. In practice, however, the work of deportation depended upon the records of the Hungarian interior ministry and the work of Hungarian local policemen. What this all meant was hardly a secret: On May 10 a *New York Times* headline read "Hungarian Jews Fear Annihilation." Between May and July 1944, some 437,000 Jews were deported from Hungary to Auschwitz, of whom about 320,000 were murdered.

Like all of Germany's allies, regardless of their actual policies towards Jews, Budapest considered the treatment of its own citizens to be a matter of its own sovereign choices. This was true even of the Hungarian rulers that the Germans chose in spring 1944, when Hungarian sovereignty had been compromised but not eliminated by the German invasion. In summer 1944, as circumstances changed, calculations changed as well. That June, the western allies landed in Normandy and the Red Army routed Germany's Army Group Center in Belarus. The Americans, after a series of warnings about Hungary's treatment of Jews, bombed Budapest on July 2. Horthy had remained head of state despite the German intervention and the change of government. He now halted the deportations, thereby sparing most of the Jews of Budapest. He tried again and failed again in October 1944 to change sides. Even as Budapest itself was besieged by the Red Army, the Germans wanted the city's Jews deported. A new fascist Arrow Cross government marked Jewish houses in the capital and created a ghetto; the advance of the Soviets made further transports to Auschwitz impossible. About a hundred thousand Jews were forced to leave Budapest, thousands of whom died in labor battalions. The Arrow Cross murdered about fifty Jews a day by the Danube River.

In the end, about half of the Hungarian Jewish population survived. Most of those killed had inhabited territories that changed hands during the war. The vast majority perished after the German intervention that compromised Hungarian sovereignty.

Bulgaria was the German ally least affected by the war. It never lost territory to any of its neighbors. Bulgarians did not experience occupation of any kind until the very end of the war. The Bulgarian army did not join in the invasion of the Soviet Union. It did, however, take part in the German campaigns against Greece and Yugoslavia in 1941, gaining some of Thrace from the former and Macedonia from the latter. Bulgaria was also granted southern Dobruja from Romania. Bulgarian authorities de-

ported about thirteen thousand Jews from Macedonia and Thrace, following German wishes, on lands they gained thanks to German help. Most of these children, women, and men were gassed at Treblinka.

The Bulgarian government also drew up plans for the deportation of the Jews who inhabited prewar Bulgarian territory, but these were never implemented. Bulgarian Jews often had friends, colleagues, or employers who could explain their value to Bulgarian society. Letters from non-Jewish Bulgarian citizens about Jewish Bulgarian citizens flooded ministerial offices. In March 1943, after the tide of the war had turned,

Bulgarian parliamentarians protested the anticipated deportations. Their resolution failed, but their public airing of the issue made a difference. Leaders of the Bulgarian Orthodox Church intervened on behalf of the Jews generally, and other Bulgarians issued public protests. In the end, the king seems to have changed his mind about the desirability of deporting Bulgarian Jews to their deaths, settling for a removal of Jews from Sofia to the countryside. In 1944, Bulgaria reversed alliances and finished the war on the side of the Allies.

All in all, about three-quarters of Jews on territory controlled by Bulgaria survived. Almost all of those who were killed inhabited territories where regimes had changed during the war.

Italy was Germany's ally, and its *Duce*, Benito Mussolini, was one of Hitler's inspirations. He, rather than Hitler, pioneered the politics of anti-communism, and the deployment of ideological paramilitaries to gain and then transform state power. Mussolini did not, however, see the Soviet Union as part of a planetary Jewish peril to be destroyed, nor did he imagine his Blackshirts as special units with the power to return Europe to some racial Eden by killing Jews. His major colonial aims and thus atrocities were in Africa. Italian troops joined in the invasion of France belatedly and almost irrelevantly, but participated in the invasion of the Soviet Union on a grand scale. Insofar as Italy and its soldiers contributed to the conquest of Soviet territory, they contributed indirectly to the Holocaust. The same, of course, is true of Romania, Hungary, Slovakia, and all of the other German allies on the eastern front. When Italy bungled its invasion of Greece in 1940, it forced the Germans to intervene. In this way Italian aggression created some of the preconditions to the Holocaust in southeastern Europe.

Although Italy did pass anti-Jewish and other racial legislation, Mussolini showed no interest in deporting Italian Jews to their deaths. Beyond Italy, Italian soldiers sometimes sheltered Jews. In general, Jews who had a choice would flee to zones of Italian occupation. As a matter of prestige and sovereignty, Italy would intern rather than deport Jews who escaped from Croatia. The Holocaust in Italy itself began, and could only begin, after Mussolini's fall. In Italy, as elsewhere, a failed attempt to change sides was a disaster for Jews. When Italy's new leaders tried to join the Allies, Germany invaded from the north and undertook the deportation and murder of Italian Jews themselves. In the end, about four-fifths of Italy's Jews survived; without German intervention, almost all of them would have.

Jews who were citizens of Germany's allies lived or died according to certain general rules. Jews who maintained their prewar citizenship usually lived, and those who did not usually died. Jews usually lost citizenship through regime change or occupation rather than by law; slow legal depatriation on the German model was the exception, not the rule. Jews from territories that changed hands were usually murdered. Jews almost never survived if they remained on territories where the Soviet Union had been exercising power when German or Romanian forces arrived. German occupation of states that were trying to switch sides led to the massive killing of Jews, including those who lived in countries where there had been little or nothing of a Final Solution. In all, about seven hundred thousand Jews who were citizens of Germany's allies were killed. Yet a higher number survived. This is a dramatic contrast to the lands where the state was destroyed, where almost all Jews were killed.

None of Germany's sovereign allies was indifferent to the traditional concern of preserving the state. Most of the sovereign states allied with Germany altered their foreign policy in 1942 or 1943 or 1944, as it became clear that Germany was losing the war. This meant reversing anti-Jewish policies, attempting to switch sides in the war, or both. If leaders slowed or halted their own anti-Jewish policies, it was in the hope that the Allies would notice the signal and would treat them more favorably after the war was over. Sometimes attempts to switch sides succeeded and thereby aided the Jews, as in Romania and Bulgaria. Sometimes they failed, as in Hungary and Italy. But it was this very ability to make foreign policy that distinguished sovereign states from puppet states created during the war and from the stateless zones.

This same capacity for diplomacy distinguished Germany's allies from Nazi Germany itself. Until 1942, the Jews of Germany were in a position not so different from that of Germany's allies. From 1942, however, the position of Germany's Jews worsened radically, whereas that of the Jews of Germany's allies generally improved (until and unless Germany itself intervened). Unlike the leaders of Germany's allies, Hitler was indifferent to the fate of his own state, and viewed the extermination of Jews as a good in and of itself. He thought that the world was a planet covered by races rather than a globe covered by states—and acted accordingly. Germany did not have a conventional foreign policy, since its *Führer* did not believe in sovereignty as such and could imagine state destruction as the proper end of the war just as easily as he could see it as the proper beginning.

When the war turned against Germany, the killing of Jews under German control was not slowed, as with Germany's allies, but accelerated. Because the German leadership was pursuing what it saw as colonial (anti-Slavic) and decolonial (anti-Jewish) campaigns from the beginning, Hitler and others could shift emphases from one war to another, and from one definition of victory to another. The leaders of Hungary, Romania, Bulgaria, and Italy had to contemplate the actual military conflict as it unfolded on staff maps. Hitler understood the minutiae of war; indeed, he grasped its details far better than any other head of state and better than most of his generals. But the way he synthesized the data was his alone. For him the German defeats revealed the hidden hand of the planetary Jewish enemy, whose destruction was necessary to win the war and redeem mankind. The extermination of the Jews was a victory for the species, regardless of the defeat of the Germans. As Hitler said at the very end, on April 29, 1945, Jews were the "world poisoners of all nations." He was sure of his legacy: "I have lanced the Jewish boil. Posterity will be eternally grateful to us."

Hitler was seeking to lift a Jewish curse from the planet. This categorical Nazi approach, once it was realized as policy, made possible ethnic cleansing from other countries, since it created a place, Auschwitz, where European Jews could be sent. The German mass murder of Jews created an unusual opportunity for ethnic cleansers elsewhere in Europe, creating possibilities for removing one (of many) unwanted minorities. Such an interaction was possible only because the makers of the Holocaust were realizing the desire to remove all Jews from the earth.

Hitler was not a German nationalist, sure of German victory, aiming for an enlarged German state. He was a zoological anarchist who believed that there was a true state of nature to be restored. The failed campaign in the East brought useful new knowledge about nature: It turned out that the Germans were not, in fact, a master race. Hitler had accepted this possibility when he invaded the Soviet Union: "If the German people is not strong enough and devoted enough to give its blood for its existence, let it go and be destroyed by another, stronger man. I shall not shed tears for the German people." Over the course of the war, Hitler changed his attitude towards the Soviet Union and the Russians: Stalin was not a tool of the Jews but their enemy, the USSR was not or was no longer Jewish, and its population turned out, upon investigation, not to be subhuman. In the end, Hitler decided, "the future belongs entirely to the stronger people of the east."

In the European states linked by military occupation to Hitler's strange sense of destiny, the proportion of Jews who survived varied greatly. The greatest confusion arises over the contrast between European states with significant prewar Jewish populations: the Netherlands, Greece, and France. About three-quarters of French Jews survived, whereas about three-quarters of Dutch Jews and Greek Jews were killed.

Here, as with Estonia and Denmark, intuitions fail to explain this enormous difference. In general, neither the Dutch nor the Greek population was regarded as antisemitic, whereas observers then and historians now chronicle a major current of antisemitism in French popular and political life. In the Netherlands, Jewish refugees were admitted without visas until 1938. In Greece, German-style antisemitism had almost no advocates. Antisemitism was less resonant in interwar Greek politics than just about anywhere in Europe. In the Netherlands, uniquely, there were public manifestations against the introduction of anti-Jewish laws after the German occupation. Persecution of the Jews in the Netherlands had almost no public support. And yet a Dutch Jew or a Greek Jew was three times more likely to be murdered than a French Jew.

The Netherlands was, for several reasons, the closest approximation to statelessness in western Europe. The sovereignty of the Netherlands was compromised in several ways that were unusual in this part of the continent. There was no head of state once Queen Wilhelmina left for London in May 1940. The Dutch government followed her into exile. The bureaucracy, in effect decapitated, was left with the instruction to behave in a way that would best serve the Dutch nation. Uniquely in western Europe, the SS sought and attained fundamental control of domestic policy. Arthur Seyß-Inquart, an experienced state destroyer, was made *Reichskommissar* for the occupied Netherlands. He had served as the chancellor of Austria during the days when that country had ceased to be. He was then deputy to Hans Frank in the General Government, the colony created from Polish lands where, according to the Nazi interpretation, there had never been a Polish state. Such reasoning was never applied to the Netherlands, whose people were seen as racially superior to the Poles, and indeed as part of the same racial group as the Germans. It was nevertheless the state destroyers of the SS who filled the vacuum of the missing Dutch government.

Amsterdam was the only west European city where the Germans considered creating a ghetto. That such a discussion even took place suggests the unusual dominance of the SS. German authorities withdrew the plan after the Amsterdam city council and the Dutch government objected. This reveals the difference between the occupied Netherlands and occupied Poland, where no meaningfully autonomous local or national authorities existed. The Dutch police, like the Polish police, was however directly subordinate to the German occupier. As in Poland, the Dutch police was purged, and its top leadership generally removed. A large number of German policemen, some five thousand, monitored Dutch subordinates. In the Netherlands, as in Poland, fragments of the previous state order—indeed, institutions that had once represented toleration—could be turned to the task of extermination. In Poland, the legal Jewish councils of the 1930s were transformed under the Germans into the *Judenräte*. In the Netherlands, all religions had been organized into communities for purposes of legal recognition, and all citizens were registered according to religion. This meant that the Germans could make use of precise preexisting lists of Jewish citizens. Dutch citizens protested, but it made little difference. The Dutch underground resisted, but this, if anything, only brought more harm to Jews. The German and Dutch police attended to districts where they believed the underground functioned and, in the process, found Jews in hiding.

The situation of rescuers and dissidents was quite different in the Netherlands than in Poland. People who hid Jews in the Netherlands, for example, were usually either not punished or punished lightly. People who protested anti-Jewish laws in public, such as Professor Rudolph Cleveringa at Leiden University, were sent to camps but were not killed. His Polish colleagues in Cracow or Lwów, meanwhile, were murdered for doing nothing other than being professors.

The Dutch were treated as citizens of an occupied country, unless they were Jewish. Because the Netherlands lacked basic institutions of sovereignty, and because Dutch institutions were fragmented on the east European model, the outcome for the Jews was similar, although not quite as awful, as in the stateless zones. The first transport of Dutch Jews to Auschwitz was in July 1942. Because there was no sovereign state functioning, there was no foreign policy, and no ability to change course in 1943. The Germans determined what happened to Jews, which meant that the trains from the Netherlands to Auschwitz kept running through 1944.

Greek sovereignty was also severely compromised, although in a different way. Greece was originally invaded by Italy in late 1940. The Greek army fought the Italians to a standstill, forcing Hitler to rescue Mussolini. The Greek dictator died at what proved to be a critical moment. Germany invaded Greece on April 6, 1941. The king and the government had fled the country by the end of the month. The Germans did not seek to destroy the state in Greece as they had done in Poland, but in these unusual circumstances created an occupation regime in which the Greek puppet government was powerless. Greece lost territory and was occupied by three separate powers: the Germans took the north, allowed the Italians to control the south, and granted part of Macedonia to Bulgaria. No Greek government exercising any real authority was formed during the war. Its head had to submit his nominations for ministerial positions to both the German and the Italian authorities. There was never a Greek foreign minister. The Germans and the Italians did not allow the Greek government to apply for the international recognition of the new regime in its new borders. Greek authorities were unable to control food supplies. Some forty thousand Greeks starved in the first year of the war.

The murder of Greek Jews proceeded where the Germans were in control. Italians saw the Ladino-speaking Jews of Greece, descendants of people who had fled centuries before from Spain, as members of their own Latin civilization. Italian officials provided many such people with bogus attestations of Italian nationality. Salonika, the major Jewish city in Greece, was under German occupation from April 1941. Although the Germans found that "for the average Greek there is no Jewish question," local political and professional elites understood that lawlessness and German priorities could be used to fulfill their own desires. If Jews were no longer citizens of what was no longer really a state, others could make good on prewar claims and satisfy half-hidden desires.

In summer 1942, as the Germans were desperate for labor, local Greek authorities suggested that it might be more politic to use only Jews. This stigmatized one section of the population and confirmed its vulnerability. Later that year in Salonika, the German authorities satisfied a long-standing local postulate by ceding the property of the Jewish cemetery to the city. Such a major property transfer generated a sense of material complicity between Germans and locals as well as a new moral barrier between non-Jewish Greeks and Greek Jews. The destruction of the ancient cemetery and the desecration of hundreds of thousands of remains was painful enough in the present, but also raised a question about the future. If Salonika's Jews were no longer welcome to die in their home city, where would they die?

In the first weeks of 1943, some of Adolf Eichmann's closest colleagues arrived in Salonika with the goal of arranging rapid deportations to Auschwitz. They found little public sympathy for their ideology, it seems, but more than sufficient willingness to exploit the separation of Jews from other Greeks. As Salonika Jews were ordered to wear stars and forced into ghettos, others took their movable property and sometimes their houses. The deportations began on March 15, 1943, the Jews exchanging their Greek drachmas for counterfeit Polish currency. Some 43,850 children, women, and men were sent from Salonika to Auschwitz between March and June 1943. The timing was unusual: right after the German defeat at Stalingrad, when German allies were generally trying to switch sides, or change their Jewish policy as a signal to the Allies. But Greece, although regarded by the Germans as an occupied state, was much more like a stateless territory. It had no army in the war that might change sides, and no foreign minister who might send peace signals.

The French case was very different. The very notion of "collaboration" with Germany, although it has taken on other meanings since, was coined by the French to denote a policy of one sovereign state choosing to cooperate with another. France, in contrast to the Netherlands and to Greece, did retain the basic institutions of sovereignty, and its leaders chose a policy of friendship with the German victors. After Hitler's armies crushed the French in spring 1940, he expressed the wish that "a French government continue to function on French territory." Because France, unlike the Netherlands and Greece, was placed under a traditional military occupation, there was no clear opening for the SS and its state destroyers. The new regime, with Philippe Pétain as head of state and with Vichy as the administrative center, was regarded as the legitimate continuator of the prewar republic, both at home and abroad. High officials in all ministries remained in their positions. Indeed, the number of French bureaucrats increased quite impressively during the German occupation, from about 650,000 to about 900,000. The contrast here with Poland is instructive: For every educated Pole who was murdered during the war, an educated Frenchman got a job in the civil service.

France did introduce anti-Jewish legislation on its own initiative. A "Jewish statute" was passed on October 3, 1940, breaking the long French tradition of treating all citizens in metropolitan France as equal members of the state. (Algeria, though at this time part of the French state, was a different story.) In March 1941, a General Commissariat for Jewish Questions was established to coordinate Jewish policy with Germany. The legalized theft of Jewish property began in France that July. In November, the French government created an official Jewish organization that all Jews in France were required to join. The prevailing idea among French authorities was that Jews could eventually be removed to somewhere distant—such as Madagascar. The new laws were implemented by people who had served the prewar republic.

The reasoning behind French Jewish policy was different than that of Nazi Germany and closer to that of, for example, Slovakia or Bulgaria. In Bratislava and Sofia, as in Vichy, a domestic constituency for ethnic cleansing found itself in an unusual situation: Another state, Germany, actually wished to take some (not all) of the people deemed undesirable. In the late 1930s, before the war, the French Republic had already passed a law permitting the creation of "assembly points," for Jewish and other refugees. The first of these camps had been established in February 1939.

Under the Vichy regime in 1940, the prewar aspiration to limit and control immigration became the open plan to make France an ethnically homogeneous state. Jews without citizenship, along with others who lacked citizenship, were to be removed. After the passage of the "Jewish Statute," foreign Jews were sent to camps. About 7,055 French Jews were denaturalized and thereby placed in the category of greater risk, that of foreign Jews. Policy in France then followed the logic of escalation that was visible in eastern Europe. Major raids and roundups of Jews by the French police were timed with the German invasion of the Soviet Union in summer 1941, with the reversal of the German offensive that winter, and then as retaliation for (very real) French communist resistance in March 1942. By summer 1942, the French roundups included Jewish women and children. Jews in Paris were taken to Drancy, where they were selected for transport to Auschwitz and death.

French and German policies met at a certain precise point. The French placed Jews without French citizenship in camps. The Germans wanted to take such people, but only insofar as the Germans themselves could consider them stateless. Crucially, Nazi malice stopped at the passport: As much as Nazis might have imagined that states were artificial creations, they did not proceed with killing Jews until states were actually destroyed or had renounced their own Jews. The French were willing to round up Jews from Hungary and Turkey, for example, but the Germans were unwilling to kill such people without the consent of the Hungarian and Turkish governments. Germany was entirely willing to murder Jews of Polish and Soviet citizenship, since it considered these states to be defunct. Germany was also willing to take and murder French Jews, but only under the condition that French authorities first stripped such people of citizenship. This the French authorities at first showed a certain inclination to do, although complications of law and bureaucracy delayed the process considerably.

In summer 1942, when the Germans demanded a greater number of French Jews, the highest French authorities reconsidered the question of depriving their own citizens of citizenship. Depatriation was not, for them, a Jewish question, but rather a sovereignty question. After the tide of war visibly turned at Stalingrad in February 1943, French authorities decided not to depatriate any more French Jews. In July 1943, efforts to strip French citizenship from Jews nationalized after 1927 (about half of the Jews who were French citizens) were abandoned. The Holocaust continued in France as a German policy executed with a certain amount of local French collaboration, bringing general terror to French Jews in hiding but achieving relatively little success. A large majority of French Jews, about three-quarters, survived the war.

The decisive matter, here as everywhere, was sovereignty. For French authorities, the Jewish question was subordinate to that of the well-being, as they saw matters, of their state. They certainly wished to remove Jews from France—foreign Jews to be sure and, no doubt, most or all Jews. But they could see the inherent problem of allowing German preferences to determine their own citizenship policy. The moment a state no longer determines internal membership, it loses external sovereignty. By the same token, French authorities had recourse to foreign policy and could react to the course of the war. Unlike the Dutch and the Greeks, who had lost these elements of sovereignty, the French could respond to Allied pressure about the Jews and anticipate a British and American occupation, which was indeed coming.

The Holocaust in France was mainly a crime against Jews who, from a French perspective, were foreign. As François Darlan, head of government in 1941 and 1942, put it: "The stateless Jews who have thronged to our country for the last fifteen years do not interest me." Jews without French citizenship were about ten times more likely to be deported to Auschwitz than were Jews with French citizenship. At Drancy, Jews were selected for deportation according to the vitality of their state. Jews in France understood this perfectly. In 1939, when Poland was destroyed by the joint German-Soviet invasion, Polish Jews living in France flocked to the Soviet embassy in Paris. This was not out of any love for the Soviet Union or communism. They simply knew that they needed state protection. Between September 1939 and June 1941, documents from Hitler's Soviet ally were of great value. But when Hitler betrayed Stalin, and Germany invaded the Soviet Union, these Jews' new papers were suddenly useless.

Considerably more Polish Jews resident in France were killed than French Jews resident in France. Statelessness followed these thirty thousand murdered Polish Jews to Paris, to Drancy, to Auschwitz, to the gas chambers, to the crematoria, and to oblivion.

The likelihood that Jews would be sent to their deaths depended upon the durability of institutions of state sovereignty and the continuity of prewar citizenship. These structures created the matrix within which individual choices were made, the constraints upon those who did evil, and the possibilities for those who wished to do good.

10

The Grey Saviors

In the world that Hitler imagined, killers felt no responsibility for what they did. There was no source of ethical authority for individual action, and no basis for reciprocal social or political relationships: There was nothing except an eternal war among races. In this struggle the Jews were the only immoral ones, since they undercut the natural justice of German victory and thereby the only order that could prevail on the planet. Where the Holocaust took place, states were destroyed, laws abolished, and the predictability of daily life undone. In this grotesque situation the Jews themselves had to bear all of the responsibility for their own lives, for taking extraordinary action, again and again, over days, months, years, in a setting beyond their understanding and their control.

Every Jew who survived the Holocaust had to fight collective inertia, abandon the familiar and the beloved, and confront the unfathomable. Every Jew had some exposure to antisemitism, but nothing in the collective experience of millions of Jews over thousands of years was preparation for what began in 1941. The synthesis of information into knowledge depends upon familiarity, and nothing like the Holocaust had ever happened before. The conversion of knowledge into action was imperiled by hope. Any Jew could imagine that he or she would be spared what was happening to others; the bare fact of life continuing from one moment to the next seemed to suggest the possibility of its further continuation. The certainty of death was hard to confront. It was often difficult to accept that simply doing nothing would be followed by murder. Even a Jew who grasped all that could be grasped of the unprecedented situation, and took every initiative that could be taken, would very likely die.

Almost every Jew who survived had some help from non-Jews, of one kind or another, and usually of many different kinds. Whether Jewish appeals for help would resound depended on both the addressee and the setting. Martha Bernstein, the wife of a cantor in Zweibrücken in southwestern Germany, was someone whose appeal was heard, in a very special set of circumstances, only some of which she understood. Her husband, Eleazar Bernstein, was a man of good deeds and social conscience, who visited prisons to bring cheer and counsel to Jewish prisoners. In one prison, Eleazar befriended Kurt Trimborn, whom he knew as a prison guard and a police captain. The two men played chess.

On November 10, 1938, Eleazar Bernstein was arrested in the wake of *Kristallnacht*, as were thousands of other Jewish men throughout Germany. Martha crossed the rioting city to find Trimborn and ask for help. She was unaware of the extent of his authority in this particular situation. He told her that they must act quickly before the SS assumed control; in fact, he was the SS. He had been a member of the Nazi party since 1923 and exemplified the interpenetration of the SS and the Criminal Police (*Kripo*) in the 1930s. He told Martha to go home and pack. Trimborn had his friend released from custody and then drove the couple and their children to the French border in his own car and got them across. He then seems to have arranged the paperwork to create the appearance that the family had been deported to a concentration camp. The Bernstein family would eventually reach the United States, where they prospered. Eleazar sent Trimborn a letter about the good that was done: He wrote of his daughter who had become a teacher in America, the sons who had become engineers, the grandchildren. All of this thanks to Trimborn.

The letter was written later, much later, in 1978, after Trimborn's trial for murder.

In *Einsatzgruppe* D, first in German-occupied Soviet Ukraine and then in German-occupied Soviet Russia, Kurt Trimborn ordered hundreds of Jews to be murdered and carried out neck shots himself. In at least one case he herded children from an orphanage into a gas van. In the East in 1942, he must have heard pleas for help, as he had in 1938 in Germany. At his trial he said that he had not liked the task of killing civilians and that he had, in some cases, allowed Jews to escape. This is quite possible. He was, after all, the same man. In one setting he was a rescuer, and in another a killer.

In 1938 in Germany, a game of war with clear rules, chess, had led Trimborn to become a friend and a protector. In 1942, in a war beyond Germany where all rules were rejected, Trimborn became a criminal. He used one automobile in 1938 to save three children; he used another in 1942 to kill hundreds: An engine starts, a gas pedal goes down, but in the one case people are driven to freedom and in the other they are asphyxiated. One of Bernstein's children lives today in California in a house full of chess sets. Trimborn's own children did not even know that their father knew the rules.

Most German Jews emigrated before the mass murder began. Most of the Jews who remained in Germany were killed, but only after being deported to a stateless zone, and thereby placed in a helpless situation. In some cases they were shot immediately; in others they joined local Jews in ghettos. Without prior human contacts, and without the local languages, German Jews once deported were almost never rescued. The East was for them a foreign land, just as it was for other Germans. One German Jewish woman, after her deportation to Riga, was brought to the death pits of the Rumbula Forest. Just before she was shot, she called out: "I die for Germany!" The local Jew who heard and recorded this exclamation was astonished by this cry from some other world.

No one can know what the doomed woman was thinking, but her dying commitment was far from absurd. The Germany from which she had been extruded was something that German Jews had helped to build. German Jews identified with Germany as strongly, or perhaps more strongly, than other Germans; its collapse into antisemitism and murder was for this reason a special sort of tragedy; their particular experience of the rise and fall of German civilization, limited to them and alien to the vast majority of European Jews, continues to structure our understanding of the Holocaust.

Only about three percent of the victims of the Holocaust were German Jews. For the Jews of eastern Europe, the vast majority of the victims, Germany was not something that Jews had cocreated but rather something that destroyed Jews. In his "Death Fugue," one of the great short poems of the last century, Paul Celan called death itself a "master from Germany."

The Polish literary critic Michał Głowiński wrote of the experience of his boyhood in his memoir *The Black Seasons:* "My image of the Germans—or rather my image of a German, since my image of the whole nation was embodied in an individual and what the individual did—was extremely straightforward: at any given moment he seeks to murder me, you, someone else. And he will carry out this desire without fail the moment you fall into his hands."

Głowiński, as a young boy in hiding, once played chess with a Polish blackmailer while his aunt sought the money that would save their lives. If his aunt had not succeeded, he would, in all likelihood, have been delivered to a German who would have made sure that he was killed. Głowiński's memory of his boyhood is an accurate presentation of how most Germans behaved in the places where German (or Soviet and then German) power had destroyed the state. These zones of statelessness became places of death for Jews who had lived there before the war as well as for Jews brought there during the war.

The degree of statelessness was so crucial to the life chances of Europeans beyond Germany in part because it was important to the behavior of Germans themselves. The mutation of the German polity after 1933—the creation of a party-state, the establishment of camps, the hybridization of institutions, the discrimination of Jews—gave millions of Germans a taste of the pleasures of lawlessness. During the war, most German policemen comported themselves in one way in Germany and in an entirely different way when dispatched to the East. German soldiers who had previously occupied the peaceful Loire Valley in France could shoot Jews right after they arrived in Belarus. The Order Police of the prosperous northern German port city of Bremen could assemble the Jews of Kyiv at Babyi Iar for the largest mass shooting of civilians in history. Literally nothing could have prepared them for it, and in any case they had no special training for such actions. Yet these policemen were among those who organized and oversaw the killing and who attended a celebratory dinner afterwards. Later they went back to Bremen and to directing traffic.

A lesser known but equally striking example is that of the millions of German women working for the German occupation authorities in the East or accompanying their husbands or lovers on assignments there. About half a million German women served as "helpers" of the *Wehrmacht*, and another ten thousand as "helpers" of the SS. Precisely because the occupied East was governed as a kind of anarchic colony, the flexibility and individual initiative of these women must have been crucial. It goes without saying that they knew about the Holocaust, since many of them saw murders, heard about murders, or wrote and transmitted the reports about murders.

A few German women were direct participants in the killing. Twenty of the guards at Majdanek, for example, were women. This was a concentration camp in the Lublin District of the General Government that became, over time, an extermination facility as well. Some fifty thousand Jews were gassed to death there. These women had their first experience of work as guards in Ravensbrück, the major concentration camp for females in Germany. There they were employed in what was, in effect, a lawless zone inside Germany itself. In Majdanek they were employed in a similar facility, but now surrounded by an anarchic German colony. They took part in the killing of Jews and other prisoners, for example by helping to select who was to labor and who was to be gassed.

Further east, in places such as Latvia and Ukraine, a few German women murdered Jews without the structure and experience provided by such facilities and indeed without any orders to do so. These women went beyond their instructions, in the spirit of what they saw and heard around them every day. German women who killed or took part in the killing of Jews during the war lived unremarkable lives in Germany before the war, and, unless they were prosecuted, which was rare, lived normal lives in Germany after the war. The role that German women played in mass killing was probably indispensable, but women were not taken seriously as actors during the war and were therefore able to shelter themselves after the war. Sometimes they spoke to their daughters.

If statelessness drew German women to the East to become murderers, the fact that Nazi Germany was a state attracted Jewish women from the East. From the perspective of Jewish women in occupied Poland or in the occupied Soviet Union, Germany could be a relatively safe place. Jewish women presented themselves to German occupation authorities as gentiles and asked for labor assignments in Germany, believing, quite correctly, that their chances for survival were higher there. If a woman had a contact in the Polish or Soviet underground (or, more rarely, with a sympathetic German) who could arrange false papers, she could work in relative security in Germany, pretending to be a Pole or a Ukrainian or someone else. For men this was much harder, since Jewish males bore an identifying mark, the circumcision, which could always be checked and would always be a source of anxiety. For Jewish women, however, false documents were a step back toward the world of recognition by the state. To be sure, they were stigmatized as racial inferiors in Germany: Those from Poland wore a patch with a *P*, those from the USSR a patch with the word *Ost*. All were required to live a life only of labor and could expect heavy punishments for breaking rules. Some died from poor working conditions, some were executed for breaking rules, a few were murdered. Nevertheless, a piece of paper that permitted a return to a zone where some kind of law functioned usually meant life.

The end of states meant the end of state protection, and the scramble for the next best thing. When whole countries ceased to be, old passports and identity documents became useless by the million. New ones had to be acquired one by one, and usually on German (or Soviet) terms. The importance of documentation and citizenship was perfectly clear at the time. In the eastern Polish city of Lwów, surrounded by Ukrainians and largely inhabited by Jews, occupied by the Soviets in 1939, the Germans in 1941, and the Soviets again in 1944, a certain lapidary bit of wisdom made the rounds: "The passport is what holds body and soul together." This meant that the people who had the power to rescue others were those who could dispense identity documents.

In eastern Europe most people understood the importance of regime transitions, and with time the western Allies also came to grasp the importance of documents. An attempt by the United States to rescue Jews depended precisely on the provision of documents and thus the extension of state recognition. In 1944, Washington appealed, under the auspices of the War Refugee Board, to European neutral states to use their diplomats to rescue Jews. Sweden cooperated with this plan, providing an amateur diplomat named Raoul Wallenberg. He was to enter Hungary in 1944, with the mission of extending to Hungarian Jews the protection of the Swedish state. Wallenberg did have backing from his own government and from the Americans, but he also knew that he was opposing German policy and provoking Hungarian fascists. Nevertheless, he issued something like fifteen thousand "protection passports," and probably saved more Jews than anyone else.

Wallenberg, an exceptional man, represented a certain class of rescuer, diplomats who, by virtue of their position, embodied state sovereignty and could confer state recognition. In general, the only people who could rescue Jews in large numbers were those who had some direct connection to a state and some authorization to dispense its protection. A diplomat could grant to a Jew a passport or at least a travel document—an invitation to return to the world of human reciprocity, in which a person must be treated as a person because he is represented by a state. Wallenberg was a businessman who chose and was chosen to act as a diplomat at a crucial moment: the German occupation of Hungary, when the largest remaining population of European Jews was under threat. Yet there were also other professional diplomats who found themselves serving in situations where the sovereignty of the states in which they worked was compromised, who understood that this was a disaster for Jews, and who chose to try to save them.

One such man was Ho Feng-Shan, the consul of the Republic of China in Vienna when Austria was incorporated by Germany in March 1938. Ho identified with the Austrian state and nation, and he sympathized with Chancellor Schuschnigg in his resistance to the Nazis, whom he regarded as "the devil." Ho took a rather unusual view of the essence of national greatness, believing that it was "only possible through inclusion and tolerance." His response to the "scrubbing parties" and pogroms that followed the collapse of Austria was to give Chinese visas to Jews. He issued at least a thousand, some of them to people whom he personally extracted from concentration camps. Ho could not have known in 1938 what fate awaited Jews who remained in central Europe, but he was responding to what was, at the time, an unprecedented outbreak of violence against them.

After the German occupation of the Netherlands in spring 1940, the Swiss consul, Ernst Prodolliet, issued Swiss transit visas to Jews. He was ignoring instructions to the contrary. When the Swiss consulate was closed in 1942, he left its funds with people who were trying to help Jews escape from Europe. As German forces reached France that same spring, French Jews fled southward, where some found assistance from diplomats who allowed them to continue their flight. In Bordeaux, the Spanish consul Eduardo Propper de Callejón issued thousands of transit documents to Jews and others. He was one of several Spanish diplomats throughout occupied Europe who worked in this direction. Aristides de Sousa Mendes, a Portuguese consul in the same city, also issued thousands of documents that allowed Jews and others to leave France. These men were assisting total strangers. They were using the authority inherent in their positions against prevailing policy.

A diplomatic rescuer whose actions were closer to official policy was Chiune Sugihara, the Japanese consul in Kaunas, Lithuania. He was assigned to Lithuania in 1939 in order to observe German and Soviet troop movements and predict the outbreak of the German-Soviet war. After September 1939, citizens of Poland, Jews and non-Jews alike, fled both the Germans and the Soviets to Lithuania. Particularly after the Soviets incorporated eastern Poland and began deportations to the Gulag, Jews sought refuge in Lithuania. The Soviet deportations of April 1940, which targeted Jews in large numbers, caused a mass flight of Jews to Vilnius and Lithuania generally. In Vilnius that month, some 11,030 Jewish refugees were registered. At the very moment when the Soviet Union occupied Lithuania, in June 1940, it was also carrying out another wave of deportations of Polish citizens, chiefly Jews. This brought a double panic among Jews: they had fled Soviet power in Poland only to find themselves pursued by Soviet power to Lithuania. They found in the Japanese consul a sympathetic listener.

In the 1930s, Sugihara had learned Russian, married a Russian woman, and converted to Russian Orthodoxy; he wanted people to call him Sergei. He spoke Russian with his colleagues in Polish military intelligence in the 1930s, as they all cooperated in the Promethean project and in other anti-Soviet plans. During the war, even after Poland was destroyed in September 1939, he continued to work with Polish officers in the Baltic states. His main contact was Michał Rybikowski, who was running an Allied spy network from neutral Sweden and reporting to the Polish government-in-exile in London. Rybikowski was posing as a Russian and using a passport from the Japanese protectorate Manchukuo, which he presumably obtained from Sugihara. (Because there were many Russian emigrants in Manchukuo, a European with such a passport, especially a Russian speaker such as Rybikowski, would not attract attention.) The cooperation between Sugihara and Rybikowski prepared the way for Sugihara's eventual action to help Jews.

One of Rybikowski's assignments was to manage the consequences of the Molotov-Ribbentrop pact and the German-Soviet invasion and occupation of Poland by aiding Polish refugees. His particular task in Lithuania was to prepare an escape route for Polish citizens who had gotten that far and wished to continue their flight from Europe. To this end he recruited two further officers of Polish military intelligence, Leszek Daszkiewicz and Alfons Jakubianec, who got passports from Sugihara and were employed by the Japanese consulate.

The scheme that the Polish intelligence officers invented for Polish refugees was to get a Japanese transit visa for a destination that did not demand an entrance visa. Jan Zwartendijk, the honorary Dutch consul, was willing to sign a declaration to the effect that entering Curaçao, an island in the south of the Caribbean Sea that was a Dutch colony, did not require a visa. The two Poles created a template for a special Japanese transit visa for travel to Curaçao as well as two special visa stamps, one for themselves and one for Sugihara. The original idea, as seen from the perspective of the Polish government-in-exile, was to save Polish citizens who were particularly valuable. Since transit was to be by train across the Soviet Union to Japan, the intelligence officers no doubt hoped to gather useful information from their handpicked refugees.

In the chaos of the summer of 1940, as the Soviets deported masses of people from eastern Poland and established their new regime in Lithuania, the three men gave visas to everyone who asked. Of the 3,500 or so visas they issued to Polish citizens, about two-thirds were given to Polish Jews. Since one visa sufficed for a family, some eight thousand Jews left Europe thanks to these documents. Like Ho in Vienna two years earlier, Sugihara could not have known what would happen to Jews if they remained in Lithuania. He was reacting to the refugee crisis brought on by the German occupation of western and central Poland and the Soviet occupation of eastern Poland and Lithuania. Nevertheless, he clearly felt sympathy for refugees and wished for them to survive; in this sense he consciously rescued Jews. He described the source of his actions at least once, in a brief memoir written in Russian, "as my sense of humanity, from love for my fellow human being." Daszkiewicz, not at all a sentimental man, wrote later that Sugihara was "a man who had a good heart."

Once they had done what they could, Sugihara and his two Polish employees left Kaunas for Stockholm and traveled from there to Germany. Sugihara's mission was to predict when the Germans would attack the Soviet Union—which he estimated correctly within a few days. Shortly after Operation Barbarossa began on June 22, 1941, one of his two Polish confederates, Jakubianec, was discovered by the Gestapo in Berlin, and shot as a spy. Although Jakubianec was working with the Japanese, he was reporting to his superior Rybikowski, who was serving the Polish government-in-exile and thus Britain and the United States. His execution was the end of a man who had invented a scheme that had saved thousands of Jews. But he was not executed for that, or remembered for that, or indeed for anything. His refugee scheme had nothing to do with sympathy for Jews; it was a clever manipulation of the artifacts of collapsing statecraft.

Daszkiewicz continued working for Sugihara, now in Prague, within the Protectorate of Bohemia and Moravia and thus in the Reich. He tried to make contact with the Czech underground. The discovery and death of his friend Jakubianec forced him to leave Europe. He chose to work in Palestine, a traditional terrain for Polish intelligence operatives.

During the Second World War, Palestine was still under a British Mandate, and Poland was a British ally. Before the war, Poland had been pursuing an anti-British policy in Palestine, preparing Jewish revolutionaries for their moment of opportunity: a war or a moment of British weakness. The prewar Polish consul, Witold Hulanicki, remained in Jerusalem during the war, working for the British, while maintaining his relationship with his main Jewish contact and friend, Avraham Stern. It was Stern, ever the seeker of risk and glory, who saw the Second World War as the chance to defeat the British, even going so far as to solicit the help of

Nazi Germany (without success). In a tiny group known as Lehi, Stern exploited Polish training and probably Polish weapons in a campaign of violence against the British. He was fulfilling his political program, but also pursuing a spectacularly enunciated death wish. He met the ideal fate of the Polish Romantic rebels whose martyrological ideas he deepened in his own poetry. After Stern was shot and killed by a British policeman in 1942, the work of Lehi was continued by Yitzhak Shamir. The next year Shamir's partner in anti-British violence would be Menachem Begin, who in 1942 was on his way to Palestine by a very circuitous route.

In the late 1930s, Begin and the young men of Betar had planned to create a State of Israel by descending upon Palestine to support an uprising initiated by Irgun. This was an operation that was to be carried out by Jews who were Polish citizens with the support of the Polish authorities. The destruction of the Polish state in 1939 made such schemes impossible, as Polish aid to Irgun collapsed and the leaders of Betar did their best to flee to Vilnius. Some were placed in ghettos by the Germans; others were arrested and deported by the Soviets. Begin himself was among the Betar activists deported to the Gulag in 1940.

When Nazi Germany attacked the Soviet Union in 1941, Stalin altered his attitude towards the male Polish citizens in his custody. They were to be allowed to leave the Gulag and form a Polish army to fight against the Germans. Stalin had no interest in Polish citizens fighting on the eastern front, where they might later pose a problem for Soviet power. The Red Army had, after all, invaded Poland once already during the war, and these were precisely the people who had experienced oppression by the NKVD. Best then to force them to fight on the western front, far from the USSR and Poland, where ideally they could kill Germans and die themselves. In order for Polish citizens to travel from the Gulag to the western front, they had to journey from one end of the Eurasian landmass to the other, from the Soviet north, far east, or Kazakhstan through India and Iran and Palestine to western Europe.

This new Polish armed force, created at the sufferance of Stalin and subordinate to the Polish government in London, was commanded by Władysław Anders and so known as the Anders Army. Many of the commanders of the Anders Army had little interest in Jews or held antisemitic stereotypes about their value in combat. But Jews were, nevertheless,

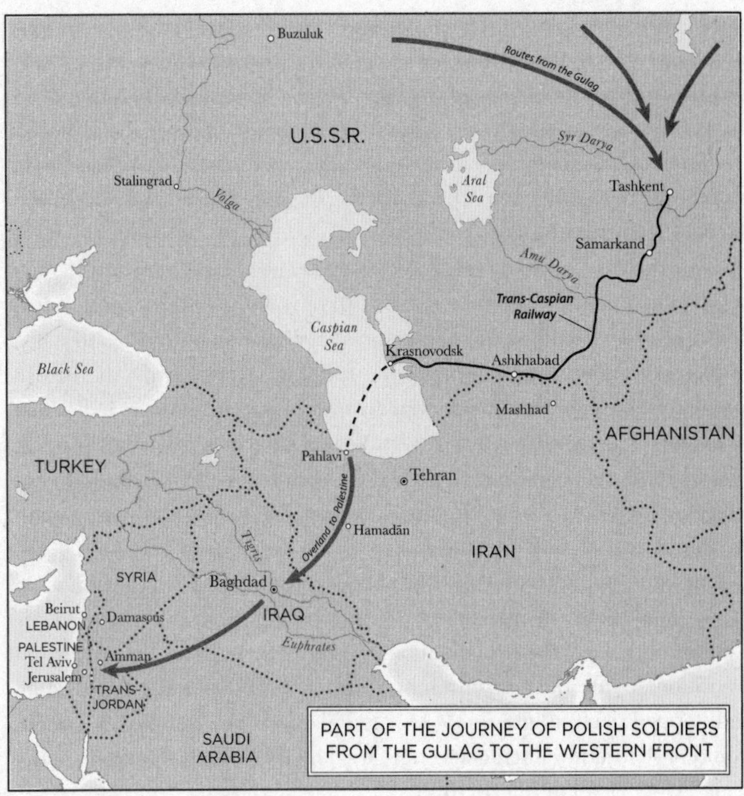

among the Polish citizens who joined its ranks. For whatever reason—because they were more likely to be targeted by Stalin, because they were more eager to fight, or because they had better relations with Polish officers—Betar members and Revisionist Zionists were present in the Polish army in considerable numbers. In this way many right-wing Zionists did make their march from Poland to Palestine, if by a very long and indirect route. The British stopped Jews who tried to come to Palestine by sea during the war, but they could hardly stop Jews who came by land in Allied uniforms.

The arrival of these Jews in Palestine revitalized Irgun. Begin reached Palestine with the Polish army in May 1942. There he encountered Wiktor Drymmer, who as director of Poland's Jewish policy in the late 1930s had been Begin's patron. Drymmer had worked to create the conditions for a large migration of Polish Jews to Palestine by way of supporting Betar and Irgun. Now he helped to arrange Begin's honorable discharge from the Polish army, so that he need not face the shame of desertion as he left a conventional armed force to serve an unconventional one. When Begin was chosen to lead Irgun in October 1943, the only clothing he owned was his Polish army uniform.

Now that the war had turned decisively against Nazi Germany, Begin's Irgun joined Shamir's Lehi in anti-British terrorism. This meant that two Polish Jews were leading the anti-colonial resistance against Poland's ally. In February 1944, Begin declared the revolt of Irgun against the British mandatory government. Begin was in every conceivable way a product of Poland. His deputy in Irgun was Yaakov Meridor, who had lived in Poland until 1936 and had returned for training by Polish military intelligence in 1939. Moshe Nechmad, responsible for Irgun operations in the Haifa district, had also taken part in the exercises in Poland in 1939. Eliahu Lankin, the Jerusalem commander of Irgun who led the attack on British intelligence in July 1944, was another Polish product. Lehi under Shamir organized the assassination of Lord Moyne that November, on the rationale that the British minister of state had opposed a Jewish state and stopped the immigration of Jews to Palestine. The techniques learned from Polish military intelligence were used by Irgun in the bombing of the King David Hotel in July 1946.

During the Second World War the Polish state existed only in the echoes of its former policies and in its flight from its own territories. The efforts made by Polish diplomats and intelligence officers in the late 1930s to create the conditions for a State of Israel did bear fruit, but only after the war. Though some of these pro-Zionist Poles, such as Hulanicki, remained active in Europe or Palestine, the Polish government itself had to flee the European continent. It evacuated Warsaw with what was seen as scandalous haste in September 1939, and made its way to Paris through Romania. After the German invasion of France, it moved again to London. There Polish ministers found themselves in a curious position. The British had entered the war on their behalf, to protect the sovereignty and borders of Poland. That objective had not been met. Poland was Britain's only ally between the fall of France in June 1940 and the entrance of the Soviet Union into the war a year later. But after the Soviet Union and then the United States entered the war in 1941, the Polish connection counted for much less.

Poland remained a formally sovereign state thanks to the legal continuity of its government-in-exile. The Germans did not recognize this government, since it claimed to represent a state that the Germans maintained had not existed. Neither did the Soviets, except for a period in the middle of the war, between the German invasion of the Soviet Union in 1941 and the visible turn of the tide of war in 1943.

The London exile government exercised formal command over the underground state in Poland and its armed forces. The Polish armed resistance, best known as the Home Army, was a vast umbrella organization that included dozens of fighting groups from the center right to the center left of the political spectrum. In principle, its chain of command was subordinate to civilian control in London. In fact, the connections with the people who ran the military and civilian organizations in Poland were slow and irregular, dependent upon couriers making long and dangerous journeys across occupied Europe. For the most part, Polish sovereignty in London meant the ability of Polish authorities to communicate with their British allies. But even such a highly constrained form of sovereignty did have some significance for Polish Jews.

The Polish government in London, unlike the Polish prewar government, comprised all of the major political parties, including the antisemitic National Democrats. It was facing a German occupation of Poland that was bloody beyond the imaginations of British politicians and public opinion. It was also confronted with a domestic Polish population who had been taught to expect, under the previous Polish regime, that one day most Jews might leave Poland. The arrival of the Germans in half of Poland in 1939 had led to the disappearance of Jews in most of the places they had lived for hundreds of years: as they were concentrated in ghettos in 1940 and 1941, and then as they were murdered in gas chambers in 1942. Poles from the eastern half of Poland, invaded by the Soviets in 1939 and reinvaded by the Germans in 1941, had seen the Jews there murdered in the open air in and after 1941; some of them propagated the version of events that the Nazis also preferred: that the Jews had earned their fate as Soviet collaborators. This was a convenient fiction, but it was often believed by Poles in western and central Poland. As the commander of the Polish underground wrote to the Polish prime minister in London, the "crushing majority" of the Polish population under German occupation was antisemitic. The Polish government in London, which did have direct sources of information on the mass shooting and then the mass gassing of Jews, sometimes blurred this information into general reports of German terror against Polish citizens.

All the same, Polish authorities did convey accurate information about the mass murder of Jews to their British and American allies and to the wider public in 1942. The Polish prime minister, Władysław Sikorski, was quite unambiguous about the significance of the clearing of the Warsaw ghetto that summer: "This mass murder has no precedent in the history of the world; all known cruelty pales in comparison." Polish information undergirded Allied press briefings and reports in the British press and on the BBC. Poles and Polish Jews alike believed that the Germans would stop murdering Jews when their actions were made known to the world; in this sense the Polish government did take the action that it believed would halt the killings. Warnings did have some effect on Germany's allies, but not on Germany itself.

On November 27, 1942, the Polish National Committee, a kind of ersatz parliament supporting the government abroad, demanded that the Allies intervene to stop the killing of Jews. On December 4, the *Times* of London reported that Germany planned a "complete extermination" of Jews under its control. On December 10, the Polish foreign ministry added its own pleas to the Allies to act. In unmistakable language, the Polish government demanded immediate action to prevent the Germans from completing their project of "mass extermination." This statement led to a firestorm in the British press and in the House of Commons, whose members stood for a moment of silence in recognition of the deliberate murder of millions of European Jews. In this way, Poles contributed to the declaration issued by the British and their American and Soviet Allies on December 17, 1942, demanding that the Germans and their partners cease killing Jews.

This warning, issued not long before the German defeat at Stalingrad, was no doubt understood by Germany's allies as providing the way to signal that their own loyalty to Berlin was conditional. It helps to explain why Slovakia, Romania, and France all changed their policy towards Jews quite significantly in 1943, and why Sweden began to demonstrate its willingness to help Jews. In this way, even limited Polish sovereignty—the ability of Polish authorities to convey credible information to their British and other Allied counterparts—was significant to the Jews.

The availability of plausible firsthand information about the mass murder of Polish Jews depended upon the courage of extraordinary individuals, who tended to be rather close to the state in both its prewar and wartime incarnations. One of these was Jan Kozielewski, known as Jan Karski, the only man in the history of the Holocaust with direct access to both the lowest of the horrors and the highest of the powers. Karski was twenty-five years old when the war began, but was already well informed about the Jewish question in Poland. As a talented young diplomat he worked first in the emigration section of the Polish foreign ministry, the unit charged with finding ways to reduce the number of Jews in Poland. From May through August 1939, he worked as the personal secretary for Drymmer, the man in charge of the support for Betar and Irgun, and this at the most intense time of Polish-Zionist contacts. Karski was Drymmer's secretary when Britain publicized its policy of restricting Jewish immigration to Palestine and Irgun began its actions against the British, and when Polish weapons were loaded onto ships bound for Palestine.

In August 1939, Karski was mobilized to the Polish military base at Oświęcim. He fled with his unit eastward, where he was taken prisoner by the Red Army. He escaped execution as a Polish officer by pretending to be an enlisted man and then jumping from a train. He found his way back to Warsaw, where he saw his brother, the commander of the Warsaw police. His brother faced the dilemma of all police officers at a moment of foreign occupation: collaborate and risk serving the interests of a foreign power, or refuse to collaborate and risk chaos and lawlessness. In order to try to resolve this question for his brother, Karski traveled as a courier to seek the Polish government-in-exile, at the time in France.

Upon his return to Poland, Karski began to attend with pained interest to the fate of the Jews. He seems to have felt quite keenly the connection between the National Democrats' desire for a Poland without Jews, the policy of the prewar Polish government to promote emigration, and the Nazi elimination of Jews from Polish life. Although the means the Germans used were alien to Polish politicians, the result corresponded to a vision that had been widespread in Poland after 1935: a country without 90 percent of its Jews. The imaginary social revolution of the second half of the 1930s, the fantasy of taking all of those Jewish homes and businesses, was actually fulfilled in the early 1940s. German rule broke the previous Polish social order by punishing the elites and killing the Jews, largely destroying the prewar middle and upper classes. Karski wrote to the Polish government that the transfer of property had created a "narrow bridge" between the Polish population and its German masters. The attitude of Poles to Jews he described as "generally severe, and often ruthless."

Most of the Jews of Warsaw were deported to the death facility of Treblinka and murdered in the *Grosse Aktion* of July–September 1942. In October, Karski entered the Warsaw ghetto, led by a Bundist through a tunnel dug by Revisionist Zionists, the group that had been the clients of Karski's superiors in the foreign ministry. Some of the people he met on the other side, members of Betar, had been part of Karski's brief three years before, when he had been Drymmer's secretary and presumably handling the paperwork on the planned emigration of Jews from Poland. Now the men of Betar were planning to fight the Germans (although some of them were still serving, in Warsaw as around the country, in the Jewish police that had just completed the deportations). Leaving the tunnel, Karski entered the building where, a few months later, the Revisionists would raise, following their own tradition, both the Zionist and the Polish flags as they rose against the Germans in the ghetto. Karski was told exactly what had happened to Warsaw Jews. His contacts asked him to help by pleading with the western Allies for action and revenge.

In October 1942, Karski reached London—no simple undertaking for a Polish courier in occupied Europe in the middle of the war. He brought with him his own observations and experiences as well as three written reports on the murder of Jews in Poland. In London, he spoke to Polish authorities and to British intellectuals and public figures: Gerald Berry, Victor Gollancz, Ronald Hyde, Allen Lane, Kingsley Martin. One aspect of his message was a simple repetition of prewar Polish foreign policy: that Polish Jews should be allowed to go to Palestine. In strong contrast to the interwar years, this plea expressed the desperate hope of the Jews themselves, who were facing a German policy of total murder. But London was far from the Warsaw ghetto, a different world. Karski was told in no uncertain terms that Jewish immigration to Palestine would not be allowed. Thus British policy, like Polish policy, remained in a sense unchanged from 1939. Karski also spoke to the American ambassador, who told him that quotas allowing Jewish immigration to the United States were unlikely to be increased. In fact, the number of Jews admitted would actually decrease. Between July 1942 and June 1943, only 4,705 Jews were admitted to the United States—fewer than the number of Warsaw Jews who were killed on a given day at Treblinka in summer 1942.

In all of his discussions, as in his memoir of 1944, Karski was unusual in drawing a clear line between the German policy of social decapitation and mass terror towards Poles, and the German policy of the total extermination of Jews. His efforts contributed to the Polish information campaign that preceded the Allied warning of December 1942. Karski himself believed that he had failed, but the observations he made and the risks he took contributed to actions that had the effect of allowing Jews to live.

Rescue was usually grey.

By the time of the warning of December 1942, most Baltic, Soviet, and Polish Jews under German occupation had already been murdered. The shooting of Jews in the occupied Soviet Union that began the previous year had continued throughout the spring and summer of 1942; Operation Reinhard, the gassing of the Jews of the General Government at Bełżec, Sobibór, and Treblinka, was complete that fall. As the Red Army pressed forward after its victory at Stalingrad in February 1943, it was overrunning the death pits (and in some cases finding them). Before long, Soviet soldiers would reach the killing facilities in the east of occupied Poland.

Under this pressure, the center of Germany's murderous campaign would shift west to Auschwitz.

The concentration camp Auschwitz was established in 1940 on the site of the Polish military base at Oświęcim, the very place where Karski had reported for duty as a Polish officer in September 1939. In summer 1940, Polish males, often politically active, began disappearing from the streets of Warsaw, dispatched to Auschwitz. Another member of the Polish underground volunteered to learn the truth about this mysterious place. As the Germans were raiding Warsaw neighborhoods regarded as elite and intellectual, Witold Pilecki walked into a roundup. Pilecki was a farmer, local activist, and reserve officer with combat experience in the Polish-Bolshevik War. He had been a member of the Polish Military Organization. Though now a married man with children, he volunteered for Auschwitz. He was dispatched on the second Warsaw transport of 1,705 men, among people who would be registered at the camp under the numbers 3821-4959 and 4961-5526. He described his own entry into the camp as the moment when he "finished with everything that had been on earth and began something that was beyond it." Pilecki remained in Auschwitz for almost three years, seeking to organize an underground within the camp and smuggling out notes. He escaped in 1943, and two years later wrote a long, detailed report of life at Auschwitz. He described the punishment and murder of Poles in 1940 and 1941, the imprisonment and gassing of Soviet prisoners of war in 1941 and 1942, and finally the transformation of the camp into a major killing facility for Jews.

Pilecki was a patriot, who believed that Auschwitz was simply one more test of Polish character, a test that some people failed and some people passed. Pilecki's major preoccupation was the possibility of Polish resistance, within the camp and without. Indeed, once he had escaped he immediately rejoined the Polish underground, and fought in 1944 in the ranks of the Home Army in the Warsaw Uprising. Nevertheless, Pilecki had no difficulty seeing and recording the distinct horror of German policy towards the Jews. At the time the gassings of Jews began, Pilecki had a labor assignment that allowed him to walk from the barracks to a tannery. He wrote of the murdered Jews from this perspective: "Over a thousand a day from the new transports were gassed. Their corpses were burned in the new crematoria." And then of everyone else: "As we marched to the tannery, raising dust from the gray path, we could see the beautiful sunrise, pinkening the lovely flowers in the orchards and the trees by the path. On the way back we saw young couples taking a stroll, inhaling the charm of spring, or women peacefully pushing their children in strollers. And then arose a thought that would stay in the mind, knock against the inside of the skull, disappearing perhaps for a moment, but then again stubbornly seeking an exit or an answer to the question: 'Are we all people?' The ones walking through the flowers and the ones going to the gas chambers? The ones marching beside us with rifles and we who have been prisoners for years?"

Karski and Pilecki were men whose primary loyalty was to a Polish state, or to the traditions that they associated with a Polish state, open to redefinition after its destruction and fragmentation. They always claimed that what they did was entirely uninteresting, a matter of duty, nothing more than anyone would or at least should have done in their place. They were curiously unaffected by the absence of actual state institutions, internalizing the obligations arising from membership in a polity while constantly reconsidering for themselves just what those obligations meant—always in the direction of demanding more rather than less of themselves. Their entire posture makes no sense without Polish statehood, but their actions went far beyond what anyone but they themselves expected.

A third outstanding member of the Polish underground, Władysław Bartoszewski, would later make the point, repeatedly and with some irritation, that individuals who worked on behalf of Jews did not first ask the Polish nation for permission to do so. As it happened, the young Catholic activist Bartoszewski was on the same transport to Auschwitz as Pilecki and 1,703 other Polish men on September 22, 1940. While Pilecki remained at Auschwitz to organize and to report, Bartoszewski was released in April 1941 (as some people were) and returned immediately to the Polish underground in Warsaw. Among many other commitments, he became active in Żegota, an umbrella group of organizations in Warsaw and other cities that worked to rescue Jews.

Some 28,000 Jews were hiding in Warsaw on the Aryan side, beyond the ghetto; of these, some 11,600 survived. Of the 28,000, some 4,000 received help in the form of money, food, shelter, and emotional support from members of Żegota. Most of the money came from the Joint, an

American Jewish nongovernmental organization, but was delivered in the money belts of Polish paratroopers dropped from British planes. Żegota was a Polish government organization, and as such represented the first state policy (and one of very few) designed to keep Jews alive. Once the money was delivered, which was no minor undertaking, everything depended upon the people of Żegota.

Among Żegota's leaders in Warsaw there was a certain dominance of members of the Polish Socialist Party. It had been the largest party in Warsaw before the war, counting many Jewish members and voters, and had opposed the prewar regime and its policy of Jewish emigration. A good deal of rescue involved socialists helping fellow party members whom they had known before the war. In general, Żegota's leaders had experienced German oppression. Its director, Julian Grobelny, was arrested by the Germans and then spent much of the war in hospital. Irena Sendlerowa, who along with other women rescued a large number of Jewish children, had been imprisoned by the Gestapo. Bartoszewski and Tadeusz Rek had both been in Auschwitz; Adolf Berman had escaped the Warsaw ghetto.

At the same time, a number of people active in Żegota were also from the antisemitic Right. The most outspoken of these was Zofia Kossak. She was the founder of the civil organization that preceded Żegota, and her significance as a rescuer is indisputable. She was concerned for the souls of Catholics who could stand by and do nothing while mass murder took place before their eyes. She was also worried that after the war Jews would blame the killing on the Poles. Antisemitic rescue was not as contradictory as it might appear. Almost no one rescued Jews from a sense of obligation to Jews; a few people rescued Jews out of a sense of obligation to fellow human beings. The antisemitic rescuers tended to dislike Jews and want them out of Poland, but nonetheless regarded them as human and capable of suffering. In some cases, antisemites who rescued Jews thought of themselves as protecting Polish sovereignty by resisting German policy; in other cases they were acting from a sense of charity.

The most effective rescuers were, and had to be, people who had good contacts with assimilated Jews, who, in their turn, had further contacts with other Jews. Such people were not antisemites. A good example was a leading Żegota activist in Warsaw, the well-connected Maurycy Herling-Grudziński. An impressive figure, he was widely known in Warsaw among

Poles and Jews alike as an outstanding lawyer before the war. Using money from the Polish government-in-exile, he was able to aid more than three hundred Jews on an estate beyond Warsaw. The first people he rescued were his professional peers, jurists, and intellectuals. Then came Jews who were more socially distant.

Like Pilecki, Karski, and Bartoszewski, Herling-Grudziński was a member of the Home Army, the military arm of the Polish underground. He fought in its ranks in the Warsaw Uprising of 1944, where he was wounded in battle. Like Pilecki (from eastern Poland), Karski (arrested by the Soviets in 1939), and Bartoszewski (who would later spend years in a Stalinist prison), Herling-Grudziński also felt the effects of Soviet power. Gustaw Herling-Grudziński, the chronicler of the Gulag, was Maurycy's brother. While Maurycy was hiding Jews in Warsaw, Gustaw was felling trees in a camp in the Soviet far north.

After the war was over, Maurycy would become a leading jurist, while Gustaw would become an admired writer. Neither of the two Polish brothers would make much of a fact that might have been crucial to their fates: They were Jewish.

All rescue involved self-rescue.

11

Partisans of God and Man

Anszel Sznajder and his brother jumped from a train evacuating them from Auschwitz in January 1945. The two of them spoke both Polish and Russian, and intimidated the locals by suggesting that they were fighting in the ranks of the Polish Home Army or with the Soviet partisans. Depending upon their initial impressions of the people they met, the brothers decided which story to use. The essential part of the story, the part that had to be believed, was that they had comrades who would protect or avenge them, "a force backing us up." They needed to be seen not as two isolated Jews who could be killed, but as fearsome men who were part of something larger: an army or a state.

The Sznajder brothers were among the few Jews who made the threat of violence work for them. Sometimes Jews survived because they joined the forces that resisted the Germans, or pretended to have done so. More often, however, the Jews who were trying to take shelter from German killing policies were exposed to greater risks by open opposition to German rule. When French communists began to resist, the first victims of German retaliations were Polish Jews in Paris. In Serbia, the partisan resistance was used by German occupation authorities as the prompt to exterminate Serbian Jews. In the Netherlands, where there were many rescuers and many resisters, the two groups got in each other's way. Where the German police sought the Dutch resistance, they tended to find Dutch Jews. In Slovakia, a national uprising led to a German intervention and to the murder of thousands of Jews who would otherwise most likely have survived.

This bloody irony was also apparent in Poland and the western Soviet

Union, where more Jews were in hiding, where German rule was more violent, and where resistance was widespread. The Warsaw Uprising of August 1944 was the most significant urban rebellion against German rule. Although it was organized and fought in the main by the Polish Home Army, it was, perhaps, the largest single effort of Jewish armed resistance. In all likelihood, more Jews fought in the Warsaw Uprising of 1944 than in the Warsaw Ghetto Uprising of 1943 (and some fought in both). The Home Army was not technically a partisan army: Its members wore uniforms or insignia to distinguish themselves from civilians, and they were subordinate to the Polish government-in-exile in London. The official German position was that the Polish state had never existed, and German forces applied their main anti-partisan tactic by shooting civilians—at the very least 120,000 of them—in Warsaw. The defeat of the Warsaw Uprising meant the physical destruction of the entirety of Warsaw, building by building, just as the ghetto had been destroyed the previous year. Up until that point the survival chances of a Jew in hiding in Warsaw were about the same as that of a Jew in hiding in Amsterdam. When Warsaw was removed from the face of the earth its Jews had no place left to hide.

The Soviet partisans were the most significant irregular force fighting the Germans in the countryside of eastern Europe. They did not distinguish themselves from civilians. Instead, they mixed among them, knowingly bringing German reprisals upon villages, counting on this as a means of recruitment. In the hinterland behind the German advance, chiefly in northwestern Ukraine and Belarus, Soviet partisans had to compete with the Germans for the loyalty of the villages, which meant, in practice, for their food. If villagers gave food to the Soviet partisans, then the Germans killed everyone in that village, including any Jews in hiding, often by immolation in a barn. If villagers gave food to the Germans, they risked violence at the hands of the Soviet partisans. The nature of partisan warfare was fatal for Jews who were attempting to hide.

The fact that the Sznajder brothers so casually claimed to be with the Poles one moment and with the Soviets at another defies the logic of the postwar polemics. The great quarrel today is not between defenders of Nazis and defenders of the resistance. It is, rather, between the defenders of the two major groups who resisted the Germans behind the eastern front: the Polish Home Army and the Soviet partisans. Both of these groups were fighting the Germans, but both were also aspiring to control the same east European lands after the war—lands that were also the world homeland of the Jews. The German eastern empire overlapped with the territory of historic Jewish settlement, which overlapped with the interwar Polish state, which overlapped with the security zone that Stalin wished to establish between Moscow and Berlin after the war.

The Jewish question, in later polemics, became a tool in an argument about the right to rule: the Polish claim to national independence against the Soviet claim to revolutionary hegemony. Defenders of the Polish resistance claim that Soviet partisans could have liberated no one, since they were servants of advancing totalitarian repression. Defenders of Moscow maintain that the Home Army was fascist, since it was not an ally of the Soviet Union. In fact, on the Jewish question, the two groups were rather similar, since their similar form as quasi-state organizations was more important than their different ideologies.

Some distinguished soldiers and officers of the Home Army opposed both the German occupation of their country and the German policy of murdering all Polish Jews. Maurycy Herling-Grudziński, Władysław Bartoszewski, Jan Karski, and Witold Pilecki all served in the Home Army. It was not at all uncommon for people who sheltered Home Army soldiers to also shelter Jews. Henryk Józewski, the interwar governor of Volhynia who had supported both the Promethean project in Soviet Ukraine and Revisionist Zionism, spent the war in the Polish underground. One of his many hiding places was in Podkowa, west of Warsaw, with the Niemyski family, whose main project was rescuing Jews. Northeast of Warsaw, in Ostrów Mazowiecka, Jadwiga Długoborska hid both local Home Army officers and Jews until she was executed by the Gestapo. Jerzy Koźmiński, like Karski and Pilecki a Home Army member who was dispatched to Auschwitz, chose not to correspond with his family when offered the chance. He did not want to endanger the Jews who were hiding in his house by revealing his home address. Michał Gieruła was another Home Army soldier who was hiding Jews. When he was denounced, some of the Jews he was sheltering were killed in his home. He and his wife were tortured by the Germans, but did not reveal the hiding place of the remaining Jews.

They were then executed by hanging. As one of those Jewish survivors later put it, the Gierułas "sacrificed their lives in exchange for ours."

The Home Army also carried out some actions to save Jewish lives, or support Jewish struggles. Probably the most significant way the Home Army and other Polish political organizations aided individual Jews was by the production of false German documents. Their famous "paper mills" could generate German *Kennkarten,* indicating that Jews were, in fact, Poles: "Aryan papers," as Jews called them at the time. Usually Poles took money or goods for this, but not always. The Home Army had a Jewish section, led by Henryk Woliński, which supplied information to foreign media beginning in early 1942. The official press organ of the Home Army, the *Information Bulletin,* reported on the Holocaust at every stage. The paratroopers who were dropped in British planes over Warsaw, their money belts stuffed with cash to help Żegota rescue Jews, were soldiers of the Home Army.

Thousands of Jews either joined the Home Army or claimed to have joined the Home Army as an explanation for their underground existence. In general, such a strategy could work only for the minority of Jews who could pass as Poles; others would almost certainly be denounced. The Warsaw region of the Home Army supplied the Jewish fighters of the ghetto with the weapons that they used to establish their authority and then more weapons that they used in the Ghetto Uprising of April 1943. In a few minor cases, small detachments of Jews were allowed to associate themselves with the Home Army. The Jews who fought in the Warsaw Uprising in August 1944 were not so much joining the Home Army (although some had done so) as joining in a battle that they saw as for their own freedom. As one of them described the thinking: "A Jewish perspective ruled out passivity. Poles took up arms against the mortal enemy. Our obligation as victims and as fellow citizens was to help them."

In the opening days of the Warsaw Uprising, on August 5, 1944, one Home Army detachment liberated KZ Warschau (Concentration Camp Warsaw), which had been a major site of the murder of Jews and Poles. Most of its prisoners were foreign Jews, Greeks who had been transported from Auschwitz because they were deemed capable of heavy labor. Because this Home Army operation was entirely symbolic and without strategic significance, it was carried out entirely by volunteers. One of them was Staszek Aronson, a Jew who had jumped the train to Treblinka and had returned to Warsaw to fight in the Home Army. Many of the Jews liberated from the camp joined the uprising. But some of them were shot, still wearing their camp uniforms, by members of a smaller Polish underground group, the right-wing National Armed Forces (Narodowe Siły Zbrojne, NSZ).

The Home Army was a continuation of the prewar Polish army and a legally constituted organ of the Polish government-in-exile abroad. As such it was open to all Polish citizens. But unlike the prewar Polish army, which was integrated in fact as well as in principle, the Home Army was seen to be an organization of ethnic Poles. The war and the deliberate German and Soviet extermination of the Polish political nation tended to push Poles towards an ethnic understanding of armed struggle. The Judeobolshevik myth provided the moral cover for robbery and murder of Jews by units of the Home Army, which certainly took place. In 1943, as the surviving Jews of Poland were in hiding, the Home Army was instructed to treat armed Jews as bandits. Sometimes this meant that the Home Army executed them, but sometimes it did not. At the very same time, the Home Army issued death sentences upon Poles who were blackmailing Jews and carried out a few. The National Armed Forces (which Jewish survivors, understandably, often confuse with the Home Army) simply took it for granted that Jews were among the foes of the nation. Although the National Armed Forces were much smaller than the Home Army, they probably killed more Jews.

The myth of Judeobolshevism could also be murderous for the Poles who were trying to help Jews. In June 1944, Ludwik Widerszal and Jerzy Makowiecki, two members of the Home Army high command who had been most responsible for aiding Jews, were murdered by their own colleagues, apparently after a denunciation that they were working for the Soviet Union. The deed was arranged by Witold Bieńkowski, himself an antisemitic rescuer of Jews. Such incidents were possible in the political environment of occupied Poland towards the end of the war, where patriotic resistance against German occupation gave way to fear of a return of communism. The same Red Army that was now advancing as a liberator from German rule had occupied Polish territory not long before as an ally of Germany. Polish Home Army soldiers were certainly correct that people

ADVANCE OF RED ARMY
1943–1944
Summer 1944
Spring 1944
Autumn 1943
FINLAND
SWEDEN
Helsinki
Lake Ladoga
Leningrad
Jan 1944
LENINGRAD
Tikhvin
Tallinn
Baltic Sea
Novgorod
Jan 1944
3rd BALTIC
NORTH
Pskov
Demyansk
Riga
Kholm
2nd BALTIC
Volga
Kalinin
Velikiye Luki
Nevel
Rzhev
U.S.S.R.
Danzig
REICHSKOMMISSARIAT OSTLAND
Vitebsk
June 1944
1st BALTIC
Moscow
Kaunas
GERMANY
Vilnius
July 1944
Smolensk
3rd BELARUS
Oka
CENTER
Front line
Aug. 19, 1944
Białystok
July 1944
Minsk
July 1944
Ryazan
2nd BELARUS
Bobruisk
Bryansk
Warsaw
Łódź
Brest
July 1944
Orel
Pinsk
Pripiat
Homel
1st BELARUS
Polesian Marshes
Lublin
July 1944
Chernihiv
Kursk
Voronezh
Cracow
Lutsk
GENERAL GOVERNMENT
Rivne
Feb 1944
Lviv
July 1944
Zhytomyr
Kyiv
Dec 1943
Belgorod
1st UKRAINIAN
4th UKRAINIAN
Kharkiv
Aug 1943
Don
Front line
July 17, 1943
Dniester
Vinnytsia
Dnipro
HUNGARY
NORTH UKRAINE
Chernivtsi
REICHSKOMMISSARIAT UKRAINE
Dnipropetrovsk
2nd UKRAINIAN
Stalino
Don
Chisinau
Taganrog
Mariupol
Rostov
Mykolaiv
Melitopol
SOUTH UKRAINE
Odessa
Sea of Azov
3rd UKRAINIAN
ROMANIA
Crimea
Kerch
Bucharest
Danube
Sevastopol
May 1944
Novorossiysk
Sofia
BULGARIA
Black Sea
GREECE
Istanbul
TURKEY

in Poland would collaborate with Soviet power and right to fear that the Soviet Union could dominate Poland after the war. It was the identification of communists as Jews and Jews (and their supporters) as communists that was the lethal error.

Although communism had been illegal in Poland before the war, and the interwar Polish communist party had been tiny, communism did provide some Polish citizens a compelling alternative to national identity. Very often, people who were communists by conviction (as opposed to apparatchiks of a communist regime) did help Jews after the German invasion. People who were accustomed to persecution for their beliefs tended to be more generous to others who suffered during the war.

In villages where communism (or its front organizations) had been popular before the war, pogroms against Jews in 1941 were less likely. Communist party membership before the war always involved meaningful social contacts between Jews and non-Jews, and always required experience in life underground. Communism also meant, for non-Jews, a worldview that competed with the everyday antisemitic discourse of the National Democrats and the Polish Right generally in the 1930s. One Polish citizen, a nurse who worked in a hospital in Białystok before the war, befriended Jewish doctors. Like a considerable number of her fellow Belarusians who lived in Poland in the 1930s, she was sympathetic to communism and disgusted by what she remembered as "ubiquitous antisemitism."

Though communist ideology was friendlier to Jews than most varieties of patriotism, the wartime circumstances of actual recruitment to the Soviet partisans were difficult for Jews. In the places where the Soviets had ruled in 1939 and 1940, in the doubly occupied territories and in the prewar Soviet Union, the Germans carried out the Holocaust by shooting in 1941 and 1942, delegating the task when they could to Soviet citizens. This meant that in the occupied Soviet Union, the number of local young men who took direct part in the murder of Jews was high, far higher than in occupied Poland to the west. To the Soviet partisans, however, the members of the auxiliary police forces were a precious resource, to be brought over if at all possible to their own side. The result was that the Soviet partisans, behind the German lines, were fighting amidst the killing fields and recruiting the killers, sometimes by promising them amnesty. Anton Bryns'kyi, a Soviet partisan commander so friendly to Jews that he was rumored to be Jewish, recruited from the German police apparatus. Indeed, in late 1942, Ukrainian nationalists were quite concerned that young Ukrainian auxiliary policemen, whom they regarded as their future cadres, were instead leaving to fight for the Soviets. One Ukrainian policeman, in a dramatic example of this trend, saved his Jewish girlfriend from the death pits by switching sides just before she was to be shot and taking her with him to join the Soviet partisans.

Jews who knew the local terrain deliberately recruited the murderers of their fellow Jews to the Soviet partisans. Izrael Pińczuk was a young Jewish man from a tiny village called Gliny, near Rokitno, in Volhynia. When the killing began, Pińczuk did not want to be separated from his mother. Like many Jewish fathers, brothers, and sons, his first thoughts during the mass murder were of his family. His mother told him to save himself so that he could say kaddish for her. At first he disobeyed and followed the rest of the community towards death. But then the men were separated from the women at a transit camp in Sarny, and he never saw his mother again. Having listened to rabbis prophesy the return of the messiah and proclaim the need to accept death with dignity, Pińczuk ran and made his way to local peasants whom he knew and trusted. Then he joined the Soviet partisans, and turned his deep local knowledge to their purposes. "I have a whole staff of local people recruited by me," he said, "among the local people, Ukrainians, who went over to the service of the Germans, and now come over to our side. Although this is an element that served the Germans and even robbed and killed Jews, it is much better to have them as our collaborators rather than as enemies favoring and serving the Germans."

Not every local Jew working for the returning Soviet regime was so explicit about this question, but the experience was a general one. Such side switching was necessary for the existence of the Soviet partisans, who were often double or even triple collaborators. The result was a curious mixture, in the ranks of the Soviet partisans, between Jews who were seeking to save themselves from the Germans and murderers of Jews who were seeking to save themselves from Soviet revenge for their collaboration with the Germans. Some of the Soviet commanders from prewar Soviet territory were themselves antisemites, who found in the partisans an opportunity to express and act according to views that were illegal in the Soviet Union itself. Jews seeking to join the Soviet partisans had to deal with, in various measures, the kinds of people they had been seeking to escape. Many Jews who tried to join the Soviet partisans without weapons were murdered instead. Some who tried to join were first robbed of their weapons and then killed.

Nevertheless, the Soviet partisans were, for most Jews, the closest thing to a friendly army and the best opportunity for self-rescue by taking sides. The commanders of the Soviet partisans who were friendly to Jews and saved their lives were people from both sides of the Polish-Soviet border and of various nationalities. Perhaps the most warmly remembered of them was "Max," who served under Anton Bryns'kyi in northwestern Ukraine, in Volhynia. Max was rumored to be many things but was, in fact, a Pole named Józef Sobiesiak. He was one of the few, and perhaps the only, partisan commander who sought out contacts within ghettos in the hopes of rescuing Jews. On one occasion he ordered a punitive expedition against a pair of Ukrainians who had raped and turned in two Jewish girls who had been in hiding. The two Ukrainians were shot, their houses were burned down, and warnings were left for their neighbors. The partisan who led this punitive exhibition was himself a Ukrainian.

A substantial number of the Jewish men who joined the Soviet partisans and fought with vigor were from Volhynia. Like Belarus to the north, Volhynia was a terrain well suited to partisan warfare. As the Germans undertook to complete the liquidation of ghettos in Volhynia in autumn 1942, Soviet partisans were already known to be in the vicinity. In comparison to Belarus, its people were highly politicized, in all possible directions: Ukrainian, Polish, Jewish, communist, and nationalist. The much-loved Polish Soviet partisan commander Max was active in this region. A certain level of Jewish initiative resounded in the Jewish voices of wartime Volhynia. Many of the Jews who joined the Soviet partisans in Volhynia had already fled to the marshes before the Soviets arrived. Some of them had formed family camps, where women and children were sheltered and fed. Jewish men from Volhynia were articulate about their motives: "the magnificent feeling of the deed, of the struggle for victory." Or: "I am glad that I took some revenge. With every German I killed I felt better."

In the late 1930s, the Polish army had trained young Jewish men in the use of firearms in the Volhynia region, where Betar and Revisionist Zionism were popular. The Jews fighting in the swamps of Volhynia, like Jews of this part of Europe generally, lived not only in the midst of a German project to kill them all but among rival ideas of what their political future should hold: Israel, Poland, the Soviet Union. All of these Jews, so long as they lived, were touched not only by the campaign to kill them but also by all three of these visions of political life. Max remembered the names of the three family camps established by Jews: "Birobidzhan," the name of the Soviet autonomous zone for Jews; "Nalewki," the major Jewish neighborhood in Warsaw; and "Palestine," the Mediterranean land that members of Betar had promised to themselves.

In 1943 and 1944, some Jews were fighting alongside the Soviets against the Germans in the marshes of what had been remote Polish borderlands; others, sometimes their neighbors, had been deported to the Gulag, then had made their way with a Polish army through India and Iran to Palestine, where they would fight the British in the deserts of what would become the State of Israel.

Both the Soviet Union and Poland claimed the territories where Jews lived and died, and the Soviets were intent on overwhelming not just the Germans but any forces that supported Polish independence. All organized attempts to rescue Jews had to become politicized, since from a Soviet perspective any organization, regardless of purpose, was either pro-Soviet or anti-Soviet. In the Stalinist understanding of reality, there was no society as such and no space for independent action. Anything that took place had to be seen not as an element of a complicated reality but as a reflection of the basic conflict between the proletariat and its global capitalist oppressors—which meant, in practice, the Soviet leadership and those it deemed hostile at a given moment. People who rescued Jews on a large scale, regardless of their own personal sentiments, were inevitably classified one way or the other. Those who lived under Soviet rule usually understood all of this.

One such person was Tuvia Bielski, a shopkeeper and miller's son from prewar Poland's major stretch of forests and swamps in the northeast, in what is today western Belarus. Bielski was a Polish citizen who had performed military service in the Polish army between 1927 and 1929. He first experienced Soviet rule during the German-Soviet invasion of 1939, when eastern Poland was annexed to the Soviet Union. Bielski moved then to the city of Lida and worked for the Soviet trade apparatus. After the German invasion of the Soviet Union in June 1941, Bielski tried to defend Jews from mass murder. He and his brothers established a family camp in the Naliboki Forest in early 1942. Like other family camps, this was a Jewish initiative; but, as elsewhere, the leaders had to come to an arrangement with the Soviet partisans. Bielski convinced local Soviet partisans that he was one of theirs, and in late 1942 he and the men who protected the family camp were formally subordinated to Soviet command. The price of this was that Bielski and his men took part in Soviet operations against the Polish Home Army.

The Soviet Union had invaded eastern Poland in 1939 as an ally of Germany and arrived in eastern Poland again in 1944 as an enemy of Germany. Stalin explained to his British and American allies that the Soviet Union would treat the lands gained by alliance with the Germans as if they had always been Soviet. The Soviet forces that arrived in these lands, now for a second time, had amnesia among their ammunition. The previous Soviet invasion of Poland and the associated destruction of the Polish state in 1939 were to be completely forgotten. The arrival of Soviet forces in prewar Polish territory in 1944 was to be a liberation from fascism, nothing less and nothing more.

This powerful myth could admit no objection. Moscow's actual responsibility for inviting the Nazis into eastern Europe was to be purged from Soviet history, distributed instead among the enemies of the moment, people deemed to be potential opponents of Soviet power. Since the populations that fell under Soviet rule in eastern Poland had been Polish citizens before 1939 and had therefore experienced a Soviet occupation between 1939 and 1941, everyone was in some sense suspect, because their lives contradicted the political line. Bielski himself was a Zionist who named his family camp "Jerusalem." Zionism was a risky allegiance, and one that he would not have mentioned to his Soviet comrades. Fighting on the same side as the Soviets, against the Germans, was not enough to be on the right side of the story. The fact that Bielski was willing to use his men in actions against Polish forces, whatever he personally thought about it, was likely a necessary demonstration of his loyalty. Bielski had played chess with the local commander of the Home Army. His actions were no doubt dictated by his correct understanding of what the Soviets expected.

Although the Polish army, unlike the Red Army, had never engaged in combat as a German ally, the Soviets had no trouble seeing the Poles as fascists. In the Stalinist world of discourse, a "fascist" was not a Nazi or someone who had helped the Nazis; a "fascist" was someone who was deemed by the Stalinist regime not to be working in the interests of the Soviet Union. As a general rule, the Red Army would allow the Poles to engage in combat against the Germans, and then disarm them and give them a choice between subordination to Soviet command or the Gulag. In some cases, Polish soldiers, and especially Polish officers, were simply murdered. After the Red Army had reached Berlin and defeated the Germans in May 1945, it returned to the forests of northeastern Poland for a separate operation against the remnants of the Home Army. After the clearing of the Augustów Forest in June 1945, some 592 Polish men were executed. About forty thousand Polish men were sent to the Gulag at war's end, seventeen thousand of them on accusations of having served in the Home Army—which was the largest underground organization in Europe to resist the Nazis from the beginning of the war to the end.

Between 1945 and 1949, in the four years after the war, as communists supported by Moscow made their way to total power in Poland, Soviet propaganda developed the postwar line that supporters of Polish statehood, supporters of Jewish statehood, Americans, Nazis, and fascists were all somehow essentially the same people. The United States had remained politically present in Europe by extending the aid known as the Marshall Plan; Israel was established as an independent state in 1948 but did not become, as Stalin had hoped, a Soviet client; and the North Atlantic Treaty Organization (NATO) was founded in 1949 as a military alliance to the west of Stalin's empire. In the Soviet propaganda of the early Cold War, the same alignment of forces that the Red Army had defeated in 1945 were still at large in the world, ready at any moment to attack the homeland of socialism. The actual facts of the matter—who had fought against whom and who had collaborated with whom between 1939 and 1945—were largely irrelevant. History was not to be discovered and understood

Oslo
NORWAY
FINLAND
Helsinki
Leningrad
RUSSIAN S.F.S.R.
Stockholm
Tallinn
ESTONIAN S.S.R.
Novgorod
Volga
SWEDEN
Kalinin
DENMARK
Riga
LATVIAN S.S.R.
Copenhagen
Baltic Sea
Moscow
LITHUANIAN S.S.R.
Vitebsk
Kaliningrad (RSFSR)
Kaunas
Smolensk
U.S.S.R.
Bremen
Gdańsk
Vilnius
Szczecin
Minsk
Bryansk
Berlin
Białystok
BELARUSIAN S.S.R.
EAST GERMANY
Poznań
POLAND
Warsaw
Łódź
Pinsk
Kursk
Voronezh
Radom
Wrocław
Lublin
Chernihiv
Don
WEST GERMANY
Prague
Lutsk
Vistula
Cracow
Kyiv
Zhytomyr
Kharkiv
CZECHOSLOVAKIA
Lviv
Danube
UKRAINIAN S.S.R.
Dnipro
Munich
Dnister
Dnipropetrovsk
Stalino
Vienna
Bratislava
AUSTRIA
Budapest
MOLDOVAN S.S.R.
HUNGARY
Chisinau
Cluj
Odessa
Sea of Azov
Trieste
Zagreb
Venice
ROMANIA
Crimea (RSFSR)
Belgrade
Sevastopol
Yalta
YUGOSLAVIA
Bucharest
ITALY
Sarajevo
Danube
Black Sea
Rome
Sofia
Skopje
BULGARIA
Tirana
Istanbul
ALBANIA
Ankara
GREECE
TURKEY
Izmir
Athens
Konya
Adana
Aleppo
SYRIA
Mediterranean Sea
LEBANON
Beirut
Damascus
West Bank
Tripoli
ISRAEL
Tel Aviv
Amman
Benghazi
Jerusalem
Gaza
TRIPOLITANIA
CYRENAICA
JORDAN
Gaza Strip
EASTERN EUROPE AND ISRAEL c. 1949
Cairo
EGYPT
Sinai
Soviet satellites
Other communist states
SAUDI ARABIA
Nile

but to be worked into a shape that was suitable for the future of the Soviet political order. All governments do this in some measure; the Soviet aspiration was unusual because it was total.

Polish soldiers who had spent the whole war fighting the Germans were classified as fascists and sometimes even executed along with German prisoners. Meanwhile, Poles who had tortured and murdered Jews during the war joined the Polish communist party, which was reestablished under Soviet tutelage, and became supporters of the new Soviet-backed communist regime in Poland. Such double collaboration was politically explicable, since people who had carried out German policy needed protection in the new order. It was also politically necessary. Just as people who resist one form of tyranny will tend to resist another, people who have collaborated with one form of tyranny will tend to come to terms with the next. Multiple collaboration was inevitable in a country such as Poland that had first been divided between the Germans and Soviets, then completely occupied by the Germans, and then completely occupied by the Soviets.

Any Marxist could have explained why Soviet power in postwar Poland could not be pro-Jewish. Poles, like everyone else in Europe under German occupation, had taken Jewish property. Because Jews had been so numerous in Poland, and because the share of urban property owned by Jews had been high, this amounted to a dramatic transformation of the whole society. It was not that all Poles were poorer than all Jews before the war. Nor was it the case that Poles prospered during the occupation—the scale of destruction, even in the countryside, was something inconceivable in western Europe. What was telling for the future was the German politics of relative deprivation: taking something from everyone, but taking everything from the Jews, and then taking their lives. This created the gaps—the empty apartments and commercial and professional niches—that Poles filled with all the greater determination given their losses during the war and their uncertainty about what was coming next.

The Soviets entered a country devastated by war and faced a population that was generally hostile. Rather than questioning the Nazi social revolution in Poland, Soviet power sanctioned it. In effect, though not by design, the Germans had carried out the first stage of the standard two-part Soviet revolution: the transfer of property from a group deemed to have no future to another group that then becomes beholden to authority—preparatory to the completion of the revolution by collectivization. Soviet and thus Polish communist propaganda denied the special suffering of Jews and portrayed their murder as part of the general martyrdom of peaceful Soviet or Polish citizenries. If there was no Holocaust and therefore no ethnic specificity to German policy, then there could not have been an ethnic transfer of property. Property became a point of contact between the Soviet authorities and the local population, much as it had between the German authorities and the local population. The Germans allowed Poles to steal, and the Soviets allowed Poles to keep what they had stolen. The consequences of the Holocaust became part of the legitimation of Soviet rule.

Soviet-style rule in Poland as elsewhere required a monopoly on virtue as well as control over the past. Resistance to the Soviets was by definition pro-German and reactionary, since History had only two sides. Any true wartime opposition to the Germans must have been organized by the Soviets. Other forms had no right to exist, and so had to be crushed if they still existed, presented as somehow objectively pro-Nazi and "fascist." The Warsaw Ghetto Uprising of 1943 was revised as communist (and therefore not essentially Jewish) and thus acceptable; the Warsaw Uprising of 1944 was presented as fascist and consigned to oblivion. The Home Army was presented as a partner of the Nazis, even though the men and women of the Polish resistance were being tortured in Gestapo prisons while the Soviet Union was still Nazi Germany's ally.

Poles who had rescued Jews were sometimes troublesome in the new communist order, since they drew attention to the social basis of Soviet rule (the far larger number of Poles who had stolen from Jews) as well as to the hollowness of the Soviet characterization of the war (fascists against the USSR and its peaceful citizens). Thus, individual Poles who resisted the Germans *and* resisted the Soviets *and* drew attention to the special Jewish plight were a hindrance to memory policy. Witold Pilecki, who volunteered for Auschwitz and fought in the Warsaw Uprising, was shot by the Polish communist regime as a spy. Władysław Bartoszewski, who had been sentenced to Auschwitz by the Germans and who had worked ably to rescue Jews in Żegota, was sentenced to prison by the communists for his service in the Home Army. Jan Karski, who had voluntarily entered the Warsaw ghetto and had tried to explain to western leaders the character of the Final Solution, was in emigration after the war, and so beyond the reach of Polish communist authorities. Soviet propaganda slandered him as an antisemite. In Palestine, Witold Hulanicki, the Polish diplomat who supported Jewish revolutionaries, was murdered, most likely on Soviet instructions. The most effective rescuer of Jews in eastern Europe, the amateur diplomat Raoul Wallenberg, was arrested by Soviet counterintelligence and held in the infamous Lubianka and Lefortovo prisons. He died in Soviet custody, although to this day no one knows the details.

As the example of Wallenberg illustrates, the total need to allocate good and evil extended beyond the Polish and Jewish questions. The Soviet return to Europe meant the establishment of friendly, which is to say communist, regimes in Hungary, Czechoslovakia, Bulgaria, and Romania, as well as in Poland. In none of these places would the robbery of Jews be challenged, and in none of them would the murder of Jews enter history as a distinct subject. Nowhere would the people who risked their lives to rescue Jews be regarded as heroes. Those who helped Jews were portrayed as those who somehow got more money for saving them than they did by killing them. Rescuers in eastern Europe generally tried to conceal what they had done, so as not to arouse the interest of neighbors who might want to search for Jewish valuables. The powerful and enduring myth of Jewish gold and jewelry in the houses of rescuers reflects the mindset of those many Poles and east Europeans who robbed and killed Jews, not that of those who helped them. But since under Stalinism no contrary moral discourse could appear, materialism was all that remained.

Klimenty Sheptyts'kyi was another Polish citizen and rescuer of Jews who was punished by the Soviets after the war. He was a Greek Catholic churchman, an archimandrite of the Studite Order of monks, representing a faith that in its liturgy was eastern, like the Orthodox Churches of Ukraine and Russia, but in its institutional hierarchy was western, in that it was one of the many smaller Catholic churches subordinate to the Vatican. Following the instructions of his brother Andrei, who was the metropolitan of the Greek Catholic Church, Klimenty and other monks and priests hid more than a hundred Jews, many of them children, in their cathedral complex, Saint Jura, in Lwów—which they, as Ukrainians, called Lviv.

Andrei Sheptyts'kyi was the only Christian churchman of such high rank to act decisively against the mass murder of Jews. He had initially welcomed the German invasion as a liberation from Soviet rule, which had targeted not only his church but an increasing number of his flock. Without ever changing his opinion about the evil of the Soviet regime, he quickly came to believe that Nazi occupation was worse. Aside from his labor of rescue, which was of course secret, he protested to Himmler, protested to Hitler, and asked the pope to intervene to protect Jews. He told Pius XII that Jews were "the first victims" of German rule and that National Socialism meant "hatred of everything that is honorable and beautiful." He issued pastoral letters reminding his flock of the divine commandment not to murder. He also classified murder as a reserved sin, which meant that Greek Catholics who killed human beings had to confess personally to him. Because Andrei Sheptyts'kyi was aged and crippled, these confessions were his way of being informed about what he understood as a deluge of sinfulness among his people. Hearing confession required him to face the truth, time after time, of what many Ukrainian Christians were doing to Jews. He died in November 1944, not long after the return of the Red Army. The Soviets forcibly subordinated the Greek Catholic Church to the Moscow Patriarchate of the Orthodox Church, which they had long before humiliated and tamed. When Klimenty refused to renounce his faith, he was sentenced to prison in Soviet Russia, where he died in 1951.

The Sheptyts'kyi brothers were no doubt unusual human beings, and Andrei was acting from a position of some authority. As an archbishop of the Catholic Church, he was far less vulnerable to German oppression than the vast majority of the population and the vast majority of churchmen. His church was also in a special position, in that its believers had been subject to Soviet occupation in 1939–1941, when the Soviet Union annexed eastern Poland. Many of the Ukrainian nationalists whom the Germans induced to collaborate after 1941 were Greek Catholics. Although many of these young men did not heed the instructions of their metropolitan, they would have reacted negatively had the Germans arrested or killed Sheptyts'kyi. In this sense his status was something like that of a diplomat, and his ability to exploit the buildings of the cathedral complex to save Jews resembled the ability of diplomats to extend state protection.

Yet the Greek Catholic Church itself had a history of vulnerability. It was a kind of mediator between Eastern and Western Christian traditions in Europe. Established in 1596 as part of an attempt to restore unity among Eastern and Western Christians, it was known for two centuries as the Uniate Church. Its years of greatest prosperity were under the early modern Polish-Lithuanian Commonwealth, which ceased to exist in 1795. Most of the ecumenical territory of the Uniate Church then passed into the Russian Empire, which did not recognize its existence and which oversaw its merger with the dominant Orthodox Church. The Uniate Church survived, however, in the Habsburg province of Galicia. The Roman Catholic Habsburgs renamed it the "Greek Catholic Church," to emphasize its connection with Rome. Under Habsburg rule, the church became associated with a Ukrainian national revival, one of whose leaders was Andrei Sheptyts'kyi.

In 1918, the Habsburg monarchy disintegrated after its defeat in the First World War, and Galicia, with all of its Greek Catholics, was incorporated within the newly independent Polish state. Ukrainians were suddenly a national minority within a nation-state rather than within a pluralist empire. The nationally aware Ukrainians of the former Habsburg district of Galicia, accustomed to a good deal of freedom under Habsburg rule, were seen by Polish authorities as a particular threat. Roman Catholic Poles did not usually regard the Greek Catholic Church within Poland as an equally dignified part of the larger Catholic Church. Within interwar Poland, the Greek Catholic Church was the refuge of a Ukrainian national minority, many of whose members believed that they were oppressed by the Polish state. The Polish state was constitutionally secular; its policies were nevertheless influenced, especially in the second half of the 1930s, by a large National Democratic movement that associated itself with the Roman Catholic Church. For many Polish nationalists, Andrei Sheptyts'kyi was the servant of an alien cause. Within his own church, Sheptyts'kyi was known for his unusually positive attitude towards Jews and respect for Jewish tradition. He corresponded with rabbis in Hebrew.

In its experience of alienation from central authority, the Greek Catholic Church resembled other churches that rescued Jews. As a general matter, churches that enjoyed a close relationship with the state before the war were not active in rescue. With the collapse of the previous political order, their own capacity for action declined. Men of the cloth who were unaccustomed to being in opposition rarely ventured forth with interpretations of Christian teachings that might provide a basis for resisting the new Nazi status quo. In Nazi Germany itself, the major denominations tended to articulate a form of Christianity that was aligned with the new order. Although there were exceptions, such as Dietrich Bonhoeffer and the Confessing Church he helped establish, German Protestants generally allowed their churches to be nazified.

By contrast, church leaders and Christian believers who were used to a certain amount of tension with political authorities and with the surrounding population tended to be more open to the possibility of opposing German policies, and quicker to recognize a Christian mission to aid Jews. It was not the content of Protestantism, most likely, that made French Protestants more likely to aid Jews than French Catholics, but rather their own minority status and history of persecution. In the Netherlands, where Catholics were predominant in some districts and Protestants were in others, the Catholics tended to rescue Jews where Catholics were the minority, and Protestants tended to rescue Jews where Protestants were the minority. Members of smaller religions, especially, were able to trust one another in times of stress, and accustomed to seeing their homes as embattled outposts of truth in a broken world. It seems that the more alienated Christians were from authority before the war, the more likely they were to rescue Jews.

In the occupied Soviet Union, fleeing Jews sometimes found shelter with representatives of banned minor Protestant denominations. Baptists in Ukraine, for example, rescued Jews. They believed that Jews were children of Israel and liked to discuss the Bible and Zionism with them. The Krupa and Zybelberg families stayed in a Baptist's hayloft for six weeks and grew friendly with him. They promised to invite him to Palestine if they survived. They told him their dreams, and he interpreted them. The Shtundists, an evangelical Protestant denomination that arose in southern Russia and Ukraine under the influence of the Baptists and other Protestants, also tended to be friendly to Jews in distress. Lea Goldberg was a teenage Jewish girl from Rafałówka who, alone, escaped the mass shooting of the Jews of her village in August 1942. She found her way to Shtundists, who took her in. She converted. When the Ukrainian Insurgent Army

(Ukraïnsk'a Povstans'ka Armiia, UPA) attacked the Shtundists, most likely in July 1943, they captured her and used her as a nurse. She watched for six months as her UPA unit killed Soviet partisans, Poles, and Jews. When she finally escaped the UPA she made her way back to a Shtundist she knew, who hid her under the hay of his wagon. Emanuel Ringelblum, the Jewish historian who created the archive of the Warsaw ghetto, believed that minor Protestant denominations behaved similarly in Poland. Protestants who rescued Jews were not acting from the ecumenical views that have since become more common, but rather from an interpretation of Christian belief that operated more or less in isolation from the dominant institutions of spiritual and secular authority.

The dominant Roman Catholic Church in Poland took no stance against the mass murder of the millions of Jews who had lived for centuries among its adherents. Catholic doctrine at the time deemed Jews collectively responsible for the killing of Jesus, and Catholic teachings about modernity connected the blight of communism to Judaism. As a result, the motivations of Roman Catholics who rescued Jews had to arise from some sort of individualism, either their own or that of their parish priests. Such Roman Catholics tended to express religious beliefs that were unorthodox or heretical.

Wilm Hosenfeld, a Roman Catholic Nazi German officer stationed in Poland, came to regard the Holocaust as a kind of second original sin. He served as the director of sports for German officers in occupied Warsaw. For whatever reason, he saw the deportation of the Jews from the city with clear eyes and declined to apply political or ideological rationalizations to the sin of murder. For him, the crucial question was simply whether or not the Jews of the ghetto were being deported to their deaths. If so, he wrote, there "is no honor in being a German officer." After the destruction of the ghetto, he spoke of "a curse that can never be lifted." He aided several Jews and Poles, rescuing some from certain death. He is remembered for finding and helping the pianist Władysław Szpilman in the ruins of Warsaw during the final weeks of the German occupation. Hosenfeld was sentenced to twenty-five years in prison as a war criminal by the Soviets and died in captivity. Szpilman survived to tell Hosenfeld's story.

Aleksandra Ogrodzińska, a Polish Roman Catholic, believed in miracles. In 1940, she and Vala Kuznetsov were colleagues in a Soviet workplace in the middle of marshy Polesia, in what had been eastern Poland before the Soviet invasion. After the Germans drove out the Soviets in 1941, Aleksandra lied to the new authorities, claiming that Vala was her domestic help. In this way she removed one Jewish woman from public view. In the weeks and months and years that followed, Aleksandra cried when she told Vala what was happening to the Jews. "Why do we deserve this?" Vala asked Aleksandra. "Just because we are Jews?" Aleksandra wept and tried to comfort Vala, and perhaps herself, by saying that a miracle that very night could liberate them and change everything.

Wonders and visions threaten religious institutions, because they challenge the monopoly of inspiration of the clergy. Gedali Rydlewicz escaped from a transport from Biała Podlaska, on the western edge of Polesia. She found her way to a man at the edge of a forest whom the people of the area called the "Saint." Michał Iwaniuk wrote religious poetry, blessed people on his own authority, and spoke to all and sundry of his visions. It is unclear whether he was Roman Catholic or Orthodox; Jewish sources are usually mute on the differences among various sorts of Christianity. In either case, he would have been a heretic and a blasphemer; he was certainly an outsider, living beyond the reach of religious and other institutions. Iwaniuk helped something like sixty Jews over the course of the war. When asked why he did so, he said that the Virgin Mary had appeared before him and instructed him to save people.

Roman Catholic nuns were outsiders of a different kind. They and their convents were entirely subordinate to the hierarchy and the teachings of their church. They kept a distance from the everyday politics of religion—as women in an institution directed by men and in which only men can serve as priests, and as people living in isolation from the world in pursuit of specific forms of devotion. Polish Roman Catholic nuns saved hundreds, if not thousands, of Jewish children. In some cases, they wanted to convert Jewish children to the Roman Catholic faith. Michał Głowiński's mother, when she found her son alive after the war, was happy to allow the nuns to baptize him in recognition of what they had done and risked. From the theological perspective of the Catholic Church, the rescue of souls was more important than the preservation of earthly lives. In the politics of the Catholic Church, the conversion of the children made them Christians.

For the nuns in their convents—women who had left their earthly families or who had none—children had a certain special appeal that older Jews might not have. Yet, in a rather large number of cases, Polish Roman Catholic nuns also rescued young Jewish men, who for any number of reasons did not belong in a convent. Anna Borkowska, for example, the mother superior of a Dominican convent near Vilnius, aided several Jews. One of her favorites was a passionate and intelligent young man called Aryeh Wilner, whom she called "Jurek" (a Polish diminutive for Jerzy, or George). After Wilner left the convent and went to Warsaw, he used "Jurek" as his *nom de guerre* in the Jewish underground and in his contacts with Poles on the Aryan side of the city. In 1943, Wilner was entrusted with the mission of securing support and arms from the Home Army before the uprising in the ghetto. Fighting broke out while he was beyond its walls, and so his descriptions of the motives of the ghetto fighters reached Poles and thus the world. The uprising was not about preserving Jewish life, he explained, but about rescuing dignity. His Polish interlocutors understood this in their own national romantic terms: that Jewish self-sacrifice was meant to redeem the Jewish nation. Wilner seems to have meant something more general. The ghetto uprising was about the dignity of human beings, and thus a challenge to everyone who might have done more but instead did less. If it was redemption, it was also rebuke.

Jurek returned to the flaming ghetto, where he was killed as Aryeh.

Oswald Rufeisen was a young Zionist from southwestern Poland who spoke German as well as Polish. His parents had been subjects of the Habsburg monarchy and enrolled him in a primary school where German was the language of instruction. He was then sent to live with an aunt in Bielsko so that he could continue his schooling in a German-language gymnasium. There he joined Akiba, a Zionist organization, and learned to ride horses with a Polish friend. Rufeisen's family was integrated into Polish society; his father served for eight years in the Polish army. Young Oswald never experienced antisemitism. Nevertheless, the idea of Zionism—of a land for the Jewish people—gave him a sense of belonging during the years that he spent away from home. When the German army invaded Poland in September 1939, he fled eastward like hundreds of thousands of other Polish Jews, with the idea of eventually reaching Palestine.

Using the Akiba network, he tried to reach a Baltic port where he could catch a ship. He got as far as Latvia, by then a Soviet republic, but was sent back by the NKVD to Lithuania. He managed to escape the border police and make his way to Vilnius, by then the capital of Soviet Lithuania, where he looked for and found fellow Akiba members. Tens of thousands of Jewish refugees had joined the hundred thousand or so Jews who were native to the city. Rufeisen took up several trades, including shoe making, to sustain himself. He found that he liked Russians, but assumed that he and other Jewish refugees in Vilnius would eventually be deported by the NKVD, just as Jews from eastern Poland had been. Instead the Germans invaded in June 1941, and Rufeisen was arrested not long after by a Lithuanian policeman in the German service. When asked for his profession he said that he was a shoemaker; this spared him from being shot at Ponary, since the Germans happened to need shoemakers. In September 1941, he observed a roundup of Jews in Vilnius and decided to hide. Seeing an intoxicated German surrounded by Polish teenagers, he took a chance and helped the man find his way. The German confided in him that he and his comrades had shot 1,700 Jews that day; this was why he was so drunk.

Rufeisen now understood what was happening to the Jews of Vilnius and decided to leave the city. A chance acquaintance offered him work on his farm just beyond its outskirts, three kilometers from the killing site at Ponary. A Belarusian veterinarian who treated the cattle there told Rufeisen that he was welcome to join his family in a safer and more isolated place and wrote him a letter of recommendation. Rufeisen decided to go. The village was called Turets and was not safe; its Jews were all murdered in November 1941, shortly before Rufeisen's arrival. He found a job as a janitor at the school, working for meals. He took some of the clothing of the murdered Jews when it was distributed among the villagers.

The Belarusian family with whom he was living asked him to register with the police, which meant the local Belarusian auxiliary policemen serving the Germans. The police commander was so impressed with Rufeisen's German that he tried to hire him as a German tutor. Eventually,

Rufeisen came to work as a translator between the Belarusian gendarmes and the German policemen stationed at Mir. He presented himself as a Pole with a German father. He was formally employed by the German police, and wore a German uniform. Much of the work was on horseback, and he had to be present at mass shootings of Jews. At some point he met a Jew from Mir whom he had known in Vilnius, and began to pass news to him that might help local Jews. From his new position inside the German police outpost, Rufeisen warned the Jews of Mir that they were all to be killed on August 13, 1942. He even smuggled them some weapons. Some three hundred Jews escaped Mir as a result.

Denounced to the police by a Jew from Mir as the person who had provided the warning, Rufeisen admitted to his German employer that this was the case. In the course of a conversation about his motives he admitted, of his own volition, that he was Jewish. The German policeman, shocked by this confession, treated him with a good deal of sympathy, saying that Rufeisen was foolish to admit such a thing. Rather than arranging for his execution, his superior made a vague remark about how Rufeisen might somehow survive and left him unattended. Rufeisen made a break for it, and although he was pursued by the men who had been his colleagues and even fired upon, he had the impression that not all of the policemen wanted to catch him.

As he fled, Rufeisen happened to see a nun, which gave him an idea. He slipped through the gates of the local cloister of the Sisters of the Resurrection. This was an unusual order, founded by a Polish mother and daughter and devoted to the particular Polish martyrological tradition of national sacrifice. He asked the nuns for help. They were afraid. They knew that Rufeisen was a Jew and that others in the area knew this as well. They told him that they would pray for guidance. That day the homily in the sermon happened to be the parable of the Good Samaritan (Luke 10:25–37), which the two women took as a sign from God. In the story a Jew is robbed and beaten and needs help, and he is aided not by one of his own but by a member of a foreign and hostile tribe, a Samaritan. The nuns could hear the parable of the Good Samaritan as simple guidance from a place of authority to help a stranger. But as they themselves must have understood, the parable had a deeper significance. Jesus recited it while discussing with his disciples a crucial biblical passage, Leviticus 19:18: "Thou shalt not avenge, nor bear any grudge against the children of thy people, but thou shalt love thy neighbor as thyself: I am the LORD." Jesus told his disciples that "Thou shalt love thy neighbor as thyself," after the duty to love God with heart, soul, and mind, was the most important of God's commandments (Luke 10:27, Matthew 22:39, Mark 12:31). The disciples then wanted to know whom they should regard as their people and whom they should regard as their neighbor. It was these questions that Jesus answered with the story of the Good Samaritan, of the stranger who helps a stranger. Then he asked his disciples who was the neighbor in the story, and they answered: "He that shewed mercy on him." Jesus then told them: "Go, and do thou likewise."

Rufeisen was taken by the nuns to their cloister and sheltered for more than a year. "It is difficult even to imagine the subterfuges to which the Sisters had to resort in order to enable me to stay," he later recalled, "especially in the autumn and winter, and even to make my stay more pleasant." He spent his time in the cloister reading the New Testament. Still a Zionist, Rufeisen discovered in Jesus an image of the Jew at home in Palestine. In December 1943, when his presence seemed to be endangering the cloister, he agreed to leave, dressed as a nun. He encountered a Jew from Mir, who led him to Soviet partisans. The unit in question was shooting all of the Poles in its ranks, so Rufeisen was now eager to prove that he was a Jew. Other Jews from Mir whom Rufeisen had saved were with Tuvia Bielski and his family camp. So Rufeisen served with Bielski's men for a time. Then he allowed himself to be persuaded by Jews he had saved at Mir to go to work for the Soviets as the Red Army returned to the region. He served in the NKVD for three months, writing reports on the behavior of people he had known during the war. Rufeisen was one of countless people who worked for the security apparatuses of both Nazi Germany and the USSR, but of course one of the very few Jews who managed to do so. Finally he made his way to Cracow and there joined a monastery.

Andrei Sheptyts'kyi, the Greek Catholic metropolitan, referred to the parable of the Good Samaritan in his communications with his Ukrainian flock. "Understand," he wrote, "that everything that you do in the direction of loving your neighbor in this way will bring God's blessing to your family and village." Michał Iwaniuk, known as the Saint, also cited the parable, if imprecisely. Five Jews who were rescued by a Roman Catholic priest in Krosno would later cite a reference he had made familiar: "love thy neighbor." Among the thousands of individual Polish Roman Catholics who chose to help Jews, many explained their motivations by the same reference, inexact but unmistakable: the duty to "help a neighbor."

For such men and women, to be a neighbor was a reciprocal relationship: a neighbor was someone who helped another, or someone who needed help from another; someone who showed mercy, or someone who needed mercy. Humanity recognized itself in the suffering other. During the war, Oswald Rufeisen read the New Testament in hiding in a cloister, but when he joined a monastery he took an Old Testament name: Daniel, the interpreter of dreams, the prophet of calamities. The Christians who showed mercy to Jews such as Rufeisen were exceptions in the moral catastrophe that was Christianity during the Holocaust. In a time of inundation, they worked quietly against the current, surfacing to help, and then disappearing.

12

The Righteous Few

Ita Straż, a young woman of nineteen, was pulled by Lithuanian policemen to a long pit in the Ponary Forest. She had heard the firing of the guns and now could see the rows of corpses. "This is the end," she thought. "And what have I seen of life?" She stood with others naked at the edge of the trench as the bullets flew past her head and body. She fell straight backward, not feigning death, simply from fright. She remained motionless as one body after another fell on top of her. When the pit was full, someone walked on top of the final layer of corpses, firing downward into the heap. A bullet passed through Ita's hand, but she made no sound. Earth was thrown over the pit. She waited for as long as she could, and then pushed her way through the bodies and dug through the soil. Without clothing, covered only in mud and in the blood of herself and others, she sought help. She visited one cottage and was turned away, and then a second, and then a third. In the fourth cottage she found help, and she survived.

Who lives in the fourth cottage? Who acts without the support of norms or institutions, representing no government, no army, no church? What happens when the encounters in grey, of Jews needing help contacting people with some connection to an institution, give way to simple meetings of strangers, encounters in black? Most Jews most of the time were turned away, and died. When the outside world offered threats but no promises, the few people who acted to rescue Jews often did so because they could imagine how their own lives might be different. The risk to self was compensated by a vision of love, of marriage, of children, of enduring the war into peace and into some more tranquil future.

In the simplest form, this vision was one of sexual desire. In her recollections of escape from trains to both the Gulag and Bełżec, Zelda Machlowicz does not say that she was attractive; nor does she need to: Her tone and her story suffice. Zelda was a country girl, the daughter of a family of Jewish farmers in interwar Poland, in eastern Galicia, today in western Ukraine. Many Jews farmed in this part of the world. Whereas Jews in the Russian Empire had been forbidden to own land beyond the towns, Jews in the Habsburg monarchy had been allowed to farm. After the Habsburg monarchy was destroyed by the First World War and Galicia became part of Poland, thousands of Jews continued to till the soil and to raise livestock. The Machlowicz family were among these until the Soviet invasion of eastern Poland. In 1940, the NKVD deported the family as "kulaks," people who owned too much property.

Zelda jumped from the Soviet deportation train, leaving her parents behind, and made for the town of Rawa Ruska, where she hid from Soviet authorities. When the Germans arrived in June 1941, she was already accustomed to living by her wits. She sought to avoid the German shooting campaigns and then, beginning in early 1942, transport to the German death facility at Bełżec. Zelda was concealing not her person but rather her identity, frequenting places where she was not known and presenting herself as a Ukrainian girl. She did not enter the ghetto and did not wear the star by which Jews were supposed to mark themselves. She had certain advantages. As a woman, she carried no physical sign of Jewishness. She was most likely wearing clothes that revealed that she was rural but not that she was Jewish. Like other Jews from the countryside, she could speak Ukrainian well, and could perform certain feats that non-Jews believed that Jews could not, such as saddle and ride a horse. She was never recognized as a Jew by a stranger, but she was, after a time, recognized by people she knew.

Most of the police power, under German as under Soviet occupation, was local. Although Zelda was not from Rawa Ruska, she ran the risk every day that one of the Ukrainian auxiliary policemen would recognize her. One day two of them did. They stopped—teenage boys themselves—and taunted her. "Come with us to Bełżec," they said, "where you can rest." A third Ukrainian policeman ran up and joined them; Zelda recognized Pietrek Hroshko, with whom she had attended school before the war. "Don't take her," he told his colleagues. "She's my fiancée from before the war, I'll keep her." In Ukrainian, the word "fiancée" has a much broader meaning than in English: more like "girlfriend." The first two Ukrainian policemen left him to it. Then Pietrek turned to Zelda, and an exchange began that revealed not only the complexity of the death around them, but the sophistication of the young life within them.

P: "I saved your life. Be with me. I've wanted you for a long time, since before the war, when you were in sixth grade."
Z: "Listen, you could only take advantage of me. I'm a Jew and you are a German policeman. So do with me now what you like. Or wait, and later, when the war is over, perhaps we can marry."
P: "I swear I won't lay a finger on you. Come home with me."
Z: "Thank you, no. God will repay you."
P: "You'll regret this—I will hide you."
Z: "I don't want to make trouble for your career with the Germans. You know that I'm alone, I'm barely sixteen, but I'll be fine."
P: "Remember me."

Later Zelda was denounced by a fellow Jew and deported to Bełżec. She escaped from that train as well, although she was shot and wounded. She was found by a Ukrainian family who took her for a Ukrainian and nursed her back to health. The young man of the family was a policeman in the service of the Germans, and he, too, was attracted to Zelda. "Mom," he said, "you've brought me a fiancée." Zelda decided to make her way to Lwów and join a cloister. On the way she stole identity documents from a Ukrainian girl who was sitting next to her on the train. As the saying in Lwów went, the passport held body and soul together. Zelda stole the girl's identity and took on a series of jobs, one of which was falsifying German documents.

A Jewish woman might be rescued by a new lover—someone she met in hiding, who proposed marriage and so a new home and shelter. Alicja Rottenberg left the Warsaw ghetto to seek shelter on the Aryan side. She and two female cousins hid first with the secretary of her uncle. There they were denounced and had to flee. Next they found a place with a sailor, but had to leave because of unwanted sexual attention. After that they were lodged by a former prostitute, who took a liking to Alicja. The former prostitute was unable to keep the three young women for very long, but she did find them a new refuge with her sister and her sister's two daughters, who were to be paid by Alicja. The cohabitation of five young women in an unconventional situation brought tensions of the conventional kind.

A friend of the house, a young man called Zdzisław Barański, began to pay more attention to Alicja than to the two sisters. When he proposed marriage to Alicja rather than to one of them, they became jealous and denounced Alicja to her suitor as a Jew. Alicja hoped to spare Zdzisław the trouble she knew would ensue. "I could see for myself that the situation was unpleasant. I decided to tell Barański that, for our common good, we should break off the relationship. The next evening when Barański came to see me I began to speak in a delicate way about ending our understanding. He responded immediately that he already knew about everything, and that it was all of no significance to him. He promised to take care of me and to help me insofar as he could."

At that point the host family decided to steal everything from their Jewish tenants and then denounce them to the police. The decision probably arose not so much from anger as from calculation. When the sisters told Zdzisław that Alicja was Jewish, they were, in effect, denouncing their mother as someone who was illegally sheltering Jews and themselves as conspirators. In a moment of human jealousy they had endangered the lives of their mother and of themselves. The only way to ensure their own safety, to know that Zdzisław would not denounce them, was to be rid of the Jews. Alicja was safe: Her fiancé was as good as his word and found her a new shelter in the outskirts of Warsaw. Alicja's two cousins were shot the next day. Alicja and Zdzisław did indeed marry after the war. They had a daughter and were later divorced.

A wife might save a husband, or a husband a wife. Sofia Eyzenshteyn was a midwife in Kyiv, in Soviet Ukraine, known for her "golden hands." In September 1941, the Germans shot most of the Jews who had remained in the city at Babyi Iar. Sofia's husband, who was not Jewish, dug a shelter for her in the back of a courtyard. He disguised her as a homeless person and led her there. Then, continuing what must have been a family routine, he walked the dog and spoke to it. When he approached the hiding place, he addressed the flow of speech to his wife. He brought her food and water. She found the hiding unbearable and asked him to poison her. This he did not do. She survived.

Love for children could also bring about rescue.

Katarzyna Wolkotrup was a Polish grandmother. She lived in Baranowicze with her children and their families: She had a married daughter, a married son, and an unmarried son. Her daughter and son-in-law had a baby, Katarzyna's first and only grandchild. Her three children were on friendly terms with a Jewish couple, Michał and Chana, who had a baby of the same age. Michał and Chana hid in the basement of the house with their little daughter. The baby would cry, and Grandma Katarzyna, at Chana's request, would take the baby out for air. This was much safer than Michał or Chana appearing outside and indeed almost without risk: The baby was a girl and so not circumcised, and anyone watching would likely see nothing more than a grandmother with her own grandchild. There was no more typical sight in Poland, where the grandmothers raise the children.

One day when Katarzyna was out with Michał and Chana's baby, she heard loud noises back at the house and was afraid to return. When she finally did she found everyone dead: not only Michał and Chana, but also her own three children, her son-in-law, her daughter-in-law, and her baby grandchild. They had been denounced by a neighbor, who probably got the house as a reward. At the age of fifty-four, now without any of her family and without the future she had expected, Katarzyna left Baranowicze for good. She kept the little girl as her own, raising her, as the Jews who interviewed her after the war noted, to be "healthy and lovely."

Nannies also raise children, and love them. In Warsaw, Maria Przybylska had worked for the Lewin family as the nanny of little Regina, raising her for the first years of her life. From the Warsaw ghetto, Regina's father made contact with Maria. After he was deported to Treblinka and murdered, his wife and daughter left the ghetto for the Aryan side and found Maria. Regina's nanny took them both in, her former ward and her former employer, and found them both shelter. Regina could more easily pass as Polish, presumably at least in part because she had been raised by a Polish nanny. She lived with some of Maria's Polish friends, to whom she was introduced as Maria's niece. Regina's mother, on the other hand, was recognizably Jewish in her speech and appearance. It was agreed that Regina's mother would stay with a male friend of Maria.

Maria was now working for a German family, from whom she stole food and coal for Regina and her mother. Maria's friend gave Regina's mother his own bed and slept on the floor. A cook in a restaurant, he stole meat for the woman under his care, taking none for himself. Regina, writing from Sweden in 1946 as a seventeen-year-old, had this to say about the woman and man who saved her and her mother: "I owe to those people everything, that today I can see the sun and look at people, that I exist and enjoy life and freedom. I don't know if anyone from my own family would have made such a sacrifice and cared for us, the way that they cared for us and loved us."

Men sometimes took in children, because their wives asked them to or because they wanted to themselves. Sergiusz Siewer adopted a three-year-old orphan girl who was known in his village, near Białystok, to be one of two Jewish survivors. He loyally raised her until his wife left him, taking the child. Stanisław Jeromiński, also from the Białystok region, took in the one-year-old daughter of a Jewish acquaintance. After the war he did not want to part with the girl: "He regards her as his daughter and says that he risked his head for her"—which, in fact, he had.

Sometimes men lost their own children, and missed them, and did something about it. This was how Rachela Koch and her two daughters survived. The Koch family had lived before the war in Kołomyja, a city in Galicia where almost no Jews survived the war. Rachela and her two girls tried to escape the shooting actions by fleeing to a bunker. They were the last three in and so got the worst place, in the darkness and fetidity of the very deepest hole. As a result, they escaped the shooting when the hideout was found.

After climbing out, the three of them awaited death, in grief and misery, at the side of the road. A passing Pole, Michał Federowicz, recognized them as Jews, as most Poles could with most Jews most of the time. He asked them why they were courting death so openly; they expressed their resignation. He took all three of them in, the mother and the two daughters, and treated them as if they were his own. His three children, he told Rachela and her daughters, had been taken away by the Germans. Michał must not have been a young man, and these must have been grown children, since he regarded not only Rachela's daughters but also Rachela herself as a child. "As a protest," he told them, "it would be right and good to take in three other children."

Women lost children, and the absence was felt by those closest to them. Ewa Krcz, for example, a mother in a village not far from the Polish town of Oświęcim, lost her daughter Genia during the war. She was inconsolable. Her little boy knew how he could help. Nearby was the complex of camps and killing facilities that the Germans had built around the Polish military base at Oświęcim: Auschwitz. Here was a place where, at war's end, there were many children who desperately needed care.

The last major transports to Auschwitz were of the Jews of Hungary, most of whom were murdered, but some of whom were still working as slave laborers when the camp was closed. The adults were marched in horrible conditions toward Germany, the children left behind. Many of the boys and girls were already orphans; others were becoming orphans as surviving parents fell behind on the death marches and were shot. Some were too young to know their own names. Ewa's son, at his own initiative, walked into Auschwitz and chose a two-year-old girl who he thought would please his mother. The child was very ill, but Ewa nursed her back to health and raised her. Later the girl would seek her birth parents in Hungary. She did not find them.

Childless couples did not lose children, but they sometimes found them. A Jewish girl from Nowograd-Wołyńsk in Volhynia survived the mass shooting in a trench where her mother and sister were murdered. She ran from hut to hut in the forest, and finally found shelter with a young woman. There the girl was beaten so long and brutally that the neighbors complained of the noise and told her to seek shelter somewhere else. She finally met an older Ukrainian couple, Marko and Oksana Verbievka, who seemed sympathetic and who listened to her story: her life, the pit, the shootings, the flight, the beatings. They cried as they listened to her. And then Oksana said: "Be at peace, little child, forget all this; you will be a daughter to us, we have no children, everything will be yours."

And then, after a moment: "But you won't abandon us later, will you?" The girl stayed with Marko and Oksana for the rest of the war, and then left them.

The words of Oksana and Marko, Ukrainian peasants, convey the sadness of childlessness, the inevitability of aging, the desire to transcend death through posterity, but also the simple and present need for help on a farm. This was an age of agriculture. These eastern reaches of interwar

Poland, today western Belarus or western Ukraine, were still almost entirely agrarian. The farming was without machinery, requiring intense animal and human labor. The Great Depression had hit hard and lasted long in this part of the world, separating farmers from markets, turning them back to self-sufficiency. Economics was more about labor than about exchange—about producing enough so that humans and animals could survive the winter to produce again the next summer. There was usually enough manpower to go around; thanks to the international immigration limitations of the 1920s and 1930s, there had in fact been too much. This would change under German rule.

In the invasion of the Soviet Union of 1941, which was launched from precisely these territories, the Germans had taken many of the horses, since even the army of the famed *Blitzkrieg* moved chiefly by horsepower. When Operation Barbarossa did not go as planned, and the Germans had to send millions more of their own young men to the front, they replaced the lost labor in Germany by taking men and women from eastern Europe. At first this was by recruitment, and then by impressment, and finally in murderous campaigns. As millions of Poles, Ukrainians, Belarusians, and Russians were brought to Germany, the country became more Slavic in its population than it had been since the Middle Ages. This left parts of eastern Europe starved for labor, and countless families desperate for help in the pastures and fields. Hundreds of Jewish children, perhaps a few thousand, survived because peasant families needed labor. Most of them were orphans.

Noema Centnerschwer, from the Białystok region, was about ten when the Germans invaded and the mass killing of Jews began. She worked at seven homesteads in the countryside before she found one where she could stay. It was a large farm where the children were too small to work and where there was only one farmhand. "After a few days," she remembered, "they sensed that I was Jewish, but they let me stay anyway. They weren't kind, they brought up my Jewishness, but they didn't let me go hungry." Chawa Rozensztejn was from the same part of the world, from the town of Łomża. She survived the pogrom of Jews by Poles in the town in 1941 and then the clearing of the ghetto in 1942. At the age of six, she made her way alone to the surrounding villages. As a nine-year-old, she recalled that the peasants she found were "friendly enough when I worked conscientiously."

Szyja Flejsz was a boy of about Noema's age from Volhynia. He hid in several villages and then made for the woods with some other boys. He worked for a time as a shepherd, then followed advice to go to Woronówka, a small settlement inhabited only by Poles. During the Soviet period in 1940, the NKVD had deported two villagers. The Germans assumed control in 1941. By the time Szyja arrived in early 1943, the surrounding woods were the site of the partisan war between Soviets and Germans. By day, as he remembered, everyone tried to keep peace with the Germans, and by night with the Soviets.

Szyja was taken in by Zygmunt Kuriata. Of some forty-two huts in Woronówka, twenty-two belonged to members of the Kuriata family, which perhaps created a sense of trust. One of the two people deported from the village by the NKVD had been a member of the family, but Zygmunt seems not to have drawn any specious conclusions about Jews and communism. Zygmunt knew that Szyja was a Jewish orphan and treated him well. He wanted Szyja to learn prayers, perhaps to help him blend in, since forced recital of the Lord's Prayer was one way Christians tested Jews; or perhaps to save his soul. Perhaps neither, or both. But Szyja thought of his murdered parents: "My father was a Jew, my mother was a Jew, and I want to be a Jew." Kuriata received this with equanimity: "A Jew is a Jew, he does not want to pray."

In 1943 in Volhynia, a third force entered the partisan war. Ukrainian nationalists, in these extreme conditions, were able to establish their own partisan army. In the first months of the year, many of the Ukrainians who had been serving the Germans as auxiliary policemen went to the woods and joined the Ukrainian Insurgent Army (UPA). This formation emerged as a result of the triple occupation of Volhynia and other lands inhabited by Ukrainians that had been part of Poland until 1939. The Soviet occupation had destroyed legal Ukrainian political parties and discredited the radical Ukrainian Left. Then the German occupation offered thousands of young Ukrainian men—some of whom had already been serving the NKVD as militiamen and assisting in the deportation of Poles and others—training in methods of killing Jews and others. Then the anticipated return of Soviet power, represented in late 1942 and early 1943 by the Soviet partisans, brought these policemen and others to the woods, some of them as Soviet partisans, others to the UPA.

The commanders of the UPA, Ukrainian nationalists, meant to resist the Soviets and establish a Ukrainian state, but their immediate task in early 1943 was the ethnic cleansing of Poles. In a number of cases, this meant the death of Jews who had taken shelter with Polish families; in at least one case, a Jew who had a good hiding place rescued a Pole from Ukrainians. In 1943, Poles and Jews in small settlements such as Woronówka were amidst a three-sided German-Soviet-Ukrainian partisan war, and in an impossible position. In June, the Germans set fire to Woronówka as punishment for its supposed support of the Soviet partisans. One member of the Kuriata family was burned alive. The inhabitants who remained eked out a miserable existence among the ruins, the forest, and neighboring villages. They were repeatedly attacked by the Ukrainian partisans of the UPA, who burned down the last building in the village in November. Each time the UPA attacked, Szyja fled to the woods with his Polish family. In summer 1944, when regular Soviet forces arrived, the NKVD completed the task of ethnic cleansing that its Ukrainian nationalist enemy had begun. People of Polish and Jewish origin were registered and deported west, beyond the restored Molotov-Ribbentrop border, to a Poland that was itself being shifted to the west. The last time the Soviets had been in control, in 1939, they had deported people to the Gulag according to class criteria; this time they deported people by ethnic criteria to the country where they were thought to belong.

All of the surviving residents of Woronówka went west, and the locality, battered by the first Soviet occupation, then by the German occupation, then by Ukrainian partisans, and finally by the return of Soviet power, ceased to exist. Zygmunt Kuriata and his wife registered Szyja as a member of their family, and the three of them were transferred to distant Silesia, to lands that Poland was allowed to take from Germany after the war. Many surviving Polish Jews were resettled to Silesia after they were expelled from the lands of eastern Poland that were claimed again by the Soviet Union in 1945. So it was there, after the war, at the age of sixteen, that Szyja again met Jews. He decided to leave his Polish family and return to Jewish life. Zygmunt was clearly restraining emotions: "If you want to go, we won't hold you back; if you want to stay, we won't make you leave." Zygmunt and his wife cried when Szyja left them.

Labor could be more or less exploitative, but labor itself was no sign of hostility or alienation. This was a time and place where children worked; the labor of children would have been taken for granted, in much of the countryside anyway, in the general understanding of what a family was. Some Jewish children could thus justify their existence by what they did, and some of them, although by no means all, were loved in return. In the end, then, the working farm was a sort of institution, both economic and moral, in which Jewish children could find a place.

Like the bond between mothers and children, or fathers and children, or nannies and children, a farmstead provided a relationship where some Jewish children could fit. Like marriage, the prospect of marriage, or sexual desire, labor could generate an image of the present or the future where someone was missing, where someone was needed, where someone could be added. That someone, sometimes, could be a Jew.

All of these situations, although extreme, were not the ultimate form of self-sacrifice. In other cases of rescue there was truly no institution at all, not even a purely private one such as a farm, home, family, or love affair. What happened when there were no states, no diplomats, no armies, no churches—and no human need for a relationship, and no way for the Jew in search of shelter to provide anything useful? What happened when there was no discernible human motivation at all, no connection between the personal act of rescue and the world in which it took place, and no vision as to how the Jew might supplement the future of others? Who rescued then? Almost no one.

It seems simple: to see a person who is marked for extinction. And yet no human encounter is simple. Every meeting has a setting, partly designed by those who meet, partly designed by others, partly a matter of chance. No historical event, even the Holocaust, is of such a scale as to transcend the inherently specific character of each human interaction. No quantity of meaning, no matter how sincerely ascribed, can void the subjective quality of each meeting. The reasons why people helped or did not help often had to do with something about the first encounter with the Jew who needed their help. Since this was true, Jews sometimes survived when they were able to think, if only for a moment, beyond their own particular suffering and see the encounter from the perspective of the other.

Joseł Lewin was from near Bielsk Podlaski, on the western edge of marshy Polesia. His family had been killed, and he was wandering alone, undecided about what to do, whether he should try to survive, and how. He finally decided to take shelter in the barn of a peasant he knew, in a settlement called Janowo. When the peasant found Joseł in the barn, the peasant was surprised and frightened, as almost everyone was in these circumstances. It is always a shock to find an unexpected person on one's property, and Poles in the countryside knew that Jews were no longer supposed to exist. However they felt about that matter personally, Poles knew that they were in violation of the German order, and likely the norms of local society, the moment a Jew set foot on their land.

Seeing the peasant's reaction, Joseł stopped him from speaking and asked him for a small favor: not to do anything for thirty minutes, simply to wait for that half an hour, and then come back to the barn. Then Joseł would have something to tell him. When the peasant returned, this is what he heard from Joseł: "I don't want to live any longer; I'll commit suicide and you bury me." The peasant responded: "The earth is frozen two meters down; it will be hard to dig." It was November 1943. What were these two men, who had known each other for years, actually saying to each other at that moment? "The earth is frozen two meters down; it will be hard to dig." Perhaps, just perhaps, what the peasant meant was something like this: "I will not dig your grave; perhaps you too should wait a while and think it over." If Joseł had not given the peasant time to calm down, perhaps the peasant would have reacted differently. If the peasant had not remarked upon the hard weather, Joseł might have killed himself. The peasant gave Joseł food and shelter for the next eight months. Joseł lived.

Like Joseł Lewin, Cypa and Rywa Szpanberg thought that they had had enough of life amidst death. They were in Aleksandra, a small settlement not far from the city of Równo, in Volhynia. When Jews were ordered to the ghetto in July 1942, the two women decided to spare themselves the intermediate steps, and simply act in such a way that the Germans would kill them. In central Poland, in the Warsaw ghetto, Jews could still be fooled, or fool themselves, about what deportation meant. In places like Volhynia, however, where the public mass murder of Jews had been under way for a year, even false hope was close to impossible. So before the transfer to the ghetto, Cypa and Rywa found a place that was unknown to them, sat down together, cried, and waited for death.

The Pole who owned the land was a stranger to them. When he heard their sobbing, he took the two women to his farm in Trzesłaniec. Afterwards he took in eight more Jews. Would he have taken in any Jews at all if not for that chance encounter with two tearful women who had found their way to his property and were at his mercy? To be sure, most people in his situation did not behave nearly so honorably, and many behaved much worse. And yet without the decision of Cypa and Rywa to control the timing of their own deaths, the landowner would never have met them, and perhaps would never have undertaken to rescue Jews at all. His efforts were all the more difficult in 1943, when the UPA began to ethnically cleanse Poles from Volhynia. And yet nine of the ten Jews he sheltered on his farm survived.

There were indeed people, although precious few of them, who felt compelled by the simple need for help. Irena Lypszyc survived thanks to one such person. She was a Warsaw Jew who fled to the eastern regions of Poland to escape the German invasion of September 1939, only to find herself unexpectedly under Soviet power. Such refugees were initially helped by local Jewish communities, insofar as that was possible, but were helpless when the Germans invaded the Soviet Union in June 1941. Almost all of the local Jews were then killed, and the proportion of already displaced Jews who died must have been close to a hundred percent. After all, they had no prewar connections with the place where they found themselves, and no knowledge of the terrain.

Like most such people, Irena Lypszyc did not know much about her new surroundings. She was in Wysock, in Polesia, when the German invasion came. When the Jews of the town were rounded up for execution in September 1942, she ran into the swamps with her husband. It does not seem that she had ever previously spent much time out of doors. The two of them lived on berries and mushrooms for a few days before deciding to risk making contact with the outside world. Irena decided that she would stand on the first road she found, hail the first person she saw, and ask for help.

The man approaching her had a double-barreled shotgun on his shoulder and agreed to her request without batting an eye. As she came to understand, he was a natural rebel, living from smuggling and moonshine far away from any center of power, opposing whichever political system claimed authority over him. In interwar Poland he had hidden communists; when the Soviets invaded he had sheltered Poles from deportation by the NKVD; and now that the Germans had come he was helping Jews. He did not really seem to see a difference between one sort of rescue and another.

Irena told his story but did not betray his name.

Other rescuers, with more orderly minds and more conventional ways of being in the world, exhibited a mysterious steadfastness, a silently understood need to remake a corner of the world, to transform the overwhelming difficulty of the task into a kind of normalcy, where the labor and its presentation become something like the preoccupation of an entire personality. A private choreography of warmth and safety defied the exterior social world of cold and doom.

Rena Krainik found herself by chance in the village of Kopaniny, in eastern Galicia, not far from the city of Stanisławów. Wearing rags, she knocked on the door of complete strangers, meaning to ask for shelter for a few hours and expecting to be turned away. Instead, the Zamorski family, a homemaker and a retired Polish army officer, took her in and treated her as one of their own for the rest of the war. As Rena remembered, "They didn't ask me any questions, they didn't demand any documents, they didn't scrutinize my face to see whether I was Jewish. Mrs. Zamorska shared with me her very modest wardrobe, and the whole family shared with me every bit of food from the miserable portions allotted to the Poles." Rena understood the risks that her hosts were taking and appreciated their virtue. "I was penniless, naked, and barefoot. The sacrifice was all the greater in a locality such as Kopaniny, where every new arrival attracted attention."

In the city of Stanisławów itself, where almost all of the Jews were murdered, Janina Ciszewska took in eleven for most of the war. In a house downtown she owned two apartments that were connected by an interior door. She hid the Jews in the second apartment, the one that did not open onto the hallway. At first she took in four people on behalf of a friend. When the Jews' money ran out, she took a job with the German civilian administration, in the office that provided for the social welfare of ethnic Germans. Janina spoke German and, at the Jews' request, registered herself as an ethnic German. She stole clothes and shoes from her employers (some of which had likely been taken from the bodies of murdered Jews), took them to the countryside, sold them at markets, and used the money to feed her growing group of wards. She made light of all the difficulties. She was, as one of the Jews she rescued wrote after the war, a "brave, warm woman." She kept on a bright, beaming face, so that the Jews, as she said, would believe that she "could do anything."

When he received a request, years after the war, to provide information about his rescue of Jews, Bogdan Bazyli responded almost dismissively: "you won't believe me, ask the Teitelmans in Israel." The Bazyli family were Poles in the Pańska Dolina settlement, not far from the city of Dubno, in Volhynia. The Teitelman family had fled the murder of the Jews of Murowicz in September 1942. The Bazylis built them a dugout on the family property and kept them there for the rest of the war. Every morning, the Bazyli children brought food and took away a bucket of urine and feces. The Bazyli family took in a total of twenty-two Jews, all of whom survived the war. The Teitelmans supplied these facts from Haifa, but like most Jews they had little to say about the motives of those who saved them: "he who wanted to help in those terrible times did help." From the new world of Israel the Teitelman family wished Bogdan Bazyli "a long and healthy life."

Wanting to help was not enough. To rescue a Jew in these conditions, where no structure supported the effort and where the penalty was death, required something stronger than character, something greater than a worldview. Generous people took humane decisions, yet still failed. Probably most men and women of goodwill who were able to take the initial risk failed after a month, a week, a day. It was an era when to be good meant not only the avoidance of evil but a total determination to act on behalf of a stranger, on a planet where hell, not heaven, was the reward for goodness.

Good people broke. Mina Grycak found a peasant who sheltered her family for months and then finally yielded to the pressure. He first tried to kill the family in a clownish way that was bound to fail, and then threatened to kill himself. Had the war lasted for months rather than for years, his behavior would have been exemplary.

The nature of an encounter could end a rescue, just as it could begin one. Abraham Śniadowicz and his son stayed with a peasant for two months, and then began to share their place of shelter with two more Jews. They did not tell their host. When the peasant learned of the unannounced arrivals, he told all four Jews to leave. "I must emphasize," said Abraham, "that this Christian was a very good person."

It is very hard to speak of the motivations of the men and women who risked their lives to rescue Jews without any anchor in earthly politics and without any hope of a gainful future with those whom they rescued. To be motivated means to be moved by something. To explain a motivation usually means the delineation of a connection between a person and something beyond that person—something that beckons from the world of today, or at least from an imagined future. None of that seems pertinent here. Accounts of rescue recorded by Jews rarely include evaluations of their rescuers' motivations.

What Jewish survivors tend to provide is a description of disinterested virtue. They tend to say, in one way or another, that their rescuers were guided by a sense of humanity that transcended or defied the circumstances. As Janina Bauman put it, "that we lived with them strengthened what was noble in them, or what was base." Anton Schmid was an Austrian who employed Jews in the 1930s, defended them from repressions in Vienna after the *Anschluss* in 1938, and rescued hundreds from death as a German soldier. Those who knew him before and during the war tended to say that he was *menschlich*—humane. Joseph C., who escaped from the death facility at Treblinka, wept in his testimony when he tried to describe the one Pole who helped him in his distress. The word that he finally found to describe Szymon Całka was "humanity."

Agnieszka Wróbel, who herself survived a German concentration camp, rescued several Jews from the Warsaw ghetto, at great risk to herself. Two of the Jews who lived with her wrote long and detailed accounts of her actions, but neither tried to explain how she was capable of such choices and actions. Instead, Bronisława Znider reflected that "the role of people such as Agnieszka Wróbel was not so much that they rescued people from death, but that in the hearts of people who were chased like animals, in the spirits of Jews who were doomed to die, she aroused a bit of hope that not everything good was lost, that there were still a handful of human beings worthy of the name."

If Jews had little to say about the reasons why they were rescued, the rescuers themselves were even less forthcoming. They generally preferred not to speak about what they did. Olha Roshchenko, a Ukrainian in Kyiv, helped two of her friends to escape after the mass shooting at Babyi Iar. "I did not save them," she said. What she meant was that other people also helped her friends, and that in the end her friends saved themselves. This was of course true, and indeed was almost always true. Jews themselves had to take the most exceptional actions if they were to survive, and those who helped them were almost always a large group of people. Olha's friends reply in the same conversation: "There were a number of people who helped Jews, and don't always speak of it." And this was also true. People who did not rescue Jews claim to have done so, and people who did rescue Jews often keep their peace. There is an unmistakable tendency of rescuers, when they speak at all, towards a certain specific modesty, a diffidence that verges on a general attempt not to answer questions about motivation. When rescuers do say anything at all it is almost always uninteresting: a banality of good that is so consistent across gender, class, language, nation, and generation as to give pause.

Helena Chorążyczewska, an uneducated peasant woman, provided this explanation of why she took in Jews and kept them alive: "I always said that when I grew up I would never let anyone leave my house naked or hungry." Thus the idea of hospitality was extended to the furthest, darkest reaches of human experience. Was this imagination or a lack of imagination? The German (Austrian) soldier Anton Schmid was kind to people, including Jews. Kindness required ever greater personal risk as circumstances grew ever worse; Schmid did not change as the world changed, and was one of the few Germans to be executed for saving Jews. In the letter that he wrote to his family just before his death, he did not provide grand explanations for what he had done; he said he had simply "acted as a human being" and regretted the grief he would cause by not returning home to his loved ones. Feliks Cywiński, who helped twenty-six Jews, spoke of a sense of "obligation." Kazimiera Żuławska recalled a "purely human sense of outrage." Adam Zboromiski said that he needed to "feel like a human being."

Karolina Kobylec: "That is just the way I am."

Jan Lipke was a Latvian who aided dozens of Jews in and around Riga. One of the people who owed his life to Lipke said that the way he behaved was "far beyond the limits of heroism and common sense." Lipke placed his own life in jeopardy several times, acting on behalf of people with whom he had no prior connection. He himself said that his chosen course was nothing at all extraordinary, that it was "normal." Throughout Europe, this is what rescuers said again and again: that they were behaving normally. "We regarded it as the most normal thing to help those who needed help"—thus the verdict of a Polish family who sheltered two Jews for much of the war. They were not describing the normality that they saw around them, of course. They were not acting as others acted, or following the explicit or implicit prescriptions of those in power. Their sense of normality must have come from within, or from something learned and internalized before the war, since there were few or no external sources of the norms they exemplified.

Deep in the forests or swamps, rescuers might hide Jews without many other people noticing. But in the villages and towns, where every action was noticed and commented upon, slight alterations in the motions of everyday life could trigger everyday death. Jews could not be maintained inside a house without some change in behavior outside the house. Every transaction, every exchange, every purchase, everything that in normal times happened unremarkably at the cash nexus, carried in these times an additional social meaning. A family might be murdered because an illiterate peasant bought, as a kindness for the Jews in his home, a newspaper.

Rescuers were risking death, but not in the way people risk death in a moment of wartime heroism. There were moments, of course, when rescue resembled a battle, and these are the easiest to glorify. In the stateless zones of eastern Europe, to shelter Jews meant risking one's own life and that of one's family, at every moment, over the course of weeks, months, or even years. The choice to rescue was not a choice of the usual kind, to be followed by other choices that might undo or obviate the first. It was a choice that, once made, impinged upon every aspect of future life for multiple people over an indefinite period. It usually demanded a certain amount of planning and a capacity to think about the future in terms other than the conventional ones. A Belarusian peasant, near Minsk, chose which of his crops to sow in the spring with a thought to providing cover for his Jewish wards in the summer and fall.

Miron Lisikiewicz, who rescued Jews, asked: "What is money compared to the life of a human being?" The notion of acting in one's own economic interests—for money—has little or no place here. Again and again Jews stressed that the people who aided them were, apart from everything else, either losing money or risking their lives to get the additional money they needed to keep extra mouths fed. A Polish sewer worker fed ten Jews who were hiding in the sewers of Lwów; to pay for the food, his wife sold her clothes. Jan Lipke in Riga would get angry if anyone so much as mentioned money. Bronisława Rozmaryn, who was given shelter in Warsaw by Helena Kawka, remembered her rescuer this way: "She risked her own life and that of her two beautiful little children in order to be able to rescue us. She did this entirely without any material motivation, wanting only to save four little Jewish children, who were wandering the streets of Warsaw without any shelter." Emanuel Ringelblum, the chronicler of the Warsaw ghetto, believed that "there is not enough money in the world to make up for the constant fear of exposure." In other words, some other consideration had to be at work aside from fear and greed.

It is true that many Jewish recollections, especially those recorded long after the war, include rather formulaic statements that their rescuers did not receive material compensation. Such language was needed for people to be recognized by Yad Vashem, the Israeli memorial of the Holocaust, as "righteous gentiles," rescuers of Jews. In order to clear the hurdle of "no material considerations," Jews who wanted their rescuers to be honored sometimes simplified the story and claimed that no money was involved. Of course, it often was. But the people who rescued Jews, as opposed to those who betrayed or killed them, were almost never making money. Valuables or cash might indeed be exchanged, but not in the normal sense of a contract. There was no state to defend such contracts; indeed, the authorities offered rewards for Jews so that they could be murdered.

Money was important, since it is hard to sustain life without it. But a Jew's future depended on the individual taking the money, a person who was operating in a radically altered political and economic world. Rather than a normal market, in which individuals have property and determine their value among themselves, this was a dark market. All property relations had been destabilized, almost no one could be sure of their economic future, and some people—the Jews—were not individuals with the right to property and its exchange, but a special sort of human contraband. To have Jews at home in the stateless zones of eastern Europe, in occupied Poland and the occupied Soviet Union, was to risk one's life; to be willing to hand them over would bring salt or sugar or vodka or money and the end of anxiety and fear. Turning in a Jew meant avoiding the risk of individual and collective punishment.

Within this set of incentives, the economically rational response for a non-Jew approached by a Jew was to promise help, take all of the Jew's money as quickly as possible, and then turn in the Jew to the police. The economically rational action for someone who knew that someone else was sheltering a Jew was to denounce that person before someone else did to collect the reward and perhaps the property, and to avoid the risk of being denounced oneself as someone who knew about the rescue. It would be comforting to believe that people who brought about the death of Jews were behaving irrationally, but in fact they were often following standard economic rationality. The righteous few were behaving in a way that a norm based upon economic calculations of personal welfare would regard as irrational.

In the darkest of times and places, a few people rescued Jews for what seems like no earthly reason. These tended to be people who in normal times might seem to take ethical and social norms a bit too literally, and whose fidelity to their expressed principles survived the end of the institutions that supported and defended them.

If these rescuers had anything in common beyond that, it was self-knowledge. When you know yourself there is little to say. This is worth brooding upon as we consider how we, who know ourselves so poorly and have so much to say about ourselves, will respond to the challenges to come.

Conclusion: Our World

In the small photograph that her son keeps in his Warsaw apartment, Wanda J. radiates self-possession, a quality that stood her in good stead during the Second World War and the German occupation of Poland. She lost her husband at war's end, but saved herself and their two boys. When the Warsaw ghetto was created, she defied German orders and kept her family from resettling there. Denounced as a Jew on the Aryan side of Warsaw, she talked her way out of trouble. She moved her children from place to place, relying upon the help of friends, acquaintances, and strangers. When institutions were obliterated or warped in the aftermath of German invasion, when first the ghetto and then the rest of the city of Warsaw were burned to the ground, what counted, she thought, were the "faultless moral instinct and basic human goodness" of the people who chose to help Jews.

Most of the Jews of Warsaw did go to the ghetto and were murdered at Treblinka. Vasily Grossman, a Soviet Jewish writer working as a journalist in the Red Army who saw and described that place, wrote that "kindness, this stupid kindness, is what is most truly human in a human being." The Holocaust began with the idea that no human instinct was moral. Hitler described humans as members of races doomed to eternal and bloody struggle among themselves for finite resources. Hitler denied that any idea, be it religious, philosophical, or political, justified seeing the other (or loving the other) as oneself. He claimed that conventional forms of ethics were Jewish inventions, and that conventional states would collapse during the racial struggle. Throughout Europe, but to different degrees in different places, German occupation destroyed the institutions that made ideas of reciprocity seem plausible. Where Germans obliterated conventional states, or annihilated Soviet institutions that had just destroyed conventional states, they created the abyss where racism and politics pulled together towards nothingness. In this black hole, Jews were murdered. When Jews were saved, it was often thanks to people who could act on behalf of a state or by institutions that could function like a state. When none of the moral illumination of institutions was present, kindness was all that remained, and the pale light of the individual rescuers shone.

The state stood at the middle of the story of those who wished to kill Jews, and of those who wished to save them. Its mutation within Germany after Hitler's rise to power in 1933 and then its destruction in Austria, Czechoslovakia, and Poland in 1938 and 1939 transformed Jews from citizens into objects of exploitation. The double assault upon state institutions in the Baltic states and eastern Poland, at first by the Soviet Union in 1939 and 1940 and then by Nazi Germany in 1941, created the special field of experimentation where ideas of a Final Solution became the practice of mass murder. The Holocaust as mass shooting extended as far east into Soviet Belarus, Soviet Ukraine, and Soviet Russia as German power reached. The German policy of total killing then spread back west into territories that the Germans had conquered before the final, fateful conflict with the USSR that began in 1941. The removal of institutions had been, however, irregular throughout western, central, and southern Europe; the Holocaust spread insofar as states were weakened, but no further. Where political structures held, they provided support and means to people who wished to help Jews.

Wanda J.'s judgment about the decisive importance of a sense of humanity seems like a hopeful conclusion, but it is not. Good and evil can be rendered visible, as in memoirs such as hers, but they are not easy to summon or dismiss. Most of us would like to think that we possess a "moral instinct." Perhaps we imagine that we would be rescuers in some future catastrophe. Yet if states were destroyed, local institutions corrupted, and economic incentives directed towards murder, few of us would behave well. There is little reason to think that we are ethically superior to the Europeans of the 1930s and 1940s, or for that matter less vulnerable to the kind of ideas that Hitler so successfully promulgated and realized. A historian must be grateful to Wanda J. for her courage and for the trace of herself that she left behind. But a historian must also consider why rescuers were so few. It is all too easy to fantasize that we, too, would have aided Wanda J.

If we are serious about emulating rescuers, we should build in advance the structures that make it more likely that we would do so. Rescue, in this broad sense, thus requires a firm grasp of the ideas that challenged conventional politics and opened the way to an unprecedented crime.

Hitler was not simply a nationalist or an authoritarian. For him, German politics were only a means to an end of restoring the state of nature. To characterize Hitler as an antisemite or an anti-Slavic racist underestimates the potential of Nazi ideas. His ideas about Jews and Slavs were not prejudices that happened to be extreme, but rather emanations of a coherent worldview that contained the potential to change the world. His conflation of politics and science allowed him to pose political problems as scientific ones and scientific problems as political ones. He thereby placed himself at the center of the circle, interpreting all data according to a scheme of a perfect world of racial bloodshed corrupted only by the humanizing influence of Jews. By presenting Jews as an ecological flaw responsible for the disharmony of the planet, Hitler channeled and personalized the inevitable tensions of globalization. The only sound ecology was to eliminate a political enemy; the only sound politics was to purify the earth.

Hitler's merger of science and politics took the name *Lebensraum*: "habitat" or "ecological niche." Races needed ever more *Lebensraum*, "room to live," in order to feed themselves and propagate their kind. Nature demanded that the higher races overmaster and starve the lower. Since the innate desire of each race was to reproduce and conquer, the struggle was indefinite and eternal. At the same time, *Lebensraum* also meant "living room," with the connotations of comfort and plenty in family life. The desire for pleasure and security could never be satisfied, thought Hitler, since Germans based their consumer desires upon their perceptions of the American way of life. Because standards of living were always subjective and relative, the demand for pleasure was insatiable. *Lebensraum* thus brought together two claims: that human beings were mindless animals who always needed more, and jealous tribes who always wanted more. It confused lifestyle with life itself, generating survivalist emotions in the name of personal comfort.

Science in fact possesses and enables a certain autonomy, one which a sound politics must recognize rather than seek to subsume. The invisible forces of the world are not conspiring Jews, but physical, chemical, and biological regularities that we are ever more capable of describing. The experience of a European empire, so important to Hitler, did have a biological component, but not the one that he imagined. The unseen advantage that enabled Europeans to conquer the Americas was not their innate racial superiority but the microbes they unwittingly carried in their bodies. The rapid conquest of the New World so admired by Hitler was possible because the germs aided the conquerors. In imagining that Slavs would fight "like Indians" on a receding frontier, Hitler ignored the battle that Indians could not win: against contagious illnesses. Fighting on their home continent, Germans lacked the immunological advantages that Europeans had in North America. In eastern Europe, Germans feared diseases so much that, when they were not busy calling Jews "typhus bacteria," they spared Jewish doctors so that they could treat Germans infected with typhus. The colonialist had to bear disease in his own bloodstream, not fear it in the blood of others. He won the world not by cleansing it of imagined impurities but by bringing real impurities with him.

When science is disengaged from politics, simple analyses such as these reveal why Hitler's territorial solution to ecological crisis made no sense. As Hitler himself knew, there was a political alternative in the 1930s: that the German state abandon colonization and support agricultural technology. The scientific approach to dwindling resources, which Hitler insisted was a Jewish lie, held much more promise for Germans (and for everyone else) than an endless race war. Scientists, many of them Germans, were already preparing the way for the improvements in agriculture known as the Green Revolution. Had Hitler not begun a world war that led to his suicide, he would have lived to see the day when Europe's problem was not food shortage but surpluses. Science provided food so quickly and bountifully that Hitlerian ideas of struggle lost a good deal of their resonance. In 1989, a hundred years after Hitler's birth, world food prices were about half of what they had been in 1939 when he began the Second World War—despite a huge increase in world population and thus demand.

The compression of politics and science into *Lebensraum* empowered a *Führer* to define what was good for his race, racialize German institutions, and then oversee the destruction of neighboring states. His worldview also compressed time. There was no history for Hitler: only a timeless pattern of Jewish deception and the useful models of British and American imperialism. There was also no future as such: just the unending prospect of the double insatiability of need and want. By combining what seemed like the pattern of the past (racial empire) with what seemed like an urgent summons from the future (ecological panic), Nazi thinking closed the safety valves of contemplation and foresight. If past and future contained nothing but struggle and scarcity, all attention fell upon the present. A psychic resolve for relief from a sense of crisis overwhelmed the practical resolve to think about the future. Rather than seeing the ecosystem as open to research and rescue, Hitler imagined that a supernatural factor—the Jews—had perverted it. Once defined as an eternal and immutable threat to the human species and the whole natural order, Jews could be targeted for urgent and extraordinary measures.

The test that was supposed to confirm Hitler's idea of nature, the campaign that was to rescue Germans from the intolerably claustrophobic present, was the colonial war against the Soviet Union. The 1941 invasion of the USSR threw millions of Germans into a war of extermination on lands inhabited by millions of Jews. This was the war that Hitler wanted; the actions of 1938, 1939, and 1940 were preparation and improvisation, generating experience in the destruction of states. The course of the war on the eastern front created two fundamental political opportunities. At first, the zoological portrayal of Slavs justified the elimination of their polities, creating the zones where the Holocaust could become possible. Then, with time, Germany's uncertain fortune revealed the deep political logic of Hitler's thinking—the practical relationship between *Lebensraum* and planetary antisemitism. It was when these two ideas could be brought together—territorially, politically, and conceptually—that a Holocaust could proceed.

As the colonial war for *Lebensraum* faltered against the resistance of the Red Army, Nazis emphasized instead the struggle to save the planet from Jewish domination. Since Jews were held responsible for the ideas that had supposedly suppressed the stronger races, only their extermination could ensure victory. The SS men who had begun as state destroyers, murdering members of groups thought to be the bastions of enemy polities, now became the mass murderers of Jews. Wherever German power undid Soviet power, significant numbers of local people joined in the killing. In occupied Poland in 1942, most Jews were deported from their ghettos and murdered by gassing, as at Treblinka. Yet even at this extreme the colonial, material element never entirely vanished. In Warsaw, hungry Jews were drawn to the deportation point by promises of bread and marmalade. Himmler issued the order to kill them at the moment he decided that the labor they provided was less valuable than the calories they consumed.

The Jews of the rest of Europe would survive Hitler's murderous logic only insofar as they and their neighbors remained attached to the conventional state institutions. In the dark zones of statelessness, survivors such as Wanda J. needed good fortune and virtuous assistance. The idea of rescue seems close to us; the ideology of murder seems distant. Ecological panic, state destruction, colonial racism, and global antisemitism might seem exotic. Most people in Europe and North America live in functional states, taking for granted the basic elements of sovereignty that preserved the lives of Jews and others during the war: foreign policy, citizenship, and bureaucracy. After two generations, the Green Revolution has removed the fear of hunger from the emotions of electorates and the vocabulary of politicians. The open expression of antisemitic ideas is a taboo in much of the West, if perhaps a receding one. Separated from National Socialism by time and luck, we find it easy to dismiss Nazi ideas without contemplating how they functioned. Our forgetfulness convinces us that we are different from Nazis by shrouding the ways that we are the same.

Hitler's program confused biology with desire. *Lebensraum* unified need with want, murder with convenience. It implied a plan to restore the planet by mass murder and a promise of a better life for German families.

Since 1945, one of the two senses of *Lebensraum* has spread across most of the world: a living room, the dream of household comfort in consumer society. The other sense of *Lebensraum* is habitat, the realm that must be controlled for physical survival, inhabited perhaps temporarily by people characterized as not quite fully human. In uniting these two passions in one word, Hitler conflated lifestyle with life. For the vision of a well-stocked cupboard people should endorse the bloody struggle for other people's land. Once standard of living is confused with living, a rich society can make war upon those who are poorer in the name of survival. Tens of millions of people died in Hitler's war not so that Germans could live, but so that Germans could pursue the American dream in a globalized world.

At precisely this point Hitler's theory allowed him to join globalization with domestic politics. Hitler was right to believe that, in an age of global communication, notions of prosperity had become relative and fluid. After his pursuit of *Lebensraum* failed with the final German defeat in 1945, the Green Revolution satisfied demand in Europe and much of the world, providing not just the food needed for bare physical survival, but a sense of security and an anticipation of plenitude. Yet no scientific solution is eternal; the political choice to support science buys time, but does not guarantee that future choices will be good ones. Another moment of choice, a bit like the one Germans faced in the 1930s, could be on the way.

The Green Revolution, perhaps the one development that most distinguishes our world from Hitler's, might be reaching its limits. This is not so much because there are too many people on earth, but because more of the people on earth demand ever larger and more secure supplies of food. World grain production per capita peaked in the 1980s. In 2003, China, the world's most populous country, became a net importer of grain. In the twenty-first century, world grain stocks have never exceeded more than a few months' supply. During the hot summer and droughts of 2008, fires in fields led major food suppliers to cease exports altogether, and food riots broke out in Bolivia, Cameroon, Egypt, Haiti, Indonesia, the Ivory Coast, Mauritania, Mozambique, Senegal, Uzbekistan, and Yemen. In 2010, the prices of agricultural commodities spiked again, leading to protests, revolution, and ethnic cleansing in the Middle East. The civil war in Syria began after four consecutive years of drought drove farmers to overcrowded cities. Indirectly, and alongside other causes, climate change brings violence and south-to-north migration, which strengthens the European far right, and challenges European integration.

Though the world is not likely to run out of food as such, richer societies may again become concerned about future supplies. Their elites could find themselves once again facing choices about how to define the relationship between politics and science. As Hitler demonstrated, merging the two opens the way to ideology that can seem to both explain and resolve the sense of panic. In a scenario of mass killing that resembled the Holocaust, leaders of a developed country might follow or induce panic about future shortages and act preemptively, specifying a human group as the source of an ecological problem, destroying other states by design or by accident. There need not be any compelling reason for concern about life and death, as the Nazi example shows, only a momentary conviction that dramatic action is needed to preserve a way of life.

It seems reasonable to worry that the second sense of the term *Lebensraum,* seeing other people's land as habitat, is latent. In much of the world, the dominant sense of time is coming to resemble, in some respects, the catastrophism of Hitler's era. During the second half of the twentieth century—the decades of the Green Revolution—the future appeared as a gift that was on the way. The dueling ideologies of capitalism and communism accepted the future as their realm of competition and promised a coming bounty. In the plans of government agencies, the plotlines of novels, and the drawings of children, the future was resplendent in anticipation. This sensibility seems to have disappeared. In high culture the future now clings to us, heavy with complications and crises, dense with dilemmas and disappointments. In vernacular media—films, video games, and graphic novels—the future is presented as post-catastrophic. Nature has taken some revenge that makes conventional politics seem irrelevant, reducing society to struggle and rescue. The earth's surface grows wild, humans go feral, and anything is possible.

Hitler the thinker was wrong that politics and science are the same thing. Hitler the politician was right that conflating them creates a rapturous sense of catastrophic time and thus the potential for radical action. When an apocalypse is on the horizon, waiting for scientific solutions seems senseless, struggle seems natural, and demagogues of blood and soil come to the fore. A sound policy for our world, then, would be one that keeps the fear of planetary catastrophe as far away as possible. This means accepting the autonomy of science from politics, and making the political choice to support the pertinent kinds of science that will allow conventional politics to proceed.

The planet is changing in ways that might make Hitlerian descriptions of life, space, and time more plausible. The expected increase of average global temperatures by four degrees Celsius this century would transform human life on much of the globe. Climate change is unpredictable, which exacerbates the problem. Present trends can mislead, since feedback effects await. If ice sheets collapse, heat from the sun will be absorbed by seawater rather than reflected back into space. If the Siberian tundra melts, methane will rise from the earth, trapping heat in the atmosphere. If the Amazon basin is stripped of jungle, it will release a massive pulse of carbon dioxide. Global processes are always experienced locally, and local factors can either restrain or amplify them. The coasts are likely to flood, but where and when is impossible to say. Half of the world's cities are threatened, but which one will be lost first cannot be known. Its end will not come in one huge wave, but after countless cumulative breaches. No individual storm will be subject to prediction more than a few days in advance. Each will be unique, and yet each will belong to a cumulative trend.

Perhaps the experience of unprecedented storms, relentless droughts, and the associated wars and south-to-north migrations will jar expectations about the security of basic resources and make Hitlerian politics more resonant. As Hitler demonstrated during the Great Depression, humans are able to portray a looming crisis in such a way as to justify drastic measures in the present. Under enough stress, or with enough skill, politicians can effect the conflations Hitler pioneered: between nature and politics, between ecosystem and household, between need and desire. A global problem that seems otherwise insoluble can be blamed upon a specific group of human beings.

Hitler was a child of the first globalization, which arose under imperial auspices at the end of the nineteenth century. We are the children of the second, that of the late twentieth century. Globalization is neither a problem nor a solution; it is a condition with a history. It brings a specific intellectual danger. People have no choice but to think on a planetary scale—as Hitler and Carl Schmitt never tired of emphasizing. Since the world is more complex than a country or a city, the temptation is all the greater to find some master key to understanding everything. When a global order collapses, as was the experience of many Europeans in the second, third, and fourth decades of the twentieth century, a simplistic diagnosis such as Hitler's can seem to clarify the global by referring to the ecological, the supernatural, or the conspiratorial. When the normal rules seem to have been broken and expectations have been shattered, a suspicion can be burnished that someone (the Jews, for example) has somehow diverted nature from its proper course. A problem that is truly planetary in scale, such as climate change, obviously demands global solutions—and one apparent solution is to define a global enemy.

The Holocaust was different from other episodes of mass killing or ethnic cleansing because German policy aimed for the murder of every Jewish child, woman, and man. This was only thinkable because the Jews were understood as the makers and enforcers of a corrupt planetary order. Jews can again be seen as a universal threat, as indeed they already are by increasingly important political formations in Europe, Russia, and the Middle East. So might Muslims, gays, or other groups that can be associated with changes on a worldwide scale.

Climate change as a local problem can produce local conflicts; climate change as a global crisis might generate the demand for global victims. Over the past two decades, the continent of Africa has provided some indications of what these local conflicts will be like, and hints about how they might become global. It is a continent of weak states. In conditions of state collapse, droughts can bring hundreds of thousands of deaths from starvation, as in Somalia in 2010. Climate change can also increase the likelihood that Africans will find ideological reasons to kill other Africans in times of apparent shortage. In the future, Africa might also become the site of a global competition for food, perhaps with accompanying global ideological justifications.

Africa was a part of Germany's colonial past when Hitler came to power. The conquest of Africa was the final stage of the first globalization, at the time of Hitler's childhood. It was in sub-Saharan Africa that Germans and other Europeans relearned their lessons of race. Rwanda is an artifact of Europe's scramble for Africa in general and of German East Africa in particular. The division of its population into Hutu and Tutsi clans was the typical European method of rule: to favor one group in order to govern another. It made no more and no less sense than the idea that Poles and Ukrainians belonged to a different race than Germans, or that Slavs should be recruited from starvation camps in order to aid in the killing of Jews. Today's Africans can and do apply racial divisions and fantasies to one another, just as Europeans did to Africans in the 1880s and 1890s and Europeans did to Europeans in the 1930s and 1940s.

Mass killing in Rwanda provides an example of a political response to ecological crisis on a national scale. The exhaustion of the country's arable land in the late 1980s was followed by an absolute decline in crop yields in 1993. The government recognized overpopulation as a problem and was accordingly seeking ways to export its own people to neighboring countries. It faced a political rival associated with the Tutsis whose invasion plans involved the redistribution of precious farms. The government's policy of encouraging Hutus to kill Tutsis in spring 1994 was most successful where there were land shortages. People who wanted land denounced their neighbors. Perpetrators said that they were motivated by the desire to seize land and by the fear that others would do so before them. During the campaign of killing, Hutus did indeed kill Tutsis, but when no Tutsis were available Hutus also killed other Hutus—and took their land. Because Tutsis had been favored by the colonial powers, Hutus who killed them could cloak themselves in a myth of colonial liberation. Between April and July 1994, at least half a million people were murdered.

The starvation in Somalia and the mass killing in Rwanda are dreadful suggestions of what climate change might bring to Africa. The first exemplifies death brought directly by climate, and the second, racial conflict brought by the interaction of climate and political creativity. The future might hold the third and most fearsome possibility: an interaction between local scarcity and a colonial power capable of extracting food while exporting global ideology. Even as Africans themselves struggle for access to arable soil and potable water, their continent presents itself as the solution to the food security problems of Asians. The combination of weak property rights, corrupt regimes, and one half of the world's untilled soil has placed Africa at the center of Asian food security planning. The United Arab Emirates and South Korea have tried to control large swathes of Sudan. They have been joined by Japan, Qatar, and Saudi Arabia in consistent efforts to buy or lease agrarian terrain in Africa. A South Korean company has tried to lease half of Madagascar.

One Asian country exhibits a unique combination of enormous need for food and a commensurate ability to pursue resources: the People's Republic of China. China is a rising industrial and exporting power that cannot from its own territory ensure the basic supplies needed for the expanding prosperity that its population takes for granted. In some respects, China might be in a worse position now than Germany was in the 1930s. Its supply of arable soil per person is about forty percent of the world average, and is diminishing at a rate of about a million hectares per year. The Chinese people have experienced mass hunger. The Second World War and the succeeding civil war in China brought starvation to millions of people. A decade after the victory of the communists, the famine caused by Mao's Great Leap Forward of 1958–1962 killed tens of millions of people.

In twenty-first-century China, the gap between the two senses of the word *Lebensraum*—comfort and survival—appears to be small. There are tens of millions of prosperous Chinese today whose family members died of starvation in living memory. The Chinese populace will likely require more and more calories because prosperous Chinese, like prosperous people everywhere, demand greater food security as well as more and different kinds of food. The same Chinese communist party that starved its own people during its revolutionary phase still rules the country. Since it is responsible both for past famine and for future plenty, it is hugely sensitive to food supplies. This can be seen in the market-distorting purchases of agricultural commodities whenever global supply seems threatened. It is improbable that China, given its growing wealth, will actually run out of food. Much more likely are overreactions to momentary anxieties that punish peoples beyond China. Regardless of whether large numbers of

Chinese are actually threatened with physical hunger, the politics of national prosperity will tend towards decisive international action when a sense of threat emerges.

Facing some future crisis, perhaps a series of annual droughts, leaders in Beijing might draw the conclusion in the 2030s that leaders in Berlin drew in the 1930s: that the globalization that serves a booming export sector must be complemented by durable control of living space that ensures food supplies. The Chinese leadership has described Africa as a source of needed resources, including food. Chinese authorities demonstrated during the climate-related civil war that began in Sudan in 2003 that they would support mass murderers when doing so seemed to serve their investments. In Sudan, drought drove Arabs southward into the lands of African pastoralists. The Sudanese government sided with the Arabs and designed a policy to eliminate the Zaghawa, Masseleit, and Fur peoples as such. This Sudanese government was armed by China and Russia.

China also faces a shortage that was unheard of in the 1930s: potable water. Climate change seems to intensify the water cycle, bringing more droughts as well as more floods. Places that are drenched are getting more water; places that are parched are getting less. Close to a billion people worldwide lack the half gallon a day needed for drinking, and more than two billion lack the five gallons a day needed for hygiene. In the twenty-first century, people have rioted for water not only in China but in Bolivia, India, Kenya, Pakistan, Somalia, and Sudan. China disposes of only about a third as much freshwater per person as the global average, and much of it comes from glaciers that are melting away in the warming air. Half of Chinese freshwater and about twenty percent of Chinese groundwater are already polluted beyond potability. By 2030, Chinese demand for water will likely be close to twice the current supply. It is quite possible, of course, that China, or at least its more prosperous citizens, will be able to afford desalination of seawater in the future as technology improves.

Less peaceful approaches to the problem of uncertain water and food supplies are also possible. China has a long border with a country that has considerable supplies of water: the Russian Federation. Chinese farmers are cultivating the land on their side of the Chinese-Russian border ever more intensively, Russian farmers ever less so. In the early twenty-first century, Beijing invested more capital in eastern Russia than did Moscow.

As time passes, Beijing might look to Siberian water, just as it now looks to Siberian natural gas and oil. Beijing's preferred method of control, in Russia as in Africa, has been legal contracts on terms advantageous to itself. Russian leaders, like African ones, have been amenable to this form of submission. This Chinese approach to Moscow has worked with natural gas, and it might work with water.

Yet as climate change continues, and as unpredictable events accumulate, land in Africa and Russia might seem more precious to Africans and Russians themselves. Under pressure, the Chinese will perhaps find the ideas that seem to justify the impoverishment and death of Africans and Russians. Or perhaps Russians and Africans will find the ideas that justify putting an end to Chinese globalization and to the people who seem to be behind it.

None of these Chinese scenarios is inevitable. China's preoccupations resemble those of interwar Germany, but Chinese leaders do not exhibit Hitler's unusual opposition to scientific solutions. Whereas Hitler opposed the agricultural science that eventually resolved any sense of ecological panic in Germany, Chinese authorities fund the energy research that could slow climate change and thus lessen concern about food and water. Beijing has invested in solar, wind, fission, and fusion energy, and has committed itself to reaching voluntary targets for greenhouse gas emissions by 2030. Because it imports rather than exports natural gas and oil, China has no powerful domestic constituencies that oppose alternative forms of energy. China is a contributor to climate change and might find itself involved in Africa and Russia as climate change continues. At the same time, Chinese engineers are also developing and implementing technical solutions that slow climate change, thereby reducing the risk of these and other possible future conflicts.

Russian governments of the early twenty-first century, by contrast, have based their budgets and staked their popular support on the export of hydrocarbons to Europe and China. Because Russian governments seek to maintain demand for natural gas and oil in these great neighboring markets, they have indirectly committed themselves to a future of carbon pollution and climate change. Perhaps relatedly, the sense of coming catastrophe has been more evident in Russian culture than in China or in the West. Gifted Russian thinkers, novelists, artists, and filmmakers have presented diverse and arresting images of human decadence and downfall. Like a century ago, when Russia was riven by revolution and counterrevolution, the Russian political class surpasses any of its neighbors in formulating and transmitting catastrophist ideology.

In a new Russian colonialism that began in 2013, Russian leaders and propagandists imagined neighboring Ukrainians out of existence or presented them as sub-Russians. In characterizations that recall what Hitler said about Ukrainians (and Russians), Russian leaders described Ukraine as an artificial entity with no history, culture, and language, backed by some global agglomeration of Jews, gays, Europeans, and Americans. In the Russian war against Ukraine that this rhetoric was meant to justify, the first gains were the natural gas fields in the Black Sea near the Crimean Peninsula, which Russia invaded and annexed in 2014. The fertile soil of mainland Ukraine, its black earth, makes it a very important exporter of food, which Russia is not.

President Vladimir Putin of Russia developed a foreign policy doctrine of ethnic war. This argument from language to invasion, whether pressed in Czechoslovakia by Hitler or in Ukraine by Putin, undoes the logics of sovereignty and rights and prepares the ground for the destruction of states. It transforms recognized polities into targets of willful aggression, and individuals into ethnic objects whose putative interests are determined from abroad. Putin also placed himself at the head of populist, fascist, and neo-Nazi forces in Europe.

As migrants from the south continue to arrive in Europe, driven by climate change and associated state collapse, the European Far Right gains popularity and votes. One of the parties that Russia supports, the *Front National,* has become a leading political force in France. Its triumph, alongside the rise of similar forces, would likely mean the end of the European Union. The EU not only embodies a tradition of learning from the Second World War, it also supports sensible climate policies and bolsters the sovereignty of small states. Its collapse would thus weaken the structures that separate the Europeans of today from a history of mass killing. While supporting politicians who blame global Jews for planetary problems and applying techniques of state destruction, Moscow generated a new global scapegoat—the homosexuals. The new Russian idea of a "gay lobby" responsible for the decadence of the world makes no more sense than the old Nazi idea of a "Jewish lobby" responsible for the same, but such an ideology is now at large in the world.

As Russia demonstrated, the Second World War can shift quickly from being a cautionary tale to an instructive precedent. In 1939, Stalin made an alliance with Hitler, that is, with the European Far Right of the time, on the logic that doing so would cause Europe to destroy itself. Stalin imagined that Germany and its western neighbors would then clash and that their power would dissolve. Putin seems to have made a similar calculation. Just as the purpose of alliance with Hitler in 1939 was supposed to turn the most radical force in Europe against Europe itself, so Russian support of the European Far Right is meant to disrupt and disintegrate the most peaceful and prosperous order of the early twenty-first century—the European Union. In 2014 and 2015, Putin rehabilitated the Molotov-Ribbentrop pact, the agreement between Nazi Germany and the Soviet Union that began the Second World War and created some of the preconditions for the Holocaust.

Africa demonstrates the risks of local shortages, China suggests the problems of global power and national anxiety, and Russia shows how practices of the 1930s can come to seem like positive examples. Thanks in large measure to Moscow, state destruction and the construction of planetary enemies have returned to vogue in Europe. In the Middle East, states tend to be weak, and Islamic fundamentalists have long presented Jews, Americans, and Europeans as planetary enemies. The Russian anti-gay campaign, which associates European and American power with the hidden hand of the gay international, was targeted to the Muslim world as well as to domestic constituencies.

These forms of counterglobal thinking increase the possibility that particular groups can be blamed for planetary phenomena. In large parts of the world, hundreds of millions of Muslims are likely to face, as a result of climate change, a collapse of possibilities for life that will have no local explanation. Places that contribute almost nothing to climate change are battered by its consequences. Bangladesh, a Muslim country with half the population of the United States, is wracked by storms and floods exacerbated by the rising seas. In Libya, by contrast, the annual drought is expected to lengthen from one hundred to two hundred days. The people of Egypt depend upon the Nile, which runs four thousand miles through desert before it reaches Cairo. Forces beyond the control of Egyptians have made ours a planet where the Nile can run dry.

It is already the case that North African Muslims bring antisemitic beliefs to Europe. But what if such Muslims in North Africa and the Middle East actually blamed Jews for environmental disasters? In Exodus 4:9, a text shared by Muslim, Jewish, and Christian traditions, God warns that "the water which thou takest out of the river shall become blood upon the dry land." The Jews who live in the Middle East, citizens of Israel, might be at risk in a time of water shortages. One element of the struggle for control of the West Bank and the Golan Heights is concern about water supplies. Israelis drink from aquifers under the occupied territories. Although Israel has the military and technological capacity to protect its population from the consequences of climate change, the continuing desertification of the Middle East might generate both regional conflict and the demand for scapegoats. In a Middle Eastern war for resources, Muslims might blame Jews for both local problems and the general ecological crisis; that was, after all, Hitler's approach. Naturally, Israelis could also blame Muslims and seek to draw their American allies into a larger conflict.

Zionists of all orientations were correct to believe that statehood was crucial to future national existence. The destruction of European states in the 1930s was a precondition to all of the major Nazi crimes, including the Holocaust itself. Most Zionists of the Left and Center believed that a state of Israel could be established by some arrangement of international law. This proved to be correct, but only after the perpetration of the Holocaust. The Revisionist Zionists of the Far Right were correct in fearing an imminent catastrophe in the 1930s and reasoned that covert cooperation with the Polish state was therefore justified.

Since 1977, when Menachem Begin came to power in Israel, national terrorism has moved closer to the center of Israeli national myth. What the glorious retellings of the history of Irgun and Lehi often omit is the Polish connection. The careers of Irgun's commander Begin and Lehi's leaders Avraham Stern and Yitzhak Shamir are inconceivable without their Polish background and backers. After Begin, Shamir would serve as prime minister from 1983 to 1984 and then again from 1986 to 1992. Other comrades in arms and Polish clients resurfaced in positions of authority. Yaakov Meridor, once trained in the tactics of terrorism by the Poles, would be elected to the Israeli parliament and serve as economics minister under Begin and Shamir. Lankin, also trained by the Poles, would be Israel's ambassador in South Africa. Their political tradition, Likud, was the extension of the Revisionist Zionism that had flourished under the protection of the Polish state in the second half of the 1930s. The Polish connection might seem to have been broken with the rise of Benjamin Netanyahu, the first Likud prime minister born in Israel—and the first who is not a native speaker of Polish. Netanyahu speaks American English instead, in line with his own education and with Israel's present geopolitical affiliation. Yet even here the link to Polish policy is strong: During the high tide of cooperation with Poland, Netanyahu's father was the private secretary to Vladimir Jabotinsky, the founder of Revisionist Zionism.

The ambivalence of interwar Polish support for Revisionist Zionists suggests a similar tension within American support for an Israel governed by their successors. In the late 1930s, Polish leaders and much of the Polish population were pro-Zionist because they wanted Jews to leave Poland during an economic crisis. Some Americans of the early twenty-first century are pro-Israel because they want Jews in the Holy Land during the coming apocalypse. The United States of today resembles Poland in the 1930s in the sense that more Christians are active supporters of the Zionist idea than are Jews. Some of Israel's American political allies—evangelical Christians—tend to deny the reality of climate change while supporting hydrocarbon policies that accelerate it. Among these American evangelicals are millions of dispensationalists, who support Israel because they believe that disasters there herald the second coming of Jesus Christ. In the 1940s, dispensationalists maintained that the Holocaust was the work of God because it forced Jews to reconsider their errors and move to the Promised Land. Although such a sharp substitution of politics by apocalypse is a minority view, a displacement of the political history of the State of Israel within a story of the end times is common in American society.

As prime minister of Israel, Begin sought and found alliances with American evangelicals beginning in 1977, about forty years after he had made contact with Polish officials. In the 1930s, Revisionists such as Begin, Stern, and Shamir made the case, entirely correctly, that Jews needed state protection. Their Polish patrons supported the ideas of a state of Israel in an attempt to defuse economic crisis and mass antisemitism. The irony that confronts their successors, the second generation of Revisionist Zionists who now rule Israel, is perhaps more vexing. Some of their American patrons support policies that could hasten a catastrophe that would endanger the State of Israel, whose destruction they see as a stage in the redemption of the world. Zionists were correct that statehood protects Jews, but their allies can be people who see Israel as a means to some other end.

Americans, when they think about the Holocaust at all, take for granted that they could never commit such a crime. The U.S. Army, after all, was on the right side of the Second World War. The historical reality is somewhat more complicated. Franklin D. Roosevelt sent racially segregated armed forces to liberate Europe. Antisemitism was prominent in the United States at the time. The Holocaust was largely over by the time American soldiers landed in Normandy. Although they liberated some concentration camps, American troops reached none of the major killing sites of the Holocaust and saw none of the hundreds of death pits of the East. The American trial of guards at the Mauthausen concentration camp, like the British trial at Bergen-Belsen, reattributed prewar citizenship to the Jewish victims. This helped later generations to overlook the basic fact that denial of citizenship, usually by the destruction of states, was what permitted the mass murder of Jews.

Mass killings generally take place during civil wars or regime changes. It was the deliberate policy of Nazi Germany to artificially create conditions of state destruction and then steer the consequences towards Jews. Destroying states without such malign intentions produces more conventional disasters.

A misunderstanding about the relationship between state authority and mass killing underlay an American myth of the Holocaust that prevailed in the early twenty-first century: that the United States was a country that intentionally rescued people from the genocides caused by overweening states. Following this reasoning, the destruction of a state could be associated with rescue rather than risk. To be sure, the United States contributed to the destruction of regimes in Germany and Japan in 1945. But it also undertook to rebuild state structures. One of the errors of the 2003 invasion of Iraq was the belief that regime change must be creative. The theory was that the destruction of a state and its ruling elite would bring freedom and justice. In fact, the succession of events precipitated by the illegal American invasion of a sovereign state confirmed one of the unlearned lessons of the history of the Second World War.

The invasion of Iraq killed at least as many people as did the prior Iraqi regime. It exposed the members of the Iraqi ruling party to religious cleansing and prepared the way for chaos throughout the country. The American invaders eventually sided with the political clan they had initially defeated, so desperate were they to restore order. This permitted a troop withdrawal, which was then followed by Islamist uprisings. More than a million Iraqi refugees fled to Syrian cities. The destruction of the Iraqi state in 2003 and the political disturbances brought by the hot summer of 2010 created the space for the terrorists of the Islamic State in 2014.

A common American error is to believe that freedom is the absence of state authority. The genealogy of this confusion leads us back to the Germany and the Austria of the 1930s.

The dominant stereotype of Nazi Germany is of an all-powerful state that catalogued, repressed, and then exterminated an entire class of its own citizens. This was not how the Nazis achieved the Holocaust, nor how they even thought about it. The enormous majority of the victims of the Holocaust were not German citizens; Jews who were German citizens were much more likely to survive than Jews who were citizens of states that the Germans destroyed. The Nazis knew that they had to go abroad and lay waste to neighboring societies before they could hope to bring their revolution to their own. Had Hitler been assassinated in 1939, as he almost was, Nazi Germany would likely be remembered as one fascist state among others. Not only the Holocaust, but all major German crimes took place in areas where state institutions had been destroyed, dismantled, or seriously compromised. The German murder of five and a half million Jews, more than three million Soviet prisoners of war, and about a million civilians in so-called anti-partisan operations all took place in stateless zones. The crime of the Holocaust was unprecedented in that it was the only such attempt to remove an entire people from the planet by way of mass murder. Yet in a certain respect Nazi Germany as a regime confirms everything that we know from decades of research on mass killing. On the one hand, social scientists have shown that ethnic cleansing and genocide tend to follow state collapse, regime changes, and civil war. On the other hand, historians emphasize that certain kinds of polities, communist party-states such as the Soviet Union, the People's Republic of China, and Cambodia under the Khmer Rouge, are capable, in times of peace, of killing large numbers of their own citizens as a matter of deliberate policy. In these communist regimes the populations were not citizens in the traditional sense, since the party was the politically decisive instance, and could ordain that killing was required by the logic of history. These systems killed almost entirely their own citizens, almost exclusively on their own territory. Nazi Germany united these two logics of death, synthesizing order and chaos to produce the single most murderous outburst in human history. It was party-state that artificially generated state collapse in other countries, thereby creating a zone beyond its own prewar borders where a Holocaust was possible.

Since the Holocaust is an axial event of modern history, its misunderstanding turns our minds in the wrong direction. When the Holocaust is blamed on the modern state, the weakening of state authority appears salutary. On the political Right, the erosion of state power by international capitalism seems natural; on the political Left, rudderless revolutions portray themselves as virtuous. In the twenty-first century, anarchical protest movements join in a friendly tussle with global oligarchy, in which neither side can be hurt since both see the real enemy as the state. Both the Left and the Right tend to fear order rather than its destruction or absence. The common ideological reflex has been postmodernity: a preference for the small over the large, the fragment over the structure, the glimpse over the view, the feeling over the fact. On both the Left and the Right, postmodern explanations of the Holocaust tend to follow German and Austrian traditions of the 1930s. As a result, they generate errors that can make future crimes more rather than less likely.

On the Left, the dominant current of interpretation of the Holocaust can be called the Frankfurt School. The members of the group known by this name, largely German Jews who immigrated to the United States, portrayed the Nazi state as an expression of overgrown modernity. Theodor Adorno and Max Horkheimer, in their influential *Dialectic of Enlightenment*, began (as did Hitler) from the premise that "bourgeois civilization" was about to collapse. They reduced scientific method to practical mastery, failing (as did Hitler) to grasp the reflective and unpredictable character of scientific investigation. Whereas Hitler presented the Jews as the creators of bogus universalisms that served as façades for Jewish mastery, Adorno and Horkheimer opposed all universalisms as façades for mastery in general. The murder of Jews, they claimed, was just one instance of the general intolerance for variety that was inherent in attempts to inform politics with reason. It is hard to overstate the depth and significance of this error. Hitler was not a supporter of the Enlightenment but its enemy. He did not champion science but conflated nature with politics.

On the Right, the dominant explanation of the Holocaust can be called the Vienna School. Followers of the Austrian economist Friedrich von Hayek claim that the overweening welfare state led to National Socialism, and thus prescribe deregulation and privatization as the cure for political evil. This narrative, though convenient, is historically indefensible. There has never been a democratic state that built a social welfare system and then succumbed to fascism (or communism) as a result. What happened in central Europe was rather the opposite. Hitler came to power during a Great Depression which had spread around the world precisely because governments did not yet know how to intervene in the business cycle. Hayek's homeland Austria practiced capitalism according to the free-market orthodoxies of the time, with the consequence that the downturn was awful and seemingly endless. The oppression of Austrian Jews began not as the state grew, but as it collapsed in 1938.

The ideal capitalism envisioned by advocates of the free market depends upon social virtues and wise policies that it does not itself generate. In the particular form of capitalism generated by German policy and experienced by Jews and their rescuers during the Holocaust, every exchange depended upon personal trust, in the sense that the other party in the arrangement could betray and kill. In an extreme version of market utopianism, which Hayek himself opposed, the Vienna School merges with the thought of Ayn Rand. She believed that competition was the meaning of life itself; Hitler said much the same thing. Such reductionism, although temptingly elegant, is fatal. If nothing matters but competition, then it is natural to eliminate people who resist it and institutions that prevent it. For Hitler, those people were Jews and those institutions were states.

As all economists know, markets do not function perfectly at either the macro or the micro level. At the macro level, unregulated capitalism is subject to the extremes of the business cycle. In theory, markets always recover from depression; in practice, the human suffering induced by economic collapse can have profound political consequences, including the end of capitalism itself, before any recovery takes place. At the micro level, firms in theory provide goods that are desired and affordable. In practice, companies seeking profits can generate external costs that they do not themselves remediate. The classical example of such an externality is pollution, which costs its producers nothing but harms other people.

A government can assign a cost to pollution, which internalizes the externality and thus reduces the undesired consequence. It would be simple to internalize the costs of the carbon pollution that causes climate change. It requires a dogma to oppose such an operation, which depends upon markets and in the long run will preserve them, as anticapitalist. On the American secular right, some supporters of the unrestrained free market have found that dogma: the claim that science is nothing more than politics. Since the science of climate change is clear, some American conservatives and libertarians deny the validity of science itself by presenting its findings as a cover for conniving politicians. This is a merger of science and politics—quite possibly a dangerous one.

Though no American would deny that tanks work in the desert, some Americans do deny that deserts are growing larger. Though no American would deny ballistics, some Americans do deny climate science. Hitler denied that science could solve the basic problem of nutrition, but assumed that technology could win territory. It seemed to follow that waiting for research was pointless and that immediate military action was necessary. In the case of climate change, the denial of science likewise legitimates military action rather than investment in technology. If people do not take responsibility for the climate themselves, they will shift responsibility for the associated calamities to other people. Insofar as climate denial hinders technical progress, it might hasten real disasters, which in their turn can make catastrophic thinking still more credible. A vicious circle can begin in which politics collapses into ecological panic. The direct consequences of climate change will reach America long after Africa, the Near East, and China have been transformed. By then, it will be too late to act.

The popular notion that free markets are natural is also a merger of science and politics. The market is not nature; it depends upon nature. The climate is not a commodity that can be traded but rather a precondition to economic activity as such. The claim of a "right" to destroy the world in the name of profits for a few people reveals an important conceptual problem. Rights mean restraint. Each person is an end in himself or herself; the significance of a person is not exhausted by what someone else wants from him or her. Individuals have the right not to be defined as parts of a planetary conspiracy or a doomed race. They have the right not to have their homelands defined as habitat. They have the right not to have their polities destroyed.

When states are absent, rights—by any definition—are impossible to sustain. States are not structures to be taken for granted, exploited, or discarded, but are fruits of long and quiet effort. It is tempting but dangerous to gleefully fragment the state from the Right or knowingly gaze at the shards from the Left. Political thought is neither destruction nor critique, but rather the historically informed imagination of plural structures—a labor of the present that can preserve life and decency in the future. One plurality is between politics and science. A recognition of their distinct purposes makes possible thinking about rights and states; their conflation is a step toward a total ideology such as National Socialism. Another plurality is between order and freedom: each depends upon the other, although each is different from the other. The claim that order is freedom or that freedom is order ends in tyranny. The claim that freedom is the lack of order must end in anarchy—which is nothing more than tyranny of a special kind. The point of politics is to keep multiple and irreducible goods in play, rather than yielding to some dream, Nazi or otherwise, of totality.

Gustaw Herling-Grudziński, who endured Stalin's Gulag while his brother was sheltering Jews, wrote that "a man can be human only under human conditions." The purpose of the state is to preserve these conditions, so that its citizens need not see personal survival as their only goal. The state is for the recognition, endorsement, and protection of rights, which means creating the conditions under which rights can be recognized, endorsed, and protected. The state endures to create a sense of durability.

A final plurality thus has to do with time. When we lack a sense of past and future, the present feels like a shaky platform, an uncertain basis for action. The defense of states and rights is impossible to undertake if no one learns from the past or believes in the future. Awareness of history permits recognition of ideological traps and generates skepticism about demands for immediate action because everything has suddenly changed. Confidence in the future can make the world seem like something more than, in Hitler's words, "the surface area of a precisely measured space." Time, the fourth dimension, can make the three dimensions of space seem less claustrophobic. Confidence in duration is the antidote to panic and the tonic of demagogy. A sense of the future has to be created in the present from what we know of the past, the fourth dimension built out from the three of daily life.

In the case of climate change, we know what the state can do to tame panic and befriend time. We know that it is easier and less costly to draw nourishment from plants than animals. We know that improvements in agricultural productivity continue and that the desalination of seawater is possible. We know that efficiency of energy use is the simplest way to reduce the emission of greenhouse gases. We know that governments can assign prices to carbon pollution and can pledge reductions of future emissions to one another and review one another's pledges. We also know that governments can stimulate the development of appropriate energy technologies. Solar and wind energy are ever cheaper. Fusion, advanced fission, tidal stream power, and non-crop-based biofuels offer real hope for a new energy economy. In the long run, we will need techniques to capture and store carbon dioxide from the atmosphere. All of this is not only thinkable but attainable.

States should invest in science so that the future can be calmly contemplated. The study of the past suggests why this would be a wise course. Time supports thought, thought supports time; structure supports plurality, and plurality, structure. This line of reasoning is less glamorous than waiting for general disaster and dreaming of personal redemption. Effective prevention of mass killings is incremental and its heroes are invisible. No conception of a durable state can compete with visions of totality. No green politics will ever be as exciting as red blood on black earth. But opposing evil requires inspiration by what is sound rather than by what is resonant. The pluralities of nature and politics, order and freedom, past and future, are not as intoxicating as the totalitarian utopias of the last century. Every unity is beautiful as image but circular as logic and tyrannical as politics. The answer to those who seek totality is not anarchy, which is not totality's enemy but its handmaiden. The answer is thoughtful, plural institutions: an unending labor of differentiated creation. This is a matter of imagination, maturity, and survival.

We share Hitler's planet and several of his preoccupations; we have changed less than we think. We like our living space, we fantasize about destroying governments, we denigrate science, we dream of catastrophe. If we think that we are victims of some planetary conspiracy, we edge towards Hitler. If we believe that the Holocaust was a result of the inherent characteristics of Jews, Germans, Poles, Lithuanians, Ukrainians, or anyone else, then we are moving in Hitler's world.

Understanding the Holocaust is our chance, perhaps our last one, to preserve humanity. That is not enough for its victims. No accumulation of good, no matter how vast, undoes an evil; no rescue of the future, no matter how successful, undoes a murder in the past. Perhaps it is true that to save one life is to save the world. But the converse is not true: saving the world does not restore a single lost life.

The family tree of that boy in Vienna, like that of all of the Jewish children born and unborn, has been sheared at the roots: "I the root was once the flower / under these dim tons my bower / comes the shearing of the thread / death saw wailing overhead." The evil that was done to the Jews—to each Jewish child, woman, and man—cannot be undone. Yet it can be recorded, and it can be understood. Indeed, it must be understood so that its like can be prevented in the future.

That must be enough for us and for those who, let us hope, shall follow.

Acknowledgments

Wanda J., with the help of others, saved herself and her two sons. One of them grew up in postwar communist Poland to become a historian. He taught in the secret study circles that were known, by reference to a tradition of the nineteenth century, as a Flying University. After martial law was declared in Poland in 1981 he was interned in a camp. A decade after that, after the disintegration of the Soviet Union, he agreed to be one of my two doctoral supervisors. In that sense I owe my career as a historian to the people who aided Wanda Grosmanowa-Jedlicka, to Wanda Grosmanowa-Jedlicka herself, and to her younger son Jerzy Jedlicki. In the quarter century in which I have had the good fortune of making the study of eastern Europe a career, I have been instructed by several other people who survived the Holocaust. Among my colleagues are people who owe their lives to rescuers mentioned here, such as Sugihara, and among my students people descended from people saved by others, such as Sheptyts'kyi. It would be absurdly conceited to describe these encounters as a personal debt; I acknowledge them as a source of this book. History goes on, for better and for worse; the pale light of each rescue refracts down the mirrored passages of the generations.

Much of this book was written in Vienna and in the northeast of Poland: two places where some of the most notorious oppression of Jews took place, the discussion of which has produced outstanding histories that have preceded and informed my own. The Institute for Human Sciences (IWM) in Vienna is the special creation of my late friend, the philosopher Krzysztof Michalski. Without his intellectual welcome and without the support of his colleagues there, especially Ivan Krastev and Klaus Nellen, I would not have undertaken this book nor seen it through to completion. I am grateful to IWM fellows for a seminar devoted to this book and to Dessislava Gavrilova, Izabela Kalinowska, and Shalini Randeria for their friendship in Vienna. In the summers I was privileged to have been the guest of Krzysztof Czyżewski and Małgorzata Szporer-Czyżewska and their Borderlands Foundation in Krasnogruda, staying with my family in a house that once belonged to the family of Czesław Miłosz. The Borderlands Foundation does what so many humanists recommend: seek and find ways to understand the other.

Some of the debts go back to the years just before I began this book. Discussions of my book *Bloodlands*, a history of German and Soviet mass killing on the lands where the Holocaust took place, helped me to ask what I hope were some of the right questions about the origins of the Final Solution. The books of Peter Longerich have been significant, in that I am seeking to extend his case for politics to peoples beyond the Germans and lands beyond Germany. Christoph Dieckmann's study of Lithuania has been exemplary in its unity of theoretical understanding and regional knowledge. On the specific question of the psychic consequences of the appearance and disappearance of state power, I have been influenced for two decades by east European rereadings of Hannah Arendt, in particular that of Jan Tomasz Gross. Several of the lines of thought I pursue here were initiated in his books *Revolution from Abroad* and *Neighbors*. For almost a quarter century, Andrzej Waśkiewicz has challenged me to think more broadly about the category of politics. While I was writing *Bloodlands* I was also helping my late friend and colleague Tony Judt create a book of discussions called *Thinking the Twentieth Century*. Those conversations in New York helped me clarify some of the thinking about the state that figures in this book.

Robert Silvers of *The New York Review of Books* edited and published essays where I worked out certain ideas that feature in the middle chapters. Timothy Garton Ash, one of my doctoral supervisors, discussed structure and conclusions with me. Tina Bennett, now of WME and my agent, befriended me as we began graduate school together at Oxford. She was the first reader of this manuscript and its first editor; her discernment and her enthusiasm were hugely appreciated. Tim Duggan, my editor and publisher at Crown, took up the project with tremendous skill, energy, and devotion. Thomas Gebremedhin handled the manuscript superbly, and I appreciate the attention paid to this work by the staff at Crown. I also thank Detlef Felken of C. H. Beck for conversations between *Bloodlands* and *Black Earth,* Stuart Williams and Jörg Hensgen of Bodley Head for their reading of the full text, and Pierre Nora of Gallimard for his thoughts about tone and conclusion. My friends and colleagues James Berger, Johann Chapoutot, Fabian Drixler, Rick Duke, Susan Ferber, Janos Kovács, Hiroaki Kuromiya, Eric Lohr, Wendy Lower, Istvan Rév, Berel Rodal, Joanne Rudof, Stuart Rachels, Jeffrey Veidlinger, and Anton Weiss-Wendt were generous enough to comment upon full drafts. David Brandenberger and Joshua Goodman each commented on a chapter of this book. Andrea Böltke and Andy Morris read the text with exemplary professional care. Jonathan Wyss of Beehive Mapping added the indispensable visual element.

The arguments that appear here are also the fruit of the learning that comes from listening to students. I taught draft chapters to a special seminar at the London School of Economics in 2013–2014, and am grateful to students there as well as to my colleague Arne Westad for wonderful discussions. I learned a good deal from my students in History 987 at Yale University in 2012; a late draft of this manuscript was read by the students of History 683 in 2015. Graduate students at Yale have been my intellectual companions. While I was thinking about this book, Yedida Kanfer finished a doctoral dissertation on religion and society in Łódź, and while I was writing, Jadwiga Biskupska completed one on the German occupation of Warsaw. David Petruccelli has helped me to think about transnational history and Katherine Younger about church and state. Jermaine Lloyd kept me thinking about race as a category of transnational history. Sara Silverstein, whose dissertation bears on the relationship between rights and the state, provided thoughtful comments. I have also learned from Rachel White, whose subject is French Christians and political resistance. Aner Barzilai and Stefan Eich intervened with useful suggestions.

I am grateful to Naomi Lamoreaux, the superb chair of Yale's history department, as well as to Ian Shapiro and the MacMillan Center and Jim Levinsohn of the Jackson Institute for Global Affairs. Adam Tooze led two discussions of early chapters at Yale. I have been very fortunate to spend my career at an institution so devoted to the humanities in general and to history in particular, and where Jewish, German, and Slavic history are broadly represented in teaching, research, and library collections. I cannot stress enough the importance of the open stacks of the Sterling Library, the support of librarians at Yale, and the special resource that is the Fortunoff Video Archive for Holocaust Testimonies. New Haven has been my home over the years because my old and true friends Daniel Markovits, Sarah Bilston, Stefanie Markovits, and Ben Polak live there.

The arguments have also benefited from public presentation. I was fortunate to have been able to discuss this book at a René Girard Lecture at Stanford University, at a Philippe Roman Lecture at the LSE, at a 1939 Club Lecture at UCLA, and at the Graduate Institute in Geneva, at Sheffield University, the University of Edinburgh, St. Andrew's University, Birkbeck College London, University College London, the University of Oxford, Cambridge University, City College of New York, Princeton University, Georgetown University, Emory University, the Institute for Social Research at Hamburg, the Sorbonne, the Conrad Festival in Cracow, and at an Arendt Prize seminar at Bremen. Leon Wieseltier had an idea that took me to Ukraine at an important moment.

The arguments here rest upon the broad learning of countless colleagues in history and other disciplines, and in some measure upon my own research. In the early sections on Hitler's thought I returned to the primary sources, above all Hitler's own writings and speeches, in order to elucidate certain basic logics as clearly as possible. The intellectual debts that enabled such an attempt are too broad to be recorded, either here or in the Notes, but include my studies with Mary Gluck and Leszek Kołakowski as well as long encounters with Isaiah Berlin and Andrzej Walicki. The sections of chapters 2 and 3 on interwar Polish policy, and the sections of chapters 9, 10, 11, and 12 that discuss individual rescue, rest heavily on archival materials. The documentary evidence of rescue is largely in Russian, Polish, and Yiddish; I have been at pains these last few years to read as much of this material as possible. Generalizations, of course, are quite difficult. I have done my best to make sure that the claims about rescue are based on what Jews themselves said, with a preference for languages they knew at the time, and for dates as close as possible to the events recalled. As with many aspects of the history of the Holocaust, there remain large untapped reserves of primary materials in these east European languages. Jeffrey Burds, Wójtek Rappak, and Zbyszek Stańczyk generously shared archival documents that are cited here. Tess Davidson, Karolina Jesień, Andrew Koss, Julie Leighton, Olga Litvin, and Adam Zadrożny all helped me to find sources. The responsibility for this text is mine.

Although this is not a book about science, I do make certain claims about the relationship between science and politics. Insofar as I have made sense of these connections I owe a debt to practicing scientists, especially my friends Matthew Albert, Olivia Judson, and Carlo Maley, my cousin Steven Snyder, and my brother Philip Snyder. My brother Michael Snyder, a student of Native American literature, has expanded my own thinking about the global character of the history I aspire to recount in this book. Throughout its writing I have been grateful for the love and support of my sisters-in-law Lori Anderson Snyder and Mary Snyder and have thought often of my nieces Cora and Ivy and nephews Benjamin and Thomas. I would not be able to broach the metaphysical questions that bound this history without my parents Estel Eugene Snyder and Christine Hadley Snyder. I think also upon my grandparents and great-grandparents, to whom I owe what understanding I have of living from the land. As I wrote in the hills of Podlasie I thought of the hills of Ohio.

Mira, lily of the valleys. Marci Shore understands much of this subject better than I. She knows languages, sources, shadows that do not flee away. Her translation of *The Black Seasons* demonstrates what can be said about this history in English. Her historical writing on ideas is for me exemplary, and the philosophical questions posed here are ones that she keeps alive in my mind. I thank her for her loving-kindness: to me, and before all and after all to Kalev and Talia.

Notes

Introduction: Hitler's World

1 **Nothing can be known** Space: *Second Book,* 8. "Innere abgeschlossenheit" and desire of nature for races to separate: *Mein Kampf,* 281–82. See Chapoutot, *Le nazisme,* 428; Chapoutot, "Les Nazis et la 'Nature,'" 31. The American consul general Raymond Geist was right to speak of an antisemitic "cosmology": Husson, *Heydrich,* 121. The argument of this book proceeds from an idea of a planetary Jewish threat to the enabling condition of statelessness by way of the new forms of politics that united the antisemitic idea and the anti-political condition. Sémelin (in *Purifier,* 135) is right that the history of mass killing must be international. But in the special case of the Holocaust, it seems important first to define how its originator understood the planet. Hitler's scheme of international relations was derivative of his ecology. The ideas do seem to have been fundamentally constant; as Kershaw writes, "Hitler retained at the core an extraordinary inner consistency." *End,* 281. Burrin speaks similarly of "la consistence et la continuité étonnantes que manifesta cette vision du monde." *Hitler et les Juifs,* 19.

1 **In Hitler's world** For English and French thinkers such as Hobbes and Rousseau, an imaginary state of nature is a literary device to enable us to consider human choices about power. We are to imagine, as an exercise, what life must have been like before humans came together to make rules. Then we should think our way through to the structures we actually desire. Hitler's understanding of nature also had little to do with German traditions of thought. For Kant, perfect knowledge of an external natural world is unattainable, and wisdom consists in striving towards it in full awareness of our limitations. For Hegel, the state of nature was a barbaric stage of prehistory that gave way to institutions that man is constantly perfecting. According to Marx, nature is that which surrounds us and resists us. We know it and ourselves insofar as we work to change it. On Schmitt, see Zarka, *Un détail,* 7, 36. See also Neumann, *Behemoth,* 467.

1 **"Nature knows," wrote Hitler** Quotation: *Mein Kampf,* 140. Charles Darwin did on one occasion write that empire would eliminate "the savage races." *Descent of Man,* 1:201. From context it can be seen that his concerns in making

this remark were far from political. Darwin, the author of the powerful notion of evolution by natural selection, did not think that races were like species; on the contrary, he held that all humans belonged to a single species capable of applying reason and thereby selecting for survival on grounds other than the biological. See Tort, *L'effet Darwin,* 75–80. I am distinguishing between Marx and Engels, his friend and popularizer, who codified the "scientific" version of Marxism. On the long encounter of second-generation Darwinism with second-generation Marxism, see Kołakowski, *Main Currents,* vol. 2, *Golden Age.*

2 **Yet these liberals** "Feige Völker": *Mein Kampf,* 103. See Koonz, *Nazi Conscience,* 59. Cf. Sternhell, *Les anti-Lumières,* 666–67.

3 **Hitler's worldview dismissed** Daily bread: *Mein Kampf,* 281; *Second Book,* 15, 74. See also Hilberg, *Destruction,* 1:148. Riches of nature and commandment: *Table Talk,* 51, 141. One aim of this presentation is to avoid a problem identified by Arendt: "the failure to take seriously what the Nazis themselves said." *Origins,* 3. See also Jureit, *Das Ordnen von Räumen,* 279.

3 **Hitler exploited images** Cf. White, "Historical Roots."

3 **Knowledge of the body** See Engel, *Holocaust,* 15.

4 **When paradise falls** See Valentino, *Final Solutions,* 168, Jäckel, *Hitler in History,* 47. Cf. Sarraute, *L'ère du soupçon,* 77, and Arendt, *Origins,* 242: "The hatred of the racists against the Jews sprang from a superstitious apprehension that it might actually be the Jews, and not themselves, whom God has chosen, to whom success was granted by divine providence." On wordview as faith, see Bärsch, *Die politische Religion,* 276–77.

4 **Hitler's presentation** *Mein Kampf,* 73. This invocation of divine will, the last sentence of chapter 2 of *Mein Kampf,* was cited by Carl Schmitt as he opened his conference on the struggle of German jurisprudence against the Jewish spirit: "Eröffnung," 14. Cf. the concept of "redemptive antisemitism" in Friedländer, *Years of Extermination.*

4 **Hitler saw the species** "Unnatur": *Mein Kampf,* 69. See also *Mein Kampf,* 287; *Sämtliche Aufzeichnungen,* 462–63; Chapoutot, "La loi du sang," 391; Poliakov, *Sur les traces,* 212, 217; Bauman, *Modernity,* 68; Arendt, *Origins,* 202.

5 **Hitler's basic critique** On Himmler, see Kühne, *Belonging,* 60; Chapoutot, "La loi du sang," 374, 405. Cf. Steiner, *In Bluebeard's Castle,* 45.

5 **Any nonracist attitude** "No such thing": *Mein Kampf,* 102; "Highest goal": 103; "Eternal Right": *Mein Kampf,* 144.

5 **If states were not impressive** Hans Frank quotations: "Ansprach," 8; "Einleitung," 141. For Schmitt see "Neue Leitsätze," 516. Cf. Arendt, *Essays in Understanding,* 290, 295.

6 **Insofar as universal ideas** Child: *Table Talk,* 7. For Hitler's claim that "Jewish" ideas are all the same: *Mein Kampf,* 66 and passim. On Jesus: Bärsch, *Die politische Religion,* 286–87; on Saint Paul: Chapoutot, "L'historicité nazie," 50. See also Thies, *Architekt,* 29.

6 **Indeed, for Hitler there was** No history: *Mein Kampf,* 291. Always destroys: *Table Talk,* 314, similarly at 248; see also *Sämtliche Aufzeichnungen,* 907; Thies, *Architekt,* 42. No future: *Second Book,* 10. It is true that Hitler calls history his fa-

vorite subject in *Mein Kampf,* but what he means is his hazy intuition of the forces behind the facts.

7 **Though Hitler strove to define** Mann cited after Poliakov, *Histoire de l'antisémitisme,* 357. Stein: *Self-Portrait in Letters,* 9. See Zehnpfennig, *Hitlers Mein Kampf,* 128; Burrin, *Hitler et les Juifs,* 23.

7 **For Hitler, the conclusion** Gassing: Husson, *Heydrich,* 41.

8 **Hitler saw both the struggle** "Geistiger Pestilenz": *Mein Kampf,* 66. Healthy reaction: cited after Govrin, *Jewish Factor,* 7. Entire continent: *Staatsmänner,* 557.

8 **The fall of man** *Table Talk,* 314. Cf. Friedländer, "Some Reflections," 100.

9 **Equating nature and politics** Zehnpfennig's interpretation is similar: *Hitlers Mein Kampf,* 116. See also Neumann, *Behemoth,* 140.

9 **Hitler accepted that scientists** See Jonas, *Imperative of Responsibility,* 29.

9 **Hitler understood that agricultural** Best case, limit, scientific methods, own land: *Second Book,* 16, 21, 74, 103. "Todgefährliche Gedankengänge": *Mein Kampf,* 141. See also Fournier, *La conception National-Socialiste,* 39.

10 **Hitler had to defend** *Mein Kampf,* 282–83.

10 **The world's problem** Anarchic state: Husson, *Heydrich,* 256. "Wohin man die Juden schicke, nach Sibirien oder nach Madagascar, sei gleichgültig," July 21, 1941, *Staatsmänner,* 557.

1. Living Space

11 **Although Hitler's premise was** See Vincent, *Politics of Hunger,* 126ff; Offer, *Agrarian Interpretation,* 2, 24, 25, 59. These works emphasize moral and political discomfort brought by the blockade. Leonhard estimates 700,000 dead, which is considerably more than Vincent and Offer seem to suggest. *Die Büchse der Pandora,* 518.

11 **The world political economy** Peaceful economic war: *Second Book,* 10. Cf. Offer, *Agrarian Interpretation,* 82, 83, 217.

12 **Hitler understood that Germany** Autarkic economy: *Table Talk,* 73. German peasants: *Mein Kampf,* chap. 2.

12 **The British were to be respected** Division of the world: Hildebrand, *Vom Reich,* 654. Armageddon: *Second Book,* 76. See also *Mein Kampf,* 145.

12 **It was also reassuring** The Japanese, for example, tried without success to persuade Hitler to treat the British rather than the Soviets as the main enemy. See Hauner, *India in Axis Strategy,* 378, 383–84.

12 **America taught Hitler that need** Benchmark: *Second Book,* 21. Cf. Guettel, "Frontier." Guettel is quite right that the number of references to the United States in *Mein Kampf* is limited, though the passages are very powerfully suggestive. Hitler proclaims, for example, that the United States is the model of the new kind of empire, mastering contiguous territories by racial unity (144). The logic described here is even more apparent in the *Second Book.* And as Guettel himself notes, the treatment of Americans as masters of space was ubiquitous in the rhetoric of German colonialists; Hitler's references would have been clear. In any case the point is that America defined a global situation in which standards

of living were comparative and relative. See also Fischer, *Hitler and America,* 18, 21, 28; Thies, *Architekt,* 50.

13 **Globalization led Hitler** Wildenthal, *German Women,* 177; Sandler, "Colonizers," 436.

13 **The inevitable presence** Land as limit of science: *Second Book,* 21; also *Mein Kampf,* 282. Hitler made the point directly to Roosevelt in his *Reichstagsrede* of April 28, 1939; Franz Neumann stressed this in his *Behemoth,* 130.

13 **If German prosperity** Bleak: *Second Book,* 105. Racially pure: *Mein Kampf,* 282. Younger and healthier: *Second Book,* 111. For a contemplation of the importance of myths of the soil in the whole history of mass killing and ethnic cleansing, see Kiernan, *Blood and Soil.* On the word *Lebensraum* see Conrad, *Globalisation and the Nation,* 61.

14 **While Hitler was writing** Cf. Arendt, *Origins,* 353, 469; and Smith, "Weltpolitik," 41.

14 **The twentieth century** See Longerich, *Davon,* 160–61. More beauty: Ziegler, *Betting on Famine,* 263. Goebbels was discussing the goals of the invasion of the USSR: "für einen voll gedeckten Frühstücks-, Mittags-, und Abendtisch." Cited in Koenen, *Russland-Komplex,* 427. For an admirable comparative history, see Collingham, *Taste of War.*

15 **"One thing the Americans have"** American spaces: *Table Talk,* 707. See Guettel, "German South-West Africa," 535; Simms, *Europe,* 339, 343.

15 **All that remained** Europe itself: *Mein Kampf,* 145. May: *Table Talk,* 316. See McDonough, *Hitler,* 22; Mosse, *Nationalization,* 196. Cf. Arendt, *Origins,* 183.

15 **In the late nineteenth century** Iliffe, "Effects of the Maji Maji Rebellion," 558–59. Gerwarth and Malinowski note that the scorched-earth starvation campaign is neglected. "Ghosts," 283. Military history: Zimmerer, *Von Windhuk,* 43. Numbers of Herero and Nama from Guettel, "German South-West Africa," 543. See also Chirot and McCauley, *Why Not Kill,* 28. Trotha quotation and conditions on Shark Island: Hull, *Absolute Destruction,* 30, 78; see also Levene, *Rise,* 233. Comparison to American states by Theodor Leutwein and quotation of Bernhard Dernburg from Guettel, "German South-West Africa," 550, 524. "Vernichtungsoperation" and "Endlösung" and 70 percent figure from Lower, "German Colonialism," 5, 2.

16 **A famous German novel** Novel: Sandler, "Colonizers," 162. French: *Second Book,* 144. An extended consideration of the differences and connections is Conrad, *Globalisation,* especially 174, 177, 182. Those who apply Freudian or Girardian arguments to explain the extrusion of German Jews might also consider German relations with Poles.

16 **When Hitler wrote** Kopp, "Constructing a Racial Difference," 84–85 and passim.

17 **During the First World War** *Mein Kampf,* 144. On the Polish question during the First World War, see Niemann, *Kaiser und Revolution,* 25–36; and Rumpler, *Max Hussarek,* 50–55. On the cleansing of border zones, see Geiss, *Der polnische Grenzstreifen,* 125–46. On the politics of the German-Austrian occupation of Ukraine, see Snyder, *Red Prince.*

17 **The complete loss** See Sandler, "Colonizers," 19, 35, 149–50, and passim; Wildenthal, *German Women*, 172–73.

18 **"The Slavs are born"** Slavish mass: Zimmerer, *Von Windhuk*, 137. Last war: Kay, *Exploitation*, 40. Inconceivable: *Table Talk*, 38. Beads and dance: *Table Talk*, 34, 425. Nazi song: Ingrao, *Believe*, 117. Koch: Dallin, *German Rule in Russia*, 167. See generally the discussion in Lower, *Nazi Empire-Building*, 24–29. Conrad's *Heart of Darkness* is not actually about Europeans and Africans as races, as its opening passage makes unmistakably clear. Conrad was a Pole from Ukraine.

18 **When German occupation came** Diary: Berkhoff, *Harvest of Despair*. States: *Mein Kampf*, 140. See Jureit, *Das Ordnen von Räumen*, 219.

19 **Some states, claimed Hitler** Foreign intelligentsia and rabbits and leadership in Jewry: *Second Book*, 34, 149, 151. Rabbits: *Table Talk*, 28. Worldview: Müller, *Der Feind*, 44. See also Mazower, *Hitler's Empire*, 152.

19 **Communism was the proximate** Control point: Govrin, *Jewish Factor*, 30. Fortunate: *Second Book*, 153. Preparation for domination: *Table Talk*, 126. See also *Sämtliche Aufzeichnungen*, 163. Alexander Stein was making this point in 1936: *Adolf Hitler*, 111.

19 **Hitler's interpretation** Churchill and Wilson: Cała, *Antysemitizm*, 175; Zaremba, *Wielka Trwoga*, 71. *Times*: Schlögel, "Einleitung," 15. Destruction of German people (1936): Dieckmann, "Jüdischer Bolschewismus," 55. Immediately: *Second Book*, 152. Cards and clay: Römer, *Der Kommissarbefehl*, 204. Similar process: Kershaw, *Hitler*, 651.

20 **In this racist collage** Interestingly, the quotation about rivers is often given as "Our Mississippi must be the Volga," without the final phrase. This alters the meaning and narrows the range of reference quite substantially. See Kershaw, *Hitler*, 650. For a history of the United States that reminds us that Hitler was not wrong in every respect: Mann, *Dark Side of Democracy*, 70–98. The history of the United States also demonstrated that slaves could outnumber free settlers. McNeill, *Global Condition*, 21.

21 **The destruction of the Soviet Union** *Mein Kampf*, 73. The fundamental work on the Hunger Plan is Gerlach, *Kalkulierte Morde*. Quotation from Kay, *Exploitation*, 133; see also 162–63. On Generalplan Ost see Madajczyk, "Generalplan Ost," 13; and more recently Wasser, *Himmlers Raumplanung;* and Aly and Heim, *Vordenker der Vernichtung*.

21 **If the war did not** See Kershaw, *Fateful Choices*, 57.

22 **The Judeobolshevik myth** Cf. Koselleck, *Futures Past*, at 222, where he notes that Hitler distinguished between three levels of secrecy: what he told his immediate circle, what he kept to himself, and what even he himself did not dare to think through.

22 **From the perspective of Berlin** The Bolshevik Revolution is known as the "October Revolution" because it took place, according to the Julian calendar in force at the time in the Russian Empire, in October. By the Gregorian calendar the revolution began in November.

22 **Before the revolutions of 1917** This compresses a long and complex history that is expertly told in Polonsky, *Jews of Poland and Russia*. Lohr estimates that a

Jewish subject of the Russian Empire was 184 times more likely to emigrate than a Russian subject of the Russian Empire. *Russian Citizenship,* 86.

23 **Jews inhabited the western** Poliakov, *Histoire de l'antisémitisme,* 379; Lohr, *Nationalizing,* 14, 16, 24, 138, 139, 146. The special feature of the pogroms of 1915 was the direct role of the army: Lohr, "1915," 41–42. On theft: Wróbel, "Seeds of Violence," 131. See also Prusin, *Nationalizing,* 42, 55; Wasserstein, *On the Eve,* 309. Two of Marc Chagall's most famous paintings, *Cemetery Gates* (1914) and *Newspaper Seller* (1917) are associated with the Holocaust; in fact they portray this period.

23 **In the minds of Europeans** Creates a Jewish question: Pergher and Roseman, "Imperial genocide," 44. Begin: Shilon, *Menachem Begin,* 6; Stern: Heller, *Stern Gang,* 100. Sixty thousand: Budnitskii, *Russian Jews,* 76. See also Stanislawski, "Russian Jewry," 281. The continuities of violent practice are a major theme of Holquist, *Making War.*

24 **The other side generally** Budnitskii, *Russian Jews,* 90, 176, 213 and passim; Herbeck, *Das Feindbild,* 285–87; Beyrau, "Der Erste Weltkrieg," 103, 107; Lohr, "1915," 49; Lohr, *Russian Citizenship,* 122, 130; Lohr, *Nationalizing,* 150; Wróbel, "Seeds of Violence," 137; Dieckmann, "Jüdischer Bolschewismus," 59–64. Hitler on the *Protocols: Mein Kampf,* 302. He seems to be aware that they are not authentic, but accepts their logic. The *Protocols* are often described as a forgery. But a forgery is an imitation of something real, and here nothing is real. The *Protocols* were a fiction that enabled life within a fictional world.

24 **Germany backed** Offer, *Agrarian Interpretation,* 50; Golczewski, *Deutsche und Ukrainer,* 240ff. Some Germans found it possible even in 1918 to imagine Ukraine as empty space: see Jureit, *Das Ordnen von Räumen,* 165; but compare Liulevicius, *War Land.* German war aims in the East are still a matter of much discussion. The debate centers around Fischer, *Griff nach der Weltmacht.*

26 **Once Germany was defeated** See Abramson, *Prayer for the Government;* Dieckmann, "Jüdischer Bolschewismus," 59–61. The association of Jews, Bolshevism, and pogroms reached even the best of minds. Vladimir Nabokov, for example, explained pogroms by the prominence of Jews in the revolution. Schlögel, "Einleitung," 15–16.

26 **The vanquished adherents** January 1920: Schlögel, "Einleitung," 15. On the Soviet representative Viktor Kopps and the "destruction" (*unichtozhenie*) of the Jews: ibid., 18. On Scheubner-Richter's plans for Ukraine and Russia, see Snyder, *Red Prince,* chap. 6. See generally Stein, *Adolf Hitler,* 104–8; Kellogg, *Russian Roots,* 12, 65, 75, 218; Liulevicius, *German Myth,* 176; Dieckmann, "Jüdischer Bolschewismus," 69–75.

27 **The Judeobolshevik idea** On the adaptation of Christian images to political purposes see Herbeck, *Das Feindbild,* 105–65. For a military history of the Polish-Bolshevik War, see Davies, *White Eagle.* On the European settlement as of 1921 see Wandycz, *Soviet-Polish Relations, 1917–1921*; and Borzęcki, *Soviet-Polish Peace.*

27 **The Judeobolshevik myth seemed** I am instructed by Jäckel's judgment: "Perhaps never in history did a ruler write down before he came to power what he was to do afterward as precisely as did Adolf Hitler," in *Hitler in History,* 23. But

within Hitler's two books there is a political logic that must be explicated before the next two problems can be solved: how Hitler could come to power (a minor subject here), and how he could implement his ideas after he came to power (a major subject here). What might seem to be weaknesses in the thought proved to be opportunities in practice, and so the thought must be presented first.

28 **In Hitler's ecology** Cf. Pollack, *Kontaminierte Landschaften.*

28 **During a death march** Ozsváth, *In the Footsteps of Orpheus*, 203, translation at 207.

2. Berlin, Warsaw, Moscow

30 **In the six years after** Müller, *Der Feind,* 43.

33 **After the failure of his coup** Hitler's tactical reticence: Koonz, *Nazi Conscience,* 11, 12, 21, 25, 22. See also Mosse, *Nationalization,* 183; Confino, *World Without Jews,* 151; Engel, *Holocaust,* 20. On the actual theological compromises that later followed, see Heschel, *Aryan Jesus.*

33 **After his release** Kershaw, *Hitler Myth,* 230, 233, and passim; Sémelin, *Purifier,* 89; Koenen, *Russland-Komplex,* 390, 413, 415; Bloxham, *Final Solution,* 143; McDonough, *Hitler,* 79. On Hitler's voters, see King et al., "Ordinary Voting Behavior." Cf. Hagen's judgment that Hitler was a "dangerously self-confident, indefatigable and politically canny man." *German History,* 275.

33 **In reality, National Socialism** Quotation: *Deutschösterreichische Tageszeitung,* March 3, 1933. See Koenen, *Russland-Komplex,* 415.

35 **In 1933, Hitler emerged** For a precise discussion see Pauer-Studer, "Einleitung," 15–17.

35 **In the weeks and months** Exemptions and numbers of Polish Jews: Maurer, "Background for 'Kristallnacht,'" 49–51. Counterboycott: Weiss, *Deutsche und polnische Juden,* 169–79.

36 **An initial inspiration** *Second Book,* 27, 37, 66. See Bloxham, *Final Solution,* 59–65; Piskorski, *Wygnańcy,* 34–60; and more broadly Ferrara and Pianciola, *Migrazioni forzate,* 39–95.

36 **Hitler was, to a point** *Second Book,* 17. A sophisticated discussion is Tooze, *Wages of Destruction.*

37 **He respected the Balkan Model** Citation from Neumann, *Behemoth,* 139; "sticky mass" from Karin von Schulmann, cited in Harvey, *Women,* 119. Cf. Jäckel, *Hitler in History,* 30: "There is abundant evidence that all the major decisions in the Third Reich were made by Hitler, and there is equally abundant evidence that the regime was largely anarchic and can thus be described as a polycracy. The misunderstanding is to suppose that the two observations are contradictory and that only one of them can be true."

37 **The theoretical reconciliation** I consider the consequences of this difference in *Bloodlands.*

38 **In 1934, Hitler was** 1934: Evans, *Third Reich in Power,* 42. Civil servants: Bloxham, *Final Solution,* 156–57.

38 **The classic definition of the state** The perceptive observer Antoni Sobański

also noticed that the uniforms were a way to cover previous affiliations, especially in Berlin. *Cywil w Berlinie,* 53.

39 **Hitler's third innovation** Cf. Arendt, *Origins,* 131, 155.

40 **The outlines of this** For the larger setting of the SA-SS-*Wehrmacht* interaction, see Evans, *Third Reich in Power,* 21–39. Schmitt: Zarka, *Un détail,* 11.

40 **Whereas the SA had stood** Cf. Wildt, *Uncompromising Generation,* 127.

40 **This mission of deferred supremacy** Ingrao, *Believe,* 65, 101.

41 **After its triumph** Himmler: Wildt, *Uncompromising Generation,* 135. Iron heart: Fest, *Das Gesicht,* 139.

41 **In 1937, Himmler established** Buchheim, "Die Höheren SS- und Polizeiführer," 563, 570, 585. See Angrick and Klein, *"Final Solution,"* 41; Bloxham, *Final Solution,* 204; MacLean, *Field Men,* 12.

42 **Among the limited responsibilities** Dachau: Goeschel and Wachsmann, "Introduction," 14; Roseman, "Lives of Others," 447.

42 **Hitler's sixth political innovation** See Wildt, *Uncompromising Generation,* 128.

43 **After Hitler's takeover** This subject, at the heart of Holocaust studies, has been developed superbly elsewhere, and so is treated briefly here. These examples from Husson, *Heydrich,* 50, 65. My argument here follows the analysis of Longerich in *Politik der Vernichtung.* On Schmitt, see Zarka, *Un détail,* 19–20.

43 **At the same time** *Weltjudentum*: One of the many acute observations in Klemperer, *Language of the Third Reich,* here at 26–27. Book burnings: Confino, *World Without Jews,* 46–47.

44 **Hitler's final innovation** SS: Jureit, *Das Ordnen von Räumen,* 395. 1938: Heim, "Einleitung," 16.

44 **The German calamity of 1918** The fundamental study of statebuilding remains Polonsky, *Politics in Independent Poland.* On the National Democratic mindset, see Porter, *When Nationalism.* Porter notes the significance of chronotopes, making a case similar to the one I try to make in the opening and closing chapters. On the politics of culture, see Shore, *Caviar and Ashes.*

45 **Poland was a new state** Taxes: Rothschild, "Ethnic Peripheries," 602. Generally: Polonsky, *Jews of Poland and Russia,* vol. 3.

45 **The question of loyalty** Benecke, *Ostgebiete,* 95–100.

46 **Polish patriotism spread** Rothschild made a number of these points concisely in *East Central Europe.*

46 **Their differences** For a forthright study of antisemitic language in the interwar church, see Porter-Szücs, *Faith.*

47 **Dmowski's opponent** For introductions to the old commonwealth and the period of the partitions that followed, see Stone, *State;* and Wandycz, *Lands.*

47 **Piłsudski's moment was** The surest guide remains Polonsky, *Politics in Independent Poland.*

48 **When Piłsudski returned to power** See generally Rothschild, *Coup*; Chojnowski, *Piłsudczycy u władzy.* On Agudat, see Bacon, *Politics of Tradition.* On the BBWR and Jews: Dowództwo Okręgu Korpusu II, "Referat o sytuacji polityczno-narodowościowej DOK II," August 1, 1929, CAW, I.371.2/A.88; Dowództwo Okręgu Korpusu II, "Referat o sytuacji politycznonarodowościowej

DOK II," November 10, 1930, CAW, I.371.2/A.88; Spektor, "Żydzi wołyńscy," 570. On Ukrainians, see Snyder, *Sketches*.

48 **Piłsudski brought a fake** Tomaszewski, "Civil Rights," 125.

48 **Piłsudski's fundamental respect** The guide to the intellectual background is Walicki, *Philosophy*.

49 **For Piłsudski neither Russia** A profound study of Piłsudski's visions of Russia is Nowak, *Trzy Rosje*.

49 **Piłsudski was perfectly aware** On his relationship with Marxism and Marxists, see Snyder, *Nationalism*.

50 **Piłsudski and his comrades** I am in accord with Daniel Beauvois that the basic relationship between the early modern Polish-speaking aristocracy and the Ukrainian populations was a colonial one. But after four centuries, the end of the commonwealth, generations of common experiences under the Russian Empire, and the emergence of modern ideas of socialism and nationalism, it no longer makes sense to use this reductive framework in the twentieth century. Many of the Poles of this milieu were able to see Ukraine by analogy as a fellow nation. The National Democrats saw Ukrainians as pre-national but as human, and as such possibly assimilable to the Polish nation. Here the difference between the Polish and the German elites might be seen as postcolonial versus precolonial.

50 **After Piłsudski's return to power** See Snyder, *Sketches;* Copeaux, "Le mouvement"; and the continuing stream of publications by Kuromiya and Pepłoński. See also Mędrzecki, *Województwo wołyńskie;* Kęsik, *Zaufany Komendanta*; Schenke, *Nationalstaat und nationale Frage.*

52 **The Soviet, Polish, and German** On this transformation, see Viola, *Unknown Gulag;* Khlevniuk, *Gulag;* Werth, *La terreur;* Kotkin, *Magnetic Mountain.*

53 **In Moscow, Warsaw, and Berlin** Collectivization was the central element of the First Five-Year Plan of 1928–1933. It began in earnest in the first weeks of 1930.

53 **This policy brought massive** The sequence of events is described in Snyder, *Bloodlands,* chap. 1, which cites a number of the primary sources. On resistance, see, for example, Graziosi, "Révoltes paysannes." For a broad sample of published Soviet archival sources, see Zelenin et al., *Tragediia sovetskoi derevni.*

53 **From the beginning** A village flees: Protokół wywiadowczy, 28 March 1930, CAW, I.303.4.6982. Kiss feet and European states: "Protokół," 23 April 1930, CAW, I.303.4.6982. Misery and oppression: K.O.P., Placówka Wywiadowcza Nr. 10, "Protokól," 25 November 1933, CAW, I.303.4.6906.

54 **A deliberate mass starvation** Forces at border: Placówka Wywiadowcza 9 Czortków, K.O.P., "Wiadomości wojskowe," 3 April 1930, CAW, I.303.4.6982; "Wiadomośći zakordonowe," Równe, 1 April 1930, CAW, I.303.4.6982.

54 **Polish diplomats in Soviet Ukraine** Five million: J. Karszo-Siedlewski, "Sytuacja na Ukrainie," 2 October 1933, CAW, I.303.4.1881. Weep: J. Karszo-Siedlewski, Kharkiv, 4 February 1933. On the streets: [Józefina Pisarczykówna] to [Jerzy Niezbrzycki], 13 June 1933, CAW, I.303.4.2099. Villages: [Leon Mitkiewicz] to [Second Department, Referat Wschód, Warsaw], 6 June 1933, CAW, I.303.4.1928. Militia: Falk, *Sowjetische Städte,* 298–300. Loyal: [Jerzy Niezbrzycki] to [Piotr Kurnicki], 16 March 1933, CAW, I.303.4.1993.

54 **The withdrawal of the Poles** Ukrainians: [Piotr Kurnicki], Report on public opinion in Soviet Ukraine, 1935, CAW, I.303.4.1993, quotation at 1. The Polish government had reports from its border guards as well as from Ukrainians who had fled the famine. Its sources of information were bountiful. See, for example, the reports from Ukrainians in CAW, I.303.4.5559 and "Zagadnienie Ukrainizacji," 12 December 1933, CAW, I.303.4.2011.

55 **The Polish diplomats** "Slogans": "Oleg Ostrowski" [Zdzisław Miłoszewski] to [Jerzy Niezbrzycki], "Zagadnienie Ukrainizacji," 12 December 1933, CAW I.303.4.2011, quotation at 15.

55 **The political famine** Preemptive attack: Pasztor, "Problem wojny prewencyjnej"; Simms, *Europe,* 346.

55 **For Polish leaders** Memoirs: Müller, *Der Feind,* 75. Hitler and generals: Rossino, *Hitler Strikes Poland,* 2. See also Simms, *Europe,* 361; Cienciala, "Foreign Policy," 136.

56 **Moscow had its own** Kuromiya, *Stalin,* 141 and passim. For a longer discussion see Snyder, *Bloodlands,* chap. 3.

57 **In the five years between** See Snyder, *Bloodlands,* chap. 3. For an introduction to the Great Terror, see Gellately, *Stalin's Curse,* 34–46. On numbers of arrests, see Khaustov, "Deiatel'nost' organov," 229.

57 **As the Polish Operation began** Naumov, *Stalin i NKVD,* 299.

3. The Promise of Palestine

58 **Naturally, there were Polish** [Jerzy Niezbrzycki], 8 June 1935, CAW, I.303.4.1926.

58 **The end of a political life** I am using "National Democrats" to describe the party known as Stronnictwo Narodowe. On the goals of pogroms, see Cała, *Antysemityzm,* 349; Melzer, *No Way Out,* 22; Korzec, *Juifs en Pologne,* 247; Rudnicki, *Równi,* 148. For a first survey of their extent, see Żyndul, *Zajścia antyżydowskie.*

58 **In 1935, responsibility** Transfer of responsibility: Weinbaum, *Marriage of Convenience,* 7. OZON: Melzer, *No Way Out,* 27–29; Hagen, "Before the 'Final Solution,'" 373; Jabotinsky, *War and the Jew,* 86. Jewish wife of Miedziński: Wynot, "'Necessary Cruelty,'" 1051.

59 **The man responsible** All citizens: HI, Polish Embassy Washington, Jews alphabetical files, Refugees, Warsaw to Washington, 20 May 1938. Beck's analysis of global political economy: *New York Times,* 30 January 1937; JPI, 34/7, Józef Beck, "Wspomnienia," 143. Drymmer's analysis: "Zagadnienie żydowskie," 66. 150,000: Weinbaum, *Marriage of Convenience,* 45. First of all: *New York Times,* 14 June 1937.

59 **The question of the settlement** 1885, *Madagassez,* Blum, explorers: Brechtken, *Madagaskar,* 16, 57, 98, 120; see also Korzec, *Juifs en Pologne,* 250.

60 **Polish authorities also allowed** 1926: Friedman, *Roads,* 44. Blum's understanding: JPI, 34/7, Józef Beck, "Wspomnienia," 146. Nationalists: Drymmer, *W służbie,* 153. French nationalists: Marrus and Paxton, *Vichy,* 61. Understanding Zionism: "Palestine: Polish Attitude," NA, CO/733/352/6.

61 **Hitler's Jewish policy** 130,000: Heim, "Einleitung," 13. 50,000: Husson, *Heydrich,* 68. Riots: Morris, *Righteous Victims,* 128–38.

62 **London at first reacted** British and German position: Yisraeli, *ha-Raikh,* 2; Yisraeli, "Germany and Zionism," 158–59. German consul: Herf, *Jewish Enemy,* 27–28; Mallmann and Cüppers, *Halbmond und Hakenkreuz,* 51, 53.

62 **The Polish position differed** A good summary of the Polish position in 1937 is Szembek to London, 18 March 1937, AAN, MSZ 322/18497/35. Boundaries: Drymmer, "Zagadnienie," 66, quotation at 70. Sinai and Jordan: NA, CO/733/368/5/30 and 34; also on extension "towards the south," Aveling to Eden, 26 July 1937, NA, CO/733/352/6/46. The British were completely aware of public and official opposition to their policy, but did not seem to suspect where it would lead: Aveling to Eden, 14 July 1937, NA, CO/733/352/6. Arms and training to Haganah: Melzer, *No Way Out,* 142, 152; Weinbaum, *Marriage of Convenience,* 158. See also *New York Times,* 9 July 1937. It seems there were two distinct aspects of the Polish policy of military support of Zionism: (1) more or less open support of the Haganah, and thus the left wing, with arms and training, arranged by the general staff, with some payment from the Jewish side; and (2) clandestine support of the Revisionists, and thus the right wing, arranged by the consular section of the ministry of foreign affairs, with no payment from the Jewish side.

63 **The world Zionist movement** Evacuation plan: Melzer, *No Way Out,* 136. See also Engel, "Historical Objectivity," 578.

63 **Jabotinsky wanted Poland** Syria: Weinbaum, *Marriage of Convenience,* 113.

64 **Jabotinsky's power base** The basic work on this subject is now Heller, "Rise of the Zionist Right"; for these details see 19, 20, 35, 54, 144, 149, 158, 246. Model: Shindler, *Military Zionism,* 131, 138, 191; Shindler, *Military Zionism,* 129. Dream: Heller, *Stern Gang,* 24.

64 **Both Menachim Begin and another** Shapira, *Land and Power,* 196–202, 242. Romantic poets: Shamir, *Summing Up,* 6; Shilon, *Menachem Begin,* 11, 16.

64 **After Piłsudski's death** Heller, "Rise of the Zionist Right," 144, 145, 162. Also Heller, *Stern Gang,* 26; Weinbaum, *Marriage of Convenience,* 35. On Trempeldor: Zertal, *Israel's Holocaust,* 13–14.

65 **Yet disagreement about the meaning** Legacies of Piłsudski: Shindler, *Military Zionism,* 138, 205. Confrontation: Shilon, *Menachem Begin,* 18; Heller, "Zionist Right," 93.

65 **By 1938, the Polish ruling elite** Decisive significance of riots: Segev, *One Palestine,* 384. Origins and name of Irgun: Shindler, *Military Zionism,* 189; Shilon, *Menachem Begin,* 12; Kaplan, *Jewish Radical Right,* 9; Shapira, *Israel,* 128. Betar and Irgun: Shavit, *Jabotinsky,* 56.

66 **Irgun liaised with the Polish** Instructions to Hulanicki: Warsaw to Jerusalem, 8 April 1937, AAN, MSZ 322/B222532/35. See also Weinbaum, *Marriage of Convenience,* 128, instrument quotation at 135; and Drymmer, *W służbie,* 155–56.

66 **Avraham Stern was a child** Heller, *Stern Gang,* 100–103; Golan, *Stern,* 12. University: M. Schwabe and H. Pflaum to Dr. Magnes, Jerusalem, 19 December 1929, YMA, 1393/1/4/47/333.

66 **Although he was a talented linguist** Poems and literary exercises: YMA, 1393/1/4/43/230; YMA, 1393/1/4/45/282, 302, 303. Reality: cited in Golan, *Stern,* 17.

67 **Hulanicki, the Polish consul** Ideological leader quotation in Hulanicki to Warsaw, 5 January 1937 [1938], AAN, MSZ 322/B18516/32. Plan: Shavit, *Jabotinsky,* 229; Bell, *Terror,* 44. Landing quotation: Lankin, *To Win,* 7. The projected size of the Jewish force varies in the sources; the highest figure I have seen is 45,000: Heller, "Zionist Right," 95.

67 **Drymmer endorsed** Drymmer, "Zagadnienie," 71; Korboński, "Unknown Chapter," 374; Giedroyc, *Autobiografia,* 45; Weinbaum, *Marriage of Convenience,* 145; Heller, *Stern Gang,* 43; Spector, "Holocaust," 20; Spektor, "Żydzi wołyńscy," 573; Snyder, *Sketches,* 66; and Snyder, "Volhynian Jews."

67 **Although Polish leaders** The shift from one to the other and the attendant anti-Jewish element can be seen in Studentowicz, *Polska idea,* 12, 29, 46, 47; see also Giedroyc, *Autobiografia,* 62–63, for a frank description of the ideas of his milieu, at the time essentially the junior league of the Polish ruling class.

68 **There was some continuity** On Drymmer: Weinbaum, *Marriage of Convenience,* 125. Apostle: Józewski, "Zamiast pamiętnika," 10.

68 **The continuities were ideological** Common anti-communism: AAN, MSZ 322/18497/35, Szembek to London, 18 March 1937. Emotional appeal: "Notatka z rozmowy wicedyrektora T. Gwiazdowskiego z. p. Dr. Goldmanem," AAN, MSZ 322/B18415/21. See also Giedroyc, *Autobiografia,* 62.

69 **Yet there were some telling** See Paweł, *II Rzeczpospolita wobec ruchu prometejskiego,* 62, 65, 282.

69 **In the first Prometheanism** Porter-Szücs, *Faith and Fatherland,* 295.

70 **Unlike the Nazi regime** Hagen, "Before the 'Final Solution,'" 373, 375. Opposition: Wynot, "'Necessary Cruelty,'" 1043–44.

70 **This was a misunderstanding** May 1934: Roos, *Polen,* 151. Grand design: JPI, 34/7, Józef Beck, "Wspomnienia," 93.

71 **It quickly became obvious** Debicki, *Foreign Policy,* 90; Roos, *Polen,* 209; Müller, *Der Feind,* 64.

71 **Göring would later return to Białowieża** Beorn, *Marching into Darkness,* 97.

71 **Cults of personality are open** Quotation: Weinberg, *Foreign Policy,* 404.

72 **The hope was that if Poland** Totalistic states: Kornat, *Polityka równowagi,* 147. Stalin: Kuromiya, *Stalin,* 141 and passim.

72 **Right after Piłsudski's** Natural ally: JPI, 67/3/9, Jan Szembek, "Uwagi i obserwacje," August 1936. Propositions to join the Anti-Comintern Pact: Wojciechowski, *Stosunki,* 389; Kornat, *Polen,* 156.

72 **This was a trying time for Polish** Arrest instructions: [To Outpost E-15 in Ukraine], 7 August 1936, CAW, I.303.4.1956.

74 **General instructions from the Warsaw** Military intelligence: [To Outpost K-10, Leningrad], 19 November 1937, CAW, I.303.4.1983.

74 **In summer 1938** Göring in August and discussions of October: Wojciechowski, *Stosunki,* 423, 510. Ribbentrop-Lipski discussion: Lipski, *Diplomat in Berlin,* 453. Texts of Polish fallback negotiating positions on the highway: JPI, 67/76. Wein-

berg argues that the unwillingness to join the Anti-Comintern Pact was the key issue. *Foreign Policy,* 484.

75 **The side talk between German** Lipski, *Diplomat in Berlin,* 411, 453; Husson, *Heydrich,* 125; Loose, "Reaktionen," 48.

75 **In these negotiations** Historians of these negotiations often quote Lipski's remark that Poland would build a monument to Hitler if he found a way to resolve the Jewish question. With knowledge of the Holocaust we can find this remark even more revolting than it, in fact, was. Lipski was expressing the hope that, despite the overwhelming difficulties, Germany could induce some maritime power to open some overseas colony to Polish Jews. It never occurred to him that Hitler's "resolution" could be total mass murder. The remark is evidence of Lipski's incomplete understanding of Hitler, which was hardly unique to him, and not of Lipski's desire for a Holocaust of the Jews. See Lipski to Beck, 20 September 1938, in Lipski, *Diplomat in Berlin,* 411; and Melzer, *No Way Out,* 143. After the invasion of Poland, Lipski enlisted as a private in France and fought against the *Wehrmacht* in 1940.

75 **Most important was what the Poles** See *Staatsmänner,* 557; JPI, 67/3/14, "Krótkie sprawozdanie z rozmowy Pana Ministra Spraw Zagranicznych z p. Himmlerem w Warszawie," 18 February 1939. The Himmler quotation is from somewhat later, May 1940, but it conveys the basic difference in attitudes. Kühnl, *Der deutsche Faschismus,* 329.

76 **Warsaw's political vision reached** HI, Polish Embassy London, Jewish Emigration 1938, Consular Department Warsaw [Drymmer] to Jerusalem, 16 December 1938. See also HI, Polish Embassy London, Polish Consulate General in Jerusalem, Jerusalem to Warsaw, 4 July 1939.

4. The State Destroyers

77 **The Austria where Erika** Erika M. quotations: FVA, 2617. On the idea of *Lebensunfähigkeit*: Pauley, "The Social and Economic Background." Figures: Heim, "Einleitung," 27, 31.

78 **The contradictory Austria** These themes are developed at lurid length in the second chapter of *Mein Kampf.*

78 **Although Hitler did not** For richer discussions, contrast Steininger, "Road to the Anschluss" and Gehl, *Austria, Germany, and the Anschluss.* See also Stourzh, *Vom Reich zur Republik.* On National Socialism in interwar Austria, see Pollack, *Der Tote im Bunker.*

79 **Yet for Erika M.** See Rabinbach, *Crisis.*

79 **Beyond Vienna, the leading** On Friedrich von Wiesner and Jews and monarchism, see Vasari, *Leidenschaft,* 114; Snyder, *Red Prince,* chap. 7.

79 **Austria's major political conflict** On interwar Austrian politics, see Goldinger and Binder, *Geschichte der Republik Österreich;* and then Steininger, *Der Staatsvertrag.*

80 **The Nazis were never** Heim, "Einleiting," 31–32.

80 **The rise of Hitler** Ibid., 17.

82 **Erika M. was right** Klamper, "'Anschlusspogrom,'" 25; Botz, *Nationalsozialismus in Wien,* 136. A spiritual portrait of the moment is Stefan Zweig's *Schachnovelle,* in which the action takes place in the year between the destruction of Austria and the destruction of Czechoslovakia.

82 **The next morning the** Hecht, "Demütigungsrituale," 41, 43; Raggam-Blesch, "Anschluss-Pogrom," 112, 119; Botz, *Nationalsozialismus in Wien,* 127. Amusement: FVA, 1224, Ernest P. Journalist: Gedye, *Betrayal,* 9–10.

82 **The symbolic destruction of Jewish status** Hecht, "Demütigungsrituale," 53, 67; Heim, "Einleitung," 35.

83 **The "scrubbing parties" were** FVA, 1371, Herman R.; Gedye, *Betrayal,* 297. See also Petscher, *Anschluss,* 43–47; *Der Standard,* 2 March 2013; and Botz, "'Judenhatz,'" 19.

83 **The Austrian satirist Karl Kraus** All of a sudden: FVA, 3970, Charles H.

84 **What Austrian Nazis managed** See Dean, *Robbing the Jews,* 86, 94, 105, 109. Göring: Aly and Heim, *Vordenker,* 33.

84 **In 1938, some sixty thousand Jews** Figures: Heim, "Einleitung," 44.

85 **Avraham Stern, the radical Zionist** See Wasserstein, *On the Eve,* 371; Stern: FVA, 226, William N.

85 **On March 15, 1938** Polish approaches to the United States: HI, Polish Embassy Washington, Jewish alphabetical files, Warsaw to Washington, "Notatka do rozmowy z sekretarzem stanu," 15 March 1938; HI, Polish Embassy London, Jewish Emigration 1938, Warsaw to Washington, 20 May 1938.

85 **Polish diplomats worked** Drymmer, *W służbie,* 151; Tomaszewski, *Preludium,* 70; Weiss, *Deutsche und polnische Juden,* 195; quotation of Drymmer from Skóra, *Służba konsularna,* 582. Mechanism: JPI, 67/76, Lipski to Beck, 12 November 1938.

86 **The Nazis understood the implications** Tomaszewski, *Preludium,* 114; Weiss, *Deutsche und polnische Juden,* 200. See also chapter 3. The SS had learned lessons from two prior and smaller attempts at expulsion in 1938: Soviet Jews and Jews from the Burgenland.

86 **In European capitals in 1938** The mutual reinforcement is a theme of Wasserstein, *On the Eve.*

87 **The Grynszpan family** Kirsch, *Short Strange Life,* quotation at 82–83.

87 **Some of the top Nazis saw an** See Hilberg, *Destruction,* 1:94–95.

88 **With *Kristallnacht,* Goebbels** Benz, "Pogrom und Volksgemeinschaft," 13; Jäckel, "Der November pogrom," 67–71; Engel, *Holocaust,* 21; Husson, *Heydrich,* 100; Kershaw, *Hitler Myth,* 238; Bajohr and Pohl, *Der Holocaust,* 43.

88 **Hitler did nothing to defend** Friedman, *Roads,* 45. Göring now spoke of Madagascar: see Polian, "Hätte der Holocaust," 4; Steinweis, *Kristallnacht,* 45. See also Hilberg, *Destruction,* 1:46. Henryk Grynberg notices this chain of events: *Monolog,* 10.

90 **Czechoslovakia was thus like** Ragsdale, *Munich Crisis,* 167.

90 **Czechoslovakia was a creation** See Khlevniuk, *Stalin,* 162–63.

90 **Unfortunately for the French** 50 percent of officers killed: Wieczorkiewicz, *Łańcuch,* 296. See Ragsdale, *Munich Crisis,* 36.

91 **Even as London and Paris** Troikas: Petrov and Roginskii, "Pol'skaia operatsiia," 30–31. Completely destroyed: Jansen and Petrov, *Loyal Executioner,* 96.

91 **Throughout the territory of Soviet Ukraine** Village to village: Stroński, *Represje,* 235; Iwanow, *Pierwszy naród,* 153; Kupczak, *Polacy na Ukrainie,* 327. 1,226: Nikol'skij, "Die Kulakenoperation," 635.

92 **That was the day that Hitler** Ragsdale, *Munich Crisis,* 167.

92 **Czechoslovakia had no part** Osterloh, *Reischsgau Sudetenland,* 186–98; Husson, *Heydrich,* 84. Seventeen thousand and banking: Rothkirchen, *Jews of Bohemia,* 78–79 and 105–6.

93 **Poland bordered all parties** Artificial creation: JPI, 67/3/11, Beck to Lipski, 19 September 1938. Absurdity: Zarański, *Diariusz,* 225.

93 **Poland looked like a German** Position: JPI, 67/76, Lipski to Beck, 12 November 1938; Moltke to Berlin, *Documents on German Foreign Policy 1918–1945,* D, 5:87.

94 **The destruction of Austria** Segal, "Imported Violence," 315–17; Jelinek, *Carpathian Diaspora,* 227; Roos, *Polen,* 375. Lukacs is unusual among scholars writing in English in drawing attention to this admittedly complicated issue. *Last European War,* 34 and passim.

94 **As 1939 began, Hitler** Hitler and Beck, Memorandum of Conversation, 5 January 1939; and Ribbentrop and Beck, Memorandum of Conversation, 9 January 1939; [conversation of 6 January], *Documents on German Foreign Policy 1918–1945,* D, 5:153, 160. See also Müller, *Der Feind,* 110.

95 **Hitler's problem was** Ribbentrop and Beck, Memorandum of Conversation, 1 February 1939 [conversation of 26 January], *Documents on German Foreign Policy 1918–1945,* D, 5:168; Zarański, *Diariusz,* 484; *New York Times,* 25 January 1939. On 25–26 January as the turning point: Roos, *Polen,* 395–96; Kershaw, *Hitler,* 475.

96 **The day of Ribbentrop's return** This interpretation is more or less standard among diplomatic historians such as Roos, Cienciała, Kornat, and Karski who use the Polish as well as the German sources. These leave no doubt that Polish diplomats were working hard to keep up an appearance of rapprochement with Germany while never considering joining Germany in an offensive war. The idea of a German "illusion" also appears in Korzec, *Juifs en Pologne,* 255.

96 **Hitler decided to eliminate** Kornat, *Polen,* 158, 169, 174.

98 **On March 21, 1939,** Press coordination: Roos, *Polen,* 135. As late as 1938: JPI, 67/3/11, "Sprawozdanie P. Ministra Spraw Zagranicznych z Ministrem Propagandy Rzeszy Dr. Goebellsem w obecności Amb. R. P. w Berlinie Lipskiego," 13 January 1938. Historians of Germany often treat March 1939 rather than January as the moment of the decisive break with Poland. This confuses the mass politics with the diplomacy. In March, Hitler publicized demands that he knew that the German public would find popular and that he could expect that Western states might find reasonable, but which were already irrelevant to the German-Polish discussion, the main subjects of which had been the USSR and the Jews. This is clear from the diplomatic correspondence on both the German and the Polish sides and unmistakable in the Polish memoir material. The con-

frontation of September 1939 was never about Danzig and the corridor; presenting it that way requires an indulgently literal reading of limited German sources and the exclusion of two important contexts: Hitler's prior convictions and, of course, the subsequent Second World War.

98 **The Poles were in a relatively** Satellite status: Roos, *Polen,* 380–81. Pasture: Cienciala, Lebedeva, and Materski, *Foreign Policy,* 148. Honor: Wandycz, "Poland," 203.

99 **Yet neither the collapse** HI, Polish Embassy London, Jewish Emigration from Poland 1939, Consular Department Warsaw to Washington, 10 June 1939; HI, Polish Embassy London, Jewish Emigration 1938, Consular Department in Warsaw to Paris, 23 November 1938; HI, Polish Embassy London, Jewish Emigration 1938, "Problem emigracji żydowskiej," official policy paper, 20 December 1938. See also JPI, 67/3/14, "Krótkie sprawozdanie z rozmowy Pana Ministra Spraw Zagranicznych z p. Himmlerem w Warszawie," 18 February 1939.

99 **Polish relations with Britain** Geneva: NA, CO/733/368/5/29–31; NA, CO/733/368/5/37–39.

99 **When Beck flew to London** Ambassador in Warsaw: Kennard to Cadogan, 7 March 1939; Halifax to Kennard, 8 March 1939, in *Documents on British Foreign Policy,* Third Series, 3:203, 205. For the broader setting: Pedersen, "Impact of League Oversight," especially at 60. See also Mallmann and Cüppers, *Halbmond und Hakenkreuz,* 27; Wasserstein, *On the Eve,* 413.

100 **Despite Warsaw's new** A million: Wasserstein, *On the Eve,* 412. Make the case: Shavit, *Jabotinsky,* 221.

100 **Between February and May** Details of training: Lankin, *To Win,* 35–37; Shilon, *Menachem Begin,* 149. See also Yisraeli, "ha-Raikh," 317; Drymmer, "Zagadnienie," 71; Heller, *Stern Gang,* 46. Significance: Weinbaum, *Marriage of Convenience,* 146–49. A list of the Irgun members trained is in Niv, *M'arkhot ha-Irgun,* 172. Unfriendly quotation: Lankin, *To Win,* 32.

101 **The men to whom Stern** Bell, *Terror,* 48. For discussions among British diplomats and intelligence officers on the provenance of the weapons, see NA, CO/733/375/5.

101 **Polish military intelligence** There is a broad literature on Enigma in Polish and English. See, for example, Körner, *Pleasures of Counting,* chap. 13; Gondek, *Wywiad polski,* 262–63; Kozaczuk and Straszak, *Enigma,* and Pepłoński, *Kontrwywiad.*

101 **After 1933, Polish** *Mein Kampf,* 145.

102 **The Poles could be forgiven** Decisive: Govrin, *Jewish Factor,* 33. 20 August: Haslam, *Soviet Union,* 227. Propaganda: Herf, *Jewish Enemy,* 104. See also Weissberg-Cybulski, *Wielka Czystka,* 520. Litvinov was fired on 3 May 1939.

102 **By chance the World Zionist Congress** Wasserstein, who recalls the scene in *On the Eve,* 427, departs a bit from the quotation as reported by Yiddish newspapers at the time.

103 **Just as pertinent** On propaganda harmony: Govrin, "Ilya Ehrenburg." Equilibrium and blood: Weinberg, *World at Arms,* 25, 57.

104 **Aside from Soviet** Weber, *On the Road to Armageddon,* 92.

104 **Avraham Stern in Palestine** Stern on pact: Heller, "Zionist Right," 101. Tank: Shapira, *Land and Power,* 198. See generally Hazani, "Red Carpet, White Lilies."

104 **Stern was about to lose** Quotations: Mallmann, *Einsatzgruppen,* 54. See also Böhler, *Der Überfall,* 15.

105 **The invasion of Poland** Parade: Moorhouse, *Devils' Alliance,* 10–11. Bombing: Böhler, *Der Überfall,* 169–72. Seven thousand: Libionka, "ZWZ-AK," 18.

105 **The German invasion of Poland** Klafkowski, *Okupacja niemiecka,* 38, 41, 52, 55, 72, 73, 85, 95; Madajczyk, "Legal Conceptions," 138, 143; Mazower, "International Civilization," 556, 562. Mazower's important arguments draw from Madajczyk, who draws in his turn from Klafkowski's pioneering work, written immediately after the war. Klafkowski's study was a response to Carl Schmitt, written from the perspective of an international lawyer who had experienced firsthand the practical implications of Schmitt's arguments.

106 **The nullification of statehood** Virgin territory: Chapoutot, "Le loi de sang," 330. Italians: Madajczyk, "Legal Conceptions," 144.

106 **The destruction of the Polish** Massive extermination: Mańkowski, "Ausserordentliche," 7. See Weitbrecht, *Der Executionsauftrag,* 17. Heydrich's instructions: Husson, *Heydrich,* 201, 207.

107 **The *Einsatzgruppen* killed about** Heydrich quotation: Mazower, *Hitler's Empire,* 69. On the combination of intentions and accidental discoveries in the German progression from Austria through Czechoslovakia to Poland, Mazower's account is pioneering and persuasive. On the transition to stationary police, see Biskupska, "Extermination and the Elite."

107 **The first fragmentation** Soup and bread: Sauerland, *Polen,* 90.

108 **Much of Poland's west** More freedom of action: Mazower, *Hitler's Empire,* 227. For the pidgin German and other examples, see Epstein, *Model Nazi.*

109 **In the annexed zones** Property and professions: Salmonowicz, "Z problemów," 49; Salmonowicz, "Tragic Night," 13; Engelking and Grabowski, *Przestępczość,* 14.

109 **The creation of ghettos** Urynowicz, "Stosunki," 555; Klukowski, *Zamojszczyzna,* 135. On property acquisition and hostility: Staub, "Origins and Evolution of Hate," 52. Rape: Böhler, *Der Überfall,* 19; Löw and Roth, *Juden in Krakau,* 27–30. On ghettos, cf. Michman, *Emergence,* 95. It is worth considering Arendt's discussion of colonialism in Africa in this light: *Origins,* 206.

110 **For most Poles, the ghettoizations** Löw and Roth make similar points in *Juden in Krakau,* 19, 27.

110 **The Jews sent to the ghettos** See generally Trunk, *Judenrat;* also Löw and Roth, *Juden in Krakau,* 16.

111 **New Jewish police forces** Szeryński: Friedländer, *Extermination,* 156. Revisionists: Trunk, *Judenrat,* 490; this was the case in Lithuania as well, according to Dieckmann, *Deutsche Besatzungspolitik,* 2:1056. Duties: Engelking and Leociak, *Warsaw Ghetto,* 204, 207. Informers: Finkel, "Victim's Politics," 192.

112 **Then that order changed** Hempel, *Pogrobowcy,* 24, 20, 38, 43, 85, 87, 168, 170, 183, 184, 435. Thirty thousand: Curilla, *Judenmord,* 837. On the siege of

Warsaw, see Biskupska, "Extermination and the Elite." Racialization: Seidel, *Deutsche Besatzungspolitik,* 184ff. No punishment of Germans: Browning, *Ordinary Men,* 170.

113 **Jews, not seen as a race** Rickshaws: Engelking and Leociak, *Warsaw Ghetto,* 108. Tourism: See Harvey, *Women,* 131. There was a Baedeker guide to the General Government.

113 **The Nazi racial policy** See Rutherford, *Prelude,* 56–88.

113 **In practice, Himmler** Figures from Rutherford, *Prelude,* 9. Heydrich: Brandon, "Deportation," 77–78, 86. Eichmann: Polian, "Hätte der Holocaust," 3, 4, 19.

114 **The ghettos became** Eichmann: Husson, *Heydrich,* 253. Cf. Müller, *Der Feind,* 107–10.

114 **This was the latest surprise** Planning for Madagascar: Kershaw, *Fateful Choices,* 447.

115 **When Hitler understood that** Quotations: Lukacs, *Last European War,* 105; Mazower, *Hitler's Empire,* 133. 31 July 1940 preparations for attack on USSR instead: Müller, *Der Feind,* 216–21; Megargee, *War of Annihilation,* 22.

5. Double Occupation

117 **During the war** Arendt, *Eichmann,* 240; see also Arendt, *Origins,* 22. It is interesting to note that the scholars who were most influential in the foundation of Holocaust studies did not themselves use east European languages, including Yiddish. Hilberg's parents spoke Polish but he did not. Friedländer hails from Prague but does not use Czech. No major historian of the Holocaust learned an east European language after 1989, even as a vast wealth of sources became available and new secondary literatures emerged. Some of the consequences of this are the subject of my "Commemorative Causality."

117 **Like succeeding historians** Arendt, *Origins,* 447. See also Bloxham, *Final Solution,* 283.

117 **In 1939, when Hitler** On state destruction by proxy, cf. Stein, *Adolf Hitler,* 99. Hitler on Soviet practices: *Mein Kampf,* 320. On Himmler: Kühnl, *Der deutsche Faschismus,* 329.

118 **The Germans found the conditions** See Levin, *Lesser of Two Evils,* xi. A body of sociological literature supports the kindred thesis that strong local institutions prevent crime. See Lafree, "Social Institutions," 1349, 1367.

118 **When the Germans and the Soviets** Numbers from Morris, "Polish Terror," 759. This subject is treated in Snyder, *Bloodlands,* chaps. 2 and 3. See also Gurianov, "Obzor," 202; Nikols'kyi, "Represyvna diial'nist'," 337–40; Martin, "Origins."

119 **In 1938, Stalin** In the Ukrainian NKVD, for example, sixty of the ninety ranking officers were Jewish in 1936. Zolotar'ov, "Nachal'nyts'kyi sklad," 326–31. Other figures from Gregory, *Terror,* 63. Stalin achieved here one of his great political successes, the consequences of which are still felt today. Ethnic operations that he ordered were blamed on Jews, because Jews were among the officers who

carried them out; but immediately thereafter Jewish officers were purged from the NKVD. Thus, people who oppose communism but do not wish to oppose Stalin, the Soviet Union, or Russia can always combine it with antisemitism; this opportunity for National Bolshevism or east European fascism was opened then, and remains open today.

119 **It was this NKVD** See Gross, *Revolution from Abroad,* 37–44, and Carynnyk, "Palace," 266–67; and for primary sources HI, Anders Collection, 209/1/4835; 209/6/5157; 209/6/2411; 209/6/4724; 209/7/4112; 209/7/799; 209/7/6601.

120 **Against this backdrop** Calm after chaos as policy: "Komandiram, Komissaram, i Nachpolitorganov Soedinenii," 24 September 1939, CAW, VIII.800.7.15; as experienced: HI, Anders Collection, 209/13/3960. Majorities: Głowacki, *Sowieci,* 292; Khlevniuk, *Gulag,* 236.

120 **Unlike the Germans** Total figure from *Deportatsii pol'skikh grazhdan,* 29. 139,794 and percentages: Hryciuk, "Victims 1939–1941," 184, 191; Wnuk, *Za pierwszego Sowieta,* 13, 372.

121 **One of the individuals** Herling, *World Apart,* 39, 65, 131, 132. On spontaneity, see Arendt, *Origins,* 438.

122 **From the Soviet perspective** Quotations: Cienciala, Lebedeva, and Materski, *Katyn,* 118, 140.

122 **In April 1940** For Strasman: Korboński, "Unknown Chapter," 375. For the Engelkreis, Brandwajn, and Proner families, see Spanily, *Pisane miłością,* 49, 112, 387.

123 **With one exception** Social background and Blokhin: Cienciala, Lebedeva, and Materski, *Katyn,* 25, 124. Deportation of families: Goussef, "Les déplacements," 188; Jolluck, *Exile,* 15 and then passim on the experience of women; Cienciala, Lebedeva, and Materski, *Katyn,* 173–74. Strasman: Korboński, "Unknown Chapter," 375. Jewish neighbor helps: Spanily, *Pisane miłością,* 187. Janina Dowbor, a daredevil glider and parachutist, was the one woman. She trained as a pilot in 1939, and enlisted in the Polish air force reserve. Her plane was apparently shot down by the Germans. After parachuting to safety, she was arrested by the Soviets as a Polish second lieutenant. On 21 or 22 April 1940, she was shot at Katyn, and buried along with 4,409 men.

123 **There was also continuity** On the Great Terror in Moscow: Schlögel, *Terror und Traum,* 602; Baberowski, *Der rote Terror,* 195.

123 **The Soviets, at least some** Moral sublimity: Fest, *Das Gesicht,* 162. For further reflections on similarity and difference, see Snyder, *Bloodlands.*

124 **In western and central** Frank quotation: Longerich, *Unwritten Order,* 47.

125 **An empire on Nazi principles** Prison to power: HI, Anders Collection, 209/1/10420, 209/1/2660, 209/1/3571, 209/1/3817/19, 209/1/3517, 209/1/6896 (Dubno County); 209/3/6238 (Horochów); 209/6/5157, 209/6/2376, 209/6/2652, 209/6/4303, 209/6/4284, 209/6/9083 (Kostopol); 209/11/4217, 209/11/3887, 209/11/4049, 209/11/3238, 209/9/6105 (Krzemieniec); 210/14/10544, 210/14/4527, 210/14/2526 (Zdołbunów); 209/13/2935, 209/13/8034 (Luboml); 210/12/1467, 210/12/9728, 210/12/5945.

125 **The Soviet decapitation** See Danylenko and Kokin, *Radians'kyi orhany,* 233–55, for examples of agents at work. See also Wnuk, *"Za pierwszego Sowieta";*

Nowak-Jeziorański, "Gestapo i NKVD"; revealing though on a later period: Burds, "Agentura."

126 **After the obligatory** Butchers: Margolin, *Reise,* 14.

126 **The Soviets behaved** RAF: Moorhouse, *Devils' Alliance,* 154–55. Song: Kuromiya, *Freedom and Terror,* 258.

127 **In putting an end to capitalism** Revisions: HI, Anders Collection, 310/14/4908. Cygielman: HI, Anders Collection, 210/9/4061. Kovel shops: HI, Anders Collection, 209/7/4775. Arms searches: HI, Anders Collection, 210/12/8117.

127 **The end of the Polish** On the rapid change in property regime, see Gross, *Revolution,* 37; Sauerland, *Polen,* 72. Szef: HI, Anders Collection, 210/1/5331.

128 **The massive scale of Soviet** Gunpoint: HI, Anders Collection, 209.

128 **Most Jews in eastern Poland** Volhynia figures from 1937 in "Omówienie wydawnictwa Wołyńskiego Urzędu Wojewódzkiego p. t. 'Wołyń,'" June 1937, CAW, I.371.2/A.100. Abolition of the złoty and generally: Bender, *Jews of Białystok,* 60–62, 70, 83.

129 **In altering the character** Cf. Mędykowski, *W cieniu,* 243.

129 **In other ways Soviet policy** For a theoretical reflection on the Polish historiography of double occupation, see Shore, "Conversing with Ghosts," 5–28.

130 **Even as Soviet power** Excellent examples in Wnuk, *'Za pierwszego Sowieta';* see also Gross, *Sąsiedzi,* 35.

131 **In the Ukrainian case** See Martin, *Affirmative Action Empire;* and Snyder, *Sketches.*

131 **That said, the Ukrainian** Ideological confusion: Dowództwo Okręgu Korpusu II, "Sprawozdanie o ruchu komunistycznym na terenie DOK. Nr. II za czas od dn. 15 VI do 15 X 1933 r.," 13 November 1933, CAW, I.371.2/A.91; Dowództwo Okręgu Korpusu II, "Sprawozdanie o ruchu komunistycznym na terenie DOK. Nr. II za czas od dn. 15 X 1934 do 15 I 1935 r.," CAW, I.371.2/A.92; "Nastroje wśród oddziałów 13 D.P.," Równe, 14 April 1937; CAW, I.371.1.2/A.103. Szprynger and "Hitler": Dowództwo Okręgu Korpusu II, "Sprawozdanie o ruchu komunistycznym na terenie DOK. Nr. II za czas od dn. 15 VII 1937 do 15 X 1937 r.," CAW, I.371.2/A.92. This is a subject of Snyder, *Sketches.*

132 **The Soviet invasion of eastern** Destruction of legal parties and UNDO: Danylenko and Kokin, *Radians'kyi orhany,* 214–18, 251. Every village: Il'iushyn, *OUN-UNP,* 17.

132 **During the first few months** Jewish mayors: Levin, *Lesser of Two Evils,* 44. On collectivization and changing attitudes: "Meldunek specjalny—Sprawa Ukraińska," 25 November 1941, SPP, 3/1/1/1/1. For an example, see Shumuk, *Perezhyte i peredumane. Revolution from Abroad* is the title of Gross's classic study.

133 **All in all, Soviet occupation** Arrests of Zionists: "Calendar of Pain," *Sefer Lutsk.* Begin: Shilon, *Menachem Begin,* 25, 29; Shindler, *Military Zionism,* 218. NKVD and Irgun: Hrynevych, *Nepryborkane riznoholossia,* 296.

134 **Betar was quickly powerless** Letter of 27 December 1939, NA, KV/2/2251/7a. See Lankin, *To Win,* 40; Bell, *Terror Out of Zion,* 52; Weinbaum, *Marriage of Convenience,* 140.

134 **Of the three European states** Shamir's hope: Shamir, *Summing Up,* 54.

134 **The appeals sent by Jewish** Stern's proposal: Yisraeli, "ha-Raikh," 315.

135 **Stern assumed that Hitler** See Bell, *Terror Out of Zion,* 69.

135 **Every method of changing** See Heller, *Stern Gang,* 19. Jabotinsky was simultaneously urging the British to accept the inevitable wave of Polish-Jewish refugees (without success). See, for example, Jabotinsky to MacDonald, 5 September 1939, NA, CO/733/368/5/9.

136 **These Jewish and Ukrainian** See Mallmann and Cüppers, *Halbmond und Hakenkreuz.*

137 **In 1940, the application** A boy called Joseph remembered that his family fled the German zone after laughing Germans had burned down the synagogue. His father had decided to flee east and take refuge with a friend. He did not want to take Soviet passports because he wanted to be able to return home after the war. The family was deported to the Gulag. First Joseph's brother died, then his parents. Gross and Gross, *War Through Children's Eyes,* 221.

137 **In the first half of 1940** NKVD: Hrynevych, *Nepryborkane riznoholossia,* 299.

137 **With the wider world unattainable** Quotation: Rabin, *Vishnivits: sefer zikaron,* 315. See Melnyk, "Stalinist Justice," 231. *The Lesser of Two Evils* is the title of Levin's classic work.

139 **Before the consecutive** Dieckmann, *Deutsche Besatzungspolitik,* 1:87, 95, 127, 128. On absence of pogroms see Sirutavičius and Staliūnas, "Was Lithuania," 146–50.

139 **By the standards of Europe** 23,000: Dieckmann, *Deutsche Besatzungspolitik,* 1:144. 1,500: Łossowski, *Kraje bałtyckie,* 145–47. Lemkin: See his *Totally Unofficial,* 29.

139 **As a result of the German-Soviet** On the pogrom, see Dieckmann, *Deutsche Besatzungspolitik,* 1:142.

140 **In late 1939 and early 1940** Quotations: Levin, *Lesser of Two Evils,* 198; Klarman to Levin, 8 November 1939, NA, KV/2/2251/4a; NA, KV/2/2251/1a. Zionists: Bender, *Jews of Białystok,* 66; also the memoir of Good, "'Jerushalayim,'" 13–14. Base: Hrynevych, *Nepryborkane riznoholossia,* 294. On the Lithuanian-Polish question in Vilnius, see Snyder, *Reconstruction of Nations,* chaps. 1–4.

140 **The position of Jews** Ezergailis, *Holocaust in Latvia,* 63, 69, 83. Angrick and Klein, *Final Solution,* 12. On the Agudat movement see Bacon, *Politics of Tradition.*

141 **The subsequent and rapid** Weiss-Wendt emphasizes humiliation in his account of Estonia (*Murder Without Hatred,* 39), as does Plavnieks in his fine dissertation "Nazi Collaborators," 41. Dieckmann favors the notion of shame: *Deutsche Besatzsungspolitik,* 1:114.

142 **The political resource included** Repatriation: MacQueen, "White Terror," 98. Lithuanians: Dieckmann, *Deutsche Besatzungspolitik,* 92–95. Weiss-Wendt estimates at least 1,821 Latvians (and 2,055 Estonians; Estonia will be discussed in a later chapter). *Murder Without Hatred,* 36.

142 **The timing of the Soviet** Dieckmann gives a range of 16,989 to 17,500: *Deutsche Besatzungspolitik,* 1:152. A Soviet report gives the figure of 9,817 shot in prison, 1,439 shot on the convoys, and another 1,059 who died on the convoys for an unspecified reason. Vladimirtsev, *NKVD-MVD,* 67–68.

6. The Greater Evil

144 **"The epoch of statehood"** In his famous *Der Begriff des Politischen* of 1932, discussed in Jureit, *Das Ordnen von Räumen,* 358. It is true that Schmitt was criticized from within the party for being too attached to the conventional state. But what he meant by a "total state" is not an ever larger one, but rather one that is defined by the animal, pre-political energy of the racial party, which is to create a "total revolution." See Faye, "Carl Schmitt," 164, 171.

144 **Beyond manipulation itself** Quotations: Schmitt, "*Grossraum* Order," 105, 124, 101. See Gross, *Carl Schmitt and the Jews,* 147–49, and Nunan, "Translator's Introduction." Cf. Sternhell, *Les anti-Lumières,* 618.

145 **Schmitt believed that the** Infection: Schmitt, "Eröffnung," 15. Jurists: Chapoutot, "Le loi de sang," 310–12. Seyss-Inquart quotation: Liulevicius, *German Myth,* 171.

145 **Frank, Hitler's personal** Frank quotations: Frank, "Einleitung," 141–42; Frank, "Ansprach," 9. Theft of silver: Snyder, *Red Prince,* chap. 9. His wife's robbery of the ghetto: Löw and Roth, *Juden in Krakau,* 27.

145 **Lawyers were extremely** Mallmann, *Einsatzgruppen,* 23.

146 **Germany at war remained** This argument from politics is influenced by Longerich's *Politik der Vernichtung;* what seems crucial is to extend political argument beyond the borders of the prewar Reich to the lands where the Holocaust took place, and beyond German actors to those with whom they interacted.

146 **As the *Einsatzgruppen* followed** Churchill quotation: Saviello, "Policy," 24.

146 **The Holocaust has** Calculation of one million: Brandon, "First Wave." See Benz, Kweit, and Mathäus, *Einsatz,* 33. In March 1941, Heydrich proposed to Göring a plan for the deportation of Jews to Siberia. Gerlach, *Kalkulierte Morde,* 747; Kay, *Exploitation,* 109.

147 **Sometimes the *Einsatzgruppen* who followed** Basic task is state destruction: Husson, *Heydrich,* 310.

147 **Antisemitism cannot fully** Benz, Kweit, and Mathäus, *Einsatz,* 73. See Angrick, *Besatzungspolitik.*

149 **Even the most hidebound Nazis** This nazified line of reasoning is resonant today. I try to explain why in Snyder, "Commemorative Causality." On Lithuanian pogroms: Dieckmann, *Deutsche Besatzungspolitik,* 2:1512 and passim.

149 **After the war, Soviet** On the postwar campaigns against Ukrainian and Lithuanian nationalists, which form the backdrop for these arguments, see Snyder, *Reconstruction.*

150 **It is tempting to imagine** The most useful synthesis is now Polonsky, *Jews in Poland and Russia,* vol. 3. Cf. Longerich, *Davon,* 161; Ezergailis, *Holocaust in Latvia,* 13–15.

151 **The commencement of mass killing** What is meant is not the rationalities involved in what Foucault calls governmentality, but rather the deliberate destruction of government in a traditional sense in the name of biology and in the expectation that biology can then reassert itself. This destruction does not end politics but does create a new setting in which a new kind of politics emerges. See *Naissance de la biopolitique,* 316.

151 **In a dark irony** German beliefs: Benz, Kweit, and Mathäus, *Einsatz,* 34.

152 **To a degree** The important notion of double collaboration was introduced by Gross in *Sąsiedzi* and has since figured in local studies such as Snyder, "Causes"; Brakel, *Unter Rotem Stern und Hakenkreuz*; Penter, *Kohle;* and Weiss-Wendt, *Murder Without Hatred.* It should be the topic of detailed empirical study.

152 **The Soviet system was not** See Mędykowski, *W cieniu,* 160.

155 **What local people expected** An Organization of Ukrainian Nationalists (OUN) informer on OUN intelligence cooperation with Germany: "Komunikat Informacyjny," 3 June 1932, AAN, MSW/1040/50–57.

155 **As Ukrainian nationalists** Propaganda inside Germany: Longerich, *Davon,* 159. Himka makes the point about ethnicization in "Ethnicity and Reporting." The case of Oleksandr Kohut: Kachanovs'kyi, "OUN(b)," 220, 223. On the calculation of shooting prisoners: Carynnyk, "Palace," 280–81.

155 **In Lwów on July 25, 1941** Kill one Jew: Prusin, *Lands Between,* 158. Mizoch: HI, Anders Collection, 210/14/7746; HI, Anders Collection, 210/14/3327. On Mizoch in the Soviet period, see ŻIH, 301/1795.

156 **By reducing actual Ukrainian** Klevan: ŻIH, 301/1190, Abraham Kirschner. Dubno: ŻIH, 301/2168, Pinches Fingerhut; Adini, *Dubno: sefer zikaron,* 698–701. On German confusion in Dubno: Carynnyk, "Palace," 293. On police continuity: Bauer, *The Death of the Shtetl,* 64. For development of the double collaboration theme, see Snyder, "Causes," 208–9.

158 **Jews were ordered** This recounting draws from Curilla, *Judenmord,* 246–51; and Bender, *Jews of Białystok,* 90; see also Matthäus, "Controlled Escalation," 223; Machcewicz, "Rund um Jedwabne," 73–74. Ten men in small synagogue: FVA, 2903, Leon F.

158 **In those days of late June** Heydrich on 29 June: "*Spurenlos auszulösen, zu intensivieren wenn erforderlich und in die richtigen Bahnen zu lenken, ohne dass sich diese örtlichen 'Selbstschutzkreise' später auf Anordnungen oder auf gegebene politische Zusicherungen berufen können.*" Cited in *Justiz und NS-Verbrechen,* vol. 43, 2010, Lfd. Nr. 856, 177–78. Score settling political but not ethnic: Machcewicz, "Rund um Jedwabne," 72–73. The same was true in Romania; this will be discussed in a later chapter.

159 **If Heydrich's order** Presence of Himmler with Kurt Daluege, the head of the *Ordnungspolizei* in Białystok on 8 July: Bender, *Jews of Białystok,* 94. Himmler's disappointment: Rossino, "Violence," 6. Himmler, Heydrich, Göring interest: Dmitrów, "Die Einsatzgruppen," 127, 145, 155.

159 **The presence and preferences** Police units: Dmitrów, "Die Einsatzgruppen," 112–27; Machcewicz, "Rund um Jedwabne," 75.

160 **The Germans were learning** The empirical argument is in Kopstein and Wittenberg, "Intimate Violence," chap. 4. Local polarization seems to have general explanatory power: see Croes, "Holocaust in the Netherlands," 484.

160 **The most notorious pogrom** Conditions: Kopstein and Wittenberg, "Intimate Violence," chap. 4; Bikont, *My z Jedwabnego*; also Gross, *Sąsiedzi,* 29. Traitor: Gross, *Sąsiedzi,* 35; Sauerland, *Polen,* 83.

161 **The scenography** Flag: Gross, *Sąsiedzi,* 12. Cf. Cała, *Antysemitizm,* 433.

161 **In northeastern Poland** Machcewicz, "Rund um Jedwabne," 65, 69, 70, 72.

161 **The Jedwabne method** Sauerland, *Polen,* 66; Machcewicz, "Rund um Jedwabne," 86.

162 **The presence or absence** About 1,100 of the Jews murdered in Lithuania were killed in pogroms: less than one percent of the total number killed. Dieckmann, *Deutsche Besatzungspolitik,* 2:1512.

162 **The Germans understood** According to Łossowski, *Kraje bałtyckie,* 164, some 50,000 people left Lithuania as Germans during the Soviet period, of whom one-half returned.

162 **The Lithuanian activists arrived** Business figures from Levin, *Lesser of Two Evils,* 69.

163 **The politics of mass killing** In June 1941, the Lithuanian Communist Party was almost 40 percent Russian, about 46 percent Lithuanian, and 13 percent Jewish. The communist security police was about 46 percent Lithuanian, 36 percent Russian, and 17 percent Jewish in 1940. So in both cases Jews were considerably overrepresented by comparison to their share of the population but about a third as numerous as Lithuanians. Dieckmann, *Deutsche Besatzungspolitik,* 1:165–69.

163 **Actual political experience** Dieckmann, *Deutsche Besatzungspolitik,* 1:248–53; see also Lower, "Pogroms," 224. Communist youth: Eidintas, *Jews,* 257.

164 **Double collaboration** Wette, *Karl Jäger,* 82; Dieckmann, *Deutsche Besatzungspolitik,* 1:297.

165 **The Germans never did** Dieckmann, *Deutsche Besatzungspolitik,* 1:534. Knyrimas and Baranauskas: Eidintas, *Jews,* 256.

165 **Vilnius, the Jerusalem** On the Polish-Lithuanian-Jewish question in wartime Vilnius, see Snyder, *Reconstruction,* chap. 4.

166 **This innovation took place** Dieckmann, *Deutsche Besatzungspolitik,* 2:906, 1511. Hitler, Goebbels, marking of Jews: Longerich, *Davon,* 165–68. On perceptions in the field about the course of the war, see inter alia Römer, *Kommissarbefehl,* 204.

166 **If the Soviet Union** Ingrao, *Believe,* 236. Cf. Fritzsche, "Holocaust and the Knowledge," 603. In Germany: Longerich, *Davon,* 160–61. Filbert and translation: Kay, "Transition to Genocide," 413–25; see also Ingrao, *Believe,* 81, 158–59; Ingrao "Violence de guerre," 236–37; Römer, *Kameraden,* 410, 414, 448, 462.

168 **Their hesitations about** Kay, "Brothers."

168 **The Nazi conviction** Large numbers of Latvians return: Ezergailis, *Holocaust in Latvia,* 48; see also 155, 165–66. Liberation from the Jews: Dieckmann, *Deutsche Besatzungspolitik,* 1:513. See also Silberman, "Jan Lipke," 87.

169 **By now Stahlecker** Naturally: Breitmann, "Himmler," 436. Channeling: Wette, *Karl Jäger,* 78.

171 **The Arājs *Kommando*** On Arājs and his commando, see *Justiz und NS-Verbrechen,* vol. 43, *2010.* Lfd. Nr. 856, 173–83; Kaprāns Vita Zelče, "Vēsturiskie cilvēki," 169–70, 173–74; Plavnieks, "Nazi Collaborators," 41–49, 72–85; Vīksne, "Members of the Arājs Commando," 189–202; Angrick and Klein, *Final Solution,* 74 and

passim; Ezergailis, *Holocaust in Latvia,* 177, 183, 188. Russians: Kudryashov, "Russian Collaborators," 3. Looting: Bender, *Jews of Białystok,* 95.

172 **The *Einsatzgruppen* were a hybrid** Quotation: Ezergailis, *Holocaust in Latvia,* 206. See Bloxham, *Final Solution,* 130.

172 **Aside from the *Einsatzgruppen*** 12 August: Kruglov, "Jewish Losses," 275.

173 **Jeckeln's innovation** See Pohl, "Schauplatz Ukraine," 142–44; Angrick and Klein, *Final Solution,* 130.

174 **The easternmost part** Segal, "Beyond," 5–9, quotation at 5; Jelinek, *Carpathian Diaspora,* 234. See also Mędykowski, *W cieniu,* 287. Between 1867 and 1918, the Habsburg domains were a dual monarchy known as Austria-Hungary. The government in Budapest was sovereign in its domestic affairs. The king of Hungary was the same person as the emperor of the entire realm, Franz Josef.

174 **Hungary made Jews stateless** Vladimir P.: FVA, 2837. Béla Kun: Ingrao, *Believe,* 153.

175 **If the Judeobolshevik** Breitmann, "Himmler," 433–44. Thirty-three thousand: Kershaw, *Fateful Choices,* 456. Letter home: Schneider, *Auswärts eingesetzt,* 215. More than EG: Lower, "Axis Collaboration," 186. See also Pohl, *Herrschaft der Wehrmacht,* 152; Curilla, *Judenmord,* 851.

175 **On September 28, 1941** Pohl, *Herrschaft der Wehrmacht,* 259; Pohl, "Schauplatz Ukraine," 147; Pohl, "Ukrainische Hilfskräfte," 213. Rape and party: Schneider, *Auswärts eingesetzt,* 465, 471. Already bloodied: Dina Pronicheva, "Stenogramma," 24 April 1946, TsDAVO, 166/3/245/115–34; see also Dina Pronicheva, Darmstadt, 29 April 1968, IfZ, Gd 01.54/78/1758–76. For a description of the experience from Jewish perspectives, see Berkhoff, *Harvest of Despair,* 61–68; and Berkhoff, "Dina Pronicheva's Story."

176 **Many of the aged and infirm** More research is needed on the pogroms in the prewar Soviet Union in 1941. On Kyiv see Melnyk, "Stalinist Justice," 230, 238.

176 **At the end of 1941** Angrick and Klein, *Final Solution,* 114.

7. Germans, Poles, Soviets, Jews

178 **"The East belongs to the SS!"** Wasser, *Himmlers Raumplanung,* 51. See generally Gerwarth, *Heydrich.*

179 **Organized massacres involving** Percentages derived from Arad, *Holocaust,* 521, 524. For examples of collaboration, see the cases below. On the NKVD, see Kuromiya, *Freedom and Terror,* 268.

179 **The Germans reached** The Estonian case will be discussed at greater length in the next chapter.

180 **The prewar Soviet Union** Bemporad, "Politics of Blood," 4–5, 8.

180 **In an unhappy sequence** Three hundred thousand estimate: Pohl, *Herrschaft der Wehrmacht,* 119. Denunciations: Reid, *Leningrad,* 125. Ideological interval: Hrynevych, *Nepryborkane riznoholossia,* 111–20; Moorhouse, *Devils' Alliance,* 130. Kyiv example: Schneider, *Auswärts eingesetzt,* 462; Prusin, "Community of Violence," 1.

181 **The Judeobolshevik myth** Rabin, *Vishnivits: sefer zikaron,* 300.

182 **In doubly occupied western** Valuable on the entire period and on the question of nationalism beyond western Ukraine is Berkhoff, *Harvest of Despair.*

182 **In Zhytomyr, the major city** On the terror in Zhytomyr, see chapter 2. Leaflets: Lower, *Nazi Empire-Building,* 34.

182 **When war came to Zhytomyr** For the exchange see Lower, "German Colonialism," 22. See also Lower, *Nazi Empire-Building,* 34–35.

183 **Kharkiv was the major city** Terror and bread and salt: FVA, 3272, Pyotr Borisovich L.

183 **In any large Soviet city** Gangsters: Radchenko, "Accomplices," 445.

184 **When the Kharkiv** Radchenko, "Accomplices," 443–58; details about the march from FVA, 3270, Lydia G.

184 **The mass shooting of the Jews** Lower, "German Colonialism," 26; Radchenko, "Accomplices," 443–58, trash quotation at 454.

185 **No matter where the Germans arrived** Tyaglyy, "Nazi Occupation," 127, 141.

186 **Because Army Group South of the Wehrmacht** On the Gypsies, see Holler, *Völkermord,* 68–69.

186 **In Stalino, as elsewhere** Penter, *Kohle,* 270–81; Kuromiya, *Freedom and Terror,* 263–88.

187 **The initial German policy** Pripiat: Matthäus, "Controlled Escalation," 225; *Der Dienstkalender Heinrich Himmlers,* 189. Nebe: Gerlach, *Kalkulierte Morde,* 544, 549, 567. See Mędykowski, *W cieniu,* 231. Belarusians and Poles: Dean, "Service of Poles."

187 **With less local collaboration** Beorn, *Marching into Darkness,* 73.

188 **Not long afterwards** Ibid., 97.

188 **By October 1941** Megargee, *War of Annihilation,* 99.

188 **Unlike Operation Barbarossa** Quotation: Gerlach, *Kalkulierte Morde,* 588.

190 **Once Operation Typhoon** Beorn, *Marching into Darkness,* 7, 60, 62, 73, 120, 133.

190 **In Minsk** 7 November and other symbolic dates in Minsk: Rubenstein and Altman, *Unknown Black Book,* 238, 245, 251, 252. Communists: Rein, "Local Collaboration," 394; see also Brakel, *Unter Rotem Stern und Hakenkreuz,* 304. On Soviet Jews in Minsk, see Bemporad, *Becoming.*

191 **With the advance of Operation** Identification of Jews with partisans, beginning September 1941: Gerlach, *Kalkulierte Morde,* 566.

191 **The policy of mass** Vans: Gerlach, *Kalkulierte Morde,* 1075. The "black crow" reference is ubiquitous; see, for example, USHMM, RG-31.049/01, Evgenia Elkina. The killing with vans was also an extremely grisly business; some Germans preferred shooting. See Prusin, "Community of Violence."

192 **By the end of 1941** Rasch: Lower, "German Colonialism," 24.

192 **Whereas the Germans** Kudryashov, "Russian Collaboration," 4–5, 15; Penter, *Kohle,* 275; Reid, *Leningrad,* 125. The Germans murdered Gypsies in the outskirts of Leningrad as well; with what degree of local cooperation remains to be seen. See Holler, "Nazi Persecution," 157.

193 **In the cities of Soviet Russia** Cohen, *Smolensk,* 64, 68, 78, 79, 122.

194 **In nature, thought Hitler** German starvation policies are covered in Snyder, *Bloodlands,* chapter 5.

194 **The German invasion** Quotation: Arnold, "Die Eroberung," 35. Dieckmann develops the idea of the distribution of scarcity; see *Deutsche Besatzungspolitik,* 1:536, 579–83.

195 **Like the politics of Judeobolshevism** Cf. Gerlach, "Wannsee Conference." I agree that December was a turning point and am inclined to see it as Hitler's decision to announce an intent to eliminate all Jews rather than an explicit order to kill them all, but taken at a time when killing them was proving to be easier than deporting them. In early 1942, Heydrich and others were still discussing deportations to Siberia, which would have been senseless had there been an explicit order to murder; the failure of German offensives and Heydrich's assassination must have made such a deportation seem unrealistic. The technique of fixed gassing facilities then developed in Poland was not initially meant as a total solution, but it proved more feasible than anything else, and was pursued to the end. In my understanding, Hitler's determination from the beginning was to eliminate the Jews from the planet; it was a matter of indifference whether this was achieved through murder or through deportation to some inhospitable place. What is chilling is not a diabolical plan that was followed to the letter; there was no such thing. What is chilling is a worldview in which individuals are defined as a supernatural collectivity such that their removal is seen as ethical and the method of removal makes no moral difference.

195 **The autumn of 1941** FVA, 368, Iurii Israilovich G.

196 **The battle for Kaluga** Stieff cited after Edele, "States," 374.

196 **That very day** Common front: Herf, *Jewish Enemy,* 132 and passim. Hitler's 12 December speech as recorded by Goebbels: Mazower, *Hitler's Empire,* 376; see also Witte et al., *Der Dienstkalender Heinrich Himmlers,* 289. Cf. Friedlander, *Extermination,* 281. Once the United States was in the war it had to be presented by Hitler not as a distant model but as a fragile enemy, "half Judaized and half negrified": Fischer, *Hitler and America,* 37.

196 **In the occupied zones** Pity quotation: Mazower, *Hitler's Empire,* 376. Reckoning of the number of Jews killed by the end of 1941: Brandon, "First Wave."

196 **The lessons of the USSR** Some 1,500 Poles were among the collaborating police forces in the territories that are now Belarus. The Germans sought to reduce this number when they could, favoring Belarusians. See Dean, "Service of Poles," 6. The main collaborating Polish formations were the 107th and the 202nd *Schutzmannschaft* Battalions. In general, Poles were recruited to such formations in times and places where Ukrainian policemen deserted in 1943 to form a Ukrainian partisan army. In some cases Poles joined such formations to avenge ethnic cleansing by Ukrainian nationalists. See Snyder, "Origins," and Snyder, *Reconstruction of Nations.*

198 **On January 30, 1942** Hillgruber, "Grundlage," 286. Arendt noticed the problem with prophecy; see *Origins.*

198 **That same month** Quotation: *Table Talk,* 235. Leningrad estimate: Reid, *Leningrad,* 231. Estimate of about a million: Pohl, *Herrschaft der Wehrmacht,*

181; similarly Arad, *Holocaust,* 311. Africa and hunger motivation: Kuwałek, *Vernichtungslager,* 110–11. See also Madajczyk, "Generalplan Ost," 17. Askaren: Black, "Askaris," 279; Sandler, "Colonizers," 8. The Germans said "Askaren"; in English "Askaris."

199 **No one had to say** October: Heydrich, *Husson,* 437. See also Rieger, *Globocnik,* 60–61 and 103, where he dates the meeting to late September. For a list of the sites of oppression in the district, see Poprzeczny, *Hitler's Man,* 208.

199 **In the occupied Soviet Union** Wasser, *Raumplanung,* 61, 77; Schelvis, *Vernichtungslager Sobibór,* 32, 41; Arad, *Reinhard,* 14; Tooze, *Wages of Destruction,* 468; Black, "Handlanger der Endlösung," 315. For the ethnic groups, see Black, "Askaris," 290. Some western and Polish historians inexcusably follow the ethnicizing Soviet propagandistic and current Russian nationalist practice of referring to the Trawniki men as "Ukrainians." Ukrainians were certainly among these people, but so was everyone else whom the Germans asked, including of course Russians.

200 **From the west** Poprzeczny, *Hitler's Man,* 163, gives the figure of 94 staff from T-4; Berger, in the now-standard *Experten,* gives 120. Kuwałek in *Vernichtungslager* gives a total staff count of 453.

200 **The program of mass killing** On the process, see Arad, *Reinhard,* 44, 56; Młynarczyk, *Judenmord,* 252, 257, 260; Pohl, *Verfolgung,* 94.

200 **The practice of extermination** Rieger, *Globocnik,* 115.

201 **Many Jews yielded** Productive: FVA, 147, David L. Ten people: FVA, 404, Marion C.

202 **Most likely there was never** February 1942: Witte et al., *Dienstkalender Heinrich Himmlers,* 353. See Pohl, *Verfolgung,* 95; Friedländer, *Extermination,* 343, 430. The foundational study of Operation Reinhard is Arad, *Belzec.* I provide descriptions of the murder at Treblinka in *Bloodlands.*

202 **In Warsaw in late December** See Moczarski, *Rozmowy,* 200. The course and suppression of the Warsaw Ghetto Uprising is discussed at greater length in Snyder, *Bloodlands,* chap. 9. See especially Bartoszewski, *Warszawski pierścień;* Ringelblum, *Polish-Jewish Relations;* Engelking and Leociak, *Warsaw Ghetto;* and, for a sense of how much work remains to be done on the subject, Libionka and Weinbaum, *Bohaterowie.*

203 **The man who suppressed** Quotation: Kershaw, *Final Solution,* 66.

203 **That winter, Jews** Orpo: Curilla, *Judenmord,* 837. Lange: Kuwałek, *Vernichtungslager,* 49. Stars of David: Gerlach, *Kalkulierte Morde,* 686. See Mallmann, "Rozwiązać," 85–95; Friedländer, *Extermination,* 314–18.

204 **In the General Government** On the Łódź ghetto, see Löw, *Juden im Getto Litzmannstadt.* Main task and dogs: Grabowski, *Judenjagd,* 9, 59.

204 **In 1943 and 1944** Orpo responsibility: Browning, *Ordinary Men,* 121. Masses: Engelking and Grabowski, *Przestępczość,* 195.

204 **There was a politics** Markiel and Skibińska, *Zagłada domu,* 23, 48. Posters: Cobel-Tokarska, *Bezludna wyspa,* 90. See also Skibińska, "Self-Portrait," 469–71; Engelking, *Losy Żydów,* 162, 188; Grabowski, *Judenjagd,* 24.

205 **Poles were not always** Krosno: Rączy, *Pomóc Polaków,* 44. Żbikowski, "Night

Guard," 513, 515, 517, 520, 524; Grabowski, *Judenjagd,* 82. Chronicle of collective reprisals: Madajczyk, *Hitlerowski terror,* 9 and passim.

205 **Sometimes Poles in the countryside** Order: Engelking and Grabowski, *Przestępczość,* 194–95. Engelking gives the example of a Polish policeman who refused to shoot a seven-year-old who begged for death, and instead rescued the boy. *Losy Żydów,* 198. Examples of help in Rączy, *Pomóc Polaków;* and Hempel, *Pogrobowcy.*

206 **In these conditions** Grabowski, *Judenjagd,* 11, 69. The notion of the privatization of power, an Arendtian argument developed by Gross in *Revolution from Abroad,* might be useful applied in other settings.

206 **Wherever the state** Some Dutch Jews were sent to Sobibór, which is one more way that the Dutch situation resembles the Polish one. Almost all of the other victims of Sobibór were Polish Jews. Most Dutch Jews were sent to Auschwitz.

8. The Auschwitz Paradox

207 **Auschwitz has been a relatively** See Longerich, *Davon,* 222 and passim; on property: Aly, *Hitler's Beneficiaries.*

208 **For similar reasons** Cf. Veidlinger, *In the Shadow.*

208 **Auschwitz was one of the few** See the final chapter of Snyder, *Bloodlands.*

209 **In the history of the Holocaust** More than two hundred thousand Polish Jews were murdered at Auschwitz; they were the second largest victim group, after Hungarian Jews. The third largest was non-Jewish Poles.

209 **Auschwitz arose** Steinbacher, *Auschwitz,* 27; Steinbacher, *"Musterstadt,"* 275, 293.

210 **The purpose of Auschwitz** On the development of the camps and death facilities at Auschwitz, see Dwork and Van Pelt, *Auschwitz,* 166, 177, 219, 240, 275, 290, 293, 313, 326, 351.

212 **Intuitions fail** See Valentino, *Final Solutions,* 234 and passim; and Croes, "Holocaust in the Netherlands," 492; in another setting, Straus, *Order of Genocide,* 128. The level of antisemitism, insofar as this can be ascertained, does not seem to correlate with Jewish death rates; what does strongly correlate is the degree of state destruction. Helen Fein developed an asynchronous argument similar to the one here in her valuable study *Accounting for Genocide.* Where she writes of "the lack of counterauthorities resisting" German plans (90), I have sought in previous chapters to describe the process and consequences of the destruction of those authorities as one of the causes of the Holocaust as such. State destruction created opportunities for innovation, decapitated and perverted existing institutions, and left fragments that could be deployed for other purposes. But my findings certainly confirm her general case. As in so many other matters the suggestion for further research was to be found in Hilberg, *Destruction,* 2:572–99. See also Birnbaum, *Prier,* 130.

213 **Estonia shared the fate** Fate of leaders: Kaasik, "Political Repression," 310. Fate of ministers: Paavle, "Estonian Elite," 393. See also Łossowski, *Kraje bałtyckie,* 46–55.

213 **Soviet law was applied** Penal code: Maripuu, "Political Arrests," 326; Maripuu, "Deportations," 363. 10,200: Weiss-Wendt, *Murder Without Hatred,* 40.

214 **Double collaboration** Weiss-Wendt, *Murder Without Hatred,* 131.

214 **Former employees** Ibid., 115–16.

215 **In Estonia, as everywhere** Ibid., 132. Lithuanian policemen and POW camps: Dieckmann, *Deutsche Besatzungspolitik,* 1:525.

215 **The German occupation of Denmark** Quotation: Haestrup, "Danish Jews," 22. Vilhjálmsson and Blüdnikow, "Rescue," 3, 5, 7. *Wiking:* Wróblewski, *Dywizja,* 143–47. A field surgeon in that unit was a certain German physician named Joseph Mengele. Alongside Estonians: Strassner, *Freiwillige,* 15.

216 **When the Final Solution** Haestrup, "Danish Jews," 23, 29.

216 **There was a will** A sober accounting of these events is Herbert, *Best,* 360–72.

217 **Denmark's neighbor Sweden** German stance: Dwork and Van Pelt, *Holocaust,* 327. In custody: Haestrup, "Danish Jews," 52.

217 **Jews who were Danish** Vilhjálmsson and Blüdnikow, "Rescue," 1, 3.

218 **These lists of actions and absences** Antisemitism in the states at war with Germany and in the neutral states probably worsened rather than improved during the war; Americans, according to one public opinion poll, considered Jews during the war a greater enemy than the Germans or the Japanese. Nirenberg, *Anti-Judaism,* 457–58.

220 ***Citizenship* is the name** See chaps. 5 and 6 of Snyder, *Bloodlands.*

220 **In states allied with Germany** Frank's decree of 15 October 1941 in Paulsson, *Secret City,* 67. Compare to Moore, "Le context du sauvetage," 285–86. In the Rzeszów region of the General Government in occupied Poland, some two hundred Poles were executed for sheltering Jews. See Rączy, *Pomóc Polaków,* 61.

220 **Compare the fates of Victor Klemperer** On Jews permitted to live in Nazi Germany, see Longerich, *Davon,* 252–53. Quotation from Kassow, *Rediscovering,* 13.

221 **Because Klemperer was** Kassow, *Rediscovering,* 360. Bartoszewski makes the point about Anne Frank: "Rozmowa," 16. Cf. Fein, *Accounting for Genocide,* 33.

222 **Legal discrimination** On Schmid, see Wette, *Feldwebel,* 67.

222 **Citizenship in modern states** Soviet bureaucracy might seem to be an exception. But it is in fact an exception that proves the rule. First, the Soviet state was not, constitutionally or in practice, a traditional state bound by law. It was subordinate to the communist party, and thus in the end to the subjective reading of history by party leaders. Second, in times of massive state terror, such as 1937–1938, conventional Soviet legal practices were set aside in favor of a state of emergency.

222 **Even German bureaucracy** Bloodstream: "Endlösung der Judenfrage," in Pauer-Studer, *Rechtfertigungen,* 439. Breitman notes that it was a major mass murderer, Bach-Zelewski, who began the intellectual association of death with bureaucracy. "Himmler," 446. Wasserstein provides the startling example of a Jewish bureaucracy, a council to aid Jewish emigration, that in personnel and in mode of operation was similar to the *Judenrat* of Amsterdam. What changed in the meantime was the arrival of the German state destroyers, who had created a stateless zone to which Dutch Jews were now sent. Westerbork, at first a refugee

camp, became a transit camp for death facilities in occupied Poland. See his *Ambiguity,* passim.

224 **Bureaucracies in Germany** Gerlach, "Failure of Plans," 68.

9. Sovereignty and Survival

226 **Germany invaded Yugoslavia** See Manoschek, *Serbien,* 39, 51, 55, 79, 86, 107, 186; and Pawlowitch, *New Disorder,* 281.

228 **Croatia as a state had no hope** Korb, *Im Schatten,* 439–49 for summary of major findings; see also Korb, "Mass Violence," 73; Dulic´, "Mass Killing," 262, 273.

228 **Slovakia was the other** Ward, *Priest, Politician, Collaborator,* 209, 214, 221.

228 **Slovakia joined the Axis** Himmler and 20 October 1941 meeting: Witte et al., *Dienstkalender Heinrich Himmlers,* 278. See generally Ward, *Priest, Politician, Collaborator,* 227, 230, 233, 235.

229 **Romania, Germany's major** Tradition of "securitized" Jewish policy: Iordachi, "Juden," 110.

229 **Romania had been regarded** On Romanianization, see Livezeanu, *Cultural Politics.*

230 **Traditionally Romania had been** See Geissbühler, *Blutiger Juli,* 46, 49.

231 **When on July 2, 1941** Deportation figures: Olaru-Cemiertan, "Wo die Züge," 224. Iasi and 43,500: Geissbühler, *Blutiger Juli,* 54, 119.

231 **The Romanian political** Solonari, "Patterns," 121, 124, 130, "killing all Jews" quotation at 125. "Nobody except Jews": Dumitru, "Through the Eyes," 125. See also Prusin, *Lands Between,* 154.

232 **Romanian soldiers quickly** Glass, *Deutschland,* 144–47, 266–67; Dumitru, "Through the Eyes," 206–13; Geissbühler, "He spoke Yiddish."

232 **From the perspective of Bucharest** Numbers and analysis: Glass, *Deutschland,* 15. See also Hilberg, *Destruction,* 2:811; Bloxham, *Final Solution,* 116.

233 **Romanian policy** Ancel, *Holocaust in Romania,* 479, 486; Solonari, "Ethnic Cleansing," 105–6, 113. Hitler trying: Hillgruber, "Grundläge," 290. Diplomatic protection: Glass, *Deutschland,* 230.

234 **Under their longtime ruler** For a convincing analysis, see Case, *Between States,* especially 182–88. For an example, see Antonescu's conversation with Hitler on 23 March 1944, cited in *Staatsmänner,* 392.

235 **Budapest passed anti-Jewish** Forty thousand: Lower, "Axis Collaboration," 194.

236 **The expropriation** Gerlach and Aly, *Letzte Kapitel,* 81, 83, 104, 114, 126, 148, 188–89. *New York Times:* Bajohr and Pohl, *Der Holocaust,* 115.

237 **Like all of Germany's allies** Ungváry, *Siege of Budapest,* 286–91; Segal, "Beyond," 16; Kenez, *Coming of the Holocaust,* 244–48, 257. 320,000: Pohl, *Verfolgung,* 107. Arrow Cross: Jangfeldt, *Hero of Budapest,* 240.

240 **Jews who were citizens** Kenez comes to a similar conclusion: *Coming of the Holocaust,* 234.

241 **When the war turned** 29 April: Kershaw, *Fateful Choices,* 469. "Weltvergifter aller Völker": Hillgruber, "Gründlage," 296.

241 **Hitler was seeking to lift** Cf. Bloxham, *Final Solution,* 7; Ther, *Ciemna strona,* 19.

241 **Hitler was not** Changing character of USSR: *Table Talk,* 587, 657, 661; Hitler to Antonescu, 26 March 1944, in *Staatsmänner,* 398. Stronger man: Steinberg, "Third Reich," 648; Kershaw, *The End,* 290; see also Jäckel, *Hitler in History,* 89.

242 **Here, as with Estonia** Van der Boom, "Ordinary Dutchmen," 32, 42. Van der Boom argues that Dutch Jews were killed in such large numbers because they feared hiding more than deportation. As he points out, a Jew who tried to hide was sixty times more likely to survive in the Netherlands than a Jew who did not. But punishment for hiding was not unique to the Netherlands, and Jews survived in higher numbers elsewhere in German-dominated Europe without going into hiding. The fear of hiding might indeed be a special Dutch circumstance, but it cannot alone explain why a higher percentage of Dutch Jews were killed than, say, German or Romanian Jews. On Dutch antisemitism, see Wasserstein, *Ambiguity,* 22.

242 **The Netherlands was, for several reasons** Kwiet, *Reichskommissariat Niederlande,* 51–52.

243 **Amsterdam was the only** Michman, *Emergence,* 95, 99; Moore, *Victims and Survivors,* 191, 193, 195, 200; de Jong, *Netherlands and Nazi Germany,* 12–13; Griffioen and Zeller, "Comparing," 64. See generally van der Zee, *Om erger.*

243 **The situation of rescuers** Romijn, "'Lesser Evil,'" 13, 14, 17, 20, 22; Griffioen and Zeller, "Comparing," 59.

244 **The murder of Greek Jews** Mazower, *Salonica,* 392–96. On the cemetery, see Saltier, "Dehumanizing," 20, 27; for more direct German material interests, consult Aly, *Hitler's Beneficiaries,* 251–56.

245 **In the first weeks** Mazower, *Salonica,* 402–3. This account of the war in Greece follows generally Mazower, *Inside Hitler's Greece,* 1, 14, 18, 20, 235, 238, 240, 244, 250, 251, 259, and Rodogno, *Fascism's European Empire,* 364, 390.

246 **The French case** Hitler quotation, Vichy's foreign recognition, and number of civil servants: Rousso, *Vichy,* 15, 47. See also Birnbaum, *Sur la corde raide,* 252.

246 **France did introduce** Rousso, *Vichy,* 79–81. Madagascar: Marrus and Paxton, *Vichy,* 14, 60, 113. Same people: Bruttman, *Au bureau,* 199–201. I cannot enter here into the interesting issue of relationships between the French state's treatment of its Jewish and Muslim subjects. See Surkis, *Sexing the Citizen*; Shepard, *Invention.*

246 **The reasoning behind** 7,055: Personal communication from Patrick Weil, 11 October 2012; on the denaturalization process see his *How to Be French,* 87–122. Camps in France in 1939 and 1940: Grynberg, *Les camps,* 11, 35 and passim.

247 **Under the Vichy regime** Paris and Drancy: Wieviorka and Laffitte, *Drancy,* 21, 106, 118–19.

247 **French and German policies** Ibid., 120, 209.

247 **In summer 1942** Weil, *How to Be French,* 122; Rousso, *Vichy,* 92–93.

248 **The decisive matter** See Marrus and Paxton, *Vichy,* 325. The case of Belgium, where 60 percent of the Jews present survived, is midway between the Netherlands and France. The occupation was crucially military rather than civilian, as in France. The sovereign remained in the country, unlike the Netherlands. In Belgium, unlike in France but like the Netherlands, the Germans were able

to place their own people atop the police. Like France, in Belgium there were a large number of Jews who were not citizens; unlike in France they were not specially targeted by a sovereign authority. Unlike in the Netherlands, however, the Germans did not assemble a large police force of their own. Belgian Jews seem to have been better informed than Dutch Jews about the meaning of deportation; thus Van der Boom's explanation of the unwillingness of Dutch Jews to go into hiding would not apply to Belgian Jews. See Griffioen and Zeller, "Comparing," 54–64; also Conway, *Collaboration,* 24; Fein, *Accounting,* 156–67.

248 **The Holocaust in France** Rousso, *Vichy,* 93. Thronged: Marrus and Paxton, *Vichy,* 85, also 364. Soviet citizenship: Sémelin, *Persécution et entraides,* 208–9.

249 **Considerably more Polish Jews** Klarsfeld gives 26,300 Polish and 24,000 French Jews. Many of the 5,000 he classifies as Soviet would have been Polish Jews who took Soviet citizenship after the Molotov-Ribbentrop pact. *Le mémorial,* 19.

10. The Grey Saviors

250 **In the world that Hitler** According to Otto Ohlendorf, the commander of *Einsatzgruppe* D, Himmler said that responsibility rested with Himmler and Hitler alone. See Rzanna, "Eksterminacja."

250 **Every Jew who survived** Cf. Dwork and Van Pelt, *Holocaust,* 348.

251 **Almost every Jew** Hanna Krall recalls forty-five people who helped her, in one way or another. Bartoszewski and Lewinówna, *Ten jest,* 299.

251 **In *Einsatzgruppe* D** Christian Ingrao has developed this theme, especially in his *Les chasseurs noirs.*

252 **In 1938 in Germany** *Los Altos Town Crier,* 15 April 2009; Ralph Bernstein, personal communication, 15 April 2013; *Justiz und NS-Verbrechen,* vol. 37, 2007, Lfd. Nr. 777, 397, 398, 405, 407–9, 417, 431, 438, 439; Angrick, *Besatzungspolitik,* 422. About twenty-six thousand Jews were sent to camps in November 1938. Goeschel and Wachsmann, Introduction, 28.

252 **Most German Jews emigrated** Rumbula: Michel'son, *Ia perezhila,* 84.

252 **No one can know** See Snyder, "Commemorative Causality."

252 **Only about three percent** For this and other reckoning, see Snyder, *Bloodlands.* Experience: Głowiński, *Black Seasons,* 170.

253 **The degree of statelessness** Bremen police: *Bremens Polizei,* 124. See also Russ, "Wer war verantwortlich," 486, 494, 503. Cf. Browning, *Ordinary Men,* 165, 202.

253 **A lesser known** Maubach, "Expansion weiblicher Hilfe," 93–94.

254 **A few German women** Koslov, *Gewalt im Dienstalltag,* 482–84.

254 **Further east** Lower, *Hitler's Furies,* 163 and passim, for all of the conceptual issues.

254 **If statelessness drew** YIVO, RG 720, Hirshant Papers, 1/52, Syda Konis. For meditations on forced labor, see Pollack, *Warum;* Buber-Neumann, *Under Two Dictators,* 331.

255 **The end of states** Body and soul: Hryciuk, *Polacy we Lwowie,* 59.

255 **In eastern Europe** Matz, "Sweden," 106–9; Jangfeldt, *Hero of Budapest,* 161. Fif-

teen thousand to twenty thousand is the estimate in Dwork and Van Pelt, *Holocaust,* 316–18.

256 **Wallenberg, an exceptional** One exception is the French case of Le Chambon-sur-Lignon.

256 **One such man** Chan, "Ho Feng-Shan," 1–15, quotations at 5 and 15.

256 **After the German occupation** See Wasserstein, *Ambiguity,* 165; McAuley, "Decision," 4, 7, 32; Fralon, *Good Man,* 60, 79.

257 **A diplomatic rescuer** April 1940 number: Dieckmann, *Deutsche Besatzungspolitik,* 1:145.

257 **In the 1930s** For Daszkiewicz's memoir see MWP, Kolekcja Rybikowskiego, syg. 6233 [Leszek Daszkiewicz], "Placówka wyw. "G," 3, 4, 7–10, 18, 21, 22. On Rybikowski, see Pięciach, "Szpieg ze Sztokholmu" and for background, see Dubicki, Nałęcz, and Stirling, *Polsko-brytyjska współpraca wywiadowcza,* 100, 305, 342.

258 **One of Rybikowski's** MWP, Kolekcja Rybikowskiego, syg. 6233 [Leszek Daszkiewicz], "Placówka wyw. 'G,'" 21.

258 **The scheme that the Polish** MWP, Kolekcja Rybikowskiego, syg. 6233 [Leszek Daszkiewicz], "Placówka wyw. 'G,'" 22.

258 **In the chaos** Quotations here from MWP, syg. 1675, Sugihara memoir, 9; Rybikowski's memoir, at MWP, Kolekcja Rybikowskiego, syg. 6233 [Leszek Daszkiewicz], "Placówka wyw. 'G,' " 70.

259 **Once they had done** MWP, Kolekcja Rybikowskiego, syg. 6233 [Leszek Daszkiewicz], "Placówka wyw. 'G,' " 50–52, 64, 67. On Sugihara, his colleagues, and his actions, see also Pepłoński, *Wywiad,* 231–33; Kuromiya and Pepłoński, *Między Warszawą a Tokio,* 393; Levine, *Sugihara,* 117, 132, 218, 273; Sakamoto, *Japanese Diplomats,* 107, 114, 395.

260 **When Nazi Germany** See Gross, *Revolution from Abroad;* Gross and Grudeińska-Gross, *War Through Children's Eyes*; and Snyder, *Bloodlands,* chap. 4.

261 **The arrival of these** Begin, *Revolt,* 25; Drymmer, "Zagadnienie," 74; Korboński, "Unknown Chapter," 377. On Begin and the Polish army in Palestine: "Palestine: Counter Intelligence: Menahem Begin," 24 September 1937, NA, KV/2/2251/50a. Uniform and other details of journey: Shilon, *Menachem Begin,* 40–45.

262 **Now that the war** Shilon, *Menachem Begin,* 48. Meridor in Poland: Bell, *Terror Out of Zion,* 44–45. Lankin: Bell, *Terror Out of Zion,* 111. Nechmad and Lankin: Niv, *M'arkhot ha-Irgun,* 172. Lankin's memoir is *To Win;* on the Polish encounter 31–40. Meridor confirmed that he was number two under British interrogation: NA, KV/2/2251/14a.

262 **During the Second World War** These interactions are well described in Davies, *Rising '44.* On the reaction of Varsovians to the flight, see Biskupska, "Extermination and the Elite."

263 **The Polish government in London** Crushing majority: *"Proszę przyjąć jako fakt zupełnie realny że przygniatająca większość kraju jest nastrojona antysemicko."* Cited in Skibińska and Szuchta, *Wybór źródeł,* 397. For a sober analysis, see Brakel, "Was There a 'Jewish Collaboration'?"

264 **All the same** See Puławski, *W obliczu Zagłady,* 412 and passim; also Engelking and Leociak, *Warsaw Ghetto,* 667; and Engel, *Facing a Holocaust.*

264 **On November 27, 1942** 10 and 17 December: Stola, *Nadzieja,* 174; Bartoszewski, *Warsaw Ghetto,* 49. *Times:* Bajohr and Pohl, *Der Holocaust,* 99; "Extermination" and moment of silence: Saviello, "Policy," 1, 24, 27.

265 **This warning, issued** Significance: Fein, *Accounting,* 77.

265 **The availability of plausible** Secretary of Drymmer: Jan Karski, "Dziecko sanacji," *Tygodnik Powszechny,* 24 April 2012. Cf. Żbikowski, *Karski,* 10–11.

266 **Upon his return to Poland** Severe: *"przeważnie bezwzględny, często bezlitośny,"* cited in Skibińska and Szuchta, *Wybór źródeł,* 390. See Ringelblum, *Polish-Jewish Relations,* 77; Leder, *Rewolucja,* 23, 44; Bartov, "Eastern Europe," 575. Also worth considering is Thomas Bernhard's *Heldenplatz,* especially at 112.

266 **Most of the Jews** FVA, 1107, Jan K.

266 **In October 1942** Ibid. On Karski and his missions see Karski, *Story of a Secret State;* and Żbikowski, *Karski.*

268 **The concentration camp Auschwitz** Another English translation in Pilecki, *Auschwitz Volunteer,* 13. The Polish original can currently be found at http://www.polandpolska.org/dokumenty/witold/raport-witolda-1945.htm. German translation of the Polish original by Jan Skorup at http://pileckibericht.wordpress.com. Numbers: Bartoszewski, *Warszawski pierścień,* 124.

268 **Pilecki was a patriot** The passage is in Pilecki, *Auschwitz Volunteer,* 175; I translate here the Polish original.

269 **Some 28,000 Jews** 28,000 and 11,600: Paulsson, *Secret City,* 2, 5, 209, 212. 4,000: Bartoszewski and Lewinówna, *Ten jest,* 28. Joint and money belts: Bartoszewski, "Rozmowa," 35; Bartoszewski, *Warsaw Ghetto,* 59.

270 **Among Żegota's leaders** PPS: Bartoszewski, *Warsaw Ghetto,* 46. Individuals: Prekerowa, *Konspiracyjna Rada,* 69–75.

270 **At the same time** On Kossak and the debate over antisemitic rescuers, see Podolska, "Poland's Antisemitic Rescuers." See also Cała, *Antysemitizm,* 447. Rescue of human beings rather than Jews: also a finding of Tec, *When Light,* 176. Nucleus: Paulsson, *Secret City,* 26, 40; Peleg-Mariańska and Peleg, "Witnesses," 11; Oliner, *Altruistic Personality,* 6, 142.

271 **Like Pilecki, Karski, and Bartoszewski** Prekerowa, "Komórka," 521–25, 531.

271 **After the war was over** The phenomenon of assimilated Jews helping other Jews was, at least in Warsaw, not uncommon. Another form of Jewish self-help that saved lives was organization inside the Warsaw ghetto. See Sakowska, *Ludzie,* 117–86.

11. Partisans of God and Man

272 **Anszel Sznajder and his brother** ŻIH, 301/2953.

272 **The Sznajder brothers** The point is made in Croes, "Pour une approche quantitative," 95.

272 **This bloody irony** The complex histories of Jews in the Warsaw Uprising of

1944 are presented in Engelking and Libionka, *Żydzi w powstańczej Warszawie.* Amsterdam comparison: Paulsson, *Secret City,* 230.

273 **The Soviet partisans** See Brakel, " 'Das allergefährlichste,'" 403–16; Musial, *Sowjetische Partisanen,* 189, 202; *Verbrechen der Wehrmacht,* 495; Slepyan, *Stalin's Guerrillas,* 157.

274 **Some distinguished soldiers** On Józewski, see Snyder, *Sketches;* and his own memoir at BUW DR 3189. Długoborska: Bartniczak, *From Andrzejowo to Pecynka,* 138–40; Gawin, "Pensjonat." Koźmiński: Bartoszewski and Lewinówna, *Ten jest,* 310. Gieruła: Stanisław and Lusia Igeł, in Rączy, *Pomóc Polaków,* 280. Stanisław Igeł was in the Home Army.

275 **The Home Army also carried** Papers: FVA, 414, Alice H.; FVA, 538, Norman L.; FVA, 2700, Maria M. Woliński: Libionka, "ZWZ-AK," 36. On the *Biuletyn Informacyjny*: Libionka, "ZWZ-AK," 39, 43.

275 **Thousands of Jews either joined** Weapons from Home Army: Libionka, "ZWZ-AK," 57, 69. Quotation: Engelking and Libionka, *Żydzi w powstańczej Warszawie,* 91.

275 **In the opening days of the Warsaw** Kopka, *Konzentrationslager Warschau,* 82–115.

276 **The Home Army was a continuation** Bandits and death sentences: Libionka, "ZWZ-AK," 119–23.

276 **The myth of Judeobolshevism** Libionka, "ZWK-AK," 136.

278 **In villages where communism** Nurse: Elżbieta Burda, ŻIH, 301/2407.

278 **Though communist ideology** On recruitment of murderers, see generally Slepyan, *Stalin's Guerrillas,* 209. Amnesty: Penter, *Kohle,* 273. On Brins'kyi, see his *Po toï bik frontu.* Worry of Ukrainian nationalists: *OUN v svitli,* 82. Policeman and girlfriend: ŻIH, 301/2879. On the highly complex methods used by the Soviet partisans, see Burds, "Agentura"; Armstrong, *Soviet Partisans;* see also *Gazeta Wyborcza,* 15 April 2002.

279 **Jews who knew the local terrain** ŻIH, 301/717. For other examples of side switching, see Musial, *Sowjetische Partisanen,* 266–67. Jews also recruited Poles to the Soviet partisans; see the case of Mojżesz Edelstein in ŻIH, 301/810.

279 **Not every local Jew working** For another example of a Jewish recruiter, see ŻIH 301/1795. For encounters with antisemitism, see ŻIH, 301/53, Abram Leder; ŻIH, 301/299, Zoja Bajer; ŻIH, 301/1046, Lazar Bromberg. See also Dieckmann, *Deutsche Besatzungspolitik,* 2:1469. For general reflections, see Weiner, *Making Sense,* 376–382.

280 **Nevertheless, the Soviet partisans** Jewish and non-Jewish communists: Jakub Grinsberg, ŻIH, 301/305. Max: Zoja Bajer, ŻIH, 301/299. The punitive expedition: ŻIH, 301 5737, Rena Guz.

280 **A substantial number of the Jewish** German liquidations in Volhynia: A striking record is the inventory of gasoline and oil used exclusively for travel from ghetto to ghetto to murder remaining Jews. "Ausgabeliste," DAVO, Fond R-2, Opis 2, Delo 196. Volhynian Jewish partisans, male and female: ŻIH, 301/299; ŻIH, 301/718; ŻIH, 301/719; ŻIH, 301/1811. On family camps see Arad, "Original Form." Feeling of the deed: Aron Perław, ŻIH, 301/955. Each dead German: Leon Jarszun, ŻIH, 301/1487.

281 **One such person was Tuvia Bielski** On Bielski, see Tec, *Defiance,* 5, 40, 63, 80, 110, 145, 185, 208.

282 **This powerful myth could admit** Chess and disarmament: Libionka, "ZWZ-AK," 112. Correct understanding: Slepyan, *Stalin's Guerrillas,* 210.

283 **Although the Polish army** 592: Petrow, *Psy Stalina,* 223. Seventeen thousand: Gurianov, "Obzor," 205.

283 **Between 1945 and 1949** For surveys, see Simons, *Eastern Europe;* and Applebaum, *Iron Curtain.*

285 **Polish soldiers who had spent** Executions: Skarga, *Penser,* 28. Double collaboration at the end of the war: Skibińska, "Self-Portrait," 459; Grabowski, *Judenjagd,* 93, 109; Gross, *Sąsiedzi,* 115.

285 **Any Marxist could have explained** For articles that are suggestive of some of these interpretations, see Abrams, "Second World War"; and Gross, "Social Consequences."

285 **The Soviets entered a country** On the Soviet and communist Polish attitudes to the Holocaust, see especially Kostyrchenko, *Gosudarstvennyi antisemitizm;* Brandenberger, "Last Crime"; Szaynok, *Polska a Izrael;* Shore, "Język." For a longer discussion see Snyder, *Bloodlands,* chap. 11.

286 **Poles who had rescued Jews** Hulanicki: The case is made in Ginor and Remez, "Casualty." Wallenberg: The latest evidence is in Matz, "Cables in Cipher."

288 **The Sheptyts'kyi brothers** See Hentosh, "Pro vstavlennia," 318–25, and Motyka, *Cień Kłyma Sawura,* 80–82, for these details; the state of the art is Himka, "Metropolitan Andrei Sheptytsky." For the experiences of rescued children see Rotfeld, *W cieniu,* 53–54, 88; Kahane, *Lvov Ghetto Diary,* 118–55; Lewin, *Przeżyłem,* 155–59.

289 **Yet the Greek Catholic Church** On the origins of the Uniate Church, see Gudziak, *Crisis and Reform,* 209–22 and passim; Koialovich, *Tserkovnaia uniia,* 1:166–68 and passim.

289 **In 1918, the Habsburg monarchy** On Galicia, Ukraine, Poland, and Sheptyts'kyi, see Snyder, *Reconstruction,* chap. 3; Snyder, *Red Prince,* chap. 3; Himka, *Religion and Nationality;* Jobst, *Zwischen Nationalismus und Internationalismus.*

289 **In its experience of alienation** The case is made in Braun and Tammes, "Religious Deviance," 3, 11; Cabanel, "Protestantismes minoritaires," 455. On Germany, see Ericksen, *Complicity,* 95 and passim.

290 **By contrast, church leaders** On the famous French example of Le Chambon-sur-Lignon, see Sémelin, *Persécutions,* 717–37.

290 **In the occupied Soviet Union** Baptist rescue: Spektor, "Żydzi wołyńscy," 577; Spector, "Holocaust," 243; ŻIH, 301/397, Jakub and Esia Zybelberg, Hersz and Doba Mełamud. See also *Sefer Lutsk,* testimony of Fanye Pasht; Ringelblum, *Polish-Jewish Relations,* 242. Lea Goldberg and the Shtundists: ŻIH, 301/1011; also Siemaszko and Siemaszko, *Ludobójstwo,* 793. Cf. Cabanel, "Protestantismes minoritaires," 446.

291 **The dominant Roman Catholic Church** On the tortuous reconsiderations, see Connelly, *From Enemy to Brother.*

291 **Wilm Hosenfeld, a Roman** Confino, *World Without Jews,* 198.

292 **Aleksandra Ogrodzińska, a Polish** ŻIH, 301/2502, Wala Kuźniecow.

292 **Wonders and visions threaten** YIVO, Hirshant Papers, 3/206.

293 **For the nuns in their convents** Ringelblum, *Polish-Jewish Relations,* 226.

296 **Rufeisen was taken** This account is compiled from ŻIH, 301/3726 (also classified as ŻIH, 301/2827) and FVA, 1834; quotation from the former.

296 **Andrei Sheptyts'kyi** Sheptyts'kyi: Motyka, *Cień Kłyma Sawura,* 86. Iwaniuk: YIVO, Hirshant Papers, 3/206. Priest and Polish Roman Catholics: Rączy, *Pomóc Polaków,* 253, 100.

12. The Righteous Few

298 **Ita Straż, a young woman** Tomkiewicz, *Zbrodnia w Ponarach,* 203. Vova Gdud survived Ponary in the same way. He was helped in the first cottage. See Good, "Yerushalayim," 17–18.

298 **Who lives in the fourth** For a typical and eloquent record of being turned away multiple times, see Pese Kharzhevski-Zlotnik, "Di Kristlekhe 'hilf' far di Kolbutsker yidn," in Yasni, *Sefer Klobutsk,* 247–49.

300 **Later Zelda was denounced** YIVO, RG 104/MK547/7/200, Zelda Machlowicz-Hinenberg.

301 **At that point the host** YIVO, RG 104/II/5, Alicja Gornowski.

301 **A wife might save** Rubenstein and Altman, *Unknown Black Book,* 60–61. See Fogelman, *Conscience,* 260.

302 **Love for children could also** Romantic relationships that provided a structure for rescue could, of course, be homosexual, as in the case of the rescue of a Jew by a Polish Roman Catholic priest and his Ukrainian partner. See generally Paulsson, *Secret City,* 44.

302 **One day when Katarzyna** ŻIH, 301/1959.

303 **Maria was now working** YIVO, RG 104/MK538/1072.

303 **Men sometimes took in children** Siewer: ŻIH, 301/2259. Jeromiński: ŻIH, 301/1468.

303 **After climbing out** ŻIH, 301/2877.

304 **The last major transports** For the case, see Ostałowka, *Farby wodne.* On the death marches, see Blatman, *Death Marches.*

305 **And then, after a moment** USHMM, RG-68.102M/2007.372/21/206–47.

306 **In the invasion** Cf. Engelking, *Losy Żydów,* 117.

306 **Noema Centnerschwer** Noema Centnerschwer: ŻIH, 301/2750. Chawa Rozensztejn: ŻIH, 301/1272. On prewar Łomża, see Gnatowski, "Niepokorni," 156–57.

307 **Szyja Flejsz was a boy** On his life: ŻIH, 301/2739. On the problem of competitive recruitment: TsDAVO, 3833/1/87; AW II/1321/2K; AW II/1328/2K.

308 **The commanders of the UPA** On the origins of the UPA and its mass killing of Poles, see Snyder, "Origins"; and, above all, Motyka, *Od rzezi.* On its motivations, the primary sources are bountiful; see, for example, TsDAVO, 3833/1/86/19–20; TsDAVO, 3833/1/131/13–14. Soviet interrogation protocols offer confirmatory evidence: for example, Protokol Doprosa, I. I. Iavorskii, 14 April 1944, GARF, fond R-9478, opis 1, delo 398. For the rescue of a Pole by a

Jew, see FVA, T-1645. On the Soviet continuation of the Ukrainian nationalist project, see Snyder, *Reconstruction of Nations,* chaps. 8–10.

308 **All of the surviving residents** ŻIH, 301/2739; Siemaszko and Siemaszko, *Ludobójstwo,* 280. For additional information on Woronówka, which no longer exists, see http://wolyn.ovh.org. These partings are a wrenching subject, very present in the sources. See Shore, *Taste of Ashes.* Sometimes people who loved the children they rescued encouraged them to go, following the same moral instincts that instructed them in the first place. And sometimes they later regretted it.

310 **Seeing the peasant's reaction** ŻIH, 301/3598.

311 **The Pole who owned the land** ŻIH, 301/451.

311 **The man approaching her** ŻIH, 301/946.

312 **Other rescuers, with more** See Fogelman, *Conscience,* 73, 140.

312 **Rena Krainik found herself** ŻIH, 301/6035.

312 **In the city of Stanisławów** On Janina Ciszewska, see ŻIH, 301/2514; 301/2515; 301/4362.

313 **When he received a request** ŻIH, 301/6335.

313 **Good people broke** ŻIH, 301/1263.

313 **The nature of an encounter** ŻIH, 301/2270.

314 **What Jewish survivors** Bauman: Cobel-Tokarska, *Bezludna wyspa,* 76. Joseph Co: FVA, 1065.

314 **Agnieszka Wróbel, who** YIVO, RG 104/MK536/1064, Bronisława Znider.

315 **If Jews had little to say** Olha R.: FVA, 3268. Cf. Fogelman, *Conscience,* xvi, 6.

315 **Helena Chorążyczewska, an uneducated** Chorążyczewska: MJH, 1984.T.137. Cywiński and Żuławska: Bartoszewski and Lewinówna, *Ten jest,* 300, 330. Zboromiski: YIVO, RG 104/MK538/1066. Schmid: Wette, *Feldwebel,* 25, 27, letter at 121.

315 **Karolina Kobylec: "That is just"** "Mam już taki charakter." Bartoszewski and Lewinówna, *Ten jest,* 318.

316 **Jan Lipke was a Latvian** Lipke: USHMM, RG-68.102M/2007.372/21/165–205. Beyond the limits: Silberman, "Jan Lipke," 100. Most normal thing: MJH, 1987.T.65. This confirms a finding of Monroe, *Compassion,* 221, and de Jong, *Netherlands and Nazi Germany,* 21. Cf. Arendt: "only 'exceptions' could be expected to act 'normally.'" *Eichmann,* 26.

316 **Deep in the forests** A peasant who gambled a bit more than usual might also be thought to be taking money from Jews. See Good, "Yerushalayim," 38.

316 **Rescuers were risking** USHMM, RG-31.049.01.

317 **Miron Lisikiewicz, who** Lisikiewicz: Rączy, *Pomóc Polaków,* 282. Sewer worker: USHMM, RG-68.102M/2007.372/29/2027–164. Kawka: YIVO, RG 104/MK538/1053. Ringelblum: *Polish-Jewish Relations,* 226. Lipke and money: USHMM, RG-68.102M/2007.372/16/150–63. On the issue of money and risk, see also the recollections of Blanche C. and Liubov Svershinskaia at FVA, 262, and USHMM, RG38/49/70, respectively. See also Tec, *When Light,* 88.

317 **It is true that many** Cf. Gross, *Golden Harvest,* 81.

318 **Within this set of incentives** Ringelblum, *Polish-Jewish Relations,* 77, 121; Grabowski, *Judenjagd,* 136; Good, "Yerushalayim," 18.

318 **In the darkest of times** I was led to this formulation by a paper on Teresa Prekerowa by Jadwiga Biskupska. Similar conclusions are reached by Tec, *When Light,* 154; Oliner, *Altruistic Personality,* 6; Fogelman, *Conscience,* 58. A profound study by a historian who was once a rescued child leads in the same direction: Redlich, *Together and Apart.*

Conclusion: Our World

319 **In the small photograph** Wanda Grosmanowa-Jedlicka: Bartoszewski and Lewinówna, *Ten jest,* 487. At least fifteen thousand Warsaw Jews never entered the ghetto. See Kermish, "Activities," 374.

319 **Most of the Jews of Warsaw** Grossman, *Life and Fate,* 409. He continues: "Kindness is powerful only while it is powerless." See Monroe, *Compassion,* 258.

320 **Wanda J.'s judgment** Compare Bauer, *The Death of the Shtetl,* 97.

321 **Science in fact possesses** At a methodological level, I have opposed forms of historical writing that permit exits into prior emotional convictions or newfound teleological comfort. That said, on the substantial issue of the relationship between technique and experience, I am with the Kantians and against Heidegger. For a close historical examination of a crucial debate: Gordon, *Continental Divide,* on the issues most pertinent to this study at 15, 17, 31, 35, 217, 220, 225, 238. The rapid conquest: Hitler was formed by but did not partake in the age of the frontier. See Webb, *Great Frontier,* 280. Even the German victories over the Herero were due in part to the spread of disease in cattle. See Levene, *Rise,* 247.

322 **When science is disengaged** Food prices: Evenson, "Economic Consequences," 473. See also Federico, "Natura Non Fecit Saltus," 24. For a history of these improvements, see Olmstead and Rhode, *Creating Abundance,* especially 64–66 and 388–98.

324 **At precisely this point** Mazower, *Hitler's Empire,* 594. Cf. Maier, *Unmasterable Past,* 7: "For almost four decades the Federal Republic has lived, so to speak, by bread alone." Also Bartov, *Mirrors of Destruction,* 167: "Studying the Holocaust is the best means to prevent its mystification." On the special 1950s: Federico, "Natura Non Fecit Saltus," 21. Consider the word "calorie," which in the West almost always means something of which people get too much. In the 1930s, people and planners counted calories to ensure that a household had enough of them to survive, or that laboring men, women, and animals received enough of them to power the economy.

324 **The Green Revolution** China net importer: Aliyu, "Agricultural Development." Few months' supply: Denison, *Darwinian Agriculture,* 11. Food riots: Moyo, *Winner Take All,* 109.

325 **Though the world is not** Of course, simple deprivation of food is bad enough; in the world of today, a child starves to death every five seconds. Ziegler, *Betting on Famine,* xiii.

325 **It seems reasonable to worry** Cf. Gumbrecht, *Nach 1945,* 245, 264, 305. See also Rousso, *La dernière catastrophe;* Berger, *After the End.*

326 **The planet is changing** Internal combustion engines and factories produce gases that trap the sun's heat within the atmosphere. The ongoing destruction of forests and wetlands accelerates this warming, since plants absorb carbon dioxide and emit oxygen. A mass of global data demonstrates an increase in annual minimum temperatures of the surface of the earth, of the air at the surface of the earth, of the higher atmosphere, and of the surface of the oceans. Causality: Maslin, *Global Warming,* 1, 4, 57. Temperatures and causality: Alexander, "Global Observed Changes," 31; Rohde, "A New Estimate," 22; Rohde, "Averaging Process," 1; Zhang, "Detection of Human Influence," 461. Predictions too modest: Rahmsdorf, "Comparing Climate Projections," 1; *Economist,* 22 September 2012; *Guardian,* 27 November 2012. Nonlinear effects: Maslin, *Global Warming,* 112, 116; Mitchell, "Extreme Events," 2217; Latif, "El Niño," 20853. The basic point about regionalism in Pitman, Arneth, and Ganzeveld, "Regionalizing," 332. Species: Maslin, *Global Warming,* 99; also Clarke, "From Genes to Ecosystems," 6. Coastlines: Cayan, "Climate Change Projections," S71; Helmuth, "Hidden Signals," 191; Rahmsdorf, "Comparing Climate Projections," 1. Storms: Tebaldi, "Modelling Sea Level Rise," 1. For an extremely impressive history of climate change in an earlier period, see Parker, *Global Crisis.*

326 **Perhaps the experience** Cf. Tooze, *Wages of Destruction,* 477, 544, 549. As Mount points out, realist theories of international politics will have to account for the real changes on our real planet: "Arctic Wake-up Call," 10.

326 **Hitler was a child** First globalization: Trentmann: "Coping with Shortage," 15, 22, and passim; Federico, "Natura Non Fecit Saltus," 23. Most affected: Brown and Crawford, "Climate Change," 2. Useful in the future will be Kiernan's reminder that all historical episodes of mass killing are connected in one way or another to an account of the value of land. *Blood and Soil,* especially chap. 4.

328 **Mass killing in Rwanda** The exhaustion of: *New York Times,* 14 December 1989. 1993: Campbell, "Population Pressure," 2. Overpopulation and land motivation: Newbury, "Background," 13. Land motivation: Rose, "Land and Genocide," 64. Organization: Stanton, "Could the Rwandan," 211–15; Hintjens, "Explaining," 249, 261, 270. Organization and numbers: Straus, "How Many Perpetrators," 86–87. Loyalty to group: Sémelin, *Purifier,* 314.

328 **The starvation in Somalia** Moyo, *Winner Take All,* 32–33; *Economist,* 21 May 2009; Brautigam, "Land Rights"; Horta, "Zambezi Valley." 60 percent of world's untilled arable land: *Economist,* 4 September 2013. Madagascar: Ziegler, *Betting on Famine,* 200.

329 **One Asian country exhibits** Land and water: Diamond, *Collapse,* 362–65. Hectares: Moyo, *Winner Take All,* 29. Famine: Dikötter, *Mao's Great Famine*; Yang, *Calamity and Reform,* 21–42.

329 **In twenty-first-century China** As during the drought of 2010: Sternberg, "Chinese Drought," 8. Sensitivity: Ziegler, *Betting on Famine,* 41.

330 **Facing some future crisis** Sudan: Reeves, *Dying,* 3. Chinese involvement:

Doriye, "Next stage," 25; King, "Factoring Environmental Security," 151. See also Zafar, "Growing Relationship," 119.

330 **China also faces** Tropical regions and water cycle: Stern, *Economics of Climate Change,* 70, 74. Water shortages: Sullivan, "National Security," 15–16. General crisis by 2050, current shortages, riots: Solomon, *Water,* 368, 370, 371. China: King, "Factoring Environmental Security," 104; Moyo, *Winner Take All,* 41; Stern, *Economics of Climate Change,* 78; Solomon, *Water,* 440.

330 **Less peaceful approaches to the problem** Russia: Blank, "Dead End"; Kaczmarski, "Domestic Sources"; Lotspeich, "Economic Integration." Test case of relations: Eder, *China-Russia,* 130–131.

331 **Yet as climate change** In 2007, the number of Chinese in low-elevation coastal zones was estimated at 11 percent of the population; if that percentage held in 2015 the figure would be about 149 million. The entire population of Russia is about 145 million. McGranahan, Balk, and Anderson, "Rising Tide," 26.

331 **None of these Chinese** Voluntary targets: *New York Times,* 11 November 2014.

331 **Russian governments of the early** On Russian revenue from hydrocarbons: Gustafson, *Wheel of Fortune,* 1, 5.

332 **In a new Russian colonialism,** For maps see the newspaper *Novorossiia,* for example 1 August 2014.

332 **President Vladimir Putin of Russia** See Riabov and Riabova, "Decline of Gayropa?" For a chronicle of Russian policy to Ukraine in 2013 and 2014, see my forty or so articles in English, French, and German as collected on timothysnyder.org or in Ukrainian or Russian translation in the editions listed in the bibliography.

332 **As Russia demonstrated** I discussed this connection in several of the publications cited above, as well as in the *Frankfurter Allgemeine Zeitung* of 15 December 2014. Many of the fundamental connections were drawn by Anton Shekhovtsov in a series of important commentaries.

333 **All forms of counterglobal** Poverty: Xenopoulos, "Scenarios," 1562. Cf. Gerlach, *Extremely Violent Societies,* 263. Egypt and Libya: King, "Factoring Environmental Security," 99, 100, 117, 359; Klare, "Climate Change Battlefields," 358–59. Drought: Femia, "Climate Change," 31. ISIS and water: *New York Times,* 14 October 2014.

335 **The ambivalence of interwar Polish** Spector, *Evangelicals and Israel,* 187–88; Clark, *Allies for Armageddon,* 5, 151, 170; Weber, *On the Road to Armageddon,* 191. On attitudes towards climate change: Smith and Leiserowitz, "American Evangelicals," 4; and Anthony Leiserowitz, personal communication, 26 August 2013.

335 **As prime minister of Israel** Weber, *On the Road to Armageddon,* 148; Clark, *Allies for Armageddon,* 190, 229.

336 **Americans, when they think** For wartime antisemitism, see Abzug, *America Views the Holocaust,* 87–92, 99–103, and passim. Mauthausen trial: Jardim, *Mauthausen Trial,* 123, 144, 189, 210. Bergen-Belsen: Damplo, "Prosecuting," 24. For a balanced assessment of Roosevelt, see Breitman and Lichtman, *FDR,* 315–30.

336 **A misunderstanding about** One can infer from Collier's *Bottom Billion,* especially at 126, that military intervention makes more sense after a state has failed than with the goal of making a state fail.

336 **Mass killings generally** Regime changes and civil wars: Goldsmith and Semenovich, "Political Instability," 10.

337 **The dominant stereotype** Cf. Arendt, *Origins,* 310. In *Bloodlands,* I discuss all of these policies.

338 **On the Left, the dominant** Horkheimer and Adorno, *Dialektik der Aufklärung,* especially 212, 217; quotations at 1, 15. See also Horkheimer, *Eclipse of Reason,* 176–77. The same mistake in a less radical formulation can be found in Neumann's reports to the OSS: *Secret Reports,* 28, 30. See Habermas, *Der philosophische Diskurs der Moderne,* 135, 138; Kołakowski, *Main Currents,* 347; Zehnpfennig, *Hitlers Mein Kampf,* 129.

338 **On the Right, the dominant** See the longer discussion in Judt and Snyder, *Thinking.*

339 **The ideal capitalism** Rand: Burns, *Goddess,* 175.

339 **As all economists know** See generally Powell, *Inquisition,* 63, 98, and passim; Oreskes and Conway, *Merchants of Doubt,* 169–215; *Economist,* 15 February 2012; Tollefson, "Sceptic," 441. In 2011, the fossil fuel industry spent about $300 million to muddy the waters: Silver, *Signal,* 380. See Farley, "Petroleum and Propaganda," 40–49. See also Union of Concerned Scientists, "Got Science?," 18 October 2012; and Weart, "Denial," 46, 48. Capitalism certainly registers the data of climate change. Insurance companies keep precise records of storms as they restrict the availability of flood insurance. Parker, *Global Crisis,* 691–92. The error of the libertarian Right is echoed, in a certain way, by some members of the Christian Right. Creationists oppose the theories of Darwin, as amplified by generations of scientists, with respect to nonhuman animals, instead applying the term "science" to their static portrait of a natural order created by God. This is one more conflation of science and politics. Meanwhile, in their support of unrestricted capitalism, many creationists apply Social Darwinian concepts to their fellow human beings. Humans have the right to dominate nature, and more competitive humans have the right to dominate less competitive ones. This is yet another merger of science and politics.

339 **Though no American would deny** Hitler denial: *Hitler and His Generals,* 62. See Thomä, "Sein und Zeit im Rückblick," 285; Genette, *Figures I,* 101; Robbe-Grillet, *Pour un nouveau roman,* 133. The denial of climate science poses serious problems for the U.S. Navy, which faces the likelihood of flooding bases and the reality of competition for the waters of the melting Arctic. *Christian Science Monitor,* 2 March 2010.

340 **The popular notion** The market is not nature: Bloom, *Closing,* 84; Bauman, *Modernity,* 235. Cf. Moses, "Gespräch." At this point in the argument I am demonstrating the relationships between the concepts rather than educing the historical relationship. Cf. Moyn, *Last Utopia,* 82–83.

340 **When states are absent** Nazi Germany murdered chiefly the citizens of other countries. What about the states that carried our mass murder of their own citi-

zens? The three most horrifying twentieth-century cases—the People's Republic of China, the Union of Soviet Socialist Republics, and Cambodia under Pol Pot—were all party-states, where both ideology and practice demanded that the state institutions be secondary to party institutions, and where the legitimacy of the state was completely undercut by the ideological appeal made by party leaders to the future of the collectivity. These histories follow a different trajectory than that of Nazi Germany and its neighbors but in one respect teach the same lesson: the significance of the state in the banal conservative sense of a monopolist of violence and an object of reciprocal duties and rights. The subject is vast and requires separate treatment; some of the relevant issues are raised in the Soviet chapters of my *Bloodlands.*

341 **Gustaw Herling-Grudziński** Herling, *World Apart,* 132.

341 **In the case of climate** Only the state can create the structures within which scientists and engineers can develop fruitful technologies. Individuals might follow market incentives in developing fusion and other technologies, but only insofar as the state molds those incentives. The simple decision by a state or states to invest in science would change the mood and deepen confidence in the future.

342 **Understanding the Holocaust** For case studies of the practical dilemmas of rescue, see Power, *Problem from Hell.*

A Note on Usages

By "Final Solution" I mean the German intention to eliminate the Jews by some means from the territory under their control. By "Holocaust" I mean the version of the Final Solution that was implemented, the mass murder of Jews in Europe.

This book covers a broad linguistic territory. The Jews killed in the Holocaust generally spoke different languages than the people who write about the Holocaust today. My own coverage tilts towards the territories where most European Jews lived and died, and towards their languages at the time, including Yiddish, Polish, and Russian. These languages are written in three different alphabets, the Hebrew, Latin, and Cyrillic. The people who used them were usually multilingual and often known by different names at different stages of life. I transliterate according to simplified versions of the Library of Congress guidelines. Sometimes I spell names as the people in question preferred. I have done my best to keep the complexities arising from transliteration and translation from interfering with voices and arguments. Localities were also known by different names to their different inhabitants at the same time and by different official names as regimes changed over time. I have opted for known English toponyms where such exist and otherwise have used the official name according to the political entity that governed when a locality is first mentioned. Naturally, this does not imply any revanchism on my part. I use "Lwów," for example, because there is no good English equivalent (no one says "Leopolis"), and this was the official name of the city in Poland at the time when it enters the chronicle. Today the city is in Ukraine and is known as Lviv. I use "Stalino" to describe the major city of the Donbas because this is how it was known in

Soviet Ukraine after 1924. Today it is called "Donetsk." Translations, unless otherwise noted, are my own.

Biblical citations follow the King James Bible. In the bibliography I have indicated a date of first publication of a book when this might be of interest. In the endnotes I use brackets to indicate that encrypted archival material has been decrypted. The notes are coded to the first words of a paragraph rather than to a superscript number. They use a short citation formula of author and brief title; the full citations can be easily located in the bibliography.

Archives and Abbreviations

AAN	Archiwum Akt Nowych (Archive of New Files), Warsaw
AW	Archiwum Wschodnie, Karta (Eastern Archive, Karta Institute), Warsaw
BUW	Biblioteka Uniwersytetu Warszawskiego, Gabiner Rękopisów (Warsaw University Library Manuscript Department), Warsaw
CAW	Centralne Archiwum Wojskowe (Central Military Archive), Rembertów
DAVO	Derzhavnyi Arkhiv Volyns'koï Oblasti (State Archive of the Volyn Region), Lutsk
FVA	Fortunoff Video Archive for Holocaust Testimonies, Yale University
GARF	Gosudarstvennyi Arkhiv Rossiiskoi Federatsii (State Archive of the Russian Federation)
HI	Hoover Institution, Stanford University
IfZ	Institut für Zeitgeschichte (Institute for Contemporary History), Munich
JPI	Józef Piłsudski Institute, New York
MJH	Museum of Jewish Heritage, New York
MWP	Muzeum Wojska Polskiego (Museum of the Polish Army), Warsaw
NA	National Archives, Kew, United Kingdom
SPP	Studium Polski Podziemnej (Polish Underground Study Trust), London
SUSC	Shoah Collection, University of Southern California
TsDAVO	Tsentral'nyi Derzhavnyi Arkhiv Vyshchykh Orhaniv Vlady ta Upravlinnia (Central State Archive of Higher Organs of Government and Administration), Kyiv
USHMM	United States Holocaust Memorial Museum, Washington, DC
YIVO	Yivo Institute for Jewish Research, New York
YMA	Manuscripts and Archives, Sterling Memorial Library, Yale University
YV	Yad Vashem, Jerusalem
ŻIH	Żydowski Instytut Historyczny (Jewish Historical Institute), Warsaw

Published Sources

Published Hitler Primary Sources

Hitler and His Generals: Military Conferences 1942–1945. Edited by Gerhard L. Weinberg. New York: Enigma Books, 2003.

Hitler's Second Book. Edited by Gerhard L. Weinberg. Translated by Krista Smith. New York: Enigma Books, 2010. German edition 1961, dictated 1928.

Hitler's Table Talk 1941–1944. Translated by Norman Cameron and R. H. Stevens. New York: Enigma Books, 2000.

Mein Kampf. Munich: Zentralverlag der NSDAP, 1939. Originally published in 1925 and 1926 in two volumes.

Sämtliche Aufzeichnungen, 1905–1924. Edited by Eberhard Jäckel and Axel Kuhn. Stuttgart, Ger.: Deutsche Verlags-Anstalt, 1980.

Staatsmänner und Diplomaten bei Hitler: Vertrauliche Vertretern des Auslandes 1942–1944. Edited by Andreas Hillgruber. Frankfurt: Bernard and Graefe, 1970.

Published Nazi Primary Sources

Frank, Hans. "Ansprache." In *Das Judentum in der Rechtswissenschaft. 1. Die deutsche Rechtswissenschaft im Kampf gegen den jüdischen Geist,* 7–13. Berlin: Deutscher Rechtsverlag, 1936.

———. "Einleitung zum 'Nationalsozialistischen Handbuch für Recht und Gesetzgebung.'" In *Rechtfertigungen des Unrechts: Das Rechtsdenken im Nationalsozialismus in Originaltexten,* edited by Herlinde Pauer-Studer and Julian Fink, 141–79. Berlin: Suhrkamp, 2014.

Kühnl, Reinhard, ed. *Der deutsche Faschismus in Quellen und Dokumenten.* Cologne: PapyRossa, 2000.

Schmitt, Carl. "The *Grossraum* Order of International Law with a Ban on Intervention for Spatially Foreign Powers: A Contribution to the Concept of Reich in International Law (1939–1941). In *Writings on War,* edited and translated by Timothy Nunan, 75–134. Cambridge: Polity Press, 2011.

———. "Eröffnung." In *Das Judentum in der Rechtswissenschaft: 1. Die deutsche Rechtswissenschaft im Kampf gegen den jüdischen Geist,* 14–18. Berlin: Deutscher Rechtsverlag, 1936.

———. "Neue Leitsätze für die Rechtspraxis." In *Rechtfertigungen des Unrechts. Das Rechtsdenken im Nationalsozialismus in Originaltexten,* edited by Herlinde Pauer-Studer and Julian Find, 513–16. Berlin: Suhrkamp, 2014.

Witte, Peter, Michael Wildt, Martina Voigt, Dieter Pohl, Peter Klein, Christian Gerlach, Christoph Dieckmann, and Andrej Angrick, eds. *Der Dienstkalender Heinrich Himmlers 1941/42.* Hamburg: Hans Christians Verlag, 1999.

Other Published Documents

Abzug, Robert H., ed. *America Views the Holocaust, 1933–1945: A Brief Documentary History.* Boston: St. Martin's, 1999.

Cienciala, Anna M., Natalia S. Lebedeva, and Wojciech Materski, eds. *Katyn: A Crime Without Punishment.* New Haven, Conn.: Yale University Press, 2007.

Danylenko, Vasyl', and Serhiy Kokin, eds. *Radians'kyi orhany derzhavnoï bezpeky u 1939–chervni 1941 r.* Vol. 1. Kyiv: Kyiv-Mohyla Akademiia, 2013.

Deportacje obywateli polskich z Zachodniej Ukrainy i Zachodniej Białorusi w 1940/Deportatsii pol'skikh grazhdan iz Zapadnoi Ukrainy i Zapadnoi Belorussii v 1940 godu. Warsaw: IPN, 2003.

Documents on British Foreign Policy 1919–1939. Third Series, vol. 3. London: His Majesty's Stationery Office, 1950.

Documents on British Foreign Policy 1919–1939, Third Series, vol. 4. London: His Majesty's Stationery Office, 1951.

Documents on German Foreign Policy 1918–1945, Series D (1937–1945), vol. 5. Washington, D.C.: Government Printing Office, 1953.

Dubicki, Tadeusz, Daria Nałęcz, and Tessa Stirling, eds. *Polsko-brytyjska współpraca wywiadowcza podczas II wojny światowej.* Warsaw: Naczelna Dyrekcja Archiwów Państwowych, 2004.

Justiz und NS-Verbrechen: Sammlung deutscher Strafurteile wegen nationalsozialistischer Tötungsverbrechen. Vol. 37, 2007. Lfd. Nr. 777, 398–441.

Justiz und NS-Verbrechen: Sammlung deutscher Strafurteile wegen nationalsozialistischer Tötungsverbrechen. Vol. 43, 2010. Lfd. Nr. 856, 173–237.

Libera, Paweł, ed. *II Rzeczpospolita wobec ruchu prometejskiego.* Vol. 4. Warsaw: Centralne Archiwum Wojskowe, 2013.

Lipski, Józef. *Diplomat in Berlin 1933–1939.* Edited by Wacław Jędrzejewicz. New York: Columbia University Press, 1968.

Neumann, Franz, Herbert Marcuse, and Otto Kirchheimer. *Secret Reports on Nazi Germany: The Frankfurt School Contribution to the War Effort.* Edited by Raffaele Laudani. Princeton, N.J.: Princeton University Press, 2013.

OUN v svitli postanov Velykykh Zboriv. N.p., 1955.

Skibińska, Alina, and Robert Szuchta, eds. *Wybór źródełdo nauczania o zagładzie Żydów na okupowanych ziemiach polskich.* Warsaw: Centrum Badań nad Zagładą Żydów, 2010.

United States Department of Defense. "Quadrennial Defense Review Report." February 2010.

United States Department of the Navy. Vice Chief of Naval Operations. "Navy Climate Change Roadmap," 21 May 2010.

Vladimirtsev, N. I., and A. I. Kokurin, eds. *NKVD-MVD SSSR v bor'be s banditizmom i vooruzhennym natsionalisticheskim podpol'em na Zapadnoi Ukraine, v Zapadnoi Belorussii i Pribaltike 1939–1956*. Moscow: MVD Rossii, 2008.

Zarański, Józef, ed. *Diariusz i teki Jana Szembeka*. Vol. 4. London: Orbis, 1972.

Zelenin, I., et al., eds. *Tragediia sovetskoi derevni: Kollektivizatsiia i raskulachivanie*. Vol. 3. Moscow: Rosspen, 2000.

Diaries, Memoirs, and Correspondence

Adini, Ya'acov. ed. *Dubno: sefer zikaron*. Tel Aviv: Irgun yots'e Dubno be-Yisra'el, 1966.

Bartoszewski, Władysław. *The Warsaw Ghetto: A Christian's Testimony*. Translated by Stephen G. Cappellari. Boston: Beacon Press, 1987.

Bartoszewski, Władysław, and Zofia Lewinówna, eds. *Ten jest z ojczyzny mojej*. Warsaw: Świat Książki, 2007.

Begin, Menachem. *The Revolt*. 1948. Reprint, Los Angeles: Nash Publishing, 1972.

Bryns'kyi, Anton. *Po toï bik frontu*. Kyiv: Politvydav Ukraïny, 1976–78.

Buber-Neumann, Margarete. *Under Two Dictators: Prisoner of Hitler and Stalin*. 1949. Reprint, London: Pimlico, 2008.

Drymmer, Wiktor Tomir. *W służbie Polsce*. Warsaw: Gryf, 1998.

Giedroyc, Jerzy. *Autobiografia na cztery ręce*. Edited by Krzysztof Pomian. Warsaw: Czytelnik, 1996.

Głowiński, Michał. *The Black Seasons*. Translated by Marci Shore. Evanston, Ill.: Northwestern University Press, 2005.

Good, William Z. "From 'Jerushalayim d'Lita' and Back." Unpublished memoir, 1988.

Herling, Gustaw. *A World Apart*. Translated by Andrzej Ciolkosz. 1951. Reprint, New York: Penguin, 1996.

Józewski, Henryk. "Zamiast pamiętnika." *Zeszyty Historyczne*, no. 59 (1982): 3–163.

Kahane, David. *Lvov Ghetto Diary*. Translated by Jerzy Michałowicz. Amherst: University of Massachusetts Press, 1990.

Karski, Jan. "Dziecko sanacji." Interview by Maciej Wierzyński. *Tygodnik Powszechny*, 24 April 2012.

———. *Story of a Secret State: My Report to the World*. London: Penguin, 2011.

Klukowski, Zygmunt. *Zamojszczyzna 1918–1943*. Vol. 2. Warsaw: Karta, 2007.

Kulka, Otto Dov. *Landscapes of the Metropolis of Death*. Translated by Ralph Mandel. London: Allen Lane, 2013.

Lankin, Eliahu. *To Win the Promised Land: The Story of a Freedom Fighter*. Translated by Artziah Hershberg. Walnut Creek, Calif.: Benmir Books, 1992.

Lemkin, Raphael. *Totally Unofficial*. New Haven, Conn.: Yale University Press, 2013.

Lewin, Kurt I. *Przeżyłem: Saga Świętego Jura spisana w roku 1946*. Warsaw: Zeszyty Literackie, 2006.

Margolin, Julius. *Reise in das Land der Lager*. Berlin: Suhrkamp, 2013.

Michel'son, Frida. *Ia perezhila Rumbulu*. Israel, 1973.

Moczarski, Kazimierz. *Rozmowy z katem*. Cracow: Znak, 2009.

Peleg-Mariańska, Miriam, and Mordecai Peleg. *Witnesses: Life in Occupied Kraków*. London: Routledge, 1991.

Pilecki, Witold. *The Auschwitz Volunteer: Beyond Bravery.* Translated by Jarek Garliński. Los Angeles: Aquila Polonica, 2012.

Rabin, Haim. ed. *Vishnivits: sefer zikaron le-kedoshe Vishnivits she-nispu be-shi'ath ha-natzim.* Tel Aviv: Irgun 'ole Vishnivits, 1979.

Rubenstein, Joshua, and Ilya Altman, eds. *The Unknown Black Book: The Holocaust in the German-Occupied Soviet Territories.* Bloomington: Indiana University Press, 2008.

Sefer Lutsk. Tel Aviv: Irgun Yots'e Lutsk be-Yisrael, 1961.

Shamir, Yitzhak, *Summing Up: An Autobiography.* Boston: Little, Brown, and Company, 1994.

Shtokfish, David, ed. *Pinkes Kuzmir.* Tel Aviv: Irgunei yots'ei Kuzmir bi-medinat Yisra'el uva-tefutsot, 1970.

Shumuk, Danylo. *Perezhyte i peredumane.* Kyiv: Vydavnyts'tvo imeni Oleny Telihy, 1998.

Silberman, David. "Jan Lipke, An Unusual Man." In *Muted Voices: Jewish Survivors of Latvia Remember,* edited by Gertrude Schneider, 87–111. New York: Philosophical Library, 1987.

Spanily, Andrzej. ed. *Pisane miłością: Losy wdów katyńskich.* Vol. 3. Gdynia, Poland: Rymsza, 2003.

Sobański, Antoni. *Cywil w Berlinie.* Warsaw: Sic!, 2006.

Stein, Edith. *Self-Portrait in Letters.* Translated by Josephine Koeppel. Washington, D.C.: Institute of Carmelite Studies, 1993.

Weissberg-Cybulski, Aleksander. *Wielka czystka.* Translated by Adam Ciołkosz. Paris: Institut Littéraire, 1967.

Yasni, A. Volf. ed. *Sefer Klobutsk: Mazkeret kavod le-kehilah ha-kedoshah she-hushmedah / Yizkor-bukh fun der farpeynikter Klobutsker kehile.* Tel Aviv: Irgun yots'e Klubotsk be-yisra'el and Klobutsker landsmanshaftn fun Frankraykh un fun Oystralye, 1960.

Newspaper and Press Articles (chronological order)

"Die Weltgefahr des Bolschewismus: Rede des Reichskanzlers Adolf Hitler im Berliner Sportpalast." *Deutschösterreichische Tageszeitung,* 3 March 1933.

"Beck Says Poland Is Not Anti-Jewish." *New York Times,* 30 January 1937.

"Poles Renew Call for Exile of Jews." *New York Times,* 14 June 1937.

"Poland Seen Opposed to Palestine Plan." *New York Times,* 9 July 1937.

"Beck Says Poland Is Loyal to Allies." *New York Times,* 25 January 1939.

"Stern Gang Leader Hailed as Patriot." *Times* (London), 16 February 1967.

Perlez, Jane. "Kigeme Journal: Why Worry About Crops When Fishing's Better!" *New York Times,* 14 December 1989.

Motyka, Grzegorz. "Lachów usunąc." *Gazeta Wyborcza,* 15 April 2002.

Ridgeway, Eliza. "A Survivor's Story: Resident Reflects on Family's Escape from the Nazis." *Los Altos Town Crier,* 15 April 2009.

"Buying Farmland Abroad: Outsourcing's Third Wave." *Economist,* 21 May 2009.

Broder, John M. "Climate Change Seen as Threat to U.S. Security." *New York Times,* 9 August 2009.

Rogers, Walter. "War Over the Arctic? Climate Change Skeptics Distract Us from Security Risks." *Christian Science Monitor,* 2 March 2010.

Pięciach, Wojciech. "Szpieg ze Sztokholmu." *Tygodnik Powszechny,* 19 April 2011.

Goldenberg, Suzanne. "*Wall Street Journal* Rapped Over Climate Change Stance." *Guardian* (Manchester), 1 February 2012.

"Trouble in the Heartland: Climate-Change Skepticism." *Economist,* 15 February 2012.

Winston, Andrew. "Politicians Who Deny Climate Change Cannot Be Pro-Business." *Bloomberg: Harvard Business Review,* 7 September 2012.

"Now You Don't: Arctic Ice." *Economist,* 22 September 2012, 89–90.

Union of Concerned Scientists, "Got Science? Not at News Corporation." 18 October 2012.

"Heartland Institute." Sourcewatch.org, 26 November 2012.

Goldenberg, Suzanne. "US Coastal Cities in Danger as Sea Levels Rise Faster Than Expected, Study Warns." *Guardian* (Manchester), 27 November 2012.

Pollack, Martin. "Des is a Hetz und kost net viel." *Der Standard,* 2 March 2013.

"Cold Comfort Farms." *Economist,* 4 September 2013.

Novorossiia. 1 August 2014, map.

Davenport, Coral. "Pentagon Signals Security Risks of Climate Change." *New York Times,* 13 October 2014.

Landler, Mark, "U.S. and China Reach Climate Accord After Months of Talks." *New York Times,* 11 November 2014.

Secondary Sources

Abrams, Bradley. "The Second World War and the East European Revolution." *East European Politics and Societies* 16, no. 3 (2003): 623–64.

Abramson, Henry. *A Prayer for the Government: Ukrainians and Jews in Revolutionary Times,* Cambridge, Mass.: Harvard University Press, 1999.

Adam, Uwe Dietrich. "How Spontaneous Was the Pogrom?" In *November 1938: From 'Kristallnacht' to Genocide,* edited by Walter H. Pehle, 73–94. Oxford: Berg, 1990.

Alexander, L.V., et al., "Global Observed Changes in Daily Climate Extremes of Temperature and Precipitation." *Journal of Geophysical Research* 111 (2006): 1–65.

Aliyu, Rafeeat. "Agricultural Development and 'Land Grabs': The Chinese Presence in the African Agricultural Sector." *Consultancy African Intelligence,* 16 January 2012.

Aly, Götz. *Hitler's Beneficiaries: Plunder, Racial War, and the Nazi Welfare State.* Translated by Jefferson Chase. New York: Metropolitan Books, 2007.

Aly, Götz, and Susanne Heim. *Vordenker der Vernichtung: Auschwitz und die deutschen Pläne für eine neue europäische Ordnung.* Hamburg: Hoffmann und Campe, 1991.

Ancel, Jean. *The History of the Holocaust in Romania.* Translated by Yaffah Murciano. Lincoln: University of Nebraska Press, 2011.

Angrick, Andrej. *Besatzungspolitik und Massenmord: Die Einsatzgruppe D in der südlichen Sowjetunion 1941–1943.* Hamburg: Hamburger Edition, 2003.

Angrick, Andrej, and Peter Klein. *The "Final Solution" in Riga: Exploitation and Annihilation, 1941–1944.* Translated by Ray Brandon. New York: Berghahn Books, 2012.

Applebaum, Anne. *Iron Curtain: The Crushing of Eastern Europe 1944–1956.* New York: Doubleday, 2012.

Arad, Yitzhak. *Belzec, Sobibor, Treblinka: The Operation Reinhard Death Camps.* Bloomington: Indiana University Press, 1987.

———. *The Holocaust in the Soviet Union,* Lincoln: University of Nebraska Press, 2009.

———. "Jewish Family Camps in the Forests: An Original Means of Rescue." In *Jewish Resistance to the Holocaust,* edited by Michael R. Marrus, 234–45. Westport, Conn.: Meckler, 1989.

Arad, Yitzhak, Shmuel Krakowski, and Shmuel Spector, eds. *The Einsatzgruppen Reports.* New York: Holocaust Library, 1989.

Arendt, Hannah. *Eichmann in Jerusalem: A Report on the Banality of Evil.* London: Faber and Faber, 1963.

———. *Essays in Understanding, 1930–1954.* New York: Schocken Books, 2005.

———. *In der Gegenwart.* Munich: Piper, 2000.

———. *The Jewish Writings.* New York: Schocken Books, 2007.

———. *The Origins of Totalitarianism.* New York: Harcourt, Brace, 1951.

Armstrong, John. *Soviet Partisans in World War II.* Madison: University of Wisconsin Press, 1964.

Arnold, Klaus Jochen. "Die Eroberung und Behandlung der Stadt Kiew durch die Wehrmacht im September 1941: Zur Radikalisierung der Besatzungspolitik." *Militärgeschichtliche Mitteilungen* 58, no. 1 (1999): 23–64.

Baberowski, Jörg. *Der rote Terror: Die Geschichte des Stalinismus.* Munich: Deutsche Verlags-Anstalt, 2003.

Baberowski, Jörg, and Anselm Doering-Manteuffel. "The Quest for Order and the Pursuit of Terror." In *Beyond Totalitarianism: Stalinism and Nazism Compared,* edited by Michael Geyer and Sheila Fitzpatrick, 180–227. Cambridge: Cambridge University Press, 2009.

Bacon, Gershon C. *The Politics of Tradition: Agudat Yisrael in Poland, 1916–1939.* Jerusalem: Magnes Press, 1996.

Bajohr, Frank, and Dieter Pohl. *Der Holocaust als offenes Geheimnis: Die Deutschen, die NS-Führung und die Alliierten.* Munich: Beck, 2006.

Baker, Michael L. "The Coming Conflicts of Climate Change." *Council on Foreign Relations,* 7 September 2010.

Bärsch, Claus Ekkehard. *Die politische Religion des Nationalsozialismus: Die religiöse Dimension der NS-Ideologie in den Schriften von Dietrich Eckart, Joseph Goebbels, Alfred Rosenberg und Adolf Hitler.* Munich: Wilhelm Fink Verlag, 1998.

Bartniczak, Mieczysław. *From Andrzejewo to Pecynka, 1939–1944.* Warsaw: Książka i Wiedza, 1984.

Bartoszewski, Władysław. "Rozmowa." In *"Żegota": Rada Pomocy Żydom 1942–1945,* edited by Andrzej Krzysztof Kunert, 7–36. Warsaw: Rada Ochrony Pamięci Walk i Męczeństwa, 2002.

———. *Warszawski pierścień śmierci.* Warsaw: Świat Ksiażki, 2008.

Bartov, Omer. "Eastern Europe as the Site of Genocide." *Journal of Modern History,* no. 80 (2008): 557–93.

———. *Mirrors of Destruction: War, Genocide, and Modern Identity.* Oxford: Oxford University Press, 2000.

Bauer, Yehuda. *The Death of the Shtetl.* New Haven, Conn.: Yale University Press, 2010.

Bauman, Zygmunt. *Modernity and the Holocaust.* Ithaca, N.Y.: Cornell University Press, 1989.

Bell, J. Bowyer. *Terror Out of Zion: The Israeli Fight for Independence.* New Brunswick, N.J.: Transaction Publishers, 1996.

Bemporad, Elissa. *Becoming Soviet Jews: The Bolshevik Experiment in Minsk.* Bloomington: Indiana University Press, 2013.

———. "The Politics of Blood: Jews and Ritual Murder in the Land of the Soviets." Paper presented at Yale University, 2014.

Bender, Sara. *The Jews of Białystok During World War II and the Holocaust.* Translated by Yaffa Murciano. Waltham, Mass.: Brandeis University Press, 2008.

Benecke, Werner. *Die Ostgebiete der Zweiten Polnischen Republik.* Cologne: Böhlau Verlag, 1999.

Benz, Wolfgang. "Pogrom und Volksgemeinschaft. Zwischen Abscheu und Beteiligung: Die Öffentlichkeit des 9. November 1938." In *Die Novemberpogrome 1938: Versuch einer Bilanz,* edited by Andreas Nachama and Claudia Steuer, 8–19. Berlin: Stiftung Topographie des Terrors, 2009.

Benz, Wolfgang, Konrad Kwiet, and Jürgen Matthäus. *Einsatz im "Reichskommissariat Ostland": Dokumente zum Völkermord im Baltikum und in Weissrussland 1941–1944.* Berlin: Metropol Verlag, 1998.

Beorn, Waitman Wade. *Marching into Darkness: The Wehrmacht and the Holocaust in Belarus.* Cambridge, Mass.: Harvard University Press, 2014.

Berger, James. *After the End: Representations of Post-Apocalypse.* Minneapolis: University of Minnesota Press, 1999.

Berger, Sara. *Experten der Vernichtung: Das T4-Reinhardt Netzwerk in den Lagern Belzec, Sobibor und Treblinka.* Hamburg: Hamburger Edition, 2013.

Berkhoff, Karel C. "Dina Pronicheva's Story of Surviving the Babi Yar Massacre: German, Jewish, Soviet, Russian, and Ukrainian Records." In *The Shoah in Ukraine: History, Testimony, Memorialization,* edited by Ray Brandon and Wendy Lower, 291–317. Bloomington: Indiana University Press, 2008.

———. *Harvest of Despair: Life and Death in Ukraine Under Nazi Rule.* Cambridge, Mass.: Harvard University Press, 2004.

Beyrau, Dietrich. "Der Erste Weltkrieg als Bewährungsprobe: Bolschewistische Lernprozesse aus dem 'imperialistischen Krieg.'" *Journal of Modern European History* 1, no. 1 (2003): 96–123.

Bikont, Anna. *My z Jedwabnego.* Warsaw: Proszyński i S-ka, 2004.

Birnbaum, Pierre. *Prier pour l'état: les Juifs, l'alliance royale et la démocratie.* Paris: Calmann-Lévy, 2003.

———. *Sur la corde raide: Parcours juifs entre exil et citoyenneté.* Paris: Flammarion, 2002.

Biskupska, Jadwiga M. "Extermination and the Elite: Warsaw under Nazi Occupation, 1939–1944." PhD diss., Yale University, 2013.

Black, Peter. "Askaris in the 'Wild East': The Deployment of Auxiliaries and the Implementation of Nazi Racial Policy in Lublin District." In *The Germans and the East,* edited by Charles W. Ingrao and Franz A. J. Szabo, 277–309. West Lafayette, Ind.: Purdue University Press, 2008.

———. "Handlanger der Endlösung: Die Trawniki-Männer und die Aktion Reinhard

1941–1943." In *Aktion Reinhardt, Der Völkermord an den Juden im Generalgouvernement 1941–1944,* edited by Bogdan Musial, 309–52. Osnabrück, Ger.: Fibre, 2004.

Blank, Stephen. "At a Dead End: Russian Policy in the Far East." *Demokratizatsiya* 17, (2009): 17, 122–44.

Blatman, Daniel. *The Death Marches: The Final Phase of Nazi Genocide.* Cambridge, Mass.: Harvard University Press, 2011.

Bloom, Allan. *The Closing of the American Mind.* New York: Simon and Schuster, 1987.

Bloxham, Donald. *The Final Solution: A Genocide.* Oxford: Oxford University Press, 2011.

Böhler, Jochen. *Der Überfall: Deutschlands Krieg gegen Polen.* Frankfurt am Main: Eichborn, 2009.

———. *"Grösste Härte": Verbrechen der Wehrmacht in Polen September/Oktober 1939.* Osnabrück, Ger.: Deutsches Historisches Institut, 2005.

Borzęcki, Jerzy. *The Soviet-Polish Peace of 1921 and the Creation of Interwar Europe.* New Haven, Conn.: Yale University Press, 2008.

Botz, Gerhard. "'Judenhatz' und 'Reichskristallnacht' im historischen Kontext: Pogrome in Österreich 1938 und in Osteuropa um 1900." In *Der Pogrom 1938: Judenverfolgung in Österreich und Deutschland,* edited by Kurt Schmid and Robert Streibel, 9–24. Vienna: Picus Verlag, 1990.

———. *Nationalsozialismus in Wien: Machtübernahme, Herrschaftssicherung, Radikalisierung, 1938–1939.* Vienna: Mandelbaum, 2008.

Brakel, Alexander. "'Das allergefährlichste ist die Wut der Bauern': Die Versorgung der Partisanen und ihr Verhältnis zur Zivilbevölkerung. Eine Fallstudie zum Gebiet Baranowicze 1941–1944." *Vierteljahreshefte für Zeitgeschichte,* no. 3 (2007): 393–424.

———. *Unter Rotem Stern und Hakenkreuz: Baranowicze 1939 bis 1944.* Paderborn, Ger.: Schöningh, 2009.

———. "Was There a 'Jewish Collaboration' under Soviet Occupation? A Case Study from the Baranowicze Region." In *Shared History, Divided Memory: Jews and Others in Soviet-Occupied Poland, 1939–1941,* edited by Elazar Barkan, Elizabeth A. Cole, and Kai Struve, 225–44. Leipzig, Ger.: Leipziguniversitätsverlag, 2007.

Brandenberger, David. "Stalin's Last Crime? Recent Scholarship on Postwar Soviet Antisemitism and the Doctor's Plot." *Kritika,* vol. 6, No. 1, 2005, 187–204.

Brandon, Ray. "Deportation ins Reichsinnere." In *Naziverbrechen: Täter, Taten, Bewältigungsversuche,* edited by Martin Cüppers, Jürgen Matthäus, and Andrej Angrick, 75–88. Darmstadt, Ger.: Wissenschaftliche Buchgesellschaft, 2013.

———. "The First Wave." Unpublished study, 2009.

Braun, Robert, and Peter Tammes. "Religious Deviance and Mobilization: The Rescue of Jews in the Netherlands." March 2013.

Brautigam, Deborah, and Tang Xiaoyang. "China's Engagement in African Agriculture: 'Down to the Countryside.' " *China Quarterly,* no. 199 (1999): 686–706.

Brechtken, Magnus. *"Madagaskar für die Juden": Antisemitische Idee und politische Praxis 1885–1945.* Munich: R. Oldenbourg Verlag, 1997.

Breitman, Richard. "Himmler and the 'Terrible Secret' Among the Executioners." *Journal of Contemporary History* 26, nos. 3–4 (1991): 431–51.

Breitman, Richard, and Allan J. Lichtman. *FDR and the Jews.* Cambridge, Mass.: Harvard University Press, 2013.

Brown, Oli, and Alec Crawford. "Climate Change and Security in Africa: A Study for the Nordic-African Foreign Ministers Meeting." International Institute for Sustainable Development, March 2009.

Browning, Christopher R. *Ordinary Men: Reserve Police Battalion 101 and the Final Solution in Poland.* New York: HarperCollins, 1993.

Bruttmann, Tal. *Au bureau des Affaires juives: L'administration française et l'application de la législation antisémite (1940–1944).* Paris: La Découverte, 2006.

Buchheim, Hans. "Die Höheren SS- und Polizeiführer." *Vierteljahrshefte für Zeitgeschichte* 11, no. 4 (1963) : 362–91.

Budnitskii, Oleg. *Russian Jews Between the Reds and the Whites, 1917–1920.* Translated by Timothy J. Portice. Philadelphia: University of Pennsylvania Press, 2012.

Burds, Jeffrey. "Agentura: Soviet Informants' Networks and the Ukrainian Underground in Galicia." *East European Politics and Societies* 11, no. 1 (1997): 89–130.

———. *Holocaust in Rovno: The Massacre at Sosenki Forest, November 1941.* New York: Palgrave, 2013.

Burleigh, Michael. *The Third Reich: A New History.* New York: Hill and Wang, 2000.

Burns, Jennifer. *Goddess of the Market: Ayn Rand and the American Right.* Oxford: Oxford University Press, 2009.

Burrin, Phillip. *Hitler et les Juifs.* Paris: Éditions de Seuil, 1989.

Cabanel, Patrick. "Protestantismes minoritaires, affinités judéo-protestantes et sauvetage des Juifs." In *La résistance aux génocides: De la pluralité des actes de sauvetage,* edited by Jacques Sémelin, Claire Andrieu, and Sarah Gensburger, 445–56. Paris: Presses de la Fondation Nationale des Sciences Politiques, 2008.

Cała, Alina. *Żyd—wróg odwieczny? Antysemityzm w Polsce i jego źródła.* Warsaw: Nisza, 2012.

Campbell, David J., Jennifer M. Olson, and Len Berry. "Population Pressure, Agricultural Productivity, and Land Degradation in Rwanda: An Agenda for Collaborative Training, Research and Analysis," Rwanda Society-Environment Project, Michigan State University, Working Paper 1, 1993.

Carynnyk, Marco. "The Palace on the Ikva: Dubne, September 18th, 1939, and June 24th, 1941." In *Shared History, Divided Memory: Jews and Others in Soviet-Occupied Poland, 1939–1941,* edited by Elazar Barkan, Elizabeth A. Cole, and Kai Struve, 263–301. Leipzig, Ger.: Leipzig Universitätsverlag, 2007.

Case, Holly. *Between States: The Transylvanian Question and the European Idea During World War II.* Stanford, Calif.: Stanford University Press, 2009.

Cayan, Daniel R. et al. "Climate Change Projections of Sea Level Extremes Along the California Coast." *Climatic Change,* no. 87 (2008): S57–S73.

Cienciala, Anna M. "The Foreign Policy of Józef Piłsudski and Józef Beck, 1926–1939: Misconceptions and Interpretations." *Polish Review* 65, nos. 1–2 (2011): 111–52.

Chalecki, Elizabeth L. "He Who Would Rule: Climate Change in the Arctic and Its Implications for U.S. National Security." Paper presented at the International Studies Association, 2007.

Chan, Michelle Mengsu. "Ho Feng-Shan and the Jews He Saved." Seminar paper, Yale University, December 2012.

Chapoutot, Johann. "L'historicité nazie: Temps de la nature et abolition de l'histoire." *Vingtième Siècle,* no. 117 (2013): 43–55.

———. "Les juristes nazis face au traité de Versailles (1919–1945)." *Relations internationales,* no. 149 (2012): 73–88.

———. *La loi du sang.* Paris: Gallimard, 2014. Pagination cited according to manuscript kindly provided by the author.

———. *Le nazisme et l'Antiquité.* Paris: Quadrige, 2012.

———. "Les Nazis et la 'Nature.' " *Vingtième Siècle,* no. 113 (2012) : 29–39.

Chirot, Daniel, and Clark McCauley. *Why Not Kill Them All? The Logic and Prevention of Mass Political Murder.* Princeton, N.J.: Princeton University Press, 2006.

Chojnowski, Andrzej. *Piłsudczycy u władzy: Dzieje Bezpartyjnego Bloku Współpracy z Rządem.* Wrocław, Poland: Ossolineum, 1986.

Clark, Victoria. *Allies for Armageddon: The Rise of Christian Zionism.* New Haven, Conn.: Yale University Press, 2007.

Clarke, Andrew. et al. "Antarctic Ecology: From Genes to Ecosystems (Introduction)." *Philosophical Transactions: Biological Sciences* 362, no. 1477, 5–9.

Cobel-Tokarska, Marta. *Bezludna wyspa, nora, grób: wojenne kryjówki Żydów w okupowanej Polsce.* Warsaw: IPN, 2012.

Cohen, Laurie. *Smolensk Under the Nazis: Everyday Life in Occupied Russia.* Rochester, N.Y.: University of Rochester Press, 2013.

Collier, Paul. *The Bottom Billion: Why the Poorest Countries Are Failing and What Can Be Done About It.* Oxford: Oxford University Press, 2007.

Collingham, Lizzie. *The Taste of War: World War II and the Battle for Food.* New York: Penguin, 2012.

Confino, Alon. *A World Without Jews: The Nazi Imagination from Persecution to Genocide.* New Haven, Conn.: Yale University Press, 2014.

Connelly, John. *From Enemy to Brother: The Revolution in Catholic Teaching on the Jews.* Cambridge, Mass.: Harvard University Press, 2012.

Conrad, Sebastian. *Globalisation and the Nation in Imperial Germany.* Translated by Sorcha O'Hagan. Cambridge: Cambridge University Press, 2010.

Conway, Martin. *Collaboration in Belgium: Léon Degrelle and the Rexist Movement.* London: Yale University Press, 1993.

Copeaux, Étienne. "Le mouvement 'Prométhéen.'" *Cahiers d'études sur la Méditerranée orientale et le monde turco-iranien,* no. 16 (1993): 9–45.

Croes, Marnix. "The Holocaust in the Netherlands and the Rate of Jewish Survival." *Holocaust and Genocide Studies* 20, no. 3 (2006) : 474–90.

———. "Pour une approche quantitative de la survie et du sauvetage des Juifs." In *La résistance aux génocides: De la pluralité des actes de sauvetage,* edited by Jacques Sémelin, Claire Andrieu, and Sarah Gensburger, 83–98. Paris: Presses de la Fondation Nationale des Sciences Politiques, 2008.

Curilla, Wolfgang. *Der Judenmord in Polen und die deutsche Ordnungspolizei.* Paderborn, Ger.: Ferdinand Schöningh, 2011.

Dallin, Alexander. *German Rule in Russia, 1941–1945: A Study of Occupation Policies.* London: St. Martin's Press, 1957.

Damplo, Danica. "Prosecuting the Beasts of Belsen." Research paper, London School of Economics, 2014.

Darwin, Charles. *The Descent of Man, and Selection in Relation to Sex.* 2 vols. London: John Murray, 1871.

Davies, Norman. "The Misunderstood Victory in Europe." *New York Review of Books,* 25 May 1995.

———. *Rising '44: "The Battle for Warsaw."* London: Macmillan, 2003.

———. *White Eagle, Red Star: The Polish-Soviet War, 1919–1920.* New York: St. Martin's Press, 1972.

Dean, Martin. *Robbing the Jews: The Confiscation of Jewish Property in the Holocaust, 1933–1945.* Cambridge: Cambridge University Press, 2008.

———. "The Service of Poles in the German Local Police (Schutzmannschaft Einzeldienst) in the Eastern Districts of Poland and Their Role in the Holocaust." 2002.

Debicki, Roman. *The Foreign Policy of Poland 1919–1939.* London: Pall Mall Press, 1963.

de Jong, Louis. *The Netherlands and Nazi Germany.* Cambridge, Mass.: Harvard University Press, 1990.

Denison, R. Ford. *Darwinian Agriculture: How Understanding Evolution Can Improve Agriculture.* Princeton, N.J.: Princeton University Press, 2012.

Diamond, Jared. *Collapse: How Societies Choose to Fail or Succeed.* New York: Penguin, 2005.

Dieckmann, Christoph. *Deutsche Besatzungspolitik in Litauen 1941–1944.* 2 vols., Göttingen, Ger.: Wallstein Verlag, 2011.

———. "'Jüdischer Bolschewismus' 1917 bis 1921." In *Holocaust und Völkermorde. Die Reichweite des Vergleichs,* edited by Sybille Steinbacher, 55–81. Frankfurt: Campus Verlag, 2014.

Dikötter, Frank. *Mao's Great Famine: The History of China's Most Devastating Catastrophe, 1958–62.* London: Bloomsbury, 2010.

Dmitrów, Edmund. "Die Einsatzgruppen der deutschen Sicherheitspolizei und des Sicherheitsdienstes zu Beginn der Judenvernichtung im Gebiet von Łomża und Białystok im Sommer 1941." In *Der Beginn der Vernichtung. Zum Mord an den Juden in Jedwabne und Umgebung im Sommer 1941,* edited by Edmund Dmitrów, Paweł Machcewicz, and Tomasz Szarota, and translated by Beate Kosmala, 95–208. Osnabrück, Ger.: Fibre, 2004.

Drymmer, Wiktor Tomir. "Zagadnienie żydowskie w Polsce 1935–1939." *Zeszyty Historyczne* 13 (1968): 55–77.

Dulić, Tomislav. "Mass Killing in the Independent State of Croatia, 1941–1945: A Case for Comparative Research." *Journal of Genocide Research* 8, no. 3 (2006): 225–81.

Dumitru, Diana. "Through the Eyes of the Survivors: Jewish-Gentile Relations in Bessarabia and Transnistria During the Holocaust." In *Eradicating Differences: The Treatment of Minorities in Nazi-Dominated Europe,* edited by Anton Weiss-Wendt, 203–27. Newcastle, UK: Cambridge Scholars, 2010.

Dwork, Debórah, and Robert Jan van Pelt. *Auschwitz.* New York: Norton, 1996.

———. *Holocaust: A History.* New York: Norton, 2002.

Edele, Mark, and Michael Geyer, "States of Exception." In *Beyond Totalitarianism: Stalinism and Nazism Compared,* edited by Michael Geyer and Sheila Fitzpatrick, 345–395. Cambridge: Cambridge University Press, 2009.

Eder, Thomas Stephan. *China-Russia Relations in Central Asia.* Wiesbaden, Ger.: Springer, 2014.

Edmonds, James A., and Norman J. Rosenberg. "Climate Change Impacts for the Conterminous USA: An Integrated Assessment Summary." *Climate Change,* no. 69 (2005): 151–62.

Eichholtz, Dietrich. *Krieg um Öl: Ein Erdölimperium als deutsches Kriegsziel (1938–1943).* Leipzig, Ger.: Leipziger Universitätsverlag, 2006.

Eidintas, Alfonsas. *Jews, Lithuanians, and the Holocaust.* Vilnius, Lithuania: Versus Aureus, 2003.

Engel, David. *Facing a Holocaust: The Polish Government-in-Exile and the Jews, 1943–1945.* Chapel Hill: University of North Carolina Press, 1993.

———. *Historians of the Jews and the Holocaust.* Stanford, Calif.: Stanford University Press, 2006.

———. *The Holocaust: The Third Reich and the Jews.* Harlow, UK: Pearson, 2000.

———. *In the Shadow of Auschwitz: The Polish Government-in-Exile and the Jews, 1939–1942.* Chapel Hill: University of North Carolina Press, 1987.

———. "Poles, Jews, and Historical Objectivity." *Slavic Review* 46, nos. 3–4 (1987): 568–80.

Engelking, Barbara. *Jest taki piękny, słoneczny dzień: Losy Żydów szukających ratunku na wsi polskiej 1942–1945.* Warsaw: Centrum Badań nad Zagładą Żydów, 2011.

Engelking, Barbara, and Jan Grabowski. *"Żydów łamiących prawo należy karać śmiercią!": Przestępczość Żydów w Warszawie 1939–1942.* Warsaw: Centrum Badań nad Zagładą Żydów, 2010.

Engelking, Barbara, and Jacek Leociak. *The Warsaw Ghetto: A Guide to the Perished City.* Translated by Emma Harris. New Haven, Conn.: Yale University Press, 2009.

Engelking, Barbara, and Dariusz Libionka. *Żydzi w powstańczej Warszawie.* Warsaw: Centrum Badań nad Zagładą Żydów, 2009.

Epstein, Catherine. *Model Nazi: Arthur Greiser and the Occupation of Western Poland.* Oxford: Oxford University Press, 2010.

Ericksen, Robert P. *Complicity in the Holocaust: Churches and Universities in Nazi Germany.* Cambridge: Cambridge University Press, 2012.

Evans, Richard J. *The Third Reich in Power.* London: Penguin, 2005.

Evenson, R. E., and M. Rosegrant. "The Economic Consequences of Crop Genetic Improvement Programmes." In *Crop Variety Improvement and Its Effect on Productivity,* edited by R. E. Evenson and D. Gollin, 473–98. Wallingford, UK: CABI, 2003.

Ezergailis, Andrew. *The Holocaust in Latvia: The Missing Center.* Riga: Historical Institute of Latvia, 1996.

Falk, Barbara. *Sowjetische Städte in der Hungersnot 1932/33.* Cologne: Böhlau Verlag, 2005.

Farley, John W. "Petroleum and Propaganda: The Anatomy of the Global Warming Denial Industry." *Monthly Review* 64, no. 1 (2012): 40–53.

Faye, Jean-Pierre. "Carl Schmitt, Göring, et l'État total." In *Carl Schmitt ou le mythe du politique,* edited by Yves Charles Zarka, 161–82. Paris: Presses Universitaires de France, 2009.

Federico, Giovanni. "Natura Non Fecit Saltus: The 1930s as the Discontinuity in the History of European Agriculture." In *War, Agriculture, and Food: Rural Europe from the*

1930s to the 1950s, edited by Leen van Molle, Yves Segers, and Paul Brassley, 15–32. New York: Routledge, 2012.

Fein, Helen. *Accounting for Genocide: National Responses and Jewish Victimization During the Holocaust.* Chicago: University of Chicago Press, 1984.

Fermia, Franceso, and Caitlin Werrell, eds. "The Arab Spring and Climate Change." February 2013.

Ferrara, Antonio, and Niccolo Pianciola. *L'età delle migrazioni forzate: Esodi e deportazioni in Europa 1853–1953.* Bologna: Il Mulino, 2012.

Fest, Joachim C. *Das Gesicht des Dritten Reiches.* Munich: Piper, 2006.

Finkel, Evgeny. "Victim's Politics: Jewish Behavior During the Holocaust." PhD diss., University of Wisconsin–Madison, 2012.

Fischer, Fritz. *Griff nach der Weltmacht.* Düsseldorf, Ger.: Droste, 1961.

Fischer, Klaus P. *Hitler and America.* Philadelphia: University of Pennsylvania Press, 2011.

Fogelman, Ewa. *Conscience and Courage: Rescuers of Jews During the Holocaust.* New York: Anchor Books, 1994.

Foucault, Michel. *Naissance de la biopolitique: Cours au Collège de France, 1978–1979.* Paris: Gallimard, 2004.

Fournier, Jacques, *La conception National-Socialiste du Droit des Gens,* Paris: Editions A. Pedrone, 1939.

Fralon, José-Alain. *A Good Man in Evil Times: The Heroic Story of Aristides de Sousa-Mendes.* Translated by Peter Graham. New York: Basic Books, 2000.

Friedlander, Henry. *The Origins of Nazi Genocide: From Euthanasia to the Final Solution.* Chapel Hill: University of North Carolina Press, 1995.

Friedländer, Saul. "Some Reflections on the Historicization of National Socialism." In *Reworking the Past: Hitler, the Holocaust, and the Historians' Debate,* edited by Peter Baldwin, 88–101. Boston: Beacon Press, 1990.

———. *The Years of Extermination: Nazi Germany and the Jews, 1939–1945.* New York: HarperCollins, 2007.

Friedman, Philip. *Roads to Extinction: Essays on the Holocaust.* New York: Jewish Publication Society of America, 1980.

Fritzsche, Peter. "The Holocaust and the Knowledge of Murder." *Journal of Modern History* 80, no. 3 (2008): 594–613.

Gawin, Magdalena. "Pensjonat Jadwigi Długoborskiej." *Teologia Polityczna,* no. 7 (2013): 142–59.

Gedye, G. E. R. *Betrayal in Central Europe: Austria and Czechoslovakia: The Fallen Bastions.* New York: Harper and Brothers, 1939.

Gehl, Jürgen. *Austria, Germany, and the Anschluss, 1931–1938.* London: Oxford University Press, 1963.

Geiss, Imanuel. *Der polnische Grenzstreifen 1914–1918.* Lübeck, Ger.: Matthiesen, 1960.

Geissbühler, Simon. *Blutiger Juli: Rumäniens Vernichtungskrieg und der vergessene Massenmord an den Juden 1941.* Paderborn, Ger.: Schöningh, 2013.

———. "'He Spoke Yiddish Like a Jew': Neighbors' Contribution to the Mass Killing of Jews in Northern Bukovina and Bessarabia, July 1941." *Holocaust and Genocide Studies* 28, no. 3 (2014): 430–49.

Gellately, Robert. *Lenin, Stalin, and Hitler: The Age of Social Catastrophe.* New York: Knopf, 2007.

———. *Stalin's Curse: Battling for Communism in War and Cold War.* New York: Knopf, 2013.

Genette, Gérard. *Figures I.* Paris: Éditions du Seuil, 1966.

Gerlach, Christian. *Extremely Violent Societies: Mass Violence in the Twentieth-Century World.* Cambridge: Cambridge University Press, 2010.

———. "Failure of Plans for an SS Extermination Camp in Mogilëv, Belorussia," *Holocaust and Genocide Studies* 11, no. 1 (1997): 60–78.

———. *Kalkulierte Morde: Die deutsche Wirtschafts- und Vernichtungspolitik in Weissrussland 1941 bis 1944.* Hamburg: Hamburger Edition, 1999.

———. *Krieg, Ernährung, Völkermord: Forschungen zur deutschen Vernichtungspolitik im Zweiten Weltkrieg.* Hamburg: Hamburger Edition, 1998.

———. "The Wannsee Conference, the Fate of the German Jews, and Hitler's Decision in Principle to Exterminate All European Jews." *Journal of Modern History* 70, no. 4 (1998): 759–812.

Gerlach, Christian, and Götz Aly. *Das letzte Kapitel: Realpolitik, Ideologie, und der Mord an den ungarischen Juden 1944–45.* Stuttgart, Ger.: Deutsche Verlags-Anstalt, 2002.

Gerwarth, Robert. *Hitler's Hangman: The Life of Heydrich.* New Haven, Conn.: Yale University Press, 2011.

Gerwarth, Robert, and Stephan Malinowski. "Hannah Arendt's Ghosts: Reflections on the Disputable Path from Windhoek to Auschwitz." *Central European History* 42 (2009): 279–300.

Ginor, Isabella, and Gideon Remez. "A Cold War Casualty in Jerusalem, 1948: The Assassination of Witold Hulanicki." *Israel Journal of Foreign Affairs* 4, no. 3 (2010): 135–56.

Glass, Hildrun. *Deutschland und die Verfolgung der Juden in rumänischen Machtbereich 1940–1944.* Munich: Oldenbourg, 2014.

Głowacki, Albin. *Sowieci wobec Polaków na ziemiach wschodnich II Rzeczypospolitej 1939–1941.* Łódź, Poland: Wydawnictwo Uniwersytetu Łódzkiego, 1998.

Gnatowski, Michał. "Niepokorni i przystosowani: Stosunki polsko-żydowskie w regionie łomżyńskim." In *Żydzi i stosunki polsko-żydowskie w regionie łomżyńskim w XIX i XX wieku,* edited by Michał Gnatowski, 149–60. Łomża, Poland: Łomżyńskie Towarzystwo Naukowe im. Wagów, 2002.

Goeschel, Christian, and Nikolaus Wachsmann. Introduction to *The Nazi Concentration Camps, 1933–39: A Documentary History,* 1–28. Lincoln: Nebraska University Press, 2010.

Golan, Zev. *Stern: The Man and His Gang.* Tel Aviv: Yair Publishing, 2011.

Golczewski, Frank. *Deutsche und Ukrainer, 1914–1939.* Paderborn, Ger.: Ferdinand Schöningh, 2010.

Goldinger, Walter, and Dieter Binder. *Geschichte der Republik Österreich 1918–1938.* Oldenburg, Ger.: Verlag für Geschichte und Politik, 1992.

Goldsmith, Benjamin E., and Dimitri Semenovich. "Political Instability and Genocide: Comparing Causes in Asia and the Pacific and Globally." 2012.

Gondek, Leszek. *Wywiad polski w Trzeciej Rzeszy 1933–1939.* Gdynia, Poland: Wojskowa Drukarnia, 1982.

Gordon, Peter. *Continental Divide: Heidegger, Cassirer, Davos.* Cambridge, Mass.: Harvard University Press, 2010.

Gourevitch, Philip. *We Wish to Inform You That Tomorrow We Will Be Killed with Our Families.* New York: Picador, 1998.

Goussef, Catherine. "Les déplacements forcés des populations aux frontières russes occidentales (1914–1950)." In *La violence de guerre 1914–1945,* edited by S. Audoin-Rouzeau, A. Becker, Chr. Ingrao, and H. Rousso, 177–90. Paris: Éditions Complexes, 2002.

Govrin, Yosef. "Ilya Ehrenburg and the Ribbentrop-Molotov Agreement." *Israel Journal of Foreign Affairs* 7, no. 2 (2013): 103–8.

———. *The Jewish Factor in the Relations between Nazi Germany and the Soviet Union 1933–1941.* London: Vallentine Mitchell, 2009.

Grabowski, Jan. *Judenjagd: Polowanie na Żydów 1942–1945. Studium dziejów pewnego powiatu.* Warsaw: Centrum Badań nad Zagładą Żydów, 2011.

Graziosi, Andrea. "Collectivisation, révoltes paysannes et politiques gouvernementales à travers les rapports du GPU d'Ukraine de février-mars 1930," *Cahiers du Monde russe* 34, no. 3 (1994) : 437–72.

Gregory, Paul R. *Terror by Quota: State Security from Lenin to Stalin.* New Haven, Conn.: Yale University Press, 2009.

Griffioen, Pim, and Ron Zeller. "Comparing the Persecution of the Jews in the Netherlands, France, and Belgium: Similarities, Differences, Causes." In *The Persecution of the Jews in the Netherlands 1940–1945,* edited by Peter Romijn, et al., 53–89. Amsterdam: Vossiuspers UvA, 2012.

Gross, Jan Tomasz. *Revolution from Abroad: The Soviet Conquest of Poland's Western Ukraine and Western Belorussia.* Princeton, N.J.: Princeton University Press, 1988.

———. *Sąsiedzi: Historia zagłady żydowskiego miasteczka.* Sejny, Poland: Pogranicze, 2008.

———. "The Social Consequences of War: Preliminaries to the Study of the Imposition of Communist Regimes in East Central Europe." *East European Politics and Societies* 3 (1989): 198–214.

Gross, Jan Tomasz, with Irena Grudzińska Gross. *Golden Harvest: Events at the Periphery of the Holocaust.* New York: Oxford University Press, 2012.

Gross, Irena Grudzińska, and Jan Tomasz Gross. *War Through Children's Eyes: The Soviet Occupation of Poland and the Deportations, 1939–1941.* Stanford, Calif.: Hoover Institution Press, 1981.

Gross, Raphael. *Carl Schmitt and the Jews: The "Jewish Question," the Holocaust, and German Legal Theory.* Translated by Joel Golb. Madison: University of Wisconsin Press, 2007.

Grynberg, Anne. *Les camps de la honte: Les internés juifs des camps français (1939–1944).* Paris: Éditions La Découverte, 1991.

Grynberg, Henryk. *Monolog polsko-żydowski.* Wołowiec, Poland: Czarne, 2012.

Gudziak, Borys. *Crisis and Reform.* Cambridge, Mass.: Harvard University Press, 1998.

Guettel, Jens-Uwe. "From the Frontier to German South-West Africa: German Colonialism, Indians, and American Westward Expansion." *Modern Intellectual History* 7, no. 3 (2010): 523–52.

———. "The U.S. Frontier as Rationale for the Nazi East? Settler Colonialism and

Genocide in Nazi-Occupied Eastern Europe and the American West." *Journal of Genocide Research* 15, no. 4 (2013): 401–19.

Gumbrecht, Hans Ulrich. *Nach 1945: Latenz als Ursprung der Gegenwart.* Translated by Frank Born. Berlin: Suhrkamp Verlag, 2012.

———. "Our Broad Present." Read in manuscript, 2013.

Gurianov, A. Ie. "Obzor sovetskikh repressivnikh kampanii protiv poliakov i pols'kikh grazhdan." In *Poliaki i russkie: Vzaimoponimanie; vzaimoneponimanie,* edited by A. V. Lipatov and I. O. Shaitanov, 199–207. Moscow: Indrik, 2000.

Gustafson, Thane. *Wheel of Fortune: The Battle for Oil and Power in Russia.* Cambridge, Mass.: Harvard University Press, 2012.

Habermas, Jürgen. *Der philosophische Diskurs der Moderne.* Frankfurt: Suhrkamp Verlag, 1985.

Haestrup, Jørgen. "The Danish Jews and the German Occupation." In *The Rescue of the Danish Jews: Moral Courage Under Stress,* edited by Leo Goldberger, 13–53. New York: New York University Press, 1987.

Hagen, William W. "Before the 'Final Solution': Toward a Comparative Analysis of Political Antisemitism in Interwar Germany and Poland." *Journal of Modern History* 68, no. 2 (1996): 351–81.

———. *German History in Modern Times: Four Lives of the Nation.* Cambridge: Cambridge University Press, 2012.

Harvey, Elisabeth. *Women and the Nazi East: Agents and Witnesses of Germanization.* New Haven, Conn.: Yale University Press, 2003.

Haslam, Jonathan. *The Soviet Union and the Struggle for Collective Security in Europe, 1933–39.* Houndsmills, UK: Macmillan, 1984.

Hauner, Milan. *India in Axis Strategy: Germany, Japan, and Indian Nationalists in the Second World War.* Stuttgart, Ger.: Klett-Cotta, 1981.

Hazani, Moshe. "Red Carpet, White Lilies: Love of Death in the Poetry of the Jewish Underground Leader Avraham Stern." *Psychoanalytic Review* 89, no. 1 (2002): 1–47.

Hecht, Dieter. "Demütigungsrituale—Alltagsszenen nach dem 'Anschluss' in Wien." In *"Anschluss" März–April 1938 in Österreich,* edited by Werner Welzig, 39–71. Vienna: ÖAW, 2010.

Heim, Susanne. "Einleitung." In *Die Verfolgung und Ermordung der europäischen Juden durch das nationalsozialistische Deutschland 1933–1945.* Vol. 2, *Deutsches Reich 1938–August 1938,* edited by Susanne Heim, 13–63. Munich: Oldenbourg Verlag, 2009.

Heller, Daniel K. "The Rise of the Zionist Right: Polish Jews and the Betar Youth Movement, 1922–1935." PhD diss., Stanford University, 2012.

Heller, Joseph. *The Stern Gang: Ideology, Politics, and Terror, 1940–1949.* London: Frank Cass, 1995.

———. "The Zionist Right and National Liberation: From Jabotinsky to Avraham Stern." *Israel Affairs* 1, no. 3 (1995): 85–110.

Helmuth, Brian et al. "Hidden Signals of Climate Change in Intertidal Ecosystems: What (Not) to Expect When You Are Expecting." *Journal of Experimental Marine Biology and Ecology,* no. 400 (2011): 191–99.

Hempel, Adam. *Pogrobowcy klęski: Rzecz o policji "granatowej" w Generalnym Gubernatorstwiue 1939–1945.* Warsaw: PWN, 1990.

Hentosh, Liliana. "Pro stavlennia mytropolyta Sheptyts'koho do Nimets'koho okupatsiynoho rezhymu v konteksti dokumenta z kantseliariï Al'freda Rozenberga," *Ukraïna moderna,* 2013, 298–317.

Herbeck, Ulrich. *Das Feindbild vom "jüdischen Bolschewiken": Zur Geschichte des russischen Antisemitismus vor und während der Russischen Revolution.* Berlin: Metropol Verlag, 2009.

Herbert, Ulrich. *Best: Biographische Studien über Radikalismus, Weltanschauung und Vernunft, 1903–1989.* Bonn, Ger.: J.H.W. Dietz, 1996.

Herf, Jeffrey. *The Jewish Enemy: Nazi Propaganda During World War II and the Holocaust.* Cambridge, Mass.: Harvard University Press, 2006.

Heschel, Susannah. *The Aryan Jesus: Christian Theologians and the Bible in Nazi Germany.* Princeton, N.J.: Princeton University Press, 2008.

Hiio, Toomas, Meelis Maripuu, and Indrek Paavle. Introduction to *Estonia 1940–1945,* vol. 1 of the report of the Estonian International Commission for the Investigation of Crimes against Humanity. Tallinn, Estonia: Tallinna Raamatutrükikoda, 2005.

Hilberg, Raul. *The Destruction of the European Jews.* 3 vols. New Haven, Conn.: Yale University Press, 2003.

Hildebrand, Klaus. *Vom Reich zum Weltreich: Hitler, NSDAP und koloniale Frage 1919–1945.* Munich: Wilhelm Fink Verlag, 1969.

Hillgruber, Andreas. "Die ideologisch-dogmatische Grundlage der nationalsozialistischen Politik der Ausrottung der Juden in den besetzten Gebieten der Sowjetunion und ihre Durchführung 1941–1944." *German Studies Review* 2, no. 3 (1979): 263–96.

Himka, John-Paul. "Ethnicity and Reporting of Mass Murder: *Krakivski visti,* the NKVD Murders of 1941, and the Vinnytsia Exhumation." 2009.

———. "Metropolitan Andrey Sheptytsky and the Holocaust." *Polin* 26 (2013).

———. *Religion and Nationality in Western Ukraine.* Montreal: McGill-Queen's University Press, 1999.

Hintjens, Helen M. "Explaining the 1994 Genocide in Rwanda." *Journal of African Studies* 37, no. 2 (1999): 241–86.

Holler, Martin. *Der nationalsozialistische Völkermord an den Roma in der besetzten Sowjetunion (1941–1944).* Heidelberg: Dokumentions- und Kulturzentrum Deutscher Sinti und Roma, 2009.

———. "The Nazi Persecution of Roma in Northwestern Russia: The Operational Area of Army Group North, 1941–1944." In *The Nazi Genocide of the Roma: Reassessment and Commemoration,* edited by Anton Weiss-Wendt, 153–80. New York: Berghahn Books, 2013.

Holquist, Peter. *Making War, Forging Revolution: Russia's Continuum of Crisis, 1914–1921.* Cambridge, Mass.: Harvard University Press, 2002.

Horkheimer, Max. *Eclipse of Reason.* New York: Oxford University Press, 1947.

Horkheimer, Max, and Theodor W. Adorno. *Dialektik der Aufklärung: Philosophische Fragmente.* 1944. Reprint, Frankfurt: S. Fischer Verlag, 1969.

Horta, Loro. "The Zambezi Valley: China's First Agricultural Colony?" Center for Strategic and International Studies, Online Public Policy Forum, 20 May 2008.

Hryciuk, Grzegorz. *Polacy we Lwowie 1939–1944.* Warsaw: KiW, 2000.

———. "Victims 1939–1941: The Soviet Repressions in Eastern Poland." In *Shared History—Divided Memory: Jews and Others in Soviet-Occupied Poland,* edited by Elazar Barkan, Elisabeth A. Cole, and Kai Struve, 173–200. Leipzig, Ger.: Leipzig University-Verlag, 2007.

Hrynevych, Vladyslav. *Nepryborkane riznoholossia: Druha svitova viina i suspil'no-politychni nastroï v Ukraïni, 1939–cherven' 1941 rr.* Kyiv: Lira, 2012.

Hsiang, Solomon M., Marshall Burke, and Edward Miguel. "Quantifying the Influence of Climate on Human Conflict," *Science,* 1 August 2013.

Hull, Isabel V. *Absolute Destruction: Military Culture and the Practices of War in Imperial Germany.* Ithaca, N.Y.: Cornell University Press, 2005.

Husson, Édouard. *Heydrich et la solution finale.* Paris: Perrin, 2012.

Iliffe, John. "The Effects of the Maji Maji Rebellion of 1905–1906 on German Occupation Policy in East Africa." In *Britain and Germany in Africa, Imperial Rivalry and Colonial Rule,* edited by Prosser Gifford and Wm. Roger Lewis, with the assistance of Alison Smith, 558–75. New Haven, Conn.: Yale University Press, 1967.

Il'iushyn, I. I. *OUN-UPA i ukraïns'ke pytannia v roky druhoï svitovoï viiny v svitli pol's'kykh dokumentiv.* Kyiv: NAN Ukraïny, 2000.

Ingrao, Christian. *Believe and Destroy: Intellectuals in the SS War Machine.* Translated by Andrew Brown. Cambridge: Polity, 2013.

———. *Les chasseurs noirs: La brigade Dirlewanger.* Paris: Perrin, 2006.

———. "Violence de guerre, violence génocide: Les Einsatzgruppen." In *La violence de guerre 1914–1945,* edited by S. Audoin-Rouzeau, A. Becker, Chr. Ingrao, and H. Rousso, 219–40. Paris: Éditions Complexes, 2002.

Iordachi, Constantin. "Unerwünschte Bürge. Die 'Judenfrage' im Rumänien und Serbien zwischen 1931 und 1939." *Transit: Europäische Review,* no. 43 (2012/2013): 106–17.

Iwanow, Mikołaj. *Pierwszy naród ukarany: Stalinizm wobec polskiej ludności kresowej 1921–1938.* Warsaw: Omnipress, 1991.

Jabotinsky, Vladimir. *The War and the Jew.* New York: Dial Press, 1942.

Jäckel, Eberhard. *Hitler in History.* Hanover, N.H.: University Press of New England, 1984.

———. "Der Novemberpogrom 1938 und die Deutschen." In *Die Novemberpogrome 1938. Versuch einer Bilanz,* edited by Andreas Nachama and Claudia Steur, 66–73. Berlin: Stiftung Topographie des Terrors, 2009.

Jangfeldt, Bengt. *The Hero of Budapest: The Triumph and Tragedy of Raoul Wallenberg.* Translated by Harry D. Watson and Bengt Jangfeldt. London: I. B. Tauris, 2014.

Jansen, Marc, and Nikolai Petrov. *Stalin's Loyal Executioner: People's Commissar Nikolai Ezhov, 1895–1940.* Stanford, Calif.: Hoover University Press, 2002.

Jardim, Tomaz. *The Mauthausen Trial: American Military Justice in Germany.* Cambridge, Mass.: Harvard University Press, 2012.

Jelinek, Yeshayahu A. *The Carpathian Diaspora: The Jews of Subcarpathian Rus' and Mukachevo, 1848–1948.* New York: East European Monographs, 2007.

Jobst, Kerstin. *Zwischen Nationalismus und Internationalismus.* Hamburg: Dölling Verlag, 1996.

Jolluck, Katherine R. *Exile and Identity: Polish Women in the Soviet Union During World War II.* Pittsburgh: University of Pittsburgh Press, 2002.

Jonas, Hans. *The Imperative of Responsibility: In Search of an Ethics for the Technological Age.* Chicago: University of Chicago Press, 1979.

Judt, Tony, and Timothy Snyder. *Thinking the Twentieth Century.* New York: Penguin, 2012.

Jureit, Ulrike. *Das Ordnen von Räumen: Territorium und Lebensraum im 19. und 20. Jahrhundert.* Hamburg: Hamburger Edition, 2012.

Kaasik, Peeter, and Toomas Hiio. "Political Repression from June to August 1940." In *Estonia 1940–1945,* edited by Toomas Hiio, Meelis Maripuu, and Indrek Paavle, 310–18. Talinn, Estonia: Tallinna Raamatutrükikoda, 2005.

Kachanovs'kyi, Ivan. "OUN(b) ta natsysts'ki masovi vbyvstva vlitku 1941 roku na istorychniy Volyni." *Ukraïna moderna* 20 (2014): 215–44.

Kaczmarski, Marcin. "Domestic Sources of Russia's China Policy." *Problems of Post-Communism* 59, no. 2 (2012): 3–17.

Kaplan, Eran. *The Jewish Radical Right: Revisionist Zionism and Its Ideological Legacy.* Madison: University of Wisconsin Press, 2005.

Kaprāns, Mārtiņs, and Vita Zelče. "Vēsturiskie cilvēki un viņu biogrāfijas." *Latvijas Arhīvi* 1 (2009): 166–93.

Karski, Jan. *Wielkie mocarstwa wobec Polski 1919–1945.* Translated by Elżbieta Morawiec. Warsaw: PIW, 1992.

Kassow, Samuel D. *Who Will Write Our History? Rediscovering a Hidden Archive from the Warsaw Ghetto.* New York: Vintage, 2009.

Kay, Alex J. "Brothers: The SS Mass Murderer and the Concentration Camp Inmate." *Transit Online,* 2013.

———. *Exploitation, Resettlement, Mass Murder: Political and Economic Planning for German Occupation Policy in the Soviet Union, 1940–1941.* New York: Berghahn Books, 2006.

———. "Transition to Genocide, July 1941: Einsatzkommando 9 and the Annihilation of Soviet Jewry." *Holocaust and Genocide Studies* 27, no. 3 (2013): 411–42.

Kellogg, Michael. *The Russian Roots of Nazism: White Émigrés and the Making of National Socialism.* Cambridge: Cambridge University Press, 2005.

Kenez, Peter. *The Coming of the Holocaust: From Antisemitism to Genocide.* Cambridge: Cambridge University Press, 2013.

Kermish, Joseph. "The Activities of Żegota." In *Rescue Attempts During the Holocaust,* edited by Yisrael Gutman and Efraim Zuroff, 367–98. Jerusalem: Yad Vashem, 1977.

Kershaw, Ian. *The End: The Defiance and Destruction of Nazi Germany.* New York: Penguin Press, 2011.

———. *Fateful Choices: Ten Decisions That Changed the World, 1940–1941.* London: Penguin Books, 2007.

———. *Hitler: A Biography.* New York: W. W. Norton, 2008.

———. *The "Hitler Myth": Image and Reality in the Third Reich.* Oxford: Oxford University Press, 1987.

Kęsik, Jan. *Zaufany Komendanta: Biografia Polityczna Jana Henryka Józewskiego 1892–1981.* Wrocław, Poland: Wydawnictwo Uniwersytetu Wrocławskiego, 1995.

Khaustov, Vladimir. "Deiatel'nost' organov gosudarstvennoi bezopasnosti NKVD SSSR (1934–1941 gg.)." PhD diss., Akademiia Federal'noi Sluzhby Bezopasnosti Rossiiskoi Federatsii, 1997.

Khlevniuk, Oleg V. *The History of the Gulag: From Collectivization to the Great Terror.* New Haven, Conn.: Yale University Press, 2004.

———. *Stalin: New Biography of a Dictator.* Translated by Nora A. Favorov. New Haven, Conn.: Yale University Press, 2015.

Kiernan, Ben. *Blood and Soil: A World History of Genocide and Extermination from Sparta to Darfur.* New Haven, Conn.: Yale University Press, 2007.

King, Gary, Ori Rosen, Martin Tanner, and Alexander F. Wagner. "Ordinary Voting Behavior in the Extraordinary Election of Adolf Hitler." *Journal of Economic History* 68, no. 4 (2008): 951–96.

King, Marcus Dubois. "Factoring Environmental Security Issues into National Security Threat Assessments: The Case of Global Warming." PhD diss., Fletcher School of Law and Diplomacy, 2008.

Kirsch, Jonathan. *The Short Strange Life of Herschel Grynszpan: A Boy Avenger, a Nazi Diplomat, and a Murder in Paris.* New York: Liveright, 2013.

Klafkowski, Alfons. *Okupacja niemiecka w Polsce w świetle prawa narodów.* Poznań, Poland: Wydawnictwo Instytutu Zachodniego, 1946.

Klamper, Elizabeth. "Der 'Anschlusspogrom.'" In *Der Pogrom 1938: Judenverfolgung in Österreich und Deutschland,* edited by Kurt Schmid and Robert Streibel, 25–41. Vienna: Picus Verlag, 1990.

Klare, Michael T. "Global Warming Battlefields: How Climate Change Threatens Security," *Current History* 107, no. 703 (2007): 355–61.

Klarsfeld, Serge. *Le mémorial de la déportation des Juifs de France.* Paris: Beate et Serge Klarsfeld, 1978.

Klemperer, Victor. *The Language of the Third Reich.* Translated by Martin Brady. London: Continuum, 2006.

Koenen, Gerd. *Der Russland-Komplex: Die Deutschen und der Osten, 1900–1945.* Munich: C. F. Beck, 2005.

Koialovich, Mikhail. *Litovskaia tserkovnaia uniia.* St. Petersburg, 1859.

Kołakowski, Leszek. *Main Currents of Marxism: Its Rise, Growth, and Dissolution.* 3 vols. Translated by P. S. Falla. Oxford: Oxford University Press, 1978.

Koonz, Claudia. *The Nazi Conscience.* Cambridge, Mass.: Harvard University Press, 2003.

Kopka, Bogusław. *Konzentrationslager Warschau: Historia i następstwa.* Warsaw: IPN, 2007.

Kopp, Kristin. "Constructing Racial Difference in Colonial Poland." In *Germany's Colonial Pasts,* edited by Eric Ames, Marcia Klotz, and Lora Wildenthal, 76–96. Lincoln: University of Nebraska Press, 2005.

Kopstein, Jeffrey S., and Jason Wittenberg. "Intimate Violence: Anti-Jewish Pogroms in the Shadow of the Holocaust." Manuscript, 2013.

Korb, Alexander. *Im Schatten des Weltkriegs: Massengewalt der Ustaša gegen Serben, Juden und Roma in Kroatien 1941–1945.* Hamburg: Hamburger Edition, 2013.

———. "Ustaša Mass Violence Against Gypsies in Croatia." In *The Nazi Genocide of the Roma: Reassessment and Commemoration,* edited by Anton Weiss-Wendt, 73–95. New York: Berghahn Books, 2013.

Korboński, Stefan. "An Unknown Chapter in the Life of Menachem Begin and Irgun Zvai Leumi." *East European Quarterly* 13, no. 3 (1979): 373–79.

Kornat, Marek. *Polen zwischen Hitler und Stalin: Studien zur polnischen Aussenpolitik in der Zwischenkriegzeit.* Berlin: be.bra verlag, 2012.

———. *Polityka równowagi: Polska między Wschodem a Zachodem.* Cracow: Arcana, 2007.

———. *Polityka zagraniczna Polski 1938–1939: Cztery decyzje Józefa Becka.* Gdańsk, Poland: Oskar, 2012.

Körner, T. W. *The Pleasures of Counting.* Cambridge: Cambridge University Press, 1996.

Korzec, Paweł. *Juifs en Pologne: La question juive pendant l'entre-deux-guerres.* Paris: Presses de la Fondation Nationale des Sciences Politiques, 1980.

Koselleck, Reinhart. *Futures Past: On the Semantics of Historical Time.* Translated by Keith Tribe. Cambridge, Mass.: MIT Press, 1985.

Koslov, Elissa Mailänder. *Gewalt im Dienstalltag. Die SS-Aufseherinnen des Konzentrations- und Vernichtungslagers Majdanek.* Hamburg: Hamburger Edition, 2009.

Kostyrchenko, G. V. *Gosudarstvennyi antisemitizm v SSSR ot nachala do kul'minatsii 1938–1953.* Moscow: Materik, 2005.

Kotkin, Stephen. *Magnetic Mountain: Stalinism as a Civilization.* Berkeley: University of California Press, 1995.

Kozaczuk, Władysław, and Jerzy Straszak. *Enigma: How the Poles Broke the Nazi Code.* New York: Hippocrene Books, 2004.

Kruglov, Alexander. "Jewish Losses in Ukraine." In *The Shoah in Ukraine: History, Testimony, Memorialization,* edited by Ray Brandon and Wendy Lower, 272–90. Bloomington: Indiana University Press, 2008.

Krzywiec, Gregorz. *Szowinizm po polsku: Przypadek Romana Dmowskiego (1886–1905).* Warsaw: Neriton, 2009.

Kudryashov, Sergei. "Russian Collaboration with the Nazis and the Holocaust." Paper presented at the International Institute for Holocaust Research, Yad Vashem, 2001.

Kühne, Thomas. *Belonging and Genocide: Hitler's Community, 1918–1945.* New Haven, Conn.: Yale University Press, 2010.

Kupczak, Janusz. *Polacy na Ukrainie w latach 1921–1939.* Wrocław: Wydawnictwo Uniwersytetu Wrocławskiego, 1994.

Kuromiya, Hiroaki. *Freedom and Terror in the Donbas: A Ukrainian-Russian Borderland, 1870s–1990s.* Cambridge: Cambridge University Press, 1998.

———. *Stalin.* Harlow, UK: Pearson Longman, 2005.

Kuromiya, Hiroaki, and Andrzej Pepłoński. *Między Warszawą a Tokio: Polsko-japońska współpraca wywiadowcza 1904–1944.* Toruń, Poland: Wydawnictwo Adam Marszałek, 2009.

Kuwałek, Robert. *Das Vernichtungslager Bełżec.* Translated by Steffen Hänschen. Berlin: Metropol, 2013.

Kwiet, Konrad. *Reichskommissariat Niederlande: Versuch und Scheitern nationalsozialistischer Neuordnung.* Stuttgart, Ger.: Deutsche Verlags-Anstalt, 1968.

Lafree, Gary. "Social Institutions and the Crime 'Bust' of the 1990s." *Journal of Criminal Law and Criminology* 88, no. 4 (1998): 1325–68.

Latif, M., and N. S. Keenlyside. "El Niño/Southern Oscillation Response to Climate Change." *Proceedings of the National Academy of Sciences of the United States of America* 106, no. 49 (2009): 20578–83.

Leder, Andrzej. *Prześniona rewolucja: Ćwiczenie z logiki historycznej*. Warsaw: Wydawnictwo Krytyki Politycznej, 2014.

Leonhard, Jörn. *Die Büchse der Pandora: Geschichte des Ersten Weltkriegs*. Munich: Beck, 2014.

Levene, Mark. *The Rise of the West and the Coming of Genocide*. London: I. B. Tauris, 2005.

Levin, Dov. "The Attitude of the Soviet Union to the Rescue of Jews." In *Rescue Attempts During the Holocaust*, edited by Yisrael Gutman and Efraim Zuroff, 225–36. Jerusalem: Yad Vashem, 1977.

———. *The Lesser of Two Evils: Eastern European Jewry Under Soviet Rule, 1939–1941*. Translated by Naftali Greenwood. Philadelphia: Jewish Publication Society, 1995.

Levine, Hillel. *In Search of Sugihara*. New York: Free Press, 1996.

Libionka, Dariusz. "ZWZ-AK i Delegatura Rządu RP wobec eksterminacji Żydów polskich." In *Polacy i Żydzi pod okupacją niemiecką 1939–1945, Studia i materiały*, edited by Andrzej Żbikowski, 15–208. Warsaw: IPN, 2006.

Libionka, Dariusz, and Laurence Weinbaum. *Bohaterowie, hochsztaplerzy, opisywacze: Wokół Żydowskiego Związku Wojskowego*. Warsaw: Centrum Badań nad Zagładą Żydów, 2011.

Liulevicius, Vejas Gabriel. *The German Myth of the East, 1800 to the Present*. Oxford: Oxford University Press, 2009.

———. *War Land on the Eastern Front: Culture, National Identity, and German Occupation in World War I*. Cambridge: Cambridge University Press, 2000.

Livezeanu, Irina. *Cultural Politics in Greater Romania: Regionalism, Nation-Building, and Ethnic Struggle, 1918–1930*. Ithaca, N.Y.: Cornell University Press, 1995.

Lohr, Eric. *Nationalizing the Russian Empire: The Campaign against Enemy Aliens during World War I*. Cambridge, Mass.: Harvard University Press, 2003.

———. "1915 and the War Pogrom Paradigm in the Russian Empire." In *Anti-Jewish Violence: Rethinking the Pogrom in East European History*, edited by Jonathan Dekel-Chen, David Gaunt, Natan M. Meir, and Israel Bartal, 41–51. Bloomington: Indiana University Press, 2011,

———. *Russian Citizenship from Empire to Soviet Union*. Cambridge, Mass.: Harvard University Press, 2012.

Longerich, Peter. *Davon haben wir nichts gewusst! Die Deutschen und die Judenverfolgung 1933–1945*. Munich: Siedler, 2007.

———. *Heinrich Himmler: Biographie*. Berlin: Siedler, 2008.

———. *Politik der Vernichtung: Eine Gesamtdarstellung der nationalsozialistischen Judenverfolgung*. Munich: Piper, 1998.

———. *The Unwritten Order: Hitler's Role in the Final Solution*. Stroud, UK: Tempus, 2001.

Loose, Ingo. "Reaktionen auf den Novemberpogrom in Polen 1938–1939." In *Die Novemberpogrome 1938. Versuch einer Bilanz*, edited by Andreas Nachama and Claudia Steuer, 44–57. Berlin: Stiftung Topographie des Terrors, 2009.

Łossowski, Piotr. *Kraje bałtyckie w latach przełomu 1934–1944*. Warsaw: Instytut Historii PAN, 2005.

Lotspeich, Richard. "Economic Integration of China and Russia in the Post-Soviet

Era." In *The Future of China-Russia Relations,* edited by James Bellacqua, 83–145. Lexington: University of Kentucky Press, 2010.

Löw, Andrea. *Juden im Getto Litzmannstadt: Lebensbedingungen, Selbstwahrnehmung, Verhalten.* Göttingen, Ger.: Wallstein Verlag, 2006.

Löw, Andrea, and Markus Roth. *Juden in Krakau unter deutscher Besatzung.* Göttingen: Wallstein, 2011.

Lower, Wendy. "Axis Collaboration, Operation Barbarossa, and the Holocaust in Ukraine." In *Nazi Policy on the Eastern Front: Total War, Genocide, and Radicalization,* edited by Alex J. Kay, Jeff Rutherford, and David Stahel, 186–219. Rochester, N.Y.: University of Rochester Press, 2012.

———. "German Colonialism and Genocide: A Comparative View from Below in Africa 1904–1908 and Ukraine 1941–1944," unpublished paper, 2003.

———. *Hitler's Furies: German Women in the Nazi Killing Fields.* Boston: Houghton Mifflin, 2013.

———. *Nazi Empire-Building and the Holocaust in Ukraine.* Chapel Hill: University of North Carolina Press, 2005.

———. "Pogroms, Mob Violence, and Genocide in Western Ukraine, Summer 1941: Varied Histories, Explanations, and Comparisons." *Journal of Genocide Research* 13, no. 3 (2011): 217–46.

Lukacs, John. *The Last European War.* New Haven, Conn.: Yale University Press, 1976.

Lynch, Michael J., Ronald G. Burns, and Paul B. Stretesky, "Global Warming and State-Corporate Crime: The Politicalization of Global Warming Under the Bush Administration." *Crime, Law, and Social Change* 54 (2010): 213–39.

Machcewicz, Pawel. "Rund um Jedwabne—Neue Forschungsergebnisse polnischer Historiker." In *Der Beginn der Vernichtung. Zum Mord an den Juden in Jedwabne und Umgebung im Sommer 1941,* edited by Edmund Dmitrów, Paweł Machcewicz, and Tomasz Szarota, and translated by Beate Kosmala, 19–94. Osnabrück, Ger.: Fibre, 2004.

MacLean, French. *The Field Men: The SS Officers Who Led the Einsatzkommandos.* Atglen, Penn.: Schiffer, 1999.

MacQueen, Michael. "Nazi Policy Toward the Jews in the Reichskommissariat Ostland, June–December 1941: From White Terror to Holocaust in Lithuania." In *Bitter Legacy: Confronting the Holocaust in the USSR,* edited by Zvi Gitelman, 91–103. Bloomington: Indiana University Press, 1997.

Madajczyk, Czesław. "Legal Conceptions in the Third Reich and Its Conquests." *Michael: On the History of Jews in the Diaspora* 13 (1993): 131–59.

———. "Vom 'Generalplan Ost' zum 'Generalsiedlungsplan.'" In *Der "Generalplan Ost": Hauptlinien der nationalsozialistischen Planungs- und Vernichtungspolitik,* edited by Mechtild Rössler and Sabine Schleiermacher, 12–19. Berlin: Akademie Verlag, 1993.

Madajczyk, Czesław, and Stanisława Lewandowska. *Hitlerowski terror na wsi polskiej 1939–1945.* Warsaw: PWN, 1965.

Maier, Charles S. *The Unmasterable Past: History, Holocaust, and German National Identity.* Cambridge, Mass.: Harvard University Press, 1997.

Mallmann, Klaus-Michael. "'Rozwiązać przez jakikolwiek szybko działający środek':

Policja Bezpieczeństwa w Łodzi a Shoah w Kraju Warty." In *Zagłada Żydów na polskich terenach wcielonych do Rzeszy*, edited by Aleksandra Namysło, 85–115. Warsaw: IPN, 2008.

Mallmann, Klaus-Michael, Jochen Böhler, and Jürgen Matthäus. *Einsatzgruppen in Polen: Darstellung und Dokumentation*. Darmstadt, Ger.: WBG, 2008.

Mallmann, Klaus-Michael, and Martin Cüppers. *Halbmond und Hakenkreuz: Das Dritte Reich, die Araber und Palästina*. Darmstadt, Ger.: WBG, 2006.

Mamdani, Mahmood. *When Victims Become Killers: Colonialism, Nativism, and the Genocide in Rwanda*. Princeton, N.J.: Princeton University Press, 2001.

Mańkowski, Zygmunt. "Ausserordentliche Befriedungsaktion." In *Ausserordentliche Befriedungsaktion 1940 Akcja AB na ziemiach polskich*, edited by Zygmunt Mańkowski, 6–18. Warsaw: GKBZpNP-IPN, 1992.

Mann, Michael. *The Dark Side of Democracy: Explaining Ethnic Cleansing*. Cambridge: Cambridge University Press, 2005.

Mann, Michael E. "Do Global Warming and Climate Change Represent a Serious Threat to Our Welfare and Environment?" *Social Philosophy and Policy* 26, no. 2 (2009): 193–230.

Manoschek, Walter. *"Serbien ist judenfrei": Militärische Besatzungspolitik und Judenvernichtung in Serbien 1941/1942*. Munich: R. Oldenbourg Verlag, 1993.

Maripuu, Meelis, and Argo Kuusik. "Political Arrests and Court Cases from August 1940 to September 1941." In *Estonia 1940–1945*, edited by Toomas Hiio, Meelis Maripuu, and Indrek Paavle, 319–327. Talinn, Estonia: Tallinna Raamatutrükikoda, 2005.

Maripuu, Meelis, and Peeter Kaasik. "Deportations of 14 June 1941." In *Estonia 1940–1945*, edited by Toomas Hiio, Meelis Maripuu, and Indrek Paavle, 363–83. Tallinn: Tallinna Raamatutrükikoda, 2005.

Markiel, Tadeusz, and Alina Skibińska, *Zagłada domu Trynczerów*. Warsaw: Stowarzyszenie Centrum Badań na Zagładą Żydów, 2011.

Marrus, Michael R., and Robert O. Paxton. *Vichy France and the Jews*. Stanford, Calif.: Stanford University Press, 1995.

Martin, Terry. *Affirmative Action Empire*. Ithaca, N.Y.: Cornell University Press, 2001.

———. "The Origins of Soviet Ethnic Cleansing." *Journal of Modern History* 70, no. 4 (1998): 813–61.

Maslin, Mark. *Global Warming: A Very Short Introduction*. Oxford: Oxford University Press, 2004.

Matthäus, Jürgen. "Controlled Escalation: Himmler's Men in the Summer of 1941 and the Holocaust in the Occupied Soviet Territories." *Holocaust and Genocide Studies* 21, no. 2 (Fall 2007): 218–42.

Matz, Johan. "Cables in Cipher, the Raoul Wallenberg Case, and Swedish-Soviet Diplomatic Communication 1944–1947." *Scandinavian Journal of History* 38, no. 3 (2013), 1–23.

———. "Sweden, the United States, and Raoul Wallenberg's Mission to Hungary in 1944." *Journal of Cold War Studies* 14, no. 3 (2012): 97–146.

Maubach, Franka. "Expansion weiblicher Hilfe: Zur Erfahrungsgeschichte von Frauen im Kriegsdienst." In *Volksgenossinnen. Frauen in der NS-Volksgemeinschaft*, edited by Sybille Steinbacher, 93–111. Göttingen, Ger.: Wallstein Verlag, 2007.

Maurer, Trude. "The Background for Kristallnacht: The Expulsion of Polish Jews." In *November 1938: From "Reichskristallnacht" to Genocide,* edited by Walter H. Pehle, 44–72. Oxford: Berg, 1990.

Mazower, Mark. *Governing the World: The History of an Idea.* New York: Penguin Press, 2012.

———. *Hitler's Empire: Nazi Rule in Occupied Europe.* London: Allen Lane, 2008.

———. *Inside Hitler's Greece: The Experience of Occupation, 1941–1944.* New Haven, Conn.: Yale University Press, 1995.

———. "An International Civilization? Empire, Internationalism, and the Crisis of the Mid-Twentieth Century." *International Affairs* 82, no. 3 (2006): 553–66.

———. *Salonica: City of Ghosts.* New York: Knopf, 2005.

———. "Violence and the State in the Twentieth Century." *American Historical Review* 107, no. 4 (2002): 1147–67.

McAuley, Jr., James K. "Decision in Bordeaux: Eduardo Propper de Callejón, the Problem of the Jewish Refugees, and Actor-Network Theory in Vichy France, 1940–1941." BA thesis, Harvard College, 2012.

McDonough, Frank. *Hitler and the Rise of the Nazi Party.* London: Pearson, 2003.

McGranahan, Graham, Deborah Balk, and Bridget Anderson. "The Rising Tide: Assessing the Risks of Climate Change and Human Settlements in Low Elevation Coastal Zones." *Environment and Urbanization* 19, no. 1 (2007): 17–37.

McNeill, William H. *The Global Condition: Conquerors, Catastrophes, and Community.* Princeton, N.J.: Princeton University Press, 1992.

Mędrzecki, Włodzimierz. *Województwo wołyńskie.* Wrocław, Poland: Ossolineum, 1988.

Mędykowski, Witold. *W cieniu gigantów: pogromy 1941 r. w byłej sowieckiej strefie okupacyjnej.* Warsaw: ISP PAN, 2012.

Megargee, Geoffrey. *War of Annihilation: Combat and Genocide on the Eastern Front, 1941.* Lanham, Md.: Rowman and Littlefield, 2007.

Melnyk, Oleksandr. "Stalinist Justice as a Site of Memory: Anti-Jewish Violence in Kyiv's Podil District in September 1941 Through the Prism of Soviet Investigative Documents." *Jahrbücher für Geschichte Osteuropas* 61, no. 2 (2013): 223–48.

Melzer, Emanuel. *No Way Out: The Politics of Polish Jewry.* Cincinnati: Hebrew Union College Press, 1997.

Michman, Dan. *The Emergence of Jewish Ghettos During the Holocaust.* Translated by Lenn J. Schramm. Cambridge: Cambridge University Press, 2011.

Mitchell, John F. B., Jason Lowe, Richard A. Wood, and Michael Vellinga. "Extreme Events Due to Human-Induced Climate Change." *Philosophical Transactions of the Royal Society: Mathematical, Physical and Engineering Sciences* 364 (2006): 2117–33.

Młynarczyk, Jacek Andrzej. *Judenmord in Zentralpolen: Der Distrikt Radom im Generalgouvernement 1939–1945.* Darmstadt, Ger.: WGB, 2007.

Monroe, Kristen Renwick. *The Hand of Compassion: Portraits of Moral Choice During the Holocaust,* Princeton, N.J.: Princeton University Press, 2004.

Moore, Bob. "Le contexte du sauvetage dans l'Europe de l'Ouest occupée." In *La résistance aux génocides: De la pluralité des actes de sauvetage,* edited by Jacques Sémelin, Claire Andrieu, and Sarah Gensburger, 277–90. Paris: Presses de la Fondation Nationale des Sciences Politiques, 2008.

———. *Victims and Survivors: The Nazi Persecution of the Jews in the Netherlands, 1940–1945.* London: Arnold, 1997.

Moorhouse, Roger. *The Devils' Alliance: Hitler's Pact with Stalin, 1939–1941.* London: Bodley Head, 2014.

Morris, Benny. *Righteous Victims: A History of the Zionist-Arab Conflict, 1881–1999.* New York: Knopf, 1999.

Morris, James. "The Polish Terror: Spy Mania and Ethnic Cleansing in the Great Terror." *Europe-Asia Studies* 56, no. 5 (July 2004): 751–66.

Moses, A. Dirk, "Das römische Gespräch in a New Key: Hannah Arendt, Genocide, and the Defense of Republican Civilization," *Journal of Modern History,* Vol. 85, No. 4 (2013), 867–913.

Mosse, George L. *The Nationalization of the Masses: Political Symbolism and Mass Movements in Germany from the Napoleonic Wars Through the Third Reich.* New York: Meridian, 1977.

Motyka, Grzegorz. *Cień Kłyma Sawura: Polsko-ukraiński konflikt pamięci.* Gdańsk, Poland: Muzeum II Wojny Światowej, 2013.

———. *Od rzezi wołyńskiej do akcji "Wisła": Konflikt polsko-ukraiński 1943–1947.* Warsaw: Wydawnictwo Literackie, 2011.

Mount, Amy. "The Arctic Wake-up Call: Oil, Climate Change, and Governance in the Place of Melting Ice." Paper presented at Yale University, 2013.

Moyo, Dambisa F. *Winner Take All: China's Race for Resources and What It Means for the World.* New York: Basic Books, 2012.

Müller, Rolf-Dieter. *Der Feind steht im Osten: Hitlers geheime Pläne für einen Krieg gegen die Sowjetunion im Jahr 1939.* Berlin: Ch. Links Verlag, 2011.

Musial, Bogdan. *Sowjetische Partisanen 1941–1944: Mythos und Wirklichkeit.* Paderborn, Ger.: Ferdinand Schöningh, 2009.

Naumov, Leonid. *Stalin i NKVD.* Moscow: Iauza, 2007.

Neumann, Franz. *Behemoth: The Structure and Practice of National Socialism.* Toronto: Oxford University Press, 1942.

Newbury, Catharine. "Background to Genocide: Rwanda." *Issue: A Journal of Opinion* 23, no. 2 (1995): 12–17.

Niemann, Alfred. *Kaiser und Revolution.* Berlin: August Scherl, 1922.

Nikol'skij, Vladimir. "Die 'Kulakenoperation' im ukrainischen Donbass." In *Stalinismus in der sowjetischen Provinz 1937–1938,* edited by Rolf Binner, Bernd Bonwetsch, and Marc Junge, 613–40. Berlin: Akademie Verlag, 2010.

Nikol's'kyi, V. M. *Represyvna diial'nist' orhaniv derzhavnoï bezpeky SRSR v Ukraïni.* Donetsk, Ukraine: Vydavnytstvo Donets'koho Natsional'noho Universytetu, 2003.

Nirenberg, David. *Anti-Judaism: The Western Tradition.* New York: Norton, 2013.

Niv, David. *M'arkhot ha-Irgun ha-tseva'i ha-le'umi.* Vol. 2. Tel Aviv: Mosad Klozner, 1966.

Nowak, Andrzej. *Polska i trzy Rosje.* Cracow: Arcana, 2001.

Nowak Jeziorański, Jan. "Gestapo i NKVD." *Karta,* no. 37 (2003): 88–97.

Offer, Avner. *The First World War: An Agrarian Interpretation.* New York: Oxford University Press, 1989.

Olaru-Cemîrtan, Viorica. "Wo die Züge Trauer trugen: Deportationen in Bessarabien, 1940–1941." *Osteuropa* 59, nos. 7–8 (2009): 219–26.

Oliner, Samuel P., and Pearl M. Oliner. *The Altruistic Personality: Rescuers of Jews in Nazi Europe.* New York: The Free Press, 1988.

Olmstead, Alan L., and Paul W. Rhode. *Creating Abundance: Biological Innovation and American Agricultural Development.* Cambridge: Cambridge University Press, 2008.

Oreskes, Naomi, and Erik M. Conway. *Merchants of Doubt: How a Handful of Scientists Obscured the Truth on Issues from Tobacco Smoke to Global Warming.* New York: Bloomsbury Press, 2010.

Ostałowska, Lidia. *Farby wodne.* Warsaw: Wydawnictwo Czarne, 2011.

Osterloh, Jörg. *Nationalsozialistische Judenverfolgung im Reichsgau Sudetenland 1938–1945.* Munich: Oldenbourg Verlag, 2006.

Ozsváth, Zsuzsanna. *In the Footsteps of Orpheus: The Life and Times of Miklós Radnóti.* Bloomington: Indiana University Press, 2000.

Paavle, Indrek. "Fate of the Estonian Elite in 1940–1941." In *Estonia 1940–1945,* edited by Toomas Hiio, Meelis Maripuu, and Indrek Paavle, 391–409. Talinn, Estonia: Tallinna Raamatutrükikoda, 2005.

Panh, Rithy, with Christophe Bataille. *L'élimination.* Paris: Grasset, 2011.

Parker, Geoffrey. *Global Crisis: War, Climate Change, and Catastrophe in the Seventeenth Century.* New Haven, Conn.: Yale University Press, 2013.

Pasztor, Maria. "Problem wojny prewencyjnej w raportach belgijskich diplomatów z lat 1933–1934." In *Międzymorze: Polska i kraje Europy środkowo-wschodniej XIX–XX wieku,* edited by Andrzej Ajnenkiel et al., 313–20. Warsaw: IH PAN, 1995.

Pauer-Studer, Herlinde. "Einleitung." In *Rechtfertigungen des Unrechts. Das Rechtsdenken im Nationalsozialismum in Originaltexten,* edited by Herlinde Pauer-Studer and Julian Find, 15–135. Berlin: Suhrkamp, 2014.

Pauley, Bruce F. "The Social and Economic Background of Austria's *Lebensunfähigkeit.*" In *The Austrian Socialist Experiment,* edited by Anson Rabinbach, 21–37. Boulder, Colo.: Westview Press, 1985.

Paulsson, Gunnar S. *Secret City: The Hidden Jews of Warsaw 1940–1945.* New Haven, Conn.: Yale University Press, 2002.

Pavlowitch, Stevan L. *Hitler's New Disorder: The Second World War in Yugoslavia.* New York: Columbia University Press, 2008.

Pedersen, Susan. "The Impact of League Oversight on British Policy in Palestine." In *Britain, Palestine, and Empire: The Mandate Years,* edited by Rory Miller, 39–65. Farnham, UK: Ashgate, 2010.

Penter, Tanja. *Kohle für Stalin und Hitler: Arbeiten und Leben im Donbass 1929 bis 1953.* Essen, Ger.: Klartext Verlag, 2010.

Pepłoński, Andrzej. *Kontrwywiad II Rzeczypospolitej.* Warsaw: Bellona, 2002.

———. *Wywiad polskich sił zbrojnych na zachodzie 1939–1945.* Warsaw: MOREX, 1995.

Pergher, Roberta, and Mark Roseman. "The Holocaust—a Colonial Genocide?" *Dapim: Studies on the Holocaust* 27, no. 1 (2013): 42–73.

Petrov, Nikita, and K. V. Skorkin. *Kto rukovodil NKVD, 1934–1941.* Moscow: Zven'ia, 1999.

Petrov, N. V., and A. B. Roginsksii. "'Pol'skaia operatsiia' NKVD 1937–1938 gg." In *Repressii protiv poliakov i pol'skikh grazhdan,* edited by A. I. Gurianov, 22–43. Moscow: Zven'ia, 1997.

Petschar, Hans, ed. *Anschluss: Eine Bildchronologie.* Vienna: Christian Brandstätter Verlag, 2008.

Pfeffer, W. T., J. T. Harper, and S. O'Neel. "Kinematic Constraints on Glacier Contribution to 21st-Century Sea-Level Rise." *Science* 321, 5 September 2008, 1340–43.

Pietrow, Nikita. *Psy Stalina.* Warsaw: Demart, 2012.

Piskorski, Jan M. *Wygnańcy: przesiedlenia i uchodźcy w dwudziestowiecznej Europie.* Warsaw: Państwowy Instytut Wydawniczy, 2009.

Pitman, A. J., A. Arneth, and L. Ganzeveld. "Regionalizing Global Climate Change Models." *International Journal of Climatology* 32 (2012): 321–37.

Plavnieks, Richards. "Nazi Collaborators on Trial During the Cold War: The Cases against Viktors Arājs and the Latvian Auxiliary Security Police." PhD diss., University of North Carolina at Chapel Hill, 2013.

Podolska, Anna. "Poland's Antisemitic Rescuers: A Consideration of Apparent Contradictions." MA thesis, University College London, 2013.

Pohl, Dieter. *Die Herrschaft der Wehrmacht: Deutsche Militärbesatzung und einheimische Bevölkerung in der Sowjetunion 1941–1944.* Munich: R. Oldenbourg, 2008.

———. "Schauplatz Ukraine: Der Massenmord an den Juden im Militärverwaltungsgebiet und im Reichskommissariat 1941–1943." In *Ausbeutung, Vernichtung, Öffentlichkeit: Neue Studien zur nationalsozialistischen Lagerpolitik,* edited by Norbert Frei, Sybille Steinbacher, and Bernd C. Wagner, 135–179. Munich: K. G. Saur, 2000.

———. "Ukrainische Hilfskräfte beim Mord an den Juden." In *Die Täter der Shoah,* edited by Gerhard Paul. Göttingen, Ger.: Wallstein Verlag, 2002.

———. *Verfolgung und Massenmord in der NS-Zeit 1933–1945.* Darmstadt, Ger.: Wissenschaftliche Buchgesellschaft, 2008.

Poliakov, Léon. *Histoire de l'antisémitisme.* Vol. 2, *L'âge de la science.* Paris: Calmann-Lévy, 1981.

———. *Sur les traces du crime.* Paris: Éditions Grancher, 2012.

Polian, Pavel. "Hätte der Holocaust beinahe nicht stattgefunden? Überlegungen zu einem Schriftwechsel im Wert von zwei Millionen Menschenleben." In *Besatzung, Kollaboration, Holocaust: Neue Studien zur Verfolgung und Ermordung der europäischen Juden,* edited by Johannes Hürter and Jürgen Zarusky. Munich: Oldenbourg, 2010.

Pollack, Martin. *Kontaminierte Landschaften.* Vienna: Residenz Verlag, 2014.

———. *Der Tote im Bunker: Bericht über meinen Vater.* Vienna: Zsolnay, 2004.

———. *Warum wurden die Stanislaws erschossen? Reportagen.* Vienna: Zsolnay, 2008.

Polonsky, Antony. *The Jews in Poland and Russia.* Vol. 2, *1881–1914.* London: Littman Library, 2010.

———. *The Jews in Poland and Russia.* Vol. 3, *1914–2008.* London: Littman Library, 2012.

———. *Politics in Independent Poland 1921–1939: The Crisis of Constitutional Government.* Oxford: Clarendon Press, 1972.

Poprzeczny, Joseph. *Odilo Globocnik, Hitler's Man in the East.* Jefferson, N.C.: McFarland, 2004.

Porter, Brian. *When Nationalism Began to Hate: Imagining Modern Politics in Nineteenth-Century Poland.* New York: Oxford University Press, 2000.

Porter-Szücs, Brian. *Faith and Fatherland: Catholicism, Modernity, and Poland.* New York: Oxford University Press, 2011.

Powell, James Laurence. *The Inquisition of Climate Science*. New York: Columbia University Press, 2011.

Power, Samantha. *"A Problem from Hell": America and the Age of Genocide*. New York: Basic Books, 2002.

Prekerowa, Teresa. "Komórka 'Felicji': nieznane archiwum działacza Rady Pomocy Żydom w Warszawie." *Rocznik warszawski* 15 (1979): 519–56.

———. *Konspiracyjna Rada Pomocy Żydom w Warszawie 1942–1945*. Warsaw: Państwowy Instytut Wydawniczy, 1982.

Preston, Paul. *The Spanish Holocaust: Inquisition and Extermination in Twentieth-Century Spain*. New York: Norton, 2012.

Prusin, Alexander V. "A Community of Violence: The SiPo/SD and Its Role in the Nazi Terror System in Generalbezirk Kiew." *Holocaust and Genocide Studies* 21, no. 1 (2007): 1–30.

———. *The Lands Between: Conflict in the East European Borderlands, 1870–1992*. Oxford: Oxford University Press, 2010.

———. *Nationalizing a Borderland: War, Ethnicity, and Anti-Jewish Violence in East Galicia, 1914–1920*. Tuscaloosa: University of Alabama Press, 2005.

Puławski, Adam. "The Polish Government-in-Exile in London, the Delegatura, the Union of Armed Struggle-Home Army and the Extermination of the Jews." *Holocaust Studies* 18, nos. 2–3 (2012): 118–44.

———. *W obliczu Zagłady: Rząd RP na Uchodźstwie, Delegatura Rządu RP na Kraj, ZWZ-AK wobec deportacji Żydów do obozów zagłady (1941–1942)*. Lublin, Poland: IPN, 2009.

Rabinbach, Anson. *The Crisis of Austrian Socialism: From Red Vienna to Civil War, 1927–34*. Chicago: University of Chicago Press, 1983.

Rączy, Elżbieta. *Pomoc Polaków dla ludności żydowskiej na Rzeszowszczyźnie 1939–1945*. Rzeszów, Poland: IPN, 2008.

Radchenko, Yuri. "Accomplices to Extermination: Municipal Government and the Holocaust in Kharkiv." *Holocaust and Genocide Studies* 27, no. 3 (2013): 443–63.

Raggam-Blesch, Michaela. "Das 'Anschluss'-Pogrom in den Narrativen der Opfer." In *"Anschluss" März–April 1938 in Österreich*, edited by Werner Welzig, 111–24. Vienna: ÖAW, 2010.

Ragsdale, Hugh. *The Soviets, the Munich Crisis, and the Coming of World War II*. Cambridge: Cambridge University Press, 2004.

Rahmsdorf, Stefan. "A Semi-Empirical Approach to Projecting Future Sea-Level Rise." *Science* 315 (19 January 2007), 368–70.

Redlich, Shimon. *Together and Apart in Brzeżany: Poles, Jews, and Ukrainians, 1919–1945*. Bloomington: Indiana University Press, 2002.

Reeves, Eric. *A Long Day's Dying: Critical Moments in the Darfur Genocide*. Toronto: Key, 2007.

Reid, Anna. *Leningrad: The Epic Siege of World War II, 1941–1944*. New York: Walker, 2011.

Rein, Leonid. "Local Collaboration in the Execution of the 'Final Solution' in Nazi-Occupied Belorussia." *Holocaust and Genocide Studies* 20, no. 3 (2006): 381–409.

Riabov, Oleg, and Tatiana Riabova. "The Decline of Gayropa? How Russia Intends to Save the World." *Eurozine*, 2014.

Rieger, Berndt. *Creator of the Nazi Death Camps: The Life of Odilo Globocnik*. London: Vallentine Mitchell, 2007.

Ringelblum, Emanuel. *Polish-Jewish Relations During the Second World War.* Translated by Dafna Allon, Danuta Dabrowska, and Dana Keren. Evanston, Ill.: Northwestern University Press, 1992.

Robbe-Grillet, Alain. *Pour un nouveau roman.* Paris: Les Éditions de Minuit, 1963.

Rodogno, Davide. *Fascism's European Empire: Italian Occupation During the Second World War.* Translated by Adrian Belton. Cambridge: Cambridge University Press, 2006.

Rohde, Robert, et al. "A New Estimate of the Average Earth Surface Land Temperature Spanning 1753 to 2011." Paper presented at the Third Santa Fe Conference on Global and Regional Climate Change, 2012.

Römer, Felix. *Kameraden: Die Wehrmacht von innen.* Munich: Piper, 2012.

———. *Der Kommissarbefehl: Wehrmacht und NS-Verbrechen an der Ostfront 1941/42.* Paderborn, Ger.: Ferdinand Schöningh, 2008.

Romijn, Peter. "The 'Lesser Evil': The Case of the Dutch Local Authorities and the Holocaust." In *The Persecution of the Jews in the Netherlands 1940–1945,* edited by Peter Romijn, 13–26. Amsterdam: Vossiuspers UvA, 2012.

Roos, Hans. *Polen und Europa: Studien zur polnischen Aussenpolitik.* Tübingen, Ger.: J. C. B. Mohr, 1957.

Rose, Laurel L. "Land and Genocide: Exploring the Connections with Rwanda's Prisoners and Prison Officials." *Journal of Genocide Research* 9, no. 1 (2007), 49–69.

Roseman, Mark. "The Lives of Others—Amid the Deaths of Others: Biographical Approaches to Nazi Perpetrators." *Journal of Genocide Research* 15, no. 4 (2013): 443–61.

Rossino, Alexander B. "Anti-Jewish Violence in the Białystok District During the Opening Weeks of Operation Barbarossa." Paper presented at the United States Holocaust Memorial Museum, April 2001.

———. *Hitler Strikes Poland: Blitzkrieg, Ideology, and Atrocity.* Lawrence: University Press of Kansas, 2003.

Rotfeld, Adam Daniel. *W cieniu: 12 rozmów z Marcinem Wojciechowskim.* Warsaw: Agora, 2012.

Roth, Randolph. *American Homicide.* Cambridge, Mass.: Harvard University Press, 2009.

Rothkirchen, Livia. *The Jews of Bohemia and Moravia: Facing the Holocaust.* Lincoln: University of Nebraska Press, 2005.

Rothschild, Joseph. *East Central Europe Between the Two World Wars.* Seattle: University of Washington Press, 1974.

———. "Ethnic Peripheries Versus Ethnic Cores: Jewish Political Strategies in Interwar Poland." *Political Science Quarterly* 96, no. 4 (1981–82): 591–606.

———. *Piłsudski's Coup d'État.* New York: Columbia University Press, 1966.

Rousso, Henry. *La dernière catastrophe: L'histoire, le présent, le contemporain.* Paris: Gallimard, 2012.

———. *Le régime de Vichy.* Paris: Presses Universitaires de France, 2012.

Rudnicki, Szymon. *Równi, ale niezupełnie.* Warsaw: Midrasz, 2008.

Rumpler, Helmut. *Max Hussarek: Nationalitäten und Nationalitätenpolitik in Österreich im Sommer des Jahres 1918.* Graz, Austria: Verlag Böhlau, 1965.

Rüβ, Hartmut. "Wer war verantwortlich für das Massaker von Babij Jar?" *Militärgeschichtliche Mitteilungen* 57, no. 2 (1999): 483–508.

Rutherford, Philip T. *Prelude to the Final Solution: The Nazi Program for Deporting Ethnic Poles, 1939–1941.* Lawrence: University Press of Kansas, 2007.

Rzanna, Ewa. "Raul Hilberg, Zagłada Żydów Europejskich." Read in manuscript, 2014.

Sakamoto, Pamela Rotner. *Japanese Diplomats and Jewish Refugees: A World War II Dilemma.* Westport, Conn.: Praeger, 1998.

Sakowska, Ruth. *Ludzie z dzielnicy zamkniętej: Żydzie w Warszawie w okresie hitlerowskiej okupacji.* Warsaw: PWN, 1975.

Salmonowicz, Stanisław. "The Tragic Night of Occupation: On 'Collaboration from Below' in the General Government." *Polin* 26 (2013).

Salmonowicz, Stanisław, and Jerzy Serczyk. "Z problemów kolaboracji w Polsce w latach 1939–1941." *Czasy Nowożytne* 14 (2003), 43–65.

Saltier, Leon. "Dehumanizing the Dead: The Destruction of Thessaloniki's Jewish Cemetery in the Light of New Sources." *Yad Vashem Studies* 42, no. 1 (2014), 11–46.

Sandler, Willeke Hannah. " 'Colonizers Are Born, Not Made': Creating a Colonial Identity in Nazi Germany, 1933–1945." PhD diss., Duke University, 2012.

Sarraute, Nathalie. *L'ère du soupçon: Essais sur le roman.* Paris: Gallimard, 1956.

Sauerland, Karol. *Polen und Juden: Jedwabne und die Folgen.* Berlin: Philo, 2004.

Saviello, Hillary. "This Bestial Policy: Allied Public Condemnations of the Holocaust and the Establishment of the United Nations War Crimes Commission." PhD diss., London School of Economics, 2014.

Scheffran, Jürgen, and Antonella Battaglini. "Climate and Conflicts: The Security Risks of Global Warming." *Regional Environmental Change* 11 (2011): 27–39.

Schelvis, Jules. *Vernichtungslager Sobibór.* Münster, Ger.: Unrast, 2003.

Schenke, Cornelia. *Nationalstaat und nationale Frage: Polen und die Ukrainer in Wolhynien 1921–1939.* Hamburg: Dölling und Galitz Verlag, 2004.

Schlögel, Karl. "Einleitung." In *Die Russische Revolution und das Schicksal der Russischen Juden. Eine Debatte in Berlin, 1922–1923,* edited by Karl Schlögel and Karl-Konrad Tschäpe, 9–104. Berlin: Matthes und Seitz, 2014.

———. *Terror und Traum: Moskau 1937.* Munich: Carl Hanser Verlag, 2008.

Schneider, Karl. *Auswärts eingesetzt: Bremer Polizeibataillone und der Holocaust,* Essen, Ger.: Klartext Verlag, 2011.

Segal, Raz. "Beyond Holocaust Studies: Rethinking the Holocaust in Hungary." *Journal of Genocide Research* 16, no. 1 (2014): 1–23.

———. "Imported Violence: Carpatho-Ruthenians and Jews in Carpatho-Ukraine, October 1938–March 1939." *Polin* 26 (2013).

Segev, Tom. *One Palestine, Complete: Jews and Arabs Under the British Mandate.* Translated by Chaim Watzman. London: Abacus, 2001.

Seidel, Robert. *Deutsche Besatzungspolitik in Polen: Der Distrikt Radom 1939–1945.* Paderborn, Ger.: Ferdinand Schöningh, 2006.

Sémelin, Jacques. *Persécutions et entraides dans la France occupée: Comment 75% des Juifs en France ont échappé à la mort.* Paris: Seuil, 2013.

———. *Purifier et détruire: Usages politiques des massacres et génocides.* Paris: Seuil, 2005.

Shapira, Anita. *Israel: A History.* Translated by Anthony Berris. Waltham, Mass.: Brandeis University Press, 2012.

———. *Land and Power: The Zionist Resort to Force, 1881–1948.* Translated by William Templer. Stanford, Calif.: Stanford University Press, 1992.

Shavit, Yaacov. *Jabotinsky and the Revisionist Movement 1925–1928*. London: Frank Cass, 1988.

Shepard, Todd. *The Invention of Decolonization: The Algerian War and the Remaking of France*. Ithaca, N.Y.: Cornell University Press, 2006.

Shilon, Avi. *Menachem Begin: A Life*. Translated by Danielle Zilberberg and Yoram Sharett. New Haven, Conn.: Yale University Press, 2012.

Shindler, Colin. *The Triumph of Military Zionism: Nationalism and the Origins of the Israeli Right*. London: I. B. Taurus, 2006.

Shore, Marci. *Caviar and Ashes: A Warsaw Generation's Life and Death in Marxism*. New Haven, Conn.: Yale University Press, 2006.

———. "Conversing with Ghosts: Jedwabne, Żydokomuna, and Totalitarianism." In *The Holocaust in the East: Local Perpetrators and Soviet Responses*, edited by Michael David-Fox, Peter Holquist, and Alexander M. Martin. Pittsburgh: University of Pittsburgh Press, 2014.

———. "Język, pamięć i rewolucyjna awangarda: Kształtowanie historii powstania w getcie warszawskim w latach 1944–1950." *Biuletyn Żydowskiego Instytutu Historycznego* 188, no. 3 (1998): 43–60.

———. *The Taste of Ashes: The Afterlife of Totalitarianism in Eastern Europe*. New York: Crown, 2012.

Shore, Zachary. *What Hitler Knew: The Battle for Information in Nazi Foreign Policy*. Oxford: Oxford University Press, 2003.

Showalter, Dennis. "Comrades, Enemies, Victims: The Prussian/German Army and the Ostvölker." In *The Germans and the East*, edited by Charles W. Ingrao and Franz A. J. Szabo, 209–25. West Lafayette, Ind.: Purdue University Press, 2008.

Siemaszko, Władysław, and Ewa Siemaszko. *Ludobójstwo dokonane przez nacjonalistów ukraińskich na ludności polskiej Wołynia 1939–1945*. Warsaw: von borowiecky, 2000.

Silver, Nate. *The Signal and the Noise*. New York: Penguin, 2012.

Simms, Brendan. *Europe: The Struggle for Supremacy from 1453 to the Present*. New York: Basic Books, 2013.

Simons, Thomas W., Jr. *Eastern Europe in the Postwar World*. New York: St. Martin's, 1991.

Sirutavičius, Vladas, and Darius Staliūnas. "Was Lithuania a Pogrom-Free Zone? (1881–1940)." In *Anti-Jewish Violence: Rethinking the Pogrom in East European History*, edited by Jonathan Dekel-Chen, David Gaunt, Natan M. Meir, and Israel Bartal, 146–58. Bloomington: Indiana University Press, 2011.

Skarga, Barbara. *Penser après le Goulag*. Edited by Joanna Nowicki. Paris: Éditions du Relief, 2011.

Skibińska, Alina. "Perpetrators' Self-Portrait: The Accused Village Administration, Commune Heads, Fire Chiefs, Forest Rangers and Gamekeepers." *East European Politics and Societies* 25, no. 3 (2011): 457–85.

Skóra, Wojciech. *Służba konsularna Drugiej Rzeczypospolitej: Organizacja, kadry i działalność*. Toruń, Poland: Adam Marszałek, 2006.

Slepyan, Kenneth. *Stalin's Guerrillas: Soviet Partisans in World War II*. Lawrence: University of Kansas Press, 2006.

Smith, N., and A. Leiserowitz. "American Evangelicals and Climate Change." *Global Environmental Change*. Read in manuscript, 2013.

Smith, Woodruff D., "'Weltpolitik' und 'Lebensraum.'" In *Das Kaiserreich Transnational,* edited by Sebastian Conrad and Jürgen Osterhammel, 29–48. Göttingen, Ger.: Vandenhoeck and Ruprecht, 2004.

Snyder, Timothy. *Bloodlands: Europe Between Hitler and Stalin.* New York: Basic Books, 2010.

———. "The Causes of Ukrainian-Polish Ethnic Cleaning 1943." *Past and Present,* no. 179 (2003): 197–234.

———. "The Life and Death of West Volhynian Jews, 1921–1945." In *The Shoah in Ukraine: History, Testimony, and Memorialization,* edited by Ray Brandon and Wendy Lower, 77–113. Bloomington: Indiana University Press, 2008.

———. *Nationalism, Marxism, and Modern Central Europe: A Biography of Kazimierz Kelles-Krauz, 1872–1905.* Cambridge, Mass.: Harvard University Press, 1997.

———. "The Problem of Commemorative Causality." *Modernism/Modernity* 20, no. 1 (2013).

———. *The Reconstruction of Nations: Poland, Ukraine, Lithuania, Belarus, 1569–1999.* New Haven, Conn.: Yale University Press, 2002.

———. *The Red Prince: The Secret Lives of a Habsburg Archduke.* New York: Basic Books, 2008.

———. *Sketches from a Secret War: A Polish Artist's Mission to Liberate Soviet Ukraine.* New Haven, Conn.: Yale University Press, 2005.

———. *Ukraïns'ka istoriia, rosiis'ka polityka, ievropeis'ke maibutnie.* Kyiv: Dukh i Litera, 2014.

Sohn-Rethel, Alfred. *Industrie und Nationalsozialismus: Aufzeichnungen aus dem "Mitteleuropäischen Wirtschaftstag."* Edited by Carl Freytag. Berlin: Wagenbach, 1992.

Solomon, Steven. *Water: The Epic Struggle for Wealth, Power, and Civilization.* New York: HarperCollins, 2010.

Solonari, Vladimir. "Ethnic Cleansing or 'Crime Prevention"? Deportation of Romanian Roma." In *The Nazi Genocide of the Roma: Reassessment and Commemoration,* edited by Anton Weiss-Wendt, 96–119. New York: Berghahn Books, 2013.

———. "Patterns of Violence: The Local Population and the Mass Murder of Jews in Bessarabia and Northern Bukovina, July–August 1941." In *The Holocaust in the East: Local Perpetrators and Soviet Responses,* edited by Michael David-Fox, Peter Holquist, and Alexander Martin, chap. 5. Pittsburgh: University of Pittsburgh Press, 2014. Read in manuscript.

Spector, Shmuel. *The Holocaust of Volhynian Jews 1941–1944.* Translated by Jerzy Michałowicz. Jerusalem: Yad Vashem, 1996.

Spector, Stephen. *Evangelicals and Israel: The Story of American Christian Zionism.* New York: Oxford University Press, 2009.

Spektor, Szmuel. "Żydzi wołyńscy w Polsce międzywojennej i w okresie II wojny światowej (1920–1944)." In *Europa nieprowincjonalna,* edited by Krzysztof Jasiewicz, 566–78. Warsaw: Instytut Studiów Politycznych PAN, 1999.

Stanislawski, Michael. "Russian Jewry, the Russian State, and the Dynamics of Jewish Emancipation." In *Paths of Emancipation: Jews, States, and Citizenship,* edited by Pierre Birnbaum and Ira Katznelson, 262–83. Princeton, N.J.: Princeton University Press, 1995.

Stanton, Gregory H. "Could the Rwandan Genocide Have Been Prevented?" *Journal of Genocide Research* 6, no. 2 (2004): 211–28.

Staub, Ervin. "The Origins and Evolution of Hate, with Notes on Prevention." In *The Psychology of Hate,* edited by Robert J. Steirberg, 51–66. Washington, D.C.: American Psychological Association, 2005.

Stein, Alexander. *Adolf Hitler: Schüler der "Weisen von Zion."* Karlovy Vary, Czech Republic: Graphia, 1936.

Steinbacher, Sybille. *Auschwitz: Geschichte und Nachgeschichte.* Munich: Beck, 2004.

———. *"Musterstadt Auschwitz": Germanisierungspolitik und Judenmord in Ostoberschlesien.* Munich: K. G. Saur, 2000.

Steinberg, Jonathan. "The Third Reich Reflected: German Civil Administration in the Occupied Soviet Union." *English Historical Review* 110, no. 437 (1995): 620–51.

Steiner, George. *In Bluebeard's Castle: Some Notes Toward the Redefinition of Culture.* New Haven, Conn.: Yale University Press, 1971.

Steininger, Rolf. *Der Staatsvertrag: Österreich im Schatten von deutscher Frage und kaltem Krieg 1938–1955.* Innsbruck, Austria: Studien-Verlag, 2005.

———. "12 November 1918–12 March 1938: The Road to Anschluss." In *Austria in the Twentieth Century,* edited by Rolf Steininger, Günter Bischof, and Michael Gehler, 85–114. New Brunswick, N.J.: Transaction Publishers, 2002.

Steinweis, Alan E. *Kristallnacht 1938.* Cambridge, Mass.: Harvard University Press, 2009.

Stern, Nicholas. *The Economics of Climate Change.* Cambridge: Cambridge University Press, 2006.

Sternberg, Troy. "Chinese Drought, Wheat, and the Egyptian Uprising: How a Local Hazard Became Globalized." In "The Arab Spring and Climate Change," edited by Caitlin E. Werrell and Francesco Fermia. February 2013.

Sternhell, Zeev. *Les anti-Lumières: Une tradition du XVIIe siècle à la guerre froide.* Paris: Gallimard, 2010.

Stola, Dariusz. *Nadzieja i zagłada: Ignacy Schwarzbart—żydowski przedstawiciel w Radzie Narodowej RP (1940–1945).* Warsaw: Oficyna Naukowa, 1995.

Stone, Daniel. *The Polish-Lithuanian State, 1386–1795.* Seattle: University of Washington Press, 2001.

Stourzh, Gerald. *Vom Reich zur Republik.* Vienna: Editions Atelier, 1990.

Strassner, Peter. *Europäische Freiwillige: Die Geschichte der 5. SS Panzerdivision WIKING.* Osnabrück, Ger.: Munin Verlag, 1968.

Straus, Scott. "How Many Perpetrators Were There in the Rwandan Genocide? An Estimate." *Journal of Genocide Research* 6, no. 1 (2004): 85–98.

Stroński, Henryk. *Represje stalinizmu wobec ludności polskiej na Ukrainie w latach 1929–1939.* Warsaw: Wspólnota Polska, 1998.

Studentowicz, Kazimierz et al., eds. *Polska idea imperialna.* Warsaw: Polityka, 1938.

Subtelny, Orest. "German Diplomatic Reports on the Famine of 1933." In *Famine-Genocide in Ukraine, 1932–1933,* edited by Wsevolod Isajiw, 13–26. Toronto: Ukrainian Canadian Research and Documentation Centre, 2003.

Sullivan, Gordon R., et al. "National Security and the Threat of Climate Change." Arlington, Va.: CNA Corporation, 2007.

Surkis, Judith. *Sexing the Citizen: Morality and Masculinity in France, 1870–1920.* Ithaca, N.Y.: Cornell University Press, 2006.

Szaynok, Boz˙ena. *Z historia˛ i Moskwa˛ w tle: Polska a Izrael 1944–1968.* Warsaw: IPN, 2007.

Tebaldi, Claudia, Benjamin H. Strauss, and Chris E. Zervas. "Modelling Sea Level Rise Impacts on Storm Surges Along US Coasts." *Environmental Research Letters* 7, 014032 (2012): 1–11.

Tec, Nechama. *Defiance: The Bielski Partisans.* New York: Oxford University Press, 1993.

———. *In the Lion's Den: The Life of Oswald Rufeisen.* New York: Oxford University Press, 1990.

———. *When Light Pierced the Darkness: Christian Rescues of Jews in Nazi-Occupied Poland.* New York: Oxford University Press, 1986.

Ther, Philipp. *Ciemna strona państw narodowych: Czystki etniczne w nowoczesnej Europie.* Poznań: Wydawnictwo Poznańkie, 2011.

Thies, Jochen. *Architekt der Weltherrschaft: Die "Endziele" Hitlers.* Düsseldorf, Ger.: Droste Verlag, 1976.

Thomä, Dieter. "Sein und Zeit im Rückblick: Heideggers Selbstkritik." In *Martin Heidegger: Sein und Zeit,* edited by Thomas Rentsch, 282–98. Berlin: Akademie Verlag, 2001.

Thomson, Allison M. et al. "Climate Change Impacts for the Conterminous USA: An Integrated Assessment. Part 3: Dryland Production of Grain and Forage Crops." *Climatic Change,* no. 69 (2005): 43–65.

———. "Climate Change Impacts for the Conterminous USA: An Integrated Assessment. Part 5: Irrigated Agriculture and National Grain Crop Production." *Climatic Change,* no. 69 (2005): 89–105.

Tollefson, Jeff. "The Sceptic Meets His Match." *Nature* 475 (2011): 440–41.

Tomaszewski, Jerzy. "The Civil Rights of Jews in Poland, 1918–1939." *Polin* 8 (1995): 124.

———. *Preludium Zagłady: Wygnanie Żydów polskich z Niemiec w 1938 r.* Łódź, Poland: PWN SA, 1998.

Tomkiewicz, Monika. *Zbrodnia w Ponarach 1941–1944.* Warsaw: IPN, 2008.

Tooze, Adam. *The Wages of Destruction: The Making and Breaking of the Nazi Economy.* New York: Viking, 2007.

Tort, Patrick. *L'effet Darwin: Sélection naturelle et naissance de la civilisation.* Paris: Éditions du Seuil, 2008.

Trentmann, Frank. "Coping with Shortage: The Problem of Food Security and Global Visions of Coordination, c. 1890s–1950." In *Food and Conflict in the Age of the Two World Wars,* edited by Frank Trentmann and Flemming Just, 13–48. Houndmills, UK: Palgrave Macmillan, 2006.

Triepel, Heinrich. *Die Hegemonie: Ein Buch von Führenden Staaten.* Stuttgart, Ger.: W. Kohlhammer, 1938.

Trunk, Isaiah. *Judenrat: The Jewish Councils in Eastern Europe Under Nazi Occupation.* New York: Macmillan, 1972.

Tyaglyy, Mikhail. "Nazi Occupation Policies and the Mass Murder of the Roma in Ukraine." In *The Nazi Genocide of the Roma: Reassessment and Commemoration,* edited by Anton Weiss-Wendt, 120–52. New York: Berghahn Books, 2013.

Ungváry, Krisztián. *The Siege of Budapest: One Hundred Days in World War II.* Translated by Ladislaus Löb. New Haven, Conn.: Yale University Press, 2005.

Urynowicz, Marcin. "Stosunki polsko-żydowskie w Warsawie w okresie okupacji hitlerowskiej." In *Polacy i Żydzi pod okupacją niemiecką 1939–1945: Studia i materiały,* edited by Andrzej Żbikowski, 537–690. Warsaw: IPN, 2006.

Valentino, Benjamin. *Final Solutions: Mass Killing and Genocide in the Twentieth Century.* Ithaca, N.Y.: Cornell University Press, 2004.

Van der Boom, Bart. "Ordinary Dutchmen and the Holocaust: A Summary of Findings." In *The Persecution of the Jews in the Netherlands 1940–1945,* edited by Peter Romijn et al., 29–52. Amsterdam: Vossiuspers UvA, 2012.

Van der Zee, Nanda, *Om erger te voorkomen: de voorbereiding en uitvoering van de vernietiging van het Nederlandse jodendom tijdens de Tweede Wereldoorlog,* Soesterberg: Aspekt, 2008.

Van de Vliert, Evert, Huadong Yang, Yongli Wang, and Xiao-peng Ren. "Climato-Economic Imprints on Chinese Collectivism." *Journal of Cross-Cultural Psychology* 44, no. 4 (2012): 589–605.

Vasari, Emilio. *Dr. Otto Habsburg oder die Leidenschaft für Politik.* Vienna: Verlag Herold, 1972.

Veidlinger, Jeffrey. *In the Shadow of the Shtetl: Small-Town Jewish Life in Soviet Ukraine.* Bloomington: Indiana University Press, 2013.

Verbrechen der Wehrmacht: Dimensionen des Vernichtungskrieges 1941–1944. Hamburg: Institut für Sozialforschung, 2002.

Vīksne, Rudīte. "Members of the Arājs Commando in Soviet Court Files: Social Position, Education, Reasons for Volunteering, Penalty." In *The Hidden and Forbidden History of Latvia under Soviet and Nazi Occupations 1940–1991,* edited by Valters Nollendorfs and Erwin Oberländer, 188–208. Riga: Institute of the History of Latvia Publishers, 2007.

Vilhjálmsson, Vilhjálmur Örn, and Bent Blüdnikow. "Rescue, Expulsion, and Collaboration: Denmark's Difficulties with Its World War II Past." *Jewish Political Studies Review* 18, nos. 3–4 (2006).

Vincent, C. Paul. *The Politics of Hunger: The Allied Blockade of Germany, 1915–1919.* Athens: Ohio University Press, 1985.

Viola, Lynne. "Selbstkolonisierung der Sowjetunion." *Transit,* no. 38 (2011): 34–56.

———. *The Unknown Gulag: The Lost World of Stalin's Special Settlements.* New York: Oxford University Press, 2007.

Walicki, Andrzej. *Philosophy and Romantic Nationalism: The Case of Poland.* Notre Dame, Ind.: University of Notre Dame Press, 1994.

Wandycz, Piotr S. *The Lands of Partitioned Poland, 1772–1918.* Seattle: University of Washington Press, 1975.

———. "Poland Between East and West." In *The Origins of the Second World War Reconsidered,* edited by Gordon Martel, 187–210. New York: Routledge, 1999.

———. *Soviet-Polish Relations, 1917–1921.* Cambridge, Mass.: Harvard University Press, 1969.

———. *Z Piłsudskim i Sikorskim: August Zaleski, Minister Spraw Zagranicznych w latach 1926–1932 i 1939–1941.* Warsaw: Wydawnictwo Sejmowe, 1999.

Ward, James Mace. *Priest, Politician, Collaborator: Jozef Tiso and the Making of Fascist Slovakia.* Ithaca, N.Y.: Cornell University Press, 2013.

Wasser, Bruno. *Himmlers Raumplanung im Osten.* Basel, Switz.: Birkhäuser Verlag, 1993.

Wasserstein, Bernard. *The Ambiguity of Virtue: Gertrude van Tijn and the Fate of the Dutch Jews.* Cambridge, Mass.: Harvard University Press, 2014.

———. *On the Eve: The Jews of Europe Before the Second World War.* New York: Simon and Schuster, 2012.

Weart, Spencer. "Global Warming: How Skepticism Became Denial." *Bulletin of the Atomic Scientists* 67, no. 1 (2011): 41–50.

Webb, Walter Prescott. *The Great Frontier.* Boston: Houghton Mifflin, 1952.

Weber, Timothy P. *On the Road to Armageddon: How Evangelicals Became Israel's Best Friends.* Grand Rapids, Mich.: Baker Academic, 2004.

Weil, Patrick. *How to Be French: Nationality in the Making Since 1789.* Translated by Catherine Porter. Durham, N.C.: Duke University Press, 2008.

Weinbaum, Laurence. *A Marriage of Convenience: The New Zionist Organization and the Polish Government 1936–1939.* Boulder, Colo.: East European Monographs, 1993.

Weinberg, Gerhard L. *The Foreign Policy of Hitler's Germany.* Chicago: University of Chicago Press, 1980.

———. *A World at Arms: A Global History of World War II.* Cambridge: Cambridge University Press, 1994.

Weiner, Amir. *Making Sense of War: The Second World War and the Fate of the Bolshevik Revolution.* Princeton, N.J.: Princeton University Press, 2001.

Weiss, Yfaat. *Deutsche und polnische Juden vor dem Holocaust: Jüdische Identität zwischen Staatsbürgerschaft und Ethnizität 1933–1940.* Translated by Matthias Schmidt. Munich: Oldenbourg, 2000.

Weiss-Wendt, Anton. *Murder Without Hatred: Estonians and the Holocaust.* Syracuse, N.Y.: Syracuse University Press, 2009.

Weitbrecht, Dorothee. *Der Exekutionsauftrag der Einsatzgruppen in Polen.* Filderstadt, Ger.: Markstein, 2001.

Werth, Nicolas. *La terreur et le désarroi: Staline et son système.* Paris: Perrin, 2007.

Westerling, Anthony L., et al. "Continued Warming Could Transform Greater Yellowstone Fire Regimes by Mid-21st Century." *Proceedings of the National Academy of Sciences of the United States of America* 108, no. 32 (2011): 13165–70.

Wette, Wolfram. *Feldwebel Anton Schmid: Ein Held der Humanität.* Frankfurt: S. Fischer Verlag, 2013.

———. *Karl Jäger: Mörder der litauischen Juden.* Frankfurt: S. Fischer Verlag, 2011.

White, Lynn. "The Historical Roots of Our Ecological Crisis." *Science* 155 (1967): 1203–7.

Wieczorkiewicz, Paweł Piotr. *Łańcuch śmierci: Czystka w Armii Czerwonej 1937–1939.* Warsaw: Rytm, 2001.

Wierzbicki, Marek. "Soviet Economic Policy in Annexed Eastern Poland." In *Stalin and Europe: Imitation and Domination, 1928–1953,* edited by Timothy Snyder and Ray Brandon, 114–37. Oxford: Oxford University Press, 2014.

Wieviorka, Annette, and Laffitte, Michel. *A l'intérieur du camp de Drancy.* Paris: Perrin, 2012.

Wildenthal, Lora. *German Women for Empire, 1884–1945.* Durham, N.C.: Duke University Press, 2001.

Wildt, Michael. *An Uncompromising Generation: The Nazi Leadership of the Reich Security Main Office.* Translated by Tom Lampert. Madison: University of Wisconsin Press, 2009.

Wnuk, Rafał. *"Za pierwszego Sowieta": Polska konspiracja na Kresach Wschodnich II Rzeczypospolitej.* Warsaw: IPN, 2007.

Wojciechowski, Marian. *Stosunki polsko-niemieckie 1933–1938.* Poznań: Instytut Zachodni, 1980.

Wróbel, Piotr. "The Seeds of Violence: The Brutalization of an East European Region, 1917–1921." *Journal of Modern History* 1, no. 1 (2003): 125–43.

Wróblewski, Robert. *Dywizja Wiking w Polsce w świetle materiałow archiwalnych.* Lublin, Poland: Kagero, 2010.

Wynot, Edward D., Jr. " 'A Necessary Cruelty': The Emergence of Official Antisemitism in Poland, 1936–1939." *American Historical Review* 76, no. 4 (1971): 1035–58.

Yang, Dali L. *Calamity and Reform in China: State, Rural Society, and Institutional Change Since the Great Leap Famine.* Stanford: Stanford University Press, 1996.

Yisraeli, David. "Germany and Zionism." In *Germany and the Middle East, 1835–1939,* edited by Jehuda L. Wallach, 142–64. Tel Aviv: Tel Aviv University, 1975.

———. *ha-Raikh ha-Germani ve-Erets Yiśra'el: be'ayot Erets Yiśra'el ba-mediniyut ha-Germanit ba-shanim 1889–1945.* Ramat-Gan, Israel: Bar Ilan University, 1974.

Zagłada polskich elit: Akcja AB—Katyń. Warsaw: Instytut Pamięci Narodowej, 2006.

Zaremba, Marcin. *Wielka Trwoga: Polska 1944–1947.* Cracow: Znak, 2012.

Zarka, Yves-Charles. *Un détail Nazi dans la pensée de Carl Schmitt: La justification des lois de Nuremberg du 15 septembre 1935.* Paris: Presses Universitaires de France, 2005.

Żbikowski, Andrzej. *Karski.* Warsaw: Świat Książki, 2011.

———. " 'Night Guard': Holocaust Mechanisms in the Polish Rural Areas, 1942–1945." *East European Politics and Societies* 25, no. 3 (2011): 512–29.

Zehnpfennig, Barbara. *Hitlers Mein Kampf. Eine Interpretation.* Munich: W. Fink, 2000.

Zertal, Idith. *Israel's Holocaust and the Politics of Nationhood.* Translated by Chaya Galai. Cambridge: Cambridge University Press, 2011.

Zhang Xuebin et al. "Detection of Human Influence on Twentieth-Century Precipitation Trends." *Nature* 448 (2007): 461–66.

Ziegler, Jean. *Betting on Famine: Why the World Still Goes Hungry.* Translated by Christopher Caines. New York: New Press, 2013.

Zimmerer, Jürgen. *Von Windhuk nach Auschwitz: Beiträge zum Verhältnis von Kolonialismus und Holocaust.* Münster, Ger.: LIT Verlag, 2011.

Zolotar'ov, Vadim. "Nachal'nyts'kyi sklad NKVS USRR u seredyni 30-h rr." *Z arkhiviv VUChK-HPU-NKVD-KGB,* no. 2 (2001): 326–31.

Żyndul, Jolanta. *Zajścia antyżydowskie w Polsce w latach 1935–1937.* Warsaw: Fundacja Kelles-Krauza, 1994.

Fiction

Bernhard, Thomas. *Heldenplatz.* 1988. Reprint, Frankfurt: Surhkamp, 1995.

Conrad, Joseph. *Heart of Darkness and Other Stories.* 1899. Reprint, London: Wordsworth, 1998.

Grossman, Vasily. *Life and Fate.* 1959. Reprint, New York: Harper, 1985.

Orwell, George. *1984.* 1949. Reprint, London: Penguin, 2008.

Zweig, Stefan. *Schachnovelle.* 1943. Reprint, Frankfurt: Fischer, 2004.

Index

Page numbers in *italics* refer to illustrations.

About the Author

INE GUNDERSVEEN

TIMOTHY SNYDER is the Housum Professor of History at Yale University and a member of the Committee on Conscience of the United States Holocaust Memorial Museum. He is the author of *On Tyranny: Twenty Lessons from the Twentieth Century* and *Bloodlands: Europe Between Hitler and Stalin*, which received the literature award of the American Academy of Arts and Letters, the Hannah Arendt Prize, and the Leipzig Book Prize for European Understanding. Snyder is a frequent contributor to *The New York Review of Books* and the *Times Literary Supplement* and a former contributing editor at *The New Republic.* He is a permanent fellow of the Institute for Human Sciences, serves as the faculty advisor for the Fortunoff Archive for Holocaust Testimonies, and sits on the advisory council of the YIVO Institute for Jewish Research. He lives in New Haven, Connecticut.

BY TIMOTHY SNYDER

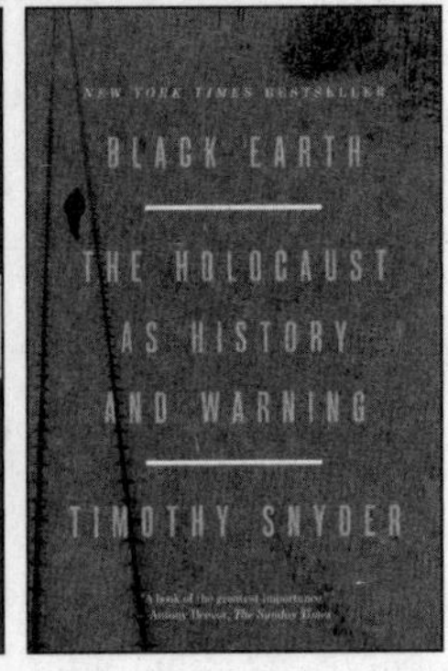

"We are rapidly ripening for fascism.
This American writer leaves us with no illusions about ourselves."

—SVETLANA ALEXIEVICH,
winner of the Nobel Prize in Literature

"Snyder reasons with unparalleled clarity, throwing the past and future into sharp relief."

—MASHA GESSEN,
author of *The Future Is History*

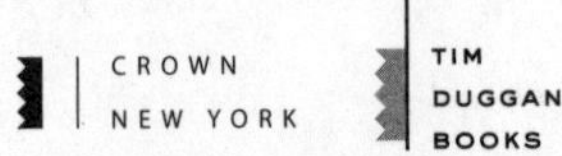

Available wherever books are sold